Mastering

Autodesk Inventor® 2009 and Autodesk® Inventor LT 2009

Mastering

Autodesk Inventor® 2009 and Autodesk® Inventor LT 2009

Curtis Waguespack

Sean Dotson, P.E.

Bill Bogan

Andrew Faix

Seth Hindman

Loren Jahraus, P.E.

Dennis Jeffrey

Shekar Subrahmanyam

Bob Van der Donck

WILEY

Wiley Publishing, Inc.

Senior Acquisitions Editor: Willem Knibbe
Development Editor: David Clark
Technical Editor: Sean Dotson
Production Editor: Rachel McConlogue
Copy Editor: Kim Wimpsett
Production Manager: Tim Tate
Vice President and Executive Group Publisher: Richard Swadley
Vice President and Executive Publisher: Joseph B. Wikert
Vice President and Publisher: Neil Edde
Book Designers: Maureen Forys and Judy Fung
Proofreader: Jen Larsen, Word One
Indexer: Ted Laux
Project Coordinator, Cover: Lynsey Stanford
Cover Designer: Ryan Sneed
Cover Image: © Pete Gardner/Digital Vision/Getty Images

For general information on our other products and services or to obtain technical support, please contact our Customer Care Department within the U.S. at (800) 762-2974, outside the U.S. at (317) 572-3993 or fax (317) 572-4002.

Wiley also publishes its books in a variety of electronic formats. Some content that appears in print may not be available in electronic books.

Library of Congress Cataloging-in-Publication Data

Mastering Autodesk Inventor 2009 and Autodesk Inventor LT 2009 / Curtis Waguespack ... [et al.]. — 1st ed.
   p. cm.
  ISBN 978-0-470-29314-0 (pbk. : website)
  1. Engineering graphics. 2. Engineering models — Data processing. 3. Autodesk Inventor (Electronic resource) I. Waguespack, Curtis, 1974-
  T353.M42 2008
  620'.00420285536 — dc22

                                                                              2008034573

10 9 8 7 6 5 4 3 2 1

Dear Reader,

Thank you for choosing *Mastering Autodesk Inventor 2009 and Autodesk Inventor LT 2009*. This book is part of a family of premium-quality Sybex books, all of which are written by outstanding authors who combine practical experience with a gift for teaching.

Sybex was founded in 1976. More than thirty years later, we're still committed to producing consistently exceptional books. With each of our titles we're working hard to set a new standard for the industry. From the paper we print on, to the authors we work with, our goal is to bring you the best books available.

I hope you see all that reflected in these pages. I'd be very interested to hear your comments and get your feedback on how we're doing. Feel free to let me know what you think about this or any other Sybex book by sending me an email at nedde@wiley.com, or if you think you've found a technical error in this book, please visit http://sybex.custhelp.com. Customer feedback is critical to our efforts at Sybex.

Best regards,

Neil Edde
Vice President and Publisher
Sybex, an Imprint of Wiley

Acknowledgments

This book is a collaborative effort involving far more people than listed on the cover. Personally, we would like to thank our families whose patience and understanding made this and all other pursuits possible. Professionally, we would like to thank the co-workers, clients, customers, and friends whose input and ideas have helped build the knowledge and experience that each of us draws from in applying concept to practice.

Thank you to the team at Wiley: David Clark, Rachel McConlogue, Kim Wimpsett, Willem Knibbe, Peter Gaughan, and Kelly Trent for their patience, focus, and professionalism, without which there would be no book. Your hard work and support have eased our efforts in turning ideas into pages.

— *The Authors*

About the Authors

Mastering Autodesk Inventor 2009 and Autodesk Inventor LT 2009 was written by a team of Inventor experts with a diverse and expansive pool of industry experience. Here is a bit more about each of them.

Curtis Waguespack served as lead author on this book. He is a senior applications engineer at D3 Technologies, was the Autodesk Partner of the Year for 2008, and is an Inventor Certified Expert and an Autodesk Manufacturing Implementation Certified Expert. His experience designing construction equipment, industrial machinery, and food service equipment, while working closely with the shop floor, has provided real-world insights into the requirements and demands of using Inventor in day-to-day design. Curtis consults with and supports manufacturing and design firms whose industries range from aerospace to consumer products to industrial machinery, each using Inventor in a specific way to meet the demands of their particular industry. Aside from work, he enjoys traveling and spending time outdoors pursuing a variety of interests.

Sean Dotson, P.E., was the technical editor and authored many of the tips and tricks found in this book. He graduated from the University of Florida with a bachelor's degree in mechanical engineering. He has more than 12 years in the custom automation and material-handling industry and is currently the president of RND Automation & Engineering, located in Sarasota, Florida. He has been involved, from a customer standpoint, with Inventor since its inception. As an Autodesk Inventor Certified Expert, he maintains both sDotson.com and mCADForums.com where he provides tutorials, macros, and other tools free of charge for the Inventor community. In his free time, he enjoys competing in triathlons and hiking with his wife and son.

Bill Bogan authored the chapter about Inventor Studio. During his career, he has designed mining vehicles and dental equipment, collaborated on a concrete finisher, and supported CAD products for an aerospace firm. Bill is in his second employment with Autodesk, for a total of nine years, as one of the original Inventor product designers and is currently a subject-matter expert. He also makes time to do animation and renderings for clients and personal interest and maintains a web page with Inventor tips and tutorials. Among his other accomplishments, he is a training instructor, is a presenter at Autodesk University, and is active in the San Diego AMUG chapter. Outside of his formal career, he has helped manufacture race cars, he builds and maintains web pages, he dabbles with remodeling and landscape projects, and he likes to travel.

Andrew Faix, author of the chapter about documentation, has been an Inventor product designer with Autodesk since 2003. Andrew has contributed to the design of Drawing Manager features and functionality from Inventor 8 through Inventor 2009. Currently, Andrew is the product design lead for Inventor core applications (part, assembly, drawings, and sketches) and works out of Autodesk's Novi, Michigan, development office. Prior to Autodesk, Andrew worked for an Autodesk MSD reseller as an applications engineer with a focus on Inventor. He has a bachelor's degree in mechanical engineering from the Rochester Institute of Technology and has held several mechanical design and engineering positions before beginning his career as a CAD/CAE expert. Andrew is a technical writer with extensive training experience. He's been a speaker at Autodesk University, a volunteer with the U.S. First Robotics program, and a regular contributor to the Inventor discussion group (`discussion.autodesk.com`).

Seth Hindman works for Autodesk's Manufacturing Solutions division and primarily focuses on the sheet metal industry, where he is responsible for the design of Inventor's sheet metal environment. He started his exploration of CAD/CAE with the R12 release of AutoCAD and in 2000 began a new relationship with the R1 release of Inventor. Before joining Autodesk in 2005, he worked in the fluid power industry, designing hydraulic components and developing systems for a variety of industries. Seth earned his bachelor's degree in mechanical engineering from Portland State University in Portland, Oregon. Seth authored the chapter about sheet metal.

Loren Jahraus, P.E., authored the chapter about Frame Generator. He has a bachelor's degree in mechanical engineering from the University of Wisconsin–Madison. He also attended Universität Stuttgart as an academic exchange student. He has designed a variety of machinery including an optical sorter for food products, an automated system to handle and monitor decommissioned nuclear weapons, and equipment to test computer chips. He has been a member of the Inventor team since 1999. He also volunteers in schools, introducing elementary-school students to engineering with the SAE A World In Motion curriculum and mentoring a high-school FIRST Robotics team.

Dennis Jeffrey coauthored several chapters of this book. Dennis is a well-known trainer, author, and consultant with 22 years supporting Autodesk manufacturing products. He has been a speaker at Autodesk University for seven years. He is an Autodesk Inventor Certified Expert and Autodesk Manufacturing Implementation Certified Expert. He has more than 40 years experience in design and manufacturing combined with 21 years of writing and training users in 3D design. His background in design includes photofinishing equipment, fixturing, and custom machinery. His varied background also includes working as a pioneer programmer and designer for microcomputers starting in 1974, with stints as a university instructor in design in 1981 through 2000. He currently consults on Autodesk manufacturing products at his firm, Tekni Consulting LLC, and is a regular columnist for the AUGI Hot News and AUGI World publications.

Shekar Subrahmanyam authored the chapter about weldment design and Inventor tools. He worked for General Electric and Computervision before joining Autodesk. He has been a member of the Inventor team since 1999. He has led several key technology projects at Autodesk that have resulted in patents. He recently attended the Executive Leadership and Management Program at Massachusetts Institute of Technology. Shekar has a doctorate degree from Rensselaer Polytechnic Institute, a master's degree from University of Texas, and bachelor's degree from Bangalore University, India, all of which are in mechanical engineering. He has organized several international conferences and seminars in CAD and solid modeling. In addition, he is the author and reviewer of several technical papers published in national and international journals. He was an invited speaker at CAD 05 and National Manufacturing Week. Shekar volunteers for the FIRST Robotics competition and the Center for Agile Manufacturing, India. He is a member of the ASME and SMA. He lives in Michigan with his wife and two daughters.

Bob Van der Donck authored the chapter about functional design in this book. He worked as a QA analyst for Inventor R1 through R10 and headed the Inventor workflow team. This team allowed Autodesk to use and look at the product in the same way Autodesk customers would use Inventor; consequently, Autodesk could test and tailor the product to these customers' specific needs. Prior to Autodesk, Bob worked for more than 10 years in the manufacturing industry. Since April 2008, he has been the worldwide technical lead for Inventor within the Product Support department. Bob started his career as a design engineer in the mold and die industry and later moved on to work as a research engineer in the telecom industry. He has a master's degree in electro-mechanical engineering from the University of Brussels and speaks four languages fluently. In his free time, he enjoys playing basketball and soccer and exploring the interesting music and film scene in the Portland area.

Contents at a Glance

Contents

Introduction

Autodesk Inventor was introduced in 1999 as an ambitious 3D parametric modeler based not on the familiar AutoCAD programming architecture but instead on a separate foundation that would provide the room needed to grow into the fully featured modeler it now is almost a decade later. Inventor 2009 marks a change of focus in the development of Inventor from an up-and-coming application to the current release with the inclusion of the design accelerator wizards and with refined core functions.

The maturity of the Inventor tools happily coincides with the advancement of the CAD market's adoption of 3D parametric modelers as a primary design tool. And although it is important to understand that 2D CAD will likely never completely disappear from the majority of manufacturing design departments, 3D design will increasingly become a requirement for most. With this in mind, we have set out to fill the following pages with detailed information on the specifics of the tools, while addressing the principles of sound parametric design techniques.

Who Should Read This Book

This book is written with a wide range of Inventor users in mind, varying from beginning to advanced users:

◆ Beginning Inventor users who are making the move from traditional 2D CAD design to Inventor 2009. These readers will have experience with AutoCAD and an understanding of basic design and engineering concepts, as well as a desire to improve their skill set and stay competitive in the market place.

◆ Intermediate Inventor users who have gone through formal Inventor training during their company's initial implementation of Inventor and are looking for more information on a specific module within Inventor. This book also targets users looking for a desktop reference to turn to when they come upon an area of Inventor that they do not encounter on a day-to-day basis.

◆ Advanced Inventor users who have mastered the Inventor tools they use over and over daily but want to conquer the parts of the program they do not utilize during their normal design tasks. This book also targets advanced users who want to add to their skill set to move up the ranks within their present company or want to expand their knowledge in pursuit of a new position with another employer.

Attempting to learn all the tools in Inventor can be an intimidating experience, because of the wide range of task-specific modules available. It was the goal of this book's authors to separate these modules into easy-to-tackle chapters relating to real-world situations for which the tools were designed, while also including chapters on general Inventor tools, techniques, and design principles.

What you will learn   The following pages will explain the Inventor settings while teaching you how each tool functions. Just as importantly, though, these pages are filled with the tips and techniques learned by the authors while spending years using, researching, and discussing the tools that are Autodesk Inventor. You should come away from reading this book with a solid understanding of the capabilities of Inventor and a strong idea of how to tackle your design challenges in the future, as well as an abundance of timesaving tips and tricks.

What you will need   To obtain the files needed to complete the tutorial files in this book, you can visit www.sybex.com/go/masteringinventor2009 and download the collection of files referenced in the following pages.

To install and run Inventor 2009, you should consult the system requirements information found on the installation media and ensure that you have a system capable of running Inventor competently. Autodesk recommends the minimum of 512MB of RAM and 1.5GB of available hard disk space for basic educational purposes dealing with small tutorial-sized assemblies. An additional 1.8GB of hard disk space is required to install Content Center. Note that these are the bare minimums to run the program, and you might see slow performance when executing operations that require heavy calculations.

We recommend a minimum of 2GB or RAM for doing production work on moderate-sized assemblies and encourage you to consider a 64-bit operating system with at least 8GB of RAM if considering large assembly design. You can find more information about workstations specs and large assemblies in Chapter 9.

The Mastering Series

The Mastering series from Sybex provides outstanding instruction for readers with intermediate and advanced skills in the form of top-notch training and development for those already working in their field as well as clear, serious education for those aspiring to become pros. Every Mastering book includes the following:

◆ Real-world scenarios, ranging from case studies to interviews, that show how the tool, technique, or knowledge presented is applied in actual practice

◆ Skill-based instruction, with chapters organized around real tasks rather than abstract concepts or subjects

◆ Self-review test questions, so you can be certain you're equipped to do the job right

What Is Covered in This Book

This is what the book covers:

◆ Chapter 1, *"Inventor Design Philosophy"*: In this chapter, you'll learn how to design the "Inventor way" when transitioning from other 2D or 3D design applications.

◆ Chapter 2, *"Data and Projects"*: In this chapter, you'll examine file structures and search paths and learn about project file types and configurations.

◆ Chapter 3, *"Sketch Techniques"*: In this chapter, you'll explore the principles of creating parameter-driven sketches for use in modeling features and parts.

◆ *Chapter 4, "Basic Modeling Techniques"*: In this chapter, you'll conquer creating parametric features and building 3D parts models.

◆ *Chapter 5, "Advanced Modeling Techniques"*: In this chapter, you'll explore complex feature creation including sweeps, lofts, and more.

◆ *Chapter 6, "Sheet Metal"*: In this chapter, you'll learn how to create accurate sheet metal models and flat patterns as well as create documentation and set up sheet metal styles and templates.

◆ *Chapter 7, "Part and Feature Reuse"*: In this chapter, you'll examine the different methods for reusing parts and features for maximum consistency and design efficiency.

◆ *Chapter 8, "Assembly Design Workflows"*: In this chapter, you'll gain a thorough understanding of this key concept of Inventor design, including the use of assembly constraints, subassemblies, and more.

◆ *Chapter 9, "Large Assembly Strategies"*: In this chapter, you'll discover the tips and techniques to getting the best performance out of your Inventor workstation and consider upgrade requirements for the future.

◆ *Chapter 10, "Weldment Design"*: In this chapter, you'll explore the Inventor weldment modeling environment and the weldment documentation tools.

◆ *Chapter 11, "Functional Design"*: In this chapter, you'll get a thorough look at this collection of Inventor design "wizards" and consider the difference between standard modeling and functional design.

◆ *Chapter 12, "Documentation"*: In this chapter, you'll learn how to use the Drawing Manager and presentation files to create both traditional, 2D annotated drawings as well as animated assembly instructions.

◆ *Chapter 13, "Inventor Tools Overview"*: In this chapter, you'll examine this collection of Inventor utilities including AutoLimits, Design Assistant, Drawing Resource Transfer Wizard, style tools, and much more.

◆ *Chapter 14, "Exchanging Data with Other Systems"*: In this chapter, you'll take a look at the available options for importing and working with solid models from other CAD packages.

◆ *Chapter 15, "Frame Generator"*: In this chapter, you'll learn how to get the most out of this utility when creating structural frames from Inventor's library of common shapes.

◆ *Chapter 16, "Inventor Studio"*: In this chapter, you'll master this powerful tool set to create photorealistic images and animations of all your Inventor models.

How to Contact the Authors

We welcome your feedback concerning *Mastering Autodesk Inventor 2009 and Autodesk Inventor LT 2009*. Please feel free to contact us via email by sending comments and questions to inventormasters@gmail.com.

Also be sure to check out www.sybex.com for additional titles and future releases in the Mastering series. Thank you for purchasing *Mastering Autodesk Inventor 2009 and Autodesk Inventor LT 2009*; we wish you happy and successful inventing!

Chapter 1

Inventor Design Philosophy

In this chapter, we will introduce the concept of design the "Inventor way," recognizing that many users of Autodesk Inventor are transitioning from the 2D world of AutoCAD or from one of the many other 3D modeling packages available today.

Change is not painful, provided you fully understand the concepts and workflows in creating efficient, accurate models and drawings.

In this chapter, you will learn how to:

◆ Manage toolbars in Autodesk Inventor

◆ Utilize the Inventor Model browser

◆ Understand the various file types used in Inventor

◆ Understand basic principles of parametric design

◆ Understand the differences between solid and surface modeling

◆ Develop best practices for using Autodesk Inventor

Moving from the AutoCAD Environment

To the experienced AutoCAD user, Inventor may seem extremely foreign and difficult to use. In actuality, Inventor is much simpler to learn and use than AutoCAD. The key to grasping the concepts of part creation in Inventor is to set aside the methods of AutoCAD design and embrace a new and more powerful way to approach computer-aided design.

The Inventor interface is clean, simple, and easy to learn.

Gone is the AutoCAD command line. Replacing the command line is the status area at the bottom of the Inventor screen. Here you will get prompts and messages relating to the current command.

Replacing a multitude of AutoCAD dimensioning tools is one General Dimension tool and one Auto Dimension tool.

Gone is the need to have a multitude of toolbars cluttering the screen. Instead, Inventor relies on context-driven tool panels that change when in different portions of the modeling process. Having fewer toolbars onscreen at any time accelerates the learning process significantly.

To the left of Figure 1.1 is the 2D Sketch panel that we use to create and dimension the sketch profiles. Upon the completion of a sketch, simply right click and then choose Finish Sketch in order to allow the creation of a part feature. When this happens, the tool panel automatically switches to the Part Features panel as shown on the right of Figure 1.1.

FIGURE 1.1
Left: the 2D Sketch
panel; right: the Part
Features panel

When working with assemblies, the tool panel changes to the Assembly panel (as shown on the left of Figure 1.2). When you create a 2D drawing of parts or assemblies, you see the Drawing Views panel, as shown on the right of Figure 1.2.

FIGURE 1.2
Left: the Assembly
panel; right: the
Drawing Views panel

As you can see, the icons on the tool panels change with every environment. There is no need to display every possible command in the user interface.

Switching Toolbars Manually

Although Inventor will automatically change the tool panel depending on what stage of the design you are in, sometimes you will want to switch the toolbars manually. To do this, simply click the arrow next to the tool panel, and select the tool panel you want from the list displayed. Once you become comfortable with the tool panel commands, you can unselect Display Text with Icons. This removes the text descriptions next to the icons, allowing you to reduce the amount of screen real estate they consume.

Using the Inventor Graphical Interface

The Inventor graphical interface is very different from what you're used to in AutoCAD. In Figure 1.3, you can explore the entire Inventor window, which shows an assembly file open for editing.

FIGURE 1.3
The complete Inventor screen in assembly mode

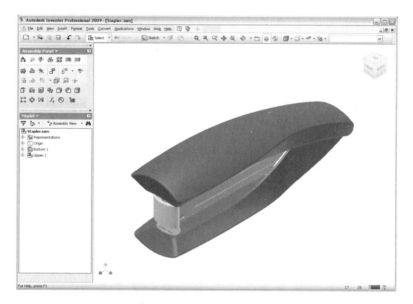

Starting at the upper left of the Inventor screen, the title bar shows the software version and the filename of the current file. Moving downward to the next row, you can see the typical File, Edit, View, Insert, Format, Tools, Convert, Applications, Window, Web, and Help pulldown menus typical in most Autodesk applications. You can go ahead and select each of the pulldown headers and examine the contents of each pulldown menu. Each of these will be covered at the appropriate time in the future pages.

The last three icons in this row are Help icons:

◆ The Help Topics icon launches Inventor's Help. You can also press F1 to access Help at any time. Pressing F1 while in a command will activate Help for that specific command.

◆ The Visual Syllabus icon activates a different type of Inventor help file that will take you through various animations that will visually describe how to follow a specific task. If you are having difficulty following text instructions, you should make it a priority to access the visual syllabus while learning to use Inventor.

◆ The Recover icon is usually grayed out. It will turn into a red plus sign when there is a problem with your file. Clicking the red plus sign will take you through several steps to attempt to correct your problem.

In the row below the menu bar are the typical Windows command options for New, Open, Undo, and Redo. Beyond the standard Windows command options, the following options are specific to Autodesk Inventor:

◆ The Select icon allows the user to set the object selection priority.

◆ The Update icon updates the file, refreshing the graphical display and recalculating all features. If the icon is grayed out, then the file does not require updating.

◆ The Sketch icon creates a new sketch on a planar face or work plane. Clicking the Sketch icon while a face or plane is preselected automatically creates a sketch on the plane or face. You can also use this icon to activate an existing sketch for editing. If a surface is preselected, the sketch will be placed on that face.

◆ Zoom All provides the standard Zoom All command option where the user view will zoom out to include all objects visible within the open file.

◆ Zoom Window provides the user with a selection method to allow zooming to objects contained within the Zoom Window box.

◆ The Zoom +/− icon provides a standard zoom in or out using the mouse button. You can also achieve this function by scrolling the wheel on a standard wheel mouse.

◆ The Pan icon allows the user to pan from one location to another within the file. You can also achieve this function by pressing and holding down the wheel of a standard wheel mouse.

◆ The Zoom Selected icon will zoom to a feature or component selected in the graphics window.

◆ The Rotate icon allows the user to rotate around the 3D model. This is not to be confused with rotating the model itself within the 3D environment.

◆ The Look At icon will orient the user viewpoint perpendicular to a selected planar face or perpendicular to a browser-selected sketch.

◆ The View Cube icon toggles on and off the availability of the 3D navigation cube that resides in the top-right corner of the graphics area. The View Cube icon allows the user to rotate around the model by clicking a face, corner, or edge of the cube, as well as allowing the user to return to a predefined home view.

◆ The Steering Wheel icon toggles on and off the availability of the navigation steering wheel. You can use this tool to zoom, pan, walk, and look around the graphics area. Also available is the ability to rewind through previous steering wheel actions. The first time the steering wheel is accessed, an introduction balloon appears to help you learn how to use this tool.

◆ The Display Mode icon has a small drop-down arrow from which you can select Shaded, Shaded with Hidden Line Display, and Wireframe Display mode. These three viewing options allow the user to toggle the display of the model in a manner that is comfortable for viewing and edge selection. Performance is typically faster in shaded mode.

◆ The View Mode icon provides the user with a choice of orthographic or perspective view. The key difference is that in perspective view parallel lines converge to a vanishing point.

◆ The Shadow icon gives the user a choice of three options: No Shadow, Ground Shadow, or X-Ray Ground Shadow.

◆ The Component Opacity icon provides the user with a toggle to turn component opacity on or off. This optional icon is available in assembly mode.

◆ The box in the upper right performs various functions. In the open assembly file, selecting a part in the graphics window will show the color style of the selected part in the list box. Once the box is active, clicking the drop-down arrow will give you a choice of the optional color styles available.

USING A WHEEL MOUSE AND 3D INPUT DEVICE

Using a wheel mouse with Inventor is recommended. Scrolling the wheel will perform a Zoom In/Out, while pressing the wheel will perform the Pan function.

Another useful tool for navigating in Inventor is a 3D pointing device. A popular brand is the Space series made by 3Dconnexion. These devices are small spheres or pucks that sit on your desk. The user grasps the sphere or puck, and by making very slight movements to the device, the model onscreen moves. Pulling, pushing, and twisting the puck allows you to zoom, pan, and orbit the model onscreen. Although many users find these devices awkward at first, most say they could never work as efficiently without one.

Tool and Browser Panels

Inventor utilizes tool panels as the default, replacing toolbars. Tool panels have the ability to switch icons inside the panel, depending upon the active file type and the specific task to be currently undertaken. Using the switching tool panels greatly simplifies usage and speeds learning. Although you could place numerous toolbars around the screen in typical AutoCAD fashion, you would reduce your efficiency and lengthen your learning cycle.

As a result, new users will benefit from resisting the urge to customize the Inventor interface and instead embrace this new approach for learning and using the intuitive features in Inventor.

In this section, we'll cover the tool panels in an assembly file, and after a few moments of use, you should begin to understand the efficiency in the Inventor approach to toolbars.

To begin, locate the assembly file with which you will be working. With Inventor 2009 open, ensure that you have no files open in the current session. Next select the File menu and then click Projects. This opens the Projects dialog box from which you can select the Samples project that Autodesk has provided for you as part of the installation of Inventor 2009. To set this project as the active one, click the Apply button toward the bottom of the dialog box. Once the project is active, you will see a check mark next to the project name. Now that the Samples project is set to be the current one, you can click Done and then close the Projects dialog box. (You'll find a more detailed explanation of working with and setting up projects in Chapter 2.)

To open the assembly, go to the File menu and click Open. To ensure that you are looking at all the files in the Samples project (and only the files in this project), click Workspace. Next browse for the file called `Stapler.iam`. This file will be located at `\Samples\Models\Assemblies\Stapler`.

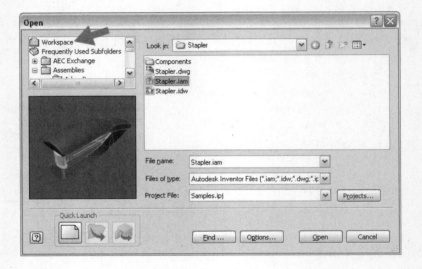

When opening your current assembly file (`Stapler.iam`), the first tool panel that you will see on the left side of your screen will be the Assembly panel because you are in assembly mode. You'll notice that in your Model browser, all items are shown in a white background, with no portion of the Model browser grayed out. You are currently in the top level of the assembly, meaning that the uppermost level of the assembly is currently active.

Double-click the subassembly called Bottom (to do this, you simply click twice quickly on the grounded assembly icon next to the word *Bottom*). Note that it is best practice to get into the habit of double-clicking the icon next to the component name, rather than the name itself, because the latter may initialize an edit of the name depending upon the speed of your clicks. Double-clicking the icon will activate the subassembly for editing in place, within the Stapler assembly. Once this subassembly is activated, all other portions within the Model browser will be grayed out.

With the Bottom subassembly activated, you will notice the Assembly panel is still visible. Next double-click the part icon for Bottom-Back. This activates the single part for editing. You will notice that the tool panel has now changed to Part Features. The tool panel change reflects that you are now editing a single part file, with part features tools ready for selection.

With the part active for editing, you will notice that the Model browser now shows all the features present in the active file. Examining these features within the active part, you can see the standard origin features, some user work planes, some additional features such as extrusions, and a fillet feature. You will also notice a red X at the bottom of the part signifying an end-of-part (EOP) marker.

USING EOP MARKERS

You can use the EOP marker to insert a feature anywhere in the model tree, where the new feature should have been created. In addition, dragging the EOP marker to the top of the part file reduces the overall part size significantly, similar to zipping a file. If you encounter a blank file in your modeling session, be sure to check the Model browser to make sure the EOP marker has been dragged to the bottom of the part file.

To return to the top-level assembly, you can simply double-click the filename (Stapler.iam) at the top of the Model browser, or you can click the Return icon at the top of your screen. Each click of the Return icon will move you up one level in the assembly. Regardless of which method you use, you will notice that the tool panel returns to the assembly tools (from the part feature tools) once you are back to the top-level assembly.

As demonstrated in this quick tour of a typical assembly structure, the Inventor tool panels are unique and intuitive to the environment you are in at the time. In addition to the toolbars you encounter in each environment, you will notice that some of the pulldown menu items will also change. In the next example, you will explore the changes encountered in the styles editor located in the Format pulldown menu.

Pulldown Menus

The pulldown menus within Inventor are similar to menus in other Windows applications. As in the previous topic, we'll discuss how Inventor changes menus and toolbars depending upon the file type that is open. In this section, we'll discuss a typical switching toolbar menu in the current assembly file.

While in an assembly file, with either the top-level assembly or a subassembly active, select the Format pulldown menu and then select Style and Standard Editor, as shown in Figure 1.4.

FIGURE 1.4
The Inventor Format
pulldown menu

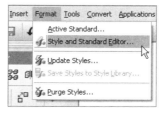

When the Style and Standard Editor dialog box opens, the styles relating to the assembly file will be shown as in Figure 1.5. You will notice that while in assembly or part mode, three style areas are available: Color, Lighting, and Material.

Next, in Inventor, create a drawing file using the standard DWG template. Note that you could also use the standard IDW template as well. With the new drawing file active, select the Format pulldown menu and then Style and Standard Editor again. You will see that the style area option reflects styles pertaining to drawings, as shown in Figure 1.6.

FIGURE 1.5
The Inventor Style and
Standard Editor
(assembly mode)

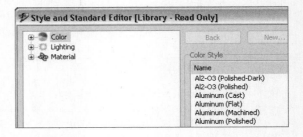

FIGURE 1.6
Style and Standard
Editor in IDW or Inventor DWG drawing mode

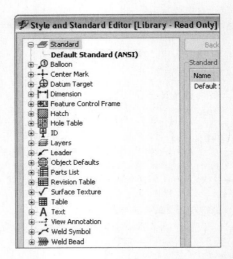

An IDW or DWG drawing style contains various dimension styles, layers and layers names, linetype settings, object defaults, text styles, and other settings related specifically to 2D drawing styles. These drawing styles relate and translate to AutoCAD drawing styles and layer names. In like fashion, the presentation file type (.ipn) style types include only Color and Lighting configurations.

The Model Browser

Inventor has what is called a *Model browser* that reflects the content in order of features, subassemblies, and parts contained within the current file. In Figure 1.7 the Stapler.iam file found in the \Samples folder of your Inventor install directory provides a good example of the Model browser contents of an assembly file. Figure 1.7 shows a representative assembly model with the browser expanded.

In this illustration, starting from the top you can see a folder containing Representations, including View representations, Position representations, and Level of Detail representations. These representations allow the user to create various view states of the assembly. For example, Figure 1.7 shows that the Position folder contains a view called Flip Open, which represents the stapler in a fully hinged open position. In Chapter 8, ''Assembly Design Workflows,'' you'll find more information about representations.

FIGURE 1.7
Stapler.iam (Inventor
sample files) illustra-
tion of Model browser
contents

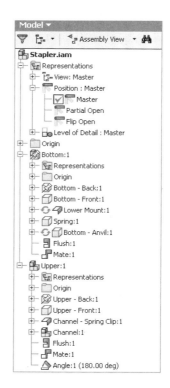

To expand any portion of the Model browser, click the plus sign to the left of the item. For example, clicking the plus sign at the left of the Representations folder expands the item to show View, Position, and Level of Detail.

Moving further down the browser tree, you'll encounter another folder called Origin. Each part and assembly file contains an Origin folder. In this example, the first Origin folder you encounter is the assembly origins. The assembly origin folder contains basic YZ, XZ, and XY work planes, work axes, and the origin's center point. These work features comprise the origin of the assembly file, and it is this origin that provides the starting point for placing files within the assembly. These work features in the origin plane are defaults and cannot be deleted; however, you can change the visibility of these planes as required.

Next in line in this example is the first file that was placed within the assembly file. In this case, it is another assembly called Bottom. An assembly placed into another assembly is typically called a *subassembly*. You will notice that there is a pushpin icon next to the filename. The pushpin represents a *grounded part*, one that cannot move within the context of this assembly. The first file inserted into an assembly file is always automatically grounded. The grounded status of a component can be turned on and off, and in fact all or none of the parts in an assembly can be grounded. However, it is best practice to ensure that at least one component is grounded in order to prevent problems generating orthographic views in the 2D drawings.

You will notice that the same Representations and Origin folders exist in this grounded assembly and in all other parts and assemblies that exist in this file. The relationships between origin planes in each of the files provide a permanent reference for downstream modifications, including 3D constraints and editing of individual parts.

In the subassembly called Bottom are additional files: Bottom-Back:1, Bottom-Front:1, Lower Mount:1, Spring:1, and Bottom-Anvil:1. Each of these files represents a separate part within the subassembly. The 1 that follows each part represents the first instance of that part name within the assembly. If a second identical part name is inserted within the same assembly, the number would be incremented according to the number of times that part is instanced within the assembly.

In the browser, note that two of the parts, Lower Mount and Bottom-Anvil, have a red and green icon preceding the part name. This icon tells the user that these two parts are set to Adaptive, meaning that these two parts will automatically adjust to changes in the part they reference. Right-clicking the Adaptive icon will display a context menu, allowing the user to turn adaptivity on or off. Next to each part name within the subassembly is a small plus sign, signifying that the part or subassembly can be expanded to show more of the contents of that specific part (see Figure 1.8). When the part or subassembly has been expanded, the plus sign switches to a minus sign, which allows the user to compress the part or assembly back to a smaller state and save room for reviewing other items within the Model browser.

FIGURE 1.8
Expanded contents in the Model browser

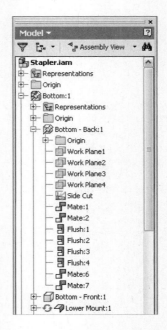

At the bottom of this section within the browser, you will see the words *Flush* and *Mate*. The Flush and Mate references are two of several 3D constraints used to "assemble and constrain" various parts. Right-clicking a constraint in the browser allows the user to locate the other part to which this part is constrained within the assembly.

Learning the File Types in Inventor

In AutoCAD, you might be used to having the DWG file format as your main file format. Inventor, on the other hand, follows the structure common to most other 3D modelers in the engineering field today. Instead of placing all information in one file, the data load is distributed into many different files. Placing the data in multiple files permits higher performance, promotes file integrity, and vastly improves performance on large designs. As you've already explored, having different file types allows you to have environment-specific tools for work with each file type.

The payoff of multiple file types is exemplified in the comparison between the way that Auto-CAD handles model space/paper space and the way that Inventor handles the same tasks. To put it simply, in Inventor the part and assembly files represent model space, and the drawing file is in effect paper space. Using multiple file types to handle the separate tasks required for modeling vs. detailing simplifies the interaction between both tasks, and as a result, you will see that all the headaches of managing model space and paper space in AutoCAD are eliminated in Inventor.

Here are the primary file formats commonly used in Inventor:

`.ipj`: Inventor project file

`.ipt`: Inventor single part file

`.iam`: Inventor assembly file

`.ipn`: Inventor presentation file

`.idw`: Inventor 2D detail drawing file

`.dwg` (Inventor): Inventor 2D detail drawing file

`.dwg` (AutoCAD): AutoCAD nonassociative drawing file

`.xls`: Excel files that drive iParts, threads, and other data

Although this list may seem intimidating, once you get used to using Inventor, having many different file types will be less of a concern. The benefit of using multiple file types to have fully associative, automatically updating designs is a cornerstone of most 3D parametric modelers. Performance and stability in the use of Inventor require good data management principles, including storing the saved files in an efficient and organized manner. We'll introduce this subject later in this chapter and expand upon it in Chapter 2.

Using DWG Files in Inventor

You can use DWG files in a number of ways in Inventor. Although Inventor does not support the creation of AutoCAD entities, AutoCAD geometry can be utilized in Inventor sketches, Inventor drawings, title blocks, and symbol creation.

When creating a new part file in Inventor, you can copy geometry directly from an AutoCAD DWG and paste it into an Inventor sketch. AutoCAD dimensions will even be converted into fully parametric Inventor dimensions. However, only minimal sketch constraints will be created when doing this. Using the Auto Dimension tool within the Inventor sketch environment, you can apply sketch constraints to the copied AutoCAD data quickly. It is important to remember that many AutoCAD drawings contain fundamental issues such as exploded or "fudged" dimensions and lines with endpoints that do not meet. Copying such drawings into an Inventor sketch will of course bring all of those issues along and will typically provide poor results.

Another way to use AutoCAD data in Inventor is in an Inventor DWG file. Often you'll have symbols in AutoCAD in the form of blocks that you want to use on a drawing in Inventor, such as a directional flow arrow or a standard note block. Although you could re-create these symbols in Inventor, you can also simply copy the block from AutoCAD and paste it into the Inventor DWG. This functionality exists only within an Inventor DWG and is not supported in an Inventor IDW. In fact, it is one of the few differences between an Inventor DWG and an Inventor IDW.

Mechanical Desktop DWG files can be opened or linked into Inventor assemblies. When the Mechanical Desktop file is opened in Inventor, options allow the translation of Mechanical

Desktop models into parametric Inventor parts and assemblies, as well as fully associative layouts into Inventor drawing files. When the Mechanical Desktop file is linked into an Inventor assembly, it behaves similarly to an AutoCAD XRef, and all edits will be maintained using Mechanical Desktop.

Creating DWG Files from Inventor Drawings

Users of Inventor may often find that they are called upon to create native DWG files from Inventor IDW files for use by customers or other people within the company. A user may create a DWG file by simply performing a Save Copy As and saving it as an AutoCAD DWG file. The newly created DWG file will not be associative to the Inventor part or assembly or IDW file and will not reflect any changes made to the part, assembly, or Inventor drawing file. It is common to use Save Copy As on an Inventor drawing and save it to an AutoCAD DWG just before making revision changes, thereby preserving a copy of the drawing in a static state at that revision level. Once the static copy is saved, revision edits can begin, and the original Inventor drawing will update automatically.

Beginning with Inventor 2008, users have the option of creating a native Inventor DWG file in place of the IDW file. This DWG file will behave exactly like an Inventor drawing file, except that the file extension will be .dwg instead of .idw. Just like an IDW file, an Inventor DWG file will update whenever parts or assemblies linked to the file are changed and updated. Note too that if you have IDW files that were created in a version of Inventor previous to Inventor 2008, you can save those files as fully associative DWG files so that your drawing library contains one consistent drawing file type. This process can even be batched and scheduled to run overnight using the Task Scheduler, which you can open by selecting Start ➤ Programs ➤ Autodesk ➤ Autodesk Inventor 2009 Tools Task Scheduler.

You can open an Inventor DWG file in AutoCAD and edit it with some limitation. The primary limitation is that the Inventor objects are protected from modification. AutoCAD dimensions and other entities can be added and will remain intact when the file is opened again in Inventor, but as a rule, objects must be edited in the application from which they were created.

Another aspect of working with an Inventor DWG in AutoCAD is that whereas the Inventor DWG does not contain a model space by default, once it is opened in AutoCAD, you can access model space. From model space in an Inventor DWG you can use the Insert command to place the Inventor drawing views of the model as AutoCAD blocks. These blocks will update automatically so long as they are not exploded and remain in the current DWG. However, you can explode the blocks and copy them into other DWGs without worrying about having a negative impact on the Inventor DWG. If objects such as these blocks are added to the DWG's model space in AutoCAD, you will then be able to access model space for that file in Inventor. However, you will be able only to view, measure, and plot the model space objects.

Moving from AutoCAD to Inventor

If you are moving from AutoCAD 2D to Inventor 3D modeling, you can have a great experience in the process if you put design concepts used in AutoCAD on the shelf while learning this exciting design tool.

If your experience is like that of many others who made the transition from the drawing board to drawing lines in AutoCAD, it was difficult to say the least. At first you may have been frustrated with spending more time creating electronic drawings than it would have taken to produce the drawing with the board. However, a key reason of the acceptance of AutoCAD was the ability to make edits far more quickly than you could with eraser and paper. Remember your first frustrating events learning AutoCAD when you embark on this great Inventor learning experience.

Sometimes your patience may be tried, and your first instinct will be to switch back to that trusted old friend AutoCAD.

Resist that temptation, and embrace your new friend with an open mind and willingness to learn new, exciting, and productive methods that will prove to be far more efficient than AutoCAD ever could hope to be. It may also be of some comfort that much of the interface of Inventor comes from the demand that AutoCAD users have made for a simple intuitive set of tools.

Making the move to Inventor successfully requires some evaluation of current methods of design in AutoCAD. The following are some of the evaluation steps in planning your successful move:

- Assessing your current directory structure of AutoCAD drawings. How do you store, name, and reuse current AutoCAD files? Will the structure be compatible for storing Inventor documents, or is it time to take a deep look at your data management structure?

- Determining how you will manage Inventor files. Inventor utilizes projects to manage assemblies, drawings, and associated part files. What worked in AutoCAD will probably not be the ideal scenario in Inventor.

- Documenting your current design workflow when using AutoCAD. Is it time to reevaluate the design process in light of the efficiencies that may be gained when using Inventor? How are revisions, engineering change orders, and production currently being managed, and how can Inventor improve on the design-to-manufacturing processes?

- Determining whether your current computer hardware and network are up to the task of implementing and using Inventor Series. What gets by for using AutoCAD seldom will work for the demands of 3D modeling in Inventor.

- Setting aside time for training and implementing Inventor. If you have multiple users, it might be best to consider phasing Inventor in over a period of time, allowing new users to acclimate themselves to a new way of design.

If you take the time to plan your leap into Inventor, your chances of success are greatly improved. The rewards of a successful transition are great!

In future chapters, we will expand on the evaluation tools needed to plan a great transition, but first you need to learn what is expected from Inventor. To do that, let's enter the world of 3D design.

Building a 3D Virtual Prototype

Common to machine design, actual prototypes are built to test or validate the design, and they help discover weaknesses or areas that require redesigning. It is a costly and time-consuming process but one that is needed when working from 2D designs.

Even the best engineer or designer cannot anticipate everything needed to create an accurate design the first time around. Mistakes are made, scrap is generated, and redesign and retooling are needed. The entire prototyping process is expensive and time-consuming.

This is the old way of doing things. It worked when we made 1,000 of something and had plenty of time and resources to lend to the project. It worked when material costs were relatively low. Today, in our ever more competitive market, we have no such luxuries of time and materials.

Time is of the essence, and we are pressed by worldwide competition for our products, jobs, and manufacturing bases.

The emphasis is on designing and building something quickly and economically, without sacrificing quality or performance. Many companies today specialize in custom machines and automation where the "prototype" is the end product. Clearly, anything you can do that reduces or eliminates prototyping will greatly influence your financial health and competitive strengths.

What Is a Virtual Prototype?

Over the years, as designs tools have evolved, so too have the ways we design. However, it is possible to use new design tools in the same manner we used the old tools if we are not careful. As companies moved from the drafting board to AutoCAD, many users continued to use AutoCAD in much the same way they used the board. Not reusing data in the form of blocks and block libraries and not employing block attributes to pack those blocks with intelligence are a couple examples of this.

In much the same way, it is possible to use Inventor like it is AutoCAD. Creating 3D models simply for the sake of generating a 2D shop print is a common example of this. To ensure that you are getting the most out of Inventor, you want to ensure that your designs are more than 3D models and are in fact virtual prototypes.

So, what is a 3D *virtual prototype*? Put simply, it's a digital prototype that has not yet been built. And although that simple answer seems obvious, it is the "not yet built" part of that description that is key. A virtual prototype is a completely digital 3D parametric model that functions the same way a real mechanism should.

The virtual prototype consists of a main assembly, containing many subassemblies, containing individual parts. All these components are constrained in such a way that fit, and the functionality of all parts and mechanisms can be visualized, tested, and proven before any parts are manufactured. Scrap and rework are virtually eliminated if the design is fully completed and proven in the digital form.

Making the virtual prototype allows the designer to explore the function of a mechanism before lengthy design and engineering time is expended on a design that just won't work. Developing the virtual prototype eliminates the part procurement and creation process, slashing the design time even further.

The virtual prototype can be proven with the use of stress analysis and dynamic motion simulation to find and correct weaknesses in the design, rather than just ensuring that everything is overbuilt and calling it a good design. Interference between components is also easily discovered while still in the design process.

The use of functional design in the prototyping process allows engineers to properly determine loads, power, stresses, inertia, and other properties before a machine is built. Weights, center of gravity, and other physical characteristics are at your fingertips during any stage of the design.

SEAN SAYS: TAKE FULL ADVANTAGE OF 3D

When I first looked at Inventor release 1, I had no idea how much it would change the way we designed machinery. We had been using Mechanical Desktop for a few years, but it was not until we were introduced to Inventor that we really realized the full potential of 3D design.

Looking back at some of our old AutoCAD designs, I wonder how we did it. All of the lines just lie on top of one another in one big messy dimension. To this day, I still try to orbit 2D AutoCAD drawings thinking (hoping?) they hold some hidden 2.5D information.

In this day and age, there is no reason why you should not be designing in 3D. One of the most obvious benefits you'll immediately see is simply the aspect of visualization. Now you can easily see that shaft

A is going to run through plate B. In AutoCAD you'd never be able to tell that you were missing that clearance hole. When my company adopted Inventor in 1999, we saw our percentage of rework drop by double digits.

Another bonus is the ability to produce parametric designs. This will be discussed in more detail later in the book, but basically parametric design allows you to drastically change designs based on only a few key parameters. Our standard machine division was able to produce engineer-to-order design in a fraction of the amount of time before the introduction of Inventor. By simply entering a few key parameters such as product height, width, and depth, we could produce a new, custom design in moments.

Finally, the ability to simulate designs, using both Inventor Professional's Dynamics Simulation modules and some of the built-in functions in Inventor Series, is priceless. By correctly constraining parts, you can quickly determine whether a linkage is going to bind, whether a part is going to collide with another, or whether there is any interference in your design. You can simulate the motion of an entire machine including air cylinder, cam, and other devices to simulate the movement of the real machine.

Just as many of us could never imagine going back to drafting boards and vellum, I cannot imagine ever going back to designing in 2D. Although it may take some time to become as proficient in 3D as you are in 2D, your patience and perseverance will be well rewarded.

Understanding Parametric Design

In 2D design software such as AutoCAD or other legacy packages, including most surface modelers or 3D modelers capable of creating static models, the ability to modify the design is typically limited. Modern 3D feature-based modelers provide the ability to easily change virtually any part of the design within the model.

This ability to change or modify a design is based on constraints that control either the shape or the size of a feature. The combination of geometric constraints and dimensional constraints allow virtually any variation within the model.

Most of today's 3D modeling systems utilize the same 2D constraint manager. As a result, the 2D constraints in use today are virtually identical from one software package to another. In like fashion, the dimensional constraint systems are similar from one software package to another, and these similarities allow you to easily learn a second 3D modeling system more easily the next time around.

Let's start on familiar territory with software that most of us have used, AutoCAD. When you create a design in AutoCAD, that design is not much different from creating the same design on a drawing board. In AutoCAD you can draw precise lines, arcs, circles and other objects, placed precisely and with accurate dimensions reflecting your design, in a way that you cannot do by hand. When a design requires modification, you erase, move, copy, stretch, and otherwise manipulate the existing geometry more quickly than you can by hand as well. But other than those gains in speed and accuracy, the workflow is much the same as working on a drafting board.

Dimensions in AutoCAD are what we call *driven* or *reference* dimensions. A driven dimension is controlled by the geometry, and it reflects the actual value of the geometry that is referenced by the dimension. If you stretch a line, for example, the dimension that is attached to the line will update to the new value. If you think about it, the only reason for a dimension on a 2D drawing is to convey the value of a feature or part to a person who is going to build it. If you import that

2D file into a CAM package, no dimensions are needed because the line work contains all the information about the part.

The workflow in a 3D model is substantially different than in 2D modeling. In a 3D model, you create sketches in 2D and then add geometric constraints such as horizontal, vertical, parallel, and so on. Adding the geometric constraints allows line work to adjust in a predictable and desired manner and helps control the overall shape of the sketch. Once geometric constraints are in place, you add parametric (driving) dimensions to the sketch geometry. By changing the value of the dimension, you change the size of the sketch object. As you can see, the Inventor dimension is far more powerful than the AutoCAD dimension because it not only conveys the value of a feature or part but also serves as a design parameter, allowing you to change the dimension to change the design.

Parametric feature-based modeling relies on the creation of numerous features within the model. By creating a quantity of features within the model, you are able to independently change or modify a feature without rebuilding the entire model. An example of editing a feature would be changing the radius of an edge fillet.

Parametric model features are typically either dependent or independent of one another. A *dependent* feature is dependent upon the existence or position of a previously created feature. If that previously created feature is deleted, then the dependent feature will either also be deleted or become an independent feature, unless it is made dependent on a different preexisting feature within the model. An *independent* parametric feature is normally based upon an origin feature such as a work plane, work axis, or work point or is referenced off the original base feature.

SEAN SAYS: DRAWING IN AUTOCAD BECOMES SKETCHING IN INVENTOR

The fundamental difference between AutoCAD and Inventor is that in AutoCAD you draw and in Inventor you sketch. The difference sounds subtle but is very important. In AutoCAD you construct lines precisely to specific dimensions to form the geometry that is required. In Inventor you create lines and geometry that reflect the general form and function of the feature and then use constraints and dimensions to massage it into the desired shape. This is probably the single biggest stumbling block that AutoCAD users face when starting to use Inventor.

Understanding Functional Design

Functional design is an Autodesk term for a knowledge content tool that moves the user from creating geometrical descriptions to capturing knowledge. Engineers and designers can use functional design to analyze the function and solve the design problems, rather than spending time on modeling a solution needed to create 3D representations.

THE V-BELTS GENERATOR

An example of functional design and its benefit is the use of the Inventor's V-belts Generator. Traditionally, to design a pulley system you would lay out the pulleys in positions as required by the design and then choose a belt that met the design requirements and came as close as possible to fitting the pulley spacing. The result oftentimes is that no common belt size fits the pulley spacing. The functional design approach to this task allows you to specify the belt from a standard catalog of belt sizes at the same time that you are creating the rest of the system. In this way, you know from the outset that the design is indeed functional and will work in the real world.

Functional design supports design through generators and wizards that add mechanical content and intelligence to the design. By using the components within Inventor functional design, you can create mechanically correct components automatically by entering simple or complex mechanical attributes inside the generator.

Using the functional design components within Inventor provides many advantages:

◆ You shorten the design and modification process through the use of wizards.

◆ You produce a higher level of design quality and accuracy.

◆ Functional design provides a more intuitive design environment, compared to creating complicated geometrical designs.

◆ Functional design can eliminate the need for physical prototypes for the purpose of analyzing stress and movement.

The following portions of Autodesk Inventor are part of the functional design system:

◆ Design Accelerator

◆ Frame Generator

◆ Inventor Studio

◆ AutoLimits

◆ Content Center

The Design Accelerator is an important component of the functional design system, providing the user with engineering calculation and decision-making support to identify and place standard components or create standards-based geometry from the input provided by the user. Design Accelerator tools automate selecting standard parts and creating intelligent geometry. The initial design quality is improved by validating against design requirements. Standardization is simplified by selecting the same components for the same tasks.

The Design Accelerator provides a set of wizards and calculators that are able to create mechanically correct standard components automatically by entering simple or detailed information.

The Bolted Connection Generator is one example of a wizard that can create and insert a complete bolted connection all at once by sizing the bolt diameter and length, by selecting the right parts and holes, and by assembling all the components together.

The Frame Generator will create internal or external frame assemblies for machines. The Frame Generator functions by creating a skeleton part to define the frame within an assembly file. You then use the skeleton to place and size the frame members. You can then use multiple skeletal models within an assembly to create frame members, and you can create frame members between skeletal models. You can also create frame members from the vertices and edges of existing subassemblies. This ability allows you to build framing between other components within an assembly.

Joining frame members together and adjusting the end treatments for connection between members is a simple matter in the use of this tool. Joining frame members with weld gaps and coped joints is supported.

Inventor Studio is an environment within Autodesk Inventor with a complete set of tools for creating and editing renderings and animations. With Inventor Studio you will be able to create animated renderings and photo realistic still images of parts and assemblies to help visualize the appearance and motion of designs before they are built.

Inventor Studio allows you to specify geometry and apply settings for background lights and cameras to create a scene for rendering or animation. Multiple animations can be created and saved within any one assembly file. Inventor constraints and parameters can be used to drive animations within the assembly file. In addition, any changes that are made in the part or assembly file will be transferred and reflected in the rendering and animation files.

AutoLimits monitor selected aspects of the design relative to boundaries that the user specifies. If results fall above or below the boundary limits, a warning indicator is displayed. AutoLimits can also be used to measure distance, length, volume, mass, and so on. AutoLimits monitor constantly to make sure the design still fits its requirements.

The Inventor Content Center libraries provide the designer with standard parts (fasteners, steel shapes, shaft parts, and so on) and part features. You can access the Content Center libraries from the Content Center in the Assembly tool panel, and you can share the libraries between users to provide a high level of standardization.

The Content Center dialog box permits you to lookup and insert standard parts and features into an assembly design. You can create custom Content Center folders to allow users to create custom parts for use within the Content Center. Content Center parts allow users to specify ANSI, DIN, ISO, and other international standard parts within the design environment.

Understanding Solids vs. Surface Modeling

Inventor provides the ability to create parametric models in either solid modeling or surface modeling form. In many cases, you can employ both techniques when creating a single part.

3D modeling began because of the desire to create a 3D wireframe representation of a part. This representation provided early users with the ability to visualize and measure the limits or boundaries of parts they were designing. Wireframes provided a minimal amount of information needed to create a part.

It soon became apparent that much more was needed in a 3D model. Software engineers devised objects called *surfaces* that could be created from the 3D wireframe model. Creating surfaces permitted the accurate definition of the faces or shapes that would be required in order to machine the design.

This new model description technology revolutionized the manufacturing industry. With surfaces, shapes could be programmed into CNC machines, producing accurate geometry to be used for creating precision parts. Surface modelers quickly jumped into the forefront of leading-edge technology. With surfaces, virtually anything could be designed or created.

However, surface modeling had some shortcomings. Creators of surface models had great difficulty calculating volumes, centroids, and mass. The development of surface modeling technology evolved into the ability to create a collection of watertight surfaces. Modeling kernels were further developed to allow the representation of the watertight collection of surfaces as a solid model composed of faces (surfaces).

Solid modeling got off to a good start in the mid-1980s. The first iteration of solid modeling was the ability to create static, base solids. Like surfaces, base solids were difficult to impossible to edit once created. If a mistake was made in the model, the user started over.

The second generation of solid modeling introduced parametric, history-based model creation with the ability to parametrically modify dimensions and constraints within the model to edit or modify the size or shape of the part. If an error was made in creating the part, users could access the history tree and retrace their steps toward the beginning of the part creation process, selecting the point to rebuild the rest of the model. Unfortunately, with history-based modeling, anything that was previously created from that point forward would be deleted and have to be re-created.

The current generation of solid modelers provides dynamic feature-based parametric modeling, where powerful features can be added, modified, suppressed, deleted, or reordered within the model without having to re-create good geometry. With the introduction of feature-based modeling, 3D became a must-have within the engineering community. Now, complex designs can be quickly created and modified to create virtual prototypes of complex machines without having to cut metal to prove the design.

The following are frequent questions among 3D users: Which is better? Should I use surface or solid modeling? Which should I use? The answer is that you should become proficient at using both and never have to limit your abilities. Both surface and solid modeling have a place in today's engineering environment. Learning to use both proficiently should be on the agenda of every aspiring modeler.

Although solid modeling is preferred by more users, primarily because it is a simpler approach to design, the ability to add surfaces to sculpt or modify a solid model, or to add faces that would be difficult to impossible to create using solid model features, adds a new dimension to creating a quality model. It's one of the little things that differentiate an expert user from the rest of the pack.

Let's look at definitions of some of the aspects of solid and surface modeling:

Wireframe A collection of curves and lines and other geometry is connected into a 3D (XYZ) construction representing the outer boundaries and features of a 3D part. See Figure 1.9 for an example of a wireframe model.

FIGURE 1.9
Representation of a
wireframe type model

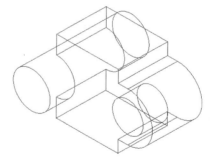

Surface A 3D mesh is composed of U and V directional wires or vectors representing a 3D face. Surfaces are generally described by a few different types: *polyface meshes* (typical in graphics modelers), representing planar faceted faces with joined edges culminating in one face; *triangulated meshes* (typical in STL files), composed of three-sided planar faces connected into one mesh; *NURBS surfaces* (based upon nonuniform rational B-splines), providing smooth, constantly evolving surfaces that can be constrained and made tangent to other adjoining surfaces and providing smooth surface transitions across a single part.

Inventor supports NURBS surface types in created or imported geometry. Figure 1.10 shows an Inventor surface model, typically displayed as a translucent object. Surfaces can be combined with solid models in a number of ways to enhance your modeling experience.

FIGURE 1.10
Representation of a
surface type model

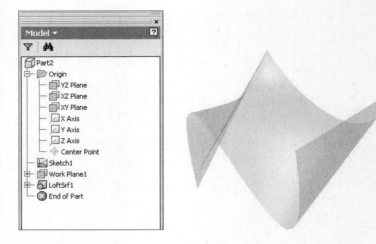

Solid   A 3D solid is composed of a collection of surfaces joined together to provide a water-tight collection with no gaps or holes. When a collection of surfaces is joined together in such a manner, it is generally considered solidified. Solids can provide the benefit of physical properties such as mass, volume, centroids, and moments of inertia or principal moments and can be tagged with other properties such as material specifications. Figure 1.11 illustrates a solid model part.

FIGURE 1.11
Representation of a solid
model in shaded mode

Best Practices in Autodesk Inventor

Every 3D modeling package follows a workflow designed to produce the best and most efficient design while retaining the stability required to update or modify the design at a later time. In addition, the workflow encourages high performance and stability within the file structure. Inventor is no different from other packages in that an efficient design workflow must be followed to ensure good results.

The following are five important areas to consider when creating an ideal workflow that will both benefit your designs and meet your company's operational requirements:

- ◆ Creating a data management structure

- ◆ Selecting the proper project file type for your designs

- ◆ Developing an efficient and stable part-modeling workflow

- ◆ Developing assembly structure for maximum efficiency

- ◆ Establishing standards for documentation

Creating a Data Management Structure

In the previous pages, we discussed the need for an efficient and practical data management structure that will fit the needs within your company. A good data management structure may be something that your company has already created or something that you may design, keeping in mind your company and customer's requirements.

Even if your company has been working in other CAD packages for many years, your filing system may be in serious need of reorganization or replacement. Many times, the file structure you find yourself working under today has simply evolved over time as changes in hardware and operating systems have come about. These evolutions range from very inefficient systems with vestiges of some long-gone setup or decision that negatively impacts the way things are done today to very efficient systems where filing is intuitive and well structured. When you're implementing Inventor, it's a good time to evaluate your system and see what changes are or are not required because of the way that Inventor uses linked files within the application. It is also important to note that parametric modelers such as Inventor create more files than traditional design software.

Redesigning a file management system for efficiency may require the skills of an outside data management consultant who also thoroughly understands the data management structure required for efficient use of Autodesk Inventor and AutoCAD. One source of a qualified individual who can tackle this task might be your local Autodesk reseller, if your reseller has an Autodesk Manufacturing Implementation Certified Expert or Certified Data Management Expert on staff. If such a consultant is not locally available, then you may want to contact Autodesk Technical Services for assistance.

We cannot overstate the need to thoroughly evaluate and correct any deficiencies in your current data management structure. Having a data management system that is set up to ensure the use of unique names for every file should be a primary goal of every Inventor user. This requires some forethought and planning in setting up a good file-naming scheme. Fixing any problems now will deliver a great payback in the use of Autodesk Inventor or AutoCAD.

Selecting the Proper Project File Type for Your Designs

Selecting the proper project file type after correcting any errors or inefficiencies in your data management structure is crucial to your success with Autodesk Inventor and, in the future, with various AutoCAD vertical applications. The next chapter of this book will introduce you to the different project file types that may or may not be suitable to your specific needs.

If you need to have multiple designers working on a single project simultaneously, it is highly recommended that you investigate Autodesk Vault. Autodesk Vault provides many benefits over other project file types when working in a collaborative system group or even when working alone. Vault is bundled with the Inventor suite and can be installed at the time of your Inventor install or at a later date. Although Vault is a highly effective tool for managing your engineering files, a poorly implemented Vault can cause a lot of headaches. Following the recommendations in this book for setting up a Vault project should keep you in the clear.

On the other hand, you may already have another product data management (PDM) database in use within your company for other applications. You may want to consider integrating Inventor into that PDM system, assuming that your existing system fully accommodates and supports Inventor at least as well as Autodesk Vault. Optionally, you might want to consider Autodesk Productstream, an upgrade of Autodesk Vault, for its additional control and management functions.

If you are working in a smaller company or have just a few users each working on individual jobs with no crossover, the Single User Project file mode might be the best way for you to work.

Developing an Efficient and Stable Part-Modeling Workflow

Paramount to the success of 3D solid modeling is developing an efficient and stable part-modeling workflow that works for your designs. Here are a few attributes of good part design:

◆ Sketched part features created from simple sketches that represent and document design intent

◆ Creation of part features that do not have a high degree of dependency upon other previously created part features

◆ Part features that are easily identified and able to be edited without creating errors

◆ Fully constrained and dimensioned sketches and features that will update and behave predictably when other features are edited

◆ Features that are properly named and identified for future editing reference

◆ Part creation workflow that is easily understood by other people, should editing be necessary in the future

◆ Practicing restraint in creating large numbers of duplicate features, when identical features could be combined into a single feature

◆ Developing a good workflow that will be repeated in future design projects, providing consistency and design, and helping others to understand and follow good design practices

SEAN SAYS: A SOLID SKETCH IS THE FOUNDATION ON WHICH STABLE PARTS ARE BUILT

Many new users do not understand the importance of having a grounded, fully constrained base sketch. It can be highly frustrating to have a model fail when you make a simple change, all because the base sketch was not properly constructed.

Developing Assembly Structure for Maximum Efficiency

Developing an efficient assembly structure is essential for success and maximum performance-break in the 3D modeling environment. Poor assembly design will plague the design process throughout the entire life of the job, often creating large assemblies that cannot be rotated for view, cannot be used to create 2D drawings, or often break down requiring many hours of repair and constant attention.

You can avoid the nightmares of poor assembly design structure with the proper use and understanding of how assembly files work. A properly designed assembly structure possesses the following qualities:

◆ A top-level assembly will be composed of numerous subassemblies constrained to one another. The use of individual parts within the top-level assembly should be limited.

◆ All components within a top-level assembly must be properly constrained to one another so that they will move or not move as they would in the real world. All adaptive components should have adaptivity turned off when adaptivity is not required at that particular moment.

◆ By limiting the number of components at the top-level assembly, the number of 3D constraints present in the top-level assembly will be limited, improving overall performance. Note that when we say *component*, we could be referring to a part file or a subassembly file.

◆ Properly created and named design views and/or level of detail (LOD) should be present within the assemblies and subassemblies of the design. Use of either or both will provide flexibility and improve performance in the assembly design as well as the 2D documentation process.

◆ Reuse of library parts, including but not limited to fasteners, purchased parts, or company standard parts used in multiple designs, will improve consistency and performance when loading assemblies. In addition, placing company standard parts will eliminate duplication of files and filenames within the data management system.

SEAN SAYS: MAKE YOUR MODELS MIMIC THE MANUFACTURING PROCESS

The simplest advice I can give to new users on the subject of assemblies is to structure them as you would in real life. If in the design you plan to assemble several parts into a transmission and then drop that transmission into a housing, then make the transmission a subassembly and insert it into the upper-level housing assembly. By making your models mimic the manufacturing process, you can also find possible flaws in your design such as fasteners that cannot be accessed or areas where parts may interfere during assembly.

Establishing Standards for Documentation

Documenting your designs in 2D drawing files should follow a standard established by your company. However, documenting 3D designs and assemblies using traditional methods and workflows might pose performance and stability issues.

Consider a workflow similar to this: establish a design workflow that encompasses the principle of "one part–one part name/number–one drawing." This establishes a link between a single part file in a single drawing file. This part could be used in many different assemblies and should be documented separately from assembly documentation. Figure 1.12 illustrates this workflow.

FIGURE 1.12
Part documentation workflow

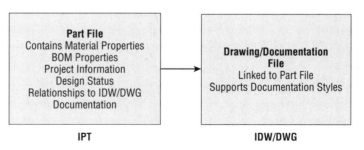

Documentation may take many forms. Inventor offers several options in this area. Your choice of methods may greatly influence productivity downstream. Aside from conventional paper prints generated from an IDW or Inventor DWG file, the Save Copy As command allows many options for creating various image formats. Figure 1.13 lists the options available in Autodesk Inventor 2009.

FIGURE 1.13
File Types Available for
Save Copy As

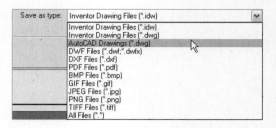

SEAN SAYS: DON'T TRY TO USE INVENTOR AS IF IT WERE AUTOCAD

Users must also realize that Inventor is not AutoCAD. AutoCAD has millions of possible ways to annotate designs and is seemingly infinitely customizable. Many companies complain that Inventor cannot mimic the output of AutoCAD. However, upon closer investigation, no one in those companies can remember why their designs are documented in that particular fashion. My suggestion is to take the time to evaluate your documentation rules and specifications. Just as design standards were changed when companies switched from the drafting board to AutoCAD, so should they be scrutinized when switching from AutoCAD to Inventor.

Digital Communication

In making the move from two-dimensional to three-dimensional design, you may want to consider modernizing all aspects of your documentation workflow. Now may be the time to move from paper to electronic documentation in all areas where the transmitted information may be utilized.

Instead of plotting paper drawings and having to manage them to make sure that the latest version of each drawing file is properly distributed to all departments, consider using the Autodesk DWF format as a method of recording and documenting IDW or DWG output.

If you are using Autodesk Vault or Productstream, you could set an option in either products to automatically generate an updated DWF file that could then be made available to all departments. A relatively ordinary PC in each department could be used to view the DWF document, apply markups and changes, and, if necessary, generate a paper print.

If you were to implement full use of Autodesk Productstream, then you would be able to manage revisions and engineering change orders electronically, documenting every change.

Using electronic files in this manner assures that every department has access to the latest, up-to-date documentation.

The Bottom Line

Manage toolbars in Autodesk Inventor   In this first chapter, you learned how the Inventor interface is designed to function efficiently, with tool panels that switch depending upon the stage of design and the environment in which you are working. The Inventor interface is designed for simplicity, ease of use, and ease of learning.

Master It   You find that using the scroll bars in the tool panels to access commands is tedious and a bit difficult to keep track of which command is where.

Utilize the Inventor Model browser   The Inventor Model browser displays information about the model in a hierarchy. When working with parts, features are listed in the browser in the order they were created, providing an evolutionary timeline of the model. In the Assembly environment, parts are organized in the model browser in subassemblies for organization and performance. Even in the drawing environment, we have browser to organize the hierarchy of views.

> **Master It**   You wish to explore an existing part model to get a better understanding of how it was created and how it might be improved.

Understand the various file types used in Inventor   You have learned that Inventor supports many different file types in its native environment, separating tasks and files to improve performance and increase stability.

> **Master It**   You have decided to use the native Inventor DWG format for all your drawing files so that you can email files without translating when sending files to customers and vendors who do not have Inventor. But you notice that when you start a new drawing, it is always an IDW file.

Understand basic principles of parametric design   Parametric design is simply a method design in which you link dimensions and variables to geometry in a way that allows the part to change by modifying the dimensions. The power of this approach lies in the fact that we can design parts, building the intent of their function right into them, as we create the model.

> **Master It**   You need to create a model based on key inputs, and want to see how changing the value of those inputs affects the relationship of the features and parts within the model.

Understand the differences between solid and surface modeling   Over time, as computing technology has progressed, so too has the way that programs approach 3D design. While surface models initially allowed the designer to visualize a design and even manufacture it from digital file, the desire to be able to extract data for calculations concerning mass and center of gravity required a solid model. The need to easily edit and modify designs without having to start over pushed solid modeling to the next step: parametric solid modeling.

> **Master It**   You need to create models that are functionally and esthetically sound.

Develop best practices for using Autodesk Inventor   You were introduced to some of the best practices in using Autodesk Inventor as your design tool. You would do well to review these best practices from time to time as you progress toward mastering this powerful design tool.

> **Master It**   You want to ensure that your implementation of Inventor is successful and in line with industry best practices.

Chapter 2

Data and Projects

In most design and manufacturing environments, teamwork has become a way of life — an essential part of getting a product to market quickly. Intelligent design requires coordination, discipline, and organization, and Inventor allows your team to work smarter rather than harder. Effort expended initially designing an efficient data system not only saves time while designing parts but can also provide safeguards against rework and downstream errors for you as a designer. When working as part of a design team, the value increases exponentially.

In this chapter, you will learn how to:

◆ Create an efficient data file directory structure

◆ Create efficient search paths

◆ Understand how Inventor uses data, library, and Content Center files

◆ Determine the best project type for your work

◆ Create single- and multiuser projects

◆ Evaluate existing parts and assemblies for inclusion in a new design

Creating a Data Structure

All design projects require planning. Part of this planning is to ensure efficient and protected access to your data. Consider where and how you store project data within your computer system. The basic directory structure defines how efficient data access will be. You don't want your design team spending hours redesigning parts because that's faster than locating existing part files. And you don't want to burden your network bandwidth with circuitous searches and repeated file resolutions. Whether you plan to work in multiuser or single-project mode, setting up an Inventor project is a good time to review the file structure that you have used in the past.

Setting Up the Ideal Directory Structure

The ideal directory structure varies based upon the type of work you do: product development, engineer to order, make to order, and so forth. In all cases, the overall goal of a directory structure should be to simplify the file structure and reduce the possibility of placing the same (or similar) file in multiple locations. You also want to create clear paths that separate your workspace from the support data and library files.

SUPPORT FILES

Examine the job-based file directory structure in Figure 2.1. You can see a folder named Engineering. This folder is intended to contain all the files used by the engineering department. Next, look at the three subfolders: 3rd Party Software, Autodesk Service Packs, and CAD files. The first two folders (3rd Party Software and Autodesk Service Packs) are intended for storing and maintaining supporting files for engineering department software.

FIGURE 2.1
Representative job-based
data structure

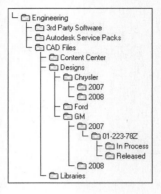

PROJECT DATA FILES

The third subfolder, CAD Files, stores all files related to individual jobs. Inside this subfolder is another folder called Designs. This folder stores all files related to individual jobs that are not part of Content Center or defined as libraries.

Designs

Within the folder called Designs, you may choose to segregate files by customer, then by year, and then individual job, or you can use any other organizational scheme that fits how you design. In the example directory structure, the Ford folder contains a subfolder for the year 2007 and beneath that another for job F150. All files that are unique to job F150 will be stored here. Additional subfolders under this folder are acceptable. Files that are shared between designs are not placed at the design level but instead in library folders.

Library Folders

Library folders contain existing, shared parts and assemblies. Designers find library folders useful as repositories for purchased parts such as fasteners, clamps, motors, connectors, and other common standard components. Library folders are also commonly used to protect designs when files will be shared in whole or in part with another project. When you designate folders as a library folder in the Inventor project, the folders and their contents are handled as read-only files. This prevents the part or assembly from being unintentionally edited or from being revised without appropriate approvals. For example, before you modify a design that was completed as part of another project, you want to determine where else that part was used. The goal is to ensure that the changes you plan will not render the part unusable for other designs.

Library folders should be located outside the main project data path. In the job-based directory structure example earlier, the Libraries folder is on the same directory level as the CAD Files folder. Placing the library folder outside the main project data path allows the path to that folder to be designated as a library path. Library folders can be located anywhere outside the primary project data path, even on different drives or mapped servers.

Content Center Folders

Before talking about Content Center project settings, let's take a moment to understand what Content Center is and how it works. The Content Center libraries are a collection of tabled data containing the definitions for how to create 800,000-plus standard parts and features. This database is managed by the Autodesk Data Management Server (ADMS) where the database libraries can be loaded in part or in full. Once the content libraries are installed in the ADMS, you can use this content in your designs. To do this, you choose a component from the database to place into your design. Understand that it is at this point that the Content Center part file is created. Up until this point, the part existed only as a definition in the database table.

In your project, you need to specify a Content Center file store location. The file store folder will include additional subfolders where Content Center files will be stored once used in your designs. These additional folders are created automatically as parts are created. The next time a part is specified from the Content Center libraries, Inventor first searches the Content Center file store directories and then creates the part from the database only if the part file does not already exist in the file store location. It is required that the Content Center file store location be outside the main project data path. From this discussion of libraries, you can see that high importance is placed on planning the correct part locations and workflow.

USING LIBRARIES

You have designed a new, custom machine or fixture for a customer. The new machine included many new, unique parts. In addition, you have included many purchased parts and components from a previously built machine. The unique parts, assemblies, and drawings were stored in files and folders in the project data path. Purchased parts and the reused components, which were library items, were not included within the project search path but instead remained in the files and folders in the library path or the Content Center subfolder paths.

Several months later, a different customer, having seen the machine on a production line, likes the design so well that they place an order for a similar machine. They would like a few modifications to suit their production needs. At this point, you may consider choosing one of two data structures for the new design: using the Library folder or allowing common files to remain within the current data structure location.

OPTION 1

You can move formerly unique parts that will be shared from the first design into a library and then include the new library path in both the old and new projects. The next time you open the old project assembly, the parts that have been moved to the new library will be located in the newly created library path, requiring resolution of the new location. If the parts are not found in the expected library path, a resolution dialog box appears for the missing parts. If you correctly resolve the new location for the parts, save the assembly, and reopen the assembly, all the parts should now be found.

Moving formerly unique parts into a library subfolder will mark those parts as normally read-only within the defined project. Placing the parts into a library subfolder will prevent unauthorized changes or revisions that would affect the documentation and creation of spare parts that would fit on the original machine design. Care must be taken when reusing parts from one machine to another. Decisions should always be made when revising a part to determine whether that revised part should be a completely new part name or number or whether the revision will fit on every machine that uses the part.

OPTION 2

You can allow the parts to remain in their original locations within the design's subfolder. However, it will be relatively easy to modify or revise that original part to where it will be no longer usable in the original design.

Project Workspace

Workspace settings are largely dependent upon whether you are working in a multiuser or single-user environment. Assuming you are working on a shared network drive in either case, your workspace will likely be located on your local hard drive. The workspace could be considered a temporary scratch area, where new and unique parts will be created and stored until finalized for a particular job or design. Once a part design is finalized, that part can be checked in (when using a multiuser project type) or simply moved/copied to the network file store that mirrors your local file structure (when using a single-user project type). We'll discuss more about project file types and workspaces later in this chapter.

PROJECT SEARCH PATHS

Inventor handles files differently than many other applications. You can think of an Inventor assembly consisting of one or more parts or subassemblies as an empty "bucket" into which parts and subassemblies are placed and assembled. Therefore, the assembly file contains only the file path references of the components it is composed of and the information about how those components are assembled. As a result, the location of referenced files is a key issue. If when opening an assembly referenced files cannot be found at the search path recorded in the assembly file, a manual file resolution process is activated. This happens most often when component files are moved or renamed outside the Inventor utilities dedicated to these tasks.

Upon manually pointing the assembly to the moved or renamed file, the new location is saved into the assembly file, assuming that the lost file is physically present within the search paths. If the file is located outside the project search path, then the File Resolution dialog box appears every time the assembly is opened. For each project, you define the search paths.

The primary search paths for Inventor projects, in order of search priority, are as follows:

◆ Libraries (read-only — absolute path structure)

◆ Workspace (normally, a local, user-specified folder)

◆ Workgroup (permanent storage area for all files except library files — relative path structure)

HOW SEARCH PATHS, PROJECT FILES, AND WORK GROUPS ARE USED

Project files are easy to create and use, provided you understand how Inventor uses them. A project file is a configuration file that lists the locations and functions of each search path. Inventor uses these definitions to resolve file links and locate the files needed for the parts and assemblies on which you want to work. Figure 2.2 shows how Inventor loads assemblies and parts inside an assembly file.

FIGURE 2.2
Inventor File Resolution
Protocol

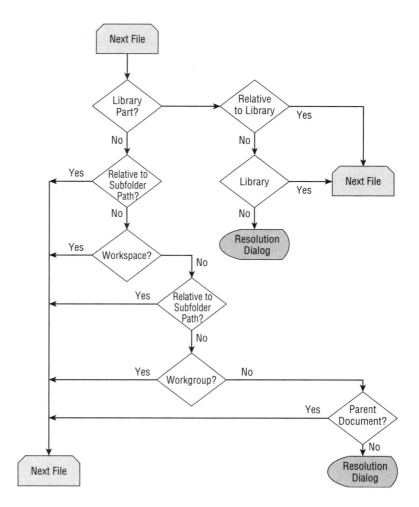

When opening a new assembly file, Inventor resolves files by searching for the first file to be located within the assembly file. Inventor first looks in the library folders for that file. If the file is not located in the library folders, then any related subfolders in the libraries are searched. Next, Inventor searches in the local workspace for the file. If the file is not located in the workspace or in any related subfolders, Inventor checks in the workgroup. If you have multiple workgroups, then the order the workgroups are listed in the project file determines the order in which they are searched. When a file is not found in any of the referenced folders, Inventor launches a manual file resolution dialog box offering you the opportunity to browse and point to the file.

WHEN NOT TO USE WORKGROUPS

Workgroups are not permitted in multiuser projects. In multiuser projects, all unique files will be stored in workspace folders.

Multiple workgroups in single-project files are not recommended for several reasons. They increase the search time when loading a large assembly and encourage you to set up additional folders to access parts in assemblies from other jobs. If parts or assemblies are to be reused, then those parts and/or assemblies should be included in a library folder so all projects have easy access.

MIGRATING FROM AutoCAD

If you are moving to Inventor from AutoCAD, you may want to consider restructuring your existing or future AutoCAD files to include them in the new data management file structure. Please note that this is not a requirement but a recommendation for future use of your AutoCAD legacy files. If you have a large number of AutoCAD files, you may choose to move only the active files into the new structure.

Within this new data management structure, you may choose to create additional folders within the structure in order to store documents, spreadsheets, emails, and other data associated with each particular job.

Preparing Parts for Reuse and Revision

As anyone who has worked in mechanical design knows, at some point in the project revisions will be needed. To protect legacy designs and avoid rework, you want to assign a team member the responsibility for revisions and library updates. Each legacy part revision request must be reviewed to determine where that part or subassembly is (or has been) used. If the proposed revision can be made without harm to any of the legacy designs, the design team reviewer updates the library part. If replacing the existing parts with a revised part causes problems with legacy designs, then the reviewer saves the existing part under a new name and updates that newly named part. This protects the existing part and prevents damage to older designs.

As discussed earlier, the team's goal is to create one unique physical part for each unique part name, with an associated 2D drawing, stored in a single location within the company's data storage system. No duplicate parts or filenames should exist anywhere within the company, except while a part is being revised. If an existing part is edited and saved as a new part name and number in the appropriate library folder, the temporary part is deleted. With this workflow, you are assured that when a part is selected for use in a design, it is the correct part.

Here are some suggested workflows for reusing designs:

Reusing existing designs for standard projects   Figure 2.3 reviews the design team's process for handling existing parts that will be reused for a new design. If the part will be reused, shared parts are moved into a library folder located outside the existing project. The next time the top-level assembly is opened, a File Resolution dialog box requests assistance in locating the moved files. If the data structure is configured correctly and the project file reflects the changes to libraries, files should need to be resolved only once.

FIGURE 2.3
Design use workflow: non-Vault project

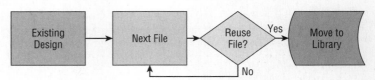

For legacy projects, you need to move the files to be reused into a folder that will be designated as a library folder within the project. Alternatively, you could simply designate the existing machine folder as a library; however, that may cause problems downstream on other designs, because the files placed into the library will be read-only in the new design. Assemblies, for example, would not be editable by adding or removing components.

As a general rule, it is better to move reusable files into a new folder that can be shared among multiple jobs as a library folder. Once these files are moved into a new folder, then the existing machine project file must be edited to include the newly created folder as a library folder location.

Once the existing project file has been properly edited to include the new libraries, the existing assemblies should be opened to verify that all files included in the assemblies may be properly located. If the files cannot be located, the File Resolution dialog box will be displayed, allowing the user to locate the moved files. If the project file was correctly created, this should be necessary only once.

Reusing existing designs for Vault projects   Autodesk Vault is a data management program that assists in the file management aspect of working with Inventor. Using Vault greatly reduces the occurrence of missing or unresolved file links because, unlike moving and renaming Inventor files with Windows Explorer, moving and renaming Inventor files in Vault automatically updates the assembly file so that file links are maintained automatically. When using Vault, it is suggested that you create a single Vault project and store all designs under it. For Vault projects, moving files to a library folder location may not be necessary, although performance can be improved by using designated library folders. Utilizing a single project path approach for all designs will simplify the reuse of files shared between jobs, as illustrated in Figure 2.4.

FIGURE 2.4
Design reuse workflow using Vault project type

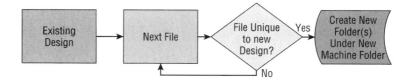

Alternatively, Autodesk Vault contains a command called Copy Design. With the Copy Design approach, you can selectively copy only the parts that need to change to the new design. Other files not copied can remain intact and referenced as fully "reused" components and/or excluded from the new, copied design. Vault's Copy Design tool also accommodates the copying of the detail drawings that accompany the copied parts.

Exploring Project File Types

As mentioned previously, file management in Autodesk Inventor is handled through the use of a project file. A *project file* is simply a configuration file set up and used to control how Inventor creates and resolves file links, where you edit files, how many old versions of the files to keep, and how Content Center files are stored and used. In the early days of Inventor, Autodesk offered two basic project types: single-user and multiuser projects. At this point, the Vault project has replaced the earlier multiuser project types.

In Inventor 2009, unless you have installed Vault, you have only one project type to choose from by default, the single-user project. The name *single-user* could be considered a misnomer, because this project is widely used by one-man shops and multiseat design departments alike. The term *single-user* does not mean that only one user may access the files in that project as it might suggest, but instead it refers to the fact that there are no means of preventing files from being accessed for editing while another user is already editing the file. This can create a "last-man-to-save-wins" situation, if care is not taken.

Many design departments use single-user projects effectively in collaborative environments because of workflows that lend themselves to this type of project or by simply maintaining good communication among the design team. For collaborative environments that require some safeguard against situations where users could potentially save over one another's work, using a Vault project is recommended.

Vault is a data management program that, as the name implies, locks down files for their protection. Once a file is in the Vault, it is checked out by a user in order to be edited. Vault typically resides on a file server where the entire design team can access it. When the file is checked out of the Vault server, it is placed on the user's local machine for editing. The next user who comes along and attempts to access that file can access only a read-only version. Once the first user is finished editing, the file is checked back into the Vault and automatically versioned.

Note that although single-user and Vault projects are the only project types offered by default, legacy multiuser project types can be enabled if required. It is also important to note that Inventor installs with a default project setup. The default project is not to be used for production work because it is not fully configurable and will almost always lead to file resolution issues.

HOW MANY PROJECTS DO YOU NEED?

Although the term *project file* may suggest you need to create a new project file for each job, customer, or machine you work with, this is not the case. Many Inventor users have found that file management is much simpler and accommodating by employing a single project to work with. Using this method, you set up one Inventor project file at the top of your file structure and organize jobs or customers under that via subfolders. It is important to note that you should use unique filenames for all your Inventor files when using one project to manage all your designs.

Creating the Project File

In Inventor 2009, three project file configurations are available: single-user, Vault, and legacy. Vault projects can be enhanced by a replacing the standard Vault product with the optional Productstream product. Two types of legacy projects, shared and semi-isolated, are available but need to be enabled by going to the Application Options dialog box and selecting the Enable Creation Of Legacy Project Types check box on the General tab.

Single-user A single-user project allows a designer to work on a job that is wholly contained on his system or on a network server location. This project file type is the simplest project file type to create and works well when users are not working on the same design concurrently.

Vault Autodesk Vault is an easy-to-use data management tool that integrates work created with Inventor, Inventor Professional, AutoCAD Mechanical, and AutoCAD Electrical. It includes features that allow design teams to track work in progress and maintain version control in a multiuser environment. Design reuse is facilitated by consolidating product information and storing it in one place. Vault is a SQL database environment. A subset of the SQL environment exists in all current Windows operating systems from Windows 2000 through Windows Vista. Vault installs separately from Inventor. The Vault installation checks to make sure that your system is compatible and that auxiliary programs required for operation are installed. Vault is included with all versions of AutoCAD and Inventor.

Productstream   Productstream adds bill of materials (BOM) management, item master, revision control, and engineering change management tools for use in Vault environments. Productstream also allows a relatively easy interface to current ERP/MRP databases. Productstream is an upgrade or add-on to Vault.

Shared (legacy)   Shared projects use network file sharing. They usually are legacy projects that rely on a fast server and on fast network connections. Files are maintained on a server and then opened, edited, and saved to the server when you are done. One disadvantage of using shared project file types is that it creates a heavy load on the server where all data is stored and increased traffic over the network. Inventor support for this project type might be removed in the future.

Semi-isolated (legacy)   Semi-isolated projects are another legacy type. These projects are similar to Vault projects, in that files are checked out from the server and copied to a local workspace for editing. Support for this project file type may be removed from Inventor in the future.

Now, which type of project is best for you?

One or more designers can use projects using Vault. Single-user projects are most commonly used when there is a single seat of Inventor in the company or when only one designer works on a particular job exclusively.

Multiuser Vault projects rely on a Microsoft SQL Server environment, which can be as simple as the Autodesk data management server, which supports up to 10 users with the default Microsoft SQL Server Express database. If you have a larger workgroup or require a higher capacity, a full version of Microsoft SQL Server 2005 is recommended. In addition, a workspace folder located on the individual user's system is required. Data servers should be a separate server with rapid data access hard drives, dedicated to the engineering department use.

Inventor 9 and earlier versions allowed you to create shared and semi-isolated project file types. If you are currently using either legacy project type, then you should consider moving to Vault or Productstream, since Autodesk may not support the legacy types in future versions. Inventor 2009 still includes legacy project types. Legacy project creation is accomplished by selecting Tools ➤ Application Options ➤ General and checking Enable Creation Of Legacy Project Types.

CREATE A GOOD DATA MANAGEMENT PLAN

We cannot stress enough that good data management is the key to using Inventor projects successfully. Using Vault will not resolve a poor project file or data management design. We'll discuss this in greater detail in the next section.

SEAN SAYS: INCLUDE IT IN YOUR HARDWARE AND SERVER DISCUSSIONS

One part of a successful Inventor deployment is the hardware and network on which the software will run. Although sitting down with your IT department sounds about as exciting as watching paint dry, it is important that the engineering group has buy-in by the IT group. You will need to discuss several things with this group including hardware for servers and workstation, the network setup (100 Base-T or Gigabit), mapped network drives, and user permissions.

A good server can be the difference between success and failure in your rollout. A server should have at least RAID 1 (RAID 5 preferable) and as much network bandwidth as possible.

Although you do need to think about your file structure, don't obsess over it. I guarantee you will end up changing the structure at least a few times before you settle on a final structure. Keep an open mind, and realize that if you have five people in a room discussing file structures, you'll end up with five different ideas. Again, involve IT in your discussions.

Finally, you should designate one person in engineering to be the engineering administrator. They need to have administrative privileges on the engineering server or network share. IT may resist; you need to keep pushing. This is important because you will need the ability to easily create, delete, and move files and folders without having to submit a help-desk ticket. Nothing will slow down a design process faster than having to wait for IT to make a simple change. Want to get on their good side? Buy them a random USB-powered object. IT folks love gizmos.

Creating a Single-User Project

Probably the best way to learn about projects is to create a single-user project. Single-user projects allow an individual to open, edit, and save files without checking the files in or out. The single-user project file is normally the choice of people who are working on their own. In the following sections, you will investigate the single-user file project mode. Once you gain an understanding of single-user projects, you will be ready to investigate the other project file options. To get the most out of this exercise, open your version of Inventor, and start the Inventor Project Wizard by going to the File menu and choosing Project. You will use the project file created here for exercises throughout the remainder of this book.

THE INVENTOR PROJECT WIZARD

Ensure that you have no file open in Inventor, and then choose File ➢ Projects to open the project file dialog box. In this dialog box, you will see various project files that were created when you installed the software. Select New. If you installed Vault along with Inventor, you will see two options in the Inventor Project Wizard, as shown in Figure 2.5. Select New Single User Project, and then click Next.

FIGURE 2.5
Creating a single-user project

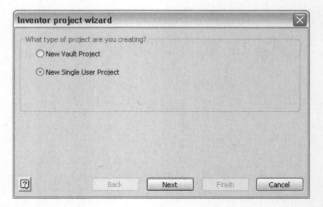

WHERE ARE MY LEGACY PROJECT TYPES?

Legacy shared and semi-isolated projects are not available unless you activated that option on the General tab in Application Options before starting the Inventor Project Wizard.

To facilitate the exercises throughout the remainder of the book, give this project the name Mastering Inventor, and place it in a folder called Mastering Inventor on the root directory of one of your local drives, such as C:\. Figure 2.6 shows a Project File screen specifying the project in C:\Mastering Inventor.

FIGURE 2.6
The Project File screen

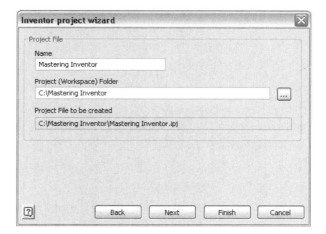

For this exercise, place all folders on a local drive. If you were creating the project in a shared network location, you would specify the workspace folder drive letter as a local drive letter and point your libraries and workgroup locations to the network drive. Once you create a location for the workspace folder, you will see that the project file will be created in that same folder. Click Next to advance to the next screen of the wizard.

If you already created a folder for your library files, and used those library folders in a previous project, those locations will appear on the Select Libraries screen, shown in Figure 2.7. When creating a new project, you can choose to include any or all of the defined library locations in the project.

Click Finish to create and save your new project file. The newly created project file link will appear in the list in the Projects dialog box.

SWITCHING AND EDITING PROJECTS

Only one project can be active at a time. To switch or edit projects, you must first close all files that are open in Inventor.

FIGURE 2.7
Select Libraries screen

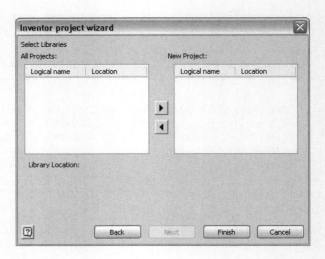

THE PROJECTS DIALOG BOX

Now that you have created your sample project file, you'll explore the options and settings available for your new project. To activate and use your new project, highlight the new project, and click Apply. You can also activate or select a new project link by double-clicking the project link. Notice that the Mastering Inventor project has a check mark next to the project name indicating that the project is now active, as illustrated in Figure 2.8.

FIGURE 2.8
Projects dialog box

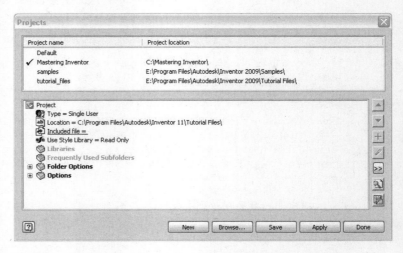

In the lower pane, you can view and access parameter settings for the following:

◆ The project type

◆ Optional included project file

◆ Style library options

- Libraries you want to use

- Frequently used subfolders

- Folder options

- Other project options

Right-click a parameter group to view the settings available within that group.

Within the Project group, you can change the project type, view the project location, and include other project files. Project types were discussed earlier in this chapter. The project location is a read-only parameter. Included files deserve some additional discussion, because the Included File parameter allows you to apply a master project to your current project.

SEAN SAYS: DOUBLE-CLICK THE DESIRED PROJECT

You can start Inventor with the project desired and preselected by double-clicking the project file (IPJ) in Windows Explorer. This loads Inventor with this project activated.

Included Files

Although not required, you can include an existing project in the configuration of the current project by right-clicking Included File. The properties and settings in the project file that you attach override the settings in the current project file. This is useful for restricting and control-ling user abilities to change the project file. Also, if you frequently create new project files, you might consider creating a master project file that contains library locations and other settings you commonly use and then include the master project file in each new project file.

Workspace

A workspace is defined as a folder existing on the local system. This folder contains all the unique files that created under this project. The workspace folder may include several subfolders that contain various aspects of the design. Examples of subfolder types might be parts, assemblies, drawings, or other subfolders as deemed necessary. To expand the project file list so you can view all the entries, click the >> icon from the tool panel on the lower-right side of the Projects dialog box and then highlight Workspace.

Workgroup

The workgroup search path specifies a location outside the current project file paths where Inven-tor can search for existing files that are not included in a library. A workgroup is specified when the project is created. Each single-user project should have a maximum of one workgroup. To expand the project file list so you can view all the entries, click the >> icon from the tool panel on the lower-right side of the Projects dialog box and then highlight Workgroups.

A NOTE ABOUT WORKGROUPS

Workgroups are not allowed in Vault or semi-isolated projects. All multiuser projects operate on the principle of checking out to edit and checking in to save and release for editing by a different user. When a file is checked out, that file is not available for editing until either it has been checked in or the checkout flag is released.

Styles Library

Inventor uses styles to specify dimensions, text, colors, materials, and other properties. This is similar to styles used in AutoCAD. However, Inventor allows you to store styles locally within the templates or in an external style library that may be used with any current or future project file.

The Use Styles Library function in projects specifies whether the project uses only local styles, local styles and the styles library, or just local styles and a read-only version of the styles library. The read-only styles library is recommended for projects where there are multiple users. With multiple users, changing or editing the styles library on the fly can cause downstream problems. To change the Use Styles Library parameter, right-click, and select the new setting.

Remember that for your projects you can right-click to select another option when it is appropriate. Click Yes if you want to be able to edit styles in this project. Click Read-Only (the default) if you want to access styles libraries and local styles without enabling style-editing capabilities. Click No if you want to restrict access to styles located within the current file and project template.

Library Options

Next on the list are libraries. Library folders are located outside the current project file path. They may be located anywhere on your system or on your server. If you are sharing library files, it is recommended that you place them on your server in a commonly accessed location.

In your newly created project file, you have not added any library folders. If at any time you want to add library folders, you can do so by right-clicking Libraries and choosing Add Path, Add Paths From File, or Paste Path, as shown in Figure 2.9.

FIGURE 2.9
Adding library paths by right-clicking

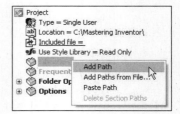

You can manually add a path, either by browsing or by typing a new file location. Be sure to give the library a descriptive name that identifies the contents of that file location. Add Paths From File permits extracting library paths from another project file. Paste Path allows the user to copy and paste. Once you have specified library paths, the Delete Section Paths option becomes available, and you can remove paths not needed by the project. Deleting unused library paths reduces search and resolution time.

Shortcuts to Frequently Used Files

Frequently used subfolders are similar to the bookmarks you can set in Internet Explorer. The subfolders must already be nested within the current project workspace, workgroup, or library. Adding frequently used subfolders to your project provides navigation links in your open, save, and placed dialog boxes so you can quickly navigate to those locations.

Folder Options

The Folder Options setting allows your project to access other file locations than are specified on the Files tab of the Application Options dialog box. Keep in mind that you may have to close and reopen Inventor in order to reinitialize the optional project file locations. You can use this option to specify different default locations for templates, design data, styles, and Content Center files. When the locations are set to the defaults, then the location and storage of the files is specified on the Files tab of the Application Options dialog box. Right-click any of the options to change the storage and access location.

SEAN SAYS: TAKE ADVANTAGE OF FOLDER OPTIONS

Folder options are useful when you have multiple customers or project types. For example, project A might contain title blocks for division A, while project B may contain title blocks for division B.

Project Options

Expand the Options heading to show the global defaults for the selected project. The option settings in a project determine file management functions; right-click an option to edit it.

Versioning and Backup

Use the Options setting to determine how many old versions or backup copies of each file to save. The Old Versions To Keep On The Save option specifies the number of versions to store in the Old Versions folder for each file saved. The first time a file is saved in a project, an Old Versions folder for that file is created. When the file is saved, the prior version is moved automatically to the file's Old Versions folder. After the number of old versions reaches the maximum in the setting, the oldest version is deleted when a newer version is moved into the folder.

INVENTOR OLD VERSIONS AND AUTOCAD .BAK FILES

Inventor versioning is similar AutoCAD's backup scheme. AutoCAD creates a *.BAK file but saves in the same folder as the design. Inventor saves the backup files in a separate directory.

All versions located in the Old Versions folder have the same name and extension, except that a number is appended after the name. The default setting of 1 creates one backup file in the Old Versions folder. If you are working with a very complex assembly or model, you can specify additional backup versions; however, remember that with each additional backup version, you are creating additional files (and using additional space) on your hard drive. Setting Old Versions to -1 will prevent Inventor from creating any backup files.

File Naming Conventions

The listing called Using Unique File Names in the Options is the area that forces the user to create unique part names for all files in the project including subfolders. Libraries are excluded in this option. The recommended setting for using unique filenames is to set this to Yes. Proper design workflow demands that each unique part have a unique name, and that name will not be used for any other part. When parts are reused, care must be taken to ensure that any revision to that part be acceptable to all designs where that part is used. If that revised part cannot be used in all the designs, then a new part name should be used, because you have now created an additional unique part.

Using Unique Filenames set to Yes forces unique filenames for every file you create within the project. Duplicating filenames results in resolution errors because the project search path is a relative path; it's relative to the location of the project file.

PROJECT DIALOG TOOL PANEL

The tool buttons along the right side of the lower pane of the projects dialog box provide access to tools that allow you add, edit, and reorder project parameter settings and paths, check for duplicate filenames, and configure the Content Center libraries used for the active project.

Use the magnifying glass icon located on the lower-right side of the Projects dialog box to check your project paths for duplicate filenames as shown in Figure 2.10.

FIGURE 2.10
Using unique filenames

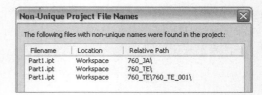

WHY RELATIVE PATHS?

An Inventor assembly file records relative paths when it links a subassembly or single parts to itself. The use of relative paths in assembly files allows the relocation of an assembly and its associated parts and subassemblies to other locations on servers or drives without requiring the resolution of a new location. Relative paths, however, introduce the danger of the assembly locating the first of two parts with the same name, with the second part never been recognized and loaded.

To prevent the possibility of the wrong part being loaded in an assembly, it is important that every part located in the search path has a unique name.

The Project dialog box supports the configuration of one or more Content Center libraries. The Content Center provides multiple database libraries that can be used in assemblies or by the Design Accelerator (Functional Design System).

If you elected to install Content Center libraries while installing Inventor, you must configure the Content Center libraries in the project before you can access them. Click the Content Center icon in the Projects editing dialog box, as shown in Figure 2.11. Then select the Content Center library you want to use, and click OK. Repeat the process for each Content Center library that you want to have available for use with the project.

Select the Content Center libraries you think you'll use. Installing all the Content Center libraries may slow your system down significantly when you are accessing Content Center because Inventor will need to index each library upon initialization.

WHERE ARE MY CONTENT CENTER LIBRARIES?

The ADMS and associated libraries must be installed if you want to use Content Center libraries. A full installation of Autodesk Vault is not required unless you plan to use Vault, but the ADMS portion is required to use Content Center and any of the Inventor utilities that utilize the Content Center libraries, such as the Frame Generator and Design Accelerator Wizards.

FIGURE 2.11
Configuring Content
Center

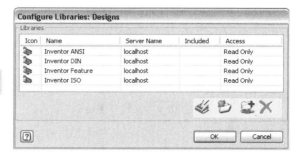

When you finish editing the project file, choose Save, and then make sure your desired project file is active before selecting Done to exit the Project dialog box.

Working in Collaborative Environments

In today's workplace, multiple designers and engineers often work as a team on a single project or job. Some create parts and assemblies, while others edit parts and assemblies, adding tubing and piping, wire harnesses, and control design. Still other users access files for documentation, CNC machining, and other processes. Sometimes you want a single individual to have sole access to the work, but let's look at team projects first. Working as a team can increase productivity many times over.

Imagine that a new, complex machine design is due at a trade show in just three months. It must be running and producing parts. Impossible? Not at all, if multiple users can work together, each assigned a different portion or subassembly within the design. Let's look in on a design team as they prepare to get to work and make it happen.

THE DESIGN TEAM

Bright and early on Monday morning, the design team has its first meeting. If this is a redesign of an existing machine, the design team will have collected all the drawings and production documents from the existing machine. At this point, the design team begins dissecting the various components to establish what portions of the existing machine could be reused in the new design and assigning particular parts or assemblies to individual team members.

If the existing machine has already been modeled in either Mechanical Desktop or Inventor, the design team will decide which portions (parts, assemblies, or subassemblies) need to be moved into the new library for read-only access during the new design.

By Tuesday, the design team should have identified the existing parts that will be used in the new machine. If the team will be working in a single-user, shared, or semi-isolated project structure, they will have moved those parts into a designated library folder or folders. These library parts and subassemblies may now be shared in the design without running the risk that modifications to any reused parts will affect legacy designs.

If the design team is working in a Vault project, the legacy files do not need to be moved. Vault uses library files differently, accessing without altering them. A single project path approach can be implemented without fear of affecting legacy designs.

By Wednesday, the design team is well on its way toward creating unique parts for the new machine. The marriage of these unique parts and the legacy parts and subassemblies creates the new machine design.

Creating a Multiuser Project

Working as a team can increase productivity many times over. In a collaborative design environment, multiple users may be working on a project at the same time. When you create a multiuser project, you have the option to choose the Vault (if Vault is installed), shared, and semi-isolated project types. As stated before, Vault works in a similar fashion to a semi-isolated project. It prevents you from working on the original version of a file located inside the Vault. Each user creates a local Vault project file that specifies a personal workspace located on the local drive and that includes search paths to one or more master projects.

To edit a Vaulted file, the user must check the file out of the Vault. The process of checking the file out copies the file to the local workspace. Whenever the file is checked out for editing, the original stored in the Vault is flagged as "checked out" to that particular user. Other users may view the checked-out files in read-only mode; they are unable to edit the checked-out file.

The user, who checked out the file, may edit and save the file in his local workspace without checking the file back into the Vault. When he saves the file, he will be prompted to choose whether he wants to check the file back into the Vault. If he chooses to check the file into the Vault, the file will be saved into the Vault and is then available for editing by a different user. Optionally, he may save the file into the Vault but keep it checked out to his local workspace, allowing other users to view the updated file without being able to edit it.

Collaborative design project files are created using the Inventor Project Wizard, in much the same manner as a single-user project file. The file resolution process within a collaborative project file functions in the same way.

A VAULT PROJECT

With Vault installed on your server or single system, you can create and configure a Vault project. If Vault Explorer is not installed on your system, then you cannot install or create a Vault project on your system. Before you create your first Vault project, verify that Vault is correctly installed and that you can open and create a new Vault file store using the ADMS console. The new Vault file store must be accessible on your local system from Vault Explorer. If Vault functions correctly, you are now ready to create a Vault project file. As with a single-user project, use the Inventor Project Wizard to name the project, specify the workspace, assign libraries for use with the project, and configure project parameters.

Choose Finish. Again, as in other project file types, you will need to edit the default settings in your project file and optionally configure your Content Center for use.

A SHARED PROJECT

Shared projects use network file sharing. Files are maintained on a server and then opened, edited, and saved to the server when you are done. To create a shared project, you must first enable legacy projects. Check Enable Creation Of Legacy Project Types on the General tab of the Application Options dialog box. Once you have enabled legacy projects, you can launch the Inventor Project Wizard and choose New Shared Project from the list, as shown in Figure 2.12.

For shared projects, notice that the new project file appears in a project workgroup folder on the drive you specify. Figure 2.13 shows the creation of a shared project.

As with a single-user project, select the libraries you want to have available in the project, and then choose Finish to access project parameters you can edit. Follow any onscreen prompts, and create the workgroup file location for your project. To complete the configuration of a shared project file, adjust the default settings to meet your project needs.

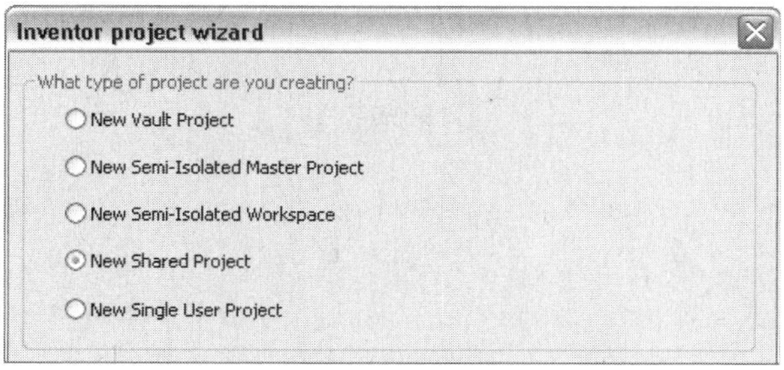

FIGURE 2.12
The project type page

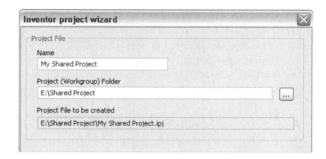

FIGURE 2.13
The project name and
location page

Just as in the single-project file creation exercise, leave Use Style Library set to Read-Only. Remember that you can right-click to select another option if it is appropriate for your project. Choose Save to save the newly created project.

SEMI-ISOLATED PROJECTS

Semi-isolated projects are stored on a server. However, in semi-isolated mode, a local workspace folder is created on each user's hard drive. When a user opens a part or assembly to edit that file, the file is checked out to that user and copied down to the user's workspace folder. The old copy of the file located on the server is flagged as checked out to the user. Other users can view the older version on the server, or the newer version, if the user has checked the file back in to the server. However, other users cannot edit the file until it is checked back in by the original user.

Semi-isolated projects may be problematic in certain environments. For this reason, using semi-isolated projects is no longer recommended. If you want to use the workflow contained in the semi-isolated mode, we recommend considering Vault instead. The workflow in Vault is virtually identical to the semi-isolated project type.

Creating a semi-isolated project is a two-step procedure. First, you must create a new semi-isolated master project. When the Inventor Project Wizard opens, note that there are two options for semi-isolated projects. Be sure to select the master project. Second, select New in the Projects window to create a new project file. In the Inventor Project Wizard, select New Semi-Isolated Master Project, as shown in Figure 2.14. Click Next.

Again, as in other project file types, name your project, and then specify a location for the project file. This is normally in the root directory of your project folder. When the project name and folder location have been specified, click Next. Add any libraries you want to have available for the project, and then click Finish. In the projects folder, select this new semi-isolated project that you have created, and double-click to make it active. Configure the project

FIGURE 2.14
Creating the new semi-isolated master project

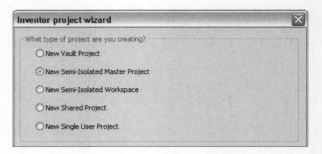

SEAN SAYS: CREATE A SEMI-ISOLATED PROJECT

Before starting a Vault project, you might want to investigate the workflow by creating a semi-isolated project. The workflows are similar, and semi-isolated projects are easier to create. If you find that the semi-isolated workflow works in your company, you might want to further investigate Vault.

SEMI-ISOLATED WORKSPACE

Once the master project is in place, a local semi-isolated workspace must be created on each client computer for each user. To create the workspace, choose New from the Projects dialog box and create a new project file specifically for the purpose of identifying the local workspace.

Using the semi-isolated project file approach, you check files out of the master project location, and they are copied down to the semi-isolated workspace for work. When you check the files back in, the completed files are copied back to the master project.

Give your workspace project file a name. Be descriptive. Then select a location for your workspace on one of your local drives. Enter the location into the box marked Project (Workspace) Folder. Browse to the location of your master semi-isolated project file, and select the master project file .ipj file that will control your project, as shown in Figure 2.15.

FIGURE 2.15
Add the semi-isolated master workspace location

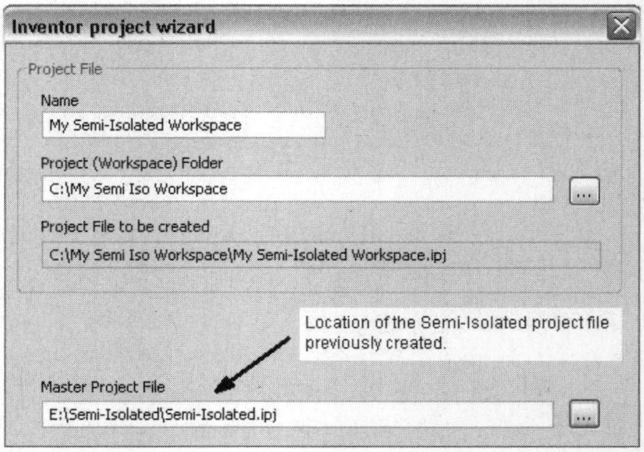

When you finish, check the Included File entry in the lower pane of the Projects dialog box. Be sure it shows that the master semi-isolated project file is included, as shown in Figure 2.16. The dialog box for this file overrides any settings for the semi-isolated workspace.

FIGURE 2.16
The workspace includes the master semi-isolated project file.

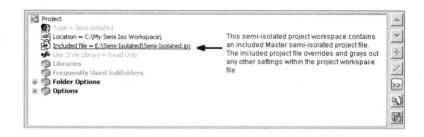

The Bottom Line

Create an efficient data file directory structure Create clear paths for support, data, and library files. Be sure to support a unique filename for each assembly and part.

> **Master It** Earlier in the chapter, you looked at a sample job-based directory structure. Now, consider a directory structure for a product-type-based directory structure to serve customers in the automotive industries. Create a directory structure.

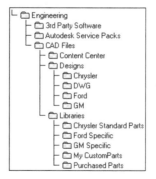

Create efficient search paths Keep your search paths isolated. For instance, keep libraries in the library path, data in the project path, and so on. Organize and group your library parts into logical folders without duplication. Make it easy to find and maintain unique parts.

> **Master It** Consider the location of the libraries in the following directory structure. How is this structure inefficient? Why is it more likely that duplicate parts will be created? How would you improve the search paths in this directory structure?

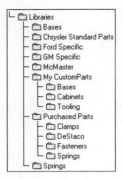

Understand how Inventor uses data, library, and Content Center files   Your project file is a XML file that lists the locations and functions of each search path. Part loads and searches begin in the library search path, then move to the local workspace, and finally move to any workgroups. Keep your paths simple to reduce search and load times. Use library files to share designs and automatically protect parts and assemblies from inadvertent revision.

Master It   What are the advantages of library files?

Determine the best project type for your work   These include the following:

Single-user projects: Single-seat or single-designer projects.

Vault projects: Single- or multiple designer workflows to track work, maintain version control, and facilitate design reuse.

Productstream: Replaces Vault and adds BOM management, item master, revision control, and change management tools to Vault type projects.

Shared projects: Require fast server and fast network connections. Legacy project support that may not be continued.

Semi-isolated projects: Similar to Vault projects, but without the advantage of database searches and management.

Master It   For a complex product that will be worked on by several design teams and updated twice a year for the next five years, which project type would you choose?

Create single- and multiuser projects   Use the Inventor Project Wizard. Customize the default settings for your work. Include only the paths and files you expect to use. You can always add more later as needed. Use a master project if you frequently create similar projects.

Master It   Why not include every library and data file in your project? What is the benefit of including a master project file?

Evaluate existing parts and assemblies for inclusion in a new design   Be methodical and thorough. Make sure that any changes made to the existing parts or assemblies will not adversely affect other products. Always consider where exiting parts and assemblies are used before revising them.

Master It   What would you do if you needed to make minor changes to an existing part for it to be used in your new project, but the changes would make the part unusable in some of the previous designs that use the same part?

Chapter 3

Sketch Techniques

This chapter will cover the principles of creating parametric sketches used in part or assembly modeling. All the skills in this chapter are based primarily on creating a single part, whether in a single part file or in the context of an assembly file.

Autodesk Inventor utilizes two types of sketches: the *2D sketch* that is created on any planar geometry and the *3D sketch* that can be created in any manner within the 3D environment. Both 2D and 3D sketches are controlled by dimensions and what we call *sketch constraints*.

As you will see in the coming pages, when you place dimensions in a sketch, the dimensions dictate the length, size, and angle of the sketch geometry. For the dimensions to do this predictably, sketch objects must know how to interact with one another. You define the interaction by placing sketch constraints on the geometry so that they know how to behave. Although the concept of dimensions driving line work may seem a bit foreign at first, you will soon come to enjoy this powerful concept.

In this chapter, you will learn how to:

Create a new part file from a template

Preserve model design intent

Perform the basic 2D sketching process

Import and convert AutoCAD drawings to Inventor sketches

Create 3D sketches in a part file

Application Options and Settings for Parts and Sketches

Before you jump into creating a part, let's look at some settings for sketches and parts. Options and settings in part files are located in different areas of Inventor depending upon whether the focus of these settings affects the application or the document. You can find the settings that control how Inventor handles all files by selecting Tools ➢ Application Options and then going to the Sketch and Part tabs in the Application Options dialog box. You can find the settings that are controlled on a per-file basis by selecting Tools ➢ Document Settings.

We'll first explore the Sketch tab of the Application Options dialog box. As shown in Figure 3.1, you can use the settings on the Sketch tab to configure how Inventor will create and manage sketches.

FIGURE 3.1
Sketch tab of Application Options dialog box

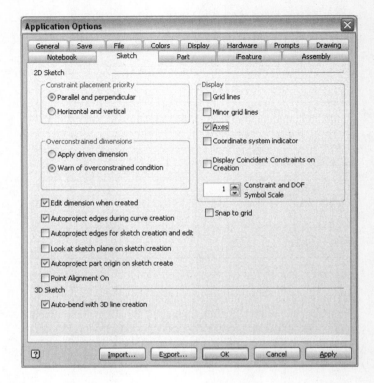

The following are the settings:

◆ The Constraint Placement Priority section determines the primary method of in-context constraint placement. Remember that in Inventor your line work employs sketch constraints to tell lines, arcs, and circles how to interact with one another. *In-context constraints* are simply automatic sketch constraints that are placed while you sketch based upon the existing geometry. The default setting will place priorities on applying parallel and perpendicular constraints while sketching. Note that if you have used Autodesk Mechanical Desktop, this is a different priority than was used in that program. There, the application priority was Horizontal And Vertical. For this lesson, leave the Parallel And Perpendicular setting selected. Holding down the Ctrl key as you sketch will suppress in-context constraint placement. For instance, if you are sketching a line that is running very close to being parallel to an existing line, you might hold down Ctrl as you sketch the line so that Inventor does not automatically constrain the line parallel to the existing line, thereby allowing you to easily place a dimension of some slight angle on the new line.

◆ The Over-constrained Dimensions area controls the way duplicate, reference, and redundant dimensions are handled in sketches. As an example, if you sketch a line of approximately 4 inches and allow Inventor to place an in-context, horizontal constraint on this line as you sketch, then you can place a dimension on the line and set the dimension to be precisely 4 inches. As a result, the line will stretch horizontally to be 4 inches. But if you apply another dimension to the line, Inventor will warn you of the overconstrained situation and ask you to make a choice to either apply the dimension as a driven dimension (think reference dimension) or cancel the dimension.

◆ The Display area in the upper-right portion of the Sketch tab gives you settings for grid lines, minor grid lines, axes, and a 2D coordinate system indicator. All of these options set different visual references in the form of grid lines and coordinate indicators. For this book, uncheck all except for the Axes box. This will ensure that your screen matches the illustrations in this chapter.

◆ The Display Coincident Constraints On Creation check box, if selected, displays a yellow dot at all sketch points where coincident constraints are placed while sketching. If the check box is not selected, these coincident symbols can still be displayed by using the F8 (Show All Constraints) button while in a sketch.

◆ The Constraint And DOF Symbol Scale setting simply controls the size of the icons present when viewing sketch constraints. Leave this setting at the default of 1.

◆ The Snap To Grid check box allows your cursor to snap to a predefined grid spacing. The grid spacing is controlled per file in the document's settings, as will be discussed in the coming pages. Again, leave this setting unchecked.

◆ The Edit Dimension When Created box permits immediate input of a dimension value while applying sketch dimensions. Ensure that this box is checked.

◆ The Autoproject Edges During Curve Creation option allows you to reference geometry that exists from your sketch plane and have that geometry automatically included in your sketch. As an example, if you sketch on the top face of a cube that has a hole on the bottom face, you might want to find the center of the hole to reference in your sketch, but since that hole exists on a different plane, it needs to be projected up into your sketch before you can do so. Enabling this option allows you to dimension to the hole center and have it automatically projected as you do. Ensure that this check box is selected.

◆ The Autoproject Edges For Sketch Creation And Edit check box will automatically project the edges of the face that you create a sketch on. Although this can be convenient in some cases, it can also become counterproductive because it places extra line work into your sketches. This can add a level of complexity to your sketches that is not required. Figure 3.2 shows the results of having this option on. You will want to uncheck this box for these exercises.

FIGURE 3.2
Results of Autoproject Edges For Sketch Creation And Edit check box being selected

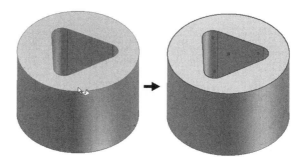

♦ The Look At Sketch Plane On Sketch Creation option reorients the graphics window so that you are always looking perpendicular to the sketch plan while creating or editing a sketch. The exercises in this book will assume this is not selected, but you may find that it is your preference to select this.

♦ The Autoproject Part Origin On Sketch Create setting will automatically project the part's origin centerpoint whenever a new sketch is created. By *origin centerpoint*, we mean the point that is zero in the X, Y, and Z directions. Projection of this point makes it easy to constrain and anchor your sketch, so proceed with this option checked.

♦ The Point Alignment On setting allows endpoints and midpoints to be inferred by displaying temporary, dotted lines to assist in lining up sketch entities. Figure 3.3 shows an endpoint being located using the Point Alignment option. If you've used AutoCAD, this is much like using the polar tracking option. You can experiment with this setting and see whether it fits your preference.

FIGURE 3.3
Point alignment inferring endpoint

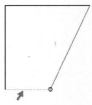

Next we'll look at the Part tab (Figure 3.4) found by selecting Tools ➤ Application Options.

FIGURE 3.4
The Part tab in Application Options

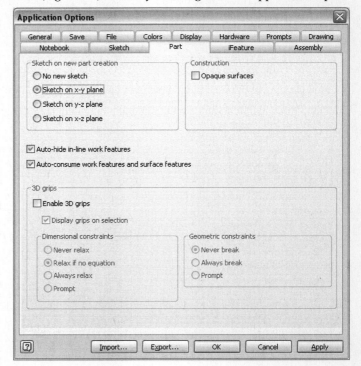

Here are the settings:

◆ The Sketch On New Part Creation area in the upper left of this tab determines the sketch plane on which the original sketch (Sketch1) will be created. Most users of Inventor utilize the XY plane for their initial sketch. Note that if this setting is switched to No New Sketch, Sketch1 is not automatically created for you. Instead, you are left to create a new sketch and specify the origin plane on which you want to sketch. You can leave this set to use the XY plane for your initial sketch.

◆ The 3D Grips area at the bottom of the Part tab controls the use and settings of 3D grips. 3D grips allow you to click a face and modify features by simply gripping them and dragging the grip to resize the feature. Although this may seem like a great way to quickly mod-ify your parts, it is important to understand the negative impact that 3D grips can have on your sketches. Because sketches are created with dimensions and sketch constraints to define and control geometry, 3D grips must "relax" these parameters in order to allow you to grip edit a feature. Typically we strive to create very well-defined and properly con-strained sketches so that our models can be edited precisely and with predictable results. Using 3D grips often works against that effort. Therefore, we recommend that you turn off this feature until you have a very strong familiarity with creating and editing Inventor sketches. And by then, as is the case with most seasoned Inventor users, you will probably see that there is very little to be gained by using 3D grips as a shortcut to editing your parts.

The remaining three options do not concern sketching, but here is a brief description of what they do:

◆ The Opaque Surfaces setting toggles the appearance of any new surface from a translucent surface that you can see through to an opaque surface.

◆ The Auto Hide In-line Work Features check box allows automatic hiding of a work feature when it is consumed by another work feature. For instance, if you create a work plane by picking a work axis and a work point, the work axis and work point will be stacked under the work plane in the browser.

◆ The Auto-consume Work Features And Surface Features check box allows Inventor to con-sume surfaces when converted to a solid, in addition to consuming work features. This keeps the browser clean and organized when working with surceases.

Creating a New Part File from a Template

Creating a 3D parametric model is vastly different from working in 2D, or even with a static 3D surface or with solid modeling. In parametric feature-based modeling, a part is composed of a series of parametric features, each describing a different segment of the part being designed. Figure 3.5 illustrates the basic steps required to create a feature-based parametric part and to document that part in a 2D drawing. This workflow will be repeated in every part you create.

Like most applications today, Inventor uses templates to create new files. However, Inventor handles this task a bit differently than what you may be accustomed to doing. Instead of des-ignating files as templates by using a unique file extension, Inventor designates a directory as a template directory and then considers all files in that directory and subdirectories to be templates. Templates are an important part of a good workflow because they allow you to begin with a con-sistent start point and because they prevent you from accidentally saving over files that you might otherwise use as start points for new work.

FIGURE 3.5
Basic workflow steps to
create and document a
part

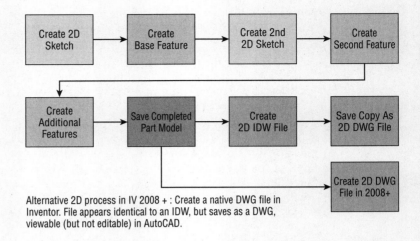

Alternative 2D process in IV 2008 + : Create a native DWG file in
Inventor. File appears identical to an IDW, but saves as a DWG,
viewable (but not editable) in AutoCAD.

Begin by making sure that your active project is the Mastering Inventor project (`Mastering Inventor.ipj`) that you created in the previous chapter and then create a new part file from a template. Select New in the Inventor File menu. For this first example, you will be creating an inch-based part file from the `Standard.ipt` part icon on the Default tab, as shown in Figure 3.6. This assumes that upon installation of Inventor, you have selected ANSI – Inch as your default standard. If you have configured for a different standard, then select `Standard.ipt` from the English tab, because this will also be an inch-based part.

FIGURE 3.6
Selecting a part file
template

If you are creating a metric-based part, you will select the Metric tab in the New File dialog box and select a millimeter-based `Standard.ipt` template. Internally, Inventor stores all data in centimeter units; however, you can set the unit of measure by selecting Tools ➤ Document Settings. Any file can have its units changed after creation by editing these document settings.

After you have selected the proper template and clicked OK, your screen should appear as shown in Figure 3.7.

FIGURE 3.7
Part file with Sketch1 active

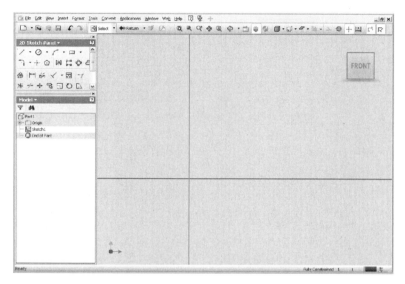

Preserving Design Intent

One of the most powerful benefits to using any 3D modeler is the ability to capture something called *design intent*. So you can better understand the concept of design intent, we'll start with a basic definition: design intent is the intellectual arrangement of features and dimensions of a design. Design intent governs the relationship between features in a part and parts in assemblies. The intent of each component of a design is to work as a solution to the final design problem.

Manual designs on paper or two-dimensional CAD do not preserve design intent beyond recording geometry and dimensional data. 3D model geometry is a virtual representation that associates design data with the actual creation of a physical part. Parametric feature data may be retrieved and modified at any time and be reflected within the complete assembly.

The preserved design intent within a complete assembly permits the use of a virtual design instead of creating actual prototypes. The preservation of design intent in sketching requires that all parametric dimensions and geometric constraints be fully utilized within each sketch. Using shortcuts and failing to fully constrain each sketch may jeopardize design intent.

SEAN SAYS: THINK ABOUT DESIGN INTENT IN YOUR MODELS

Design intent is an important concept in parametric solid modeling design. It is simple to create a 3D model, but it takes some forethought and extra steps to create a model that preserves design intent. This extra time will pay off when you or a co-worker needs to edit the model in the future.

Design intent is the act of capturing intelligence in your model by means of geometric and mathematical relationships that define the fit and function of the part.

Let's look at a simple example. Say you want to create a part that is 2 inches wide and then want to place a hole in the center of the part. There are two basic approaches.

◆ Place the hole 1 inch from an edge of the part.

◆ Place the hole on a parametric midplane of the part.

Both workflows produce the same result, and both are valid; however, they have two distinctly different design intents. The intent of the first method is to place the hole 1 inch from a side of the part (when the part is 2 inches wide, it will be 1 inch from either side). If the part becomes wider as a consequence of downstream design changes, the hole will remain 1 inch from the edge and hence will not be centered.

The second workflow keeps the hole in the center of the part. Regardless of the width of the part, the hole will remain in the center.

By expressing design intent in your part models, you not only create more robust models that withstand downstream changes to the design, but you also give others who might use these models an insight into your thinking process. You express, through dimensions, formulas, and geometric constraints, what is important and what "rules" must be followed. Encourage everyone in your design team to use these design intent guidelines, and I'm certain your projects will flow a bit more smoothly.

Creating a Basic 2D Sketch

When creating a part, we almost always start with a 2D sketch. Sketching in a 3D modeler is a very different process than you may be accustomed to using a 2D CAD program. In the 2D program, emphasis is on creating accurate geometry sized to the exact dimensions of the finished part from the outset. In Inventor and most parametric modelers, we focus on the basic geometry and then work toward a precise model.

For this example, you will employ a technique more closely resembling paper napkin sketching in which you create a simple sketch initially devoid of dimensions or accurate geometry. Sketching in this manner is simple and much faster than inputting precise values. Precise values are not needed at this point because adding parametric dimensions as you complete the sketch will bring precision. It is worth mentioning that Inventor does have an interface for drawing precisely as you might in a 2D drafting package; however, it is typically used only in special circumstances. In virtually any 3D modeler, creating a simple sketch is better than creating a complex sketch showing all the geometry that would normally be in a 2D drawing view. Performance, stability, and ease of future editing will be enhanced by simplifying sketches and eliminating detail within the sketch that will be included in future sketches. The details that are eliminated in the first sketch will be added to multiple future sketches in order to record the design intent within the part.

You should add sketch objects such as fillets, chamfers, hole features, and the like to a part as part features instead of creating those features in sketches. Your workflow should be to simplify each portion of part feature creation, adding multiple part features that can be individually edited or controlled.

Sketched or placed part features may be modified, deleted, suppressed, or reordered depending upon the need of the designer.

SHARING A SKETCH FOR USE IN MULTIPLE FEATURES

Although building features on individual sketches is a good basic workflow, there is a more advanced technique you can use. By placing the sketch geometry for multiple features in one master base sketch and then sharing the sketch, you have the ability to easily modify the part by editing one sketch. To share a sketch, simply right-click on the sketch in the browser after the first feature from it is created. Although this technique can cause problems if the sketch has not been properly dimensioned and constrained, a solid base sketch can easily be edited and allow changes to multiple features simultaneously. This technique has the distinct advantage of preserving design intent to the fullest extent.

Exploring the 2D Sketch Commands

Users moving from a 2D drawing package such as AutoCAD will find that the commands are similar to the basic 2D objects. Some hotkeys, such as L for line and C for circle, are still available. Object snaps are active and embedded within each command. For some commands, right-clicking during the command will permit you to set optional, temporary object snaps.

When viewing the commands within the 2D Sketch panel, you will notice that some commands or icons will have a small downward arrow next to the command indicating that there are additional commands hidden below the primary. It is also possible to display the commands with or without the corresponding text descriptors by right-clicking anywhere on the tool panel. Figure 3.8 shows the hidden icons in both display modes.

FIGURE 3.8
Display text with and
without icons

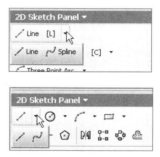

Here's a list of the available 2D sketch commands in Inventor 2009 and a short description of what each command does:

- ◆ Line permits the construction of a line between two picked points.

- ◆ Spline permits the creation of a NURBS-based spline by picking various vertex points. In a 2D sketch, these points must be created on the current plane.

- ◆ Center Point Circle creates a circle by specifying the centerpoint and a point defining the diameter.

- ◆ Tangent Circle creates a circle tangent to three selected lines, with the diameter defined by the boundaries of all three lines.

- ◆ Ellipse creates an ellipse defined by picking the centerpoint, a major axis point, and a minor axis point.

- ◆ Three Point Arc defines an arc by picking both endpoints and selecting a direction curve.

- ◆ Tangent Arc creates a tangent arc between two lines or curves.

- ◆ Center Point Arc creates an arc by defining the centerpoint and both endpoints.

- ◆ Two Point Rectangle defines a rectangle by selecting the diagonal corner points of the rectangle. The rectangle will have a horizontal/vertical orientation.

- ◆ Three Point Rectangle defines a rectangle with the first two points setting the length and direction of the first side and the third point setting the length of the adjacent side. The rectangle can be drawn at any angle orientation.

- ◆ Fillet allows the creation of a dimensioned sketch fillet. This command should be used sparingly, because it is better to create a fillet feature and keep the sketch as simple as possible.

- ◆ Chamfer allows the creation of a chamfer between two lines. Like the Fillet command, chamfers are best applied as part features rather than in the sketch.

- ◆ Point, Center Point creates either a simple point consisting of a dot or a centerpoint consisting of a dot and center cross. Centerpoints define hole centers. Use the Center Point tool on the Standard toolbar to switch between point styles.

- ◆ Polygon creates a multisided polygon inscribed or circumscribed about a reference circle or arc.

- ◆ Mirror mirrors selected sketch objects around a centerline and applies symmetric constraints between the objects.

- ◆ Rectangular Pattern creates a rectangular pattern or array defined by two edges.

- ◆ Circular Pattern creates a circular pattern defined by a distance and a centerpoint.

- ◆ Offset offsets a sketch object or closed loop.

- ◆ Place Feature places a predefined feature from Content Center.

- ◆ General Dimension allows you to place parametric dimensions such as linear, angular, radius, dimension, or aligned, replacing multiple dimension tools.

- ◆ Auto Dimension allows automatic placement of dimensions and geometric constraints in an effort to fully dimension and constrain a sketch.

- ◆ 2D Constraints places geometric relationships on sketch entities used to join multiple sketch objects together with certain characteristics. Constraints will be discussed in full later in the chapter.

- ◆ Show Constraints allows the individual selection of sketch objects to display related geometric constraints.

- ◆ Extend extends a 2D object to the next intersecting object. Pressing the Ctrl key allows the selection of a different boundary. Pressing the Shift key converts the Extend command into the Trim command.

- ◆ Trim trims a sketch object between intersecting objects. Pressing the Shift key converts the Trim command into the Extend command.

- ◆ Split converts a single sketch object into two objects by breaking the object at an intersection point.

- ◆ Move moves an underconstrained sketch object. Options permit copy and precise movement.

- ◆ Copy copies a sketch object for placement in another location.

◆ Scale scales a sketch object by scale factor or dynamically.

◆ Rotate rotates a selected sketch object around a reference point.

◆ Stretch stretches a selected sketch object around a reference point.

◆ Project Geometry copies an existing edge, work feature, or object to the active sketch. Options are available on the pulldown menu.

◆ Parameters displays the Parameters dialog box showing parameter names and values.

◆ Insert AutoCAD File allows insertion of a 2D AutoCAD drawing into the active sketch. You can also do this by using Copy and Paste.

◆ Text permits the placement of text objects into the active sketch.

◆ Geometry Text permits the alignment of sketch text along geometry such as arcs and circles.

◆ Insert Image permits the insertion of images in various formats into an active sketch for use as a reference or to create a decal.

◆ Edit Coordinate System permits the realignment of the sketch coordinate system. This is not generally recommended for frequent usage.

◆ Import Points allows the insertion of points via a Microsoft Excel spreadsheet.

WHEN TO USE SKETCH FEATURES

Although many tools are available in the sketch environment, some should be used with caution.

Fillets and chamfers should be placed as features whenever possible. Rectangular and circular arrays (known as patterns in Inventor) should also be placed as features. In these scenarios, simply create a sketch of one of the elements, turn it into a feature, and then pattern that feature.

You should also be careful when using the Auto Dimension tool. Although it will quickly fully constrain your sketch, it will not do so in a manner that preserves your design intent.

Using Sketch Object Modifiers

Sketch object modifiers are located on the top right edge of the standard toolbar, as shown in Figure 3.9. These icons are utilized to modify sketch objects prior to creation or to modify preselected existing sketch objects.

FIGURE 3.9
Sketch modifiers

Here are the modifiers:

◆ The Construction Line toggle controls the creation of construction linetypes. Construction lines are used in sketching where you required some geometry that you do not want to be part of your profile. Construction lines are filtered out of profile detection. For instance, if you have a circle with a construction line bisecting it, Inventor will ignore the line and consider only the circle for creating a solid.

- The Centerline toggle converts a standard line into a centerline. Centerlines are used to define symmetrical objects. By default, dimensioning to a centerline will produce a diametric dimension rather than a linear dimension.

- The Point toggle converts a point, from a centerpoint into a simple point, and vice versa. Centerpoints are typically automatically detected by the Hole command, whereas simple points are not.

- The Driven Dimension toggle switches a dimension from a dimension that drives the length, location, size, and orientation of sketch geometry to a dimension that simply reports or references the length, location, size and orientation of sketch geometry, or vice versa.

- The Constraint Inference toggle activates or deactivates inferred constraints. An *inferred* constraint is a term describing sketch constraints that are automatically applied as you sketch. An alternative to using the toggle is to press the Ctrl key while placing sketch objects.

- The Point Alignment toggle allows or disallows endpoints and midpoints to be inferred by displaying temporary, dotted lines to assist in lining up sketch entities. As with constraint inference, you can suppress this option during a command by holding the Ctrl key down.

Setting Sketch Constraints and Dimensions

Sketch constraints are simply attributes that define a sketch object or the relationship that the sketch object has with other sketch objects. Sketch constraints can be placed manually or automatically as you sketch. Automatic constraints are often called *in-context constraints*. When creating in-context constraints, a visual marker, or *glyph*, will appear next to the cursor as you add sketch objects. If you pick a point while the glyph is visible, then that geometric constraint will be added to the sketch object. No matter whether created automatically or manually, once they're created, all sketch constraints can be removed from the geometry to which they refer.

The recommended process for creating a fully constrained and dimensioned sketch is to first apply geometric constraints and then apply parametric dimensions. The geometric constraints control or lock down the shape of the sketch, while the dimensional constraints control the size of the geometry.

Types of geometric constraints in Inventor include the following:

- Perpendicular: Objects are constrained perpendicular to other objects.

- Parallel: Objects are constrained parallel to other objects or edges.

- Tangent: Objects are placed tangent to another object or edge. Objects can be tangent to another even if they do not physically share a point.

- Smooth: This creates a continuous curvature (G2) condition between a spline and another sketch object, such as a line, arc, or spline. The G2 condition brings the curve out past the tangency point to create a smooth transition from one curve into the next.

- Coincident: Objects or points are placed in contact with another object.

- Concentric: Arcs and circles are placed so that they share the same centerpoint.

- Collinear: A line object or ellipse axis is placed to lie on the same line as another line object or ellipse axis.

♦ Equal: This makes two objects equal in length or radius.

♦ Horizontal: This makes an object line up parallel to the x-axis. Two points may also line up horizontally.

♦ Vertical: This makes an object line up parallel to the y-axis. Two points may also line up vertically.

♦ Fix: This anchors any geometry or point in place within the part sketch. This constraint should be used sparingly.

♦ Symmetry: This creates a "mirror" constraint between two similar objects. This constraint relies upon a line to serve as a centerline about which objects are to be symmetrical.

Now that we have discussed sketch commands, modifiers, and constraints, we'll show how to create a sketch. Select the Line command from the 2D Sketch Panel. Move your cursor to the graphics window, and click a point in the top-left quadrant of the screen. Release the mouse button; move your cursor to the right in a somewhat horizontal position; and without picking, drag your cursor left and right and up and down slowly.

When you move the cursor into a position that is horizontal to the first point you clicked, you will see a horizontal constraint glyph near the cursor, as shown in Figure 3.10.

FIGURE 3.10
Sketching a line with a
horizontal constraint

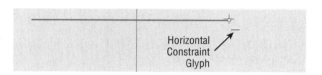

Click a point in the upper-right quadrant, while the horizontal glyph is showing. You have just created a horizontal line, placing an automatic, or in-context, constraint. Continue the line down at an angle to the right and then click to create an angled line at approximately 45°. At this point, the length of the geometry you have created does not matter. In Figure 3.11, you will notice that as you create the angled line, no constraint glyph is showing.

FIGURE 3.11
Sketching a line with no
horizontal constraint

Continue to create line geometry by dragging the cursor directly downward from the last point selected. You will notice that another constraint glyph appears showing that it will add a perpendicular constraint relationship between the top horizontal line and the vertical line you are currently creating. While the glyph is still showing, click a point in the lower-right quadrant to create the line, as shown in Figure 3.12.

You can disable the in-context placement of any constraint by holding down the Ctrl key while creating the sketch object. The glyph will disappear indicating that a constraint will not be attached to the object. If you want to change the focus of the in-context constraint from one existing geometry object to another, you simply move, or *scrub*, the cursor over the desired existing geometry to assign a new constraint type and relationship to the newly chosen geometry. For example, if the implied constraint to be added to the next line is a parallel constraint where you want a perpendicular constraint, simply scrub the cursor over the line that would normally create a perpendicular constraint. The constraint glyph will change from a parallel to a perpendicular constraint.

FIGURE 3.12
Sketching a line with a
perpendicular constraint

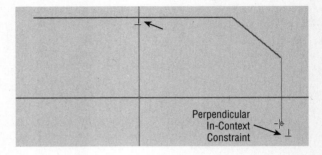

In Figure 3.13, you will continue creating a line parallel to the top line in your sketch. From the endpoint of your previous vertical line, move your cursor to the left until you are approximately below the starting point of the first line, while positioning your cursor so that you will see a parallel constraint glyph near your cursor. When your cursor is directly below the starting line endpoint, you should see a dashed point alignment tracking line indicating that you are directly below the starting point. With the horizontal glyph and the tracking line showing, click a point.

FIGURE 3.13
Sketching a line with
an implied horizontal
constraint and object
tracking

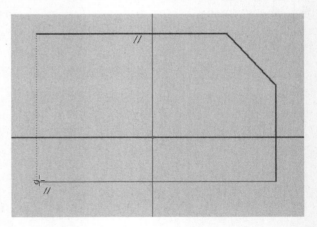

You have now created a line with an endpoint directly below your starting point. Continue sketching the final line, purposely leaving the profile open, as shown in Figure 3.12. Once you've done this, right-click select Done, or hit the Esc key. When you right-click while in a command, you will launch what is called a *context menu*. The contents of the context menus will change depending upon the active command, the state of the part or assembly, and the availability of certain commands at this point in time. As we go through the workflow of creating a finished part, we will be telling you to access the right-click menus often. Using the context menus, as shown in Figure 3.14, will save you time compared to selecting tool icons. ''When in doubt, right-click'' is a good rule of thumb throughout Inventor.

We have left our sketch profile open to demonstrate what might be called a *drag-based* constraint. Click the endpoint of the vertical line you held short, and simply drag up to the endpoint of your first horizontal line. You will see a green dot indicating the endpoint as well as a constraint glyph letting you know that you are placing a coincident constraint between the two endpoints. This is helpful when you have errantly clicked an endpoint and accidentally left a sketch profile open. You must have a closed sketch utilizing continuous linetype geometry in order to convert the sketch into a base solid feature. Open sketch geometry may be used only to create surfaces or feature paths.

FIGURE 3.14
Right-clicking launches in-context menus.

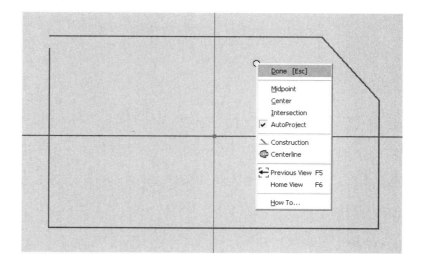

Note, too, that you can select any corner and then drag your sketch to adjust the shape. You can also click the lines and drag them to adjust the location. This drag-based editing is allowed because the sketch is not fully dimensioned and therefore is underconstrained.

Now that you have a closed sketch, it is time to check your constraints and then add dimensions to the sketch. Inventor 2009 has a very handy status line in the lower-right corner of the Inventor screen. Figure 3.15 shows that we have six dimensions or constraints needed to fully constrain our sketch.

FIGURE 3.15
Status line showing six dimensions or constraints needed

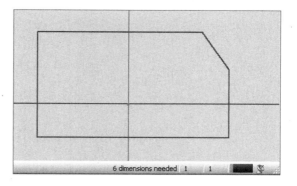

As you add constraints and dimensions to the sketch, the status line will change and reflect the number of constraints and dimensions that are still required. Good modeling practice demands that every sketch be fully constrained. A fully constrained series of sketches provides stability within the model, while delivering consistent and expected results when edited. However, it is worth noting that Inventor does not require you to fully constrain a sketch before moving on to create a solid as some other 3D modelers do. This can be useful when working out a beginning design concept or creating adaptive parts.

To check geometric constraints within the sketch, right-click anywhere in the graphic screen outside the sketch boundaries, and select Show All Constraints. Your screen should look similar to Figure 3.16. Note that when right-clicking, you get different results depending upon what you are right-clicking or what you have preselected. Therefore, it is important to ensure that nothing is selected when attempting to access the default right-click menu. You can do this by simply double-clicking any blank space in the graphics area, thereby clearing your selection.

FIGURE 3.16
Geometric constraint
display

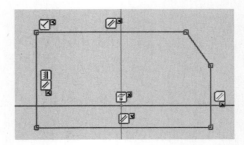

Figure 3.16 shows the geometric constraint relationships that were created in-context while sketching. Note that the coincident constraints on the corners are grouped into square grips. Hovering over the grip will show the grouped constraints. Hovering over any of the constraint icons will highlight the geometry that is referenced by that constraint. If constraints need to be deleted, select the appropriate constraint, right-click, and click Delete from the menu. To turn off the constraint display, right-click, and select Hide All Constraints.

Be aware that there is another right-click option called Constraint Visibility, which controls which constraint glyphs will display when using Show All Constraints. In the Constraint Visibility dialog box, you can choose to show or not show some or all the constraint glyphs. If you choose clear all of them, the Show All Constraints command will not show any glyphs and may appear not to be working.

New to Inventor 2009, degrees of freedom display in sketches, providing indicators of under-constrained conditions. Figure 3.17 illustrates the current degrees of freedom in our example sketch. The red arrows provide indicators of the direction(s) in which a sketch can be stretched or moved. Once the sketch is completely dimensioned, constrained, and anchored to the origin point, this display will not show any degrees of freedom. To activate degrees of freedom within a sketch, right-click and select Show All Degrees Of Freedom. To hide degrees of freedom, repeat and select Hide All Degrees Of Freedom.

Another visual indicator of a sketch's constraint status is the line color. Underconstrained lines will change color once they are fully constrained. Line color is dependent upon the color scheme you use. You can change the color scheme by selecting Tools ➤ Application Options and going to the Colors tab.

Adding Dimensions to Sketches

Dimensioning a sketch in Autodesk Inventor is simple compared to accomplishing the same thing in AutoCAD and many other design programs. It is worth noting that the placement and appearance of sketch dimensions are not as important as they are in drafting programs such as AutoCAD, because once you create a solid from your sketch, the visibility of all dimensions is turned off. Drafting dimension styles, for dimensions that will be displayed on the printed page, are managed in the Inventor drawing, as discussed in Chapter 12.

FIGURE 3.17
Selecting Show All
Degrees Of Freedom

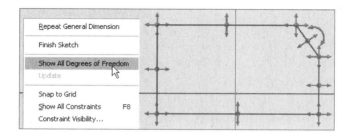

Inventor has one basic dimension command for all types of sketch dimensions, called the General Dimension command. To access the General Dimension command, choose it from the 2D Sketch panel, or right-click and choose Create Dimension. Next, click the horizontal line at the top of your sketch. Drag your cursor up, and you will see the dimension previewed. To set the dimension on the screen, click somewhere above the horizontal line. Upon clicking the screen, you will be presented with an input box. Enter a value of **1.75** inches, and click the green arrow button. You will see the horizontal line adjust to the specified length. At this point, because the General Dimension command is still active, you can edit the dimension input by clicking the dimension to open the input box again. Note that when the General Dimension command is not active, you simply double-click the dimension to open the input box.

Let's place another dimension by clicking the diagonal line. You'll note that as you drag the dimension for placement, Inventor previews either a vertical dimension or a horizontal dimension depending upon the direction you drag. Since in this case you want to place an aligned dimension, you will right-click and choose Aligned, as shown in Figure 3.18.

FIGURE 3.18
Aligned dimension
selection

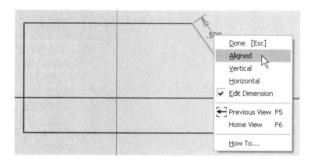

The General Dimension command makes frequent use of the right-click context menu. This context menu will change depending upon the type of geometry selected. Figure 3.19 shows the context menu options when dimensioning a circle.

Keep in mind that we use the General Dimension command to dimension all object types in Inventor. The type of dimension is dependent upon the object or objects selected. Selecting a circle or arc gives you diameter and radius options. Selecting two parallel lines gives you a distance between the two. Selecting two nonparallel lines gives you an angle dimension. Selecting a line and a circle gives you a distance between the circle's centerpoint and the line. So, you should begin to see that General Dimension is a very versatile tool that is dependent upon the selections you make.

FIGURE 3.19
Radius dimension
selection

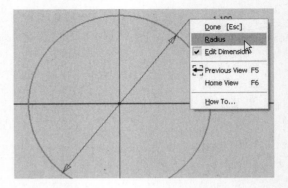

Add the remainder of the dimensions as shown in Figure 3.20. Note that if you place an errant dimension that you want to erase or simply want to practice by removing dimensions and redimensioning your sketch, you can simply select the dimensions you do not want and press the Del key on the keyboard, or you can right-click and choose Delete.

FIGURE 3.20
Dimensionally complete
sketch

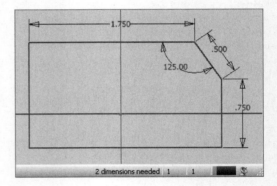

Inventor 2009 has an indicator at the bottom of the screen that shows how many dimensions or constraints are needed (you can see this in Figure 3.20). If your sketch is fully dimensioned and constrained but not yet anchored, it should display that two dimensions are needed. If the display indicates that more than two dimensions are needed, then you will need to reevaluate your sketch for missing constraints.

Anchoring the Sketch

To create an environment of consistent behavior for placement or editing of parts, the original first sketch must be anchored to the part origin. Every part file has an origin point that marks the X=0, Y=0, Z=0 point in the coordinate system. This point was automatically projected in your sketch. This automatic projection is controlled by the Autoproject Part Origin On Sketch Create option in the Application Options settings as discussed at the beginning of this chapter.

To anchor your sketch to this projected origin point, right-click, and select Create Constraint ➤ Coincident. With the command active, click the point highlighted in Figure 3.21 and then select the projected origin point located at the x-axis and y-axis intersection point. Alternatively, you can select the Coincident constraint in the 2D Sketch panel.

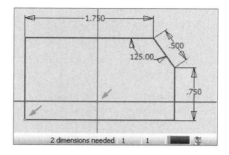

When you select the origin point as your second click, you will see the entire sketch move to the anchored origin point. Depending upon your color scheme, all the underconstrained lines should change color once the sketch is anchored. Your results should look like Figure 3.22.

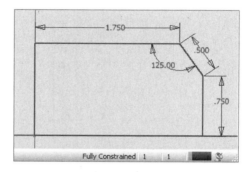

If you right-click and choose Show All Degrees Of Freedom as you did earlier, you should not see any red arrows because the sketch is fully constrained and has no degrees of freedom left. You will also note that the status bar now displays the words *Fully Constrained*. Yet another way of ensuring that your sketch is constrained fully is to select and drag a sketch object horizontally or vertically. If the sketch changes size or shape, then the sketch is not fully constrained.

All of these methods of determining whether a sketch is fully constrained should indicate to you the importance of fully constraining your sketches, unless you have a specific reason for not doing so.

CHECKING YOUR SKETCH

Grabbing parts of the sketch and moving them around is known as sketcherizing. This technique allows you to determine whether the sketch is fully constrained and, if not, how the sketch is allowed to move. It also allows you to "rough in" a sketch to meet the design intent required.

Now that the sketch is fully constrained, you can right-click and select Finish Sketch. To edit an existing sketch, simply double-click the named sketch in the Model browser, or right-click the named sketch and select Edit Sketch. When you are in Edit Sketch mode, everything in the browser except for the active sketch will be grayed out. You are now finished with this example, and there is no need to save this file for any future steps in this book.

SEAN SAYS: FULLY CONSTRAINED SKETCHES ARE THE KEY TO SUCCESS

I cannot overstate the importance of fully constrained sketches. When a sketch is underconstrained, it can cause a domino effect of errors. Although most users are very good at dimensioning their sketches, the most common mistake is to not affix the sketch to a grounded point in the sketch plane. As shown earlier, the geometry can be anchored to the origin point after it has been drawn.

Another method is to begin sketching from the origin. When you place your first line, rectangle, circle, or arc on the sketch, click the origin as a starting point. Inventor does not care in what quadrant the part is created. Only when analyzing the moment of inertia of a part is the location, with respect to the origin, a concern. Starting your first sketch element at the origin will help ensure your sketches are fully constrained.

REFINING, CONSTRAINING, AND DIMENSIONING A 2D SPLINE

As mentioned earlier in the chapter, it is important to fully dimension, constrain, and anchor all sketch geometry. Spline geometry types require a different technique than other geometry in order to control and dimension the shape to preserve design intent.

In principle, splines themselves cannot be dimensioned. Normally, only endpoints and vertices can have dimensions attached. Autodesk Inventor is one of the few 3D modelers that provide additional controls for dimensioning and modifying spline curves.

Let's examine your options with an exercise.

Create a new part file based upon the ANSI inch-based template, Standard.ipt. First sketch a horizontal construction line staring at the origin point and running to the right and then dimension it to a length of 4 inches. Next select the Spline command located underneath the Line command, accessible by clicking the small down arrow next to the Line command. Draw a spline curve starting at the origin point and ending along the x-axis, similar in shape to Figure 3.23. When you have selected the last point on the x-axis, right-click and select Create.

FIGURE 3.23
Completed 2D spline

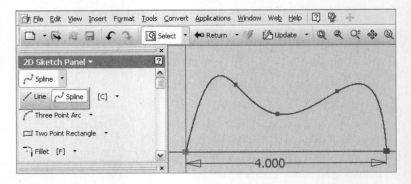

The spline curve in Figure 3.23 contains five vertex points. These are otherwise known as control points. Dimensions can be added only to control points, not to the spline itself. Additional vertex points can be added to the spline at any time by right-clicking the spline and selecting Insert Point.

Adding more control points along a spline curve has the effect of tightening control on the spline, limiting adjustments to the curve. In like fashion, points can be selected and deleted to relax the constraints upon the spline curve. For this example exercise, you will continue with the five original points.

Exit the dimension command, right-click, and then select Show All Constraints. There should be a coincident constraint anchoring the beginning and endpoints to the construction line. Right-click, and select Hide All Constraints. You have effectively limited the endpoints of the spline from movement. From this point forward, you can now add vertical and horizontal dimensions to each of the points on the spline to control the current shape. Use the General Dimension command to place dimensions, as shown in Figure 3.24.

FIGURE 3.24
Bowtie options

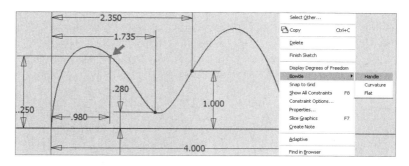

Adding more points to the spline is only one way to refine and control the curve. In addition to anchoring all the points, you have the ability to adjust various aspects of the curve by using the Bowtie option at each of the vertex points.

The Bowtie option is accessed by right-clicking a vertex point and selecting Bowtie, as shown in Figure 3.24.

There are three options for using the Bowtie command in a 2D sketch: Handle, Curvature, and Flat.

Selecting Handle allows the user to drag the handle endpoints for dynamic manipulation of the spline curve. Figure 3.25 illustrates how a handle can be stretched and rotated about the vertex to change the shape.

FIGURE 3.25
Dynamic manipulation
using the handle

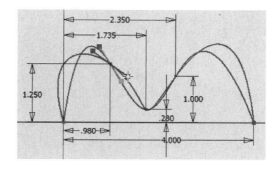

Once a Handle option has been turned on, selection of the vertex will display the handle. While the handle is visible, it can be dimensioned and anchored using any number of options, as shown in Figure 3.26.

FIGURE 3.26
Dimensions added to the
handle and vertex

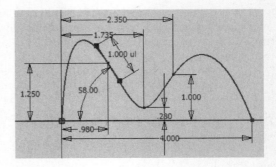

The Curvature option is another tool that will allow you to alter the spline curve but in a different manner. The Curve option acts on the portion of the curve surrounding the selected vertex. The result of changing the curvature at that selected point will also affect the rest of the spline curve, as shown in Figure 3.27.

FIGURE 3.27
The Curvature option
changes the shape.

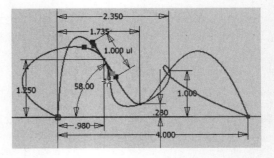

The Flat option acts on the portion of the curve surrounding the selected vertex and holds that specific area flat on the curve. Once created, this handle can also be dimensioned in the same manner as other handles. Figure 3.28 illustrates how the Flat option can affect the shape of the curve.

FIGURE 3.28
Flat option example

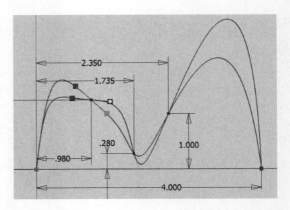

You can save your file for future reference; however, we will not be using this example again.

You can combine any number of techniques to create the desired curve. Partially dimensioning a handle allows additional control on any particular vertex point by dragging the point before anchoring the vertex. Ideally, any spline should be completely dimensioned, constrained, and anchored to assure that the curve does not change during downstream editing operations.

CREATING SKETCHES FROM A GRAPHICS IMAGE

Occasionally you may need to create a part from a scanned image or napkin sketch. To do this, you can insert the image into your sketch and sketch over the top of it. Although this is generally not a good approach for creating precise machined parts, it is a valid workflow when designing consumer products when you need to capture the general shape and feel of parts.

Place an image into a part sketch by clicking the Insert Image icon in the 2D Sketch panel. Browse for the image you want to place into the sketch, and choose Open when the image is located. Next you will be asked to click an insert point for the image. The cursor is attached to the upper-left corner of the image. Once you've placed the image on the screen, you can dimension and constrain the edges of the image like any other sketch entity.

Now you can sketch on top of the image, tracing the edges to create the profile, and then use general dimensions to tweak the sketch as required, as shown in Figure 3.29.

FIGURE 3.29
Creating a sketch from
an image file

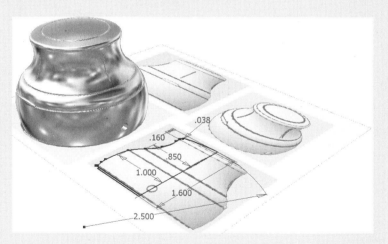

Using Construction Geometry

Using construction geometry within an Inventor sketch permits geometric control of the location and shape of objects without using parameters. Construction geometry is composed of a dashed linetype rather than a continuous linetype. Construction geometry is filtered out of boundary detection.

PRESERVING DESIGN INTENT

NTF produces a line of exhaust pipes for the automotive industry. The engineers at NTF are looking to streamline the design of pipe fittings used in their product. One particular part is a bolted flange fitting. This particular fitting is available in various sizes, designed to fit tubing diameters ranging from 2 inches to 4 inches.

The design team has decided to settle on a single design for the flange that allows for adjusting the tube size and allowing other dimensions in the overall shape to vary in relationship to the selected tube.

In this case, using construction geometry to control the size and shape will preserve the design intent of the part. The finished flange appears in Figure 3.30.

FIGURE 3.30
Finished pipe flange

Developing a good workflow in part design pays big dividends in terms of productivity and ease of editing. Using construction geometry is an essential part of that workflow. Proper use of construction geometry sets up relationships between varying objects within the sketch. That relationship is preserved when dimensions are changed or added.

Let's learn about creating and using construction geometry by making that part for NTF. We will start with creating the bulk of the sketch and then use construction geometry to anchor the sketch:

1. Create a new part file by selecting File ➢ New and then select Standard.ipt (inch).

2. Use the Line command to create a triangle with a horizontal constraint on the bottom line. Use the General Dimension command to set the length of the horizontal line to 3.5 inches. Do not be concerned with creating an exact shape at this point. Do not round the three corners, because they will be added as a part feature.

3. Add angular dimensions to the bottom corners by selecting the General Dimension command and clicking the two lines on the right side of the triangle. Set the angle to 60°. Continue by selecting the two lines on the left side of the triangle, but instead of setting the angle to 60°, clear the input box and then select the first dimension placed. You will see the name of the first dimension, such as d1, appear in the input box.

4. By referencing one dimension to the other, you have created a simple parametric function. You will notice that the new dimension shows a prefix (fx:) to indicate that its value

is a function of another dimension. The evaluated value is displayed after this prefix. The dimensioning of the triangle is now complete, and you will note that two dimensions are still required to fully constrain the sketch, as shown in Figure 3.31.

FIGURE 3.31
Sketch1 with a function linking the dimensions

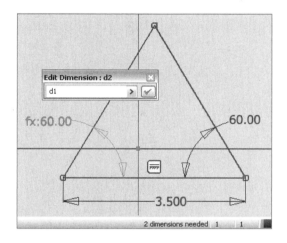

SEAN SAYS: EQUATIONS ARE POWERFUL

Equations are a powerful way to preserve design intent. In the previous example, you created a very simple equation. You made the second dimension equal ($=$) to the first. When you change the $60°$ dimension to 30 degrees, the second dimension will change to $30°$ as well. You could have just as easily have made the second equation be 1/2 of the valve. Simply click the dimension, and then add **/ 2** in the Edit Dimension dialog box (for example, enter **d1 / 2**). You can get as complex as you want using addition, subtraction, multiplication, and division operands as well as trig functions, exponentials, and more. For more information about these power equations, search for *functions in edit boxes* in Inventor's help system.

Now that the basic sketch is created, you can proceed to add some geometry that will help you set up design intent in this part. Begin by selecting the construction icon in the upper-right corner of the Inventor window, as shown in Figure 3.32. This will toggle the sketch linetype to Construction. After creating the construction circle in the next step, be sure to toggle Construction to off; otherwise, everything you create after this point will be construction geometry.

FIGURE 3.32
Change to Construction line type

Create a circle inside the triangle. Right-click, select Create Constraint, and then choose Tangent from the context menu shown in Figure 3.33. Apply a Tangent constraint to the circle and then to the closest line.

To ensure that you have nothing selected, double-click in a clean area of the graphics area, and then right-click and add choose Create Constraint. Choose Coincident from the fly-out menu and place the Coincident constraint on the centerpoint of the construction circle and the origin centerpoint. Your sketch should now be fully constrained.

FIGURE 3.33
Select a Tangent constraint

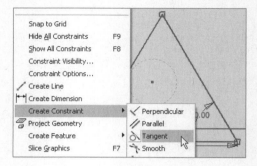

Select the Center Point Circle command from the 2D Sketch panel, and create another circle starting at the center of the construction circle to about midway between the centerpoint and the construction circle. Dimension this to a diameter of 1.625 inches. Refer to Figure 3.34 to confirm that you have created the sketch geometry correctly.

FIGURE 3.34
Using a construction circle in a sketch

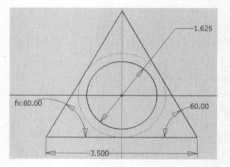

PRESERVING AND CHANGING DESIGN INTENT

Sometimes an existing dimension does not communicate the full design intent of the sketch. For example, suppose you want to control the distance between the inner circle and the outer edge of the finished part. The designers know that the minimum distance from the inside of the hole to the outer edge should be 0.25 inch. Use the General Dimension tool to add a dimension from the edge of the inner circle to the edge of the outer, construction circle.

Upon doing so, you will be warned that the additional dimension will overconstrain the sketch and therefore will be need to be placed as driven dimension. Quite simply, you have a conflict between the 3.5-inch horizontal dimension and the minimum edge distance dimension. Click the Accept button to place the driven dimension, and notice that the dimension value is (0.198) inch, as shown on the left of Figure 3.35.

To resolve this, you could delete the 3.5-inch horizontal dimension by selecting the dimension and pressing the Del key. However, you still want to know the distance of the horizontal line, so instead of deleting the dimension, you can select it and then use the Driven Dimension button, as shown on left side of Figure 3.31, to change it from a driving dimension to a driven dimension. Next select the

(0.198) inch dimension and use the Driven Dimension button to change it from driven to a driving dimension. Once it is a driving dimension, double-click it, and set the value to 0.25 inch. Note that the horizontal driven dimension adjusts as required. The right side of Figure 3.35 shows the final sketch.

FIGURE 3.35
Changing the design intent

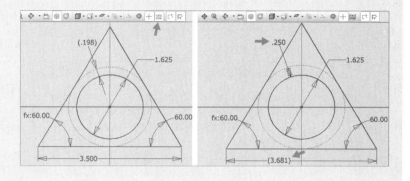

Right-click and select Finish Sketch. Save this file as flange.ipt in the Mastering Inventor folder. You may notice that the completed sketch does not reflect the shape of the finished part, as shown in Figure 3.20. To evaluate the finished part created from this sketch, open the file called flange_finished.ipt from the Mastering Inventor folder.

Notice that the radius corners and the drill holes were added as separate features on this part. Adding features in this way allows for easy editing of individual features during the design process. Use the + symbol next to Extrusion1 in the browser to locate the sketch that was created as described earlier.

PROJECTING GEOMETRY

You may have noticed that there is a Sketch2 already created in the Model browser of flange_finished.ipt. This sketch was created to allow you to explore an important concept in part sketching. Projecting geometry from a previous feature for use in new features saves you time by not having to re-create information that has already been created. But even more important is the way that projected geometry updates when the original feature updates, allowing you to maintain the design intent of a feature throughout the part. Double-click the Sketch2 icon in the browser to edit it. Notice that the sketch was created on a work plane above the original features. Once you have the sketch ready for editing, click Project Geometry in the 2D Sketch tool panel and then select the edges or faces in the original features. You will see the geometry of those features be included in Sketch2.

Creating Sketches from AutoCAD Geometry

Converting accurate, dimensioned 2D drawings eliminates redrawing of all the original geometry. Inventor allows selective importing of 2D drawings with associative geometry directly into a new part sketch. Success in importing existing drawings depends on the following criteria:

◆ The AutoCAD file must contain *accurate* original geometry.

◆ Duplicate geometry must be deleted from the AutoCAD file.

◆ Proper AutoCAD drawing techniques must be employed in creating the AutoCAD file. For example, there must be only one line segment between any two points. Two shorter lines appearing as a single line will be imported exactly as drawn in the AutoCAD file.

◆ For dimensions to be converted to Inventor parametric dimensions, the existing AutoCAD dimensions must be associative to the geometry. Disconnected dimensions (AutoCAD Def-points not snapped to the proper geometry location) will cause problems when converted to Inventor dimensions.

CONVERTING EXISTING DESIGNS FROM AUTOCAD FILES

Efficient Manufacturing Company has recently decided to convert to 3D design using Autodesk Inventor. They have more than 20 years worth of designs that were completed in standard AutoCAD. They would like to utilize existing drawings by converting those into 3D feature-based parametric parts.

They will begin this process by creating a new part file. When in active sketch mode, they can import AutoCAD sketch geometry by selecting the Insert AutoCAD File command, as shown in Figure 3.36.

FIGURE 3.36
Insert AutoCAD File
command

Let's illustrate this process by creating a new part file using the default `Standard.ipt` template. With Sketch1 active, select the Insert AutoCAD File command. Selecting this command will open a dialog box, allowing you to select the desired AutoCAD file. If you have copied the example files from the Mastering Inventor DVD, then select the `Import1.dwg` from the DWG folder. Click Open to start the conversion process, as shown in Figure 3.37.

Once the AutoCAD file opens, you will move into a series of Import Destination Options pages. The first page, as shown in Figure 3.37, is mostly grayed out except for specifying units, constraining endpoints, and optionally applying geometric constraints upon import under most conditions.

When an AutoCAD drawing is imported into a sketch, Inventor records the unit type of the AutoCAD file. By default, the unit type is displayed within the Import dialog box but is grayed out. If the unit type is not correct or the unit is of a different type than you require, you may input a different input unit type.

Checking the Constrain End Points box allows you to insert coincident constraints between sketch objects found to have endpoints that occupy the same coordinates. When the Apply Geometric Constraints box is checked, Inventor will add minimal constraints to the imported

AutoCAD geometry. You can use the Auto Dimension tool to place many constraints at once, after the geometry is imported. When doing this, it is best to uncheck the Dimensions check box and let the Auto Dimension tool place just constraints. Note, too, that although some dimensions will not be imported, those that are will be parametric Inventor dimensions. Figure 3.38 shows the result of importing file, `Import1.dwg`.

FIGURE 3.37
DWG import options

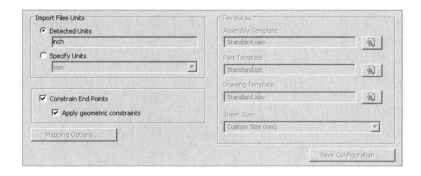

FIGURE 3.38
Original DWG file and finished imported sketch

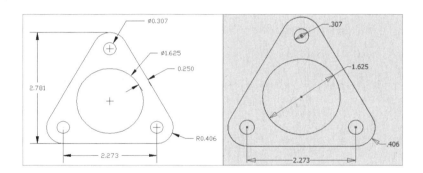

If the AutoCAD geometry was created at the 0,0 origin, then it should import into Inventor at the same origin location. If the AutoCAD geometry is not located at the origin of the sketch, then you can use the Move command, selecting both the geometry and any dimensions, to move the entire imported sketch into the proper location.

You should note that this imported drawing might be further broken down into separate features. For instance, each hole could be a separate feature. Note, too, that as you learned earlier, having the round corners modeled as features separate from the base feature allows for easier edits in Inventor.

Creating separate features from one sketch can be handled easily by sharing a sketch. If a sketch is shared and visible, it can be reused over and over to create new features. To share an existing sketch in a new part file, you will first have to create a feature from that sketch before it can be shared. This has been done for you in the `SharedSketch.ipt` file in the Mastering Inventor folder.

Open this part and look at the Model browser. Notice that Extrusion1 has been created from an imported sketch, much like the one you just imported. Use the + symbol in the browser, and expand Extrusion1 so that you can see Sketch1. Right-click Sketch1, and choose Share Sketch. Upon doing so you will see that Sketch1 becomes visible in the graphics area and is shown as shared above and below Extrusion1 in the browser, as illustrated in Figure 3.39. From here you could create another extrusion from the shared sketch to cut the holes out of the part. If you were to do so, Sketch1 would be permanently shared. However, if you want to unshare a sketch that has not been used after it was shared, you can do so by right-clicking and choosing Unshare.

FIGURE 3.39
A shared sketch

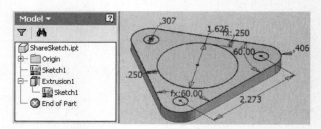

Although using the Import "wizard" as described works without having AutoCAD open or even installed, you can import AutoCAD geometry in an even more efficient manner by simply copying from an open AutoCAD file straight into an Inventor sketch.

From an open AutoCAD file, you can select the geometry you want to import and then right-click and choose Copy, thereby copying the selected objects to the Windows clipboard. Next, from within Inventor, with a 2D sketch active for editing, simply right-click and choose Paste. You will be presented with a bounding box preview of the pasted entities. At this point, you can right-click and choose Paste Options and ensure that the insert scale is correct, or you can simply click the screen and place the pasted geometry.

Although importing geometry from AutoCAD can be an efficient way to reuse existing Auto-CAD files, experienced Inventor users will tell you that you are almost always better off to model parts from scratch rather than import from AutoCAD. Consider the part you just imported. Importing it from AutoCAD does not give you results that are aligned with our design intent in this example.

Creating and Using 3D Sketches

3D sketches permit the creation of nonplanar 3D features. 3D sketches are created in part files. 3D sketches are comprised of geometry located in various XYZ locations or points within the file. Although a 3D sketch may lie upon a 2D plane, in most designs that will not be the case. 3D sketches should never be used for creating geometry that could be created within the 2D sketch environment.

The 3D Sketch command is accessible only from within the part environment. Although this may seem like a limitation, a designer can create a part within the assembly environment in order to utilize the 3D sketch command.

3D sketches can be utilized to create a 3D parametric path for lofts and sweeps. Using the command in this manner allows a designer to create complex tubing and wire paths, add other complex geometry to existing parts, or create complex loft features.

This command can also be used to assist in creating parting lines on nonplanar geometry often used for molds, dies, and fixtures. Complicated cuts in die blocks and saddles is possible when 3D paths are used in this manner, along with parting surfaces.

Creating a 3D Spline

Let's explore some of the commands in the 3D Sketch panel. Open the file called **3DSketch.ipt** in the Mastering Inventor folder. Although this is a part file, you will notice that this file has some reference surfaced in it already. This was included simply to emulate a situation where you might be creating a part within the context of an assembly. We will talk more about creating parts within an assembly in the chapters to come.

There is also a 2D sketch called Profile1 already in the browser. You'll use this sketch at the end of this exercise, but for now let's create a new 3D sketch by accessing the 3D Sketch icon from the flyout next to the 2D Sketch icon, as shown in Figure 3.40. Once the 3D sketch is created, you will see that the tool panel displays the list of 3D sketch commands. First in the list is the Line command. Note that at the end of the line icon there is a down arrow indicating that other commands are listed under that icon. Clicking the down arrow reveals both the Line and Spline commands.

FIGURE 3.40
Creating a 3D sketch

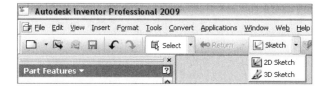

Our goal is to create a 3D sketch running from the center of the connection input of the box through each of the large holes in the flange brackets. Start the Spline command, and the Inventor Precise Input toolbar appears along with the 3D coordinate triad. The triad displays the X, Y, and Z planes and the corresponding axis in the form of three arrows. The red arrow indicates the x-axis, the green arrow indicates the y-axis, and the blue arrow indicates the z-axis. You will notice that the triad is first positioned at 0,0,0.

Specify a start point for the spline by clicking the front, circular edge of the connection input. Next click the center of the first triangular flange bracket. Do the same for the other two flange brackets. Right-click and choose Create to complete the spline. Then right-click again and choose Done to exit the spline command. Your screen should look similar to Figure 3.41.

FIGURE 3.41
3D sketch spline

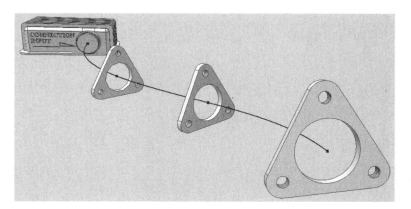

Using the 3D Coordinate Triad and Precise Redefine Functions

Let's take a moment to explore the 3D coordinate triad and its functionality. Each part of the triad is selectable for different tasks, as you will explore in the coming paragraphs. Figure 3.42 shows the anatomy of the triad.

FIGURE 3.42
Inventor Precise input and the 3D coordinate triad

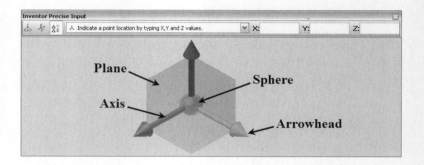

While still in the 3D sketch, start the Line command. You will notice the return of the triad and Precise Input toolbar. Click the endpoint of the spline to set the start of the line on this point. You will see the triad move the spline endpoint. Notice that the triad is not lined up with the bracket flange. To remedy this, you will use the Precise Redefine button found on the Precise Input toolbar. Once you have clicked the Precise Redefine button, select the shaft of the red arrow and then the bottom edge of the triangular flange bracket toolbar, as shown on the left of Figure 3.43. Click the Precise Redefine button again, and this time click the green arrow shaft and the small edge, as indicated in center of Figure 3.43. The triad orientation should now resemble the far right of Figure 3.43.

FIGURE 3.43
Precise Redefine command

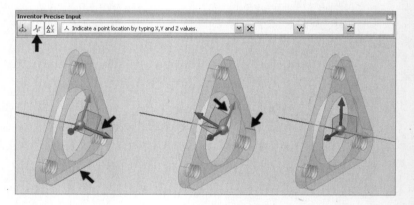

Next, click the triad plane between the blue and green arrows to isolate that plane on which to sketch. It should turn red when selected, and you will see a 0 placed in the X cell of the Precise Input toolbar. Fill out the rest of the input cells so that you have X = 0, Y = 6, and Z = 0.5 and then press Enter on the keyboard. Note you can hit the Tab key to switch between the X, Y, and Z input cells. Values will be input as relative coordinates. Recall that with relative coordinates the new input coordinate point is based on the previous point rather than the absolute 0,0,0 origin point.

You will now have a line running from the end of the spline out at 6 inches in the y-axis with a slight rise in the z-axis. Still in the Line command, right-click and ensure that Auto-bend is checked in the right-click menu. Auto-bend will place a radius at the corners in your line route. You can set the default radius size by selecting Tools ➤ Document Settings and going to the Sketch tab. Once you've placed the bends, you can edit them like any other dimension.

With the Line command still active, click the plane between the green and red arrows on the triad to isolate the XY plane, and set X = 4, Y = 4, Z = 0. Press Enter on the keyboard to set this line. You will see a small dimensioned radius at the corner of your two line segments. This is a result of the Auto-bend option. Right-click and choose Done to exit the Line command. Your 3D sketch should resemble Figure 3.44.

FIGURE 3.44
3D sketch path

Typically pipe and tubing are dimensioned from axis intersection to axis intersection, so you will now add dimensions to each of the line segments to follow that workflow. Select the General Dimension command in the 3D Sketch panel, and add dimensions as shown in Figure 3.45. Notice you want to edit the bend radius that was created with the Line command. Right-click, and choose Finish 3D Sketch.

FIGURE 3.45
3D sketch dims

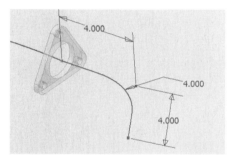

As a test to see whether you have successfully created your 3D sketch for its intended purpose, let's run a sweep along the path. Recall that there is a 2D sketch in the browser named Profile1. This will be your sweep profile, and your 3D sketch will be your path. Find and click the Sweep button in the Part Features tool panel. Profile1 will be automatically selected as the sweep profile unless you have another unconsumed, closed profile sketch in your part, in which case you will need to select Profile1 manually. Once you've selected the profile, ensure that the Path option in the Sweep dialog box is selected, and then click the 3D sketch you just created. Your sweep should preview as shown in Figure 3.46.

As a final note, we should point out that the connection box and triangular bracket flanges have been derived into this part file as a reference feature. In the real world, once you were done with your part, you would locate that feature in the browser and turn off the visibility. To do this, locate and expand the feature in the browser called DerivedPart1.ipt. Right-click the feature called Derived Work Body1, and uncheck the Visibility box. If you'd like, you can save and close the part.

INCLUDING 3D GEOMETRY

You might need to use edges of parts as a path for another feature, in much the same way that you project geometry in a 2D sketch. In a 3D sketch, however, you are not really projecting the geometry onto a sketch plane but simply including it for use in your 3D sketch. To see how this works, open the file named `IncludeGeometry.ipt` in the Mastering Inventor folder. The file has a sketch named Lip Profile already created and ready to be used in a sweep feature. However, before you can do that, you must define a path along which to sweep the profile.

FIGURE 3.46
Sweeping along a 3D sketch

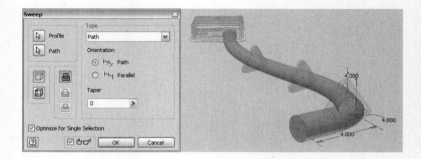

To do this, create a new 3D sketch. In the 3D sketch tools, click the Include Geometry command. Next click each edge as shown in Figure 3.47 to define the sweep path. Once the edges are selected, right-click and choose Finish Sketch. Next, choose Sweep from the Part Features panel and use the 3D sketch for the path.

FIGURE 3.47
Including geometry in a 3D sketch

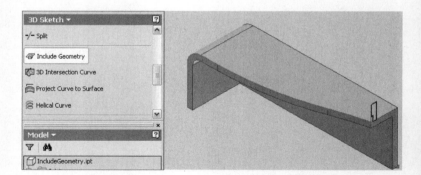

WORKING WITH CURVES IN 3D SKETCHES

You can use a 3D sketch to find the intersection of two surfaces, sketch profiles, work planes, or some combination thereof. The resulting sketch is fully associative and will update automatically should the curves change, as shown in Figure 3.48.

Similarly, you can find intersections of curves and faces using the Project Curve To Surface tool in a 3D sketch. This tool has three variations of output. Geometry created using these commands will adjust if the original geometry changes. Or, if desired, the link can be broken from the parent geometry to prevent it from adjusting automatically.

FIGURE 3.48
3D Intersection Curve
dialog box

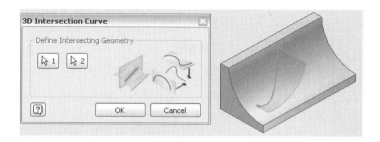

The first output, Project Along A Vector, requires a face, a curve, and a direction. Projecting to a continuous face such as a cylinder results in a 3D sketch entity that follows the surface as if the curve were slicing straight down through the face.

The second output is called Project To Closest Point, and projects curve in the shortest possible path normal to the surface. The result of a 3-inch line to a convex surface would be a curve less than 3 inches because the endpoints of the line would take the shortest path to the curve, rather than wrapping about it.

The third output is Wrap To Surface. This output creates a curve that will be the same overall dimension as the curve from which it was created. Consider wrapping a string around a cylinder; the string stays the same length. Figure 3.49 shows all three outputs.

FIGURE 3.49
Project Curve To Surface
dialog box

You can also create 3D helical curves such as thread paths and coils by using the Helical Curve tool within the 3D sketch tools. Helixes can be specified by pitch and revolution, pitch and height, revolution and height, or a true spiral. A helix can be combined with other 3D sketch objects to compose a complex path as required.

REFINING AND CONSTRAINING A 3D SKETCH

You can use various methods to anchor and constrain a 3D sketch in much the same fashion as you do with a 2D sketch. In the case of 3D spline curves, users are presented with the ability to add constraints, vertex points, work features, and handles. Further refining can take place with the ability to adjust the fit method and spline tension to create the exact curve shape desired.

Although Curvature and Flat handles cannot be applied to a 3D spline, constraints can reshape a spline to fit to adjacent geometry, as illustrated in Figure 3.50. In this example, a spline was created between the bottom corner and the top corner. Then a Tangent constraint was added between the spline and the bottom curved edge and between the spline and the top edge, reshaping the curve to fit.

FIGURE 3.50
3D Sketch modified by Tangent constraints

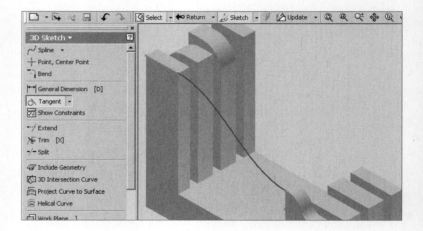

The Bottom Line

Create a new part file from a template   In this chapter, you learned how to choose an appropriate template for creating a new part file. You also explored the Application Options and Document Settings options that control sketch-related settings in Inventor.

Master It   Let's assume you have opened an inch-based template file to create a new part and have created some sketches and features within the file. You now realize that this should have been a metric part and that you should have opened a metric-based template.

Preserve model design Intent   Establishing and preserving design intent is a powerful benefit of 3D design. Every design should be created with the possibility that the design will be modified at a later date, and changes to the design may not affect only a particular part; the changes may also affect the function of an entire machine or related components.

Master It   You have created a flange part used to join one 2-inch pipe to another section of 2-inch pipe. Future designs will call for many variations of this design.

Perform the basic 2D sketching process   We explored sketching in Inventor by concentrating on the use of sketch constraints on sketch objects to establish relationships between them and on the use of parametric dimension to then drive the sketch entities. Recall that you can have both driving and driven dimension in a sketch.

Master It   You have been tasked with redesigning a shop fixture from a previous design but are unsure of some of the dimensions at the onset of your design.

Import and convert AutoCAD drawings to Inventor sketches   This chapter discussed reusing and importing existing AutoCAD files into Inventor for part creation.

Master It   You have many existing 2D AutoCAD drawings detailing legacy parts. You want to reuse these designs as you convert to 3D modeling. You need to create numerous features within the model so that the model can be easily edited while preserving design intent.

Create 3D sketches in a part file Much of working with a 3D parametric modeler can be done by sketching in a two-dimensional plane and then giving depth to the sketch to create 3D features. However, sometimes you need to create paths or curves that are not planar. In those cases, you use the 3D sketch tools.

Master It You need to create a three-dimensional sketch for a complex model. The design of this model precludes the exclusive use of 2D sketches.

Chapter 4

Basic Modeling Techniques

This chapter covers the principles of creating a 3D parametric part, which makes it probably the most important chapter in this book. Unless you thoroughly learn and adopt the principles covered in this chapter, you will be forever handicapped in the 3D design process.

All the skills in this chapter are primarily based around creating a single part, whether it be in a single part file or in the context of an assembly file. Do yourself a favor and learn or review these basics before jumping into the more complex features.

In this chapter, you will learn how to:

◆ Create basic part features

◆ Create and use work features in part mode

◆ Place and configure hole features

◆ Pattern and mirror features

◆ Modify existing part features

Exploring Application Options and Settings for Part Modeling

As in previous chapters, you should make sure that your settings in Application Options match the approach we're using in this book. This will ensure that the examples you work on will match the results you see here.

Specifying Global Settings

You maintain global settings for Autodesk Inventor within the Application Options dialog box. For this section of the chapter, we will be concentrating on the Part tab in Application Options, which allows you to maintain part-specific settings. Figure 4.1 shows the Part tab of Application Options. Please adjust all your settings to match Figure 4.1.

The Sketch On New Part Creation section allows you to predetermine which origin plane in the first sketch will be placed. If No New Sketch is selected, then Inventor will create a new part file without an initial sketch. You can then determine the origin plane for the first sketch

The Construction setting determines whether created surfaces will be translucent by default or opaque similar to a part.

The Auto-hide In-line Work Features option allows automatic hiding of a work feature when it is consumed by another work feature. For instance, if you create a work plane by clicking a work axis and a work point, the work axis and work point will be stacked under the work plane in the browser. The Auto-consume Work Features And Surface Features option allows Inventor to consume surfaces when converted to a solid, in addition to consuming work features.

FIGURE 4.1
The Part tab

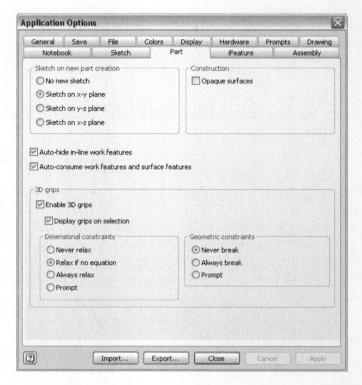

The 3D Grips settings affect how 3D grips can modify a part file. In normal use, 3D grips allow you to modify part features by selecting and dragging a grip. If a dimension is controlling the feature, then the dimension will update to reflect the changes in the part. If Never Relax is selected, then any features controlled by the dimension will not change.

When Relax If No Equation is selected, then a dimension value will update, unless that dimension value is determined by an equation. Selecting Always Relax will always allow the use of 3D grips, even when controlled by an equation. The Prompt setting will prompt you to accept any changes during drag operations.

The settings in the Geometric Constraints area control how constraints will be handled during drag operations. Leave the Never Break option selected.

Specifying Document-Specific Settings

To change the options in a specific part file, you'll need to access the part's Document Settings dialog box by selecting Tools ➤ Document Settings. The Document Settings dialog box allows specific settings for an individual file in the following areas:

- ◆ Lighting styles

- ◆ Materials

- ◆ Units

- ◆ Modeling dimension display values

- ◆ Individual sketch settings

- ◆ Model values

◆ Bill of materials (BOM)

◆ Default tolerances

Any changes made in the part's Document Settings dialog box will be applied only to the current document. Current document settings will not affect the settings in other parts within the assembly.

Figure 4.2 shows the part's Document Settings dialog box with the Standard tab active. The Standard tab controls the active lighting style of the current graphics window. In addition, you can set the physical material properties of the current part here.

FIGURE 4.2
The Standard tab in the part's Document Settings dialog box

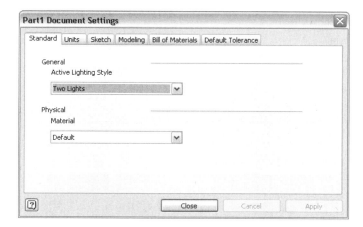

You can set the input measurement units on the Units tab, as shown in Figure 4.3. Internally, Inventor stores and calculates all values as centimeters. The settings on this tab allow you to change the unit specification values. As an example, you could open a metric (mm) part and change the input settings to inches.

FIGURE 4.3
Units tab in Document Settings

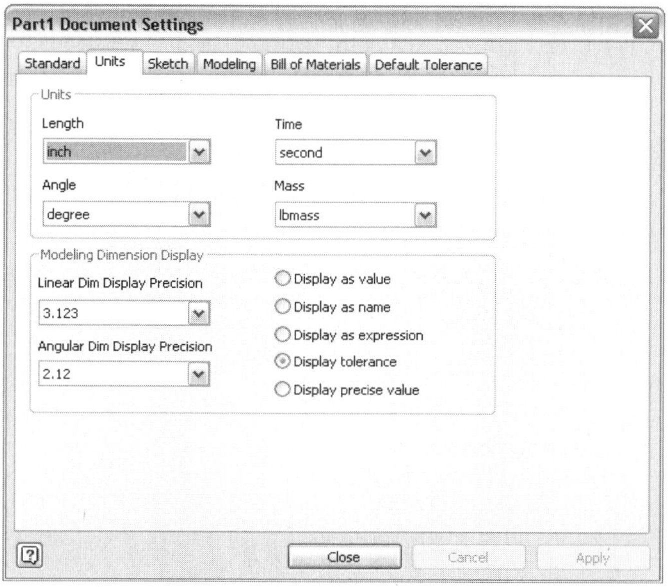

On this tab, you can also define the model dimension's display precision by the number of decimal places and define how that dimension will be displayed. Many people prefer the Display As Expression setting because it shows the dimension name along with any expression that exists in the dimension; if no expression exists, then the dimension name and dimension value are displayed.

On the Sketch tab, as shown in Figure 4.4, you can adjust how the 2D sketch tools work and appear in an active sketch. In addition, you can change the preset value for Auto-Bend Radius in the 3D Sketch area.

FIGURE 4.4
The Sketch tab in
Document Settings

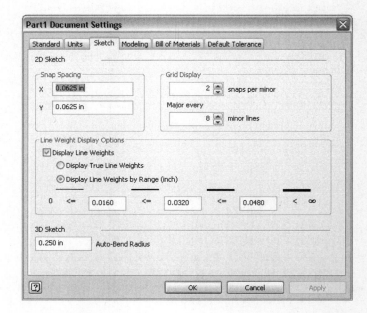

Figure 4.5 shows the Modeling tab, which allows changes to the behavior while modeling the current active part. Checking the Compact Model History box allows Inventor to purge all roll-back document history when you save the current file. Compacting the model history improves performance in large assembly files. You should select this option only when performance is affected in large assembly files or when existing disk space is limited. Otherwise, leave this unchecked.

Checking the Advanced Feature Validation box permits Inventor to use a different algorithm to compute features. Using this option can produce more accurate feature results in rare cases such as Shell, Draft, Thicken, and Offset features. However, this option is slower in calculation than the default option and should be used only on rare occasions where the accuracy of the model may be in question.

The Tapped Hole Diameter setting determines how the size of tapped hole features are controlled. Thread representations in drawings are generated correctly only when Tapped Hole Diameter is set to Minor.

The 3D Snap Spacing values are also set on the Modeling tab. These values have significance only when using 3D snap.

FIGURE 4.5
Modeling tab in
Document Settings

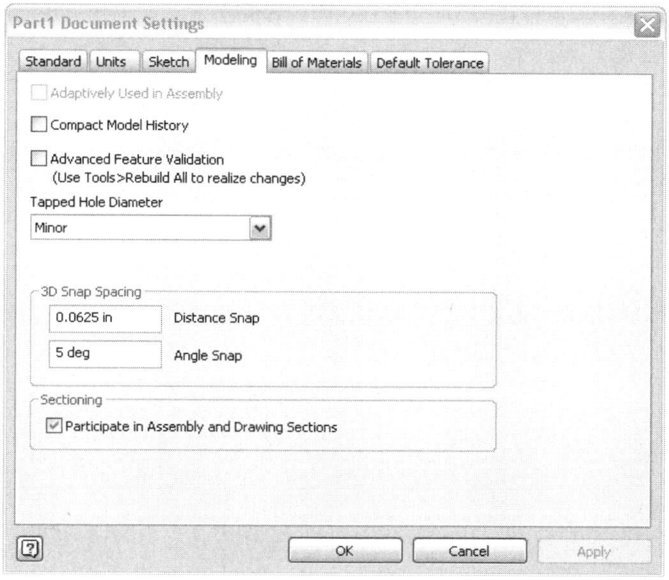

The Participate In Assembly And Drawing Sections setting controls whether the part is sectioned in the assembly and drawing environments. This box is typically unchecked in standards fastener parts that would normally not be sectioned according to traditional drafting standards.

The Bill Of Materials tab determines the structure of the current file and how that structure relates to the bill of materials in an Inventor assembly. Figure 4.6 shows the default settings for structure and quantity.

FIGURE 4.6
Bill Of Materials tab in
Document Settings

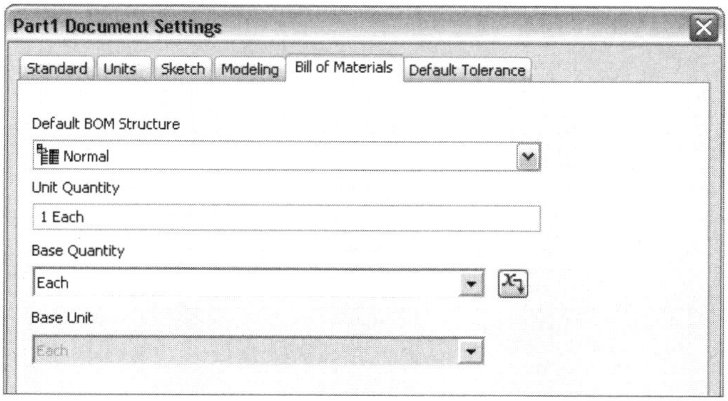

You can add BOM structure properties to individual parts in the Document Settings dialog box. Figure 4.7 shows the choices available in a model or assembly file for setting individual file properties.

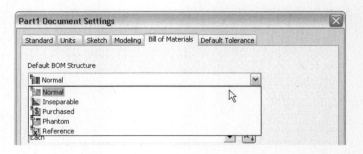

You'll use the Normal setting (the default) for most components. Parts designated as Normal are given an item number and included in quantity calculations. The placement of normal parts in the bill of materials is determined by the parent assembly properties. A normal subassembly may be composed of any combination of inseparable, phantom, purchased, and reference parts without having any affect on how those parts list in the BOM.

Inseparable components are assemblies that allow the inclusion of press fit, glued, welded, or riveted components that might be damaged if taken apart. A good example is a hinge that is fully assembled but should be listed in the BOM as a single part. Although the Inseparable structure is listed in the part's Document Settings dialog box, it is intended as an assembly property.

Purchased components are parts that are not normally fabricated or manufactured by your company but instead purchased from vendors. Any purchased component, whether part or assembly, will be listed in a parts-only parts list. A purchased component assembly will not normally have the component parts listed in the BOM, since that component will be purchased as a single unit.

Phantom components exist in the design but are not included as specific line items in the BOM. A construction assembly that exists as a container (subassembly) within a higher-level assembly, simply to hold a number of components together for assembly purposes, can be set to Phantom. When this assembly is set to Phantom, it will not appear in the parts list; however, the parts included within the construction assembly will be listed as individual parts.

Phantom components are ignored by the BOM. No item number is assigned, and no quantity calculations are performed on the phantom assembly. However, the quantity of individual parts contained within the phantom assembly will be multiplied by the quantity of the phantom component included in the top-level assembly.

A reference component designation is used to provide reference information within an assembly design. An example of a reference part might be a product container placed in a conveyor assembly. The conveyor components are the parts and assemblies you are designing, but the container is required to ensure clearance and function of your design. In a drawing, reference parts will be indicated in the view as hidden line geometry. Reference components are excluded from the BOM and are excluded from quantity, mass, or value calculations.

Figure 4.8 shows the Default Tolerance settings. Creating tolerance values affects sketches and parts only. Adding tolerance values to a part file requires that you select either Use Standard Tolerancing Values or Export Standard Tolerance Values, or you can select both options.

You can check the Standard Tolerancing Values box to use the precision and tolerance values set in this dialog box. You can check the Export Standard Tolerance Values box to export tolerance dimensions to the drawing environment.

Once you've selected an option, you can then add linear or angular tolerance values. You can add any number of tolerance values by precision to this part. When you have added your values to the part, click Apply to stay in the dialog box and apply the new settings to this tab, or click OK to apply the settings and exit the dialog box.

FIGURE 4.8
Default Tolerance tab in
Document Settings

Creating Basic Part Features

Inventor 3D part modeling is based upon the principle of creating a base feature and then adding features to finish out the part. Figure 4.9 illustrates the basic workflow for creating a part composed of many features.

FIGURE 4.9
Part creation workflow

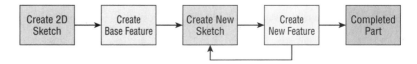

In general, it is good modeling practice to keep each sketch as simple as possible. Standard 2D drafting practice requires that you place all part details or components within a single view. It is not good practice to use the same 2D drafting workflow within any feature-based 3D modeler. Complicated sketches can drag down sketching performance and virtually eliminate easy changes to features. Consider the part shown in Figure 4.10. On the left is the part created from a single complex sketch; on the right is the same part created from a simple base feature and then several dependant features. The version on the left would prove difficult to modify, while the one on the right would be a snap because each feature is broken out into its own sketch. Of course, sometimes creating a more complex sketch is required, but if you follow the simple sketch rule of thumb, you will find Inventor much more accommodating, and you will quickly master part creation and will be ready to tackle complex sketches when they are needed.

FIGURE 4.10
Complex Sketch vs
Simple Sketch

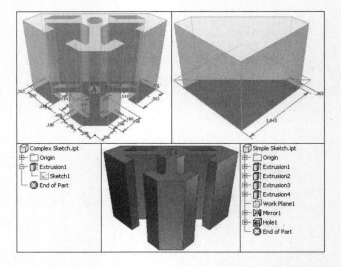

The base feature in a 3D model should always be anchored to the origin of the part for easy placement of that part in the future. The base feature will generally be the largest feature in the part, unless there is a specific reason for not making it so.

Feature dependencies can affect the extent to which you can modify a part in the future. Features are dependent upon other part geometry when you cannot delete or modify a portion of the part or feature without affecting another feature built later in the part. As an example, if you were to create a new face on a part and then create an additional feature on that face, then you could not delete the face without also deleting the new feature.

Although feature dependencies can be edited or broken, good design practice will eliminate the need to adjust dependencies later in the design. To preserve design intent, you should never break dependencies; instead, you should edit the underlying sketch geometry and anchor that geometry that created the feature to a different part feature. Broken dependencies will create a part that is not fully parametric.

Simplifying Your Sketches

In Figure 4.11 you can see a U-shaped block with a machined ridge surrounding a triangular opening, with threaded holes in different locations. Although you could create a single sketch to capture most of these features, this would make changing the part parametrically difficult, and would require a great deal of editing in the sketch.

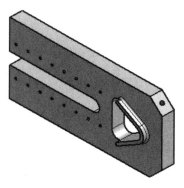

Using numerous features within a 3D model allows simplified control over modifications of the model in the future. Separate features may be suppressed or modified to alter the design, without having to make changes in a complicated sketch.

Instead of attempting to create all the geometry in a single sketch, we'll analyze the proposed part first. One good method for determining how well parts should be created in Inventor is to mimic the steps required to machine such a part.

In the shop, a machinist would first cut a rectangular shape to the proper size. Then the machinist would probably machine the slot and the chamfers at the end. Once that was completed, the machinist would probably mill the face of the part to create the triangular pocket and the extending lip around the pocket. The machinist then would create the threaded holes on the face and finish with the threaded holes in the chamfers.

SEAN SAYS: CONSIDER MODELING VS. MACHINING

Although the "design as you'd manufacture" paradigm is a great philosophy to follow when creating 3D parts, there is a major difference between modeling and machining. The difference is that when modeling you have the ability to add material, whereas a machining operation only takes away material.

This is a subject to consider when designing parts. It is easy to design a part that is impossible (or at least very expensive) to make in a normal machining center. Consider the location of features in relation to the parent features. In some cases, although the part may be easier to make as one piece, it might be less expensive to machine as multiple pieces. Also consider the size of the end mills and drills when creating parts. You can create very small fillets or square corners in a design, but try to machine a 0.010" fillet in a cavity that is 3" deep, and you'll quickly earn the ire of your local toolmaker.

Since a majority of the parts you'll be designing will one day need to be created out of metal and plastic, it pays to take the time to consider both your design and your real-world creation methods.

Creating a Part Using the Same Workflow

Start a new inch-based part file. Figure 4.12 details the geometry that should be included in Sketch1 of the part. In this case, a simple rectangle constrained to the origin will become the base feature by using the Extrude command after selecting Finish Sketch.

FIGURE 4.12
Initial sketch

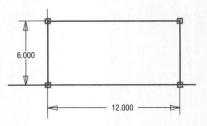

Take a look at the Extrude command before we show how to extrude Sketch1. When working in 3D modeling, it's always best to view the model in isometric mode so that you can easily preview the effect the command will have prior to execution. Right-click, and select Isometric View. Next select the Extrude command from the Part Features panel. Figure 4.13 shows the Part Features panel and the active Extrude command's dialog box.

FIGURE 4.13
Extrude feature options

The Extrude command permits you to create solid or surface geometry by checking the appropriate Output box. The default of this box will be solids if the unconsumed, visible sketch contains closed geometry. If the sketch geometry is not fully closed, then the Output box will automatically switch to surface, or a red plus icon might appear indicating that the sketch an open profile.

When extruding the base feature in a part, you will have only one option for extrusion, Join. The other two extrusion options, Cut and Intersect, are unavailable for the first feature. Other extent operations will be available for use on additional features within the same part. This menu is context-based, meaning that only certain commands are available during certain stages of operation.

Extrude extent options on the base feature include Distance, To, and From-To. When the Distance option is selected, you can input any unit value or parameter name/tag. When the To option is selected, you are prompted to select a face for the termination of the extrusion. When the From-To option is selected, you're prompted to select a start face and a termination face. If a termination face is smaller than the extrude profile, then you will need to check the Extended Face option, as shown in Figure 4.14.

The direction icons at the bottom of the Extents area allow extrusion in a forward, backward, or midplane direction. When a button is selected, the graphics screen will preview the direction and final size of the extrusion. If Midplane is selected, the extrusion will be equidistant in both directions.

FIGURE 4.14
Extrude to an extended face

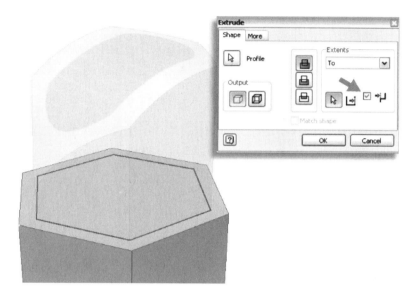

At the top of the dialog box, you will see a tab named More. Selecting this tab will permit you to set the Minimum Solution and Angle Of Extrusion properties. Selecting Minimum Solution allows extrusion termination on the nearest distance face when options for termination faces are ambiguous. An example of an ambiguous face is an extrusion terminating on a circular face where either side of the circular face could be considered the termination face, as shown in Figure 4.15.

FIGURE 4.15
Minimum Solution

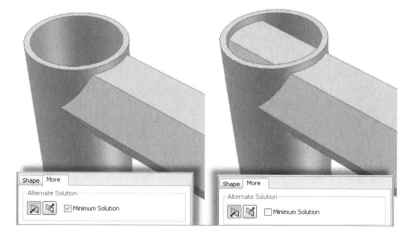

At the bottom of the More tab you can set a taper angle for the extrusion. Setting a positive value for the Angle option will result in the extrusion increasing in cross section as it is extruded. Setting a negative value for the Angle option will result in a smaller cross section at the end of the extrusion.

Creating the Second Feature

Once the base feature extrusion is created to a thickness of 1 inch, you can add a second feature to create the round end slot. To create a second feature, you will first need to create a new sketch. Click the large front face of the part, right-click, and select New Sketch, as shown in Figure 4.16.

FIGURE 4.16
Create a new sketch
on a face

You can also select Sketch and then select the face upon which to create the sketch. If you want to create a sketch off a known face, select Sketch and then a face. Before releasing the right mouse button, drag a plane off the face to create a new work plane and a sketch at the same time.

Sketch2 is now created and active. Click the Look At icon at the top of the screen next to the Orbit icon; then click Sketch2 in the Model browser to orient the active sketch plane perpendicular to your screen.

Sketch a rectangle on the face selected for the sketch. You can place this rectangle in the middle of the face for now; you will relocate it using a sketch constraint later. Sketch a circle at the end of the rectangle starting with the midpoint of the vertical line and snapping to the endpoint of the top or bottom line. You don't need to trim the circle before converting this sketch into a feature, and in fact unneeded trimming of sketch entities often works against you because it may remove sketch constraints.

Add dimensions as shown in Figure 4.17 and then constrain the midpoint of the rectangle to the midpoint of the left edge of Extrusion1 using the Coincident Constraint option. If Sketch2 is properly created and constrained to the edge, then the edge of the sketch rectangle and edge of the first extrusion will be collinear. Right-click, and choose Finish Sketch. Then right-click and select Isometric View.

FIGURE 4.17
Creating and dimension-
ing geometry in Sketch2

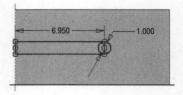

SEAN SAYS: USE WORK FEATURES TO ANCHOR YOUR SKETCHES

Another way to anchor this sketch to the midplane of the rectangle is by using work features. Before starting this sketch, select the Workplane feature tool. Select one side of the rectangular feature and then the other. This will create a parametrically centered work plane.

Now create a sketch on the surface of the features as shown in Figure 4.14. Use the Project Geometry tool, and select the work plane created in the previous step. This will project a line onto the sketch plane. Now use this line as a centerline in your sketch creation sequence. If you were to ever change the size of the base feature, then the work plane, the projected line, and hence this sketch would all update and remain centered.

While in isometric view, select the Extrude command from the Part Features panel. Select both the rectangle and the circle to be extruded. Since you are removing material from this part, you need to select the middle button, Cut, to cut the slot into the base feature.

You will notice that additional options have been added into the Extents pulldown menu: To Next and All. The To Next option tells Inventor to extrude to the next termination face if one is available.

The All option extrudes the profile through all the current features of the entire part in the specified direction or in both directions if you chose the Midplane option. If the size of the base part features change, then the cut extrusion feature will update accordingly.

In the case of a part like this, you will always want the slot feature to cut completely through the part. Since that is the desired result of this extrusion, you will want to select All, as shown in Figure 4.18, for the termination value. Click OK to complete the extrusion.

FIGURE 4.18
Extruding (cutting) the second feature

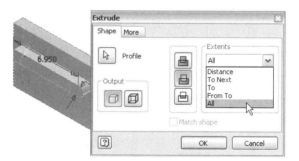

The previous two part features were constructed using the Extrude command on a sketch. These features are called *sketched features*, because they are based upon a preexisting sketch. Another type of feature is the placed feature. Placed features do not necessarily rely upon a preexisting sketch but are solely dependent upon existing part geometry.

Creating a Placed Chamfer Feature

Ordinarily, a designer would create chamfer and fillet features at the end of the overall part creation process. Creating chamfers and fillets at the end of the process reduces errors because of feature dependencies associated with these features. In this model, however, you will need to create the chamfers at this point, because threaded holes rely on the face created by the chamfers.

Select the Chamfer command from the Part Features tool panel. When the Chamfer dialog box appears, you will notice that there are three options for chamfer creation.

The first option is the Distance option, where the distance on each adjoining leg of the selected edge will be offset the same distance, creating a 45°-angle chamfer. The second option allows for setting a distance and an angle that will determine the shape of the chamfer. The third option allows you to specify two distances that determine the final shape.

In Figure 4.19, you will see that additional options are exposed to allow setback options on corner treatments when three converging edges come together. The two icons shown represent the end effect of selecting the particular corner treatment option.

FIGURE 4.19
Create chamfered corners

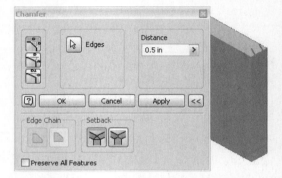

For the example design, you will select the first option, Distance, and enter a distance of 0.5 inch. The result will be a 45° chamfer where both legs of the chamfer are equal. So, click the two edges as shown in Figure 4.19, set the distance, and click OK to complete the chamfer feature.

Creating a Sketch-Based Hole Feature

Hole features are very powerful components of Inventor. Many methods are available for creating hole features. Hole features can be created by utilizing existing sketches containing sketch center points, by distance from two planar edges, on a face by referencing concentric edge, or by using a work point feature.

Looking at the existing model, you can see that the two newly created chamfers were placed on opposing sides of the same edge. Since the chamfers are equal in size, their placement sets up a situation where you can create a single hole on one of the chamfers and then mirror the whole feature onto the other chamfer.

The design intent of the hole feature requires that the hole remain centered in the chamfer face. Therefore, placing a hole by edges will not easily retain this intent. Instead, you will create a sketch for the hole placement. To do this, click the face that was created by the chamfer feature; then right-click, and select New Sketch.

To find the center of the chamfer face, draw a diagonal construction line from one corner of the face to the other, as shown in Figure 4.20. Ensure that the Construction icon is unchecked, and select the Point, Center Point icon in the 2D Sketch panel. Place a centerpoint at the midpoint of the construction line just created. A centerpoint locates the position of a sketched hole feature automatically. It is important to understand the difference between a point and a centerpoint and how the two are used by the Hole command. Onscreen, a centerpoint is displayed as a point and crosshair, where as a point is displayed as a simple dot. Much like you can toggle a standard line to be a construction line, you can also toggle a centerpoint to be a simple point. You can do this by using the Center Point icon next to the Construction icon. As with the Construction icon, you can do this prior to placing the point/centerpoint or after the fact. The Hole tool, as you are about to see, will automatically pick up the centerpoints in a sketch but will not automatically pick up simple points.

FIGURE 4.20
Placing a centerpoint

When the sketch is complete, right-click, and choose Finish Sketch. Click the Hole command in the Part Features panel, and set Placement to From Sketch if that is not default. If your center-point was not automatically selected by the Hole tool, then you can select it now. Note that if you have more than one unconsumed sketch in your part, the Hole tool will not automatically pick up the centerpoints because the application has no way of knowing which sketch you intend to use. With the centerpoint selected, click the Tapped Hole option and set the size to 0.375. After you set the size, the Designation pulldown will provide a list of thread types for the selected size. Set the designation to 3/8-16 UNC. For the hole depth, set the value to 25.4 mm. Note that although this is an inch-based part, you can enter values in any type of unit measurement, and Inventor will automatically calculate the default equivalent, which is inches in this case. Keep in mind that entering 25.4 without a unit suffix will result in a 25.4-inch hole because Inventor assumes the default unit for any value that is not specified. At this point, your screen should look like Figure 4.21. Click OK to create the hole feature. Note that this feature is listed in the model browser.

FIGURE 4.21
Placing a threaded hole feature

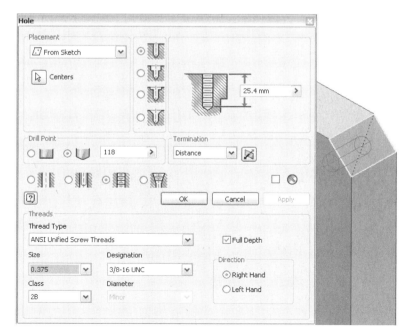

Mirroring Features

Now you want to mirror the hole across the center of the part. To do so, you require a face or place to use as a mirror reference. So, you will simply create a work plane to serve as this reference.

In the Part Features panel, select Workplane. To create a midpart work plane, you can simply choose two parallel faces, and a bisecting work plane will automatically be centered between them. If the position of one of the faces should ever change, thereby changing the distance between the two faces, the bisecting work plane will adjust automatically to stay centered between the two faces. For this part, choose the two opposing faces, as shown in Figure 4.22. Additional work features types will be introduced and explained later in this chapter.

FIGURE 4.22
Creating a midpart work
plane

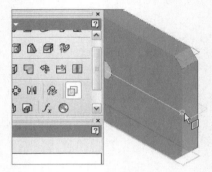

Now that you've created the work plane, you'll mirror the hole across the part. Choose the Mirror command in the Part Features panel. Select the hole feature from the Model browser, or click the feature itself in the graphics window. Switch the selection focus from features to mirror plane by clicking the Mirror Plane icon in the Mirror dialog box, and select the work plane you created previously.

Figure 4.23 shows the expanded dialog box obtained by clicking the >> symbol that appears in many dialog boxes within Inventor. Expanded dialog boxes reveal options for that specific dialog box. In this case, you'll see the Creation Method options. (Every dialog box also contains a Help icon that provides additional information on a specific subject.)

FIGURE 4.23
Mirroring features

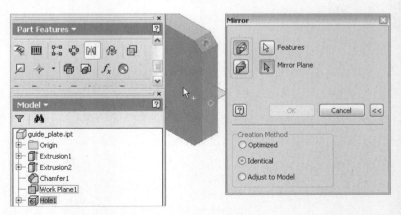

Since the mirror will occur on a different face, the Identical method will be used. Although Optimized is the fastest method when used to create a mirrored feature, it is best used when mirroring complex features that might otherwise take a long time to compute and only when the mirror occurs on the same face.

Note too that had you decided to create only half of this part, you could set the Mirror method to Mirror The Entire Solid. There is an option in this method to remove the original as well.

Once you've set the work plane to Mirror Plane, click OK to create a second hole feature on the opposite chamfer. Right-click the work plane, and uncheck Visibility to hide the work plane. As a matter of best practice, Workfeature Visibility should be turned off when the work feature is no longer in use.

Creating a Placed Hole Feature

When examining the original model, note that there are two rows of threaded holes on the front face of the part. The specifications for this part indicate that each row of holes is evenly spaced from hole to hole. The left hole is spaced 0.75 inches above the top edge of the U-shaped groove and 0.5 inches from the left edge of the part. Although you could create a sketch to place the hole as you did with the first hole, this time you will go directly into the Hole dialog box to create a placed hole feature.

With the Hole tool, select Linear for the placement method. Select the front face where the holes will be created. Once the front face has been selected, the dialog box will toggle to a selection of Reference 1. Click the top horizontal edge of the groove, and type **0.75** inch for the offset value. Click the left vertical edge of the part, and type **0.5** inch for the offset value. You will now create a threaded hole with a Termination setting of Through All and a Designation setting of 5/16-18 UNC. Once you have set the dialog box to match Figure 4.24, click OK.

FIGURE 4.24
Hole placement by linear method

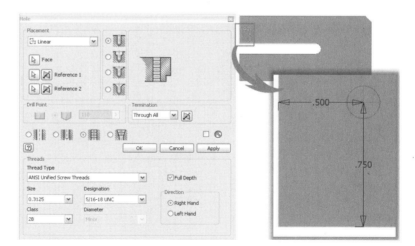

LEARNING MORE ABOUT HOLE FEATURES

Additional placement methods and hole types are available within the Hole dialog box. Some of these additional methods and types are covered in future exercises. You are encouraged to explore every dialog box encountered during the scope of this book so that you learn about the potential uses for these options. As you hover over each option segment, a tool tip will appear describing the option.

One good way to learn about the options that are available is to create a "play part" consisting of rectangular and circular objects. This way, you can explore all the hole options by trying the options without fear of making a mistake or unconsciously modifying a real part. This problem-solving technique allows you to eliminate variables and isolate the geometry specific to the tool on which you are focusing.

Creating a Rectangular Hole Pattern

You will notice on the original part shown in Figure 4.10 that there seems to be a pattern of holes surrounding the U-shaped cut. A quick way to create all the holes needed for this part is to pattern the placed hole you just created. There are actually two reasons to consider a rectangular pattern:

◆ A pattern saves time when creating spaced, multiple instances of a feature.

◆ Using a pattern in a part allows you to later use that pattern to create a component pattern in an assembly and follow the original part pattern. For instance, if you placed this part into an assembly, you could pattern a bolt to occupy every hole within the pattern by simply constraining one bolt into the original hole feature, and then use the component pattern tool to automatically pick up the hole pattern count and spacing. The pattern component command is available only within the assembly environment.

Let's determine the pattern spacing first. From the creation of the second feature, you know that the round and slot has a width of 1 inch. From the creation of the placed hole, you know that the offset from the slot edge is 0.75 inches. From this information, you will determine that the spacing of the two rows of holes are (2 × offset value) + 1 inch, or 2.5 inches.

The original design specification shows eight holes in each row spaced at a distance of 1 inch apart. With this information, you are now ready to proceed with creating the hole pattern.

Figure 4.25 shows the Rectangular Pattern dialog box. Although some options are available within this dialog box, they will not be used for this simple pattern. Select the placed hole from the Model browser or by selecting the hole in the graphics window.

FIGURE 4.25
Rectangular pattern preview

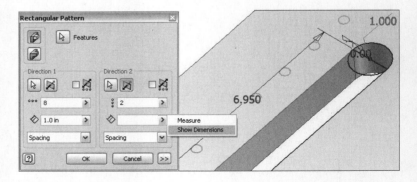

Click the arrow icon under Direction 1, and select the top horizontal edge of the part. You can select any horizontal edge for this purpose since you're determining only the direction for the pattern. You will notice that a direction arrow appears indicating the direction that the pattern will follow. If the direction is not following into the part, then click the Direction icon next to the arrow you just selected. This will toggle the direction of the pattern.

Change the Quantity box under Direction 1 to 8. Change the Column Spacing box to 1 inch (default). Notice that there are options under the Spacing pulldown menu. Leave the setting at Spacing.

Once the first direction has been determined, click the arrow icon under Direction 2. Select any vertical edge of the part to determine the vertical pattern direction. Change the direction if needed. Change the quantity box under Direction 2 to the value of 2 (default).

Although you could just change the Row Spacing value to 2.5 inches and complete the pattern, you might want to consider what would happen if the width of the slot feature were to change. If that were to happen, then the hole pattern spacing would stay at 2.5 and no longer remain symmetric to the slot width. To avoid this, you will make the pattern Row Spacing parametric by calling the dimensions of earlier features into our pattern spacing and building a formula right into the pattern so that if those dimensions change, the Row Spacing setting will follow.

To do this, first clear the Row Spacing input box. Next click the arrow at the right of the Row Spacing box, and click Show Dimensions from the flyout. Now choose the slot feature from the graphics area. This will display all the dimensions you created when sketching that feature, as shown in Figure 4.25. Note that if you accidentally select the wrong feature, you can return to the Row Spacing input and choose Show Dimension again. Once the dimensions are shown, you can select the diameter dimension, 1.0 inch.

Once you select the shown dimension, the dimension's name will appear in the Row Spacing box. Inventor automatically gives each dimension a name starting with d0 and incrementing up. Type a plus sign next to the dimension name. Next, click the arrow at the right of the Row Spacing box, and select Show Dimensions from the flyout again. This time choose the hole, and choose the 0.75 offset dimension. To compete the spacing expression, add *2 so that you are multiplying the 0.75 × 2. The result should look similar to Figure 4.26; note, though, that dimension names may vary from what is shown here depending upon the order in which you placed your dimensions. Click OK to set the pattern.

FIGURE 4.26
Rectangular pattern with a formula

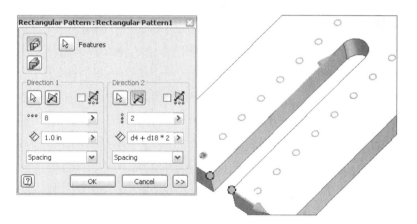

Exercise caution when using patterns. Although they can be very powerful, they can also be used in place of proper design intent. If there is a possibility that these holes might change to become nonequidistant in the future, the part should be designed with parametrically placed individual holes. Although this is more time-consuming, it is the proper way to construct the part. However, if the pattern will always remain, the pattern tool is a quick and powerful way to accomplish the task.

Creating a Second Extruded Cut and Associated Lip

The process of creating the triangular extruded cut is similar to creating the slot within this part. The triangular cut will form the basis of the associated extruded lip.

Starting a new sketch on the front face of the part, select the Polygon command from the 2D Sketch panel. Enter **3** in the Number Of Sides input box, and click the part face to set the center of the three-sided polygon. Note that after selecting the center, you can click the screen again to size the triangle. Use a parallel constraint to orient the triangle, as shown in Figure 4.27. Use the Sketch Fillet tool to place the 0.5-inch fillets on the corners, and place a dimension on one of the side so that your sketch matches Figure 4.27. Take special note that you create a construction line from the midpoint of the vertical triangle edge to the midpoint of the right-side part edge.

FIGURE 4.27
Sketch4 complete

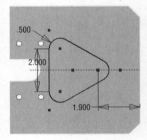

Another approach to creating this sketch is to use the Line tool, which has the capability of drawing arcs at the end of the line. You construct the arc within the Line tool by clicking the end of the current line while dragging the cursor away from the endpoint. Figure 4.28 illustrates the procedure. It may be helpful to exaggerate the arc when dragging from the end of the circle in order to get the arc direction correct.

FIGURE 4.28
Using the Line tool to
create arcs

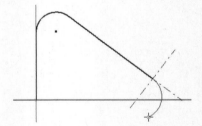

Once the sketch is fully constrained and dimensioned, you can finish the sketch and extrude the sketch through the part. You are now ready to construct the extruded lip on the part by using projected part geometry.

Projected sketch geometry allows the reuse of existing part geometry from the current features. When in an assembly file, you can also project geometry located on other parts.

Note that depending upon your sketch settings in Application Options, some projected geometry may be automatically created upon sketch creation. Before going to the next step, look at your settings by selecting Tools ➤ Application Options and clicking the Sketch tab. Note the setting highlighted in Figure 4.29 called Autoproject Edges For Sketch Creation And Edit. Having this checked will automatically project the edges of the face on which you sketch. Note that although this can be convenient in some cases, it can also become counterproductive because it places extra line work into your sketches. This can add a level of complexity to your sketch constraints as well. Ensure that this is unchecked at least for the next step of this exercise so that you can explore how to project geometry in a controlled manner.

FIGURE 4.29
Project edge settings

You will need to create another sketch for the projected lip. Click the front face once again, right-click, and select New Sketch. Using the Project Geometry command in the 2D Sketch panel, select the two right edges of the triangle and the arc between the two edges. You will notice that Inventor has created the projected reference geometry on the selected edges, as shown in Figure 4.30.

FIGURE 4.30
Projecting these three edges

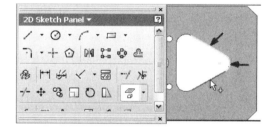

This projected geometry is different from ordinary sketch geometry, and it is now associated with the cut edges. The projected geometry can be deleted in the future but cannot be edited unless you right-click and select Break Link. When the link is broken, the geometry reverts to ordinary lines. In this example, you will want to preserve the link so that any changes to the triangular shape will also alter the associated lip.

Select the Offset command from the 2D Sketch panel, and select the projected geometry in your sketch, dragging it away from the triangular opening. Place a dimension between the projected geometry and the offset geometry and then dimension the distance between the offset lines at a value of 0.25 inch.

Using the three-point Arc command in the 2D Sketch panel, select the two endpoints between the projected and the offset geometry. Once the two endpoints are selected, drag your cursor out until you see the two implied tangent constraint glyphs. Repeat the Arc command on the other two endpoints. When completed, press F8 to show all constraints. Your screen should look similar to Figure 4.31. To clear the constraint view, press F9.

FIGURE 4.31
Showing all sketch
constraints

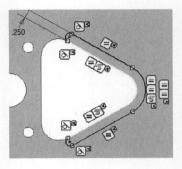

Your sketch is now complete, so finish the sketch, and extrude the lip away from the front face 0.375 inch, as shown in Figure 4.32.

FIGURE 4.32
Extruding the lip feature

One final step remains to finish this part. In the Part Features panel, select the Fillet command, and place a 0.25 radius fillet on the bottom-outer intersecting edge of the lip. Many dialog boxes such as for the Fillet command allow you to select the geometry but do not contain a selection icon. In these dialog boxes, you are given the option of selecting Selected or Click To Add within the dialog box. Note that in the Fillet dialog box if you set the fillet size before selecting the edges, the arrow icon will turn into a pencil icon. To set the focus back to selected edges so that you can click edges onscreen, simply click the pencil, and it will change back to an arrow indicating that edge selection is on.

In Figure 4.33, you will see that five edges have been selected by clicking the intersecting edge. The five edges that were selected are the end arcs, the two straight line edges, and the large arc between the lines.

FIGURE 4.33
Fillet preview on the lip

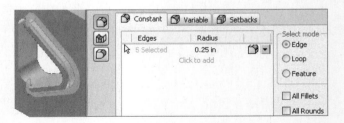

If you had additional edges to click, you could either click the word Selected to add filleted edges with the same radius value or add radius values and edges by clicking Click To Add.

Your part is now complete, and you can save this as guide_plate.ipt. Leave the file open for the next section of this chapter.

Modifying Existing Part Features

Perhaps the greatest power of parametric modeling is the ability to modify existing features as needed. Making a change in a 2D drawing can be tedious, time-consuming, and above all error prone if changes are not followed through to all drawings involved. In Inventor, by contrast, changes to the model will automatically propagate through to the drawings in all views, on every sheet. If a parametric model is properly created using multiple features to capture the design intent, then a modification more often than not is affected by merely editing a feature or the underlying sketch that created the features.

In the guide_plate.ipt example just completed, you created many features. This example represents good part creation workflow in that every feature that exists within the model can be easily modified.

Models are modified by isolating the feature to be edited. You will be making a determination whether the feature or the underlying sketch will be edited. Figure 4.34 shows the process of selecting a feature for edit. In the Model browser of guide_plate.ipt, click the plus sign to the left of Extrusion 1. You will notice that the browser expands to show Extrusion 1 and the underlying Sketch1.

FIGURE 4.34
Right-click/edit feature

Let's edit the extrusion distance of Extrusion 1. Right-click Extrusion 1 in the browser, and select Edit Feature. Set the extrusion distance by changing the extrusion value to 2 inches. Click OK to update the part. Let's also edit the width of Extrusion 2. To do this, you need to edit the sketch rather than the feature. Right-click Extrusion 2 in the browser, and select Edit Sketch. Double-click the diameter dimension, and change the value from 1 to 0.75.

Once the part is updated, examine the part to make sure that all design intent has been preserved. If this is the case, you will notice the following:

◆ The U-shaped extrusion extends completely through the part. If you incorrectly specified the extrusion depth, rather than selecting the option of All, then the extrusion probably stopped at 1 inch, which was the original value of Extrusion 1. If that is the case, you will need to edit Extrusion 2 and change the extrusion setting to All.

◆ The rectangular pattern of holes should extend through the back side of the part. If the rectangular pattern has a fixed depth, then you will need to edit Hole 2 and change the termination to Through All. If the triangular shaped cut does not cut through the entire base part, then you will need to change the extrusion depth of that feature as well.

◆ Examine the holes that were created on the chamfers. If the holes are not centered on the chamfer faces, then you have incorrectly created the sketch that placed the Hole 1 feature. You will need to go back and correct the underlying sketch to fix this problem.

PRESERVING DESIGN INTENT

A part may change many times before a machine design is completed. Often the overall part size may need to be changed, a feature will need to be resized, or additional features will need to be added. If the part has been properly constructed, changes to the part are easily and quickly accomplished.

Often you may need to change the overall size of a part to accommodate a redesigned component that pushes change down through the assembly. In changing the size, you may also have to adjust some of the other features as well. Designing a part with an eye toward preserving design intent will reap great rewards in accuracy and productivity. For instance, you might have a choice in the sketch environment of pulling a dimension from the outside edge of the part, or of pulling the dimension from an existing feature. Although the result may seem the same initially, anticipating edits begins to distinguish the difference.

When developing a part design, you should consider many factors. One factor is functionality. Determining how a part will function within the design helps the engineer determine the overall size and shape, what material will be needed for the part, and how that part will interact or interfere with other parts contained within the machine design.

Another factor might be overall mass or total weight of the combined design. Overall mass may affect the amount of power required to make the machine function. Reducing the mass of each part while retaining overall strength will normally reduce the machine's power requirements or allow more start/stop functions in a given time frame.

Quite often, parts will be modified many times in order to meet design parameters. Creating independent features allow the preservation of design intent and the modification of the part without breaking the design.

The redesign of the guide_plate.ipt requires that the drilled, threaded holes be changed. You will need to change the designation of the rectangular arrayed holes to counterbored clearance holes.

Right-click Hole 2, and select Edit Feature. Change from Drilled hole to Counterbore in the upper portion of the dialog box. When making this change, examine the options for the hole type. This dialog box will create drilled holes, counterbores, spotfaces, and countersunk hole types. You can combine these options with other options within the dialog box. An example is that you could create a counterbored hole with or without threads or a counterbored clearance hole as your change requires.

Select Clearance, as shown in Figure 4.35. You will notice that the bottom portion of the Hole dialog box has changed and now shows fastener information.

Thread values are determined by an Excel spreadsheet called Threads.xls. The thread listings on Hole2 when it was set to Threads rather than Clearance was determined by the values in the spreadsheet. If the specific thread values that you require are not contained within the current spreadsheet, then you can edit this spreadsheet as required. Of course, anytime you start to make edits to a system file, you should back up the original to give you a place to return should your edits not go well.

Clearance values are determined by a different spreadsheet called Clearance.xls. Like the thread value spreadsheet, you can edit this one as well. Both spreadsheets are located in the \Inventor(version name)\Design Data folder under Program Files.

With the clearance option selected, determining the fastener standard, type, size, and fit is very simple. Once the proper options have been indicated, the clearance spreadsheet will determine all the values.

Set all values as shown in Figure 4.35. When the values have been input, click OK to update the model. Figure 4.36 shows the result of this change.

FIGURE 4.35
Editing Hole2 feature values and settings

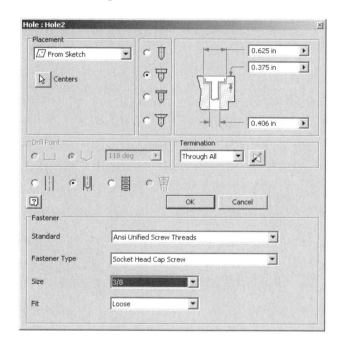

FIGURE 4.36
Updated guide plate

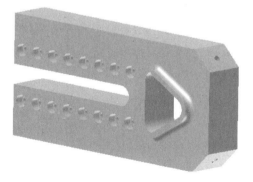

Creating and Using Work Features

Earlier in this chapter, you created a work plane as a reference for a mirror function. Placing this work plane was a simple procedure, easily understood. Unfortunately, not all parts are rectangular in shape. Creating complex, nonplanar parts requires a good understanding of using and creating work planes, work axes, and work points.

Work features do not directly create other features but are instead considered reference type geometry. Using work features assists you in creating or placing features or components where there is no other point of reference.

There are three environments in which work features can function. The creation of work features within each of the environments remains local to that environment, with few exceptions. The three environments where work features are created and function are parts, assemblies, and 3D sketches.

Let's address the work features within parts first. As you have discovered, you can easily create a new sketch on the flat faces of a part. 2D sketches require a planar face for their existence, so a curved or spherical face cannot be selected to create a 2D sketch. However, many times you are required to do just that. Work planes come to the rescue because they are planar and can be created on just about any type of geometry. The key to creating any work plane is to specify a location and an orientation.

Work Plane Tangent to Cylinder

Let's look at the problem of creating a drilled hole on the circular face of a cylinder. Creating a drilled hole on the ends of a cylinder is not a problem because the ends of the cylinder are planar; however, creating a drilled hole in the cylindrical face is not straightforward. Creating a work plane tangent to the face of the cylinder allows you to then create a sketch referencing the work plane, from which you can then place the hole. This section shows how it's done.

Create a new metric part file by selecting the Standard (mm).ipt template from the Metric tab in the New File dialog box. If your Inventor software was installed using the ANSI (inch) standard as the default, then the Metric tab will appear at the top of the dialog box, as shown in Figure 4.37.

FIGURE 4.37
Selecting Standard
(mm).ipt

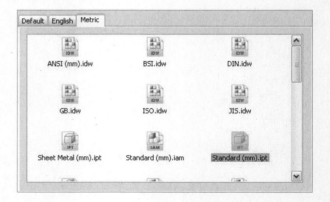

In Sketch1, create a circle starting at the origin point, and give it a dimension of 45 mm. Right-click and then select Finish Sketch. Switch to isometric view, and extrude the circle to a distance of 1.5 inches. Mixing unit types is simple in any Inventor file because the unit type determined in Document Settings will convert any input value to the preset unit equivalent. When using alternate unit types, be sure that your value is followed by the unit type. The cylinder is now created. Save this file as WP-Cylinder.ipt, and leave this file open.

SEAN SAYS: UNDERSTAND UNITS IN EQUATIONS

One stumbling block people often encounter when entering units in a dimension dialog box is the case of the characters. The proper abbreviation for inches is in, not IN. Millimeters is mm, not MM. If you enter the case incorrectly, the equation will remain red and will not be accepted. You can also mix units. For example, 25.4 in/23.1 mm * 2 ft is a perfectly valid equation. To see a list of all the acceptable equations in Inventor, select Help ➤ Help Topics and enter **units, equations** in the index search box.

In the next step, select the Work Axis icon in the Part Features panel. Select the circular face of the cylinder, and a work axis will be created through the center of the cylinder. This axis will be used to help anchor the sketch that you will create in the next step. It is important to note that each part has three default origin axes and three default work planes, as well as the default origin point, all of which exist in the Origin folder. Since you created the circle in your sketch on the origin point, you could have just turned the visibility on for the default z-axis, rather than creating a new axis at the center of the part. We have created a user axis here to illustrate how you might create a work axis on a part feature that is not placed at the part origin, but keep in mind that in the real world it is best practice to use origin geometry when you can.

You will now need to create a work plane to reference a new sketch. Click the Workplane icon, and select the YZ plane from the Origin folder in the Model browser and then the front of the circular face. A work plane is created parallel to the YZ plane and tangent to the circular face. Again, a work plane is defined by a location and an orientation. Here the cylindrical face supplies the location, and the YZ plane supplies the orientation. Figure 4.38 illustrates a correctly placed user work plane.

FIGURE 4.38
Creating an offset/
tangent work plane

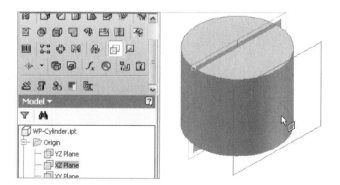

You will notice that work planes have a different color on each side of the work plane. The yellow colored side is called the *normal* side and is typically the side that faces in the positive Z direction. However, you can flip the normal side if required by simply right-clicking the edge of the work plane and choosing Flip Normal. Note that you always select work planes by clicking the edges; clicking in the center of the work plane does not select the work plane but instead the objects behind the work plane. This is so work planes can remain visible without getting in your way.

Sketching on a Work Plane

Right-click the edge of the work plane created in Figure 4.38, and select New Sketch. Click the Look At icon and select Sketch 2 in the Model browser to orient your view perpendicular to the screen. Use the Project Geometry command in the 2D Sketch panel to project the axis in the center of the cylinder. You will be using this projected work axis as construction geometry for the purpose of positioning and anchoring a centerpoint.

Remember, you can convert any selected object in the sketch to construction geometry by preselecting the geometry and then selecting the Construction icon at the top of the screen. Of course, just as you can when sketching construction lines, you can also select the Construction icon before projecting geometry so that all your projected objects will automatically be construction objects. Remember, though, that if you select the Construction icon when projecting an axis or edge, then you will need to deselect the icon before returning to regular geometry.

In sketch view, with the Construction icon toggled on, project one circular edge of the cylinder. Projecting this edge will give you an additional reference point for locating the point and center-point in the next step. Turning off visibility on the work plane by right-clicking should allow you to see the dashed construction lines, if they are not visible to you at this point.

While in sketch mode, select the Point, Center Point icon in the 2D Sketch panel. Click the construction line created from the work axis, and place the centerpoint directly on the construction line. Be careful to click to one side or the other of the midpoint of the construction line to avoid placing a coincident constraint on that midpoint. Placing the point directly on the construction line should have added an implied coincident constraint between the centerpoint and the line. Press F8, or right-click and select Show All Constraints, to see whether the implied constraint exists on the placed point. If the implied constraint does not exist, then right-click and select Constraints from the menu. Use the Coincident constraint. Select F9, or right-click and select Hide All Constraints.

Add a general dimension between the projected edge and the centerpoint by using the value of 21 mm. Your sketch should look like Figure 4.39.

FIGURE 4.39
Anchoring the point and
centerpoint

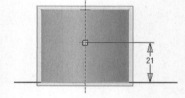

Place an M2 × 0.4 counterbore, threaded hole on the centerpoint, as shown in Figure 4.40. Use the values in the dialog box for reference.

Creating Text in a Sketch

You'll now create an embossed feature 90° from the existing hole. An *embossed* feature is created from a 2D sketch. In the first work plane example, you created a tangent work plane by selecting the YZ origin plane. To create the new work plane, simply select the XZ origin plane (orientation) and the outer tangent face of the cylinder (location). You may need to right-click and select Flip Normal to position the normal side of the work plane away from the cylinder. Once the yellow, normal side is facing out from the cylinder, right-click the edge of the work plane and select New Sketch.

FIGURE 4.40
Metric threaded hole values

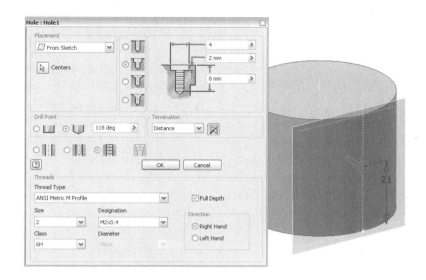

Select the Look At icon, and click the work plane you just created. The screen should now orient to the work plane. You just learned a second way to orient the screen, perpendicular to your sketch view.

You will be embossing your name onto the part in this step. Select the Text icon from the 2D Sketch panel. Click a point that is inside the current area occupied by the cylinder to place the text. In the Text dialog box, change the font type to Arial and the type size to 6.10 mm. Set the type style to Bold, and type your first name. Click OK to exit the dialog box. You should now see your first name in the current sketch, surrounded by a text box or reference line. If the text appears inside out, as if reading it in a mirror, then your work plane normal needs to be flipped.

The text line/box aids in the placement of text within Inventor. The edges of the text box may be constrained and dimensioned like any other geometry. You will use this capability to anchor and center the text box within the part. You will first need a reference for constraining purposes, so you will need to project the work axis into this sketch. Even though the work axis was projected in the previous sketch, every sketch where it is needed for reference will require another projection.

After you have projected the work axis, you will then need to create a vertical construction line through the center of the text line/box. While in the active sketch, click the construction icon and then the Line tool, and draw a line vertically from the midpoint of the text line/box to the other midpoint. Right-click and select Create Constraint. Using the coincident constraint, click the midpoint of the center vertical line in the text box and then click the projected work axis construction line. Your text box will now be centered about the axis.

Using the General Dimension command, click the horizontal line in the text box and the referenced circular edge of the cylinder. Type a value of 0.75, and accept the value by selecting the check box. You will see that the value of the dimension you just created has changed to 19.05 mm, because you are using a metric unit template. At this point, click Finish Sketch, and click Save.

Because Inventor does not have an autosave function, you should save frequently during the construction of a model or assembly. Your part should look similar to Figure 4.41.

FIGURE 4.41
Text on a tangent work plane

Embossing Text

Using the Emboss command from the Part Features tool panel, select your name, and change the direction arrow to point toward the cylinder. Select the Wrap To Face box, and select the face of the cylinder. There are three options for the Emboss command: Emboss From Face (add), Engrave From Face (remove), and Emboss/Engrave From Plane (which will add and remove material as needed when embossing across an uneven face). Select the Engrave From Face option. With the depth set at 1 mm, click OK.

As an option, you can also preselect the face color by clicking the button just below the Depth setting. Changing the face color will make the emboss feature more visible to the eye. You can change the color of features or faces within any part by right-clicking any feature in the Model browser or by right-clicking an individual face within the graphics window and changing properties to the desired color. See Figure 4.42.

FIGURE 4.42
Embossing text

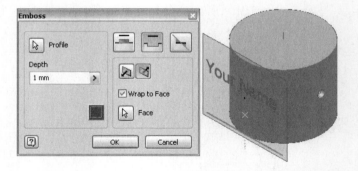

We'll show additional techniques for creating and using work features at appropriate times in later chapters. Information and examples on work features and usage is also available within the Inventor help files. Autodesk Inventor contains a wealth of information available at your fingertips by simply selecting one of the help icons, such as the Visual Syllabus shown in Figure 4.43. Don't forget to consult the command specific How To information found by right-clicking while in any command and selecting How To.

FIGURE 4.43
The Visual Syllabus
within Inventor

The Bottom Line

Create basic part features   In this chapter, you lerned how to plan a workflow that allows you to create stable, editable parts that preserve design intent.

Master It   You need to create a fairly complex part consisting of many extrusions, revolves, sweeps, or lofts. In addition, you will need to create holes, fillets, chamfers, and other part modifiers. This part may need significant modification in the future by you or by other designers.

Create and use work features in part mode   Using work features, work planes, work axes, and work points enable you to create virtually any part or feature. Work features are the building blocks for sketch creation and use.

Master It   Your design will require creating features on spherical and cylindrical faces. You need to precisely control the location and angle of these features.

Place and configure hole features   There are several approaches for creating and modifying existing holes.

Master It   You are required to design a part with several types of clearance and threaded holes, some of which may be custom thread designations and all of which are likely to change in size, designation, or fit.

Pattern and mirror features   In this chapter, you looked at how to pattern and mirror features on a part. Using both commands can streamline your part design.

Master It   You are tasked with creating a complex part with a group of features that are not only symmetrically distributed across the part center but are also evenly spaced along the length of the part.

Modify existing part features   History-based modeling provides access to previously created sketches and features for ease of editing.

Master It   You are collaborating on designing a new variation of a standard component. You anticipate changes to your design as the collaborative team collects information and works through design challenges.

Chapter 5

Advanced Modeling Techniques

Chapter 4 introduced some of the basic modeling techniques required when creating a 3D parametric part. Modern parametric modeling utilizes numerous features to create stable, editable parts. The basic workflow in creating a part is to create a base feature and then build upon the base.

In this chapter, you will be exploring more complex and curvy modeling techniques that will enable you to build far more real-world parts. Now that you have mastered creating simple parts, you are ready to move on to the fun stuff.

All the skills in this chapter are primarily based on creating a single part, whether in a part file or in the context of an assembly file. You should learn or review these basics first before jumping into the more complex features.

In this chapter, you will learn how to:

◆ Create complex sweeps and lofts

◆ Design turned parts and threads

◆ Utilize part tolerances

◆ Understand and use parameters and iProperties

◆ Analyze parts and work with base solids

◆ Troubleshoot modeling failures

Complex Sweeps and Lofts

Now that you have moved from creating simple parts, you will explore the use of sweeps and lofts to create complex parts. Both sweeps and lofts require one or more profiles to create a flowing shape. Sweeps require one sketch profile and a second sketched sweep path to create 3D geometry. Lofts require two or more sketch profiles and optional rails and/or points that assist in controlling the final geometry.

Creating and Using Sweeps

You can think of a sweep feature as an extrusion that follows a path defined by another sketch. You can utilize a 2D or 3D sketch path to create a sweep feature. You can use sweeps to add or remove material from a part, or you can use the Intersect option as you can with the Extrusion command. As with most Inventor geometry, a sweep can be created as a solid or a surface.

CREATING 2D PATHS

When creating a sweep feature, you can first create the path sketch and then create a profile sketch that will contain the geometry to be swept along the path. Normally, this geometry will be perpendicular to one end of the sweep path. To create the sketch, you will need to create a work plane at the end of your path. This work plane will be referenced to create a new sketch.

A basic rule of sweep features is that the volume occupied by the sweep profile may not intersect itself within the feature. Self-intersecting features are not currently supported. An example of a self-intersecting feature is a sweep path composed of straight-line segments with tight radius arcs between the segments. Assuming that the sweep profile is circular in nature with a radius value larger than the smallest arc within the sweep path, the feature would self-intersect, and the operation would fail. For a sweep to work, the minimum path radius must be larger than the profile radius. In the 2D sketch path example shown in Figure 5.1, the path radius is set at 0.5 inch. Knowing that the minimum path radius value is 0.5 inch, you can determine that the sketch profile radius must be less than or equal to this value.

FIGURE 5.1
2D sketch path

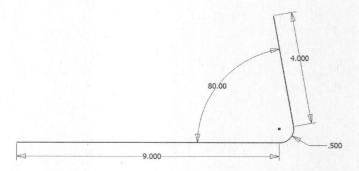

Start a new part file using the Standard.ipt template, and create a 2D sketch as shown in Figure 5.1.

CREATING THE SWEEP PROFILE

Once you've created the sketch path, right-click and choose Finish Sketch; then click Workplane in the Part Features tool panel. Select the endpoint of the 2D sketch path and then the path itself to create the plane. This creates a plane on the point orthogonal to the selected line. Observe that the created work plane displays a color to indicate the normal direction of the work plane. The normal direction (positive Z) will be a beige or yellowish color, while the backside is light blue. Figure 5.2 shows the created work plane.

Once you've created the work plane, right-click the work plane, and select New Sketch. Alternatively, you can select the work plane and then the 2D Sketch button to create the new sketch.

In the new sketch, use the Project Geometry command to project the 9-inch line into this new sketch. It should come in as a projected point. Next, create a circle anchored to the projected point, and give it a value of 1 inch in diameter. Finish the sketch, and select the Sweep command. If you have a single sweep profile, then it should automatically select the profile and pause for you to select a path. Note that you can select either Solid or Surface for the feature. The sweep type will default to Path, and the orientation will default to Path also.

The Sweep command also has an option to taper the sweep feature, as shown in Figure 5.3. A number less than zero for the taper will diminish the cross section as the profile follows the path. A positive number will increase the cross section. If the taper increases the cross section at the radius of the path to a value that exceeds the path radius value, then the feature will fail. If the taper decreases the cross section to zero before the end of the path, then the sweep will also fail.

FIGURE 5.2
Creating a work plane on which to sketch

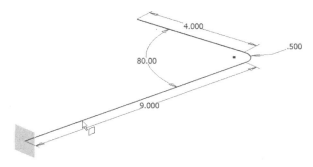

FIGURE 5.3
Sweep dialog box options

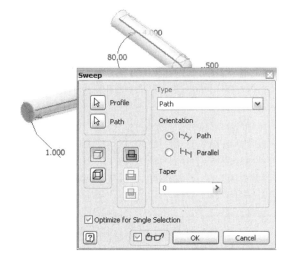

Sweep Type Options

Although sweeping along a path is the default option, you can also utilize Path & Guide Rail or Path & Guide Surface to control the output of the Sweep command. These options provide additional control for more complex results. Normally these options are utilized on sweeps based upon a 3D sketch path.

PATH & GUIDE RAIL OPTION

The Path & Guide Rail option provides a means to control the orientation of a profile as it is swept along a path. In Figure 5.4, the rectangular sweep profile will be swept along the straight path but controlled by the 3D helical rail. This approach is useful for creating twisted or helical parts.

The 3D helical rail is guiding the rotation of the profile even though the sweep profile is fully constrained with horizontal and vertical constraints. Creating this part starts with creating the sweep path as the first sketch, followed by creating a second sketch perpendicular to the start point of the sweep path.

FIGURE 5.4
Sweep profile, Path &
Guide Rail option

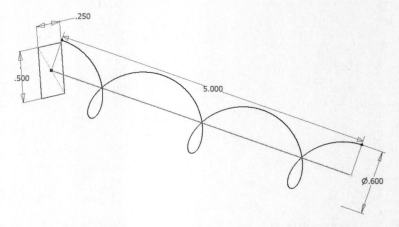

The 3D helical rail is created using the Helical Curve command in a 3D sketch. Open the file called Sweep-GuideRail.ipt, and create the sweep feature as shown in Figure 5.5 by using the straight line as the path and the helix as the guide rail.

FIGURE 5.5
Sweep with Guide Rail
option

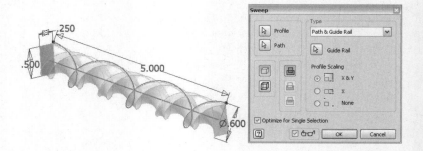

PATH & GUIDE SURFACE OPTION

At times you will need to sweep a profile that will conform to a specific shape and contour. In the past, you might have looked at the Loft command instead of the Sweep command so that you could create a rotation of the profile as it follows the path. If the cross section profile does not change along the path, the sweep with Path & Guide option will create the desired feature.

Figure 5.6 illustrates the Path & Guide Surface option. In this example, the designer wanted to create a semicircular molding that would also conform to the walls of a circular room. The design specifications are that the outer edges of the molding must conform to the wall without gaps.

The first step will be to create an environment for the sweep. You do this by creating an extruded surface as a reference for the final part. In this example, the surface was created by extruding a half circle, dimensioned to the size of the room wall. The extrusion length should exceed the height of the molding when created. The surface sketch was created on the XY plane, with the arc center constrained to the centerpoint origin.

A second 2D sketch is created on the XZ plane. The first step is to project the surface edge as a construction line. The half-circle profile of the molding is created at the construction line center and dimensioned to the proper arc radius. This sketch will be used to create a projected 3D sketch.

FIGURE 5.6
Curved sweep with
Guide Surface option

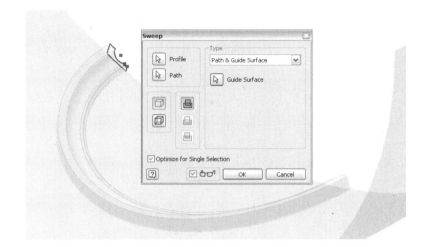

Next, create a 3D sketch by right-clicking in the feature environment and selecting New 3D Sketch. The 3D Sketch panel will appear. Select the Project Curve To Surface command from the 3D Sketch panel and then select the surface, followed by the curve. You will notice that there are three Output options and a Direction option in the Project Curve To Surface dialog box. In the example shown in Figure 5.7, the designer chose the first output option, Project Along Vector, to project the 2D arc onto the surface.

FIGURE 5.7
3D sketch, Project Along
Vector option

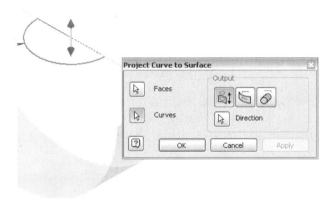

Once you've created the 3D sketch, create a work plane at the endpoint of the 3D path, perpendicular to the path. Use this work plane to create a new sketch located on the end of the 3D path. The designer is now ready to sketch the sweep profile.

While in the active sketch, select construction geometry, and project the curved edge of the surface into the sketch. The imported profile is now rotated to be coincident to the projected construction curve. The alternative is to create new profile geometry constrained to the sketch origin and the construction curve. The profile geometry should be fully dimensioned and constrained before exiting the sketch. Figure 5.8 shows the completed sweep profile.

FIGURE 5.8
Sweep profile

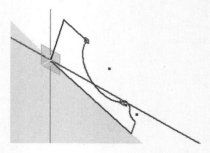

After the sweep profile is completed, the designer is ready to utilize the Path & Guide Surface option. To examine the Path & Guide Surface option, open the file called Path-GuideSurf_Sweep.ipt, and click the Sweep command. The sweep profile will be selected for you automatically. Select the Path & Guide Surface option and then select the path and surface.

Loft Features

Often, sweep features do not allow the creation of complex shapes. The nature of lofted features allows the creation of multiple cross-sectional profiles that are utilized to create a lofted shape. The Loft command requires two or more profile sections in order to function. Rails and control points are additional options to help control the shape of a lofted feature.

One good example of lofted shape is a marine boat hull. Another example is an exhaust manifold cavity. A third example is the product design of a cosmetic bottle. Each of these examples illustrates a different type of loft.

LOFT WITH RAILS

Figure 5.9 shows the completed wireframe geometry to create a section of a boat hull. The geometry includes four section sketches, each composed of a 2D spline. There are two rails: the top and bottom composed of 3D sketch splines. Open the file called BoatHullLoft.ipt to examine these sketches.

Since the four section sketches are open profiles, the Loft command will automatically create a lofted surface. To create the loft, select the four cross section sketches in consecutive order, front to back or back to front; then click Click To Add in the Rails section of the dialog box; and select 3D Sketch 1 and 2 as the two rail curves.

If you have the Preview option checked at the bottom of the dialog box, you should see a preview of the surface indicating the general shape, as shown in Figure 5.10. When you click OK, the surface will be created.

AREA LOFT

Autodesk Inventor 2008 introduced area loft as an option in the standard Loft command. Area loft is used in the design the components where the flow of a gas or liquid must be precisely controlled. Area loft is a different way of controlling the finer points of creating a loft shape.

FIGURE 5.9
Loft with rails geometry

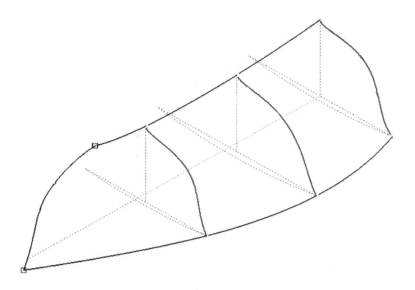

FIGURE 5.10
A surface loft with rails

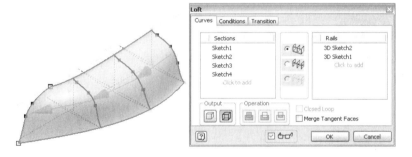

Figure 5.11 illustrates the geometry required to create an area loft. Open the file called AreaLoft.ipt, and click the Loft button to explore these area loft options.

The Area Loft option is accessed in the standard Loft dialog box, as shown in Figure 5.12. Area loft requires two or more sketch sections and the centerline in order to work.

Select the three sections in consecutive order starting with the rectangular sketch, progressing to the circular sketch. Once the sketch sections are selected, along with the centerline selection, you can select additional locations along the centerline to generate additional sections for area control at the selected locations. Once the centerline sketch has been selected, you should see text appear in the graphics window indicating the position and area of each cross section.

When you click Click To Add in the Placed Sections area, you can then click a location along the centerline to place additional area sections.

FIGURE 5.11
Area loft profiles

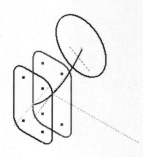

FIGURE 5.12
Loft dialog box with
Area Loft option

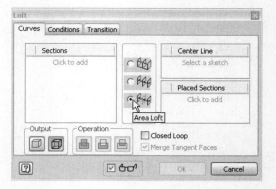

Once a location is clicked, the Section Dimensions dialog appears, as shown in Figure 5.13, giving you control over the position and section area of the placed section. Any number of placed sections can be used to create precise control of the feature.

FIGURE 5.13
Section Dimensions dia-
log box

While still in the Loft dialog box, you can right-click existing section text to edit that section's dimension values. Note that right-clicking one of the three dimensioned original sketch profiles will not permit you to edit those profiles. Instead, you will need to edit each sketch and change the dimensions or geometry of the sketch. Figure 5.14 illustrates an added position within the area loft shown in red that is editable.

CENTERLINE LOFT FEATURE

The centerline loft feature allows you to determine a centerline for your loft to follow. Open the file called CenterlineLoft.ipt, and click the Loft button. Select Click To Add in the Sections portion of the dialog box, and choose the two ellipses and the work point for sections. Next, select the Center Line radio button, and choose Sketch2 for the centerline. You screen should look like Figure 5.15.

FIGURE 5.14
Creating an area loft

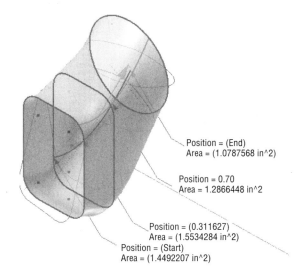

Position = (End)
Area = (1.0787568 in^2)

Position = 0.70
Area = 1.2866448 in^2

Position = (0.311627)
Area = (1.5534284 in^2)
Position = (Start)
Area = (1.4492207 in^2)

FIGURE 5.15
CenterLineLoft.ipt

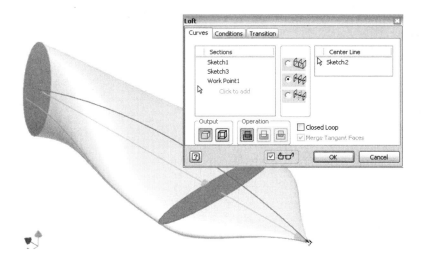

Before you click OK to finish the loft, go to the Conditions tab in the Loft dialog box. This tab is available in all three loft styles and controls how a loft will behave at the beginning and the end of the loft feature.

As shown in Figure 5.16, the Conditions tab provides control over the tangency, angle, and weight at the boundary. Click the Workpoint1 pulldown, and set the condition to Tangent. Notice the difference in the shape of the loft, as shown in Figure 5.16.

The full list of conditions depending upon the geometry type include the following:

◆ *Free Condition*: No boundary conditions exist for the object.

◆ *Tangent Condition*: This condition is available when the section or rail is selected and is adjacent to a lateral surface, body, or face loop.

◆ *Smooth (G2) Condition*: This option is available when the section or rail is adjacent to a lateral surface or body or when a face loop is selected. G2 continuity allows for curve continuity with an adjacent previously created surface.

◆ *Direction Condition*: This option is available only when the curve is a 2D sketch. The angle direction is relative to the selected section plane.

◆ *Sharp Point*: This option is available when the beginning or end section is a work point.

◆ *Tangent*: This option is available when the beginning or end section is a work point. Tendency is applied to create a rounded or dome-shaped end on the loft.

◆ *Tangent To Plane*: This is available on a point object, allowing the transition to a rounded dome shape. The planar face must be selected. This option is not available on centerline lofts.

FIGURE 5.16
Conditions tab

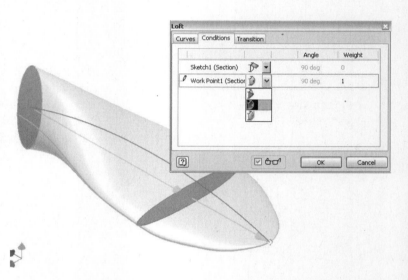

The angle and weight options on the Conditions tab allow for changes to the angle of lofting and the weight value for an end condition transition. In this example, if the endpoint condition is changed to tangent on the work point, the weight is automatically set to 1 and can be adjusted. Click the weight, and change it to 3 to see how the end condition will change in the preview. Experiment with the weight to see the changed conditions. If a value is grayed out, then the condition at that point will not allow a change.

Turned Parts and Threads

Creating turned and revolved parts is a regular occurrence in many engineering departments because of the types of parts designed and manufactured. The parts consist of circular features around a common axis. There are actually two different workflows for creating circular parts, each with its own advantages and disadvantages. Creating threads on a part presents another challenge.

Circular parts can be created using a single sketch and revolving it around a centerline axis. Alternatively, multiple circular extrusions can be created to produce the same part.

There are also two different workflows for creating thread features on a part. Threaded features can be added to any circular component by means of the *thread* feature, which creates cosmetic threads on the part, or through the use of the *coil* feature, which creates physical threads. Typically physical threads are created only when that geometry is required for the model. Generally, using cosmetic threads is sufficient because they are an intelligent feature that can be retrieved in the detail drawing of the part and called out as per the specifications of the feature.

Revolved Cylindrical Parts

Revolved cylindrical parts utilize a sketch with a center axis. Figure 5.17 illustrates two ways to create the same sketch. The view on the left side shows a sketch profile anchored at the origin and dimensioned from the origin. The view on the right side illustrates the same sketch, anchored at the origin but dimensioned from a created centerline, which creates diametric dimensions. The two sketches will create the same revolved feature, the difference being that the centerline allows you to dimension the sketch using diameter dimensions if to maintain the design intent of the part.

FIGURE 5.17
Dimension to the sketch vs. centerline

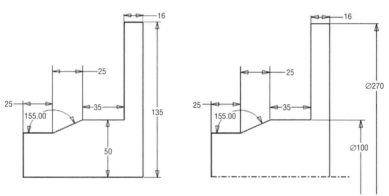

The centerline is created with the use of the Line command with the Centerline tool toggled on. In this example, the centerline was created starting at the origin point and continuing to the right of the sketch, extending beyond the sketch for selection ease. When dimensions are created on the sketch and terminated at the centerline object, they will actually extend to the other side of the revolved part diameter.

The advantage of creating a revolved profile, rather than creating stacked circular extrusions, is that the relationship of every portion of the sketch can be easily visualized from the start. The disadvantage is that a contour sketch is not always easily edited to remove or change a portion of the feature. In addition, if the sketch is not fully dimensioned and constrained, it can create errors down the line with faces and edges. For this reason, you should always fully dimension and constrain your sketches. Figure 5.18 shows the finished revolved feature.

FIGURE 5.18
Revolved circular features

Extruded Cylindrical Parts

An alternate method, using extruded circular features, provides better control and can allow for editing of each individual portion of the cylindrical part. Essentially this is the building-block approach of creating one feature after another until the entire cylindrical part is created. Figure 5.19 shows the finished extruded feature.

FIGURE 5.19
Extruded circular features

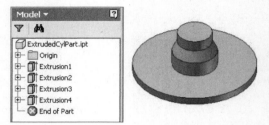

The advantage to this approach is that the same part design is comprised of four separate features, each one individually editable without affecting other portions of the part.

The disadvantage with this approach is that it takes a small amount of additional time to create the part and creates features that are dependent upon the previously created feature. If any extrusion in the middle of the part is deleted, then, prior to deletion, the next feature down the model tree will need to be reassociated with a different face.

SEAN SAYS: SHOULD YOU USE REVOLVED OR EXTRUDED CYLINDRICAL PARTS? IT DEPENDS!

Although neither revolved nor extruded cylindrical parts are inherently better, each has its place and its pros and cons. The extruded method is typically easier to edit and follow, but you may end up with many features to create a simple part. Also, editing one section of the cylinder may require editing several other features (for example, if you shorten one section by 1 inch but want to keep the overall length unchanged, you will have to edit other features to add back this 1 inch. The revolved method, on the other hand, allows you to parametrically link the dimension of the sketch so that changing one of the dimensions will change the others. I think that revolved cylindrical features hold more design intent than extruded parts. However, there is nothing wrong with either method.

Creating Threaded Features

Inventor offers the option of creating cosmetic threads that represent actual threads in the part, and it creates 2D geometry information for detailing those threads. Cosmetic threads are created with a threaded hole feature. Or you can use the Thread tool on the Feature panel bar to add threads to existing part features. The thread features is added to the model browser as a separate feature.

COSMETIC THREADS

Creating cosmetic threads on a circular part is a relatively simple procedure. Open the part named CosmeticThread.ipt, and click the Thread button in the Part Features tool panel. In the Thread dialog box, you will notice the option of creating a thread along the full length of the feature. By unchecking that option, you can create a specific length defined by an offset and a length.

Figure 5.20 shows the result of a 1-inch thread on the part. You can go to the Specification tab to change the thread type.

FIGURE 5.20
Cosmetic thread feature

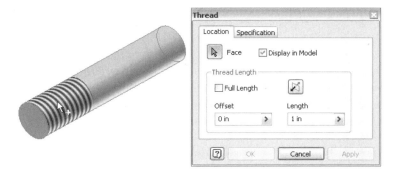

Click OK to create the thread feature, and notice that the crests and valleys of the thread are not created, but instead the thread is just a graphic wrapped around the face.

Using the Split command on a circular face allows even more control over the placement of cosmetic threads along what might otherwise be a continuous face.

SEAN SAYS: COSMETIC THREADS ARE USUALLY SUFFICIENT

Unless you are going to actually cut threads directly from your 3D model, cosmetic threads are usually sufficient. The advantage of these threads is that they contain all the thread information in the model that can later be extracted in a drawing without carrying the burden of complex modeling features.

PHYSICAL THREADS

Physical threads can be created using the coil feature. Physical threads create large models and can seriously affect performance and assemblies. As a result, physical threads should be used only where absolutely necessary, such as the design of a bottle or jar top or other geometries such as a worm gear.

Open the file called PhysicalThread.ipt, and notice the sketch called tooth profile. You will use this sketch to cut a thread using the coil feature. Click the Coil button in the Part Features tool panel to start the Coil command. Since there is only one unconsumed sketch in the part, the profile is selected automatically for you. Use the z-axis to define the coil axis.

Once the axis is selected, you will see a preview of the default coil settings. If the coil preview is showing the direction going away from your part, flip the direction of the axis using the Flip Direction button. Click the Cut button to ensure that the coil feature is removing material from the part. When the preview shows the correct direction, click the Coil Size tab in the dialog box, as shown in Figure 5.21.

This tab allows you to control the type of coil that will be created. The available coil types are Pitch And Revolution, Revolution And Height, Pitch And Height, and Spiral. You will use the Pitch And Revolution, which is the default option, setting your pitch at 0.145 and your revolutions at 8. Once set, you can click OK, and your result should be the same as shown in Figure 5.22.

FIGURE 5.21
Coil Size tab in the Coil
dialog box

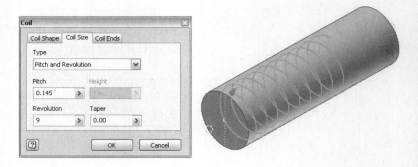

FIGURE 5.22
Completed coil thread

Cast and Plastic Parts

Designing cast and plastic parts require special consideration for modelers. The process of creating parts that will shrink during the manufacturing process can be a daunting task, particularly if the shrinkage is nonlinear.

Autodesk Inventor can help you create parts that can be adjusted to provide associative models that change dimensional characteristics to suit each stage of the process design. Inventor provides this through the use of derived parts.

Deriving an existing part into a new part file permits the overall scaling of the part as it is being created. Nonlinear scaling is accomplished using an add-in available in the Inventor installation directory. Carefully planning and using both approaches can achieve the goal of creating accurate cast and molded parts. You can also use these techniques to create forging dies and similar products.

Derived Part Creation

The design of cast, forged, and plastic parts is aided through the use of derived parts. Derived parts are based solids that are linked to the original feature-based part. Modifications are allowed to the derived part in the form of additional features. Original features are modified in the parent part, and changes in modification to the parent part are moved to the derived part upon save and update.

There is no reasonable limit to the number of times the parent part or succeeding derived parts can be again derived into more variations. Intelligent use of derived parts can create children usable for molds and dies and machining purposes.

LINEAR-DERIVED PART SCALING

Linear scaling of the original part is easily achieved by using the Derived Component command. To create a derived part, save the original part, then create a new single part file, and finally close the active sketch.

In the Part Features panel, select Derived Component, and browse to the original saved part. When you select the part and click Open, you will be presented with the screen shown in Figure 5.23.

FIGURE 5.23
Two percent scaling with derived part

The Inventor 2009 version permits deriving any or all of the components listed within the dialog box. The components with the grayed-out buttons indicate that those components will be ignored and not shown within the final derived part. The button with the + sign indicates that the solid body will be shown in this derived part.

For the purposes of this chapter segment, you are concerned only with the Scale Factor box shown at the bottom of the dialog box. A scale factor of 1.0000 indicates that the derived part will be created at the original part size. This factor is a multiplier so that a 2 percent increase would be designated as 1.02 scale factor. Scaling using this dialog box creates a linear scale in all X, Y, and Z directions.

The scale factor can be edited at any time by right-clicking the part name in the Model browser and selecting Edit Derived Part, as shown in Figure 5.24.

NONLINEAR-DERIVED PART SCALING

You can accomplish nonlinear part scaling in Autodesk Inventor by using an add-in that you can find at C:\Program Files\Autodesk\Inventor 2009\SDK\UserTools\DerivedPart_SP. From that location, run the Install.bat file. After installing the macro, a Part Features tool panel icon will be available called Derived Part (Scale/Position).

Selecting the Derived Part (Scale/Position) icon will introduce a new dialog box shown in Figure 5.25, permitting you to browse to the part file that will be scaled and allowing individual X, Y, and Z scale value inputs.

FIGURE 5.24
Editing a derived part

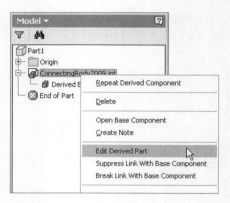

FIGURE 5.25
Nonuniform scale settings

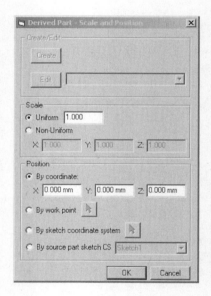

Part Tolerances

Autodesk Inventor allows you to analyze parts in a manner that ensures valid fit and function at dimensional extremes. When the parts are assembled within an Inventor assembly file, you can check to ensure that the parts can be assembled without interference. By specifying dimensional tolerances within parts, you are capturing valuable design data that will assist in manufacturing and assembly.

You can add tolerances to any individual sketch dimension by right-clicking and setting individual precision and tolerance values. Altering the dimension to adjust for tolerance and procession will not affect any other dimension within the part. Alternatively, global tolerancing can be specified within a part and will affect every dimension within the model.

Depending upon the particular design, allowable tolerances will be specified to ensure that the entire assembly will be within reasonable tolerances after manufacture and assembly. Inventor templates can be created, storing tolerance types and other settings for each standard. When the part is created using such a template, standard tolerance values can be overridden for specific dimensional values. If needed, you can override all tolerances within a file or just a specific dimension.

When considering part designs for manufacturing, be careful not to apply precise tolerance values where they are not necessary for the design and assembly. Excessive and unneeded tolerancing during the design phase can substantially increase the cost to manufacture each part. The secret to good design is to know where to place tolerances and where to allow shop tolerances to occur.

Setting Global File Tolerances

Global tolerance values within a single part will be created and modified by accessing Tools ➢ Document Settings and then clicking the Default Tolerance tab within an active part file or template. By default, a file will not be using any tolerance standards. In Figure 5.26, the Use Standard Tolerancing Values box has been checked to enable the addition of new standards for the file. If you want to export the tolerance values to your drawing files, you will want to also check Export Standard Tolerance Values. After you have selected Apply, you can close the dialog box.

FIGURE 5.26
Document settings for tolerance

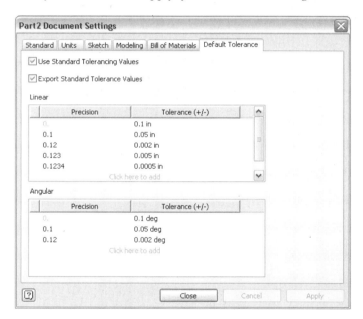

Figure 5.27 shows a simple sketch created using the template created in the previous step. Since the document settings are defaulted to three places, all sketch dimensions are in three places, with the appropriate tolerances. To change the tolerance values of a sketch dimension, simply select the dimension, right-click, and change the precision through the dimension properties of any specific dimension.

The default tolerances are set to +/- tolerances. To select another tolerance standard, simply override the existing tolerance values in the dimension properties or change the precision of a sketch dimension.

You will notice that the global tolerance settings apply tolerances to all dimensions. This is controlled by the global values in the document settings and will normally result in an overtoleranced part. For normal design, it is better to apply tolerance values individually rather than applying them by the rules defined in the standard.

When this part moves forward into the drawing environment, retrieved dimensions will reflect the nominal value except for dimensions where precision and tolerance are overridden. A better workflow for the drawing environment would be to create multiple dimension styles with various precision and/or tolerance options.

The designer must keep in mind that the tolerance settings in the part are designed to function with the assembly environment and calculating tolerances and stack up within the assembly. They are not meant to provide tolerancing in the drawing environment.

FIGURE 5.27
Sketch showing tolerances

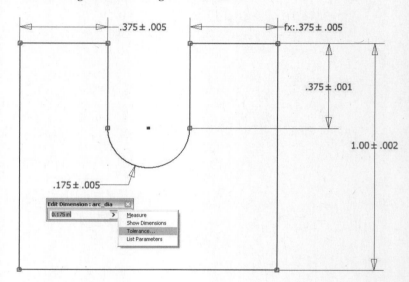

Overriding Current Tolerances

Not all sketch dimensions will require tolerance values. Normally, mating faces and corresponding values will be the ones that require tolerancing to avoid stack-up issues. Other faces may also require tolerancing to avoid interference type issues. The document's settings will allow you to set a default precision for all dimensions within a sketch.

When dimensioning in a sketch, you can select on any dimension, right-click, select Dimension Properties, and change precision and tolerance values for that individual dimension. If you retrieve model dimensions within the drawing environment, any changes to the model tolerance value (overrides) will be reflected in the drawing views.

Parameters and iProperties

Parameters in part and assembly files can provide powerful control over individual parts and assemblies while also improving efficiency within designs. Part parameters enable the use of iParts, which are a form of table-driven part. Assembly parameters enable the use of table-driven assemblies and configurations. Parameters are accessed through the Tools menu and within the Part Features and Assembly tool panels.

iProperties, generically known as *Windows file properties*, allow the input of information specific to the active file. The iProperties dialog box is accessed through the File pulldown in Inventor. The dialog box contains several tabs for input of information:

◆ The General tab contains information on the file type, size, and location. The creation date, last modified date, and last accessed date are preserved on this tab.

◆ The Summary tab includes part information such as title, subject, author, manager, and company. Included on this tab are fields for information that will allow searching for similar files within Windows.

◆ The Project tab stores file-specific information that along with information from the Summary, Status, Custom, and Physical tabs can be exported to other files and used in link information within the 2D drawing file.

◆ The Status tab allows the input of information as well as the design state and dates of each design step.

◆ The Custom tab allows the creation of custom parameters for use within the design. Parameters and exported from the Parameters dialog box will also appear in the list. Formulas can be used within a custom parameter to populate values in preexisting fields within the Project and Status tabs.

◆ The Save tab determines the behavior of the current file upon save.

◆ The Physical tab allows for the changing of material type used in the current file and displays the calculated physical properties of the current part such as mass and moment of inertia, as determined by the material type.

Active use of iProperties will help the designer in improving overall productivity as well as the ability to link part and assembly information into 2D drawings. Adding search properties in the Summary tab will assist the user in locating similar files.

Part Parameters

Part parameters are composed of model parameters, user parameters, reference parameters, and custom parameters. Model parameters are automatically embedded as a part is dimensioned and features are created. Most are a mirror image of the sketch creation process. As each dimension is created on a sketch, a corresponding model parameter is created, starting with a parameter called d0 and continuing with the label value being incremented each time a new parameter is created. To access the list of parameters, you can click the Parameters button in the 2D and 3D Sketch tool panels as well as the Part Features tool panel. Figure 5.28 represents a typical parameter list.

Looking at the columns across the top of the dialog box, you will see columns for the parameter name, unit type, equation, nominal value, tolerance type, model value, parameter export, and descriptive comments. Let's look at each of these columns in turn:

◆ *Model Parameters*: The values in this column correspond to the name of the parameters assigned as the part is built. Each parameter starts with a lowercase *d* followed by a numeric value. Each of these parameters can be renamed to something that is more familiar such as Length, Height, Base_Dia, or any other descriptive single word. Spaces are not allowed in the parameter name. Hovering over a name will initiate a tool tip that will tell you where that variable is used or consumed.

◆ *Unit type*: The unit type defines the unit used in the calculation. Normally, the unit type will be set by the process that created it. When a user parameter is created, you will be presented with a Unit Type dialog box when clicking in the Unit column. This will allow you to select a particular unit type for the user parameter.

◆ *Equation*: This either specifies a static value or allows you to create algebraic style equations using other variables or constants to modify numeric values.

◆ *Nominal Value*: This column displays the result of the equation.

◆ *Tolerance*: This column shows the current evaluated size setting for the parameter. Click the cell to select Upper, Lower, or Nominal tolerance values. This will change the size of tolerance features in the model.

◆ *Model Value*: This column shows the actual calculated value of the parameter.

◆ *Export Parameters*: These check boxes are activated to add the specific parameter to the custom properties for the model. Downstream, custom properties can be added to parts lists and bills of materials by adding columns. Clearing the check box will remove that parameter from custom properties. After a parameter is added, other files will be able to link to or derive the exported parameter.

◆ *Comment*: This column is a descriptive column used to help describe the use of that parameter. Linked parameters will include the description within the link.

FIGURE 5.28
Part parameter list

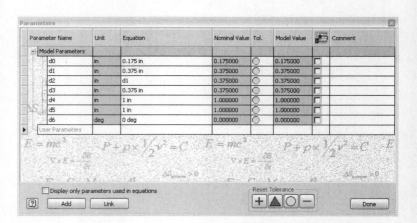

User parameters are better defined as user-created parameters. They are parameters that are created by clicking the Add button in the lower-left portion of the Parameters dialog box. User parameters can be used to store equations that drive features and dimensions in the model. The user-created parameter can utilize algebraic operators written in the proper syntax that will create an expression in a numerical value. To see a complete list of the functions available for use with parameters, search the help files for the word *functions*.

SEAN SAYS: SET UP USER PARAMETERS IN YOUR TEMPLATES

User parameters are especially powerful when creating *template parts*. Template parts are part files where geometry has already been created and are then placed in the template directory. Users can then start new parts files with this geometry predefined.

For example, let's say your company uses a standard sensor bracket in several locations. Although the basic shape remains the same, some critical dimensions such as width and hole size change depending on the application. To handle this situation, you would create the part and then create two user parameters named Hole_Size and Width. In the model parameters, you would link the dimensions that control these features to your newly created user parameters.

It's often a good idea to keep all parameters that the user "should" edit in the User Parameter section. This way the user knows exactly where to go to edit the file. After editing the parameters, the user updates the model, and the changes are applied to the model.

Reference parameters are driven parameters that are created through the use of reference dimensions and sketches and the use of derived parts, attached via a linked spreadsheet, and created by table-driven iFeatures or created through the use of the API. Inventor 2009 sheet metal creates part extents, which are stored as reference parameters.

Custom parameters are either created manually in the custom tab of iProperties or created automatically by exporting individual parameters from the list. Custom parameters may be linked to drawings and assemblies for additional functionality.

Assembly Parameters

Assembly parameters function in much the same way as part parameters, except that generally they will control constraint values such as offset and angle. When authoring an iAssembly, other parameters will be exposed for usage such as assembly features, work features, iMates, and component patterns, as well as other parameters that may exist within an assembly.

Part Analysis

Imported data commonly contains some errors in the part structure, primarily because of errors in translation, poor modeling technique at the source, or inclusion of construction data that may interfere with the creation of a good part.

Translated data may come into Autodesk Inventor as surfaces, base solids, or solid bodies. When a part is translated into Inventor as a body solid, it usually means that the quality of the part is low because of poor edge or face quality within the solid. Your chances of working with a body are slim within a mold or die environment where boolean operations are needed. Quite often, the time involved in attempting to repair a body will exceed the time required to completely remodel the part.

When remodeling a part referencing a body solid, utilize the existing geometry to create a part around the body solid, duplicating the features. When this is complete, simply delete the body solid from the part file.

Construction Environment

Part analysis is done on base solids within the construction environment. Please note that the construction environment cannot be used on feature-based parametric models. However, an imported base solid that has additional parametric features will permit the editing of the base solid within the construction environment.

Use the support.stp file as an example. To open this STEP file, select File ≻ Open, set the Files of Type pulldown to STEP Files (*.stp, *.ste, *.step), and then select the support.stp file. Click the Options button, and you will be presented with the Import Options dialog box. Using the options shown in Figure 5.29, note that the inset is the final imported geometry and will not display in your options dialog box. Normally, when importing translated files, you would have different settings to ensure that the import process would properly heal the imported geometry. However, for this example, we will be using the raw translated geometry. The imported part should resemble the inset of Figure 5.29. Once the geometry has been imported, save the file as support2.ipt.

FIGURE 5.29
Import Options settings and inset of imported part

When examining the newly translated part, you can see that some changes will be required in order to use this part in a new design. The new design will require the part to have four mounting holes at the corners and the chamfer angle changed by 5°. To accomplish this on the base solid, you will first edit the solid within the construction environment and then change the angle of the chamfer parametrically.

To access the construction environment, you must first right-click the base solid in the Model browser and then select Copy To Construction. This will copy all the geometry in the base solid to the construction environment. Figure 5.30 illustrates the changes in the Model browser.

FIGURE 5.30
Contents of the construction folder

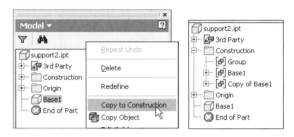

The contents of the construction folder will be different, depending upon whether the part is a base solid, surfaces, or other objects. The purpose of the construction folder is to analyze and/or repair construction geometry. To activate the Construction command environment, right-click the construction folder, and select Edit Construction. You'll notice that the Part Features panel switches to the Construction panel.

QUALITY CHECK

Click the Quality Check button in the tool panel to investigate this command. When you select Quality Check for this part, there should be no issues revealed. However, on a part that may have errors, Quality Check will do Topology Analysis, Geometry Analysis, and Modeling Uncertainty checking.

Topology refers to the relationship between geometric components. You should always start with geometry errors when repairing a part. Geometry errors can cause errors within the model, including topology errors. Geometry Analysis lists bodies or surfaces with geometry errors, grouped by error type. Modeling Uncertainty checking also lists bodies or surfaces with error, but the error is of an unknown type. Using this part within the design may not allow proper updating of the design.

Figure 5.31 shows an example of the Quality Check dialog box. The Help icon in the dialog box provides a wealth of information on using Quality Check. When using this dialog box to analyze the quality of a base part, start with Geometry Analysis. This will be the basis for repairing any potential errors within the base part.

A number of geometry errors can potentially cause Quality Check to fail. Geometry errors can cause topology errors. The Geometry Analysis will list bodies or surfaces with geometry errors and group them by error type. Repairing geometry errors is the first step in the correction process. The following is a list of the geometry errors that you may encounter when doing a quality check:

◆ *Self-intersecting surfaces*: A surface or face that intersects itself is considered a self-intersecting surface.

◆ *Self-intersecting curves*: Curves are constructed using lines arcs or splines. Curves cannot reverse, twist, or intersect the same curve.

◆ *Irregular curve*: An irregular curve occurs when the math data is inconsistent within the curve or when a curve vector has a value of zero. This error often occurs when the

approximating surface does not fit within the system tolerance settings of the defining surface within a STEP or IGES file. The error can occur when a normal point on the surface is
not facing in the same direction as the rest of the surface.

◆ *Curve discontinuities*: Curves are comprised of lines, arcs, or splines. A curve must be
smooth without abruptly changing direction causing a G0 condition (sharp edge) and
cannot have an abrupt transition between curves.

◆ *Surface discontinuities*: This happens when the normal direction or curvature of the surface changes abruptly. This error may be caused by disconnected geometry. Surfaces must
be smooth and cannot have an abrupt change in direction, causing a G0 condition (sharp
edge).

◆ *Degenerate surface*: Points defining a surface are compacted into a small area. As a result, a
degenerate surface is created.

◆ *Singularity surface*: A point on the surface factor is poorly defined, and as a result, the normal of the surface cannot be determined from existing geometry.

FIGURE 5.31
Quality Check dialog box

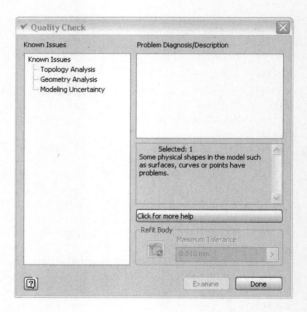

The dialog box has a context-sensitive help bar that can be selected to get more information for
analyzing and repairing errors. If you have selected Geometry Analysis and then clicked the Click
For More Help button, you will be presented with the specific help files for that area.

REPAIRS AND MODIFICATIONS

You will notice various commands within the Construction panel that will allow you to perform
repairs on your model. Some of the commands will be familiar from the Part Features panel environment. Some commands are available only within the Construction environment. Remember to

use the in-context help icon available within every command to develop a workflow for repairing your part. Some of the unique commands within this environment are listed here:

◆ *Unstitch*: This provides the ability to unstitch individual surfaces forming the base part and moving those selected surfaces into a folder within the Model browser according to data type.

◆ *Reverse Normal*: Parts and surfaces have a normal direction, commonly called the *machining direction*, which determines how a machine tool will react with that face. Parts that have inconsistent face normals will not usually behave predictably within a design. This command will flip the normal direction of any selected face or surface.

◆ *Extend Faces*: This extends surfaces within the construction environment. This will not work on solids.

◆ *Intersect Faces*: This command allows the breaking or trimming of intersecting surfaces. The Trim option will trim two surfaces at their intersection. The Break option will split two surfaces at their intersection.

◆ *Edit Regions*: This allows the editing of translated regions to reverse the trim side of a surface or to remove inner loops on a surface.

◆ *Extract Loop*: This extracts one or more loops by and trimming the surface, leaving edge wires intact. The command attempts to repair poor-quality trimming curves and saves them to wires for use in reconstructing surfaces.

Continue to examine the model. The easiest way to remove the two existing holes is within the construction-editing environment. You will notice that within the Edit Construction environment there is a copy of Base1. It is now safe to delete the original Base1 feature that resides outside the construction environment. There is no need to worry about the deletion of the original feature because you have a copy of that geometry in the construction group. You will not need to exit the construction environment before deleting the base feature. Simply right-click Base1 within the gray area of the Model browser, and select Delete.

Deleting this feature will allow you to copy the repaired feature back into the model environment when you have finished editing. In addition, the deletion will ensure that you are working totally within the construction environment.

The geometry you currently see after deletion is the copy. Using the Unstitch command, select the front face of the base portion containing the holes. Click Apply to unstitch. Next, click the two cylinders representing the hole walls, and click Apply. Finally, rotate the part, unstitch the back face of the base portion, and click Done to finish. You have now broken out the selected faces of a model, and they can now be selected and deleted within the construction environment. Select each of the unstitched faces, right-click, and Delete.

Using the Boundary Patch command, select the outer edge of the back face and then the inner cylindrical surface creating a boundary surface with a circular open center, as shown in Figure 5.32.

Create a boundary surface on the front side of the base by selecting the outer edges and then the outer cylindrical surface. If you have created both boundary surfaces correctly, then rotating the model will reveal a through hole in the center of the part.

Using the Stitch Surface command, select all three surfaces within the part, and click Apply. Select Done to exit the command. Under the folder called Copy of Base1, the Surfaces objects will disappear and be replaced by Solids.

FIGURE 5.32
Creating boundary
patches

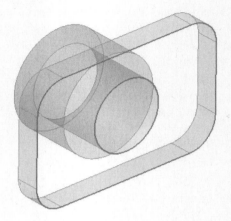

Right-click Solids, and select Copy Object. You will be presented with the dialog box shown in Figure 5.33. With the options selected as shown, click OK to create Base2 in the model environment. Right-click the construction folder, and select Finish Construction. When you have completed all repairs and modifications, you can delete the construction folder. Save the completed part as Base1.ipt.

FIGURE 5.33
Copy completed solid

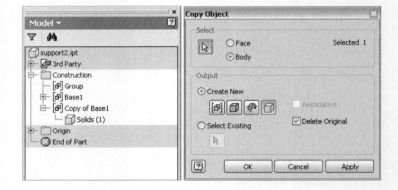

The process explained earlier can be used to repair or modify virtually any type of part. The construction environment is also highly suited to the purpose of editing and finishing a surface model. The construction environment may not completely repair a model that has yours in the Modeling Uncertainty portion of the quality check. If you have numerous errors in that portion of the checked geometry, then you will probably be better off remodeling the part.

Working with Base Solids

Base solids are normally created from imported geometry and derived parts and do not possess individual features in their original state. The designer is often called upon to modify the base solid in various ways. Autodesk Inventor provides basic tools for editing an existing base solid, as well as the ability to add features to the original model.

Activating the Solids-Editing Environment

When a base solid is encountered that requires editing, right-click the base solid in the Model browser. Select Edit Solid to activate the solids-editing environment. The Solids Editing panel now replaces the Part Features panel. The following commands are available within the Solids Editing panel:

◆ *Move*: This provides the ability to move one or more faces on a solid by specified distances and direction. In the solids environment, moved faces are not parametric.

◆ *Extend or Contract Body*: This command will expand or contract a base solid along an axis perpendicular to the selected face or plane. Expanding or contracting a base solid does not add any new features to the part.

◆ *Work features*: This environment allows the creation of work planes, axes, or points.

◆ *Toggle Precise UI*: This command activates the Precise Input dialog box for use with the solids-editing commands.

Aside from the specific solids-editing commands listed earlier, the designer has the option of using all available modeling commands in the Part Features panel bar. Figure 5.34 shows a support bracket as a solid body in a solids-editing state.

FIGURE 5.34
Base solid part

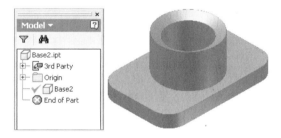

To continue open the file called Base2.ipt. This file picks up where you left off in the previous steps. Suppose you received this part from a customer and need to modify it to fit a different design. In the new design, you will need to change the chamfer angle by 5° and add through holes at each of the corners.

The first step will be to add the through holes concentric to each corner radius. Click the Hole tool in the Part Features tool panel, and set the placement option to Concentric. For the plane, select the top face of the base of the part and then choose one of the radius corners for the concentric reference. Set the hole diameter to 8 mm, and set the termination to Through All. Then click Apply. Repeat the Plane and Concentric Reference selections for the remaining three radiused corners.

Next, activate the Face Draft command, and select the planar face once again to determine the pull direction. Toggle the pull direction until the arrow faces away from the face and toward the front of the cylinder. Change your selection mode to Faces, and select the outer edge of the cylinder so that the chamfered face as highlighted. Change the draft angle to 5°, and click OK to apply the draft. Figure 5.35 shows the proper orientation for the draft. Save this file as Base3.

As shown by this example, virtually any feature may be added to the base solid without the requirement of redesigning the entire part. Any parametric features added to a base solid may be edited or suppressed at any time.

FIGURE 5.35
Application of the face draft

Troubleshooting Failures

Once in a while, even the most experienced design engineer experiences a modeling or design failure. The part may be supplied by a customer or co-worker, and you may find that editing of the part will produce failures or unexpected results.

One of the best ways to troubleshoot a part and determine exactly how the part was originally modeled is to use the End of Part marker to step through the creation process. In the Model browser, drag the End of Part marker to a location immediately below the first feature. This will effectively eliminate all other features below the marker.

Often when making modifications to a part, you might change a feature that causes errors to cascade down through the part. Moving the End of Part marker up to isolate the first troubled feature allows you to resolve errors one at a time. Oftentimes, resolving the topmost error will fix those that exist after it. Figure 5.36 shows a model tree with a series of errors. On the right, the End of Part marker has been moved up.

FIGURE 5.36
Using the End of Part maker to troubleshoot feature errors

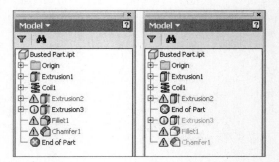

STEP 1

Normally, the first feature will start with a sketch. Right-click the first feature, and select Edit Sketch. Examine the sketch for a location relative to the part origin point. Normally, the first sketch should be located and anchored at the origin and fully dimensioned and constrained. If the sketch is not fully constrained, then add dimensions and constraints to correct it.

Drag the End of Part marker below the next feature, and repeat the step. Continue through the part until all sketches are properly constrained.

STEP 2

If all features are properly created, the next step will be to analyze the workflow used to create the part. One recommended approach to design is to create the major features first and then add secondary features such as holes, fillets, and chamfers at the end of the part. This workflow mimics normal machining practices.

On occasion, loft and sweep features may fail or produce incorrect results because fillets and chamfers were created before the failed feature. To determine whether this is the case in your model, suppress any holes, fillets, chamfers, or any other feature that you might think is causing the failure.

Once the failed feature is corrected, introduce one suppressed feature at a time until you encounter a failure. This will identify the cause. You may then attempt to move the offending feature below the failed feature and examine the result. If you are unable to move the offending feature, then reproduce the same feature below the failed feature, and leave the original suppressed.

Once the problems are corrected in a part, you can go back and delete the suppressed offending features.

If you encounter problem parts within your own modeling experience, then it may be time to seriously examine your workflow and feature creation techniques.

SEAN SAYS: USE THE END OF PART MARKER TO TIME TRAVEL

The End of Part (EOP) marker is a powerful yet often neglected tool. With this tool you can go "back in time" and edit or add features to your model. It's a great way of fixing mistakes that may have been made in the modeling process. A perfect example of using the EOP marker is to preserve design intent. Let's say you created a base feature, placed some holes down the center of the part (based on dimensions), and then altered the side faces of the part. The holes are linked to the unaltered edges of this part. You want to now make the holes tied to the midplane of this part regardless of the feature size. You could do this by placing a centered work plane down the part. However, you cannot do this now because when you went back to edit the hole sketch, the work plane will not be available for projection onto the sketch plane. You also cannot drag the work plane above the holes as it was created on the new, altered base feature faces. In this case, you'll want to drag the EOP marker above the hole feature. Now you can place the work plane centered on the two faces. Drag the EOP marker back down to the bottom of the tree. Now edit the hole feature and project the work plane so that the hole centers can be constrained to it. Easy. And we didn't even need a flux capacitor.

The Bottom Line

Create complex sweeps and lofts   Complex geometry is created by using multiple work planes, sketches, and 3D sketch geometry. Honing your experience in creating work planes and 3D sketches is paramount to success in creating complex models.

Master It   You want to model a piece of twisted flat bar.

Design turned parts and threads   Turned parts and threaded features can be developed using revolves or extrudes. Both have advantages and disadvantages in usage.

Master It   You need to cut a profile out of a part as it would be done in the shop using a radial face cutter.

Utilize part tolerances   Dimensional tolerancing of sketches allows the checking of stack-up variations within assemblies. By adding tolerances to critical dimensions within sketches, parts may be adjusted to maximum, minimum, and nominal conditions.

Master It   You want to create a model feature with a deviation so that you can test the assembly fit at the extreme ends of the tolerances.

Understand and use parameters and iProperties   Using parameters within files assist in the creation of title blocks, parts lists, and annotation within 2D drawings. Using parameters in an assembly file allow the control of constraints and objects within the assembly. Exporting parameters allows the creation of custom properties. Proper usage of iProperties facilitates the creation of accurate 2D drawings that always reflect the current state of included parts and assemblies.

Master It   You want to create a formula to determine the spacing of a hole pattern based upon the length of the part.

Analyze parts and work with base solids   Inventor provides tools to analyze translated geometry. These tools provide a quality check on the geometry and permit repair or modification of geometry within the construction environment.

Master It   You need to import a part from a vendor file and remove features in the part.

Troubleshoot modeling failures   Modeling failures are often caused by poor design practices. Poor sketching techniques, bad design workflow, and other factors can lead to the elimination of design intent within a model.

Master It   You want to modify a rather complex existing part file, but when you change the feature, errors cascade down through the entire part.

Chapter 6

Sheet Metal

The sheet metal functionality in Inventor 2009 is extremely powerful, centered around productivity and capturing your manufacturing intent. When you first begin working in the sheet metal environment, you may feel overwhelmed; however, a mastery of some basic fundamentals can make Inventor sheet metal straightforward and highly integrated with your manufacturing environment.

In this chapter, you will learn how to:

◆ Take advantage of the specific sheet metal features available in Inventor

◆ Understand sheet metal templates and rules

◆ Author and insert punch tooling

◆ Utilize the flat pattern information and options

◆ Understand the nuances of sheet metal iPart factories

◆ Model sheet metal components with non-sheet-metal features

◆ Work with imported sheet metal parts

◆ Understand the tools available to annotate your sheet metal design

◆ Harvest your legacy sheet metal styles into sheet metal rules

Getting to Know the Features

The Inventor sheet metal environment contains numerous specialized features to help you design components that obey your sheet metal manufacturing guidelines and process restrictions. The following sections describe general feature classifications and capabilities that will provide you with a quick road map to the features that will help you achieve your design intent.

Starting with a Base

Out of all the sheet metal features provided, only two of them create what is referred to as *base features*. Base features are simply the first features that appear in the feature history, and they function as the platform for which all other features are built upon.

CONTOUR FLANGE

The Contour Flange tool is a sketch-based feature (open profile) that has the ability to create multiple planar faces and bends as the result of a single feature, as shown in Figure 6.1. Profile sketches should contain only arcs and lines; if sketch intersections are not separated by an arc, a fillet will be automatically added at the intersection equal to the parameter BendRadius, which is driven by the sheet metal rule. To create base features with a profile sketch, contour flanges have a width extent option called Distance, which allows a simple open profile to be utilized to create a sheet metal condition extrusion of the thickened, filleted profile.

FIGURE 6.1
Base feature contour flange that has defined an enclosure/housing

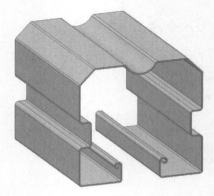

SEAN SAYS: USE THE CONTOUR FLANGE TOOL TO CREATE SHEET METAL PARTS

The Contour Flange tool is perhaps the simplest and fastest way to create sheet metal parts that are common in cross-section-like extrusions and formed channels. It is also a quick way to create models of parts when you have an existing AutoCAD sketch. By importing the AutoCAD sketch and using the Contour Flange tool, you can easily create the sheet metal part.

FACE

The Face tool is also capable of creating base features; it utilizes a closed profile to produce a simple extrusion equal to the parameter value Thickness. The profile can be constructed out of any shape and can even contain interior profiles that you don't want to participate in the result, as shown in Figure 6.2. Profiles for face features are often generated from the edge projections of planar faces or surfaces, and this capability enables numerous assembly-based and derived workflows.

FIGURE 6.2
Face base feature containing an omitted internal profile

Creating Flanges

Several sheet metal features create flanges, which are simply planar faces connected by a bend. Each of the features discussed produce constituent flange features, meaning flanges that are built on top of a base feature using a referenced edge selection. Depending on the flange-producing feature selected, you can either meticulously control very granular options or allow Inventor to apply predefined relationships and values.

FLANGE

The Flange tool creates a single planar face and bend for each edge selected with granular controls for defining the flange height, bend position, and relief options at the edge intersections. For flanges referencing a single edge, numerous width extent options are also available by clicking the >> button in the Flange dialog box. For cases in which multiple edges have been selected to specify flange locations, the automatic mitering of adjacent flanges and corner relief placement is accomplished as shown in Figure 6.3. Inventor 2009 also introduces a new method for customizing the multiflange result with the introduction of corner edit glyphs. Using the glyph allows you to customize the corner overlap type, percentage of overlap, mitering gap, corner relief shape, and corner relief size (if applicable) on a per-corner basis.

FIGURE 6.3
A multiedge flange feature preview, with visible corner edit glyphs

CONTOUR FLANGE

The Contour Flange tool supports the creation of more complicated geometry that needs to contain one or more planar faces with connecting bends in between. The Contour Flange tool is a sketch-based feature, which is ideal for quickly creating complex shapes and enclosures designs. As a base feature, as discussed earlier, the Contour Flange tool can either automatically fillet non-tangent sketch junctions or can honor specific arc radius information that has been included in the sketch. Contour flanges can create base feature flanges (previously discussed), constituent flanges (those attached to a reference face), or multilump flanges. The sketch profile consumed by the Contour Flange tool does not need to be coincident with a reference edge; it simply needs to be sketched on a plane that is perpendicular to the referenced edge. For single or zero reference edge cases, if the sketch profile is not coincident with a reference edge, a bend will automatically be positioned to connect the sketch profile to the reference face. If the sketch is not coincident with a reference edge and the width extent option is changed to Distance, the result will be a second free-floating lump body in the part.

Identical to the flange feature, cases in which multiple edges have been selected to specify contour flange locations will introduce the automatic mitering of adjacent flanges and the placement of corner reliefs, as shown in Figure 6.4. The new glyph-based corner-editing method described for flange features is also available for multiedge contour flange features. Using the glyph allows you to customize the mitering gap, the corner relief shape, and the corner relief size (if applicable) on a per-corner basis.

HEM

The Hem tool is like a contour flange because it has the ability to create multiple planar faces and bends for a selected edge, but it is restricted to predefined common hem profiles and geometric relationships. Hem does not support the selection of multiple edges, but it does contain the full array of width extent customization options if you click the >> button.

FIGURE 6.4
A multiedge contour flange feature with automatic mitering and large radius bend support displayed

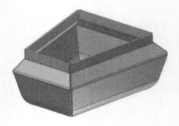

USE CONTOUR FLANGE FOR MITERED HEMS

Since all hem results can be replicated with the careful creation of a contour flange sketch, when automatic mitering is required, consider using a multiedge Contour Flange tool instead of the Hem tool.

FACE

The last feature capable of creating flanges is the Face tool. The Face tool is a closed profile sketch consumption feature but also has the ability to create attaching bends by using edge selection controls or automatically when two face features share a common edge. This automatic case is actually incredibly powerful because it allows you to create a skeletal surface model of your design, project the planar surfaces, and consume those sketches with individual face features and all the face features to manage the placement of the bends. The manual controls can be utilized to connect face features to preexisting geometry, create double bends (joggles), or even deselect edges that have been automatically inferred because they share a common edge.

An additional use of the face could also be the reuse of 2D flat patterns that had been created in another application such as AutoCAD. By importing the 2D flat pattern extent profile, the Face command can be used to thicken it to the desired value. A flat pattern can be produced for a planar face (no unfolding needs to actually occur), which enables the use of special translation tools, Drawing Manager consumption, and a variety of other uses.

Adding, Removing, or Deforming Material

Once the general shape of a sheet metal component is roughed in, material will need to be either removed or deformed in almost every design. Several sheet metal–specific features have been created to optimize these workflows because sheet metal manufacture is typically nuanced with the requirement that these operations create sheet metal conditions (normal to surface). The current capabilities of Inventor assume that these manufacturing operations are in reality applied to the flat pattern prior to folding and therefore should not interfere with unfolding (Inventor does not support post-folding manufacturing operations such as gussets, for example).

CUT

The simplest feature to accomplish cutting is the Cut tool, which is like a special sheet metal extrude. The Cut tool is a sketch consumption feature, allowing you to leverage any defined closed profile. The Cut tool was created to help simplify the options of the regular Extrude command for sheet metal designers and predefine the parameter Thickness for the cut depth to ensure a robust parametric result. The Cut tool also contains an ability to wrap the sketch profile across planar faces and bends, as shown in Figure 6.5. This option is particularly helpful because it allows you to force a uniform cut across multiple planar faces and bends with a value greater than zero and equal to or less than Thickness.

FIGURE 6.5
Cut feature utilizing
Cut-Across-Bend option

SEAN SAYS: USE CUTS

I recommend you use the Cut tool whenever possible rather than creating voids in the base sketch. Although this might go against the design philosophy I have touted in other chapters (put everything in the base sketch), with sheet metal parts it is often more robust to create your base features and flanges and then apply the cuts as required. I have found that this provides a more stable model when creating a flat pattern.

PUNCH TOOL

You can use the Punch tool to either remove material or deform it by placing predefined Punch tool geometry, as shown in Figure 6.6. Punches are special versions of iFeatures and can be predefined with additional manufacturing information and can be built using a variety of standard and sheet metal features. The "Authoring and Reusing Punches" section discusses punch features in detail.

FIGURE 6.6
Multiple instance punch
feature placing a footing
dimple

CORNER ROUND AND CHAMFER

Corner Round and Corner Chamfer are special sheet metal commands that allow you to remove or break edges similar to filleting and chamfering. Edge selection has been optimized within the two features, filtering out edges that are not normal to the sheet top and bottom faces for easy application.

FILLING IN THE GAPS

The remaining sheet metal commands fill in the blanks of the designer's tool palette (in our case the Sheet Metal Features panel bar), providing specialized functionality. The following features modify geometry that has already been introduced into the model, providing "fit and finish" in some cases and allowing the union of multiple lumps or the deformation of planar faces.

CORNER SEAM

The Corner Seam tool allows you to extend (as shown in Figure 6.7) or trim flange faces in order to manage the seam between them and select corner relief options. The Corner Seam dialog box contains numerous options for specifying your preferences and contains two fundamentally different distance definition methodologies: Maximum Gap and Face/Edge. Prior to Inventor 2009, only the Face/Edge method was available for the Corner Seam tool and was an older definition scheme that originally appeared in MDT. The face/edge method works for many situations but also tends to suffer from an inability to maintain a constant seam gap between planar faces that do not have an identical input angle. The maximum gap method was developed from the perspective of a physical inspection gauge, where the nominal value of the seam is exactly the value entered at ever point; you just might need to twist the tool as you draw it through the seam.

FIGURE 6.7
Corner seam
feature, applying
coplanar-overlap seam
type

FOLD

The Fold command enables you to design a flange with a unique profile by allowing you to sketch the position of the bend centerline on a planar face, as shown in Figure 6.8. The Fold command is a sketch consumption feature and contains numerous controls for specifying exactly how a planar face should be manipulated into two planar faces connected by a bend. The sketch bend centerline must be coincident with the face extents, requiring you to project edges and constrain the sketch. When utilizing the Fold command, remember that the feature works from an opposite perspective of other sheet metal features, where bend allowance is actually consumed, not added to the resulting folded feature. The Fold command can be combined with the Face tool to help import preexisting 2D flat patterns and then deform them into their final shape if leveraging and updating legacy designs is desired.

BEND

The Bend command allows you to connect two planar faces by selecting a pair of parallel edges. Since Inventor supports the modeling of multiple lumps, the Bend command can add either a single bend or a double bend (*joggle*) depending on the number of selections you make. For design situations in which multiple lumps have been produced, the Bend command is often used to combine the lumps into a single contiguous body.

FIGURE 6.8
Fold command being applied to a face with a spline contour

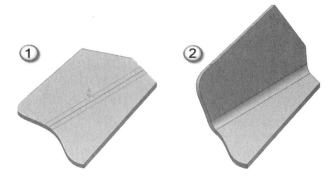

PROJECT FLAT PATTERN

A well-hidden segment of sheet metal–specific functionality is a special version of sketch projection called *project flat pattern* (nested at the end of the sketch projection flyout). Project flat pattern is available from the folded model environment and is utilized to include the projected edges of the flattened sheet metal component, oriented to the sketch plane that is active. This option is very powerful when combined with the Cut-Across- Bend option because it allows you to create parametric dimensions and constrained relationships from the perceptive of the flattened sheet. When utilizing the project flat pattern option, it isn't necessary to select every face; just pick the ones at the extremities (ensuring that they're on the same flattened side of the part as your sketch), and all of the connecting planar faces and bends will automatically be included.

CONVERT

While the main toolbar command Convert is not exclusive to sheet metal, there is a specific option within its flyout called Sheet Metal. The purpose of the Convert to Sheet Metal tool is to take a component that has been designed with a regular template and convert that document to a sheet metal subtyped document. This means all the sheet metal reference parameters and the default sheet metal rule and unfold rule that were available at installation will automatically be embedded within the document. In reality, this command is most commonly used to switch the features panel bar between Part Features and Sheet Metal Features, which is a fundamental misuse of this option because the panels can be changed by simply using the list to the right of the panel name. Using Convert to navigate back and forth can have undesirable effects, most notably the deletion of your flat pattern and the breaking of associations with downstream documentation; use the Convert Sheet Metal tool sparingly.

Using Sheet Metal Templates and Rules

The most significant change in Inventor 2009 sheet metal is the ability to create sheet metal rules that can be stored in the Inventor style library. If you aren't new to sheet metal, you might be wondering why this is a big deal since the sheet metal environment has always had great style support and definition capabilities by using special-case, template-based styles. The simple answer is that the move to the style library makes sheet metal definition information more manageable, reusable, and powerful.

What Are Sheet Metal Rules?

The new sheet metal *rules* that have been added to Inventor 2009 are a direct evolutionary step from the template-based sheet metal styles that have been available in previous releases. The sheet metal environment uses the predefined information within sheet metal rules to apply design and process information to your sheet metal component. Sheet metal rules have the ability to capture design intent that may not affect your component currently (such as bend transitions, relief options, and so on) but during the parametric design and editing process could be applied when necessary. Sheet metal rules are referenced by sheet metal features to help predefine their values and options with plausible choices based upon your manufacturing requirements.

This capability really makes sheet metal that only true rule-based design environment within the standard Inventor product suite. Sheet metal rules differentiate themselves from sheet metal styles in that their information can be published to a style XML file. One benefit of library-based styles/rules is that their definition information can be pulled into your design only when necessary, allowing your document to remain as light as possible and devoid of unneeded style information. Changing the style library architecture has also enabled a broadening of access to sheet metal rule information, allowing specialized sheet metal unfolding rules to be drawn into your design from within feature dialog boxes but no longer requiring predefinition within a style interface.

As an example of some of these enhancements, prior to Inventor 2009 many sheet metal customers would create a sheet metal template that contained all the styles used by a company. This template-based process often meant that as many as 30 sheet metal styles would be embedded into a sheet metal component even though only one would be set as the active style. The style enhancements in Inventor 2009 mean that you can select the sheet metal rule you want to use, and that rule (and its associated material style and unfold rule) will exclusively be drawn into the sheet metal document for use during the design process. Once the style information is drawn in, it gets stored in the local document and resides there until you decide to purge it.

CREATING SHEET METAL RULES VS. CREATING SHEET METAL STYLES

Before Inventor 2009, sheet metal templates were exclusively used to define sheet metal design and manufacturing preferences (sheet metal styles). The sheet metal styles were organized in a simple format, where the sheet metal style was dominant and material styles could be linked to the sheet metal style, but the relationship was parent-child. Additionally, unfolding preferences (that is, K-factor or bend table) as well as sheet thickness information were also driven by the selection of a specific sheet metal style. In Inventor 2009, the sheet metal styles have been replaced with style library sheet metal rules, but the familiar parent-child relationships established in previous releases continue to be organized in the same order; they're just a little more sophisticated.

When you first look at the sheet metal rule within the Style And Standard Editor dialog box (as shown in Figure 6.9), you will notice that the general layout is almost identical to that of the legacy Sheet Metal Styles dialog box. The linked material style (the Material value) and the Thickness value are prominently located at the top of the Sheet tab. The unfolding rule list control is used to predefine a linked sheet metal unfold rule, which is something new for Inventor 2009 that we'll talk about it in more depth later in this chapter. The Bend and Corner tabs are actually identical to Inventor 2008 and aren't changed except the move to a new home.

WHAT IF YOU STILL PREFER TEMPLATES?

Nothing is stopping you from leveraging your templates in the same way as you have used them in the past. Some customers may not like the idea of using a style library and still prefer the familiarity of template-based deployments in which all the style information is populated into a sheet metal template; this workflow is still completely supported. Although the interface has changed a little, editing values in the Style And Standard Editor dialog box affect only those values stored in the active document because Inventor does not automatically edit the style library files. So, although the interface has changed from a Sheet Metal Styles dialog box to a category within the Style And Standard Editor dialog box, edits to rules still affect only the active document.

FIGURE 6.9
Style And Standard
Editor dialog box,
Sheet Metal Rule page
displaying active rule
10 GA Galvanized

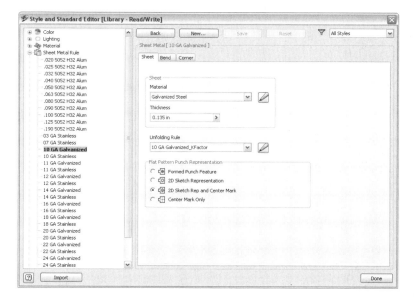

SHEET METAL DEFAULTS DIALOG BOX

Another change to the way you can interact with sheet metal rules is facilitated by the introduction of the Sheet Metal Defaults dialog box, as shown in Figure 6.10. In previous releases, the command button located at the top of the Sheet Metal Features panel bar was used to access the Sheet Metal Styles dialog box. This command has been replaced with a new one that brings up a small dialog box that reflects the current state of styles, rules, and options being applied to your sheet metal design.

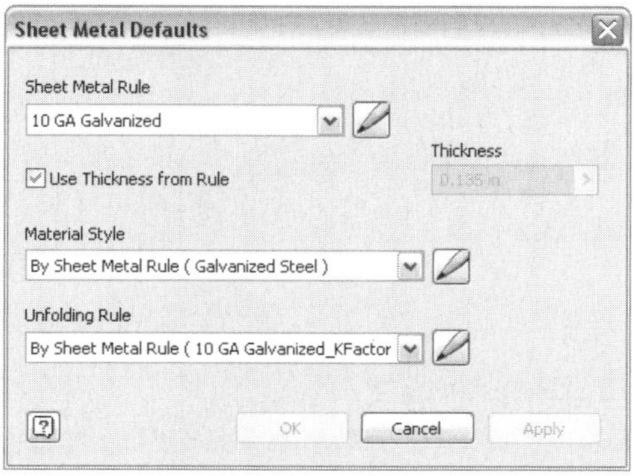

FIGURE 6.10
Sheet Metal Defaults
dialog box with no
style/rule overrides
applied

The new Sheet Metal Defaults dialog box can be used for a number of purposes. As an example, it can be used to directly access and draw into your document new styles/rules, its edit command buttons can be used to navigate to the Style And Standard Editor categories, and it can be used to perform document-level overrides of styles, rules, and thickness values. As a best practice, it's suggested that you allow the sheet metal rule to control all the information in the Sheet Metal Defaults dialog box, meaning you should allow the thickness to be driven by the referenced sheet metal rule as well as use the By Sheet Metal Rule list control option for defining the material style and unfold rule. It's also important to remember that the preferences set within the Sheet Metal Defaults dialog box affect the document; this means that whatever state the dialog box is in when you save will be persisted within the document when you reopen it in the future. If you are creating a template file and overrides have been selected within the Sheet Metal Defaults dialog box, when referencing the template file in the future to create a new design, it will start with those overrides in place. Changing the active sheet metal rule does not wipe the overrides in the Sheet Metal Defaults dialog box because these overrides are managed at the document level, not at the style library.

SHEET METAL RULES AND PARAMETERS

One mechanism used to drive manufacturing and design preferences into sheet metal features is the association of sheet metal rule values with Inventor parameters. In previous releases, these sheet metal parameters had been exposed as regular model parameters, but this convention has changed with the move of styles out of templates and rules into the style library. Sheet metal parameters are now exposed within the parameter editor as special reference parameters, as shown in Figure 6.11. The one notable exception is the Thickness parameter, which can be changed from reference to model by deselecting the Use Thickness From Rule option box in the Sheet Metal Defaults dialog box. One reason for changing sheet metal parameters into reference parameters was based upon a legacy ability to actually drive sheet metal styles from the parameter editor edits. This practice could in certain cases cause stability issues when parameters were orphaned, but some workflows were actually very powerful. We briefly discuss this type of workflow in the "Harvesting Legacy Sheet Metal Templates" section.

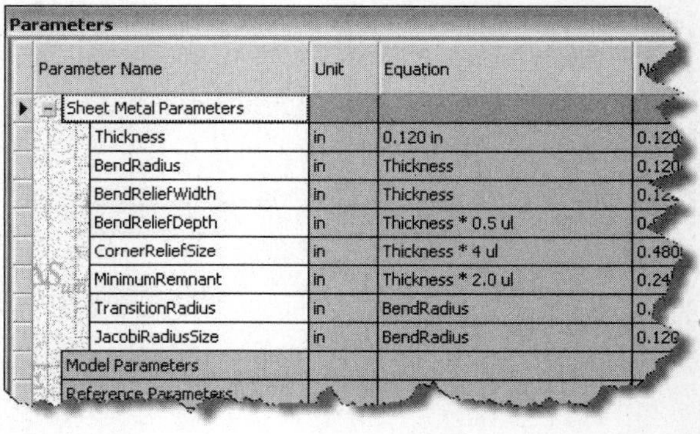

FIGURE 6.11
Sheet metal reference parameters within Inventor's parameter editor

Unfolding Your Part

With the transition of sheet metal styles into sheet metal rules, sheet metal unfolding options have also evolved and are now exposed as their own fully established rule category: sheet metal unfold rules. Two unfolding options have been traditionally supported within Inventor: linear unfolding using a K-factor and bend tables that use experimentally derived bend deduction values. Both methods continue to be embraced within Inventor 2009 with some notable style library enhancements.

The Mechanics of Unfolding

Before getting too deep into the unfold rule enhancements, an overview of the mechanics of unfolding might be helpful. Linear unfolding is accomplished by determining the bend allowance (the amount of material required to produce a bend) for a given bend by using the sheet thickness, the bend angle, the inner bend radius, and a K-factor value. For a given bend, there exists an offset surface position (within the bend cross section) that represents the neutral surface of the bend. The location of this neutral surface is most likely positioned somewhere between the 25th and 50th percentile of the cross section. The reason that this surface is referred to as the *neutral* surface is that it defines a measurable position within the bend that has the same length value in the folded and unfolded states. The K-factor is the ratio of the neutral surface position divided by the thickness of the sheet. The K-factor you use will depend on numerous factors, including material, thickness, and tooling. Most likely you will need to perform a number of test bends on a specific press brake to determine the ideal K-factor for you. Out of the box, Inventor has an unfold rule example that utilizes a K-factor value of 0.44, which means the neutral surface is expected to be positioned 44 percent through the cross section of the bend.

The second unfolding method is accomplished by using sheet metal bend tables. Bend tables support the refinement of your unfolding results by allowing you to customize the calculated developed length with experimentally determined values. Instead of using a constant K-factor value, bend tables enable you to customize the unfolding result for any combination of thickness, inner radius, and bend angle. The bend deduction values entered into the table are based upon a specific sheet thickness and are referenced to the coordinate intersection of inner bend radius and bend angle values. The granularity of the experimental values is up to you. It could be based upon 15-degree increments or perhaps 0.5-degree increments; it depends on how much experimental data you have. To create a bend table, you need to measure a sheet metal sample prior to folding and then once again after folding. By measuring the folded sample using virtual sharp locations, the values obtained will inherently be too large. The overmeasurement of the test fold sample needs to be compensated for by deducting an amount of length. By subtracting your combined measurements from the initial measurement of the sample taken prior to folding, you will be able to determine the value of excessive length (overmeasurement); this is what gets entered into the bend table and is where the method name *bend deduction* comes from.

Sheet Metal Unfold Rules

Within the Style And Standard Editor dialog box is a new Inventor style category called *sheet metal unfold rules*. Although the functionality supported within this rule type was available in previous releases, the creation of a separate unfold rule type has allowed the exposure of new user interface to help create, manage, and utilize sheet metal unfolding options as never before. Within the new unfold rule interface, an Unfold Method list control option allows you to choose between creating a linear unfold rule and a bend table unfold rule. The linear rule is simple and requires only the definition of a K-factor value. The bend table unfold rule, however, exposes a completely new user interface for Inventor 2009, where actual bend deduction values can be visualized as well as edited, as shown in Figure 6.12. The new interface will allow you to see bend table information that was previously embedded in your document but not visible to you. Bend tables can be created manually by entering values or even copying and pasting data from Excel. The Import command located at the bottom-left corner of the Style And Standard Editor dialog box now allows you to change the file extension to `.txt` so that legacy bend tables can be imported into Inventor and visualized within the new unfold rule interface. As a final capability, the Export Table command not only supports the `.xml` file format; it also supports a `.txt` format in case you need to share your bend table with others using older versions of Inventor.

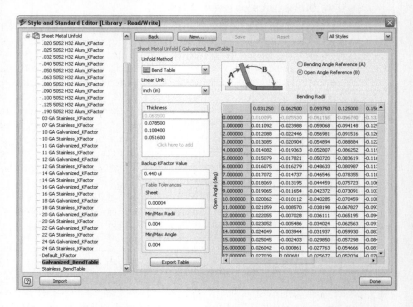

FIGURE 6.12
Style And Standard Editor dialog box, Sheet Metal Unfold Rules page displaying active rule Galvanized_BendTable

The layout of the Bend Table interface emulates the data structure of the legacy `.txt` bend tables. It has provisions for setting the unit type of the bend table as well as the bend angle reference. These options are important to understand, because they do not change any data entered into your table; they simply change how the data is interpreted when used for unfolding. Changing the linear unit from inches to feet won't affect data, but it will dramatically reduce the amount of deduction applied to your developed length calculation. As a bit of odd history on the bend table, it was designed to reference an "open angle" datum structure (which is still default) for measuring bends, whereas Inventor sheet metal features exclusively use a "bending angle" datum structure to create bent features. As a means to bridge this disparity in measurement convention, the new Bend Angle option at the top of the Bend Table interface allows you to declare in which structure your values were measured; Inventor will use this option to convert the values internally if necessary. Just to reaffirm, the angular values are not altered within the table when this option is changed.

The Thickness list collection allows you to create a number of bend tables for a given material, where the selected Thickness value will direct which bend table is being edited or viewed. A Backup K-factor value is also stored within the bend table, which is used when a bend angle/bend radius combination exceeds the boundaries of the table for a given sheet thickness. You can imagine this like an insurance plan that allows you to obtain a flat pattern even if you bend table doesn't define what deduction to use for smaller or large combinations of bend angle and radius. For combinations that fall within the table boundaries but not exactly at angle/radius coordinate values, Inventor use linear approximation to derive a value; this infers that the more granular your bend table, the better your results can be.

Working with Styles and Templates

If your project location is set to use the style library, then it is key to understand what has been defined within your template and what has been stored within the style library. As an example, if you have a sheet metal rule named MyRule1 with the Thickness value equal to 0.2 stored in your template file and a sheet metal rule named MyRule1 with the Thickness value equal to 0.5 stored in your style library, every time you start a new design from the template referencing MyRule1, you will see a Thickness value of 0.5 being applied. The reason for this is that the style library is the "published" source of your standards; its definition will always win. After saving your design, if you want to make changes to the Thickness value of MyRule1, you can apply the changes without fear that they might be automatically overwritten, because this occurs only when creating a new document using the template. (As a side note, if you did want to overwrite the local/document definition with the style library's definition, right-clicking an existing rule will present a context menu from which you can select the command Update Style, which will manually refresh the rule's definition in the document.) It is a good practice when using the style library to have perhaps a single sheet metal rule embedded in your template file. Once you know what sheet metal rule you want to apply to your model, selecting it either in the Style And Standard Editor dialog box or in the Sheet Metal Defaults dialog box will automatically draw the information into the active document. This process keeps extraneous information out of your document, providing a smaller footprint, and helps reduce the chance of style information mismatch. If you have a template file that has a numerous sheet metal rules stored within it, after publishing them to the style library, you can use the purge functionality with the Style Management Wizard to remove them.

Authoring and Reusing Punches

The most common method to cost effectively cut or deform sheet metal is by using a punch machine. Since this process is so fundamental to the sheet metal manufacturing environment, Inventor sheet metal contains a special Punch tool feature. Inventor Punch tools are a specialized subtype of iFeatures that embody unique capabilities and a simplified placement process.

Punches and iFeatures

The process of creating a punch is almost identical to a standard iFeature, but you will need to be aware of a few key differences. Different from regular iFeatures, punches require the inclusion of a sketch point (center point) in the insertion sketch; this is the highest-level sketch consumed by a feature that you are including in the published punch feature. The iFeature extraction dialog box actually checks for the inclusion of this sketch point to ensure you don't go to the trouble of publishing punches that cannot be placed. After you have created your Punch tool geometry, you will need to select Tools ➤ Extract iFeature from the main toolbar to begin the publishing process. Located at the top of the Extract iFeature dialog box is a type group that contains a Standard iFeature option and a special subtype Sheet Metal Punch iFeature option; select the Punch option.

The vast majority of the iFeature extraction dialog box is generic to standard iFeatures and punches, but once you have selected the Punch subtype option, you will see that the Manufacturing and Depth fields become enabled. Punch tools have the ability to store additional manufacturing information that is introduced during the creation process. The Punch ID field is where you can store a string that represents the Punch tool number. The simplified representation selection control allows you to select a 2D sketch representation or symbol that you want to display in the flat pattern instead of the actually formed shape. The sketch mush also contains a center mark so that it can be oriented with the punch's insertion center mark; there is more information pertaining to simplified or alternate representations later in this section. The Punch Depth field is where you can enter a value that reflects the intended throw depth of your tool into the sheet face. For example, when creating a dimple or a half shear, you need to specifically call out a Punch tool depth to ensure that the formed feature turns out exactly as you expect. The Punch Depth field allows you to enter a value or even a parametric expression that specifies this tooling depth.

REFERENCING PARAMETERS

If you want to create a parametric expression that references a parameter, that parameter must be consumed within the Punch tool's definition. A good example of such a parameter is Thickness.

Since published Punch tools are in fact just special versions of iFeatures, they are saved with .ide file extensions and can be opened within Inventor for edit. Once the Punch tool is opened, utilize the Edit iFeature command to alter embedded information or add information that was not originally included. This capability could enable you to add Punch tool numbers as well as punch depth information to Punch tools that had been published prior to the availability of these data sources.

Creating Successful Punches

When deciding how to create the geometry and parametric relationships for your punch, you may want to follow a few guidelines to improve the potential for successful authoring, ease of placement, and the computational result. Creating successful punches (and iFeatures) takes a little longer than regular modeling since you're trying to anticipate conditions in which your tooling will be placed and establishing expectations on how it will react. The following sections touch on two areas that are commonly the root of punch problems.

AVOIDING WORK GEOMETRY

Although it's a common practice to use work geometry to model features, this practice is never a good idea when creating punches (or iFeatures). The most problematic type of work geometry is the work plane, which has a defined normal direction that cannot be robustly persisted or recovered within the authored punch. Work planes are often ideal when modeling your punch tooling because you require a midplane in order to sketch a uniform cross section that can be swept. Sometimes a careful progression of additional features can help you compensate for this work plane requirement. For example, in the process of creating a dimple, you might need to cut out material and then sweep a deformed cross section in its place. Instead of cutting out the entire round, cut out only half of the profile so that a planar detail face is created in the center. You can sketch your dimple cross section upon the detail face before cutting away the remaining half round. The dimple can be finished by sweeping the profile around the original cut profile. During this process, it's critical to remember that any projections or sketch references must exclusively be made to the top face, or unintentional orientation references might be inferred. This solution didn't require a work plane but utilized the same references that you might have obtained by creating one. Since all the features were based on the geometry originally defined from the punch's insertion face, the computation is stable.

THE PARAMETERS WITHIN YOUR PUNCH

Punch features (and iFeatures) consume parameters that can be utilized to vary the size of the families of punches or help adapt your punch to different conditions. Sheet metal in particular has a number of reference parameters that are guaranteed to be in any sheet metal document since the sheet metal rule ensures their creation. These parameters can be either useful or detrimental, depending on how you utilize them. For example, when we made the round cut while creating the dimple, we utilized the parameter Thickness to define its cut depth. In the case, this is a good idea since you would want the cut depth to be able to accommodate a variety of sheet thickness for which it might be placed upon in the future. Defining the various radii in the dimple cross-section sketch is a very different situation. If you reference a sheet metal parameter when creating the cross section, it might change significantly when utilizing different sheet metal rules with a variety of sheet thicknesses. The tool may fail, since the value might change in an unexpected way that cannot be computed. Although tooling generally has well-known radius values, sometimes it seems convenient to define these values as a proportion of a parameter. Resist this practice, and choose all parameter values carefully.

Alternate Representations

Punch tools have a unique ability to change between formed and 2D representations in the flat pattern; this capability is enabled by a technology called *alternate punch representations*. To enable the alternate representation functionality, during the punch-authoring process you are afforded the opportunity to select a 2D sketch that depicts a representation you desire. The sketch geometry can be something similar to the formed geometry; it can be constructed of the projected edges of the formed geometry (this representation can change if it interacts with other features), or it can be a simple sketch that represents the Punch tool symbolically. To orient the 2D representation sketch to the insertion sketch of the Punch tool, you must insert a single center mark. You can in fact use the same sketch for both inserting the Punch tool and defining the alternate representation.

Regardless of whether the Punch tool represents removed or deformed material, the 2D alternate representation (2D Sketch, 2D Sketch and Center Mark, Center Mark Only) is displayed on the flat pattern after the Punch tool has been removed and then filled in, as shown in Figure 6.13. The formed Punch tool can be completely removed as long as the punch does not interfere with the outer contour/profile of the flat pattern. If the tool does intersect the flat pattern outer contour and a 2D alternate representation is selected, you will be prompted with a notification that will alert you to the fact that these punches could not be replaced. The punch alternate representation is set within the active sheet metal rule within the options on the Sheet tab. The punch representation can also be overridden from within the flat pattern environment using the Flat Pattern Definition dialog box's Punch Representation tab controls.

FIGURE 6.13
Sample electrical box flat pattern with formed punch knockouts and 2D alternate representation knockouts displayed

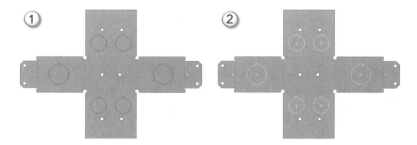

Placing Your Punch

The process of applying a published Punch tool to your sheet metal design is fairly straightforward. In fact, the reason why Punch tools are special versions of iFeatures instead of standard iFeatures is to make the placement process faster and more reliable. As discussed in the previous section, when authoring a Punch tool, the first sketch-based feature referenced to create the Punch tool needs to contain a single sketched center mark. To place a Punch tool, another sketched center mark is all that is needed. To place a Punch tool, follow these steps:

1. Create a 2D sketch containing a sketched center mark.

2. Launch the Punch tool from the Sheet Metal Features panel bar.

3. Once the Punch Tool Directory dialog box appears, select a Punch tool file from the catalog list.

4. Once you've selected the tool, the interface will change to the Punch Tool dialog box and display options for changing the punch, geometry, and size (if available within the punch definition); select Geometry.

5. On the Geometry tab, enter an angle to rotate the Punch tool preview.

6. Click Finish to complete the command.

ADDITIONAL INPUTS WHEN PLACING A PUNCH

If you run into a situation in which your Punch tool needs additional geometric inputs to orient it properly, Punch tools can be authored with these additional inputs predefined. The inputs will be automatically captured during the authoring process, which may or may not be your intention, and displayed on the Geometry tab during placement.

PATTERNING YOUR PUNCH

You can use a few methods to pattern punches within a sheet metal design. Since a sketched center mark (center point) is required for inserting the punch, you can create an array of center marks within a sketch to apply numerous punches at the same time. When you launch the Punch tool, it will attempt to automatically select all visible center marks in your sketch as long as only one sketch is visible. This method also allows you to utilize the Geometry tab, which "centers" selection control to either add center marks that were not participating or deselect center marks that you do not want a punch placed at, as shown in Figure 6.14. One powerful capability of patterned sketch center marks is the creation of irregular patterns that are produced by deselecting specific center marks in symmetric array. The sketched pattern method works, but it is limited to patterning within a single plane (2D sketch plane) and has some performance impacts when patterning large numbers of punches.

The second method for patterning punches is to insert a single punch feature and then use the rectangular or circular patterning features to create additional punch instances. Although the definition process is similar, nonplanar arrays can be created, and additional performance enhancements can be achieved. When you click the >> button of the Rectangular Pattern and Circular Pattern dialog boxes, a computational option called Optimize is available. Whenever you are trying to pattern large numbers of punches, features, or iFeatures, this option should be enabled to improve performance. Irregular punch patterns can also be produced using this method but must be computed as a symmetric array first, and then individual child occurrences can be suppressed using the feature browser.

FIGURE 6.14
Sample back bracket folded model with irregular punch pattern created using center mark deselection of a symmetric sketch array

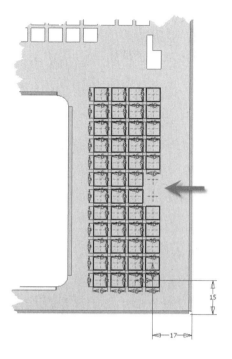

Leveraging the Flat Pattern

The flat pattern derived from the folded model ties the design to the manufacturing environment. Within Inventor, the flat pattern model is an actual flattened version of the folded model vs. a sheet that has been pieced together and thickened. Numerous tools, utilities, and data sources have been provided to enable the flat pattern to suit your individual manufacturing and documentation needs. The following sections detail these capabilities and tools.

Flat Pattern Edit Features

The flat pattern environment has its own panel bar containing a customized set of modeling tools drawn from the Part Features panel bar and the Sheet Metal Features panel bar. The flat pattern tools are referred to as *flat pattern edit features*, because they are intended to apply small alterations to the flat pattern model instead of large-scale modeling. Flat pattern edit features are applied only to the flat pattern, whereas folded model features are applied first to the folded model and then carried over to the flat pattern when the folded model is unfolded. The flat pattern can be imagined as a derivative of the folded model, establishing a unidirectional relationship (flat pattern edit features are not reflected in the folded model). There are many situations in which the generated flat pattern is not exactly what you need for manufacturing; flat pattern edit features are ideal for making small associative tweaks that previously may have had to be applied in an external (disassociated) file.

What's Stored Inside?

The flat pattern contains a wealth of manufacturing information that is stored progressively during the design process. Punch and bend information is stored within the flat pattern model specifically so that customers working with drawings, customers working with the API, or those who want to translate the flat pattern to a different file version can control all their options in a common location; the flat pattern is commonly referred to as the *jump off point* for all downstream consumers.

FLAT PATTERN DEFINITION DIALOG BOX

The flat pattern model can be manipulated by using a command called Edit Flat Pattern Definition, which is available by right-clicking anywhere is the graphics area and selecting Edit Flat Pattern Definition. The Flat Pattern Definition dialog box allows you to control a number of aspects pertaining to the flat pattern's orientation and the information stored within it.

The first tab of the Flat Pattern Definition dialog box relates to the flat pattern orientation. The selection control allows you to select either an edge or two points to define a vector that is utilized to set either a horizontal orientation or a vertical orientation. The orientation of the flat pattern is very important, because the implied x-axis is utilized to calculate the rotational angle of Punch tools that have been applied to the model. By orienting the flat pattern to your specific punch equipment, the required tool rotation angle should be directly available from your flat pattern.

Since the flat pattern base face is going to be either the face already selected or the backside face, the control of the base face has been simplified to a "flip" option. Base face definition is critical because it establishes a directional reference for bends and punch tooling as well as an association with the Front navigation tool view and the Default Drawing Manager view.

The second tab is the Punch Representation tab, which allows you to override the representation setting in the sheet metal document without having to edit the active sheet metal rule.

The third tab is the Bend Angle tab, which allows you to declare how bend angles should be reported to the API and Drawing Manager. As an example, this means that by changing the Bend Angle option to an open angle, Drawing Manager annotations of your flattened bends will recover the complementary angle of the bending angle.

SETTING OPEN ANGLE AS THE FLAT PATTERN DEFAULT

The flat pattern Bend Angle option is set to Bending Angle upon flat pattern creation by default. For companies that exclusively need to document their flat patterns using an open angle, this default condition could lead to errors because the option has to be manually edited for each flat pattern and may introduce a lack of confidence in the angular option applied. To avoid this situation, you can create a registry setting that will automatically change this setting during flat pattern creation. To create the registry setting, use the following steps:

1. Launch the REGEDIT command from the Windows Run dialog box found by selecting Start ➢ Run.

2. Once the Registry Editor is open, navigate to the following folder location: HKEY_CURRENT_USER\ Software\Autodesk\Inventor\RegistryVersion13.0\System\Preferences\SheetMetal. If you haven't created any sheet metal components, the folder might have not been created yet; simply add a folder named SheetMetal in the Preferences folder.

3. Once at the SheetMetal folder, create a new DWORD entry named EnableOpenAngle.

4. For the value data, set it to 1, as shown in Figure 6.15.

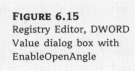

FIGURE 6.15
Registry Editor, DWORD
Value dialog box with
EnableOpenAngle

Manufacturing Your Flat Pattern

There is a very close association between sheet metal design and manufacture and the flat pattern solution within Inventor embraces this relationship. Inventor generically supports the ability to translate models to a variety of file formats, but Inventor sheet metal actually has its own utility to support the translation to .sat, .dwg, and .dxf formats. After selecting the flat pattern browser node, you can right-click and select Save Copy As; this command launches the Flat Pattern Translation dialog box. For .sat files, a simple option defining the file version will be presented. For .dwg and .dxf file formats, an extensive list of options and file-processing capabilities are made available to you.

Within the Flat Pattern Translation dialog box, you will find standard options for file type, but there is also a Layer tab that supports granular layer naming and visibility control. The last tab is the Geometry tab, which allows you to decide whether you want to apply a variety of manufacturing-specific options to the translation. The first of these options is for spline simplification, because many CNC profile manufacturing centers cannot leverage splines and are restricted to arcs and lines. This utility allows you to apply faceting rules to break the outer contour of flat patterns into linear segments. The second options group relates to the post-processing of the translated file, allowing you to force the 2D result into positive coordinate space and to merge interior and outer contours into polylines, which may be critical for a path-based tool. Sometimes you'll need additional tool path manufacturing information in your .dxf/.dwg output. For this, the flat pattern has the ability to export unconsumed sketches created on the flat pattern. Only visible sketches are exported, and a layer called IV_UNCONSUMED_SKETCHES was added to support the collection of these sketches.

Sheet Metal iPart Factories

iParts have traditionally not been very sheet metal friendly, but several enhancements in Inventor 2009 have made sheet metal iParts incredibly flexible and powerful. True sheet metal configurations and flat pattern support within member files represent that core of this new functionality.

Consuming Sheet Metal Rules

In a previous section about sheet metal rules and unfold rules, we discussed a number of advantages related to the move from templates to the style library. An additional advantage that was not discussed was that this evolution also makes sheet metal rules and unfold rules consumable by iPart factories. In a nutshell, this means configurations of sheet metal parts can be differentiated exclusively by referencing different rules. So, from the perspective of the folded model, identical fit and function designs can be made with completely different manufacturing processes reflected per member file. For example, a bracket could be designed and configured in basic mild steel or optionally in an upgraded stainless steel version. Sheet metal configurations via iParts could be very beneficial and profitable to a company that deals in varieties of components that need to fit into the same space but utilize different materials and/or manufacturing processes. On the other front, the folded model might be identical for all members, but a different sheet metal unfold rule could be used to accommodate different manufacturing locations of your component.

With the addition of flat pattern edit features and named flat pattern orientations being added to the iPart definition (the new Sheet Metal tab within an iPart author table), full support for sheet metal manufacturing configurations can also be realized in Inventor 2009. There has been a great deal of discussion about Autodesk's digital prototyping strategy within the CAD/CAE community, but the enhancements in Inventor 2009 with regard to sheet metal configurations and manufacturing configurations really deliver on the promise of this concept.

SEAN SAYS: WHAT YOU SHOULD KNOW WHEN WORKING WITH REAL-WORLD EQUIPMENT AND MATERIALS

In the real world, different machines will produce a different bend radius. Different materials will have different K-factors. If your designs are critical and you use a number of different machines and material suppliers, you may need to take these variations into account. By using a sheet metal iPart, you can create a design that utilizes the correct parameters such as bend radius and K-factor for a given machine and/or material combination.

Folded and Flat Members

The next significant enhancement to sheet metal iParts was alluded to in the discussion of flat pattern edit features: flat patterns models are now included within member files. In the past, a single flat pattern was computed for the iPart factory, changing the active folded member simply forced the flat pattern to be recomputed. Although this might not sound so bad from the perspective of the factory, once a folded member file was generated to disk, this limitation becomes apparent. Before Inventor 2009, factory member files did not contain a flat pattern model, only the factory did. When you created a drawing of an iPart factory flat pattern, you were actually documenting the active factory member's flat pattern. This meant you would need to defer updates of your drawing so that you could ensure that when editing you had the correct folded member selected so as to not change the result of the flat pattern view. In Inventor 2009, both the folded and flat pattern models are generated to disk, allowing you to create flat pattern documentation referencing the member file flat pattern instead of the factory.

For sheet metal designers who already have iPart factories with sheet metal member files on disk, a number of provisions have been added to help get the additional flat pattern body out to the instantiated member files. The first thing to remember is that Inventor migration has changed over the years to have a minimalistic impact on files; this has been done to reduce the performance impact of opening a legacy file or files in a newer version of Inventor. This also means that aspects such as getting the newly available flat pattern information into an instantiated file will not be automatic. There are a number of scenarios in which is it is fundamentally detrimental to have these updates automatically push out, most notably for a situation in which Vault or Product

Steam have to be utilized for data management. The iPart factory member nodes support a context menu command called Generate Files, as shown in Figure 6.16. This command is intended to support the batch creation of member files on disk; it can also be used to force updates, such as the flat pattern, out to the member files already in existence. In addition, a pull model vs. a push can be used. If you open the iPart factory and execute the Rebuild All operation and then save the rebuilt and migrated data, the member files when individually opened will see that they are out of date with the factory. Selecting the now-enabled Update command within the individual member file will then draw in the flat pattern information automatically.

FIGURE 6.16
Sheet metal iPart factory example, displaying Generate Files command for a selected member file

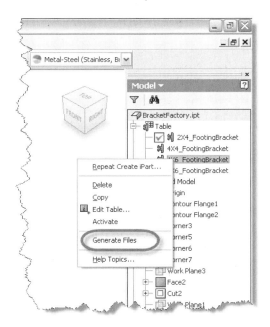

Modeling with Non-Sheet-Metal Features

Although the sheet metal feature set is extensive, sometimes using non-sheet-metal features can be helpful or possibly even required to accomplish your design. The challenge when using non-sheet-metal features is to honor the guiding principles of sheet metal design so that the resulting component can be unfolded as well as incorporate sheet metal conditions so that the features are manufacturable and therefore cost effective.

Selecting Problematic Features

Although it's possible to design sheet metal components using lofts, solid sweeps, and shells, these features can produce unpredictable and hard-to-control results. The Loft command, unless highly restricted, produces doubly curved surfaces that cannot be unfolded properly. Although it's possible to utilize rails to control loft curvature, it's time-consuming and invariably frustrating. Solid sweeps are a measure better than lofts, but these too can create unintended doubly curved surfaces. The Shell tool can be used nine times out of ten to successfully create a legitimate sheet metal feature, but the tenth time, when it doesn't work and it's not clear why, will be confounding. If you use the parameter Thickness to shell your component, you'll probably be in fairly good shape, but there are certain situations in which the Shell command cannot assure uniform thickness after the shell. These situations are not always simple to predict.

Surface-Based Workflows

By far, the most successful non-sheet-metal feature workflows typically leverage a surface that is later thickened. The reason that these workflows are so successful is that it's often easier to ensure that the resulting model embodies sheet metal conditions (the side faces are perpendicular to the top and bottom faces) since the part can be thickened normal to the surface. When constructing surfaces that will be thickened, the Extrude and Revolve commands are excellent choices because they have a restricted directions in which features are created, which can help ensure that only cones, cylinders, and planes are created (these can be unfolded). The Sweep command is possibly another good choice, but care needs to be taken to ensure that the profile and the sweep path do not contain any splines or ellipses that might prevent unfolding. For each of three previously mentioned features, the sketch profile geometry should ideally be limited to arcs and lines to help ensure the creation of unfoldable geometry. Another common surface-generating workflow is to use Derived Component, where you select the Body as Work Surface option when placing the derived component into the sheet metal file. This workflow can be combined well with either a thicken feature or a sheet metal face feature after creating projected sketches for each planar surface.

One of the biggest benefits of working with surfaces is that you can apply complicated alterations to the surface prior to thickening. Some of the most common features utilized to create cutting surfaces are Extrude, Revolve, and Sweep. The Split command (and perhaps Delete Face) can be utilized to remove faces from the thickened surface selection. When using the Sweep command, the Guide Surface Sweep option is ideal because the swept profile is rotated along the path to ensure that it remains normal to the guide surface. Sometimes a thickened sheet metal component needs to be trimmed with a complicated profile. For these situations, a swept surface combined with the sculpt feature can result in a model that still has sheet metal conditions.

Working with Imported Parts

The Inventor sheet metal environment has been designed to work with imported geometry, because its solid unfolder is concerned with topology, not with features. This means that imported parts can be drawn into Inventor and unfolded as well as modified with additional features. To be successful working with imported sheet metal models, you must follow a few general guidelines.

Setting Yourself Up for Success

There are two main methods for importing parts into Inventor: the Open command and the Insert ➤ Import command. If you are able to use the Open command (which is preferred), a standard part template is going to be utilized by default to embed initial styles and document options, so the first step will be to use the Convert ➤ Sheet Metal command to draw in the sheet metal subtype options and rules into the document. If you use the Insert ➤ Import command from within an empty sheet metal document, the imported geometry will be in the form of a surface. To work with this geometry, you will need to thicken each surface, which can be a time-consuming process. It is recommended, when possible, to "open" imported parts so that a solid body can be recovered.

The next step you need to accomplish is the measurement of the sheet thickness of your imported model; once you have this value, you can match it with an appropriate sheet metal rule (or create a new one). With the enhancements in Inventor 2009, matching the thickness can be as simple as taking a measurement from the sheet and overriding the Thickness value within the Sheet Metal Defaults dialog box with a simple copy and paste. Since the solid unfolder works with evaluated topology to facilitate unfolding, the thickness of the actual part must match the thickness of the active sheet metal rule exactly. If the imported part contains portions that are not of uniform thickness, proper unfolding may not be possible; spend some time evaluating your imported model to ensure that it conforms to sheet metal conditions. If your imported model contains faces defined by splines or ellipses, you are not going to be unfold your part. In these cases, removing these faces and replacing them with faces defined by tangent arcs may be an acceptable modification.

Annotating Your Sheet Metal Design

The Drawing Manager environment contains several tools and functions specifically focused on helping you document your sheet metal design. A quick overview of sheet metal–specific tools might help you understand them a bit better.

Creating a View of Your Sheet Metal Design

The first step in creating your documentation will be to choose which model file to reference, but sheet metal has the added requirement of deciding between a folded model and a flat pattern view, as shown in Figure 6.17. Once a sheet metal model file is selected on the Component tab, a sheet metal view options group will appear immediately below the file's path information. The displayed options allow you to choose between creating a folded or flat pattern view and, in the case of a flat pattern, choosing whether you want center marks to be recovered for any embedded Punch tools. The default view options will change based on your selection, because the flat pattern has a clear distinction between its top (Default) face and its bottom (Backside) face. The actual orientation of the 3D flat pattern defines what is a top and what is a bottom face. This also impacts bend orientation with respect to what is reported as up and what is reported as down. All punch angular information is based on the virtual x-axis previewed during flat pattern orientation.

FIGURE 6.17
Drawing Manager: Drawing View dialog box's Component tab with options displayed for sheet metal view creation

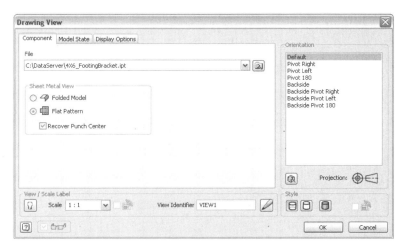

The Model State tab may also be of interest, because sheet metal iPart members can be individually selected when a factory file is referenced, as shown in Figure 6.18. Choosing between a folded model and flat pattern is also necessary when creating a drawing view of the sheet metal iPart member. If the member has not already been instantiated to disk, selecting the member from the Drawing View dialog box will automatically cause this file creation to occur.

FIGURE 6.18
Drawing Manager: Drawing View dialog box's Model State tab with options displayed for sheet metal iPart member view creation

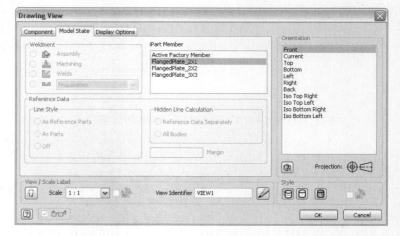

The last tab is the Display Options tab, which is important because it controls whether sheet metal bend extents should be drawn in the view as well as other annotations such as work features and tangent edges, as shown in Figure 6.19.

FIGURE 6.19
Drawing Manager: Drawing View dialog box's Display Options tab with options displayed for sheet metal bend extents

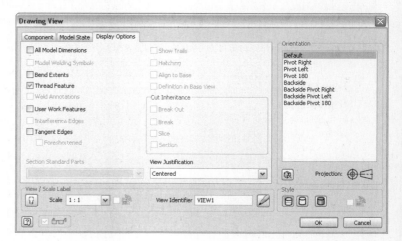

Bend, Punch, and Flat Pattern Annotations

Once you've created the view of your sheet metal component, you can switch to the Drawing Annotation panel bar to complete the documentation of your design. The sheet metal annotation commands within the Drawing Manager specifically and exclusively support views of the flat pattern model. Two leadered sheet metal annotations are available, as well as bend notes and punch notes, as shown in Figure 6.20. Bend notes allow you to recover bend angle, bend direction, bend radius, and K-factor (not on by default) for any bend centerline. The punch note allows you to select a formed punch, center mark, or 2D alternate punch representation in order to recover the punch angle, punch direction, punch ID, and punch depth (punch ID and depth need to be added to the Punch tool description when authored). When editing the punch note, you will also see a quantity command that allows you to recover the number of instances of the same Punch tool in the view.

FIGURE 6.20
Drawing Annotation panel bar with Bend Notes and Punch Notes commands displayed

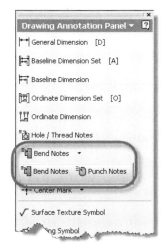

You can utilize the Table Annotation command to create a Drawing Manager bend table (not to be confused with bend tables utilized for unfolding) that documents all the bends in a selected view. To create a bend table, follow these steps:

1. Select the Table command from the Drawing Annotation panel bar.

2. Use the selection control to select an existing flat pattern view.

3. Decide whether the chosen columns are acceptable (bend direction, angle, and so on); if not, alter the selected columns.

4. Choose the Bend ID format, and enter a prefix if desired.

5. Click OK to create the bend table.

Punch table creation is a little different, because it has been incorporated within the preexisting Hole Table annotation commands. The reason that punch support was combined with hole tables is that you most likely used the Hole tool out of convenience, not necessarily to convey a manufacturing process. To make sure all of this tool-based information is consolidated together, an enhancement to hole tables was made. After invoking the Hole Table - View command and selecting a flat pattern view, you will see that the standards in the toolbar have changed to reflect predefined hole table standards. Within this list (as shown in Figure 6.21) is an example standard for punch tables, which prevents you from having to first create a standard hole table and then editing it to add all the punch information columns.

FIGURE 6.21
Drawing Manager active
style toolbar showing
punch table style preset

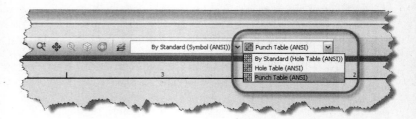

From within the Text command, you can reference the sheet metal flat pattern extent values by selecting a new sheet metal properties option from the Type list control, as shown in Figure 6.22. Once you've selected the sheet metal properties type, the Property list control will provide options for entering the flat pattern extents area, length, or width in the text box.

FIGURE 6.22
Drawing Manager Text
dialog box displaying
sheet metal properties
options for flat pattern
extents

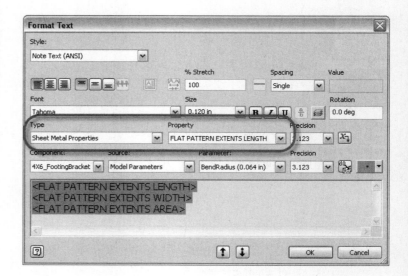

The last annotation command that can interact with sheet metal properties is the Parts List command. To recover flat pattern length and width extents within the parts list, follow these steps:

1. From within your sheet metal model, access the custom iProperties menu by selecting File ➢ iProperties ➢ Custom.

2. Create a new custom iProperty named Length.

3. Ensure the type is set to Text.

4. Enter a value of = <**FLAT PATTERN LENGTH**> **cm**.

5. Repeat steps 2–4 for a custom iProperty named Width and with a value of = <**FLAT PATTERN WIDTH**> **cm**.

6. Save the sheet metal model file.

7. From within the Drawing Manager, launch the Parts List command.

8. Using the Select View tool, select a flat pattern view of the sheet metal model containing the custom iProperties, click OK, and place the parts list on your drawing

9. Right-click your parts list, and select the Edit Parts List command.

10. Right-click the table, and select Column Chooser.

11. Select the New Property command, and enter **Length**.

12. Repeat step 11, creating an additional property named **Width**.

13. Once complete, click OK.

14. Select the new column named Length, right-click, and select the Format Column command.

15. Change the formatting and precision of the length to match your needs.

16. Repeat step 15 for the Width column, clicking OK when complete.

SAVING TIME WITH CUSTOM IPROPERTIES

If this information is something you might routinely want to access, create the custom iProperty values in your sheet metal template file so that they are always available.

Harvesting Legacy Sheet Metal Templates

Within the whole discussion concerning the move from a template-based style environment to a style library, you may have been wondering how to actually go about making the plunge. Luckily, some tools ship with Inventor that can help extract your previously defined sheet metal style information. To determine whether these tools can work for you, the following sections detail some challenges that you might run into while harvesting your styles as well as some information pertaining to the tools that can help you through the process.

Parameter Indirection

One aspect of legacy sheet metal styles that has no precedence in the style library relates to parameter indirection. In previous versions of Inventor, sheet metal users were able to build sheet metal styles that were driven by referenced parameters that in turn referenced externalized data sources (in other words, an Excel file). Within the XML-based style library, there is no way to ensure that the externalized file containing the parameter information will be found, so parameter indirection has never been supported. However, numerous sheet metal customers have leveraged this capability quite successfully to construct sheet metal configurators. With this in mind, Inventor 2009 continues to support the use of linked parameters within the sheet metal rule definition; it simply doesn't allow sheet metal rules containing parameter indirection to be published to the style XML library. Since sheet metal rules exist as document-level objects as well as published style XML entries, there's no reason why externalized parameters can't be used with the sheet metal template.

The Hidden Tools of Harvesting

When discussing the sheet metal transition to the style library, a common question is often asked: what happens to my data? The good news is that Inventor 2009 has been designed to preserve and migrate all the sheet metal style information that is stored in each sheet metal document, whether the style is active or not. Once users see that the data is still all there, the next questions generally is this: how do I move my sheet metal template styles to the style library? As a means to sort through and publish your sheet metal styles as sheet metal rules, two additional tools have been provided: the style library manager and the Style Management Wizard. These utilities work in conjunction with Inventor and are fundamentally intended to support the process of make the big change away from templates and toward the style library. This also means these tools are typically used infrequently since it's not every day that new style information is made ready for consumption in the style library. With this in mind, we'll walk through these tools to ensure that you understand how to successful publish your data.

STYLE MANAGEMENT WIZARD

Sheet metal style information has never been published to the style library before, so the Style Management Wizard is the only tool you will need to make the transition from templates to the style library. The Style Management Wizard, also known as the *harvester*, allows you to select specific target files that contain style information and either purge that style information or publish it to style library XMLs. Although the harvester supports that capability to search all the files in a given project, most sheet metal customers use a single template that contains every bit of sheet metal style information they've ever thought of. This consolidation of information is one of the main problems that influenced the move away from templates and toward the style library, because most customer sheet metal files are chocked with style information that has never and will never be used. So, with this in mind, the harvester also allows individual files to be added to queue, irrespective of the project location in which they reside. For the majority of sheet metal customers, a single targeted file might contain all the style data you want to harvest and publish into the sheet metal rule style XML file. The harvester then needs to know what to do with the extracted information. You can either create a new style library destination or select an existing style library (for example, your Inventor 2009 design data folder), but be cautious because this will overwrite any styles or rules that have an identical name. This is in fact an important aspect of the Style Management Wizard — the last imported style definition for a given style name wins. Once you initiate the harvesting of style information, you will have to wait about five minutes because Windows, Inventor, and the harvester all have to work through some processes; don't exit — it will succeed. . .just give it some time. When the harvesting is finished, you will see a log entry that reflects that the target file was successfully harvested.

BE CAREFUL WHEN HARVESTING

Different from the Style and Standard Editor dialog box within Inventor, the harvester will allow you to publish sheet metal rules that contain parameter indirection (in other words, a linked Excel file or references to model parameters), but the published rule will fail when referenced. Be careful to preview the contents of files from which you intend to harvest style/rule information.

To successfully accomplish the harvesting of your sheet metal style information, you will need to complete a few preparation tasks. First, the file or files that you intend to extract styles information from must be migrated to Inventor 2009. The next step is that you should ensure that the project file containing the referenced file(s) has its Use Style Library option set to Yes. Lastly, ensure that the location that you will be writing style information to is not read-only. It is not uncommon for the Design Data folder (under Start ➤ Programs ➤ Autodesk ➤ Inventor 2009) to be set to read-only; if you're going to edit the styles in this location, you might want to verify that they're editable. If you want to harvest the style information from a specific file, follow these steps:

1. Launch the Style Management Wizard from the following location: Program Files ➤ Autodesk ➤ Autodesk Inventor 2009 ➤ Tools ➤ Style Management Wizard.

2. Once you arrive at the welcome screen, click Next.

3. Select a project file location that contains a file that you want to harvest sheet metal style information from, and then click Next.

4. Select the folder icon in the upper-left corner in order to add a specific file to the harvesting queue.

5. Once selected, you will see the filename and file path in the harvest queue; click Next.

6. The next page allows you to select between harvesting and purging styles information; we will use the default option, which is Harvest Styles Into A Target Style Library.

7. Next you must choose whether you want to create a new style library based on your target file or edit an existing style library. For this example, we will edit the Inventor 2009 ➤ Design Data library, but you may want to create a new library to verify the results. Click Next.

MY NEW LIBRARY IS MISSING STYLES

When you create a new library based upon a target file, only the styles located within that specific file will be used. Material, color, and various other styles may not be present within your target file and may appear absent.

---

8. The last step is to click Start to begin the process of extracting your sheet metal style information.

9. When the harvesting log says it has finished and the Pause command button changes to Finished, you have completed the harvesting process.

Style Library Manager

The Style Library Manager is a utility that allows you to manipulate styles that have already been published to a style XML file. Different from the Style Management Wizard, the Style Library Manager allows you to copy, rename, and delete styles. For the purposes of sheet metal library management, the Delete function will most likely be the most utilized. An important key to remember when working with the Styles And Standard Editor dialog box is that style information can be added to the library only from within Inventor; there is no support within Inventor to delete items from the style XML files. Although there is a command named Purge Style within the right-click menu of a style (as shown in Figure 6.23), all of these commands are from the perspective of the document-level version of the style, the cached style. Update Style, for example, overwrites the cached style information with whatever is in the style file. If the style existed only in the cache, the Update Style command would never become enabled. The only command in the Style right-click menu that adds information to the style XML file is Save To Style Library. For any editing of the style XML that requires renaming or deleting, you will need to utilize the Style Library Manager. To access the Style Library Manager, select Program Files ➤ Autodesk ➤ Autodesk Inventor 2009 ➤ Tools ➤ Style Library Manager.

FIGURE 6.23
Style And Standard Editor dialog box's right-click menu for managing document and library styles

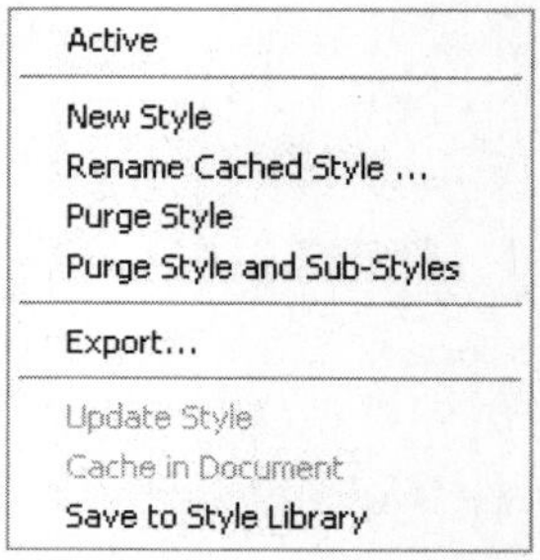

Active
New Style
Rename Cached Style ...
Purge Style
Purge Style and Sub-Styles
Export...
Update Style
Cache in Document
Save to Style Library

The Bottom Line

Take advantage of the specific sheet metal features available in Inventor   Knowing what features are available to help realize your design can make more efficient and productive use of your time.

Master It   Of the sheet metal features discussed, how many require a sketch to produce their result?

Understand sheet metal templates and rules   Templates can help get your design started on the right path, and sheet metal rules and associated styles allow you to drive powerful and intelligent manufacturing variations into your design; combining the two can be very productive as long as you understand some basic principles.

Master It   Name two methods that can be used to publish a sheet metal rule from a sheet metal part file to the style library.

Author and insert punch tooling   Creating and managing Punch tools can streamline your design process and standardize tooling in your manufacturing environment.

Master It   Name two methods that can be utilized to produce irregular (nonsymmetric) patterns of punch features.

Utilize the flat pattern information and options   The sheet metal folded model captures your manufacturing intent during the design process; understanding how to leverage this information and customize it for your needs can make you extremely productive.

Master It   How can you change the reported angle of all your Punch tools by 90°?

Understand the nuances of sheet metal iPart factories   Sheet metal iPart factories enable you to create true manufacturing configurations with the inclusion of folded and flat pattern models in each member file.

Master It   If you created sheet metal iPart factories prior to Inventor 2009, any instantiated files contain only a folded model. Name two methods that you could use to drive the flat pattern model into the instantiated file.

Model sheet metal components with non-sheet-metal features   Inventor doesn't always allow you to restrict yourself to sheet-specific design tools; understanding how to utilize non-sheet metal features will ensure that your creativity is limitless.

Master It   Name two non-sheet-metal features that can lead to unfolding problems if used to create your design.

Work with imported sheet metal parts   Understanding the way in which Inventor accomplishes unfolding as well as how to associate an appropriate sheet metal rule are keys to successfully working with imported parts.

Master It   Name the one measured value that is critical if you want to unfold an imported part.

Understand the tools available to annotate your sheet metal design   Designing your component is essential, but it's equally important to understand the tools that are available to efficiently document your design and extract your embedded manufacturing intent.

Master It   What process is required to recover flat pattern width and height extents within your Drawing Manager parts list?

Harvest your legacy sheet metal styles into sheet metal rules   Using the harvesting utilities provided, you can extract your legacy sheet metal styles and publish them into style library sheet metal rules, preassociated to material styles, sheet thickness values, and sheet metal unfold rules.

Master It   How can you extract sheet metal style information from a legacy part files or template files for the purpose of publishing it with a Sheet Metal Rule?

Chapter 7

Part and Feature Reuse

The ability to reuse parts and features in other designs is an important step to increasing productivity. Inventor provides this ability through several different workflows. This chapter is intended to introduce you to several methods that will assist you in achieving your goal.

Developing the proper workflow for your company will depend on several criteria. Depending on your involvement with the functional design aspect of Inventor, you may be converting some iParts to Content Center components. Additionally, you may decide to utilize iParts and iFeatures for design development if your design needs require them.

In this chapter, you will learn how to:

◆ Create iParts from existing designs

◆ Create and use iFeatures

◆ Copy sketches and part features to create additional features and designs

◆ Configure, create, and access Content Center parts

Working with iParts

iParts differ from standard parts in that they are essentially table-driven part factories, allowing for many different variations to be generated from the same basic design. When an iPart is inserted into an assembly, a dialog box appears and allows you to specify a variation of the original part from the table.

Within the iPart factory, you can configure feature sizes by specifying different values for the same parametric dimension, you can choose to include or suppress entire features, and you can configure the iProperties of a part. In addition to these general configuration controls, you can configure thread features and work features such as work planes, axes, and points. There are two basic forms of iParts: table-driven and custom. Both basic forms may be combined to create a table-driven part that allows custom input.

Each original iPart, called a *factory part*, generates individual derived, noneditable member parts. Member parts placed within an assembly can be substituted with a different member part through the Replace Component editing process. When a member part is replaced, generally all existing assembly constraints will be retained.

iParts bring several advantages of use within assemblies. They essentially function as completely different parts, allowing dimensional changes, feature suppression, transfer of iProperties, and other values.

Creating and Modifying iParts

iParts are created from an existing part. Existing parts already contain features and parameters. Although you can modify a standard part by changing the parameter values, this will affect the part wherever it is used. To create configurations of a standard part, you must first convert the part into an iPart.

You can publish iParts to a custom content folder for use as Content Center components or as additional content for functional design such as Frame Generator and Bolted Connections. Published iParts can also be used in other aspects of functional design where allowed.

MODIFYING THE PARAMETER LIST

Before converting a standard part into an iPart, you must first modify the parameter list. For this example, you will be using a file called `spacerblock.ipt` from the Mastering Inventor folder. To access the Parameters dialog box, go to the Tools menu and choose Parameters. Figure 7.1 displays the contents of the parameters within this file.

FIGURE 7.1
Parameters dialog box

Parameter Name	Unit	Equation	Nominal Value	Tol.	Model Value	Ex	Comment
Model Parameters							
Width	in	3 in	3.000000	○	3.000000	☑	
Height	in	2 in	2.000000	○	2.000000	☑	
Thickness	in	0.005 in	0.005000	○	0.005000	☑	
d3	deg	0 deg	0.000000	○	0.000000	☐	
d4	in	0.255 in	0.255000	○	0.255000	☐	
d5	in	0.255 in	0.255000	○	0.255000	☐	
d6	in	0.5 in	0.500000	○	0.500000	☐	
d7	deg	3 deg	3.000000	○	3.000000	☐	
d8	in	0.625 in	0.625000	○	0.625000	☐	
d9	in	0.375 in	0.375000	○	0.375000	☐	
d10	in	0.125 in	0.125000	○	0.125000	☐	
d12	deg	0 deg	0.000000	○	0.000000	☐	

Rename each model parameter, giving it a descriptive name to be used as a column header within the table. In the example shown in Figure 7.1, we have renamed d0, d1, and d2 to Width, Height, and Thickness, respectively. These names will be used as column header names in the iPart table. Parameters to which we have assigned new names will automatically be pulled into the iPart table. You can manually add unnamed parameters to the iPart table; however, it is best practice to give all parameters to be used in the iPart meaningful names. It is also important to note that parameters should always be named before being included in the iPart table in order to maintain consistency. Note too that spaces are not allowed in parameter names but can be substituted with underscores when required.

In the Export column, check all parameters that you have renamed. Checking the export column permits creation of custom iProperties within the part file. By exporting parameters as iProperties, you can easily access them in the parts list and bill of materials. Click Done to save and exit the parameter settings.

SEAN SAYS: TAKE ADVANTAGE OF THE DEFAULT PARAMETER NAME

All parameters that have been renamed from the default parameter name will be automatically included as an iPart parameter column. Use this to your advantage when creating your base part that will be converted into an iPart.

CREATING THE IPART

After you've modified the parameter list, go to the Tools menu and choose Create iPart to launch the iPart Author dialog box. This dialog box allows you to create and modify the table that will generate iPart members.

In the iPart Author dialog box, the initial table has already been constructed. The Member and Part Number columns have been added to the three automatically included named parameter columns: Width, Height, and Thickness.

For this example, add a Description column to the table by selecting the Properties tab at the top of the dialog box and expanding the Project folder. Select Description in the left window and then click the >> button between the windows to add Description as a column in the table. Figure 7.2 shows the end result. You can add properties at the same time to fully define your bill of materials and parts list.

FIGURE 7.2
iPart Author dialog box

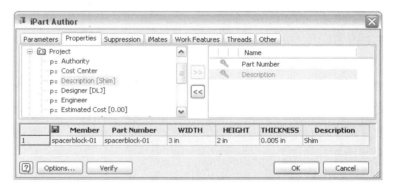

You can also add a column to suppress existing features within the part. Clicking the Suppression tab will reveal the available features within the active part. Features moved to the right side of the iPart Author will appear as an additional column or as a column marked Compute or Suppress. Do this for the feature called Fillet1 in your spacer block, as shown in Figure 7.3. You can change the value from Compute to Suppress by typing **compute** or **suppress** into the feature cell for that row, by typing **C** or **S** into the cell, or by entering a **1** or **0** for compute or suppress, respectively.

FIGURE 7.3
Computing or suppressing a feature

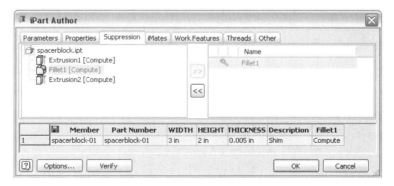

You can use the iMates, Work Features, Threads, and Other tabs (Other includes manually typed information) to add these items to the iPart in the form of columns.

Authoring Options

The Options button located in the lower-left corner of the authoring dialog box allows you to create and edit part numbers and member names for iParts. You will typically want to set these naming options before you begin adding rows to the iPart table so that as rows are added, they are automatically named according to these options. Set the Options dialog box in your part to match Figure 7.4. Click OK to set the changes to the table, and click Yes when prompted to apply these changes to all the members in the table.

FIGURE 7.4
Options dialog box

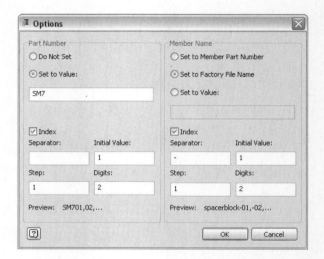

Once the first row in the table has been created, you can create additional rows within the part by right-clicking the row header and selecting Insert Row. Rows represent your iPart members in your table. Continue creating as many rows as needed for your iPart by completing the Description column and altering other values as needed. Figure 7.5 shows the completed table for this example.

FIGURE 7.5
iPart table with added rows

	Member	Part Number	WIDTH	HEIGHT	THICKNESS	Description	Fillet1
1	spacerblock-01	SM701	3 in	2 in	0.005 in	Shim	Suppress
2	spacerblock-02	SM702	3 in	2 in	0.005 in	Shim	Compute
3	spacerblock-03	SM703	3 in	2.25 in	0.020 in	Shim	Suppress
4	spacerblock-04	SM704	3 in	2.25 in	0.020 in	Shim	Compute
5	spacerblock-05	SM705	3 in	2.5 in	0.040 in	Shim	Suppress
6	spacerblock-06	SM706	3 in	2.5 in	0.040 in	Shim	Compute

Notice the disk symbol located in the Member column header in Figure 7.5. This indicates that the member column will be used as the filename for each of your iPart members. If you prefer to have the Part Number column used for the filenames, you can right-click that column header and select File Name Column.

Establishing a Key Column

To be able to specify which member of your iPart factory you want to use in an assembly, you must set up a key column. An iPart should generally have at least one primary key and can have up to eight secondary keys. In this example, set the Thickness column as the primary key and the Fillet1 column as a secondary key.

In the iPart Author dialog box, flip to the Parameters tab and locate Thickness in the right pane of the dialog box. Notice there is a gray key next to each parameter listed in the right pane. Click the key next to Thickness to set it as the primary key. You will see the key turn blue and a 1 appear to inform you that this is the first key. You will see the small blue key symbol added to the column header for Thickness, also as shown in Figure 7.6. Repeat this process to set Fillet1, found on the Suppression tab, to be key 2. You can change the order of the keys by clicking the key number and selecting from the list.

FIGURE 7.6
Creating a key

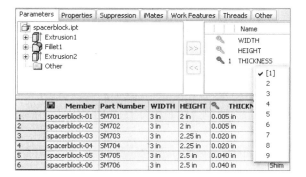

Figure 7.7 shows the completed iPart, with a primary key column of Thickness and a secondary key of Fillet1. When this iPart is inserted into an assembly, a dialog box will appear allowing the thickness value to be selected from the available thicknesses as defined in the rows of the iPart. Then you can choose between parts that have the same thickness values by selecting whether Fillet1 will be suppressed or computed.

FIGURE 7.7
Completed iPart dialog box

	Member	Part Number	WIDTH	HEIGHT	THICKNESS	Description	Fillet1
1	spacerblock-01	SM701	3 in	2 in	0.005 in	Shim	Suppress
2	spacerblock-02	SM702	3 in	2 in	0.005 in	Shim	Compute
3	spacerblock-03	SM703	3 in	2.25 in	0.020 in	Shim	Suppress
4	spacerblock-04	SM704	3 in	2.25 in	0.020 in	Shim	Compute
5	spacerblock-05	SM705	3 in	2.5 in	0.040 in	Shim	Suppress
6	spacerblock-06	SM706	3 in	2.5 in	0.040 in	Shim	Compute

SEAN SAYS: KEY SELECTION IS IMPORTANT WHEN CREATING IPARTS

You should take time to consider how your users will utilize the parts. For example, consider a socket head cap screw iPart. In the iPart, you might have diameter (1/4", 5/16", 3/8"), pitch (UNC or UNF), length (2", 3", 4", 5"), and material (stainless steel, alloy steel). Each of these columns could be key 1, but you should consider what makes it easiest to navigate to the correct part. In many cases, you might want to make the material the primary key with the diameter, pitch, and length as the second, third, and fourth keys. This means that the user will first select the material and only then be presented with the remaining diameters, pitches, and lengths for that given material. It would be a poor choice (in most cases) to have the pitch as the primary key because this is usually not the first descriptive factor when choosing a fastener.

Custom iParts

A custom iPart is an iPart factory that has one or more columns designated as a custom parameter column. A custom parameter column allows input of any value and, in turn, generates a custom iPart with infinite variations. Custom iParts are valuable for creating tube and pipe lengths, structural steel members, and other parts that require unique size input at the time of insertion.

To designate a column as a custom parameter column, simply right-click the column and select Custom Parameter Column. Columns that are set as keys are not permitted to be custom columns. Rather than setting an entire column to be custom, you may want to set just the column entry for a single member to be custom. To do this, you can right-click any cell in a nonkey column and choose Custom Parameter Cell. Once set to custom, columns and cells can be set both to restrict input to a specified range and to increment by right-clicking once again. An example of setting a range might be the spacer block width. You set the width column to be custom and then set the range so that it can be placed only in widths from 1 inch to 6 inches, as shown in Figure 7.8. You might then set the increment to be 0.25 so that the widths are set only to 8-inch increments. Key columns can also be set to have an increment.

FIGURE 7.8
Custom column settings

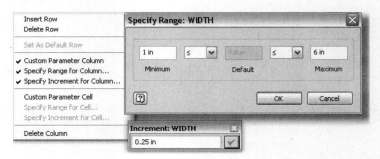

Testing the iPart

Before placing a completed iPart into production by storing it in a project library or converting it to a Content Center part, test the accuracy and interface of your part by inserting the iPart using Place Component within a blank assembly file. Using place component, insert every member in the table, and inspect and/or measure the placed component.

Moving the test forward, create an IDW file with a base view of your assembly. Generate a parts list with the desired columns, and verify the accuracy of each cell.

Do not attempt to create a zero-value dimension as a method of suppressing certain features. Zero-value dimensions will cause errors within iPart generation. It is better to create a column to suppress individual features, rather than attempt to do so through dimensions.

Once you are assured of having accurate member components, you can then place this iPart into a project library folder. If you will be using this iPart in conjunction with the functional design features of Inventor, you will need to publish the factory iPart to a custom Content Center library.

File Management and iParts

When used in an assembly, regular iPart factories generate part files that have fixed values. Because these parts are often used over and over in many assemblies, it is recommended that they be stored in a library folder. Recall that folders that are designated as libraries in your project file are handled as read-only by Inventor.

The library directory where you want to save the iPart members is set up by you, and it is required to have the same name as the factory library but preceded with an underscore. As an example, if you store the iPart factories in a library named Fasteners, Inventor will automatically place all iPart members generated from that library in a second library named _Fasteners, provided you've created one.

However, you are not required to store iParts in libraries. If you do not use libraries and you place an iPart member into an assembly, Inventor will create a folder of the same name, at the same level as the iPart factory, and store the iPart members there. For example, if you have your spacerblock iPart stored in a file at `C:\Mastering Inventor\`, then when you place an iPart member in the assembly, a subdirectory called spacerblock is created (`C:\Mastering Inventor spacerblock`), and the iPart member file is created there. Custom iPart members are always stored in a location specified by the user.

EDITING THE IPART FACTORY

Editing an original iPart factory follows the same workflow as creating an iPart. If you've placed the original iPart factory into a project library folder, then within that same project, it will not be able to be edited. Instead, create a new project file for the purpose of editing library parts. When creating a new project file, define the workspace for the project file by locating the project file in the main Libraries subfolder. Any subfolder within the library path will now be editable with this specific project file.

With the new Library Edit project file active, open the iPart you want to edit. Locate the table in the Model browser, and either double-click or right-click to activate the iPart Author dialog box. At this point, you can edit any part of the table. When you have completed your editing, you can save the part to its original location.

You can convert an iPart factory component into a standard parametric part by deleting the table attached to the iPart. Simply right-click the table from within the Model browser and select Delete. The part will revert to a parametric part with no history of the iPart functionality in the part.

Using iParts in Designs

Using an iPart in an assembly design is a little bit different from creating parts within an assembly. With standard parts, you can edit any feature by activating the part. An iPart member or child cannot be edited since it is a derived component created by the factory or parent part.

To change between iPart members, locate and expand the iPart in the assembly browser tree, right-click the table, and choose Change Component. This opens the iPart placement dialog box, which allows you to specify a new member to be used in place of the existing one. Figure 7.9 shows the specific selection path for changing the component. This replacement procedure will replace only the selected component instance.

FIGURE 7.9
Changing the component

If you want to replace all exact duplicate members of the iPart within this assembly, right-click the part within the graphics window or the Model browser, select Component, and then choose Replace All. A dialog box will appear allowing you to select the same iPart factory. Once the original iPart factory is selected, you will be prompted with the iPart placement dialog box to allow you to select the specific member to be used as the replacement.

When a component is replaced with a different member of the same family, as with iParts, normally all assembly constraints will be retained. If the replaced component is of a different family, then the assembly constraints might be broken. The same is true of parts in the same family if the original part used a certain feature to constrain to and the replacement part has that feature suppressed.

Working with iFeatures

iFeatures are features that have been extracted from an existing part file and configured for reuse in other parts. If you are familiar with AutoCAD, you might relate iFeatures to blocks, in that you can write out blocks for reuse in other drawings. Any feature based upon a sketch can be used as an iFeature. Once extracted, the iFeature is stored in a catalog and can be placed into any other part file. Inventor is supplied with a number of standard iFeature parts. iFeatures cannot currently be published to Content Center.

Using iFeatures in your designs can greatly simplify your workflow and accelerate productivity, especially if your designs contain repetitive features. Figure 7.10 shows an example of a sheet-metal part that could be created in less than 10 minutes using iFeatures.

FIGURE 7.10
Sheet metal part with
iFeatures

iFeatures support sheet-metal features as well as normal part features. iFeatures are stored in the Catalog subfolder of the Inventor program in four subfolders. You can create additional subfolders as required. iFeatures are also available online from such locations as http://cbliss.com, www.sdotson.com, and others.

Creating iFeatures

Once you have a part that consists of a feature or features that you want to reuse during the design of other parts, you can easily extract those features and place them into the catalog. The chief advantage of using iFeatures is that the original part does not need to be open in order to copy the feature. In addition, you can alter any of the parameters at will when inserting the feature into a new part.

To reuse a part feature, select the Extract iFeature option on the Tools pulldown menu. Select the feature to be reused from the Model browser or the graphics window. If additional features exist that are dependent upon the selected feature, they will be added to the iFeature as well but can be deleted during iFeature creation if not needed. Figure 7.11 illustrates how to remove a dependent feature while creating an iFeature.

FIGURE 7.11
Removing a dependent
feature

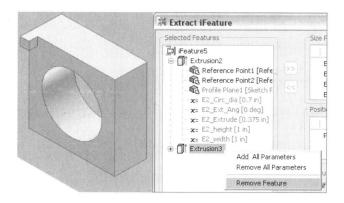

A standard iFeature similar to this will require a profile plane only in order to position the geometry onto a new part. In this example, you will notice that the named parameters and values are transferred from the existing part into the new iFeature. In Figure 7.12, you will notice that prompts will be added for each of the named parameters. When inserting this iFeature into a different part, you will be prompted to enter new values for these parameters if desired.

FIGURE 7.12
Parameters and prompts

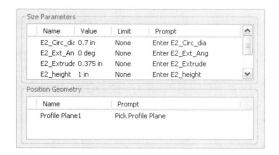

PLACING A STANDARD PART IFEATURE

To see iFeatures in action, open FeatureReuse1.ipt in the Mastering Inventor folder. Go to the Tools menu and choose Extract iFeature. You will be presented with the Extract iFeature dialog box. From the Model browser, click Extrusion2, and the dialog box will be populated with the parameter information found in that feature. In this case, the parameters have been renamed previously using the Parameters dialog box. However, you can adjust parameter names and the corresponding prompts at this point if needed.

You can also adjust the default values for the parameters without adjusting the current model. You can add lists and ranges to each parameter using the Limits column. You can remove parameters from the list as well. Click the parameter named E2_Ang, and use the << button to remove it from the parameter list.

For this example, accept the default for the rest of the parameters as shown in Figure 7.12, and click Save. Notice that Inventor takes you straight to the Catalog folder. Choose a location under Catalog, or create your own subdirectory and name this iFeature SquareSocket.ide. If warned about saving outside of the project path, choose Yes.

Now, let's place the iFeature back into the model as a test. In the Part Features tool panel, click the Insert iFeature icon. Clicking the Browse button will take you to the Catalog folder automatically. Locate the SquareSocket feature you just created, and click Open.

Select the top face of Extrusion1 to use as the profile plane. Once selected, set the angle to 45 degrees, and click Next. Enter **0.5** for the E2_Circ_Dia parameter and then click the Refresh button to see the diameter of the feature adjust. Once the size parameter has been adjusted, as shown in Figure 7.13, click Next. You will be presented with two options for placing the iFeature: Activate Sketch Edit Immediately and Do Not Activate Sketch Edit. Choose Activate Sketch Edit Immediately, and click Finish.

FIGURE 7.13
Inserting an iFeature

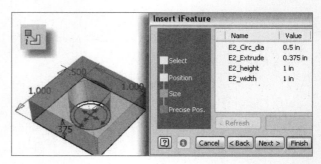

You will see that the iFeature sketch is set ready to be edited. You should also notice that the sketch is currently underconstrained. In particular, it has no dimensions or constraints holding it in position. You can place general dimensions into the sketch to anchor it place.

When you create iFeatures, you often intentionally leave them underconstrained so that the iFeature sketch will not bring along relic geometry from the original part. It is also good practice to create a separate part file from which to generate an iFeature rather than attempting to use a part file designed for production. You can copy the part features from a production part into your iFeature test part using one of the copy or cloning methods discussed in the coming pages.

EDITING IFEATURES

Once iFeature files (.ide) have been extracted and tested, you can open them in Inventor and edit them much like iParts. Locate and click the Catalog icon in the Part Features tool panel. This will take you directly to the Catalog folder in the Inventor program files where all iFeatures are stored. Locate and open the file named SquareSocket.ide. From here, you can use the Edit iFeature icon to refine parameter names, sizes, and instructional prompts for the placement of iFeatures. If the iFeature has dependent features, they can be edited also.

The iFeature Author icon allows a table to be added to the iFeature so that rows and columns can be added to configure the iFeature in the same way that you configured a part file using the iPart Author dialog box. Once you've added the table to the iFeature, you can further edit it by clicking the Edit Using Spread Sheet icon to open the table in Microsoft Excel.

When creating iFeatures, it is usually a good idea to keep the original IPT that you used to create the IDE file. This is often useful if you want to totally redesign the iFeature or make a similar iFeature.

Creating Punch Features

Punch features behave differently than standard iFeatures. Punch features require a single sketch center point during iFeature creation. The sketch center point will be used to locate the punch feature upon insertion. The destination part will require an active sketch containing sketch center points for the location of the punch feature.

The punch feature is differentiated from the standard iFeature because it is intended for use on sheet-metal parts. Sheet-metal parts are often constructed using a punch press that will locate a punch feature by XY coordinate points. Standard iFeatures are anchored differently, usually by dimensions.

When creating a punch feature, consider that in normal use most features extend through the thickness of the sheet metal. Therefore, it is important to use the Thickness parameter when creating the iFeature. Constructed properly, the punch feature will adjust to the thickness of any sheet-metal part where it is applied.

The procedure for creating a punch feature is demonstrated in `PunchFeat1.ipt`. Locate and open this file from the Mastering Inventor Folder. This part is a simple sheet-metal construction with one Cut feature. Figure 7.14 shows the sketch underlying the Cut feature. The sketch was created utilizing a single center point and a circular pattern. There is no need to anchor the sketch.

FIGURE 7.14
Sheet-metal sketch

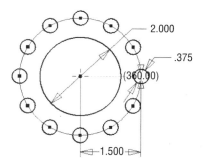

Converting the Cut feature into a punch feature utilizes a similar procedure as a standard iFeature. If you desire text-based parameters as prompts, be sure to name the parameters by going to the Tools menu and choosing Parameters before creating the punch feature. Once that is done, you are ready to create your iFeature.

Access the Extract iFeature dialog box from the Tools menu. Use the radio button at the top of the dialog box to toggle the iFeature type to Sheet Metal Punch Feature. This signals the dialog box to search for an insertion point. If you have created multiple center point locations within your sketch, you will receive an error message when trying to create the punch feature. Recall that you can switch extra center points in your sketch to standard points so that they will not interfere by using the Center Point icon next to the Construction icon. In this example, you have only one center point within the sketch, even though there are other points locating the various circles.

Figure 7.15 shows the end result of creating the punch feature described earlier. Note that there are three items in the Size Parameters list in the dialog box allowing the punch to be adjusted according to these design parameters. Because all named parameters referenced by the sketch come in by default, you might have an extra Thickness parameter listed. Under the manufacturing portion, specify a punch ID that will be used to denote tooling on the shop floor. If included, this punch ID can be retrieved and placed onto the drawing in the form of a punch note or a punch table. Enter **K775** in the Punch ID text box for this example.

You can also select a sketch for a simplified representation prior to placement in a different part so that the flat pattern can be shown in a simple manner for easy interpretation of punch locations. Click the Simplified Representation button, and select Sketch3 from the Model browser.

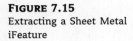

FIGURE 7.15
Extracting a Sheet Metal
iFeature

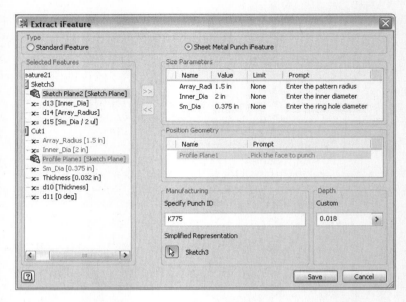

Since this is a sheet-metal part, the depth will be determined by thickness as mentioned earlier. However, you might need to specify alternate punch depths for punches in cases where your intent is to deform the material rather than truly punch it. Again, this value can be extracted later in punch annotations and tables in the drawing environment. Enter **0.018** for the custom depth for this example.

When your dialog box resembles Figure 7.15, click Save, and select the Punches folder in the Catalog directory. Name the punch feature K775.ide. If warned about saving outside the project path, choose Yes.

SEAN SAYS: iFEATURES ARE POWERFUL TOOLS

These tools allow you to quickly create standard features in your models. Examples include o-ring grooves, louvers, bosses, ribs, electrical connector punches, patterns of holes, and an infinite number of other features. Another major advantage of iFeatures is that they enforce standards. Since the iFeature can be designed to allow the user to select predefined sizes only, the possibility of error is greatly reduced. Take a few moments to examine your designs, and you'll likely see many opportunities for iFeatures.

PLACING A SHEET-METAL FEATURE

When working on a sheet-metal part, you can access iFeatures through the PunchTool or the Insert iFeature options in the Sheet Metal Features tool panel. Prior to placing a feature, you must have an unconsumed, visible sketch containing one or more center points from which the punch will position itself. In PunchFeat1.ipt, Sketch4 has been prepared for you so that you can use it to place your new punch. Locate Sketch4, and turn the visibility on via right-click.

Next locate and select the PunchTool from the Sheet Metal Part Features tool panel. Select K775.ide from the Punches folder, and click Open. For ease of use, the PunchTool option takes you directly to the Punches folder and, upon selection of the folder, displays a list of punches. You will notice that every unconsumed center point within the sketch will be populated with the selected punch.

If you want to reserve a sketch center point for some other feature, click the Geometry tab in the PunchTool dialog box, and hold down the Ctrl key while selecting the center point to be removed. If you have more than one visible, unconsumed sketch, the center points will not be automatically selected because you will need to tell Inventor which sketch to use.

Click the Size tab, and set Array_Radius to 1 inch. Click the Refresh button to preview the results. Click the Finish button to complete the punch action. Double-click Flat Pattern in the Model browser to view the flat pattern, and notice the simplified representation of your punches.

Note that when the Insert iFeature option is used within the sheet-metal environment, the same PunchTool will not display the same placement options. Instead, it will behave similar to a standard iFeature, requiring constraining of the placed punch by anchoring it to the base feature.

Reusing Existing Geometry

Geometry reuse is a productive technique in Inventor. You can reuse existing features and sketch geometry to create additional features within the same part or even on other open parts. You don't need to create additional new sketches to utilize this technique. The following sections will cover how to copy sketches and features while developing dependent and independent relationships between the features.

Copying Features

Copying features in Inventor is a relatively simple procedure using the Model browser. In an existing model, simply right-click a feature within the browser and select Copy. Next, select a different face within the model, right-click, and select Paste. Figure 7.16 shows a preview of the placement and the Paste Features dialog box.

FIGURE 7.16
Copied features

There are two questions to consider when copying a feature: what should Inventor do with features that are built based on the feature you are copying, and what should Inventor do with the dimensions for your new feature? We'll explore the features first.

Open the file FeatureReuse2.ipt in the Mastering Inventor folder. Right-click Extrusion2 in the Model browser, and choose Copy. Next, right-click anywhere, and choose Paste. Drag your cursor over any face of the part, and you will see a preview of the copied feature. In the Paste Features dialog box, set the Paste Features pulldown to Dependant, and you will notice that the fillets are now in the preview as well, because they are dependants of Extrusion2.

Click the front face of the part to position the new feature as shown in Figure 7.16. Use the +-shaped arrows to move the feature around the selected face. Use the C-shaped arrow to rotate the new feature, and notice the rotation angle is reflected in the dialog box and can be adjusted there as well.

By default, the dimensions of the new feature will be independent, meaning that because the original feature has a width of 1 inch, the new feature will have the same value, but the two will not be linked. However, if you set the parameter pulldown to Dependant, the dimensions of the new feature will reference the original feature so that if the original width changes from 1 inch to 2 inches, the new feature follows.

Set the parameter pulldown to Dependant, and click Finish. Locate and edit Sketch2 in Extrusion2, and set the diameter dimension to 0.25 inch. Finish the sketch, and notice that the new feature follows the edits of the original.

Once you've copied the feature, you should edit the copied feature sketch to properly anchor the sketch on the destination face. When editing a dependent sketch, notice that the dimensions indicate that they are being driven by a parameter from the original feature. If you change the dimensions from a parameter value to numeric value, you will break the dependency with the original sketch.

Cloning

Cloning is the process of copying feature geometry from one open part to another. The cloning process creates independent features, meaning that the new feature in the new part will have no relationship to the original feature in the original part unless set up manually.

To clone a feature from one part to another, you must first have both parts open in Inventor. From the source part, right-click the feature to be copied in the Model browser, and choose Copy. Next, switch to the destination part, right-click anywhere, and choose Paste. Drag your cursor over the face of the part you want to paste onto, and you will see a preview of the copied feature. Click the face and then click Finish when the part has positioned to your liking.

The primary difference between copying features within the same part and cloning features between two parts is that parameters can only be set to be independent during the cloning process.

It will be necessary to fully constrain and anchor the feature sketch to the new part once the feature has been copied. To accomplish this, simply edit the new feature sketch and project construction geometry from the new part base feature to serve as anchor points.

FIGURE 7.17
Linking parameters

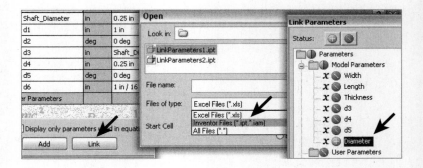

LINKING PARAMETERS

A relationship can be established between two parts, between two assemblies, or between a part and an assembly by linking the files' parameters. This can allow you to place all the design information in one file and link other files to it so that design intent is maintained.

Open the file called LinkParameters2.ipt in the Mastering Inventor folder. This is a simple pin, the shaft diameter of which you require to be linked to a hole diameter in another part. To do this, locate and click the Parameters icon in the Part Features tool panel. In the bottom of the parameters dialog box, click the Link button as shown on the left of Figure 7.17.

Adjust the Files of Type pulldown to show Inventor files and then select the file called LinkParameters1.ipt from the Mastering Inventor folder. This opens the Link Parameter dialog box, allowing you to choose which parameters to link to this part. Click the button next to the parameter named Diameter and then click OK.

This will add the selected parameter to the user parameters in your current part. Locate Shaft_ Diameter in the list, activate the cell in the Equation column, and clear the existing value. Click the arrow as shown in Figure 7.18, and choose List Parameters from the flyout. Select Diameter from the Parameters lists, and choose Done at the bottom of the dialog box. Lastly, click the Update button at the top of the graphics area to see the model update.

FIGURE 7.18
Setting a parameter to reference a linked parameter

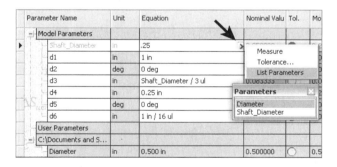

Now the shaft diameter is linked to the hole diameter in the part called LinkParameters1.ipt. You can open this part and change the diameter value to see the change carry through to the shaft of the pin. Linking parameters in this way allows you to place design information in one location and pull it into many other parts for automatic updates.

You can see this concept carried through to the assembly level by opening the file called LinkParameters3.iam, where all the parts in this simple box employ linked parameters from the base part for determining their own lengths. Edit the base part, and the sides will follow.

Copying Sketches

Quite often it is desirable to copy existing part sketches to another location within the same part or a different part. A good example of this would be creating a loft feature where each profile sketch may simply change size.

In the example shown in Figure 7.19, the part contains one unconsumed sketch and multiple work planes parallel to the XY origin plane. To copy an existing sketch, simply right-click the target sketch and select Copy. Then, select the destination work plane, right-click, and select Paste. Pasted sketches are always independent of the original sketch and will create additional parameters for each copy.

FIGURE 7.19
Copying Sketch1

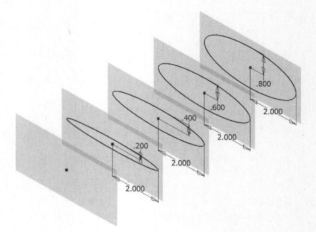

In the example file called `copysketch1.ipt` found in the Mastering Inventor folder, copy the original Sketch1 to each of four user work planes spaced 2 inches apart in the positive Z direction. Create a fifth user work plane spaced 2 inches from the last work plane. On this work plane, create a new sketch, projecting the origin point to the sketch.

Edit each sketch and adjust the minor axis on each of the sketches, decreasing the dimension value by 0.2 inches on each succeeding sketch. Create a loft utilizing all the sketches including the projected origin point. Apply a tangent condition to the projected point to achieve the result, as shown in Figure 7.20.

FIGURE 7.20
Finished loft

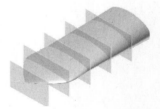

In the previous example, you copied a sketch within the same part. The procedure to copy an existing sketch to another part requires that both parts be open at the same time. Select the Arrange All option from the Window pulldown at the top of the screen to view both files at the same time. Activate the original part by selecting the top window bar. Right-click the original sketch, and select Copy. Then, after selecting the destination part work plane, right-click and select Paste.

You may also employ the standard Ctrl+Tab method of switching between open Inventor files when copying between files. No matter the method of getting from one file to the next, once the sketches are pasted, they can be edited at any time by adding additional geometry, changing dimensions, or simply using the pasted geometry for reference.

At times you may find that your sketch "flips" when pasting it onto a work plane. In many cases, you can easily fix this by right-clicking the work plane and selecting Flip Normal. This flips the positive axis of the work plane. Now, when you paste the sketch onto the work plane, it should no longer be flipped.

Introducing Content Center

The Inventor Content Center is set of database libraries based in Microsoft SQL. These libraries provide standard content in several common international standards, such as ANSI, ISO, and DIN just to name a few. Figure 7.21 shows the complete list. Once properly configured and populated, the Content Center provides an organized method for part and feature reuse.

FIGURE 7.21
Content Center libraries

You can think of these libraries simply as recipes for creating parts, because no actual parts exist in the Content Center libraries. Once these library databases are installed, you can access them from Inventor and place common parts into your designs.

Understand that it is at this point that the Content Center part file is created. Up until this point the part existed only as a definition in the database table. Content Center part files are typically stored on a network server so that as users collaborate on designs, they have access to the same part files used within the assemblies. Because the Content Center library database files are just definitions of the files, they can be installed on the user's local machines or on a network server, or both.

Content Center provides support for functional design using the Design Accelerator, Frame Generator, and other features within Inventor. When using these tools, the parts generated are pulled from the Content Center libraries. You can use Content Center in conjunction with standard iParts and iFeatures organized within libraries in the project.

Configuring Content Center

Inventor's Content Center loaded with all the standard libraries provides in excess of 800,000 variations in parts. To optimize loading, you will want to configure only the appropriate standards for your use. Installing all libraries will cause Inventor to take more time to search and index the data.

The content libraries are installed in the Autodesk Data Management Server (ADMS). The ADMS is essentially just the interface with which you interact with the SQL database program. Once the ADMS is installed and the required Content Center libraries are loaded, users log into ADMS through Inventor.

INSTALLING ADMS SERVER AND LIBRARIES

To use the Inventor Content Center application, you will need to first install the ADMS as well as the collection of Content Center databases. Be sure to plan your installation to suit your network environment.

You have the option of installing and managing the Content Center libraries on a network server or installing them locally. Unless you plan to create and use a custom library, there may not be much difference to you. Because standard Content Center libraries are all read-only databases, they cannot become out of sync; therefore, two users can access two different instances of the standard libraries and work without issue. If you plan to create custom Content Center libraries, however, it is recommended that you install on a network server so that as the library is updated over time, all users are pulling from the same source.

If required, you might install the ADMS on a network server and on the local machine and have the Content Center libraries loaded in both installs of ADMS. The user simply logs in and out of the two instances of ADMS as his location requires. This enables users to work remotely where no network connection is available.

MANAGING YOUR MEMORY FOOTPRINT

Installing all libraries into ADMS will increase your overall memory usage substantially. As mentioned earlier, installing only the libraries you use will keep the Content Center efficient. As we will discuss in the coming pages, you can create a custom Content Center library based on the standard libraries and include only what you require. Once the custom library is created, standard libraries can be removed from ADMS. You can add this at any time by reinstalling them from the Inventor installation disks.

CONFIGURING CONTENT CENTER LIBRARIES IN THE PROJECT FILES

Once ADMS and the required libraries have been installed, you will need to configure the project file to ensure that all required libraries are included in the project. To do this, you will want to close all files so that the project file can be edited.

From Inventor, go to the File menu and choose Projects. Click the Configure Content Center Libraries button at the lower right of the Projects dialog box to open the Configure Libraries dialog box, as shown in Figure 7.22. Use the buttons at the bottom of the dialog box to update, import, add, or remove libraries for the project. Removing libraries from a project will speed up the interaction between Inventor and Content Center when placing a part because fewer library tables are required to be read, searched, and indexed. Once a library is removed, you can add it to the project again at any time.

If you only occasionally access a certain library because you typically do not work with that standard, you might install it into ADMS but remove it from your Inventor project. When you do need to access this library, simply use the Configure Libraries dialog box to load it for use and then unload it once you are finished. Although the suggestion to add and remove libraries may seem like a hassle, it will pay off in time savings because you will not find yourself waiting for the libraries to index every time you access Content Center.

Using Content Center

Content Center is used in many areas of Autodesk Inventor 2009. Content Center components are used in functional design tools, such as the Shaft Generator, as well as in the use of individual, reusable components in general assembly design. Content Center is also available for use within the part environment using the Place Feature command.

FIGURE 7.22
Configuring Content
Center libraries

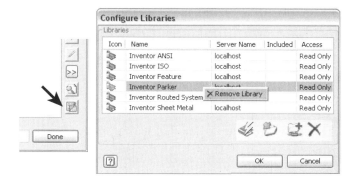

New to Inventor 2009 is the use of Content Center in Frame Generator environments. Content Center replaces the Access database environment that was used in previous versions. You can customize Frame Generator components by creating new Content Center components.

Let's take a closer look at placing components into an assembly from Content Center. You must have ADMS installed and the ANSI Content Library loaded to continue with this example. Ensure that you are logged in to ADMS by going to the File menu and selecting Autodesk Data Management Server ➢ Log In. If you are already logged in, Log In will be grayed out and will not be an option in your menu.

Enter your login information, if known. By default ADMS installs with a user account called Administrator with no password set. You can also check the Content Center library Read-Only check box to access content without logging in. Specify the name of the server on which you installed ADMS. If you have installed in on your local machine, enter **localhost**, as shown in Figure 7.23. In the Database text box, enter the name of the ADMS database; the default is Vault.

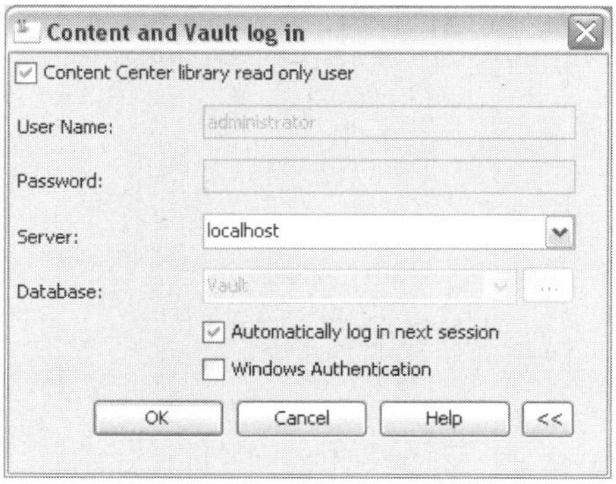

FIGURE 7.23
Logging in to ADMS

Once logged in to the ADMS, you are ready to place parts from the Content Center. In Inventor, open the file called ContentCenter1.iam in the Mastering Inventor folder. Zoom in to one of the castor wheel assemblies, and take note of the empty holes.

From the Assembly panel tools, click the Place From Content Center icon. Check to see that the three buttons as indicated in Figure 7.24 are selected. From left to right these buttons are Filters, AutoDrop, and Tree View. For the Filters button, select the ANSI to filter out all other standards. Note to turn the filter off after this exercise, simply click the Filters button again and uncheck ANSI. The AutoDrop button turns on the ability to automatically size components based on geometry in the model. The Tree View button simply splits the screen so that the Category View pane is accessible on the left of the dialog box.

FIGURE 7.24
Content Center Settings

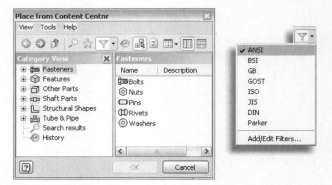

Next, select the Fasteners category, browse to Bolts and then Round Head, select Cross Recessed Binding Head Machine Screw – Type I, and click OK.

In the model, pause your cursor over one of the holes on the castor plate. You will see the AutoDrop icon activate and flicker as Inventor indexes the database for an appropriate size. If no matching size can be found in the database a cursor note will appears saying so. If an appropriate size is found, a cursor note will display it and a preview of the part will be shown. Once the size appears click the edge of the hole to set the screw in place. The AutoDrop toolbar will appear along with the red grip arrow.

Drag the grip arrow up or down to specify the length of the screw. Note that only lengths found in the database are available. In Figure 7.25 there are four icons on the AutoDrop toolbar. The first, called Insert Multiple, is available when Inventor identifies multiple targets that are like the selected target. In this case, the other hole in the plate is picked up previewed. If you apply the screw now, four screws will be placed at once. If you do not want for the multiples to be placed, you can click the Multiple Insert icon to turn it off.

FIGURE 7.25
Placing a screw with
AutoDrop

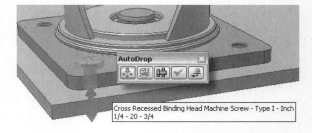

The second icon, called Change Size, is grayed out while Multiple Insert is on. It inserts the part and opens the Part Family dialog box, which allows you to edit the component. The next icon is the Bolted Connection icon, which opens the Bolted Connection Component Generator and allows you to place bolts, nuts, and washers sets as a group.

The last two icons are Apply and Done, respectively. Apply sets the previewed component(s) and allows you to continue placing more components of the same family. Done sets the component(s) and exits the AutoDrop mode. The AutoDrop toolbar is context sensitive, meaning that the icons may vary depending upon the component to be placed and the geometry it is being placed on. If you press F1 on the keyboard while the AutoDrop toolbar is displayed, Inventor will open the help file and list all the icons and their descriptions.

Click the Apply button, and continue placing screws as you see fit. Experiment with placing the cursor over one of the large diameters in the castor assembly to watch AutoDrop attempt to find an appropriate size.

When finished, let's examine where Inventor is filing the newly generated Content Center files. Go to the Tools menu and choose Application Options; then click the File tab. Look for the file path indicating the Default Content Center files, as shown at the top of Figure 7.26. This is where Inventor will place all standard parts placed from Content Center by default. You should change this path to a path that is on the network server, particularly if you're working in a multiuser environment.

FIGURE 7.26
Content Center files storage path

If this path is left to the default, Content Center part files will be saved on your local machine. This causes a problem when a co-worker opens an assembly you created, because the Content Center part files reside on your machine. There is one more place that this path may be set, and that is in the project file under Folder Options, as shown at the bottom of Figure 7.26. It is important to note that a path set in the project file takes precedence over a path set in Application Options. If the project file is set as Content Center Files = Default, then the files are stored at the Application Options path.

Only standard Content Center files are stored at this location. Custom-sized Content Center part files, such as standard steel shapes, pipes, and so on, are stored at a path chosen by you at the time of their creation.

Customizing Content Center

Standard Content Center libraries supplied with Inventor are designated read-only and cannot be modified. If you have a need to create custom part libraries or modify standard content such as adding part numbers or material types, you can do this by creating a custom Content Center library.

CREATING CUSTOM LIBRARIES

Custom libraries are initially set as read-write libraries so that you can add and modify content. Figure 7.27 shows how to create a custom library. Libraries must be added from the Autodesk Data Management Server Console. Access the ADMS by going to Start ➤ All Programs ➤ Autodesk ➤ Autodesk Data Management ➤ Autodesk Data Management Server Console.

Once logged into the ADMS Console, expand the folder in the top of the left pane, right-click the libraries subfolder, and select Create Library. Create a new library called Mastering Inventor 2009. This read-write library will be used to customize your Content Center.

After the final configuration of custom libraries, you can protect them from modification by right-clicking the selected library and clicking the read-only toggle.

FIGURE 7.27
Creating a custom library

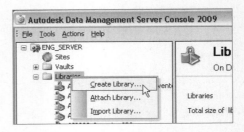

COPYING EXISTING LIBRARIES INTO CUSTOM LIBRARIES

After creating a custom library, you can copy entire or partial contents of existing standard libraries into your custom library. You might use this process when you want to simplify one of the standard libraries, remove portions of the library that are not needed in your work environment, or edit component properties such as part numbers.

To copy part families or libraries into your custom library, access the Content Center Editor from within Inventor by going to the Tools menu and choosing Content Center Editor. This editor looks similar to the Content Center dialog box. Extensive help accessed from this dialog box will further assist you in procedural details for creating custom libraries.

Locate the library or the part family within a library that you want to copy. The library must be included in the project file configuration list in order to be visible within the editor.

If you copy an entire library to your custom library, then the entire folder structure and contents will be replicated in your custom library. If you copy an individual part to your custom library, then only the affected category structure will be replicated in the custom library along with the copied part.

To copy only a portion of the category structure, browse to the last hierarchical portion of the structure that you want to replicate. Otherwise, starting from the top to copy the structure will replicate the entire structure.

CATEGORY PROPERTIES

Each category within Content Center contains category properties. Within the category properties are general information regarding the category itself. The General information tab contains the category name, category image, and source library.

The Parameters tab contains parameters used within the category to assist in the description of parts located within that category. Figure 7.28 illustrates the parameter list in the ANSI Socket Head category.

You will notice that within the parameters shown earlier some are optional and some are required. If you are placing a part within this category, you must map your part properties to all required fields for proper operation. Optional fields do not require mapping.

What this means is if you are planning on publishing a large number of your own parts to Content Center, then your part parameters must match the category parameters. If you are unable to match the parameters, then consider creating a new category.

Right-clicking an individual Content Center part will allow you to view the family properties and mapping of that part. Compare the category parameters of the part with the parameters of the intended category. Matching the two parameter lists ensures that the part will map easily into that category.

FIGURE 7.28
Socket head parameters

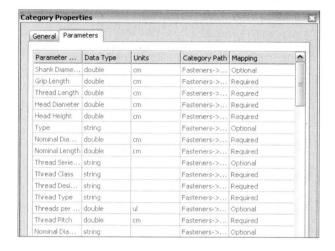

EDITING A CUSTOM CONTENT CENTER FAMILY

A Content Center family is an individual part, similar to an iPart. The part consists of a standard factory part with a family table attached that generates any of the optional table values.

You can edit any individual part by first switching the library view to your custom library designation, as shown in Figure 7.29.

FIGURE 7.29
Editing a Content Center part

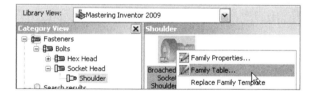

In the previous example, we switched the library view to the Mastering Inventor 2009 custom library. Right-click a part located within the custom library, and select Family Table. This launches a dialog box that allows the user to modify values, copy/paste, add/delete rows, or suppress existing rows within the table. The dialog box also allows the addition, deletion, and modification of columns and properties.

PUBLISHING EXISTING PARTS TO CONTENT CENTER

Developing a process workflow for reusing parts within your company's design environment is essential for standardization and improved productivity. Part of that workflow may include publishing existing Inventor parts that might currently be stored in project libraries. Both normal parts and iParts can be published to a custom Content Center library.

The act of publishing a standard part into the custom library adds a family table to the published part. Exported Part parameters will be converted to table parameters when published to the Custom Content Center. iPart tables are converted to family tables when published.

PREPARING THE PART FOR PUBLISHING

The easiest method to prepare a part for publishing is to convert that part to a table-driven iPart. Once you have a workable iPart that behaves correctly, you can then open the original factory iPart and publish the part. The iPart may be a custom iPart or a fully table-driven factory. iParts containing multiple row definitions in the table will convert to a fully table-driven Content Center part.

PUBLISHING THE PART

Once the iPart factory has been validated, the factory can be published to a custom Content Center library. You must have a custom library with read-write capability created prior to publishing. Your current project file must also be configured to include this custom library. In this example, you have created and configured a read-write library called Mastering Inventor 2009.

Open the file `spacerblockforCC.ipt`, and verify the table accuracy by right-clicking the table within the Model browser and selecting Edit Table. This part is similar to the part created in the iPart section of this chapter. Click OK to exit the iPart editor.

Select Publish Part from the Tools menu, and you will be presented with a Publish Guide dialog box, which will allow you to select the read-write library for publishing and the language to be used within the family. Clicking Next will allow you to select the category for publishing.

The selection of category is important because it will not only determine where the family table will be placed, but it will also determine the parameter properties that will be utilized in the creation of the Content Center family table for this part. For this example, we have selected the Spacers category that we created in the Other Parts subfolder using the Content Center Editor.

After the Spacers category is selected, define the family key columns that you will be using within the Content Center component. Figure 7.30 shows the selected key columns.

FIGURE 7.30
Defining family key columns

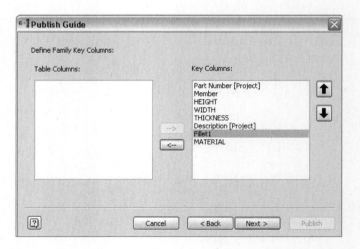

Proceeding through the Publish Guide Wizard, another screen appears, permitting the input of a description for this family table, as shown in Figure 7.31.

On the final page of the Publish Guide Wizard, you will get a preview of the component thumbnail image and the opportunity to load an alternate image for this component. Clicking Publish will publish this new family table into your custom library.

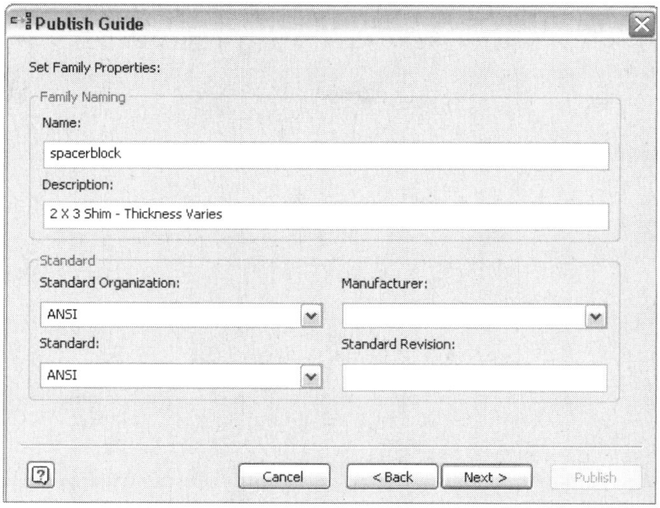

FIGURE 7.31
Setting family properties

Publish Guide

Set Family Properties:

Family Naming

Name:

spacerblock

Description:

2 X 3 Shim - Thickness Varies

Standard

Standard Organization: Manufacturer:

ANSI

Standard: Standard Revision:

ANSI

Cancel   < Back   Next >   Publish

TESTING THE NEW COMPONENT

Before using this newly published Content Center component in production, test the part in a blank assembly for proper function. Using this example, you should get an Insert Spacerblock dialog box similar to Figure 7.32.

FIGURE 7.32
Insert Spacerblock dialog
box

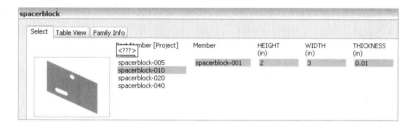

Extensive help files are located in Inventor 2009 for assisting you in publishing, editing, and using Content Center components. To locate the entire list, select Content Center in the Index tab, and browse to the specific help that you need.

The Bottom Line

Create iParts from existing designs   iParts are the solution to creating parts that allow for an infinite number of variations without affecting other members of the same part family already used within your designs.

Master It   You use a purchased specialty part in your designs and would like to create the many size configurations that this part comes in ahead of time for use within assembly design.

Create and use iFeatures   Creating a library of often used features is essential to standardization and improved productivity within your design workflow.

Master It   You want to be able to place common punches, slots and milled features quickly, rather than having to generate the feature sketch every time.

Copy sketches and part features to create additional features and designs   You do not have to create iFeatures in order to reuse various part features in your designs. If a part feature will have limited use in other designs, it is often better to simply copy it from part to part or from face to face on the same part.

Master It   You have the need to reuse features within a part or among parts. You consider iFeatures, but realize that reuse is often specialized and doesn't lend itself to setting up an iFeature.

Configure, create, and access Content Center parts   Content Center provides a great opportunity to reuse database-created geometry within assemblies and within functional design modules. The Content Center Editor provides the means to add custom content into Content Center. Custom libraries can be created within the Autodesk Data Management Server Console and added to your current project file. Content Center performance can be improved by creating selective project files that load only certain Content Center libraries.

Master It   You would like to change the part numbers in some Content Center components to match the part numbers your company uses. You would also like to add proprietary components to the Content Center, so that the design team can access them from the same place.

Chapter 8

Assembly Design Workflows

Developing a good assembly design workflow is paramount to achieving performance, flexibility, and stability in your designs. In this chapter, you will be exploring several types of workflows to achieve that goal.

Included in this chapter is a discussion on how to use subassemblies to enhance performance. Using subassemblies within your design can substantially improve performance and ease of constraining.

Large assembly design is an achievable goal with Inventor 2009. Inventor 2009 removes the limitations of memory with a true 64-bit version. Running the 64-bit version on Windows XP 64 or Windows Vista allows almost unlimited amounts of RAM to be utilized on your design. Component count can now be in the hundreds of thousands of parts, as long as you have sufficient memory on your system.

Performance in large assembly design assumes that you understand the principles and proper use of subassemblies and the role that adaptivity plays in performance. Armed with that understanding, you can configure your system for performance and develop a good workflow that allows you to design large assemblies without suffering slow system performance.

In this chapter, you will learn how to:

◆ Organize designs using structured subassemblies

◆ Use positional reps and flexible assemblies together

◆ Copy designs

◆ Substitute a single part for entire subassemblies

Understanding Subassemblies

As you will see in this chapter, you create assemblies by placing 3D constraints between parts in order to position and hold those parts together. When working with small assemblies, you can often assemble all the parts together at one level. Working with larger assemblies, however, often requires the use of multiple levels of assemblies for the sake of organization and performance. Lower-level assemblies are referred to as *subassemblies*.

The Power of Subassemblies

Imagine a common caster wheel assembly. Although it may seem like a simple component, it is of course made up of many small parts. If you had the need to use this caster in an assembly multiple times, you wouldn't place all the small parts into an assembly individually over and over. Instead, you would package them as a subassembly and place multiple instances of the subassembly throughout the top-level assembly. Figure 8.1 shows a caster wheel assembly ready to be placed as a subassembly.

FIGURE 8.1
Caster wheel assembly

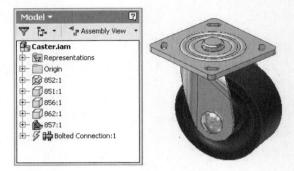

Most things that you design and build are typically made from subassemblies of some sort. In manufacturing it makes sense to create subassemblies of common parts to make the assembly process easier. It makes sense to design in exactly the same fashion. In the caster example, it saves you from having to duplicate the work of assembling the caster parts repeatedly for each instance of the caster that exists in the top-level assembly.

A second benefit to using subassemblies is the flexibility that they add to the bill of materials. Using the caster as a subassembly rather than as loose parts provides the ability to count the caster as a single item, to count the total of all the caster parts, or to do both.

SEAN SAYS: KNOW WHEN TO USE ASSEMBLIES

Although it is often necessary to create parts as assemblies (to have a correct bill of materials or to provide the correct motion), it is not always the best choice. For example, in the caster example, unless you need the casters to swivel in your assembly, consider modeling the caster as a single part or deriving the assembly into a single part. This will lower the overhead of your models as well as reduce the number of parts to track throughout your design.

There is a third and very important concept to consider when working with subassemblies. This is model performance. Imagine that you decided to place four instances of the caster into an assembly as loose parts rather than as a subassembly. For the sake of simplicity, say it takes 28 constraints among the caster parts and 2 constraints between the caster and the top-level assembly, for a total of 30 constraints. You do this for all 4 casters for a total of 120 constraints in the top-level assembly. Had you assembled the caster as a subassembly and then placed that subassembly into the top-level assembly, you would have used just 28 in the caster subassembly and 2 per caster for a total of only 36 constraints, as shown in Figure 8.2.

If you consider assembly constraints to be nothing more than calculations that Inventor must make to hold the assemblies together, then by using subassemblies you have required Inventor to create and maintain 86 fewer calculations overall. This reduction in constraints can have a significant impact on the assembly's performance and make the task of editing the assembly much easier.

FIGURE 8.2
Reduced assembly
constraints

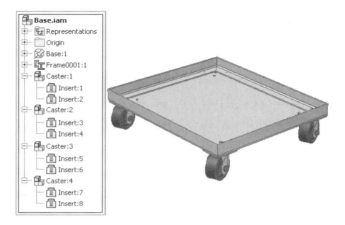

Flexibility

When multiple instances of the same subassembly are used within a design, each instance can be made flexible, relaxing constraints within the assembly to allow for changes in position within the top-level assembly. The caster assemblies in Figure 8.3 have been made flexible so that they can be swiveled and positioned independently as they would in the real world. Compare the caster positions in Figures 8.2 and 8.3, and you will notice that in Figure 8.2 all instances of the caster were required to maintain the same position because they had not yet been made flexible.

FIGURE 8.3
Flexible subassemblies

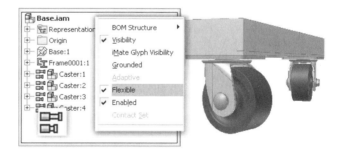

A subassembly instance is made flexible by right-clicking the instance within the browser and checking Flexible. Flexible subassemblies are displayed with an icon next to the instance name in the browser so that you can easily determine which instances are flexible.

Flexible assemblies can be nested into other subassemblies and will still update whenever the original assembly is changed. Common usages of flexible assemblies are hydraulic cylinders requiring different length extensions when used in multiple locations within a top-level assembly. When each instance of the assembly is made flexible, then each cylinder can move accordingly within the top-level assembly.

If a subassembly with nested flexible subassemblies is to be placed into a top-level assembly, then you simply right-click that subassembly to bring forward the flexibility of the nested flexible assemblies. Consider the example of the hydraulic cylinder. Multiple instances of the cylinder might be placed into an extension arm assembly and each instance made flexible so that they can be allowed to adjust as they are constrained to the extension arm parts.

If two instances of the extension arm are then placed into a top-level assembly, those instances of the extension arm need to be made flexible as well in order to allow the cylinders to demonstrate flexibility.

Top-Down Design

Inventor allows you to approach the creation of parts and assemblies in three basic ways. Figure 8.4 shows these three distinctive workflows for assembly design.

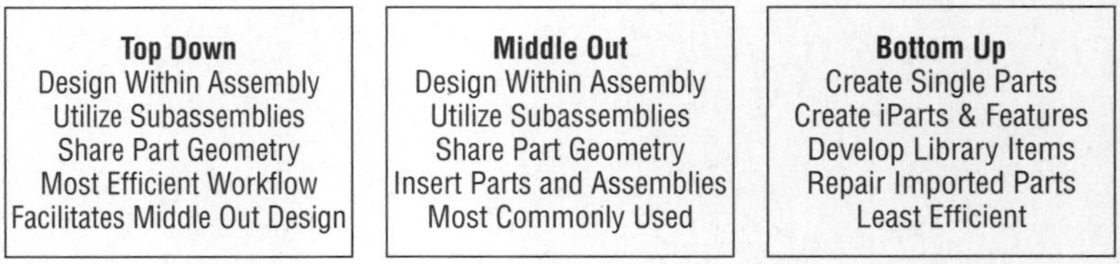

FIGURE 8.4
Design workflows

Top Down	Middle Out	Bottom Up
Design Within Assembly	Design Within Assembly	Create Single Parts
Utilize Subassemblies	Utilize Subassemblies	Create iParts & Features
Share Part Geometry	Share Part Geometry	Develop Library Items
Most Efficient Workflow	Insert Parts and Assemblies	Repair Imported Parts
Facilitates Middle Out Design	Most Commonly Used	Least Efficient

The first of these methods is called *top-down* design. In the purest sense, top-down design is performed completely within the top-level assembly of a machine or device. Parts and subassemblies are created from within the uppermost assembly, as opposed to creating components outside the top-level assembly and then placing these components later. Using this approach, you can reference and project geometry from other parts within the assembly into new parts, thereby ensuring the fit of the new parts. Another benefit to top-down design is that the designer can better visualize how each part relates to others within the assembly. When properly utilized, you minimize the number of overall assembly constraints required and allow for a stable design.

The second method works by creating parts independently and then placing and constraining them into the assembly. This method is called *bottom-up* design. Bottom-up design is common when creating parts from existing drawings and new pencil sketches. This workflow environment is ideal for repairing imported geometry, creating standard parts for your library, and converting standard parts into iParts and iFeatures. Working in the single-part environment does not easily allow you to create or reference other parts that will be utilized within your assembly design. As a result, this is probably the least efficient workflow for 3D design but is often the one employed by new users.

The third method is some combination of top-down and bottom-up design and is the most common. This approach might be called *middle-out*. This is top-down design with the ability to add existing subassemblies and parts as needed. Utilizing various functions such as Parts Libraries, Frame Generator, Bolted Connections, and Content Center components within an assembly file is an example of middle-out design.

Developing an Efficient Assembly Workflow

Let's consider an example of a top-down workflow to better understand the benefits and efficiency of this type of design. Within this workflow, you will first create the top-level assembly file. Start a new assembly file using the Standard.iam template from the default tab.

Once your new assembly is open, right-click and select Create Component. The default option in the Create In-Place Component dialog box is to create a new component as a standard single-part file. Instead, click the drop-down arrow in the Template area, and select Standard.iam.

The choices available in the pulldown are the standard templates from the default tab. If you will be selecting an alternate standard, click the Browse Templates button instead. Once you click the Browse Templates button, you will be presented with the Open Template dialog box, which gives you a choice of standards and templates.

Give this new assembly component a name corresponding to the second-level subassembly such as 2nd Level Assembly. The origin planes of the new assembly will be anchored to the selected top-level assembly origin plane upon creation and will be grounded to the top-level origin plane.

If known at the time of creating the subassembly file, determine the bill of materials (BOM) structure for this subassembly. Note that you can change this later as needed. Figure 8.5 illustrates the selection choices for the BOM structure.

FIGURE 8.5
BOM structure options

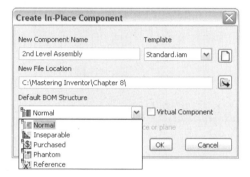

The choices for BOM structure are listed here with a brief description. You'll take a more in-depth look at BOM structure settings later in this chapter:

◆ *Virtual Components*: These components require no geometry, such as paint, grease, and so on.

◆ *Normal*: This is the default structure for all parts that are intended to be fabricated.

◆ *Purchased*: These are parts or assemblies that are not fabricated in-house.

◆ *Inseparable*: Generally, these are assemblies that cannot be disassembled without damage, such as weldments, riveted assemblies, and so on.

◆ *Phantom*: Typically, this is a subassembly created to simplify the design process by reducing assembly constraints and to roll parts up into the next highest assembly level.

◆ *Reference*: This is used for construction geometry or to add detail and references to the top-level assembly.

In this top-down design example, you will be using Normal components. Upon selecting the Normal BOM structure, click OK to exit the dialog box. You will then be prompted to select a sketch plane for the base component of this assembly. In the Model browser, expand the assembly origin folder, and select the XY Plane option. This will place and anchor the new assembly to the top-level assembly origin. This new, second-level assembly will be activated within the Model browser, ready for editing, as shown in Figure 8.6.

With the second-level assembly active, select Create Component once again, and this time use the Standard.ipt template to create a new part. Name this component Rotary Hub, and locate it in a subdirectory called Parts within your workspace, as shown in Figure 8.7. If the subdirectory does not exist, you will be prompted to create it. Use the Normal BOM structure for all parts in this example.

FIGURE 8.6
Second-level assembly active

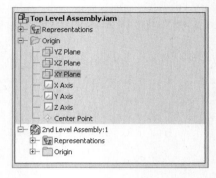

FIGURE 8.7
Creating Rotary Hub.ipt in the Parts subdirectory

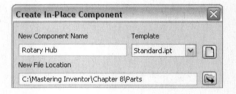

You will then be prompted once again to select a sketch plane for the base feature of this part. Locate the origin folder in 2nd Level Assembly.iam, and click the XZ plane. Because the XZ plane is perpendicular to the screen, you will need to realign the view to the current sketch plane. Click the Look At icon at the top of the screen, and locate Sketch1 in the Model browser; then click the Sketch1 icon. When clicking this icon, you will notice that Sketch1 is active and everything else within your assembly is grayed out. You should now be properly oriented to view Sketch1. Create and dimension the sketch, as shown in Figure 8.8.

FIGURE 8.8
Rotary Hub sketch

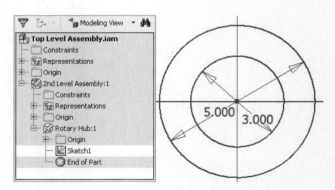

Finish Sketch1, and extrude the outer ring to a length of 1 inch. Next, create a sketch on the top face of the ring with a circle offset 0.5 inch to the inside of the overall diameter. Place a center point on the offset circle and use this to place a sketched-through hole feature with a diameter of 0.375 inch. Create a circular pattern of the hole feature with six instances, as shown in Figure 8.9.

FIGURE 8.9
A circular pattern of the through hole feature

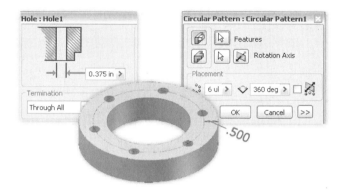

This part is now complete and located in the second-level assembly file. Click the Save icon. Remain in your file at the current level. The part will be saved, but the subassembly and overall assembly will be in a rolled-back state. Saving in a rolled-back state means you have saved at a level below the top-level assembly.

Adaptivity

Cross-part adaptivity is a powerful feature of Autodesk Inventor. Unlike some other 3D modelers, creating relationships between parts in an assembly is a simple task. In Inventor, adaptivity can be turned on or off at will. Other modelers may require that the relationships be deleted in order to turn off an adaptive feature.

Although adaptivity is a powerful tool when properly used in Autodesk Inventor, it can cause performance problems when used indiscriminately in large assemblies or when an adaptive part is utilized in another assembly without its related part. But you can fix both situations with very simple methods.

Performance issues in large assemblies can be caused by active adaptive parts. As a result, adaptivity should be turned off after use. If a related part is edited, adaptivity on the associated part should be turned on, and the assembly should be updated to reflect the changes on the related part. Once this is done, that adaptivity should be turned off once again.

SEAN SAYS: TRACK ADAPTIVITY

As we have discussed, it is a good idea to turn off adaptivity when not in use. However, Inventor does not have a good method to tell you what parts *were* adaptive. I suggest you rename the browser nodes so that you can tell what parts were adaptive. A simple way to do this is to append -A on the browser node. Simply "lazy double-click" the browser node, and edit the part name to read Browser Node -A. Now you'll know what parts were adaptive even where they are not currently adaptive.

If an adaptive part is to be used in other designs, then it is suggested that you save the part as a different filename and remove the adaptivity from the new part. Otherwise, the adaptive relationships will carry over into the other design, preventing the ability of shared parts to be edited.

CREATING ADAPTIVITY

Continuing the example, you will create an adaptive part that is related to `Rotary Hub.ipt`. To exit the level at which you created the Rotary Hub sketch, simply click the Return icon once at the top of the screen. This will move the design state from the Rotary Hub sketch and activate the second-level assembly, ready for editing at the assembly level. Select Create Component, and name the new part file as `Gasket.ipt`. Place this new part in the Parts subdirectory as you did the previous part.

Notice in the Create In-Place Component dialog box that there is a Constrain Sketch Plane to Selected Face check box. Ensure that this box is checked and then click OK to exit the dialog box. Continue by selecting the top face of the Rotary Hub sketch. When the top face is selected, a flush constraint is added between the two parts, and the new part is created. You will notice that Sketch1 is activated within the newly created Gasket part and the existing part becomes transparent. This is controlled by the Component Opacity setting found by selecting Tools ➤ Application Options and going to the Assembly tab.

Locate the Project Geometry command in the 2D Sketch panel, and project the top face of the Rotary Hub into the Gasket sketch. Note that clicking the edges of the Rotary Hub will project just that edge; clicking the face will project the entire face. Observe that `Gasket.ipt` and Sketch1 have become adaptive automatically, as shown in Figure 8.10. Adaptive parts, features, and sketches will have the red and green circular icon at the beginning of each line item. If adaptivity is turned off on any part, feature, or sketch, then the icon will disappear. Making the particular item adaptive again will redisplay the icon.

FIGURE 8.10
Gasket sketch showing adaptivity

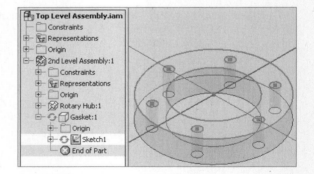

Because the Gasket sketch is adaptive, it will follow the shape and size of the Rotary Hub. Finish the sketch by selecting Finish Sketch from the right-click menu, as shown in Figure 8.11. Do not click Finish Edit because Inventor will not only finish the sketch in that case but will also move your design up one level.

Extrude the gasket to a thickness of 0.040 inch, click the Return icon once to move up to the second-level assembly design state, and then click Save.

To see how adaptivity works, double-click the Rotary Hub to activate that part for editing. You can double-click the part in the graphics area or the icon next to the part name in the Model browser to activate any part for editing. In the Model browser, right-click Extrusion1 and select Edit Sketch. Change the overall diameter from 5 to 7, and click OK.

FIGURE 8.11
Selecting Finish Sketch,
not Finish Edit

You will notice that the overall diameter and the diameter of the hole pattern of the Rotary Hub have changed, but the corresponding Gasket part remains unchanged. Click Return to move up to the second-level assembly design state once again. Click Update from the standard toolbar at the top of the screen to update the Gasket part. The Gasket part will now update to adapt to the changes made in the Rotary Hub.

REMOVING ADAPTIVITY FROM PARTS

Once a design has been approved and released for production, you should completely remove adaptivity from all parts within your assembly. Removing the adaptivity ensures that the part can be reused within other designs without conflict.

If you decide to retain adaptivity within your original assembly but plan on using the adaptive part in other assemblies, the adaptive icon will not display on those instances of the part. This is because only one occurrence of a part can define its adaptive features. However, all occurrences reflect changes and adaptive updates, including occurrence in other assemblies. It is for this reason that you must use adaptivity carefully.

To completely remove adaptivity from a part, either activate or open the adaptive part and activate the adaptive sketch. Expand the sketch and right-click Reference to select Break Link, as shown in Figure 8.12.

FIGURE 8.12
Breaking the adaptive
link

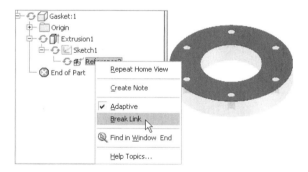

When the adaptive link is broken, the reference geometry is converted to normal sketch geometry. This geometry will need to be fully dimensioned and constrained. Once the geometry has been converted to normal sketch geometry, the part will no longer be able to be adaptive.

MAKING TEMPORARY USE OF ADAPTIVITY

Use adaptivity to find mounting holes for positioning hardware components on a base part. For example, consider a mounting clip and a base plate.

Constrain the clip to the base plate; then make the base plate active for editing, and create a sketch on the plate surface. With the sketch active, project the mounting holes, locating holes, and other needed geometry from the mounting clip to the base plate. This creates adaptive relationships in the base plate to the mounting clip.

Once the design is finalized and all the mounting clips are properly located, simply turn adaptivity off on the base plate. When the design is released for production, or at any other desired time, convert the reference geometry created when you projected geometry to normal sketch geometry. Then dimension and constrain the mounting holes as you would any other feature.

3D Constraints

3D constraints are the glue and nails of construction when it comes to 3D modelers. Properly using 3D constraints will permit the construction of stable assemblies, assist in developing stack-up tolerances, and allow parts to be driven to show the animation of a process.

Improperly using 3D constraints can create a nightmare of broken and/or redundant constraints, preventing assemblies from functioning properly, destroying assembly performance, and creating rework. Understanding how 3D constraints function in an assembly will help assure success in building and editing your design.

How Constraints Work

In a 3D modeler, constraints are used to attach parts or subassemblies together, creating assembly relationships between the components. In practice, constraint function follows real-world assembly techniques where fasteners, adhesives, and welds attach one component to another.

Using the Mate constraint as an example, three Mate constraints can function like glue in the real world, permanently binding components together. The net effect within an assembly is just like glue in that if you move one component, the other component will move also. Unlike glue, however, this joint is editable at any time.

Applying one Mate constraint between two components will remove one direction in which those components can be moved freely. The result of the Mate constraint is dependent upon the geometry selected. Consider two simple blocks with a single hole in each of them. If you apply a single Mate constraint between the top face of one block and the bottom face of the second block, they would no longer be free to travel in the Z direction but would still be free to travel in the positive and negative X and Y planes. Adding a second Mate between the centerlines of the holes would reduce the ability of the parts to travel freely in the X and Y planes but would still allow the blocks to rotate around the z-axis. Another constraint could then be added to remove that rotation if required, or it could be left unconstrained if that was the intent of the design.

Some 3D constraints permit the use of an offset distance to separate two components by a specified amount. This allows the precise control of clearance between parts.

Motion constraints create rotational relationships between parts, allowing the simulation of geared or driven movement. Transitional constraints can allow one component to move along an exact path, maintaining a perfect alignment relationship to the path.

When using 3D constraints, remember that a minimum of two and a maximum of three constraints are required to fully constrain two components together. Components fully contained within a subassembly will not figure into the constraint analysis when the top-level assembly is opened or modified.

Degrees of Freedom

Each unconstrained component existing within an assembly file possesses six degrees of freedom. The degrees of freedom are bidirectional and consist of three axial degrees of freedom along the x, y, and z origin axes, as well as full rotational freedom around the same axes.

For ease of use when learning and applying 3D constraints, you may make the degrees of freedom visible through the View menu by clicking Degrees Of Freedom. As constraints are applied to your component, the Degrees Of Freedom icon will change to reveal the remaining degrees of freedom. When the component is fully constrained, the icon will disappear. Figure 8.13 illustrates the activation process.

FIGURE 8.13
Activating Degrees Of
Freedom view

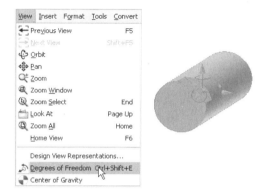

Types of 3D Constraints

Activating the Place Constraint dialog box, you will notice that there are four basic types of assembly constraints: Mate, Angle, Tangent, and Insert. Each of these assembly constraints has more than one solution, allowing great flexibility in joining two components together.

MATE CONSTRAINT

Exploring the Mate solutions, you will see that one solution option is Mate, which permits two opposing faces to mate together, similar to joining two physical objects together. The other solution option is the Flush constraint, which allows two component faces to be made flush to each other. With either option, offset distances will affect how the two faces are positioned. Figure 8.14 shows a Mate/Mate solution with no offset.

FIGURE 8.14
Mate constraint options

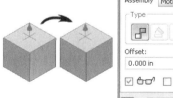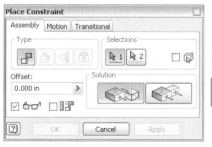

Within the Place Constraint dialog box in Inventor 2009, you have three check boxes. First, the Pick Part First check box, indicated by the small red cube, is useful when parts are partially obscured or are positioned in such a way that clicking a face or edge is difficult. This option filters the selectable geometry to a single component.

SEAN SAYS: MONITOR CONSTRAINTS WITH COLORS

Notice that in the Place Constraint dialog box the first and second geometry selection buttons are blue and green. Also notice that when you select the faces/edges, they also appear blue and green. This is very useful when helping diagnose or edit constraints.

Second, the Show Preview check box, indicated by the glasses icon, previews the constraint based upon the geometry selected once both selections are made. If the Show Preview check box is not checked, underconstrained components move into place only when the OK or Apply button is clicked. If either component is adaptive, constraints are not previewed even when the Show Preview box is checked.

Third, the Predict Offset And Orientation check box, found next to the Show Preview check box, captures the current offset location value when the object is selected. When unchecked, the offset location value is assumed to be zero.

To apply a Mate constraint between two components, select an edge, face, circular feature, or work feature on the first component. Note that you can cycle through the available selections using the Select Other tool, as shown in Figure 8.15.

FIGURE 8.15
Using the Select Other tool

Next, select the geometry on the second component to be mated. If the Show Preview box is checked, the components will move to reflect the results of your selection. If you make an incorrect selection, you can choose the selected geometry again by simply clicking the arrow buttons that correspond to selection 1 or selection 2.

Entering a value in the Offset text box will adjust the preview according to the value you specify. To preview the Flush solution, click the Flush button in the Solution area of the Place Constraint dialog box. To set the constraint, you can click either the OK button or the Apply button. Note that clicking Apply allows you to continue placing constraints as required, whereas clicking OK sets the constraint and exits the dialog box.

ANGLE CONSTRAINT

The Angle constraint permits three solutions within this constraint type. The solutions are Directed Angle, Undirected Angle, and Explicit Reference Vector. The Directed Angle solution always applies the right-hand rule, meaning that the angle rotation will function in a counterclockwise direction.

The Undirected Angle allows either counterclockwise or clockwise direction, resolving situations where a component orientation will flip during a constraint drive or drag operation.

New for Inventor 2009, the Explicit Reference Vector solution allows for the definition of a z-axis vector by adding a third click to the selection. This option will reduce the tendency of an Angle constraint to flip to an alternate solution during a constraint drive or drag. Figure 8.16 illustrates the selections required for this solution.

SEAN SAYS: USE THE RIGHT-HAND RULE

A good way to visualize the Explicit Reference Vector command is to use the right-hand rule. Take your right hand and make a "gun" shape with your index finger pointing out and your thumb pointing up. Now point your middle finger to the left, 90 degrees to the index finger. Your hand will then be making the three major axes. You can then use the thumb to determine the positive axes of the cross product of the x- and y-axes (the index and middle finger).

FIGURE 8.16
Explicit reference vector

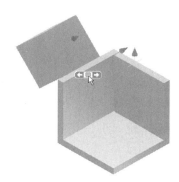

TANGENT CONSTRAINT

A Tangent constraint results in faces, planes, cylinders, spheres, and cones to contact at a point of tangency. Tangency can exist inside or outside of a curve depending on the direction of the selected surface normal. A Tangent constraint will remove one degree of linear freedom from the tangent set. When a Tangent constraint is applied between a cylinder and a planar face, the constraint will remove one degree of linear freedom as well as one degree of rotational freedom from the set. Figure 8.17 shows the placement of a Tangent constraint.

FIGURE 8.17
Tangent constraints

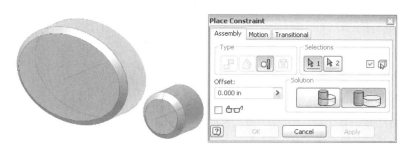

INSERT CONSTRAINT

The Insert constraint is probably the best choice for inserting fasteners and other cylindrical objects into holes or for constraining any parts where circular or cylindrical geometry is to be constrained to one another. A single Insert constraint will replace two Mate constraints, retaining one rotational degree of freedom. Options for the Insert constraint are Opposed and Aligned. The Insert constraint also allows for specifying offset values between components. Figure 8.18 shows common uses of Insert constraints.

FIGURE 8.18
Insert constraints

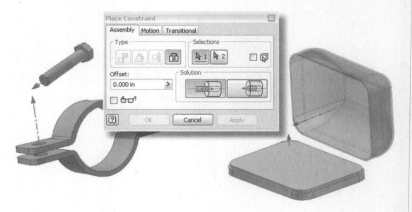

Motion Constraints

Within the Place Constraint dialog box is the Motion tab. The tab allows you to add a Rotational constraint between two components such as gears, simulating a ratio-based rotation.

To create a simple Rotational constraint, first place two components constrained around their axis. Neither component should be grounded; instead, they should be constrained to allow rotation around the axis. The rotation constraint applies a forward or reverse solution, as shown in Figure 8.19, to the two components, along with a ratio that will determine rotation speeds.

FIGURE 8.19
Rotational constraint
options

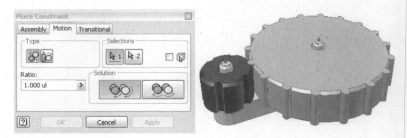

Transitional Constraints

Transitional constraints allow the movement of an underconstrained component along a path in a separate part. To create a Transitional constraint, you will first select a moving face on the underconstrained component. Then you will select a transitional face or edge on a fully constrained or grounded part.

Figure 8.20 illustrates a pin following a spline curve acting as a guide face. To drive the pin along the path, a second Mate constraint with an offset will be applied between the origin work plane in the pin and the end of the part.

FIGURE 8.20
Transitional constraint

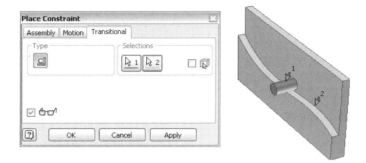

Driving Constraints

It is often desirable to simulate motion by driving a constraint through a beginning position and an ending position to confirm the intent of the design. In general, Offset and Angle constraints may be selected to drive components within an assembly. To accomplish this, simply right-click the desired constraint, and select Drive Constraint (as shown in Figure 8.21).

FIGURE 8.21
Driving a constraint

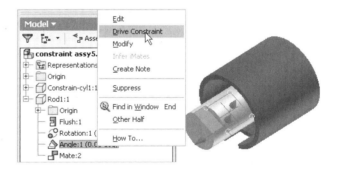

The Drive Constraint dialog box will appear, allowing you to alter the constraint by specifying steps between the start position and the end position. When a constraint is driven, any components constrained to the driven component will move in accordance to their particular shared constraints. The motion may be set to forward or reverse, stopped at any time, and even recorded by clicking the Record button prior to activating the move. If any of the affected components are constrained to a grounded component, or if the movement will violate any existing constraint, then the drive constraint will fail.

Expanding the dialog box as shown in Figure 8.22 by pressing the >> button will reveal additional controls over the drive constraint. The increment of movement can be controlled by a value or by a total number of steps from beginning to end. The length of a particular driven constraint can be controlled by the number of allowable repetitions from Start to End or can be reversed by using the Start/End/Start option. For a continuous revolution by degrees, you may exceed

360° by specifying the total number of degrees of revolution or by including an equation such as 360 deg *3.

FIGURE 8.22
Drive Constraint dialog
box options

Other parts properly constrained within the driven assembly that are adaptive will adjust to changes if the Drive Adaptivity option is checked. This particular option allows determination of a maximum or minimum condition for the adaptive part.

Checking the Collision Detection option allows for determination of an exact collision distance or angle between the driven parts. Using the Collision Detection option will help you determine interferences between moving parts so that those parts can be modified before manufacturing.

SEAN SAYS: USE THE CONTACT SOLVER FOR COLLISION DETECTION

If you have parts that interfere (such as a dowel pin in a hole) and have the Collision Detection option checked, the drive constraint command will stop immediately because it will have detected this interference. If you really need to test the collision of parts, look into using the Contact Solver.

Redundant Constraints and Constraint Failures

Excessive constraints are considered redundant when you have overconstrained components. Redundant constraints will interfere with the proper operation of your assemblies and can cause constraint failures and performance issues.

Two toggles will assist in flagging bad constraints; you can find them by selecting Tools ➤ Application Options and going to the Assembly tab. Enabling Constraint Redundancy Analysis allows Inventor to perform a secondary analysis of assembly constraints and notifies you when redundant constraints exist.

Enabling Related Constraint Failure Analysis allows Inventor to perform an analysis to identify all affected constraints and components, if a particular constraint fails. Once analysis is performed, you will be able to isolate the components that use the broken constraint(s) and select a form of treatment for individual components.

Because analysis requires a separate process, performance can be affected if these two check boxes are active. Because of this, it is advisable to activate the analysis only when problems exist.

Contact Solver

Another method for driving components within an assembly involves the Contact Solver option. With this option, only minimal constraints are required to drive a number of components. Components are not required to be constrained to one another for the Contact Solver to work.

The Contact Solver works in much the same way as parts interact within the real world. Without the Contact Solver applied, moving parts can be run through one another, creating interference. With the Contact Solver applied, parts will stop when they contact one another. A simple example of this is the slide arm pictured in Figure 8.23. On the left, you can see that the arm segments have been extended past the point that they could be in reality, allowing the slide stops to run through the slide slot. On the right, the parts have been added to a contact set, and the Contact Solver has been turned on, preventing the slide stops from running through the slots.

FIGURE 8.23
With and without
Contact Solver

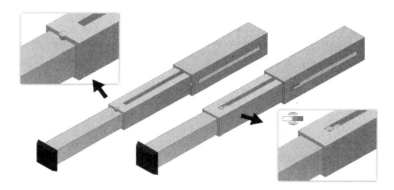

To add parts to a contact set, simply right-click the part, and click Contact Set in the context menu. An icon will appear before each component showing when a component has been added to the contact set. In addition to adding parts to a contact set, you must also ensure that the Contact Solver is turned on by going to the Tools menu and clicking Activate Contact Solver. Once all active participants within the contact set are selected and the Contact Solver is activated, then a single-driven constraint can provide a real-life simulation. Note that it is best practice to turn the Contact Solver off when performance is a consideration.

Assembly Features

An *assembly feature* is a feature created and utilized purely within the active assembly file and environment. Because this feature was created within the assembly file, it does not exist at the single part or subassembly level.

A good example of an assembly feature in use is the technique of creating drilled holes through a standard tabletop within an assembly. Common practice is to place brackets on the tabletop in order to find the mounting hole locations. This allows the holes to be drilled at the same time, ensuring an exact match and placement. Assembly features in Inventor mimic this approach.

Examining the individual tabletop file reveals that the part file does not contain the drilled holes, simply because the drill operation was performed at the assembly level rather than the part level. To understand the reasoning behind this, you might consider that the tabletop is a common part stocked in the shop and then machined as required for each assembly in which it is used. Although the stock part might exist as a cataloged item with no holes, it may exist in many different assemblies with holes of various sizes and locations. Using assembly features allow you to work in this manner.

Other examples of assembly features are contained within the weldment environment, where preparations used to facilitate welding components together are at the assembly level. Preparation features allow trimming of soon-to-be-welded components to eliminate interferences between welds and other parts of the weldment.

Care must be taken when creating geometry within the context of the assembly, because it is easy to create an assembly feature when intending to create a part feature. Although this is a common mistake that new users will make, it is one that anyone can experience. In a multilevel top-down design, always make sure you are working in the proper assembly or component by double-clicking the assembly or component in the Model browser for the purposes of opening that component for editing.

Assembly features in Inventor can be created by clicking the 2D Sketch icon in the Inventor Standard toolbar located at the top of your screen. Once you click the icon, selecting any planar face within the assembly will initiate the sketch environment. Examining the browser reveals that the newly created sketch is located above the End Of Features portion of the Model browser and that all components located within the assembly are grayed out. Note that the End Of Features marker replaces the expected End Of Part marker at the end of each part feature creation or edit. In addition, the Assembly panel has replaced the 2D Sketch panel.

Once assembly features have been created, components can be removed from the impact of those features by expanding the assembly features in the browser, right-clicking the component, and choosing Remove Participant from the menu. Components can be added to an assembly feature by right-clicking the feature, choosing Add Participant from the menu, and then choosing the component from the browser. On the left of Figure 8.24, component 1247 is being removed from the Hole feature so that the hole does not go through the part. On the right, the same component is being added to the feature.

FIGURE 8.24
Adding/removing participants from assembly features

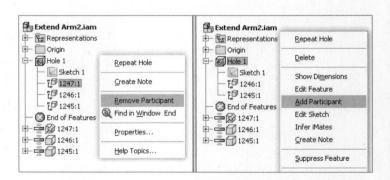

In addition to sketch-based assembly features, Extrudes, Revolves, Holes, Sweeps, Fillets, Chamfers, and Move Face features can be created as assembly features. Note that assembly features are allowed only to cut or remove material. Other commonly used assembly feature commands within the Assembly panel environment include Mirror and the Patterns commands.

SEAN SAYS: THERE ARE OTHER USES FOR ASSEMBLY FEATURES

Another novel use of the assembly feature uses no features at all. It is often useful to create an assembly sketch to determine the range of motion of parts. For example, if you have a shaft that has an arm on the end and this arm rotates through a certain angle, you can use an assembly sketch to show the envelope of this arm's movement. Simply start a new assembly sketch and project the center point of the shaft. Next project a segment of the arm that is farthest from the shaft. Now draw a circle centered on the shaft that is coincident with the project arm geometry. You now have an easy way to view the envelope of the rotating member. By using the Include Model Sketches command, you can even show this envelope in your detail drawing.

Managing the Bill of Materials

In Inventor, the BOM is the internal, real-time database that exists within every assembly. *Real-time* means that as components are added to the assembly, they are automatically added and counted in the BOM. Although you might be accustomed to referring to the tabled list of parts on the 2D drawing as a bill of materials, in Inventor such a table is called a *parts list*. Parts lists pull from directly from the assembly BOM.

The BOM is controlled at two different levels: the part level and the assembly level. Both levels factor in certain aspects of how the bill of materials is generated, how components are represented, and ultimately how the parts list is generated within the drawing environment.

Parts-Level BOM Control

In the part environment, the designer has the ability to define the BOM structure of just that part. At this level, the structure can be defined as Normal, Inseparable, Purchased, Phantom, or Reference. Determining the default setting at the part level allows control of how the part is identified within the overall assembly (or assemblies) BOM. By setting the structure at the part level, you can control the assembly BOM display according to the part settings. Any structure settings at the part level can be overridden and changed to Reference at the assembly level.

Another important structure setting at the part level is the Base Quantity property. This setting controls how the part is listed in the BOM. If the Base Quantity is set to Each, the part is tallied by count. This is the default for most standard parts. The Base Quantity can also be set to reflect the value of any given model parameter. This is most often set to a length parameter so that the Base Quantity will tally the total length of a part used in an assembly. Parts pulled from the Content Center and the Frame Generator have their Base Quantity property set to pull a length parameter by default. The Base Quantity property is set by selecting Tools ➢ Document Settings and going to the Bill Of Materials tab.

Assembly-Level BOM Control

BOM control accelerates at the assembly level. You can access the Bill Of Materials dialog box by selecting Tools ➢ Bill of Materials or by clicking the Bill of Materials icon in the Assembly Panel toolbar. In the drawing environment, the BOM Editor dialog box is accessible by right-clicking the parts list and selecting Bill Of Materials.

The Bill Of Materials dialog box allows you to edit iProperties, BOM properties, and the BOM structure; override quantities for components; and sort and create a consistent item order for the generation of parts lists. Figure 8.25 shows the Bill Of Materials dialog box.

FIGURE 8.25
Bill Of Materials dialog
box

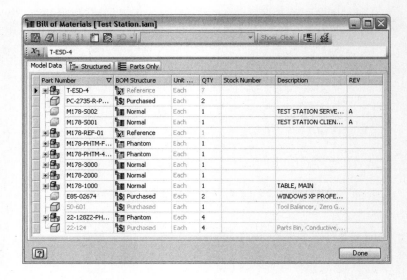

ABOUT THE BILL OF MATERIALS DIALOG BOX

Exporting a bill of materials is a straightforward process, with icons across the top of the dialog box allowing the export of the BOM data in a structured or parts-only view in formats such as MDB, dBase, or various Excel formats. The Engineer's Notebook icon permits the export of database information as a note.

Adding and Removing Columns

You can add columns to the model in any of the three tabs in the Bill Of Materials dialog box by clicking the Choose Columns icon, which will display a dialog box list in which you can drag a desired column to a specified location, as shown in Figure 8.26. To remove a desired column, simply drag the column to be removed back to the dialog box list.

FIGURE 8.26
Choose Column dialog
box

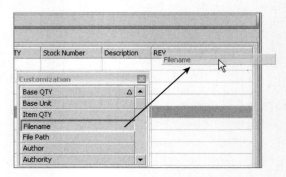

Custom Columns

The next icon at the top of the Bill Of Materials dialog box allows you to add custom iProperty columns. The pulldown list shown in Figure 8.27 within the Add Custom iProperty Columns dialog box will display a combined list of all the available custom iProperties contained within the assembly.

FIGURE 8.27
Custom iProperty list

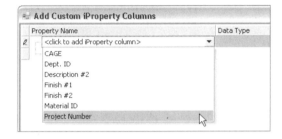

If a desired custom iProperty does not exist within the list of components, you can add it manually by selecting the <Click To Add iProperty Column> option displayed in the list box. Be sure to set the data type to the correct format when manually adding a custom iProperty to the assembly file. Manually added iProperties will be stored in the assembly file. Figure 8.28 shows the addition of a custom iProperty column called Assembly Station.

FIGURE 8.28
Creating a new custom iProperty

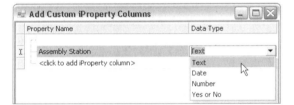

Once custom iProperty columns have been added to the assembly bill of materials, individual parts can be populated with custom iProperties as needed. Individual parts that already contain those iProperties will show the values within the respective row and column. iProperties that are edited or added to a respective part row will be pushed down to the part level; therefore, filling out iProperties at the assembly level is often the most efficient way to populate part iProperties.

The Create Expression icon located at the beginning of the Formula toolbar launches the Property Expression dialog box so you can create an iProperty expression. The newly created expression can contain a combination of custom text and iProperty names in brackets. The iProperty expression will be substituted for the field in which the expression was created, once the expression is evaluated. In Figure 8.29, the expression is created in the Description field.

FIGURE 8.29
Creating property expressions

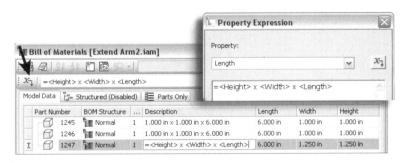

Looking across the top of the Bill Of Materials dialog box, the two icons to the far right are Part Number Merge Settings and Update Mass Properties Of All Rows. The Update Mass Properties Of All Rows icon recalculates the total mass for all components within the assembly.

Clicking the Part Number Merge Settings icon will allow different components possessing the same part number to be treated as the same component. For instance, say six base plates of the same size are used in an assembly. Four of these plates have holes drilled upon installation, and two have holes placed during fabrication. As far as the shop is concerned, all six are the same part, but in the design both plate types exist as separate part files.

To have the BOM count the total number of plates, you set the Part Number property to match on both items and then use the Part Number Merge Settings to have these files counted as a single item.

BOM Structure Designations

There are five designations from which to choose when assigning BOM structure to components: Normal, Inseparable, Purchased, Phantom, and Reference. Any part or assembly file can be assigned one of these designations within the BOM. That designation is then stored in the file, meaning that if a part is marked as Purchased in one assembly, it will be designated as Purchased in all assemblies. The structure designations are as follows:

◆ *Normal*: This is the default structure for most components. Placement and participation in the assembly bill of materials are determined by the parent assembly. In the previous example, you are creating an assembly file rather than a single part. As a result, you will be determining the characteristics of how this assembly file will behave in the top-level assembly bill of materials. With a Normal BOM structure, this assembly will be numbered and included in quantity calculations within the top-level assembly.

◆ *Inseparable*: These are generally assemblies that cannot be disassembled without damage. Examples of inseparable assemblies might include weldments, glued constructions, and riveted assemblies. In a parts-only parts list, these assemblies will be treated as a single part. Another example is a purchased part such as a motor.

◆ *Purchased*: This designation is typically for parts or assemblies that are not fabricated in-house. Examples of purchased components are motors, brake calipers, programmable controllers, hinges, and the like. Purchased components are considered as a single BOM item, regardless of whether it is a part or a subassembly. Within a purchased assembly, all child parts are excluded from the BOM and quantity calculations.

◆ *Phantom*: Use Phantom components to simplify the design process. A Phantom component exists within the design but is not shown as a line item in the BOM. A common use for a Phantom component would be a subassembly of parts that are grouped for ease of design. Setting the subassembly to be Phantom allows the parts to be listed in the BOM individually. Other examples of Phantom components could include hardware sets, screws, nuts, bolts, washers, pins, and various fastener-type components. A good example of a Phantom assembly would be a collection of parts that are normally assembled onto the machine one at a time. However, in the interest of reducing the overall number of assembly constraints within the design, the engineer might choose to preassemble the various components within a Phantom assembly. That assembly could then be constrained as one component instead of multiple parts.

◆ *Reference*: Mark components as Reference when they are used for construction geometry or to add additional detail and references to the top-level assembly. A good example of a

Reference component is a car body and frame that represents the outer shell for placement of a power train. In the 2D documentation, the car body and frame would be shown as hidden lines illustrating the overall design while highlighting the power train as the principal component within a view. Reference geometry is excluded from quantity, mass, or volume calculations regardless of their own internal BOM structure. As a result, they are not included within the parts list. They are placed only within the overall assembly to show design intent and position.

In addition to these five BOM structure designations for component files, you also have the ability to create a virtual component, which has no geometry and does not exist as an external file. A virtual component can have a complete set of properties similar to real components but that are primarily used to represent bulk items such as fasteners, assembly kits, paint, grease, adhesive, plating, or other items that do not require creating an actual model. A virtual component can be designated as any of the previous BOM structure types and can contain custom properties, descriptions, and other aspects of the BOM data like any other component.

A virtual component will be shown in the Model browser as if it were a real part. They can be created by selecting the check box next to the BOM structure pulldown in the Create In-Place Component dialog box, as shown in Figure 8.30.

FIGURE 8.30
Creating a virtual component

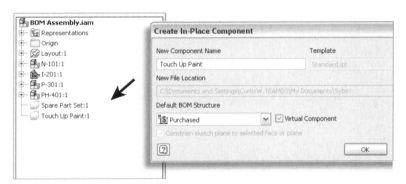

BOM View Tabs

Each tab in the Bill Of Materials dialog box represents a different BOM view. All tabs permit ascending or descending sorting of the rows in the BOM by clicking the respective column header. You can also reorder rows by simply clicking and dragging a component's icon.

Model Data Tab

With the Model Data tab active, you see the components listed just as they exist in the Model browser. You can add or remove columns to populate the Model Data tab independently of the other BOM view tabs. In this tab all components are listed in the BOM, regardless of BOM structure designation. Item numbers are not assigned in this Model Data tab. The model data is not exportable or available for placement as a parts list. Instead, this tab is typically used for organization of the BOM and assignment of BOM structure designation.

Figure 8.31 shows a bill of materials in the Model Data view. Notice that there are no item numbers listed and that all component structure types are displayed including Reference and Phantom components. Notice too that the last two parts listed are virtual parts and have been given different BOM structure designations.

FIGURE 8.31
BOM Model Data tab

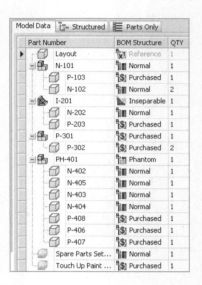

Structured Tab vs. Parts Only Tab

In addition to the Model Data tab are the Structured and Parts Only tabs. These tabs are disabled by default. To enable them, right-click the tab, and choose Enable BOM View; alternatively, click the View Options button along the top of the Bill Of Material dialog box.

The Structured tab can display all components of the assembly, including subassemblies and the parts of the subassemblies. When in structured view, additional icons will be active on the toolbar, allowing you to sort by item and renumber items within the assembly BOM. The ordering of the BOM item numbers is stored in the assembly file.

The View Options icon permits enabling or disabling the BOM view and allows modification of the Structured view. This dialog box contains two pulldown lists defining the level, the minimum number of digits, and the assembly part delimiter value. If the level is set to First Level, subassemblies are listed without listing the components contained within. If set to All Levels, each part is listed in an indented manner under the subassembly, as shown in Figure 8.32.

FIGURE 8.32
Structured Properties
dialog box

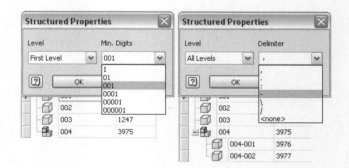

The Parts Only tab lists all components in a flat list. In this BOM view, subassemblies desig-nated as Normal are not listed as an item, but all their child components are displayed. By contrast, Inseparable and Purchased subassemblies are displayed as an item, but their child components are not displayed.

Bill of materials settings that are modified by the Bill Of Materials dialog box will carry forward into the drawing parts lists contained in the assembly. Note that if both the Structured and Parts Only views of the BOM are enabled, the same part may have a different item number in each view.

Figure 8.33 shows a bill of materials in the Structured view compared to the same assembly in the Model Data view. The first thing to note is that all the components have been assigned item numbers in the Structured view. You might also notice that the Reference and Phantom components that are listed in the Model Data view are filtered out of the Structured view. Closer inspection reveals that although the Phantom subassembly named PH-401 is not included in the Structured view, all of its child parts (N-402 through P-407) are listed, each with an arrow next to the icon to denote that they are part of a subassembly. Recall that Phantom subassemblies are used to group parts for design organization and to reduce assembly constraints while allowing the parts to be listed individually.

FIGURE 8.33
BOM structured view

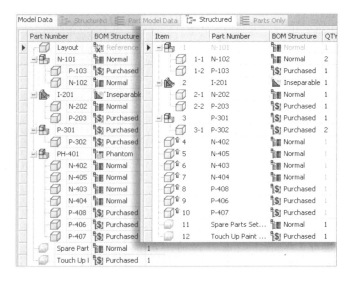

Figure 8.34 shows a bill of materials in the Parts Only view. This BOM view filters out Ref-erence and Phantom components just as the structured view does. Notice too that although the subassemblies are not listed as items, their child parts are. The exceptions to this are Purchased and Inseparable assemblies. In the illustration, the Purchased subassembly lists as a single item, since it is a Purchased component comprised of two Purchased parts and is assumed to be Purchased as one item. Note that if you had the need to list the parts as items rather than the subassembly, you would designate the subassembly as Phantom rather than Purchased.

Take a look also at the Inseparable subassembly named I-201. It lists as an item along with one of its child parts named P-203. This child part lists because it is a Purchased item and needs to be ordered. Had both children of the Inseparable subassembly been Normal parts, neither would list in the Parts Only view.

FIGURE 8.34
BOM Parts Only tab

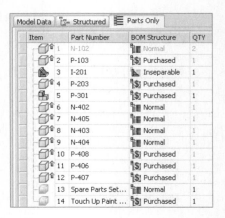

Assembly Reuse and Configurations

Quite frequently, existing assemblies are used in other designs or are used in multiple locations within the top-level assembly. There are three basic workflows for reusing assemblies in design:

◆ Copying designs

◆ Flexible and positional representations

◆ iAssemblies (table-driven assemblies)

Copying Designs

Quite often you need to copy a previous design with the intent of creating a similar design based on the original design. Part of the challenge of doing this with Inventor is creating copies of only the parts that will be modified in the new design while reusing parts that do not incur changes, all the while maintaining healthy file links. To do this effectively, you employ the Copy Components tool from within the assembly to be copied.

To begin this process, first select the top-level assembly from the browser tree and then click the Copy Components button from the tool panel. You will be presented with the Copy Components: Status dialog box, which lists the top-level assembly and the components within, as shown in

Figure 8.35. Use the Status buttons next to each component to set the component to be copied, reused, or excluded from the copy operation.

FIGURE 8.35
Copy Components:
Status dialog box

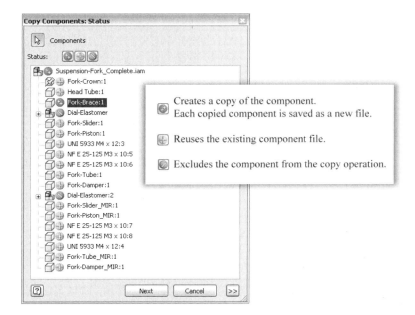

In the example in Figure 8.35, the Fork-Brace is the only part that needs to be redesigned for the new assembly; therefore, it is the only part set to be copied. In the original design, there are two instances of a subassembly called Dial-Elastomer. You can see that both instances have been excluded in this copy operation because they will be swapped out for another dial assembly that you have on file already. You will notice that all other components except the top-level assembly are set to be reused. Once the copy status of each part is set, click the Next button to move to the Copy Components: File Names dialog box, as shown in Figure 8.36.

FIGURE 8.36
Copy Components: File
Names dialog box

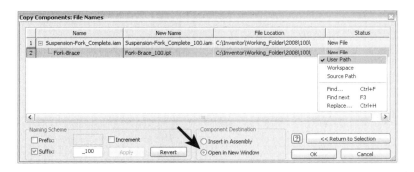

In the Copy Components: File Names dialog box, you want to set the destination button to Open In New Window in order to create a new, separate assembly file. You can then use the Prefix and/or Suffix controls to modify the existing filenames, or you can type in new names as required.

By default, the File Location is set to Source Path, meaning that the new files will land right next to the existing ones. If that is not desirable, you can right-click each File Location cell and choose User Path or Workspace. Care should be taken to ensure that file location paths are not set outside the project search path. When the filename and paths are set, click OK.

The new assembly file will open in a separate window. Interrogation of the Model browser should reveal that the components set to be reused are listed just as they were in the original assembly, the components set to be copied are listed as specified, and the components set to be excluded are not present at all.

SEAN SAYS: COPY DESIGNS WITH VAULT

If you need more advanced control over copying designs (and copying designs between projects), you might want to look into Autodesk Vault. Vault has a Copy Design tool that is very powerful and allows you to also copy and relink the detail drawing files (IDWs and DWGs) at the same time.

Representations

Inventor provides the ability to create and store three basic types of representations within an assembly file. *Representations* allow you to manage assemblies by setting up varying views, positions, and levels of detail for your models. Each of these allows for the creation of user-defined representations, and each has a master representation. Note that although user-defined representations can be renamed and deleted as required, master representations cannot. Using representations enhances productivity and improves performance in large assembly design.

Once representations are created in an assembly, that assembly file can be opened in any combination of those representation states by clicking the Options button in the Open File or Place Component dialog box, as shown in Figure 8.37. Keep in mind that although you can open or place a file by typing the filename rather than scrolling and clicking the icon, you cannot access the Options button without explicitly scrolling and selecting the file in the dialog box.

FIGURE 8.37
Opening a file in a representation

View Representations

View representations, also known as *design views* and *ViewReps*, are used to configure the display of an assembly and save that display for later use. View representations control the visibility state of components, sketch features, and work features. Also controlled by view representations are component color and styles applied at the assembly level. The enabled/not enabled status of components can be controlled in a view representation as well. In addition to these component properties, a view representation controls the onscreen zoom magnification and orientation. In effect, view representations allow "snapshot views" of portions of an assembly file. Each view representation is saved within the assembly file and has no effect on individual parts or subassemblies.

View representations are relatively simple to create and use. While in the assembly, simply zoom and rotate your model until you have the desired view showing in the current graphics window. Then, expand the Representations folder, and right-click View to select New, as shown in Figure 8.38. Now, turn off the visibility of a few parts; these visibility changes will take place only within this view representation.

FIGURE 8.38
Create a new view representation

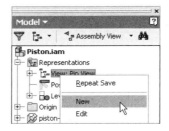

After creating the new view representation, click Save to preserve the newly created representation. You can protect the view representation you create from accidental edits by right-clicking it and choosing Lock. View representations can be accessed either by double-clicking the desired representation or by right-clicking the desired representation and selecting Activate. Private view representations are views created in early releases of Inventor and are not associative.

SEAN SAYS: ACTIVATE A NEW VIEW REPRESENTATION TO PREVENT ERRORS

Probably one of the most misunderstood "errors" in Inventor is the "The current Design View Representation is locked" message. It tells you that changes will not be saved. This alarms a lot of new users. What this means is that you have turned off the visibility (or enabled status or any number of other things) while in the Master view representation. Since the Master is locked, these changes will not be saved, and the next time you open the file, the model will be back at the previous state. To circumvent this issue, be sure to activate a new ViewRep and then make your changes and save. This way your visibility and other settings will be saved in the ViewRep. You might even consider creating a default ViewRep in your assembly template files.

Positional Representations

Positional representations, often referred to as *PosReps* for short, can be employed to set up and store components in various arrangements and are used to aid in the testing and analysis of assembly motion. Positional representations work by overriding assembly constraints, assembly patterns, or component properties.

To create a new positional representation, expand the Representations heading in the browser, right-click the Positional Representations heading, and then choose New. Continue by right-clicking the component, pattern, or constraint in the Model browser that you want to change. Choose Override from the right-click menu. The override dialog box will open to the tab that is appropriate to the entity on which you right-clicked. Figure 8.39 shows the override options for each tab. You can rename the new representation from the default name to something more meaningful; however, you cannot rename the master representation.

FIGURE 8.39
Positional representation overrides

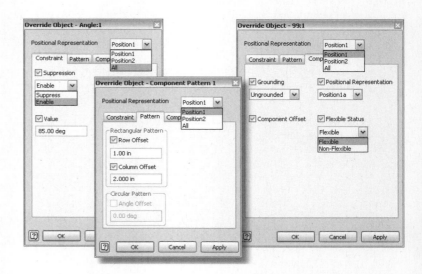

Open the file called PosReps1.iam from the Mastering Inventor folder. Locate and expand the subassembly called K130.iam in the Model browser. Notice the constraint called Angle1 and its current value of 180 degrees. You will create positional representations in this assembly by overriding this constraint.

First locate and expand the Representations folder in the browser and then find and expand the Position folder. Right-click the top level of the Position folder, and choose New. This will create a positional representation called Position1. Right-click slowly on the name Position1 and rename it Open. Next locate the Angle1 constraint, right-click, and choose Override. In the override dialog box, select the Value check box, and enter **60** in the text box. Click OK. Your positional representation has been created. You can switch between the Master and Open positional representations by double-clicking them in the browser. Follow the proceeding steps to create additional positional representations for practice.

Positional representations also allow the reuse of identical subassemblies within a top-level assembly file. When using positional representations in conjunction with flexible assemblies, you can illustrate a subassembly in different positions. Figure 8.40 shows an assembly containing two instances of the flex2.iam subassembly. The original instance, flex2:1, has the positional representation set to up. The second instance has its positional representation set to down.

To help manage positional representations, the browser can be set to display only the overrides present in each positional representation, as shown in Figure 8.41. The buttons along the top of the Representations browser allow you to create a new positional representation, validate the overrides ensuring that no errors are created in the representations, and manage the overrides via Microsoft Excel.

FIGURE 8.40
Positional
representations

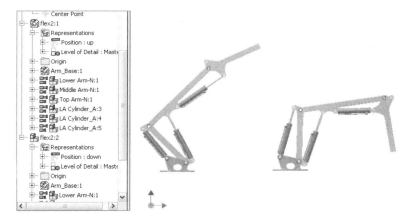

FIGURE 8.41
Representations browser

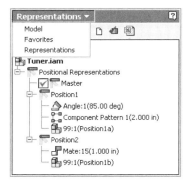

Because the positional representation properties of an assembly are stored separately, multiple views can be created in the drawing environment representing different positions of the same assembly. Figure 8.42 shows an example of an overlay view showing both available positions of this arm.

FIGURE 8.42
Overlay view of a
positional representation

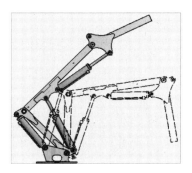

Level of Detail Representations

Proper use of level of detail (LOD) improves speed and reduces the memory required to load and navigate large assemblies. When working with a large assembly, you suppress components that are not required for a certain aspect of working with the design and then save that suppression state as a level of detail representation. For instance, if you are designing a large material-handling unit, you might open the unit in an LOD representation with everything suppressed except the frame while you work on the frame skins, thereby significantly reducing the number of parts loaded into memory.

SEAN SAYS: VIEWREPS VS. LODREPS

It is a common misconception that making parts invisible reduces the overhead of your assemblies. The models are still loaded into memory. To unload them from memory, you must utilize LODReps. Also, when using LODReps on *very* large assemblies, we have found it is better to open the assembly with the built-in All Components Suppressed state and then turn on the parts you want as opposed to opening the entire model and unloading the parts you do not want. In our tests, less RAM is consumed in the former method than the latter.

Another common example of LOD representations might be to suppress external components while working on internal components simply for convenience. In addition to this standard method of suppressing components to create LOD, Inventor 2009 introduces substitute LOD representations that allow you to trade out a large multipart assembly with a single part derived from that assembly.

Just as view and positional representations have a master representation, so too does the LOD. However, there are three additional default LOD representations: All Components Suppressed, All Parts Suppressed, and All Content Center Suppressed. These system-defined LODs cannot be removed or modified.

The All Components Suppressed representation suppresses everything within the assembly, allowing you to quickly open the assembly and then unsuppress components as required. The All Parts Suppressed representation suppresses all parts at all levels of the assembly; however, subassemblies are loaded, allowing you to examine the assembly structure without loading all of the part files. The All Content Center Suppressed representation suppresses any component in the assembly that is stored in the Content Center Files directory as designated by the IPJ (project) file.

To create a user-defined LOD, expand the Representations heading in the browser, right-click the Level Of Detail heading, and then choose New Level Of Detail. Continue by right-clicking the component or components you want to suppress, and choose Suppress from the menu. Once this is done, you must save the assembly while still in the LOD. After saving the assembly, you can create more LOD representations or flip from one to another to compare the results.

To create a substitute LOD, expand the Representations heading in the browser, right-click the Level Of Detail heading, and then choose New Substitute. There are two methods for creating substitutes. The first method simply prompts you to select any existing part file to swap out for the assembly file in the LOD, and the second creates a derived part from the source assembly. When using the Derive Assembly method, you are asked to specify a part template to use and then are brought right into the derive assembly process. The derived part is automatically marked as a substitute during the derive process and placed into the LOD.

On the left, Figure 8.43 shows an assembly in its master LOD with 304 component occurrences in the assembly and 81 unique files open in the Inventor session. On the right, the same assembly is set to a substitute LOD and reduced to a single component in the assembly and only two unique files open in the Inventor session. As you can imagine, a significant savings in memory use can be achieved by placing an assembly with a substitute LOD active into a top-level assembly.

FIGURE 8.43
Substitute LOD representation

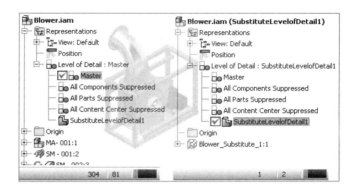

It is important to understand that substitute LODs are intended to be used by either excluding components during the derive process or in combination with user-defined LODs to exclude components. Simply making a substitute LOD of an assembly with all components included may not give you the performance gain you anticipated unless you have made the substitute from another LOD that has parts suppressed or have excluded parts while creating the substitute LOD.

LOD states are created automatically when you suppress components while in the master LOD. To save suppressions to a new LOD representation, click Save, and you will be prompted to click Yes or No to save the LOD. If you choose Yes, you can specify a name for the LOD. If you choose No, the suppression states of the component are discarded, and the assembly is saved in master LOD.

Temporary LOD representations are created in subassemblies when a subassembly component is suppressed from a top-level assembly. A tilde and index number are listed after the subassembly name to denote a temporary LOD state. Note that the subassembly is not modified. You can open the subassembly on its own and save the suppression states as a named LOD if desired.

It is important to understand the difference between LOD representations and iAssembly configurations with respect to how they affect the bill of materials. Although you can suppress features at will and substitute part files for assemblies with the use of LOD representations, Inventor still understands that all the parts in the master LOD will be included in the bill of materials. When you suppress a component in an LOD representation used in a drawing view, the view updates, and any balloons attached to that component are deleted. However, the parts list will still list the component because it always refers to the master bill of materials.

If your intent is to create an assembly configuration where some parts are to be listed in the bill of materials and others excluded, iAssemblies is the correct tool.

iAssemblies

An iAssembly is a table-driven assembly file that allows the use of component part configurations to build variations of a design. Some of the strengths of assembly configurations of this type are the abilities to swap out one component for another, to include or exclude components all together, and to adjust assembly constraint offset values to create various configurations of the original assembly.

It is important to understand that when you create an iAssembly, you create what is called an iAssembly *factory*. The configurations that will be output from this factory are called the iAssembly members. It may help to think of the factory as the parent file and the members as children.

To create an iAssembly, most often you start with an assembly composed of iParts. First, the iParts are created for all parts that will vary in size or configuration of features. Next, create the assembly using iPart members where required. Once the basic assembly is created, you add the configuration table, turning the assembly into an iAssembly.

Open the file named PB800.iam from the Mastering Inventor folder. This assembly file represents a simplified push button panel. Your goal is to create an assembly configuration with variations in the number and type of buttons used, as shown in Figure 8.44.

FIGURE 8.44
Four configurations of a push button panel

To convert the assembly into an iAssembly, go to the Tools menu and choose Create iAssembly. This will open the iAssembly Author dialog box, as shown in Figure 8.45. The first thing you should do is consider the naming conventions for the iAssembly members. Click the Options button at the bottom of the dialog box to bring up the naming options. Here you would typically configure the name for the member part number and member names so that, as you add rows to the iAssembly table, the naming drops out automatically. In this case, we'll simply click OK to choose the defaults.

FIGURE 8.45
iAssembly Author dialog box

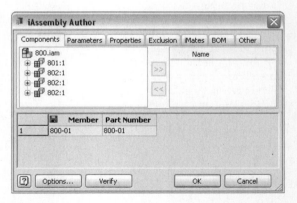

Either column can be set to be the filename column from which member part numbers are generated. This can be done by right-clicking the Member or Part Name column headers and choosing File Name Column from the menu. The filename column is indicted by the save or disk symbol.

Next, let's examine the Components tab and expand the tree next to part 801:1. In the tree of each part are four different nodes that you can use to add a column to the table. Select Table Replace from the tree and use the >> button to add it as a column in the table. Now that you have added a column to the table, you will add a row. Right-click anywhere on row 1 in the lower pane of the dialog box, and choose Insert Row. Your table should now resemble Figure 8.46.

FIGURE 8.46
Configuring an iAssembly table

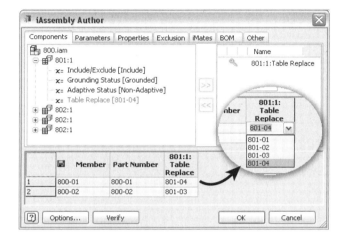

The table replace column allows you to replace an iPart member for another iPart member within the assembly. In this case, the part named 801 is the sheet-metal cover plate. This plate is an iPart that has four different sizes within the iPart table. Click the cell in row 1 in the 801:1 Table Replace column to activate a pulldown menu. From the menu, select 801-04, as shown in the inset of Figure 8.46. Click OK to exit the dialog box.

You will notice that the model has changed from a three-hole plate to a four-hole plate. This is a result of the having set the Table Replace cell to use the iPart member 801-04, which is predetermined in the iPart to be a four-hole plate. Examine the Model browser, and you will notice that a table has been added to the browser. Expand the table, and you will find a listing of the iAssembly members, 800-01 and 800-02.

WORKING WITH IASSEMBLIES

Many iAssemblies require only a few size variables and a few components that can be interchanged. Although in this example both the plate and buttons are iParts, often an iAssembly requires only a few components to be iParts for configuration.

It is typically best to tackle iAssemblies in a very structured manner, configuring only one part of the table at a time and then returning to the model to test that change. Making many changes in the table at once may make it difficult to determine how changes affect the model.

Once a couple of rows are added using the iAssembly Author interface, you can edit the table with Microsoft Excel to add many rows at once and quickly make changes to the column entries. Also in Excel, you can create formulas to concatenate column entries, calculate entries, or use if/thens to determine entries.

800-01 will have a check mark next to it informing you that this is the active member of the iAssembly. To set 800-02 as active, right-click it and choose Activate, or simply double-click it. Then double-click 800-01 to set it back as the active member of the table.

Now that you have used a different size plate, you will need to add another button to the assembly. To do this, simply select one of the existing instances, and use Copy and Paste to add a new instance. Next, place an Insert constraint between the new instance of the button and the empty hole on the plate, as shown in Figure 8.47.

FIGURE 8.47
Adding an Insert constraint

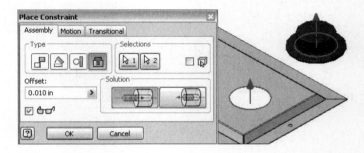

Once the new button is constrained, set 800-02 active again in the table tree, and notice that you are presented with an error message warning you that the new constraint is looking at geometry that is no longer present. Click Accept in the error dialog box, and notice the new button remains even though the hole it was constrained to is gone.

To address this, you need to edit the table further and configure the iAssembly to suppress the extra button when not needed. Do this by right-clicking the Table icon in the Model browser and choosing Edit Table. Locate part 802:2 in the tree as shown, and use the >> button to place Include/Exclude in the table as a column. Next set the value for this column to be Exclude for row 2, as shown in Figure 8.48. Click OK to return to the model, and activate both members to see that no constraint errors occur.

FIGURE 8.48
Exclude/include components in an iAssembly

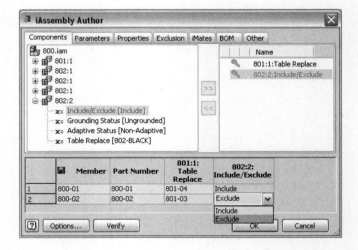

Next, you will change out the black buttons in member 800-01 to use a second green and a second red button. Edit the table, and choose the last two instances of part 802 (the button) from the tree in the top-left pane. Locate the Table Replace parameter for each, and use the >> button to include them in the table. Set the Table Replace values in row 1 to Red and Green, as shown in Figure 8.49. You do not need to change the values in row 2 because one of the buttons is already set to Black as required and the other as you recall you excluded so that it does not show in the row 2 configuration. Click OK to exit the table authoring dialog box and note the changes to configuration 800-01.

FIGURE 8.49
Table Replace in the iAssembly Author dialog box

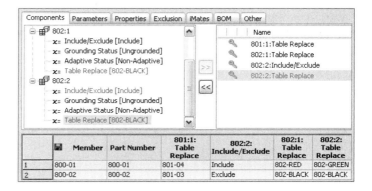

Lastly, let's set one of the buttons to be in a different position. Edit the table to return to the iAssembly Author dialog box again, and locate and activate the Parameters tab. Expand the Constraints folder, select Insert:1, and use the >> button to add it as a column in the table. Set the value of this column to 0.25 inch for row 1 of the configurations. Click OK to exit the dialog box, and notice the first button is shown pushed in because you have modified the constraint offset value.

The Bottom Line

Organize designs using structured subassemblies   Subassemblies add organization, facilitate the bill of materials, and reduce assembly constraints; all this results in better performance and easier edits. One of the habits of all Inventor experts is their effective use and understanding of subassemblies.

   Master It   You need to hand off an accurate BOM for finished designs to the purchasing department at the end of each design project.

Use positional reps and flexible assemblies together   Often you may need to show a design in various stages of motion to test interference and/or proof of concept. Copying assemblies so that you can change the assembly constraints to show different assembly positions becomes a file management nightmare. Instead, use flexible subassemblies and positional representations.

   Master It   You need to show your assembly in variations dependent upon the position of the moving parts and the task the machine is accomplishing at given stages of its operation.

Copy designs   Because of the live linked data that exists in Inventor assemblies, using Windows Explorer to copy designs and rename parts is difficult and often delivers poor results. Using the tool provided in Inventor will allow you to copy designs and maintain the links between files.

Master It   You need to duplicate an existing design in order to create a similar design.

Substitute a single part for entire subassemblies   Working with large assemblies, particularly where large, complex assemblies are used over and over as subassemblies within a top-level design, can tax most any workstation if not approached in the correct manner.

Master It   You would like to swap out a complex assembly for a simplified version for use in layout designs or to use in large assemblies in an attempt to improve performance.

Chapter 9

Large Assembly Strategies

Inventor 2009 makes working with large assemblies more manageable than ever before with fully native 64-bit support, removing the memory limitations related to the Windows XP 32-bit platform. Large assembly design on 32-bit systems is improved with Inventor 2009 using the new component substitution level of detail (LOD) representations. Substitute LODs allow you to swap out complex subassemblies with single substitute parts, all while maintaining model detail and an accurate bill of materials.

Although every design department may have a different view on what a large assembly is, everyone can benefit from the large assembly tools and strategies discussed in this chapter. Creating fully functional digital prototypes ranging from 10 to 100,000 components can be achieved if you approach the task with an eye to the topics covered here.

In this chapter, you'll learn how to:

◆ Select a workstation

◆ Adjust your performance settings

◆ Use best practices for large assembly

◆ Manage assembly detail

◆ Simplify parts

Selecting a Workstation

Ensuring that you have an adequate system to accomplish the type of design work you intend to do is an important, but often overlooked, step in achieving successful large assembly design with any parametric modeler. Understanding the capabilities and limitations of your computer and then budgeting for upgrades is an important part of working in today's design world.

If you consider the time you spend waiting and the loss of work experienced when working on an undersized computer, you will likely determine that a workstation upgrade will pay for itself within a year. If you budget for upgrades every two years, then you could argue that the upgrade is actually paying for itself in the second year of use. Although this scenario might not fit your actual situation, it demonstrates the idea that operating costs (hardware and software alike) should be budgeted and planned for and always measured against lost work and downtime.

Physical Memory vs. Virtual Memory

When your system runs low on physical memory (RAM) and requires more to complete an operation, Windows begins writing to the system hard drive in order to continue. This is known as *virtual memory* and is often referred to as a *page file*.

When considering a workstation for doing large assembly design, it should be your goal to always work in RAM as much as possible, because when Windows begins to write to virtual memory, you will notice a considerable drop in performance. One of the weakest links in terms of speed on even the most adequate workstation will be the hard drive. Accessing data from RAM can be thousands of times faster than accessing data from the hard drive. Therefore, one of the best ways to beef up a workstation is to simply add more RAM.

If you are running an older computer or skimped on RAM when you upgraded, you will notice that as you attempt to load large assemblies or drawing files of large assemblies in Inventor, you quickly use up available RAM. You will find yourself waiting for Windows to write and then read data to the hard drive. Although the unknowing user might think that Inventor has suddenly become slow, you should understand that no application can overcome the hardware and operating system limitations upon which it is installed.

If you run out of RAM on a 32-bit system, you have a limit of 4GB of virtual address space. Windows reserves 2GB of that space for the operating system by default, thereby leaving just 2GB for all the other running applications. If you work on extremely large assemblies, you might exceed the available 2GB of address space.

To resolve this, it is possible to configure Windows to reserve only 1GB of address space for the operating system and leave 3GB for the applications to use. This is referred to as "flipping the /3GB switch." Depending upon the size of the assemblies you work on, the configuration settings you adjust in Inventor, and the techniques you employ within Inventor, the extra 1GB of virtual memory might be adequate for your needs for those instances when you need a bit more memory. However, as stated earlier, it should be your goal not to be working in virtual memory but instead to always be working in RAM.

64-bit Systems vs. 32-bit Systems

The maximum amount of RAM that is supported on a Windows XP Professional 32-bit system is 4GB. If you determine that your needs currently exceed or will soon exceed the limits of a 32-bit system, you should consider a 64-bit workstation; 64-bit systems can handle up to 128GB of RAM and are faster because of the ability to handle twice as much data with each clock cycle.

Most processors purchased by the time this book is published will be 64-bit. Understand that you must also run a 64-bit operating system, such as Windows XP Professional 64 or Windows Vista, in order to gain the performance increases attributed to a 64-bit system. Although Inventor 2008 was compiled to run on a 64-bit operating system, Inventor 2009 is the first fully native 64-bit version. And therefore it's the first version of Inventor to take full advantage of a 64-bit system.

Hardware

Hardware upgrades are an important part of any design department. Budgeting properly and knowing what components to allocate more money on can make these upgrades more manageable. Dollar for dollar, you should give priority to the following components in the order listed.

RAM

Although the minimum system requirement for Inventor 2009 is 1GB, you should always consider adding as much RAM as you can afford to your workstation. If making the move to a 64-bit system, you will require a minimum of 4GB of RAM, and you should consider at least 8GB.

GRAPHICS CARDS

To ensure that your graphics card is set at the optimal settings, select Tools ➢ Application Options and go to the Hardware tab. Direct3D graphics hardware is the default setting for Windows XP Professional 32- and 64-bit versions as well as Windows Vista 32- and 64-bit versions.

Inventor 2009 will use either OpenGL or the default DirectX 9 hardware acceleration modes when running Windows XP. Windows XP 64 uses DirectX 9 only. Windows Vista 32 and 64 support DirectX 9 and 10. Inventor will automatically detect the appropriate level for your card. All configurations have OpenGL software emulation.

It is recommended that you consider a midrange graphics card for an Inventor workstation and save the money for frequent upgrades rather than investing in a high-end card, because of the rapid changes in video card technology. For recommendations on graphics cards and other hardware, refer to the following websites:

Autodesk Inventor hardware

www.inventor-certified.com/graphics/

Certified workstations

www.inventor-certified.com/graphics/cert_ws.php

Autodesk Inventor hardware graphics database

www.inventor-certified.com/graphics/registries.php

HARD DRIVES

In Inventor, working from your local drive is the preferred method, and Autodesk recommends you avoid working on Inventor files across a network. Autodesk Vault is set up to store files on a server and copy those files locally when checked out for editing. When working in this manner, Inventor has a higher-performance requirement than standard office applications, and the hard drive workload is very heavy. Therefore, upgrading your hard drive to a higher-speed SATA or serial attached SCSI (SAS) type drive may be worth considering.

PROCESSORS

When considering processors for an Inventor 2009 workstation, the chief question should concern multicore processors. As a minimum, you should consider a dual-core processor even though Inventor is not truly a multithreaded application. *Multithreaded* means that the operating system or the application will spread the processing load across the processor. If you opt for a dual-core processor, you can still take advantage of it, because Inventor will run on one core and other applications will run on the other.

There are parts of Inventor, such as Inventor Studio's rendering engine, that are multithreaded, so if you plan to do a lot of image and animation rendering in Inventor, you may want to opt for a quad-core processor. Otherwise, if you are trying to decide between a dual-core and quad-core processor, it will probably be more cost effective to go with a faster dual-core processor rather than a quad-core processor. This will likely change as the rapid pace of technology continues.

SEAN SAYS: CALCULATE THE ROI OF NEW HARDWARE

It's often hard to convince management (especially nontechnical managers) that you really do need that new computer to get your job done. After all, you're currently getting your work done, right? So why do you need the faster computer? This is where a return on investment (ROI) calculation will come in handy.

Let's say you routinely have to open, modify, and print large assembly drawings. Measure how long it takes to do this process on your old machine. Next, look at some benchmarks or talk to others who have faster machines, and make a conservative estimate at how long it would take you to do the same operations on the faster machine. Subtract the two. You now have your timesavings per operation.

Next, multiply this time by the number of times in a day or week you perform these tasks. Then multiply it by an hourly rate for your industry (you can always use your hourly salary) to get the dollar savings per time period (per week, month, and so on). Now you can take the cost of the new system and divide it by this cost savings per unit of time. This gives you the amount of time it will take to pay off that new computer.

Furthermore, once this time period has passed, you are actually *making* money because you are saving the company money once the investment has been paid off. Once you can show that the hardware will pay for itself relatively quickly, you should have fewer problems convincing management to upgrade your equipment.

Working with Performance Settings

Whether or not upgrading workstations is an option, you should ensure that your system is set up for optimal performance when working with large assemblies. A number of options in Inventor will facilitate better performance when working with large assemblies.

Working with Drawing Settings

Generating and hiding lines when creating and editing drawing views in Inventor can be some of the most processor-intensive tasks in Inventor. To help ease the demand on the system, you should be aware of several setting when working with large assembly drawings. You can find these settings by selecting Tools ➤ Application Options and going to the Drawing tab, as shown in Figure 9.1.

FIGURE 9.1
Drawing application options

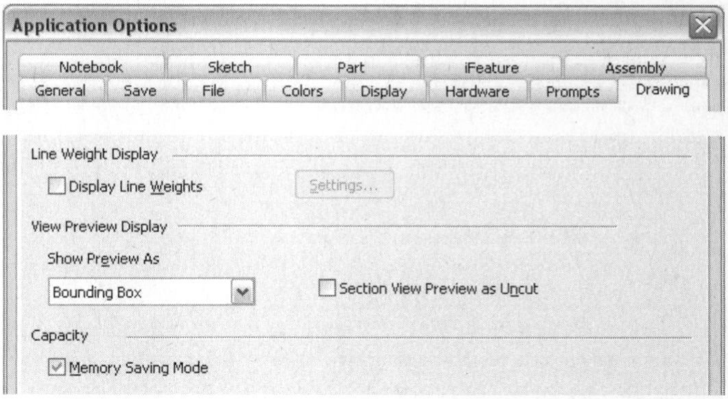

DISPLAY LINE WEIGHTS

The Display Line Weights check box enables or disables the display of unique line weights in drawings. Uncheck the box to show lines without weight differences. Line weights will still print correctly even with this box checked. Unchecking this box will speed up the performance of your drawing during edits and annotation work.

VIEW PREVIEW DISPLAY

The options in the Show Preview As pulldown box set the type of preview you get when creating a view. All Components is the default, but you will find that selecting the Partial or Bounding

Box option will improve performance because Inventor will not be required to create and update the preview as you drag your mouse around the screen. The Preview setting does not affect the drawing view result. Bounding Box previews a simple rectangle during the view creation, and Partial previews a simplified representation of the view. Bounding Box is the most efficient.

The Section View Preview As Uncut check box will also provide some performance improvements when checked. This option will allow Inventor to display the section view preview as unsectioned in order to be more efficient. The section view will still be generated as normal.

MEMORY SAVINGS MODE

Memory Saving Mode sets the way that Inventor loads components into memory during view creation. When this option is turned on, Inventor loads components into memory before and during view creation and then unloads them from memory once the view is created.

Although memory is conserved using this mode, view creation and editing operations cannot be undone while this option is enabled. You'll notice the Undo/Redo buttons will be grayed out after a view creation or edit. This option will also have a negative impact on performance when editing and creating views because the components must be loaded into memory each time. Because of this, you should consider setting this option as an application setting only if you always work with very large assemblies.

It is generally preferred to set this option per document by selecting Tools ➢ Documents Settings and going to the Drawing tab, and then setting the dropdown to Always, as shown in Figure 9.2.

FIGURE 9.2
Drawing document settings

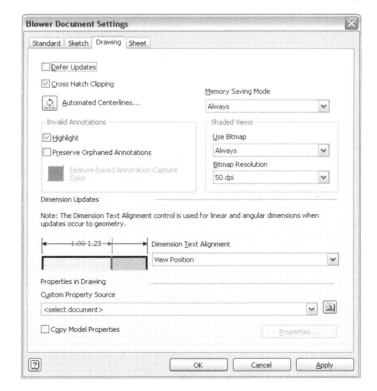

SHADED VIEWS

Also in the document settings, you can adjust the way that shaded views are displayed. Setting the Use Bitmap pulldown to Always as shown in Figure 9.2 improves performance by applying raster shading as opposed to a vector style. The difference impacts the display but typically does affect printing.

You can also adjust the bitmap resolution; setting it lower conserves memory and speeds up performance. The default is 100 dpi. Setting the dpi to 200 or higher will invoke a prompt, warning you that increasing this setting for large assemblies may not be possible.

Working with Model Display Settings

When working within the modeling environment, you can adjust several settings to have a positive impact on performance. You can access these settings by selecting Tools ➤ Application Options and going to the Display tab, as shown in Figure 9.3.

FIGURE 9.3
Display application options

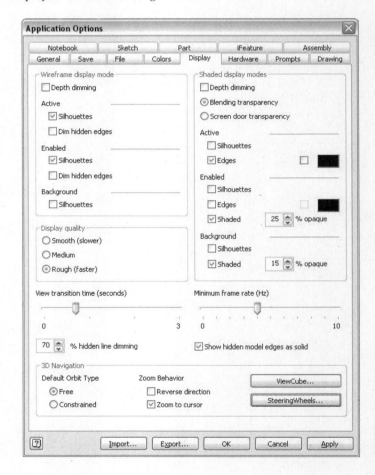

EDGE DISPLAY

Clearing the check box for edges for Enabled components in the Shaded Display Modes area of the Display tab will lighten the amount of graphics rendering required to display and update the display of your large assemblies.

DISPLAY QUALITY

Setting the Display Quality setting to Rough as shown in Figure 9.3 will speed up performance by simplifying details. Navigation commands such as zooming, panning, and orbiting are particularly affected by this setting. If you find that the rough display is not to your liking, you can toggle back and forth according to the size of the assembly model you are working with.

Working with General Settings

The following are a few general settings that can be adjusted to help large assembly performance. You can access these settings by selecting Tools ➤ Application Options and going to the General tab, as shown in Figure 9.4.

FIGURE 9.4
Default application options

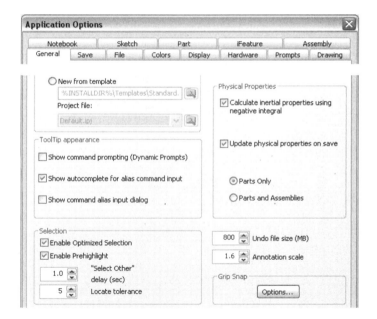

ENABLE OPTIMIZED SELECTION

This setting improves the performance of graphics during prehighlighting in large assemblies. When activated, the algorithm for the Select Other function filters for only the group of objects closest to the screen. If you click through this first group of objects, the next group is considered for highlighting.

UPDATE PHYSICAL PROPERTIES ON SAVE

When checked, this setting recalculates the mass properties of the model when you save the file. This ensures that mass properties are up-to-date. Setting this to Parts Only will ensure that the parts are all up-to-date without requiring you to wait on the recalculation for large assemblies. Note that this setting is disabled altogether by default but is recommended to be set to Parts Only if you find it helpful. Note too that the same function can be performed manually from the Bill Of Materials Editor and the Tools menu.

UNDO FILE SIZE

This option sets the maximum size of the temporary file that records changes to a file so that actions can be undone. It's typically required to increase the size of this setting when working with large models and drawings, because each undo action is typically a larger calculation. Autodesk recommends adjusting this in 4MB increments.

CAPACITY METER

The Capacity Meter is displayed at the bottom-right corner of the Inventor screen, as shown in Figure 9.5. The meter has three memory use indicators. The number to the left is the total number of occurrences in the active document. The next number is the total number of files open in the Inventor session. The last indicator is a colored bar graph that displays the amount of memory used by the session. When hovering over the Capacity Meter, a tool tip will display the details of used and available memory. In 32-bit systems, the meter can be used in two modes: Inventor Only and Physical Memory. In 64-bit systems, the Inventor Only mode is not available.

FIGURE 9.5
Capacity Meter in Inventor Only mode

| 6322 | 443 |

INVENTOR ONLY

In this mode, the display is set to look at just the Autodesk Inventor process. The bar color will change from the normal green to yellow when more than 60 percent of the allotted address space has been used. It will then turn red at 80 percent and prompt you to close documents in an attempt to free up memory, as shown in Figure 9.6.

FIGURE 9.6
Warning received at 80 percent capacity

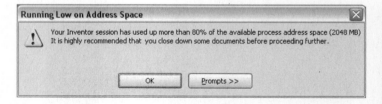

As a rule, you should not habitually work when the meter indicates that you have passed the 60 percent mark. When you do see the bar turn yellow, you should stop and create an LOD representation or close some files.

PHYSICAL MEMORY

In the Physical Memory mode, the display indicates the entire system's RAM. The green portion represents the Inventor session, while the yellow portion is all other applications. This mode is disabled if you do not have administrative rights on your workstation or if process monitors have been restricted on your system.

You can switch the modes or turn the Capacity Meter on and off by selecting Tools ➢ Customize and then going to the Toolbars tab. In the lower-right corner, select the Capacity Meter check box.

Working with System Settings

You can adjust several settings in the operating system to help with performance. Setting the page file to twice the amount of RAM is common among Inventor users in order to gain performance. There are also many visual effects that you may have grown accustomed to that actually cost you resources. If you are serious about turning your workstation into a large assembly workhorse, it is advisable to disable these features.

ADJUSTING THE VIRTUAL MEMORY PAGING FILE SIZE

To change the size of the virtual memory paging file in Windows XP Professional, right-click the My Computer icon, and choose Properties. On the System Properties tab, click the Advanced tab, then click Performance Options, and finally under Virtual Memory click Change.

In Windows Vista, right-click the Computer icon, and choose Properties. On the System Properties tab, click the Advanced System Settings tab, then click Performance Options, and finally under Virtual Memory uncheck Automatically Manage Paging File Size For All Drives. Then click Change.

Select Custom Size, set both the Initial Size and the Maximum Size to twice the available RAM, and click Set, as shown in Figure 9.7.

FIGURE 9.7
Setting the page file size in XP

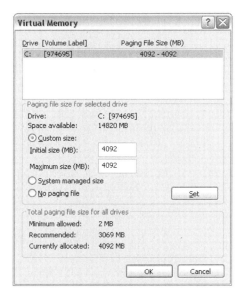

DISABLING COMMON VISUAL EFFECTS

Windows provides many options to set the visual effects of your computer. Many of them have a surprisingly high impact on performance when memory is scarce. Here are a few you might consider disabling in order to conserve resources:

◆ **Screen saver:** Select Control Panel ➤ Display and go to the Screen Saver tab. Set the Screen Saver pulldown to None. While you are working, screen savers are just another running process. You may want to set the Power Saving Mode option to turn off the monitor after a certain amount of time. If you use an LCD monitor, understand that screen savers do nothing to save an LCD screen.

◆ **Visual settings:** Right-click the My Computer icon, and select Properties. Go to the Advanced tab, and click the Settings button under Performance. Select Adjust For Best Performance. Windows will set back to a classic look and run much faster overall.

◆ **Appearance effects:** Select Control Panel ➤ Display and then go to the Appearance tab. Click the Effects button. You can uncheck everything in this box and probably never miss any of it.

◆ **Screen resolution:** If you're fortunate enough to have a nice, large-screen monitor, you probably have set the screen resolution up to maximize your space. However, this may be working against your large assembly pursuits. Experiment with setting the screen resolution back down to a lower setting such as 1024 × 768 to see whether you gain any performance when working with large assemblies.

Large Assembly Best Practices

Oftentimes Inventor users don't think about large assembly performance until it has already become an issue with the model they are working on. It is possible for two Inventor users working on two identical workstations to create two seemingly identical models, and yet those two models might perform in dramatically different ways.

If the first user has been mindful of large assembly management all along, his model and drawings will be much easier to open and work with. If the second user concentrated only on her design and gave no thought to the memory demands of the files she was creating, her model will be slow to open and work with and ultimately more likely to cause application crashes and data corruption. When the next job comes along, user 1 can reuse his model to create a similar design, while user 2 will likely re-create the assembly model because she does not trust the integrity of the first model she created.

Understanding where performance savings can be gained as you create the model will help pay off once the large assembly is created and will make it much more manageable to work with along the way. And of course, a large assembly model can be revisited and cleaned up according to best practices to make it more manageable as well. Either way, having a model that is manageable and can be reused for similar work in the future should always be your goal.

There are three stages at which you should be considering large assembly performance: creating and editing the model, opening the model, and detailing and annotating the model.

Working with the Model

You can use several methods to ensure that your large assembly will not become unmanageable. It is important to remember that the words *large assembly* are subjective. To you, a large assembly may be 200 components, whereas to someone else it may be 20,000. Either way, following best practices ensures that you are developing good procedural habits and that you are prepared for the day when you are asked to design a much larger assembly than you typically do today.

As was discussed earlier in this chapter, hardware limitations might be an obstacle that you cannot overcome even if you follow every best practice, but you'll need to follow these practices to know that for certain. Conversely, even if you have a workstation that is extremely capable, you will still benefit by developing good work habits and making your models easier to handle on less capable workstations of others you collaborate with.

Reducing Assembly Constraints

In Chapter 8, you learned about the use of subassemblies within upper-level assemblies to reduce assembly constraints. The importance of this concept cannot be overstated. Reducing assembly constraints can eliminate the number of redundant calculations Inventor must make to solve your model, and therefore it pays off immediately in that respect. The increased organization and ability to reuse components already organized into subassemblies is a benefit that may be realized in future.

To reorganize an assembly that has not been created using subassemblies, you can use the Demote option. To explore this concept, open the file called `Demote_Stapler.iam` found in the Mastering Inventor folder. Although not a large assembly by anyone's standard, this assembly has been created without using subassemblies to demonstrate the ability to demote components into subassemblies from the top down.

Your goal is to restructure this assembly into three subassemblies so that you can reduce constraints and create subassemblies that can be used in other stapler designs. From the Model Browser, select all the components with a prefix of 100. Once you've selected those components, right-click, choose Component, and then choose Demote, as shown in Figure 9.8.

FIGURE 9.8
Demoting components
to a subassembly

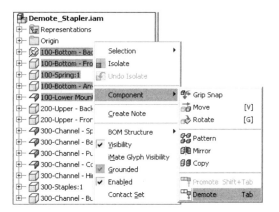

You will be presented with a Create In-Place Component dialog box, where you can specify the name of the subassembly, the template file, the file location, and the default BOM structure. Enter **100** for the name, and click OK. You will now be prompted with a warning stating that assembly constraints, features, and notes may be deleted if you restructure these components, as shown in Figure 9.9.

Although this warning may seem ominous, it is actually a good thing. Consider the five components you selected to demote in the stapler. If these components all had just one assembly constraint each relating it to some part that will not be in the new subassembly, then those five constraints will be discarded. In essence, this warning is telling you that it is cleaning up constraints that you no longer need. To do this, click OK in the warning dialog box.

FIGURE 9.9
Restructuring
components'
warning

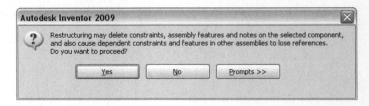

You should now see the subassembly named `100_stapler.iam` in the Model Browser. Right-click this component, and click Grounded to set it in place. Continue to demote the components prefixed with a 200 and 300 into subassemblies of the corresponding name, just as you did with the 100 prefixed components. When finished, your browser should look like Figure 9.10.

FIGURE 9.10
Subassemblies created
by demoting

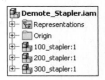

You will note the 200_stapler and 300_stapler subassemblies are ungrounded, because you have discarded all the constraints that may have related the parts between our new subassemblies together. In this case, the number of discarded constraints was about a dozen, and you can replace those with just three.

You can use insert constraints to reconstrain the subassemblies if you'd like. Note that there are three sets of color-coded faces to help you place the three required insert constraints. The green constraint set will require you to flip the insert and use the aligned solution.

Components may be restructured by dragging a component within the assembly browser from in and out of a subassembly. Moving components up out of a subassembly is called *promoting* rather than demoting. It is also important to understand that when you demote and promote components, you may need to edit the subassembly and ensure that components are constrained properly within that subassembly.

ADAPTIVITY

Too many cross-part adaptive features can cripple the performance of even a modest-sized assembly if used without discretion. As discussed in Chapter 8, adaptivity should generally be turned off once the adaptive feature or part is created.

Often features and parts are made adaptive during the early design stages of a model, when changes are made quickly and you want many parts to follow these changes. Turning off the adaptive status in the part ensures that your assembly performance will not be affected. If the adaptive part needs to be edited, you can turn on its adaptive status so that you can make adjustments.

SELECTION TOOLS

When working with a large assembly, combing through all the many parts within that assembly that you want to select for a given task can be time-consuming and difficult if you attempt to locate them using the standard Pan, Zoom, and Orbit methods. Instead, make yourself familiar with the options in the assembly Selection tool.

You can use Selection tools to suppress sets of components based on such factors as size or on internal components that are not visible because of the presence of external housings, and so on. For instance, to maintain performance, you may not want to load all the internal components into memory when they are not important to your current design task. Once you've selected the internal components, you can suppress them and create an external part-only LOD representation.

Another use of assembly Selection tools is to create view representations in the assembly to aid in the creation of views in the drawing file. As an example, when you place a view in the drawing using a design view that was created using the All In Camera tool, only the components in the screen view plane are calculated. This increases performance and memory capacity. Figure 9.11 shows the available Selection tools.

FIGURE 9.11

Available selection tools

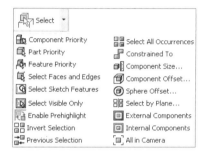

The following are the Selection tools:

◆ **Component Priority:** Sets the selection to pick up the topmost structure level of components. If set, this will pick up subassemblies and not their children.

◆ **Part Priority:** Sets the tool to select parts no matter their subassembly structure.

◆ **Feature Priority:** Selects individual features rather the parts that contain them.

◆ **Select Faces And Edges:** Allows you to highlight and select faces or the curves that define those faces.

◆ **Select Sketch Features:** Allows you to highlight and select sketches or the curves that define those sketches.

◆ **Select Visible Only:** Selects only visible components in a selection set.

◆ **Enable Pre-highlight:** Displays prehighlighting when your cursor moves over an object. This does not affect the Select Other tool, which always shows prehighlighting.

◆ **Select All Occurrences:** Selects all instances in the current file of the selected component.

◆ **Constrained To:** Selects all components constrained to a preselected component or components.

◆ **Component Size:** Selects components by the percent set in the Select By Size box. Size is determined by the diagonal of the bounding box of the components. Click the arrow to select a component and measure its size to use as a scale. Figure 9.12 shows the Component Size Selection tool.

FIGURE 9.12
Select By Size box

◆ **Component Offset:** Selects components fully or partially contained within the bounding box of a selected components plus a specified offset distance.

◆ **Sphere Offset:** Selects components fully or partially contained within the bounding sphere of a selected components plus a specified offset distance.

◆ **Select By Plane:** Selects components fully or partially intersected by a specified face or plane.

◆ **External Components:** Selects external components based on a percentage of the component's viewable surface.

◆ **Internal Components:** Selects internal components based on a percentage of the component's viewable surface.

◆ **All In Camera:** Selects all components in the current view screen based upon a percentage of the component's viewable surface.

SEAN SAYS: USE THE FEATURE SELECTION FILTER TO SELECT WORK PLANES

It can be a major pain to try to select a work plane while in a busy assembly file. To make it easier, use the Feature Selection filter as explained. Your cursor will no longer select parts but only features, making it easy to select even the most obscured work planes.

VIEW REPRESENTATIONS

View representations are often used in large assemblies to navigate to a predefined viewing angle so that you do not have to tax your system with heavy graphics regeneration. For instance, if you have an assembly that contains an entire production line of material-handling equipment, you may find it difficult to orbit around to the backside of the assembly in order to complete a simple task such as selecting a face or just looking at the assembly. If you set a design view before orbiting and then set another once you have orbited to the desired view, you can then easily toggle between the two views of this assembly, thereby increasing performance during navigation between these predefined views.

View representations have other large assembly benefits as well. When creating a drawing view of a large assembly, you can specify a preset view representation and reduce the time it takes to create the drawing view. If you have turned the visibility of some components off in the assembly view representation, the drawing view can generate even faster and provide you with a clearer and more concise view. Of course, if you already have the assembly open when creating the drawing view, the components are likely already loaded into memory.

Another way that the experienced Inventor user may use view representation is to navigate the Model Browser. For instance, if you set up a view representation to zoom in on a particular subassembly so that you can navigate to that component quickly, you can save that view representation while the entire model tree is rolled up and only the subassembly of interest is expanded. This browser state will be saved within the view representation.

Once a view representation is created, you can right-click it and choose Copy To Level of Detail to copy the view representation to an LOD representation. This allows you to transfer the visibility settings from the view representation to the LOD where they will be suppressed. In this way, you do not have to duplicate the process of turning parts off.

FIND

Navigating a large assembly Model Browser can be a chore. To help with this, you can employ the Find tool to define search criteria for constraints, components, features, sketches, and welds. When searching the model, all components that contain searched objects are expanded in the browser to make selections more visible. Searches can be saved for future use and recalled as needed using the Open Search button, as shown in Figure 9.13.

FIGURE 9.13
The Find tool in an assembly file

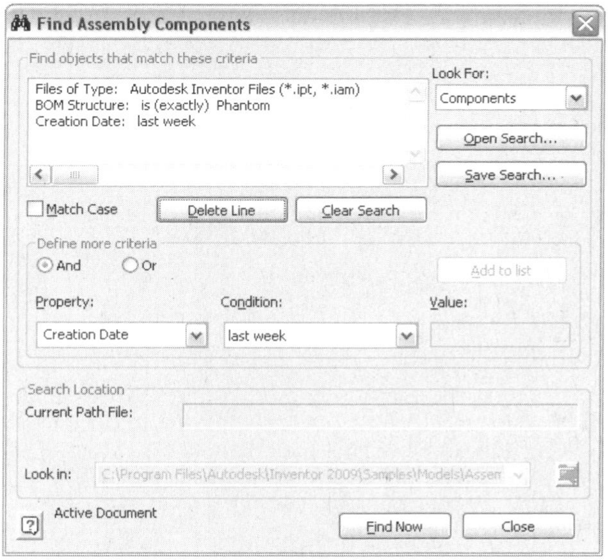

You can access the Find tool in the following ways:

◆ From within a file, click the binoculars icon in the Model Browser.

◆ In the Inventor Open dialog box, click the Find button.

Opening the Model

One of the most important aspects of working on a large assembly file is being able to open the file. Although this seems an obvious statement, many Inventor users seem to approach opening a model as an afterthought. Consider it in this way — if you were tasked with carrying a pile of stones up a flight of stairs, you would probably be unlikely to attempt to carry them all up the stairs at once. But this is exactly the kind of heavy lifting you are asking your workstation to do when opening a large assembly.

To allow your workstation to make multiple trips when opening an assembly file, you will use LOD representations. As you might recall from Chapter 8, you create LOD representations by suppressing components in an assembly. Once the LOD is created, you can access it the next time you begin to open the file by using the Options button, as shown in Figure 9.14. Once the assembly file is open, you can unsuppress components as required, and those components will then be loaded into memory. We'll cover more about creating LODs later in this chapter.

FIGURE 9.14
Opening LODs

LOD IN SUBASSEMBLIES

Often you might create a complex assembly model as a stand-alone design because you need to insert that model into an upper-level assembly as part of a larger system. Because the original design was required to generate production drawings and an accurate BOM, it includes all the components in the design.

However, because you will be placing multiple instances of this subassembly, you want to avoid placing it at the full level of detail. You might create a LOD in the subassembly where all internal components, all external hardware, and all internal and external fasteners are suppressed, leaving only the external housing and frame components.

LOD representations of subassemblies can be accessed from the Options button in the Place Component dialog box when placing them into upper-level assemblies. By placing a subassembly at a reduced level of detail, you have created a much smaller top-level assembly file and yet still have the ability to pull an accurate BOM even from the top-level assembly.

Working with Large Assembly Drawings

Not only do large assembly files require some forethought and management, but so do the drawing files of these large assemblies. Because Inventor generates the line work from the models that you create views from automatically, it is easy take the large number of calculations required to do this for granted. Stop for a moment and consider all the hidden lines, sectioned parts, and so on, that Inventor has to consider in order to render your drawing views accurately.

It is for this reason that you will want to adopt slightly differently techniques than those you use to make part or small assembly drawings.

CREATING LARGE ASSEMBLY DRAWING VIEWS

When creating drawing of large assemblies, it is advised that you do so from an LOD representation already created in the model. Doing so reduces the number of files Inventor is required to access to create and update the line work in the view. To create views from assembly representations, you simply specify the representation(s) you want to use in the Drawing View dialog box, as shown in Figure 9.15. Keep in mind that when browsing for the file to create a view of, if you use the Options button in the Open dialog box to specify the representation, you will reduce the time it takes to create the view preview.

FIGURE 9.15
Creating a drawing view from an LOD

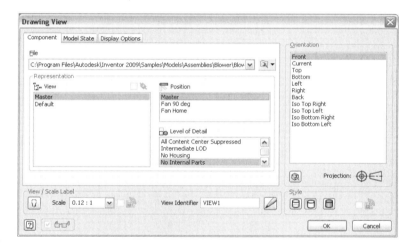

REDUCING HIDDEN LINES

Hidden line generation can be one of the most memory-intensive aspects of creating a drawing view. Generally, with large assemblies, it is not desirable to show the hidden lines of all components. Instead, you typically will want to enable hidden lines for just those components where hidden lines add clarity.

Rather than selecting the Hidden Line style in the Drawing View dialog box, first create the view with no hidden lines. Next locate and expand the view you just created in the browser, and select the components you intend to be shown with hidden lines. Right-click the components, and choose Hidden Lines.

You will be prompted with a message box informing you that you are changing the view style to show hidden lines and that any children of this view will be granted an independent view style based upon their current setting, as shown in Figure 9.16. The result will be that only the components you chose will be displayed with hidden lines.

FIGURE 9.16
Managing hidden lines

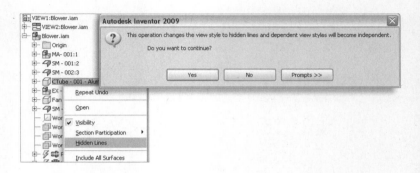

CREATING TITLE BLOCK LOGOS

A sure way to slow down your drawing's performance is to create an unnecessarily complex title block. If you have included a bitmap of your company logo in your title bock, ensure that the bitmap file is reduced in resolution and file size as much as possible. You can use any photo editor to do this.

Once you've reduced the bitmap file as much as possible, consider embedding the file into the title block rather than linking it. Although linking the bitmap does give you greater flexibility in updating the logo independent of the title block, Inventor will be required to locate the bitmap each time the drawing is loaded. To embed rather than link the logo bitmap, simply uncheck the Link check box when inserting the bitmap.

If you have pasted the logo in from AutoCAD, ensure that the logo is as clean as possible. You may be better off removing the hatches from the logo in AutoCAD and then adding them using the Fill/Hatch Sketch Region tool in Inventor.

REDUCING THE NUMBER OF SHEETS AND VIEWS PER DRAWING FILE

Although it is possible to create a large number of sheets in a single drawing file, it is generally accepted that this is not good practice. Instead, you should consider making a new file for each drawing sheet when possible. Or at the very least, keep the number of sheets per file as low as possible. There are two primary reasons for doing this.

The first reason is simply to keep the file size down. If you have a drawing of a large assembly file that includes four sheets and has a file size of 80MB, you could spilt this into two files, each with two sheets and a file size of approximately 40MB. In this way, you do not have to load the extra 40MB in sheet 3 and 4, just to make an edit to sheet 1.

The second reason to minimize drawing sheets is so you are not guilty of placing "all your eggs in one basket." Creating multiple tab or sheet files in any application can be risky. Imagine you created a load calculation spreadsheet and you developed the habit of adding a tab for each new calculation you do, rather than creating a new file for each calculation. If the file becomes corrupt, you've lost all your calculations rather than just one set of calculations. The same thing could happen with your Inventor drawing if you habitually create new sheets instead of new files.

Managing Assembly Detail

In Chapter 8, you learned about creating LOD representations within your assemblies in order to reduce the memory requirements of working with large assemblies. Here you will consider how using these LOD representations can be implemented to make you more successful in your large assembly pursuits.

Level Of Detail Strategies

All Inventor assemblies have four default LODs predefined and ready for you to use. These are Master, All Components Suppressed, All Parts Suppressed, and All Content Center Suppressed. Mastering the use of these and creating your own LODs is an important part of working with large assemblies.

The Master LOD will show your assembly with no parts suppressed. You can think of this as the highest level of detail for any assembly. The All Components Suppressed representation suppresses everything within the assembly, and you can think of it as the lowest level of detail for any assembly. The All Parts Suppressed representation suppresses all parts at all levels of the assembly, but subassemblies are loaded. And the final default LOD, All Content Center Suppressed, suppresses any component in the assembly that is stored in the Content Center Files directory as designated by the IPJ (project) file.

When opening a large assembly, you can use the All Components Suppressed LOD to quickly open the file and then manually unsuppress components as required. However, it is more practical to create your own LODs and use them to efficiently open your assemblies. Consider creating intermediate LODs based upon your design process.

For a closer look, open the assembly file called `Blower_LOD.aim` found in the Mastering Inventor folder. Expand the Representations folder browser to display the Level of Detail folder. Right-click the Level of Detail header, and choose New Level Of Detail. Rename LevelofDetail1 to MediumLOD.

Use the Selection Tool pulldown to set your selection focus to Component Priority if it is not already; then use the same pulldown and choose Internal Components, as shown in Figure 9.17. Next, set the slider to 88 percent, and finally click the green check mark.

FIGURE 9.17
Selecting internal components

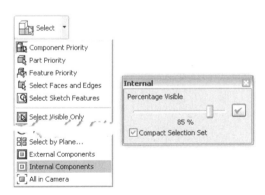

Right-click anywhere onscreen, and choose Isolate to get a better view of the components you selected. Your screen should look similar to Figure 9.18.

Next locate and select the components called MA- 001:1 in the browser, and then right-click and choose Visibility. You should see the motor subassembly become visible. Select all the components onscreen (you can use a crossing window to do this quickly), then right-click, and finally choose Suppress. Right-click anywhere, and choose Undo Isolate to bring back the visibility of the remaining components.

FIGURE 9.18
Isolated internal
components

Now that you have selected and suppressed the correct parts, save the assembly to ensure that the changes to your newly created level of detail are recorded. You can switch back and forth between the master LOD and your MediumLOD to observe the differences. To modify the MediumLOD, activate it and suppress any component you'd like; then save the assembly.

Substitution Level Of Details

Inventor 2009 introduces substitute LOD representations that allow you to trade out a large multipart assembly with a single part derived from that assembly. Substitute LODs improve efficiency by reducing the number of files Inventor is referencing and, if created from other LODs, can also reduce the amount of geometry required.

For example, in the blower assembly, you could create a substitute LOD from the entire assembly and then place that substitute into a top-level assembly as needed. You would certainly gain some efficiency by doing this because the top-level assembly is referencing only one file. However, if you created a substitute from another LOD with some complex components suppressed, you would be maintaining an even higher level of performance in the top-level assembly.

To create a substitute LOD, open the file called `Blower_LOD2.iam` from the Mastering Inventor folder. Expand the Representations folder browser to display the Level of Detail folder. Right-click the Level of Detail header, and choose New Substitute and then Derive Assembly. Notice that Inventor is asking you to specify a filename, a file template, and a location to create this file. Enter **Blower_LOD2_Substitute_1** in the New Derived Substitute Part dialog box, and leave the template and file location at the defaults. Then click OK.

Inventor will then open a new part file and take you directly into the derived assembly process. In the Derived Assembly dialog box, click the Representation tab, and select SimplifiedLOD from the Level Of Detail pulldown. Ensure that Reduced Memory Mode is selected at the bottom of the dialog box, as shown in Figure 9.19. When selected, this option allows the derived part to be created using less memory. This is done by excluding source bodies from the memory cache, and no component source bodies appear in the browser.

FIGURE 9.19
Deriving a substitute LOD

Click OK to continue. Inventor will save the derived part and return you to the blower assembly. If you examine the browser, you will notice the assembly now contains just the single substitute part, derived from the assembly. You will also notice that a new LOD, called SubstituteLevelofDetail1, has been created in the LOD representations tree, as shown in Figure 9.20. You can rename this to something of your choosing.

FIGURE 9.20
Substitute LOD

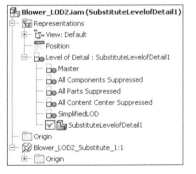

Recall that all LODs maintain an accurate BOM listing. To confirm this, select Tools ➤ Bill Of Materials and interrogate the BOM to see that even though the substitute LOD consists of a single part, Inventor still maintains the BOM information for the entire assembly.

Subassembly Level of Details

Subassembly use is where LOD representations really begin to pay off in terms of performance. Once LOD representations have been created in your assembly, you can then either place them into a top-level assembly by using the Options button or, once placed, switch the LOD in the subassembly from the Model Browser.

Creating a standard naming scheme for LODs is helpful when working with subassembly LODs. For instance, if you create all your assemblies with LODs named High, Moderate, and Low to denote the amount of detail in each LOD representation, then you can easily go through and set all these assemblies to use the matching LOD standard when placed as subassemblies.

SEAN SAYS: USE LOD NAMING CONVENTIONS

There are an infinite number of naming conventions for LODs including the one suggested here (High, Moderate, and Low). In my experience, I have also found that making LODS that have certain parts of the design turned on can be useful as well. Examples of names of LODs that I use include Frame Only, Frame & Transmission, Transmission Only, Conveyors Off, No Robots, and so on. By giving them descriptive names, users can select the appropriate LOD for the work they need to complete.

In Figure 9.21, all the subassemblies have LODs named High, Moderate, and Low set up within them. Then within each nested level, you can quickly set the LOD to correspond to the level above it. Once these are set up, you can switch all the subassemblies by changing the LOD in the uppermost level of detail. The LOD name is set in parentheses next to the assembly name.

FIGURE 9.21
Nested LODs with a consistent naming scheme

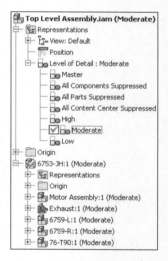

You might take this concept one step further and edit your assembly templates to automatically have High, Moderate, and Low LODs already in them. This way you do not have to create the LODs, but instead you can simply activate them and then suppress parts as required to "fill them out."

Recall that Inventor specifies your template location on the File tab of the Application Options dialog box. Note that this can be overridden in your project file. Check this by selecting File ➤ Projects, and look in the Folder Options section of the Project File Editor. If a path is specified there, that is where your templates are located. If it shows = Default, then the path found in Application Options is where your templates are located.

Simplifying Parts

Albert Einstein once suggested that things be made as simple as possible, but not simpler. This is a good concept to keep in mind when creating models in Inventor. Adding extraneous details to common parts can have a negative impact on large assembly performance. Of course, if the part file is to be used for fabrication, then a certain level of detail is required. Oftentimes, though, we create models of common parts to be used in an assembly for the end goal of getting an accurate bill of materials. Your assembly performance could most likely be improved by reducing the amount of detail in those types of parts.

Removing or Suppressing Unneeded Features

Reducing the number of edges and faces in a part is a sure way to minimize the size of the part file. Removing fillet and chamfers for purchased parts is good way to eliminate extra faces. If you have common parts that are used in large numbers throughout your assemblies, you might consider creating two versions of these parts: one version for use in large assemblies and another from which you create production drawings and Inventor Studio rendering. In Figure 9.22, you can see two versions of the same part. The file on the left is more than 900 KB, whereas the one the right is less than 200 KB.

FIGURE 9.22
A simplified part

Use Save As to create a simplified version from the original. Then edit the iProperties and set the part number property to be the same as the original. Then suppress or delete as much detail as is practical. To help manage these dual files, you can link the simplified model to the detailed version, making it easy to locate for edits. You can do this by opening the detailed version and selecting Insert ➤ Object ➤ Create From File; then browse to and select the simplified part file. Select the Link check box, and then click OK.

You will see a listing in the Model Browser called 3rd Party. Expanding this will be an embedded link to the other part file. You can click this and then Edit to open it, as shown in Figure 9.23.

FIGURE 9.23
Creating and using a link to a simplified IPT file

Working with Colors

Adding a reflective color to a part can increase the file size as well; therefore, you should consider using a flat color for simplified parts you intend to use over and over again in large assemblies. It is good practice to purge all unused color style definitions for common parts as well. Each time you change a material or color in a part file, the style definitions are cached in the file. If the file is used many times in an assembly, the unused definitions can have an impact on memory. To purge unused style definitions, select Format ➤ Purge Styles.

SEAN SAYS: USE STYLE LIBRARIES

At this point, we hope you are using style libraries to manage your material, color, and lighting style definitions. If not, then you need to take the time to do so. By tasking all the color and material information from the file itself, you really can speed up the processing of your files.

The Bottom Line

Select a workstation   Having the right tool for the job is the key to success in anything you do. This is true of selecting a large assembly workstation. You have learned that for optimal performance you should strive to keep your system working in physical memory (RAM).

> **Master It**   You notice that your computer runs slowly when working with large assemblies and want to know whether you should consider a 64-bit system.

Adjust your performance settings   You have learned that there are many settings in Inventor and in Windows that you can use to configure the application to work more efficiently with large assemblies.

> **Master It**   You want to make your current workstation run as efficiently as possible for large assembly design.

Use best practices for large assembly   Knowing the tools for general assembly design is only half of the battle when it comes to conquering large assemblies. Understanding the methods of large assembly design and how they differ from a general assembly design is a key to success.

> **Master It**   You want to create adaptive parts so that you can make changes during the initial design stage and have several parts update automatically as you work through the details. But you are concerned about how this will adversely affect your assembly performance.

Manage assembly detail   Inventor includes several tools to help manage assembly detail so that you can accomplish your large assembly design goals.

> **Master It**   You want to reduce the number of files your large assembly is required to reference while you are working on it and yet maintain an accurate bill of materials.

Simplify parts   Creating highly detailed parts may be required for generating production drawings or Inventor Studio renderings, but using those high-detail parts in large assemblies may have an adverse affect.

> **Master It**   You want to create a lower level of detail part files for common parts to be reused many times over in your large assemblies but are concerned about managing two versions of a part.

Chapter 10

Weldment Design

This chapter assumes you have a good understanding of parts, assemblies, and drawings. In this chapter, we will cover the various aspects of weldment design. Starting from weldment work-flows, design methodologies, we will cover preparations, weld beads, machining features, and weld symbols, as well as how to document the weldment design. You will also learn some tips and tricks along the way.

Weldments are available in the assembly environment as a subtype of the assembly document. Most of the topics in this chapter require an assembly to be open. Therefore, this chapter is not applicable if you only have Inventor LT installed.

In this chapter, you will learn how to:

◆ Select and use the right weldment design methodology

◆ Create and edit weld preparations and machining features

◆ Create and edit different kinds of weld beads such as cosmetic, fillet, and groove

◆ Document weldment stages in drawings

◆ Generate and maintain a consistent set of BOM across welded assemblies, drawings, and presentations

---

WELDMENT WORKFLOWS

You are a designer working for a company in the packaging industry. The entire packaging system consists of several functional units that form its structure. You are interested in the high-level core packaging unit that consists of three subassemblies: A, B, and C. Let's say it contains parts consisting of a boxed container (A), a lift-arm mechanism (B) for the boxed container, and railings (C) on which the container moves from one station to another. Each subassembly is comprised of structural steel shapes and/or tubes that are bent and plates that are welded together.

You want to analyze subassembly A, which forms the container in the context of the top-level assembly to check for interferences. For this, you need accurate solid weld beads to analyze the interference. You want to pattern these solid weld beads and its components and create a drawing of this subassembly.

On subassembly B, which forms the lift-arm mechanism, the weld beads are very complex, and you're interested only in modeling with lightweight — in other words, cosmetic — welds. For these subassemblies, you need mass analysis of welds. You do not require any solid beads as long as you can assign mass values to the cosmetic weld beads in the assembly. You want to extract properties of the cosmetic weld beads for analysis and costing. The weld beads in the subassembly need to be documented in a drawing.

On weld subassembly C, which forms the railings on which the container moves, you are interested neither in interference analysis nor in mass properties in assemblies. For C, you are interested only in quickly documenting the weldments in drawings. You need a streamlined interface to document the welds in drawings. Besides, you want to generate any weld bead or symbol regardless of the weld standard.

Exploring Weldment Design Methodologies

One of the basic questions in weldment design is, What design methodology should be used to create weldments? Unfortunately, there is no "one-size-fits-all" strategy. The design methodology you use depends on your individual needs and requirements. We will start with some definition of terms that are useful to explain the different design methodologies.

As-assembled means a view of the assembly with no weld preparations, beads, or machining features. This represents a stage in the weldment design. *As-welded* means a view of the assembly with weld preparations and weld beads but no machining features. *As-machined* means a view of the final welded assembly with the machining features that goes through the weld beads. All these represent the various stages in weldment design. Once the weldment design is done, it helps to document the various stages of weldment design in the drawing.

Depending on the need for documentation, interference analysis, mass properties, and other design criteria, you can group the weldment design methodologies into the following three broad categories:

Part files and part features You can create a weldment design using part features in part files. With this approach, you use the rich modeling features of the part (sweeps, chamfers, fillets, and lofts) to create a wide variety of weld bead shapes. However, this will be one big mess of a design that has no logical partitions. You see, the main difficulty is creating drawings with different stages — for example, as-assembled, as-welded, and so on — from a single design. You will not be able to see certain edges separating weld beads and components in drawings because they will not even exist (be merged out) in the part design. In addition, the bill of materials will not list all the individual components needed to assemble the welded structures. Still, this might be an acceptable strategy for small weldment designs that have minor design changes over a period of time. Besides, the assumption is that the designer does not need to create the different stages in design documentation from a single weldment assembly. You could place the part weldment into an assembly and then create presentations and drawings of that assembly. (However, in drawings you will not be able to create the different stages of weldment design.) Figure 10.1 shows this methodology.

Weldment assembly and derived technology You can create the part components and constrain them in a weldment assembly. With this approach, you can derive the weldment assembly (.iam) into a part file (.ipt) and model the welds in the derived assembly file using part features. Optionally, you can derive the part file into another part file to show machining on welded assemblies. Similar disadvantages exist as mentioned in the first method; however, you can modify assembly constraints to create different variants of weldment assemblies with this approach. The preparations, welds, and machining features will all exist in the derived component files. This might be a good strategy for weldments where BOM listing is needed and there is no need to document different stages of weldment design from a single weldment assembly. Figure 10.2 shows the document layout of this methodology.

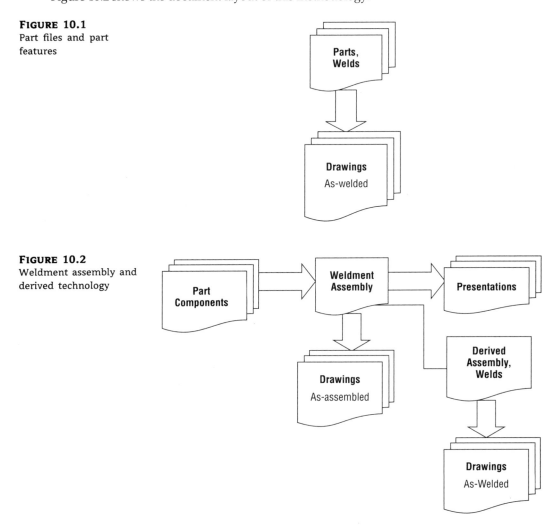

FIGURE 10.1
Part files and part features

FIGURE 10.2
Weldment assembly and derived technology

Weldment assembly   You can create the part components and constrain them in a weldment assembly. You use a mixture of cosmetic, fillet, and groove welds with preparations, machining features, and weld symbols. The main advantage is that the weldment can be documented as-assembled, as-welded, and so on. The BOM outlines the different part components. It does not preclude Finite Element analysis since the weldment assembly can be derived into a part. You might find this approach difficult initially, but you can see large gains in productivity later while documenting the weldment. This is the recommended approach for large weldments (examples are structural frames, piping, industrial gates, fences, and steel furniture) that need mass properties, interference analysis, and complete documentation. You can use a combined approach of all three methods if that's what works best for your needs. However, when new enhancements are made to weldments, this approach lends itself to easily leverage the new functionality. Figure 10.3 shows the document layout of this design methodology. (The figure doesn't show the various subassemblies that the weldment assembly might contain by breaking it into logical pieces.) Good planning helps in generating a well-built design that can be understood and easily maintained by designers. All in all, you should use this design methodology if you cannot decide on one of the other two methods.

FIGURE 10.3
Weldment assembly design methodology

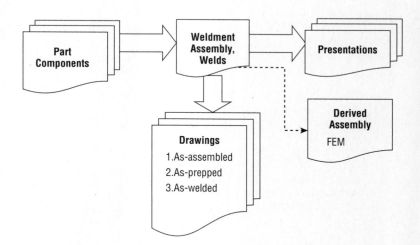

You can create a weldment assembly in two ways. First, you can create a new weldment assembly by selecting any of the weldment templates provided by Inventor (just select File ➤ New ➤ English ➤ `Weldment (ANSI).iam`). Second, you can convert an existing assembly document into a weldment assembly (just select Convert ➤ Weldment). Once you convert an assembly into a weldment, it is not possible to convert it into a regular assembly, however.

In a weldment document, you cannot create new positional representations or use flexible assembly functionality. Once you've created a weldment assembly, you can then go to the next logical step of modeling preparations.

SEAN SAYS: COMMUNICATION IS THE KEY TO DEAL WITH WELDMENTS

Depending on your needs, weldments can be as simple as single part files or as complex as weldments with preparations, welds, and machining. Talk to the group that is going to be manufacturing your parts (whether it is farmed out or in house), and find out what level of detail the group requires when making the parts to your prints. Often you will find that what is important to the designer is often not as important to the welder (and vice versa). By speaking with these groups, you'll get a better understanding of what path you should take for your weldment models and drawings.

Modeling Preparations

Let's say you've created the weldment assembly for the boxed container (subassembly A in weldment workflows section) and want to add weld beads. Before adding the weld beads, the assembly needs weld preparations to create space for the weld bead to be deposited. You can model a variety of preparation features (mostly cuts). These are the most useful preparation features:

◆ Extrude

◆ Revolve

◆ Hole

◆ Sweep

◆ Chamfer

◆ Move Face

Figure 10.4 shows the preparations environment and the relevant commands. To create the features in the previous list, you use the same set of steps that you used in part (Chapter 4) or assembly modeling (Chapter 8). The Move Face functionality is primarily intended for weld preparation in the assembly environment and is available in both the part and assembly environments.

FIGURE 10.4
Weldment features
panel

Groove welds are classified by the different kinds of weld preparations. Figure 10.5 shows the commonly used weld preparations. Figure 10.5 (in the left column, from top to bottom) shows the Square Groove Weld, Bevel Groove, and U-Groove types. In the right column, from top to bottom, Figure 10.5 shows the Double Bevel Groove, V-Groove, and Double-U types. Observe that these preparations might be referred to by slightly different names in the welding industry. Although most groove welds require nothing more than a simple chamfer, all groove welds in most cases require some sort of material removal before welding.

FIGURE 10.5
Types of weld preparations

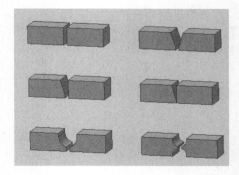

The alternative to weld preparation is to build the shape of the preparation using the sketch and then a swept volume (Extrude, Revolve, and Sweep) cut using that sketch to create the feature shape. However, it is recommended that you use the weld preparation feature, which helps show the manufacturing process. In addition, it aids in documenting the weldment in a drawing with just the components and preparations. Another advantage is that the designer, weld fabricator, or manufacturing instruction–generating program can easily find these features in one place, in other words, in the Preparations folder. This might be useful for generating the desired manufacturing information.

For editing any of the features in the Preparations folder, right-click the folder in the Model browser, and select Edit. You can also double-click the Preparations folder and edit the individual features. You have to think of the Preparations folder as a separate environment with its own set of commands. CAD environments typically tend to be a group of relevant commands with some special behaviors. The End of Part (EOP) node in the browser works differently than in the part modeling browser. In the part modeling browser, when the EOP is moved around, it sticks at that location even after an update. In the preparations environment, the EOP can be moved to above or below any feature location in the Preparations folder just like in part modeling. However, when you leave the preparations environment — either by double-clicking the top-level assembly node in the weldment assembly or by right-clicking and selecting Finish Edit in the Model browser or Graphics window — the EOP is rolled all the way to the end in the Preparations folder. It might be visualized as a browser node that does not stick in its dragged browser location, unlike parts. The EOP has similar behavior whether you are in the preparations, welds, or machining environment.

Cosmetic Welds

The weld bead and related commands are available by double-clicking the Welds folder in the Model browser in a weldment assembly. (You can see the Welds folder in the earlier Figure 10.4.) Figure 10.6 shows the available features in the welds environment.

The *cosmetic weld* feature is available by clicking the Cosmetic Weld command in the Weldment Features panel. Figure 10.7 shows the Cosmetic Weld feature dialog box. When using the cosmetic weld feature, you must input the edges of the model. These edges can belong to part components or other weld beads.

FIGURE 10.6
Weldment Features
panel

FIGURE 10.7
Cosmetic Weld
dialog box

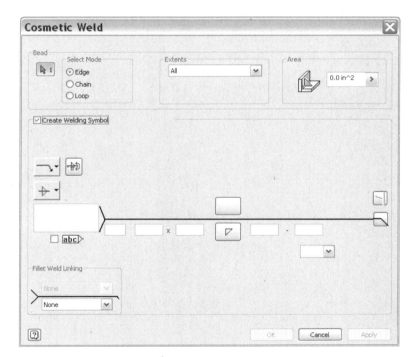

You have just designed the lift-arm mechanism (subassembly B in weldment workflows section) and you want to create cosmetic welds. Cosmetic welds are recommended for use when you have the following:

◆ A need for lightweight representation

◆ No requirement for interference analysis

◆ No need for the estimated total mass of the assembly with solid weld beads. However, you could optionally have the cosmetic weld participate in mass property calculations.

Note that the bead (the upper portion of the weld dialog boxes) and the weld symbol (the lower portion of the weld dialog boxes) are decoupled; in other words, optionally you can create the weld symbol. This applies to all types of weld beads. In addition, you can use a single weld symbol to denote multiple welds involving cosmetic, fillet, and groove welds. Cosmetic welds can represent a wide variety of welds. You can create them using edges (the Edge option), tangent continuous set of edges (the Chain option), or loops (the Loop option).

To create a cosmetic weld feature as shown in Figure 10.8, follow these steps:

1. Double-click the Welds folder in the Model browser to activate the weld bead features, or right-click the Welds folder and select Edit.

2. Click the Cosmetic Weld command in the Weldment Features panel.

3. Select the Chain option, and select the edges. The Chain option is similar to the Automatic Edge Chain option in the Fillet dialog box in part modeling. It collects all the tangent continuous edges in a loop on a single face.

4. You can enter a suitable bead cross-section area based on the leg lengths. The bead cross section can be calculated using the equation shown below and the bead cross section area value can be entered in the Area control.

$$\text{Bead cross section} = (1/2 \times \text{Leg Length1} \times \text{Leg Length2})$$

FIGURE 10.8
Creating a
cosmetic weld

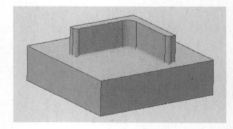

For the lift-arm mechanism (subassembly B) referenced in weldment workflows, this bead cross section area value is critical to enter and later (in the Bead Property Report and Mass Properties section), we will show how to use this for mass properties calculations.

In certain cases when there is no edge to click as input, you can split the faces of the components in the part file (.ipt) at the location where it is welded and use the split edges as input to the cosmetic weld feature. In Figure 10.9, for example, there are no explicit edges to click at the intersection of the planar face on the hollow tube and the cylindrical face on the cylinder. Therefore, you can edit the cylindrical part and use the split feature to split the cylindrical face of the cylindrical part so that you can use those split edges to create the cosmetic weld feature. Figure 10.9 shows such a cosmetic weld feature on split edges. Work points cannot be clicked as part of the cosmetic weld feature. The edges need to have finite length in order to be clickable for the cosmetic weld feature.

SEAN SAYS: WELD BEADS ARE PREFERRED

Although cosmetic welds provide designers with the information they need, users unfamiliar with the tools may not understand the intent. Whenever possible, unless there is reason to avoid them, use weld beads. In the next section, we'll discuss weld beads and explain some of their advantages.

FIGURE 10.9
Cosmetic welds using split edges

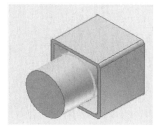

You can specify extents with parallel planes or planar faces. The extent trims the cosmetic weld bead between the From and To termination planes or planar faces. To generate the From-To cosmetic weld in Figure 10.10, follow these steps:

1. Open the weldment assembly.

2. Double-click the Welds folder in the Model browser.

3. Click Cosmetic Weld, and select an edge.

4. In the Extents pulldown in the Cosmetic Weld dialog box, select From-To.

5. Click the From button, and select one of the assembly work planes.

6. Click the To button, and select the other assembly work plane.

7. Click OK in the Cosmetic Weld dialog box.

FIGURE 10.10
Cosmetic welds with extents

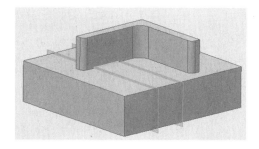

Creating Weld Beads

A *weld bead* feature is a parametric, solid representation of the real-world weld bead. It can be generated from input faces of a single component or from input faces of multiple components including bead faces in a weldment assembly. In other words, you can select faces from weld beads too as input faces to generate new weld beads. You can also create a weld on a single part that is placed in a weldment assembly. Some examples are as follows:

◆ *Example 1*: Place a single sheet metal part in a weldment assembly, and create fillet welds to create a container.

◆ *Example 2*: Create a fillet or groove weld between two plates (two parts or one part that has two Extrusion features for the plates).

◆ *Example 3*: Create a fillet or groove weld between two plates and another weld bead.

Weld beads contribute to mass property calculations and can take part in interference analyses. If you are creating solid weld beads for the boxed container (subassembly A) shown in weldment workflows section at the beginning of the chapter, the following sections on fillet and groove weld beads are highly useful. All weld bead features create an independent body that does not take part in boolean operations with the assembly components. Other machining features can cut into welds beads. There are two major weld features to create physical 3D welds:

◆ *Fillet weld feature*: A fillet weld builds up corners by adding weld material between faces. Fillet welds are the most commonly used type of weld in industrial machinery. You should use this feature when there is no gap between the components. A specialized kind of fillet weld with a gap is supported.

◆ *Groove weld feature*: A groove weld feature predominantly fills gaps between components. However, you can also use it when the components are touching each other. There are many opportunities to combine cosmetic, fillet, and groove welds to generate the desired weld beads.

◆ The weldment environment also has the Plug and Groove Weld calculators (not shown) only if the Design Accelerator add-in is loaded.

Creating Fillet Welds

The basic idea behind a *fillet weld* is that you are joining two sets of faces. The weld bead definition can be controlled parametrically by using the parameters shown in Figure 10.11. This is known as *leg length measurement*. You can enter the two leg lengths used to generate the bead and also specify the throat measurement. You just enter the throat length, and Inventor calculates the rest of the size of the weld bead. The offset value has relevance only when you declare the weld to be concave or convex. Figure 10.11 shows the two leg lengths and the two types of measurement.

The top shape of a fillet weld can be flat, convex, or concave, as shown in Figure 10.12 (from left to right). For flat, the offset is 0.0. For concave or convex based on the offset, Inventor calculates the necessary bump or depression shape.

FIGURE 10.11
Fillet weld definition

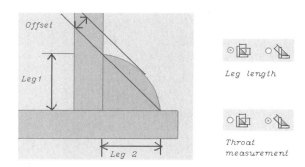

FIGURE 10.12
Flat, convex, and concave shape for fillet welds

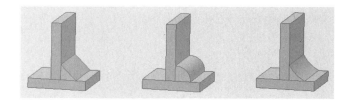

To create a simple fillet weld, follow these steps:

1. Open the weldment assembly.

2. Double-click the Welds folder.

3. Click Fillet Weld. You will get the dialog box shown in Figure 10.13.

FIGURE 10.13
Fillet Weld dialog box

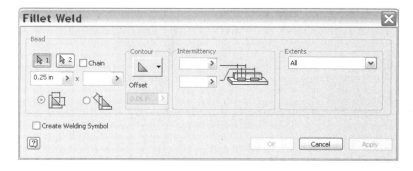

4. Enter the leg length value for the Leg1 control, **0.25 in**. Leg2 is assumed to be same as Leg1, in other words, 0.25 in, if not entered.

5. Select one single face in each of the two facesets. The mating and perpendicular horizontal and vertical faces (see the triangle preview) are the input faces for the weld, as shown in Figure 10.14.

6. The OK button is now enabled, and the left side of Figure 10.14 shows the lightweight weld bead preview. You should see three triangles per edge (see the left image of Figure 10.14) of the intersection edges of the two facesets. Click OK.

FIGURE 10.14
Fillet weld preview
and fillet weld

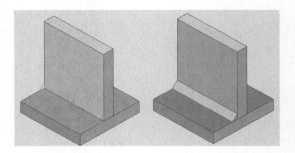

7. The fillet weld bead is created, as shown on the right of Figure 10.14.

Fillet welds are not designed to handle gaps in general. A groove weld is the most used feature to fill gaps. However, Inventor supports the case of a shaft through a plate with a hole (see Figure 10.15). The geometry of the shaft need not be cylindrical. The hole gap can be comprised of any shape consisting of multiple edges.

FIGURE 10.15
Shaft through plate

Figure 10.15 shows a hole gap through which the cylinder is passing. The fillet weld should work even if the two components are separated by a gap at some places and touch at other places.

To create these fillet welds, you still click the two facesets, as shown in Figure 10.15. Inventor infers the gap and generates the fillet weld bead. To fill the gap between the two mating cylindrical faces of the components, you should use groove welds.

Figure 10.16 shows another variant of two components that are separated by a gap. This case is no different from the case of Figure 10.15. Here the gap is not fully filled. Figure 10.16 shows the input faces and the components and shows the weld bead between the components.

In both cases of Figure 10.15 and Figure 10.16, the gap is not filled below the bead. Figure 10.17 shows the fillet weld bead cross section for the weld bead in Figure 10.15.

FIGURE 10.16
Shaft through
hollow tube

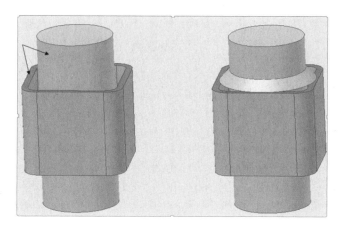

FIGURE 10.17
Fillet weld bead
cross section

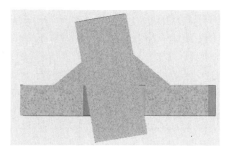

SEAN SAYS: DON'T FORGET TO SPEAK WITH THOSE MANUFACTURING THE PARTS

Inventor provides just about every possible option that you could possibly want as a designer with regard to weld sizes, shapes, and contours. However, again I urge you to speak with those who will be manufacturing the parts. It would be unfortunate to spend a lot of time with specific contours, sizes, and finishes if the weld shop is just going to give you a standard fillet weld regardless of the details you call out. You'll need to decide whether it's time to find a new welder or whether you are putting too much information into the part. More than one designer has found this out the hard way when that $10 bracket suddenly ends up costing $100 because of the demanding weld callouts placed on the print.

Creating Intermittent Fillet Welds

Intermittent fillet welds essentially produce patterns of the weld bead along a set of edges. Figure 10.18 shows an example of an intermittent fillet weld.

FIGURE 10.18
Intermittent fillet weld

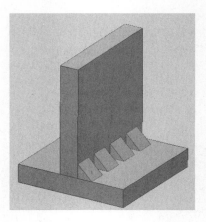

For the ANSI standard, you must specify the bead length, in other words, the length of each bead and pitch (the distance between centers). For ISO/BSI/DIN/GB, you must specify the bead length, the spacing between beads, and the number of beads. For JIS, you must specify the bead length, the distance between bead centers, and the number of beads. Figure 10.19 shows these parameters.

FIGURE 10.19
Intermittent fillet weld
parameters

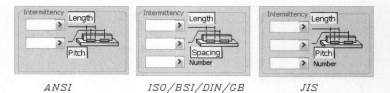

The Extents control allows you to select the beginning and ending planar faces or planes between which the weld bead will be created. The steps to produce a From-To fillet weld bead are similar to the steps outlined for extents and cosmetic welds. When welding a long piece of metal, often intermittent welds are both cost-effective and reduce warping in the part.

Creating Groove Welds

You have just designed the boxed container (subassembly A in weldment workflows section) and have created some fillet welds. You want to add some groove welds to fill gaps. Once such gaps are filled you might top it with a fillet weld. A *groove weld* is primarily used to fill gaps between two sets of faces. Figure 10.20 shows some examples.

Like fillet welds, a groove weld needs two sets of faces. The Full Face option, when checked, specifies whether to use the full face to generate the weld. The Full Face option when unchecked specifies to use only a portion of the face. Inventor calculates the specific portion of the face by projecting the smaller face set to the larger faceset (if the two facesets are the same size, Inventor picks one of them to project). Figure 10.21 shows the resulting weld bead. Since on the left of Figure 10.21 the Full Face option is disabled for Part1, only part of the face of Part1 is used for the weld bead. On the right of Figure 10.21, the Full Face option is enabled for Part1. This implies that the full face of Part1 be used to generate the weld bead.

FIGURE 10.20
Groove weld examples

FIGURE 10.21
Full Face option

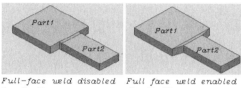

The Ignore Internal Loop option controls whether to ignore or consider the internal loop to generate the weld bead. When checked, it results in a "hollow" (Figure 10.22, left) groove weld; selecting the option results in a "solid" weld bead (Figure 10.22, right).

FIGURE 10.22
Ignore Internal Loop option

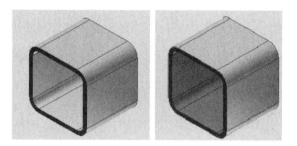

The fill direction is used to project one set of faces to another to generate the groove weld bead. In Figure 10.23, you can see the difference between the resulting weld bead shapes.

FIGURE 10.23
Fill direction

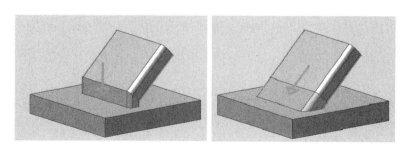

Observe that Inventor can create welds that would produce a good belly laugh from your local weld shop. Just because Inventor can produce the weld doesn't mean it's a manufacturable part. You can select the following for the fill direction:

◆ Planar faces and work planes (specifies the direction normal to chosen face/plane)

◆ Cylindrical, conical, or toroidal faces (specifies the direction of the surface's axis)

◆ Work axes

◆ Linear part edges

One of the questions that comes up frequently is, What direction should be selected for the fill? One guideline you can use is to imagine the average geometric center of faceset1 and the average geometric center of faceset2. The line connecting the two geometric centers will be the fill direction to generate the groove weld bead. You are not required to calculate the geometric centers of the facesets. It is advisable to try different fill directions to get the desired weld bead shape that are separated across a gap.

To create a simple groove weld, follow these steps:

1. Open the weldment assembly.

2. Double-click the Welds folder.

FIGURE 10.24
Groove Weld dialog box

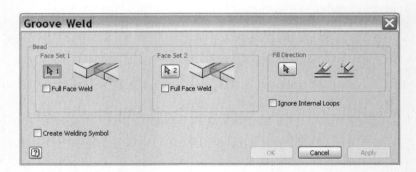

3. Click Groove Weld command.

4. Select the two face sets (two opposing planar faces), as shown in Figure 10.25. The full-fidelity preview comes up as shown in Figure 10.25 on the left.

5. Check the Full Face Weld option on both facesets since you want to use the entire face of both facesets to generate the groove weld bead.

FIGURE 10.25
Groove weld preview and groove weld

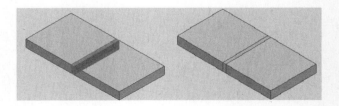

6. Click OK.

7. The groove weld bead is created, as shown on the right of Figure 10.25.

If the preview comes up, it is almost certain that the bead will succeed.

Performing Machining Operations

You have created all the welds for the boxed container (subassembly A in weldment workflows section). Now, you need to add some drilled holes that go through the welds and the components. You are also familiar with the Preparations environment having created weld preparations for groove welds.

The features available for machining are similar to the preparations environment. In terms of operations, they are performed after the generation of weld beads. One of the main advantages of providing the machining operations in a separate environment is that in drawings you can document them in the as-machined state. Holes and extrude cuts are typical post-weld machining features.

Figure 10.26 shows a welded assembly with machining operations performed on it. To create the machining features, follow these steps:

1. Open the weldment assembly.

FIGURE 10.26
Machining features on
a weldment assembly

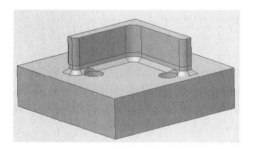

2. Double-click the Machining folder in the Model browser.

3. Create a new sketch, and place two hole centers corresponding to the two holes shown in Figure 10.26.

4. Right-click Finish sketch, and select the Hole feature in the Weldment Features panel.

5. Double-click the top-level assembly to exit from the machining environment.

Holes that are important to the location of welds should be placed into the parts that are being welded together. Because the machined view of the weldment is a subset of the welded view, you cannot refer to "machined" holes when detailing an as-welded model.

Machining features include but are not limited to the following:

◆ Extrude

◆ Revolve

◆ Hole

- ◆ Sweep
- ◆ Chamfer
- ◆ Move Face

Exploring Weld Properties and Combinations

The following sections cover the additional aspects of weldments. Specifically we will cover Weld Properties, replication, and how to combine fillet and groove weld beads to produce the desired weld bead shape.

Weld Properties

To turn off the visibility of all weld beads in an open assembly, select View ➢ Object Visibility ➢ Welds from the main menu. You can also right-click the Welds folder in the Model browser and uncheck Visibility to turn off the weld beads of a particular assembly. You can suppress individual weld bead features in the Model browser; the suppress feature is similar to part feature suppression.

You can choose the weld material during the initial conversion of an assembly to a weldment. Welded Aluminium-6061 is the default material. Let's say, for the boxed container (subassembly A in weldment workflows section) you need to select a different weld material than the default. To select another material to appear in the Weld Bead Material pulldown in the Convert To Weldment dialog box, follow these steps:

1. From the main menu, select Format ➢ Styles And Standards Editor.

2. Expand the material, and select a material, such as Aluminium-6061 AHC.

3. On the right side of the Style And Standard Editor dialog box, check the Use As Weldment Material. It is recommended that you save these changes to the style library. Go to any non-weldment assembly, and from the main menu, select Convert To Weldment.

4. Aluminium-6061 AHC should appear in the Weld Bead Material pulldown in the Convert To Weldment dialog box, as shown in Figure 10.27.

In existing weldments, you can change the weld color styles using the weld properties. In the Model browser, right-click the item Welds, select Properties, go to the Weld Bead tab, and choose the weld bead color style or the end fill color style. You can use the weld bead color style to assign different color styles to the weld bead. Similarly, the end caps (faces) that you selected in the weldment assembly can be assigned an end fill color style.

Replication

Welds (cosmetic, fillet, and groove beads) can be copied or mirrored in assemblies through the Copy Components and Mirror Components commands. Both sets of components that support the weld need to be copied or mirrored for the welds to be copied or mirrored. For example, if a cosmetic weld exists only on component C1 and if C1 is copied or mirrored, the cosmetic weld is also copied or mirrored. You cannot copy or mirror the weld beads without its components being copied or mirrored. For the boxed container (subassembly A in weldment workflows section) if you need to replicate the solid weld beads, ensure that you select all the plates and/or tubes that hold the welds together also to be included in the set that is being copied or mirrored.

FIGURE 10.27
Converting To Weld-
ment dialog box

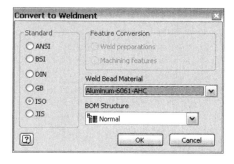

FIGURE 10.27
Converting To Weld-
ment dialog box

Weld beads can be derived from the assembly into another part document using the Derived Component command in parts.

Groove and Fillet Weld Combinations

Most welds can be generated using a combination of groove and fillet welds. Figure 10.28 shows an example of welding two hollow tubes. The horizontal tube (C1) is welded with a vertical tube (C2). Faceset1 (F1) of C1 is comprised of two faces, as shown on the left of Figure 10.28. Faceset2 (F2) of C2 is comprised of a single mating face on C2. This is shown separately in Figure 10.28 as a loop since it is difficult to show the face on C2 in the shown view. On F1 of C1, select the Full Face Weld option unchecked since we want to use only part of the face for the weld. On F2 of C2, select the Full Face Weld option checked since we want to use the full face to be used to generate the weld bead. The fill direction (shown as a downward arrow) will be the face normal of face set2, in other words, the vertical direction going down. Figure 10.28 shows the resulting groove weld bead on the right.

FIGURE 10.28
Generating the groove
weld bead

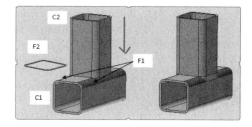

In Figure 10.29, we generate the fillet weld: Faceset1 (F1) is composed of three faces. Faceset2 (F2) is composed of three component faces and two small weld bead faces on one side (total of five faces) from the groove weld bead generated in Figure 10.28. Only four of the five faces are shown on C2. A fillet weld is generated on the other side too.

On the right of Figure 10.29, you can see the resulting fillet weld bead that is generated on the groove weld bead.

Split Technique

We will now show two examples to explain how the Split technique helps in generating the welds you need.

FIGURE 10.29
Generating the fillet
weld bead

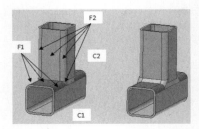

EXAMPLE 1

Since welds work on input faces (the two facesets that you select to do the weld), it is imperative in certain situations to split the input faces to have the weld bead only on a certain portion of the face. Essentially you are helping Inventor use the partial face that is generated from the split.

In certain situations using fillet welds, involving multiple possibilities (the weld can appear this side or that side or both sides) as in the case of a cylinder touching a flat plate (Figure 10.30), it might be difficult to control the placement of welds. In such situations, use the Split command in parts to split one or more faces. Follow these steps:

1. Create a flat plate and the cylinder as part files. See the left of Figure 10.30. Insert the two parts into a new weldment assembly file. Constrain the cylinder to the flat plate using a Tangent constraint. The cylinder and flat plate will have a line contact.

FIGURE 10.30
Using a split to create
multiple fillet welds

2. In the cylinder part file, use the split feature to split the cylindrical face into two equal pieces using a work plane. See the middle of Figure 10.30. One of the split lines will be collinear with the line contact.

3. You can now create a weldment on each side of the cylinder:

   a. In the weldment assembly, double-click Welds in the Model browser to go to the Weldment Features panel.
   b. Open the Fillet Weld Feature tool.
   c. Select one of the split faces on the cylinder and the planar face of the flat plate to create FilletWeld1. See Figure 10.30 on the right.
   d. Select the other split face on the cylinder and the planar face of the flat plate to create FilletWeld2. See Figure 10.30 on the right.

You can turn off the display of a split edges while creating a drawing view in a drawing (.idw) file. In the Drawing View dialog box, select Options, and ensure Tangent Edges is deselected. See the left of Figure 10.31. The resulting drawing for the welded assembly in Figure 10.30 is shown in Figure 10.31 on the right.

FIGURE 10.31
Turning off split edges
in a drawing

EXAMPLE 2

A common weld example is a hollow (optionally) cylindrical tube going through a hole in a block. The split technique is useful in generating the all-around groove weld. Figure 10.32 shows the various steps that are used to construct this overall weld.

FIGURE 10.32
All-around weld

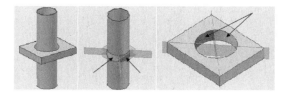

You start with one of the components, a hollow cylindrical tube, as shown on the left of Figure 10.32. Several splits are made in this component to generate four small faces of equal size shown on the middle of Figure 10.32. We show only the two split faces in middle of Figure 10.32. The hole in the block is shown on the right of Figure 10.32. You generate corresponding four splits in the second component. Only two split faces are shown on the right of Figure 10.32.

Figure 10.33 shows the top view of the four groove welds generated between the opposing split faces between the two components. On both facesets, the Full Face Weld option is checked, and the Ignore Internal Loop option is unchecked.

FIGURE 10.33
Four groove welds

Figure 10.34 (on the left) shows the resulting groove weld from the four individual groove welds of Figure 10.33. A fillet weld is topped using the groove weld faces and the cylindrical face of the hollow cylindrical tube. The resulting fillet weld on top of the groove weld is shown in Figure 10.34 (on the right).

FIGURE 10.34
Groove and fillet weld

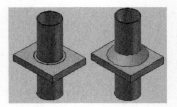

You could also use the split technique to generate an intermittent fillet weld at a user-controlled location.

Using the Weld Symbol

You can create the Weld Symbol in assemblies by clicking on the Welds folder and using the Weld Symbol command. In drawings you can find this command in the Drawing Annotations Panel. The weld symbol can be created for any of the three subassemblies that make up the core packaging unit (weldment workflow section) in assemblies and/or drawings. You have to make a decision to create them in the right place (assemblies or assemblies and drawings) based on your communication with the welding and other departments that are involved in producing the weldment. The weld symbol, which is optional in the assembly environment, has certain key characteristics:

◆ It cannot be created without a weld bead consuming it.

◆ The primary bead is the weld bead to which the welding symbol is attached.

◆ You're allowed to activate the weld symbol grips and reattach the weld symbol to any other visible bead edge from that symbol's group.

◆ Multiple weld beads (including cosmetic weld beads) can be grouped under a single weld symbol.

◆ The weld symbols are listed in a separate folder below the Weld Beads folder.

◆ A bead can be consumed by only one welding symbol object at any given time.

◆ A linked bead that is moved out of its welding symbol group causes the parent welding symbol to become unassociated.

◆ Cross-highlighting is supported for both the bead objects and the welding symbol object. If you select a welding symbol node in the Model browser, the welding symbol and all the beads consumed by that welding symbol will be cross-highlighted in the graphics window. Alternatively, if you select a bead node from either the welding symbols portion of the browser or the Beads folder portion of the browser, the bead will be cross-highlighted in the graphics window.

◆ A new welding symbol can be created for an already created weld feature.

◆ Welding symbols have visibility control.

◆ If a weld symbol references a weld feature, then it is consumed. Otherwise, the bead is unconsumed by any weld symbols. Therefore, three browser filtering options are available from the Beads folder context menu: Show All, Show Consumed Only, and Show Unconsumed Only.

Figure 10.35 shows a single weld symbol for the five welds (Fillet Weld 3 and Groove Welds 2 through Groove Weld 5) created for the single all-around weld. To add multiple welds beads to the same symbol, right-click the desired weld symbol, choose Edit Welding Symbol, and add weld beads by selecting them in either the model window or the Model browser. Only unconsumed weld beads should appear highlighted in the model window. Right-clicking the browser or model window lets you select weld beads and quickly see which weld beads have been unconsumed. To disassociate a weld bead from its symbol, right-click the bead in the Model browser, and choose the Unconsume Bead command from the context menu.

FIGURE 10.35
Single weld symbol for five welds

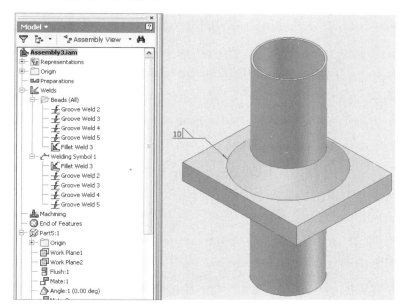

Bead Property Report and Mass Properties

To estimate accurate weld rod usage, fabrication time, and bead weights, the weld property reporting tool is available in assemblies which helps estimate costs. This tool allows you to query the mass, volume, length, type, and name of individual beads in the assembly. Through an option (available after you select Tools ➤ Weld Bead Report from the main menu), you can retrieve this data for the current assembly and all its children weldment assemblies. This information will be exported to a standard Microsoft Excel spreadsheet. Figure 10.36 shows an example. In the weldment workflow, we can generate a weld bead report for the core packaging unit that contains the three subassemblies.

FIGURE 10.36
Weld bead property reporting in assemblies

Document	ID	Type	Length	UoM	Mass	UoM	Area	UoM	Volume	UoM
C:\temp\weldbeadreport										
	Groove Weld 1	Groove	N/A		0.013	kg	28.387	cm^2	4.916	cm^3
	Fillet Weld 1	Fillet	7.62	cm	0.01	kg	26	cm^2	3.81	cm^3
	Cosmetic Weld 1	Cosmetic	1.27	cm	N/A		N/A		N/A	

Tip: To calculate the total length of weld beads, you can sum up the total length using the Microsoft Excel Sum functions. Length and Area values are not reported for groove welds. The default "save to" location is the parent assembly's directory location. You can override this location, though. Weld properties are at best estimates. Many factors can change the weight of a weld bead. If the weight of a part is critical, consider machining the part to meet the criteria after welding.

The cross section entered in the Cosmetic Weld dialog box is multiplied by the length of the cosmetic weld bead and is optionally considered in the mass properties to calculate volume. When the File, iProperties, Physical, Include Cosmetic Welds option is checked, this volume is included in the calculations. The mass is determined by the selected weld material. This option is useful for the lift-arm mechanism (subassembly B) referenced in the weldment workflows section where you only need lightweight representation but at the same time need the welds to participate in mass properties.

Drawing Documentation

The Weld Symbol dialog box, being the same in assemblies and drawings, is specific to the engineering standard you're using. Figure 10.37 shows an example of Welding Symbol (ANSI) dialog box in drawings, and the tool tip shows the title of the different input controls. The various controls in this dialog box and their meanings are explained in Table 10.1.

SEAN SAYS: BE EXPLICIT WITH SYMBOLS

Although you can refer to any textbook on welding for the correct use of the symbols listed in Table 10.1, keep in mind that many shops have their own "shorthand" versions of weld symbols. It is imperative that you communicate with the welders to make sure you agree on the symbols. Many weld shops do not know the "standard" yet still produce excellent parts.

A perfect example is the "all-around" symbol. Some shops take this to mean only opposite sides of the indicated line, while others interpret this symbols to mean you want all contiguous surfaces welded. When in doubt, you should be explicit with your symbols.

FIGURE 10.37
Welding Symbol
dialog box

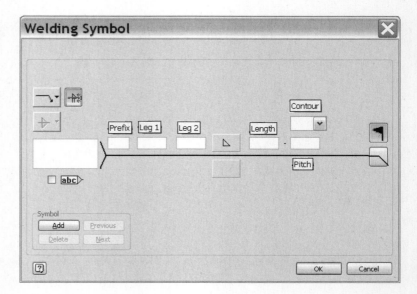

TABLE 10.1:   Welding Symbol Dialog Box Controls

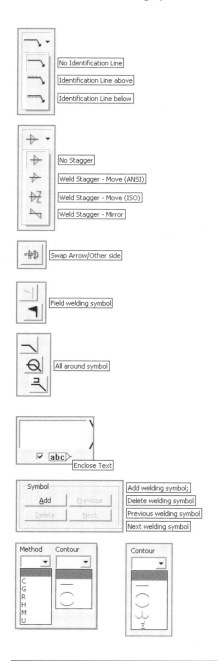

Select this option to have the identification line above or below or to omit it.

Select this option for fillet weld symbols when they are set on both sides of the reference line.

Toggle this to switch the values and options from above the reference line to below the reference line, and vice versa.

Use this option to add the field weld flag to the welding symbol.

The All Around Symbol tri/state toggle allows users to add an all-around symbol to the welding symbol. Note that the third (bottom) selection is presented only in the GB standard — all other standards will present a dual-state toggle.

Select this option to specify text to be associated to the welding symbol. The Enclose Text option will enclose the note in a box at the tail of the symbol.

Use these controls to specify multiple welding symbols attached to a single leader.

Left: These are the contour pulldown options for the fillet weld for the ANSI standard. Right: These are the contour options for the ISO/BSI/DIN/GB standard. You can set the contour using the Contour pulldown in the Welding symbol dialog box.

TABLE 10.1: Welding Symbol Dialog Box Controls *(CONTINUED)*

	The weld symbol pulldown lets you select different types of welds such as VGroove Weld, Flare-Bevel Weld, Seam Weld, Spot Weld and so on.
Prefix	Enter a prefix for the symbol.
Leg1, Leg2	Enter the leg lengths for fillet weld.
Length, Pitch	Enter the number of instances, the length of each instance, and the spacing between instances.

Weldment Design Stages

You are done with the weldment model design for the core packaging unit referenced in the weldment workflows section. Now you need to create the four major stages of weldment design in the drawing. You can create a weldment drawing in the following stages:

◆ *Assembly*: As-assembled with no assembly features

◆ *Preparation*: As-prepped

◆ *Welds*: As-welded

◆ *Machining*: As-machined

Figure 10.38 (left) shows the weldment assembly. Figure 10.38 (right) shows the weldment assembly with preparations.

FIGURE 10.38
Welded assembly and preparations

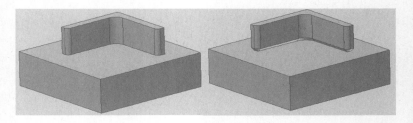

Figure 10.39 (left) shows the two weld beads, in other words, one groove weld to fill the gap and another fillet weld that goes around the groove weld. Figure 10.39 (right) shows the welds and the machining features. Figure 10.40 shows the four drawing views with weldment assembly, preparations, weld beads, and machining features.

FIGURE 10.39
Weldment assembly

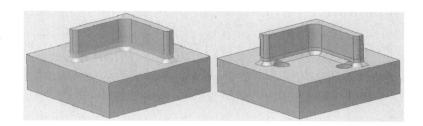

FIGURE 10.40
Four stages of the weld-
ment assembly

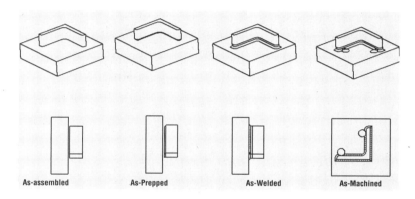

As-assembled   As-Prepped   As-Welded   As-Machined

To create a model state view as shown in Figure 10.40, follow these steps:

1. Create a new drawing.

2. Select Base View, and select the weldment assembly (.iam) file on the Component tab, under File in the Drawing View dialog box.

3. On the Model State tab, select Assembly, Machining, Welds, or Preparation.

4. In the Reference Data area of the Model State tab, Select one of the Line Style options. The three options are As Reference Parts, As Parts, Off.

5. Select any needed display options on the Display Options tab. For example, the views shown in the previous figures have weld annotations turned on.

You can retrieve associative weld symbols from the model by right-clicking the drawing view and selecting Get Model Annotations ➤ Get Welding Symbols. You can retrieve associative weld end fills in the model by right-clicking the view and selecting Get Model Annotations ➤ Get Weld Annotations. You can also add nonassociative weld annotations to your drawing. You can access cosmetic weld symbols through the Drawing Annotation panel by clicking the Caterpillar tool. Figure 10.41 shows the annotation retrieval tools in drawings.

FIGURE 10.41
Retrieve weld symbols

End Fill

In the Drawing Annotations panel, you will see the End Fill command, which is used to represent seam weld end fills and the gap/groove process shape (concave and convex). Clicking the End Fill command brings up the End Fill Dialog box, as shown in Figure 10.42. Note that you can create any weld process shape that is desired in drawings without generating the specified weld in the model.

FIGURE 10.42
End Fill dialog box

To create a seam weld process shape, follow these steps:

1. Click the End Fill tool in the Drawing Annotations panel.

2. Select the preset shape, for example, Seam Weld.

3. Select two points that represents the shape's arc chord length to create an arc. You can drag above or below the chord line to have the arc above or below.

4. Select the Options tab, and select Check Solid Fill.

5. Select a color, such as orange.

Figure 10.43 shows two examples of the present Seam Weld shape. These are custom groove weld process shapes.

FIGURE 10.43
End fill shape generation

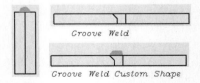

Groove Weld

Groove Weld Custom Shape

In the End Fill dialog box, the fillet process shape has Leg1 and Leg2 as parameters. The J-Type, V-Type, and U-Type Preset Shape has controls for the width and depth.

Drawing Weld Symbol

In the railings (subassembly C) example, referenced in the Weldment workflows section, you can just create the weld symbol in drawings without having to create any weld beads in the assembly. Though this saves a lot of work in assemblies, you cannot perform any interference analysis or mass properties calculations that involve welds. Observe that you can also create the weld symbol for any of the subassemblies A, B, C for the core packaging unit in assemblies and/or drawings.

To create a welding symbol in the drawing, follow these steps:

1. Select the welding symbol command in the Drawing Annotations Panel.

2. This activates the selection. The command message string displays the text Click on a location.

3. Select an entity or location in the graphics area to define the location of the welding symbol.

4. Right-click within the graphics area, and select Continue from the context menu.

5. The Welding Symbol dialog box appears.

6. Specify the desired welding symbol.

7. The welding symbol preview dynamically updates.

8. Click OK, and the specified welding symbol appears at the specified location.

Caterpillar

You can create and use caterpillars in drawings when you want to use a lightweight representation for solid weld beads. As long as the welder is comfortable with this representation, you can use caterpillars. Figure 10.44 shows the dialog box for the Weld caterpillars command in drawings. You can create weld caterpillars using the boundary (extent) edges of the welds. This drawing annotation is not associated with weldments in the assembly model. In other words you can create the caterpillar on any edge without the presence of any corresponding weld bead in the assembly. This is useful for the railing example in the weldment workflows section where you want to quickly document it in drawings. The caterpillar could be used in addition to the weld symbol to make the documentation better.

FIGURE 10.44
Weld caterpillar
dialog box

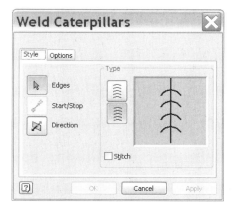

To create a caterpillar, follow these steps:

1. Select the Caterpillar command in the Drawing Annotations panel.

2. Click Edges, and select one of the long edges (the lateral edge) of the groove weld.

3. Click Options, and enter the width parameter. Adjust other parameters such as Angle, Arc %, and Spacing.

4. Click the direction to change the shape to concave or convex.

5. Start and Stop option in the dialog box which are specified by points are useful to terminate the caterpillar between the From and To locations. The caterpillar preview shows the effect of changing options.

Figure 10.45 shows the resulting caterpillar for a groove weld.

FIGURE 10.45
Weld caterpillar

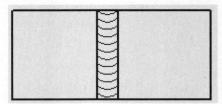

Caterpillars can be useful when you want to represent a weldment using a single part file and create a drawing out of it. You can then indicate the position and detail of the welds along the edge. Use the Split command, which will allow you to create edges where none may exist.

Bill of Materials and Parts List

For the core packaging unit in the weldment workflows example, now that the weldment design is done you need to generate a BOM and a parts list. Also you want to customize the BOM to represent a weldment.

You can automatically generate and maintain a consistent bill of materials across welded assemblies, drawings, and presentations. Components that are deemed "inseparable" are typically weldment assemblies that cannot be taken apart without doing damage to one or more of their components. Manufacturing processes treat inseparable assemblies like purchased components and are represented as a single line item.

Inseparable components also have the following two characteristics:

◆ Some child components are considered part of the parent. Hence, they don't need to be tracked or revised separately.

◆ It's a part such as a purchased assembly in a parts-only parts list.

When documented in its own context, an inseparable assembly is treated as a standard one. Figure 10.46 shows the BOM for Test Station.iam in the Samples folder that comes with

Inventor. You can find it in the \\Program Files\Autodesk\Inventor 2009\Samples\Models\Test Station folder. We have converted the assembly into a weldment assembly.

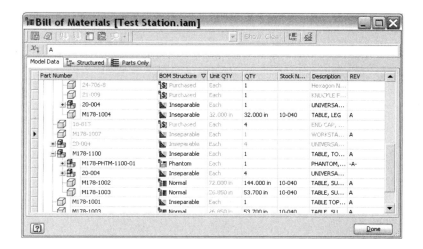

To generate the BOM, follow these steps:

1. Open the weldment assembly.

2. Click the Bill of Materials command in the Weldment Assembly Panel.

3. In the BOM Structure column, select the pulldown for each component, and select Inseparable. You can Shift-select and select multiple components to change the BOM structure type.

4. Click Done in the Bill of Materials dialog box.

Figure 10.47 shows the Parts List dialog box in drawings.
To generate the parts list for Test Station.iam, follow these steps:

1. Open Test Station.idw located in the same directory as the assembly file.

2. Go to the Drawing Annotations Panel.

3. Click Parts List.

4. Select Test Station.iam.

5. Select any table wrapping options.

6. Click OK.

Figure 10.48 shows the resulting parts list.

FIGURE 10.47
Parts List dialog box

FIGURE 10.48
Parts list

Parts List			
ITEM	QTY	PART NUMBER	DESCRIPTION
1	1	M178-1000	TABLE, MAIN
2	1	M178-2000	CABINET, PC
3	1	M178-3000	WORKSTATION HUTCH
4	4	22-124	Parts Bin, Conductive, Small
5	1	50-601	Tool Balancer, Zero Gravity, 2.6~5.7 LBS
6	1	M178-S002	TEST STATION SERVER SOFTWARE
7	2	M178-3502	SWING ARM MOUNT BRACKET
8	1	M178-S001	TEST STATION CLIENT SOFTWARE
9	1	M178-4000	TOOL CADDY
10	4	22-128Z2	PARTS BIN, FLAT MOUNT BRACKET
11	2	PC-2735-R-P4-2U	PC, RACK MOUNT, 2U
12	1	LCD-1234-SA	SWING ARM, LCD FLAT PANEL

Tip: If you derive your weldment assembly into a derived part, then the question is, How do you generate the parts list? Since the parts list is dependent on a selected view and the view is based on a single derived part, the parts list does not show any components of the derived assembly. To list components from a derived component of a weldment assembly in the parts list, place a view of the weldment assembly off to the side of your sheet and make your parts list based on that view.

The Bottom Line

Select and use the right weldment design methodology   I have shown you three weldment design methodologies. Before starting on any weldment design, it is imperative to keep the documentation, interference analysis, mass properties, and other design criteria in perspective and select the right design methodology.

> **Master It**   What is the right weldment strategy for you? If you don't need to document the weldment design stages, you could consider the part files and part features methodology or the weldment assembly and derived methodology. With the weldment assembly methodology you get to document the different stages of weldment design and reap the benefits of any new enhancements.

Create and edit weld preparations and machining features   Following the weldment methodology, you need to plan on creating the gaps needed (weld preparations) to deposit the weld beads. You need to create post weldment machining features that go through the weld beads.

> **Master It**   Where can you find these and when do you use it? Weld preparations and machining features are similar to part modeling features. Based on the weld bead shape needed, you need to plan for creating the preparations in advance. Once the welds are done, you need to create the features for the machining processes.

Create and edit different kinds of weld beads such as cosmetic, fillet, and groove   I have described the relative advantages and disadvantages of cosmetic and solid weld beads. Weldment design involves the optimal mix of these weld beads based on needs and requirements.

> **Master It**   You have the need to only create the weld annotations in drawings without any need to create them in the model. You have weld subassemblies which only needs lightweight representation in both model and drawings. In situations involving accurate interference and mass properties you need accurate weld beads. The question is: What type of weld beads should you use?

Document weldment stages in drawings   Welds need to be documented in assemblies or drawings. It is important to show the different stages of weldment design in drawings to get a good idea of how to manufacture the weldment. You can use the drawing tools effectively to annotate the welds in drawings. This will help the welder to understand the design intent better.

> **Master It**   What are the different tools used for weld documentation? You can annotate the welds in assemblies. If you prefer to document the welds in drawings, you could document the four stages of weldment design: As-assembled, As-prepped, As-welded and As-machined stages in drawings. Besides, you could use other drawing manager tools to customize weld documentation.

Generate and maintain a consistent set of BOM's across welded assemblies, drawings, and presentations   You have been shown how to generate and maintain a consistent bill of materials for weldment assemblies and a parts list in drawings. Mark parts or assemblies as Inseparable to designate them as weldments.

Master It   How do you generate the BOM and parts list for your weldment? You can generate the bill of materials and mark the components as Inseparable. In the drawing you generate the parts list for the weldment assembly.

Chapter 11

Functional Design

In this chapter, we will introduce the concept of functional design by using a CAD tool such as Inventor. The functional design tools in Inventor allow you to generate complex geometry by entering some input data. Before any geometry gets created, you can verify whether the design meets the requirements by performing a diverse set of calculations. The formulas used for the calculations are fully documented in the Engineer's Handbook. This allows the user to deviate from the built-in rules when experience dictates to override or ignore certain calculations.

In this chapter, you'll learn how to:

◆ Use Inventor's Design Accelerators

◆ Use Inventor's Design Calculators

◆ Understand the interaction of these tools with Content Center

◆ Develop best practices for using these tools

A 15-TON HOIST MACHINE

Many of the examples in this chapter are taken from the real-world 15-ton hoist machine depicted in Figure 11.1. The hoist has a full gearbox and brake system, which is situated in the front-left side of the machine. The different components of the machine were generated through classic part and assembly modeling. However, for the dynamic study of the different components and the analysis of the forces and the power transmission, Inventor's Gear Generator was extensively used.

FIGURE 11.1
A 15-ton hoist machine

Geometric Modeling vs. Functional Design

In most industries, product requirements and design criteria drive the engineering process. As its name implies, *functional design* favors function over geometry. Rather than modeling geometry first and then hoping that the form satisfies all the design criteria, in the functional design method, the designer or engineer makes sure the product operates correctly given the design criteria *prior* to finalizing the product's shape. If functional design is done well, the geometry will be the result of the design process rather than the input to it.

This chapter will concentrate on the design accelerator tools that Inventor offers to mechanical and electrical engineers so they can concentrate on the product requirements rather than spending most of their time generating the geometry of the product.

Most of the topics in this chapter require an assembly to be opened. Therefore, this chapter is not applicable if you have only Inventor LT installed.

Design Requirements

You've probably been confronted with several of the design criteria listed here. They are typical for the requirements that a design engineer will have to satisfy (in no particular order):

- Strength (material, size, weight, load conditions, mechanical behavior, safety factors)

- Power (speed, torque, momentum, power transmission, lubrication, safety)

- Temperature (cooling, heat dissipation)

- Vibration and motion (frequency response/eigenvalues/damping)

- Wear resistance (surface treatments, plating, tolerances/life cycle/wear/durability /lubrication)

- Sound restrictions/considerations (insulation/packaging)

- Optical characteristics (color, surface characteristics, refraction, transparency, chromatic aberration, aesthetics)

- Electrical and magnetic characteristics

- Cost (materials, packaging, eco-sustainability, spare parts, stock parts, standard sizes vs. custom made, maintenance, manufacturing and assembly methods, time restrictions)

Oftentimes, these requirements will conflict with each other; for example, improving strength or durability often will increase cost, and so on.

As a design engineer, you often use tools that help make the right trade-off by attempting to verify and optimize the design by using lab tests, calculations, stress analysis or rendering, and animations.

In this chapter, you will use the built-in calculation rules of the Design Accelerators in combination with animations and the Engineer's handbook to satisfy the strength, power, wear, and temperature requirements of a particular design. While doing so, we will show some real-world examples to illustrate functional design concepts. To underline the diversity of the tool, we will show examples spanning various industries, such as engine design (springs and cams), and power transmission design (gearbox).

Design Accelerators General Introduction

Inventor's Design Accelerators can be overwhelming at first because of the sheer number of accelerators and because the user interface is slightly different from the rest of Inventor. Therefore, we'll look at the dialog boxes, the browser structure, and the user interface for these tools.

Design Accelerators Input

Inventor's Design Accelerators are available only in the assembly environment. Design Accelerator dialog boxes are tabbed dialog boxes, as shown in Figure 11.2. The Design tab and the Calculation tab appear in most of the dialog boxes. Two particular areas in these dialog boxes are worth pointing out. The Results window displays the calculated values for a particular design. The Summary window will indicate whether a design is acceptable with the given parameters.

FIGURE 11.2
A typical Design Accelerator dialog box

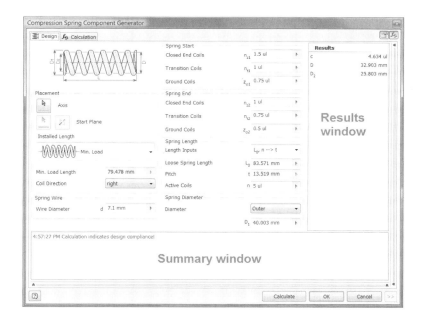

The calculation is not an automatic operation; for example, if a calculation fails and the values turn red, you typically change the parameters to correct the problem. You will not see the result of your change unless you explicitly click the Calculate button. Many calculators offer different types of calculations. Choosing a particular calculation method will disable certain fields (driven values) and enable some other fields (input values). Some calculators allow entering custom values (with, of course, a cost aspect associated with custom parts). Figure 11.3 and Figure 11.4 show an example dialog box (belt) that shows how its fields will look like if you are calculating the power from the torque and speed (Figure 11.3) vs. calculating the torque with the power and speed as inputs (Figure 11.4).

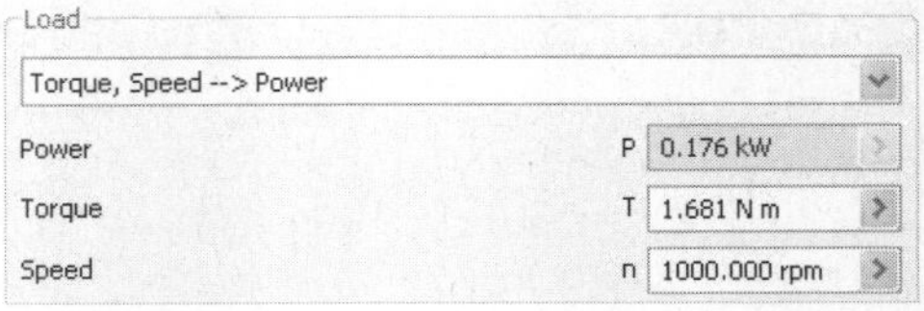

FIGURE 11.3
Torque, Speed -->
Power calculation

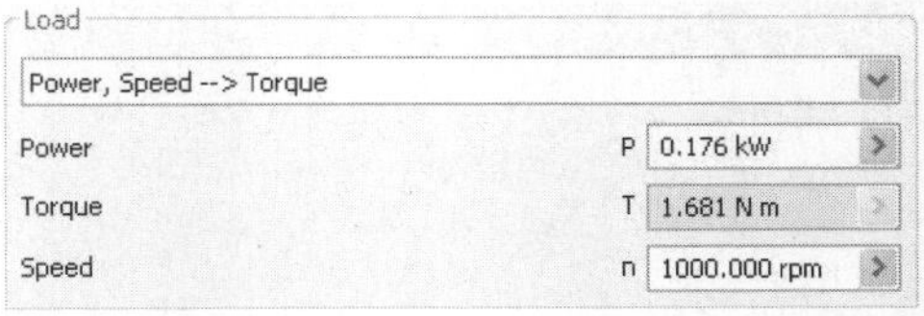

Load
Torque, Speed --> Power
Power   P 0.176 kW
Torque   T 1.681 N m
Speed   n 1000.000 rpm

FIGURE 11.4
Power, Speed -->
Torque calculation

Load
Power, Speed --> Torque
Power   P 0.176 kW
Torque   T 1.681 N m
Speed   n 1000.000 rpm

SEAN SAYS: REMEMBER TO CALCULATE

One common mistake is not clicking the Calculate button. The Design Accelerators will not update simply by changing values. You *must* click the Calculate button.

USING DEFAULT VALUES

The values used in the last calculation of a Design Accelerator component will be reused when you create a new Design Accelerator component with the same generator. If you want to use the default values of a Design Accelerator, hold down the Ctrl key when starting the Design Accelerator command.

Table 11.1 shows the icons and buttons that appear in all the Design Accelerator dialog boxes. It will help a lot if you familiarize yourself with their meaning before diving into the rest of this chapter. The border of the Design Accelerator window turns red to indicate a design failure or to flag a more general error.

Design Accelerators Output

There are two sorts of functional design tools: accelerators and calculators. It is important to understand the difference between these two categories. The output generated by Design *Accelerators* consists of subassemblies with actual geometry in them. The output generated by the Design *Calculators* (that is, the weld or plate calculators) consists only of a subassembly browser node. The calculators don't generate any geometry, but the result of the calculation can be edited and repeated with different values. The solve state of the subassemblies is indicated by an icon in the browser (Manual Solve is the default, as shown in Figure 11.5).

There are three solve states that can be changed in the Component context menu, as described in Table 11.2.

TABLE 11.1:   Common Design Accelerator Dialog Box Elements

ICON	FUNCTION
	Export to template
	Import template
	File naming
	Disable/enable calculation
	Reset calculation data
	Results displayed in HTML format
	Expand/collapse summary window
	Expand/collapse result window
	More options
	Selecting a different size or different properties
	Selecting a different type
	Deleting a selection

The possible solve states are reflected in the context menu, as shown in Figure 11.6.

The difference between Manual Solve and Automatic Solve is simple. Let's take the example of a V-belt. When the distance between the axes changes, a V-belt will automatically readjust the pulley positions if Automatic Solve is on. If Manual Solve is on, the user will have to update the pulley position by clicking the Manual Solve menu. A red lightning bolt will appear in the browser, as shown in Figure 11.7. Manual Solve (and not the more convenient Automatic Solve) is used as the default for performance reasons only.

FIGURE 11.5
Synchronous belt in Manual Solve mode

TABLE 11.2: Solve States of Design Accelerator Components

STATE	EXPLANATION
Solve Off	Change to Design Accelerator input conditions has no effect on Design Accelerator component
Manual Solve	Change to Design Accelerator input conditions only has effect after editing Design Accelerator component
Automatic Solve	Change to Design Accelerator input conditions immediately affects Design Accelerator component

FIGURE 11.6
Possible solve states

FIGURE 11.7
Out-of-date manually solved V-belt after moving one of its axes

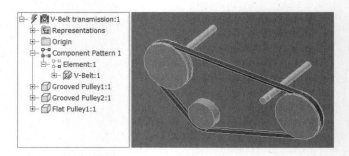

SEAN SAYS: AUTOMATIC (FOR THE PEOPLE)

Although it might be tempting to set all your accelerators to Automatic Solve, keep in mind that these tools can be very taxing on your system, especially if you are using multiple accelerators or if you are working in a large assembly. If you are going to be tweaking the position of a feature that affects the accelerator, then leave it set to automatic. However, once the design is somewhat firm, turn it to Manual Solve. It's the same advice that's given for adaptivity and the contact solver.

THE LIGHTNING BOLT ICON

The use of the yellow lightning bolt icon for a manual solve might be a bit misleading. Generally, in Inventor, this icon indicates that something is out-of-date. For Design Accelerator components, a yellow lightning bolt in the browser does not mean the component is out-of-date. An out-of-date Design Accelerator component is indicated by a red lightning bolt icon.

It is also interesting to note that the Manual Solve and Automatic Solve menus are mutually exclusive, whereas the Calculate menu is a toggle between two states.

The Calculate menu is the equivalent of the Calculate button at the top right of each Design Accelerator dialog box. It is a switch that enables or disables the Calculation tab. When calculation is turned off, the performance of the generator is faster.

The Solve Off menu does exactly that, turning off the solver completely so the Design Accelerator component is frozen until the next edit.

Because Design Accelerator assemblies typically are comprised of multiple parts that are constrained together, Inventor offers specific edit, delete, promote, and demote commands to handle these more complex entities. Figure 11.8 shows the edit and delete commands.

FIGURE 11.8
The special edit and delete commands

Figure 11.9 shows the promote and demote commands that are available on some generators only: gears, belts, cams, and shafts. Use these commands to demote Design Accelerator components out of their original Design Accelerator subassembly. This allows the grouping of components of different Design Accelerator assemblies into a single subassembly. The edit of a demoted component continues to be done on the original Design Accelerator assembly through the Edit Using Design Accelerator command.

FIGURE 11.9
The special promote and demote commands in the Component context menu

Be sure to set the Inventor selection priority to Components before you select Design Accelerator components; otherwise, you won't see the special commands.

We discourage editing the subassembly itself, but components in the subassembly can be edited under certain circumstances. Copying or patterning Design Accelerator assemblies will maintain the geometry, but you will lose the ability to edit the copied assembly with the Edit Using Design Accelerator command, which basically means you lose the Design Accelerator intelligence on the copy.

Design Generators and Content Center

Most design generators use Content Center parts, but not all. Consult Table 11.3 when you don't have access to Content Center and still want to use some of the Design Accelerators.

TABLE 11.3:   Design Accelerator's Use of Content Center Database

GENERATOR/ACCELERATOR	NEEDS CONTENT CENTER
Bolted Connections	Yes
Weld Calc	No
Tolerance Stack Up Calc	No
Limits and Fits Calc	No
Beam Calc	No (but recognizes section properties of Content Center and Frame Generator parts; see Chapter 15)
Column Calc	No (but recognizes section properties of Content Center and Frame Generator parts; see Chapter 15)
Plate Calc	No
Shaft Generator	No
Cam Generator	No
Gear Generator	No
Bearing Generator	Yes
Key Connection Generator	Yes
Spline Generator	No
Belt Generator	No
Sprocket and Chain Generator	Yes
Spring Generator	Yes (but only for belleville springs)
Pins Generator	Yes
Seals and O-rings Generator	Yes
Engineers Handbook	No

Prerequisites for This Chapter

For the remainder of this chapter and to successfully complete the exercises and the design challenges, please activate the project file called Chapter11.ipj that sits in the Start Design folder. If you want to look at the finished designs, activate the project called `Chapter11 final.ipj` from the Finished design folder. In both projects, we created frequently used folders that point to the different paragraphs and that facilitate browsing through the designs discussed in this chapter.

You will also need to have Inventor's Content Center library hooked up for many of the Design Accelerator tools that we will use in this chapter.

To access the Design Accelerator functionality, open any assembly document, and in the panel bar switch from the Assembly panel to the Design Accelerator panel.

Bolted Connections

This generator is the most popular of all Design Accelerator tools because it is able to make an entire set of bolts, washers, nuts, and the necessary holes in the supporting geometry an all-in-one operation, as the complexity of the command's dialog box in Figure 11.10 testifies. Because of its popularity, you will find that the Bolted Connection icon is also available in the regular Assembly panel bar.

FIGURE 11.10
Placement options in a bolted connection

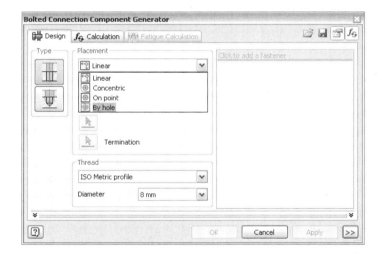

There are four placement options:

◆ Linear allows the creation of a bolted connection without any preexisting sketch by selecting a distance to two different linear edges.

◆ Concentric uses any circular edge (the edge does not have to be part of a hole feature; the edge can be part of a cylindrical extrusion) to make a bolted connection with a larger or smaller hole size.

◆ By Hole requires an existing hole, and the bolted connection will incorporate the existing hole.

◆ On Point requires an existing work point or vertex as input.

When you want the position of the holes of a bolted connection to be precisely defined and controlled, it is better to create the holes first with the regular Hole command in Inventor and then use the By Hole option rather than using the Linear or Concentric option. The disadvantage of the latter two options is that it creates only a point in a sketch, but the point is not dimensioned and could easily move. When the sketch point moves, the bolted connection will *not* follow the new position of the hole. When using By Hole, the bolted connection will automatically follow any *positional change* of the preexisting holes but will not follow *diameter changes* automatically. Keeping the diameter of the holes, generated by the bolted connection, in sync with the diameter changes in the preexisting hole requires manually selecting a different diameter in the Diameter field of the bolted connection. The reason this was done is to give you a choice because you don't necessarily want all your bolts to increase in diameter when the underlying hole diameter increases.

Enough theory, let's concentrate on an actual example. Open the assembly called `turret_handle.iam` from the Bolted Connection folder. You need to connect the brown cap with the blue plate. The cap has three holes drilled in it, and they form a circular pattern. The plate has no holes yet, and this can be verified by activating the view representation called Section. The design problem you are trying to solve is the following: considering an axial force of 750 N and a tangential force of 300 N, will three bolts be sufficient to hold the cap on the plate?

As mentioned, to respect the existing hole pattern in the cap and create the necessary holes in the plate, you start the Bolted Connection command first and take following steps:

1. Select the By Hole option.

2. Select the top face of the cap as the start plane.

3. Once you have a pattern of holes selected, the Follow Pattern option will become available, as shown in Figure 11.11. Check the Follow Pattern option.

4. Select the Termination option, and click the bottom of the blue plate as the termination face.

FIGURE 11.11
Following holes of an existing pattern

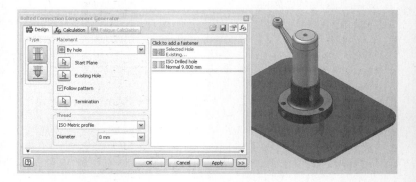

Note that there are three drilled holes automatically added to the blue plate. You could select a different hole type (counter bore), of course, by clicking the down arrow. The Bolted Connection Generator is clever enough to filter out countersink hole types for holes on faces that are not exposed. Because the holes in the cap have an 8 mm diameter, select a diameter of 8 mm as well for the hole in the blue plate. Also note that when you edit the plate, the holes in the plate have a lock symbol next to their icon in the browser indicating that they are generated by a Design Accelerator and can be modified only by that same Design Accelerator. Proof of this is that the Edit Feature command or the "double-click to edit" behavior is absent for these type of holes. If you want the hole in the plate to be independent from the Design Accelerator they were generated by, use the Explode context menu on the hole.

At this point, you can add all necessary hardware to finish the connection. It is important to note that the order of the icons in the pane on the right represents the stacking order of the bolted connection starting from the start plane down. If you want to place a bolt on the start plane, you just click the area marked with Click To Add A Fastener. You select an M8 × 45 bolt from the DIN6921 family in the Content Center database. The default proposed bolt length should be sufficient to protrude through the backside of the plate and accommodate the nut and washer, but if you desire, you can change the length of the bolt by dragging the red arrow glyph, as shown in Figure 11.12.

FIGURE 11.12
Adding bolt and adjusting bolt length via arrow glyph

If you wanted to thread the plate to avoid adding a nut and washer, you could do so by clicking the . . . icon in the ISO Drilled hole section of the pane, as shown in Figure 11.13.

FIGURE 11.13
Adding a hole thread

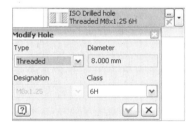

You can finish the connection by adding a washer and nut at the end of the bolt. You therefore choose the Click To Add A Fastener area at the bottom of the stack in the right pane of the dialog box, as shown in Figure 11.14.

Do you meet the design criteria with just three bolts? It all depends on the material you choose for the bolts. There are a few strength calculations on the Calculation tab:

- Bolt diameter design

- Number of bolts design

- Bolt material design

- Check calculation

FIGURE 11.14
Adding the washer and
bolt

Select the number of bolts design calculation and enter **750 N** for the maximal axial force and **300 N** for the maximal tangent force. Assuming that you are working in an environment where high conductivity between the different components is required, this forces you to use a copper alloy for the bolt material. To select a different bolt material, first check the box in front of the User Material pulldown list. To narrow down the material search to copper materials only, type **Copper** in the text field below the Material column header.

Select Copper-Nickel C96200 as the material, exit the Materials dialog box by hitting the OK button hit, and hit the Calculate button. You will see that the calculator indicates in Figure 11.15 through the value z in the Results pane that with this material you would need four bolts to guarantee sufficient strength in your construction.

FIGURE 11.15
Calculator advises four
bolts

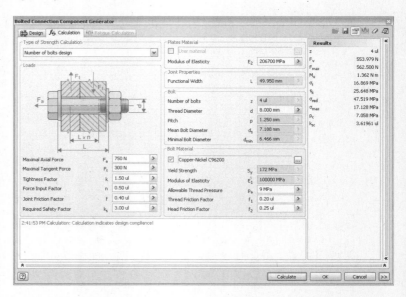

To comply your design to the calculation, you need to update the hole pattern in the cap from three to four members, and the bolted connection pattern follows accordingly, as shown in Figure 11.16 (if Automatic Solve is on) or after clicking the Component ➤ Manual Solve menu (if Manual Solve is on).

FIGURE 11.16
Final result with four
bolted connections

FIGURE 11.16
Final result with four
bolted connections

Like many Design Accelerator assemblies, the bolted connection subassembly shown in Figure 11.17 is a phantom subassembly so that only its subcomponents are shown at the parent level in the BOM.

FIGURE 11.17
Bolted connection
assembly does not par-
ticipate in BOM

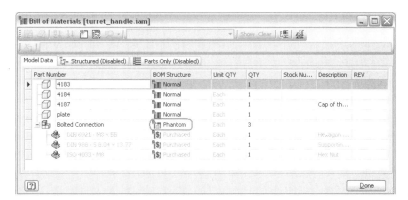

As explained earlier, the bolted connection makes the holes automatically for you. In a similar fashion, if you remove a bolted connection, you have the choice to remove the associated holes or not, as shown in Figure 11.18.

SEAN SAYS: USE BOLTED CONNECTIONS WITH CAUTION

While the Bolted Connection Design Accelerator can make quick work of adding a number of fasteners, you can get yourself into trouble easily. Because the fasteners do not adapt automatically to the diameter of the holes, you can easily find yourself out on the shop floor with boxes of fasteners that do not fit your parts. When changing the diameters of holes, you *must* go back and change the fastener diameter in the Design Accelerator.

FIGURE 11.18
Deleting the holes of a
bolted connection

Calculators

Inventor has several Design Calculators perform a specific calculation without generating any geometry. The dialog box for calculators is also restricted to one tab, the Calculation tab. Calculators do generate a node in the assembly browser, which allows you to repeat the calculation with different input values. We'll cover one calculator in more detail than the others because all calculators are very similar (weld, solder and hub joints, power screw, tolerance calculator).

Weld Calculator

Here is the functional design problem that you can solve with the weld calculator: what combination of weld material and weld height should you use for a given safety factor so that the weld withstands a lateral point force (3000 N) at a distance of 50 mm from the weld plane?

As a guide to this section, open the weld1.iam assembly from the Weldments folder. You will see that the assembly contains a rectangular tube, fillet welded to a plate. Because of this fillet weld, you'll use the fillet weld calculator.

After opening the Fillet Weld (Spatial Load) calculator, select a rectangular shape in the Weld Form pulldown. Deselect the default Weld Loads Of Axial force perpendicular to the weld plane, and select the Bending force parallel with the weld plane Weld Load instead.

Enter a bending force of **3000 N**, and enter the force arm of **50 mm**. This gives you a dialog box like in Figure 11.19. Note that we haven't chosen the Joint (or Weld) material yet and that the three dimensions defining the weld bead shape still need to be entered.

Use the Fillet Weld (Connection Plane Load) calculator instead of the Fillet Weld (Spatial Load) calculator when the loads are situated only in the plane of the weld.

There are a few interesting things to note about this calculator:

◆ There is no automatic link between the weld assembly and the weld calculator. To obtain the beam height, beam width, and weld height, use the Measure pulldown menu under the right arrow of the real value edit controls *inside* the calculator window, and proceed with measuring the weld bead in the model. Do not use the Measure commands in the Tools menu because this will exit the Design Accelerator dialog box.

An alternative is to measure and copy these distances to the clipboard prior to entering the calculator and then pasting them into the calculator.

◆ The actual weld results get stored as a subassembly without any geometry in the main assembly.

◆ Weld loads can be combined. The example in Figure 11.20 shows a combination of axial force, bending force, and torque.

◆ Weld results can be edited or can be exported to HTML files for viewing in a web browser.

◆ Fatigue calculation is not on by default and has to be explicitly turned on with the second icon at the top right of the dialog box.

FIGURE 11.19
Fillet Weld calculator

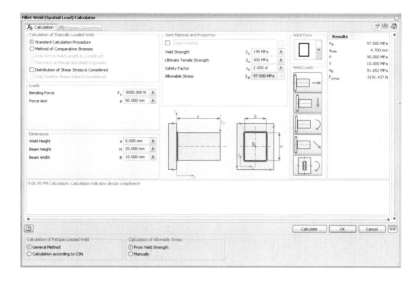

FIGURE 11.20
Weld load types

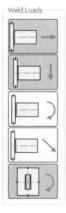

Enter **5 mm** for the weld height (a), **20 mm** for the beam height (H) and **10 mm** for the beam width (B).

As the last step, you choose the weld material by filtering out any materials that are not classified as weld material. Do this by entering **W** in the Type column, as shown in Figure 11.21. Be careful — these columns are case sensitive, so using a lowercase w will result in filtering out everything because there is no type that starts with w. Select Electrode E51xx as the material.

You can now finally click the Calculate button, and all values will be displayed in black (not red) in the Results window, as shown in Figure 11.22. At the same time, the message ''Calculation indicates design compliance!'' will show up in the Summary window.

FIGURE 11.21
Choosing a weld material in the weld calculator

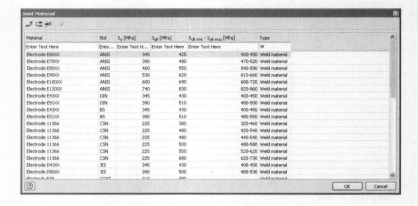

FIGURE 11.22
Weld calculator indicating a satisfactory design

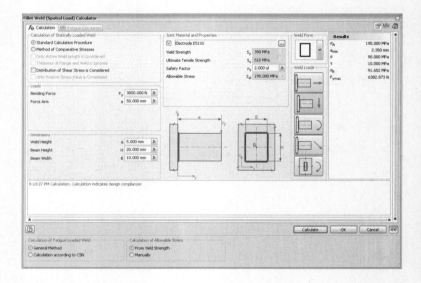

We will now explore an additional what-if scenario. What will happen if the anticipated force of 3000 is higher and you have a force of 8500N? You will most likely have to increase the weld height or the weld material to avoid breakage if you pursue the same safety factor of 2x. Well, the weld calculator will help you figure out exactly what the adequate weld height or the adequate material would be in this new situation.

Edit the existing Fillet Weld calculation, and enter **8500N** as bending force. When one or more result values show up in red, an error message will be displayed in the Summary window. The example in Figure 11.23 shows that the choice of a 5 mm weld height violates the minimum recommended weld height (a_{min}) of 6.658 mm, resulting in unacceptable stress levels.

Changing the weld height in your design to 6.658 or higher will guarantee safe stress levels. If you set the weld height to 7 mm, the calculation would pass. An alternative is to use a different weld material in the Joint Material and Properties pulldown. If you change Electrode E51xx to Electrode 120xx, a material that has a higher yield strength S_y of 740 MPa, the calculation will pass as well.

FIGURE 11.23
Weld calculator flagging
a bad design

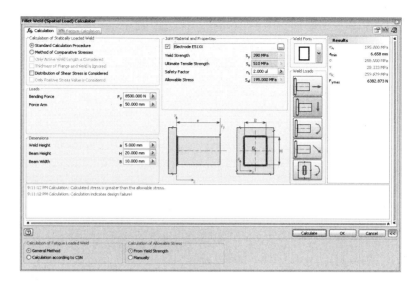

It is interesting to note that there is no relationship between materials as defined in the Design Accelerator dialog boxes and materials as defined in the Inventor style library.

To complete the exercise and to keep the calculator in sync with the actual assembly, two things need to happen. First, it would be good to also create the material E51xx in the Style And Standard editor, as shown in Figure 11.24, mark it as a weldment material, and assign this material to the weld bead properties. If you are planning on using this material on a regular basis, it would be even a better idea to add this material to the style library so you can use it in every weldment assembly via a template file.

FIGURE 11.24
Definition of Electrode
E51xx as weldment
material

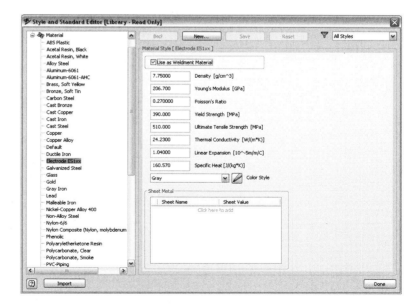

Second, if we plan to use our original material Electrode E51xx, we need to change the weld height to 7.5 mm in the weld beads of our assembly.

You used only one type of weld calculator. In Inventor there are different weld calculators for each weld type (fillet weld, butt weld, plug and groove weld, spot weld, bevel joint, lap joint, tube joint), but all use methods similar to the one explained earlier. So, it should be pretty straightforward to find your way around in the other weld calculators.

SEAN SAYS: SAVE CALCULATIONS

Once you click OK, you will be prompted to save an assembly (IAM) file. Once you save this file in your project directory, an assembly node is created in the browser. This assembly node has no geometry but contains all the information you used in your calculations. This is useful to both keep track of the calculations you have performed but also to allow others to see how you arrived at the current design. In some cases, this information might even be useful for legal purposes if the safety of your design is ever called into question.

Generators

The majority of the modules in the Design Accelerator add-in are generators. Generators not only perform calculations, but they also automatically generate the underlying geometry. This can be a real time-saver especially when you are talking about complex geometry such as helical gears or chains or synchronous belts. You will take an in-depth look at several of these generators.

Gear Generator

There are three gear families in Inventor: Spur Gears, Bevel Gears, and Worm Gears. We will explain the use of spur gears in the design of a gearbox. Therefore, open first the assembly called `Hoistgearbox.iam` from the Gears folder, and activate the view representation called Top-section. This will produce a cross-section view, as shown in Figure 11.25.

FIGURE 11.25
Top section view of the gearbox

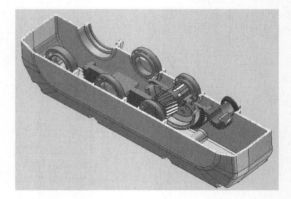

The work axis on the left depicts the driving or input axis (motor side), and the work axis on the right depicts the driven or output axis (load axis). The design challenge in this gearbox is to add the remaining gear pair to connect to the output axis while fulfilling the power requirements on that axis (7.5 kW) and the speed requirements (260 rpm) and to select a gear material that guarantees a minimum life cycle of 15000 hr.

To complete this exercise correctly and to get the same values as shown in the different figures, it is important to choose the same options as explained in this section. Start the Spur Gears command, and in this example, you will add a gear pair between the left work axis and the middle work axis, as shown in Figure 11.25. The gear (Gear2) on the left axis will be the larger gear. The gear on the middle work axis will be the smaller gear (Gear1).

Let's first make our geometrical inputs by selecting the cylindrical faces from the bearings to determine the axes of the two gears and by selecting the end face of an existing gear with name Gear 4 as the start plane for Gear1.

To determine the transmission ratio and the size of the gears, choose the Module Design Guide, and in the advanced options (by using the >> button), select Gear Ratio as the input type. This design method allows you to enter a helix angle of 8 degrees, a gear ratio of 3.6, and the number of teeth on the first gear. You can pick 19 teeth for the smaller first gear (because of the lack of space in the middle of the gearbox). The number of teeth can also be set on the graphical screen by dragging one of the four red dots on the small gear. Double-clicking the red dot gives you yet another way of entering the number of teeth. Set the face width for both gears to be 20 mm. The result on the graphic screen should look like Figure 11.26.

FIGURE 11.26
Smaller Gear 1 on the
left, larger Gear 2 on the
right

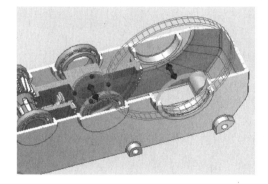

Leave pressure angle and face width unchanged, and when clicking the Calculate button, the design should be compliant like in Figure 11.27. The center distance is automatically calculated from the two cylindrical faces that you picked.

By choosing the Module Design Guide, you also unambiguously determined the module value (this value is read-only in this method, which is indicated by its field that is grayed out).

After satisfying the space and position requirements, you'll now concentrate on selecting the right material for the gears to satisfy the power and speed requirements. Activate the Calculation tab, and perform a calculation according to the ISO 6336:1996. Expand the advanced options by hitting the >> button; for the type of load calculation, you use the option Power, Speed -->

Torque because power and speed are known inputs. Also choose 37Cr4 with a face-hardened heat treatment for Gear 1 and 30CrMoV6 4 alloy materials for Gear 2.

FIGURE 11.27
Gear design shows compliance

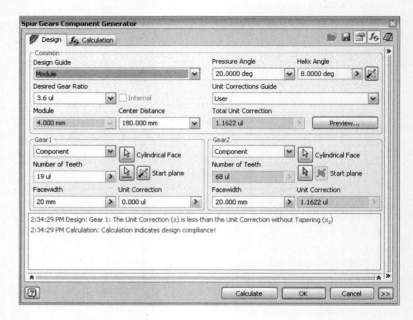

Enter **7.5 kW** for the power and **260 rpm** for the speed.

Use the Accuracy buttons if you want to adjust the precision of the calculation.

Select the Factors button to change load and lubrication parameters. The only modification you will make in this dialog box is to the Kinematic diagram of your gear. Select the diagram as shown in Figure 11.28. This diagram corresponds best with the gearbox situation.

After entering these values and clicking Calculate, you will notice in Figure 11.29 that you exceed the safety factors for pitting and tooth breakage.

To avoid breakage, you can make your gears stronger by making them wider. On the Design tab, you change the face width of Gear 1 to 60 mm and the face width of Gear 2 to 58 mm. If you also think that the contact safety factor 1.2 in the Advanced Options of the Calculation tab is overly cautious, you can reduce it to 1.0. When you repeat the calculation, you now get compliance, as indicated in Figure 11.30.

Finish off the Gear 1 by adding a couple of cylindrical extrusions and chamfers to the Spur Gear 1 part so that it fits nicely between the two ball bearings. You also make a 60 mm hole in Gear 4 so that it can slide over the shaft of Gear 1. Figure 11.31 shows the smaller Gear 1, while Gear 4 has been made invisible.

Gear design in Inventor is limited to a pair of gears at a time. When designing a gear train of five helical gears, you will have to perform three different gear set calculations and make sure you use the same units in each set.

You can lock a gear's position by turning off the flexibility on the gear set assembly.

FIGURE 11.28
Kinematic diagram of
the gear set

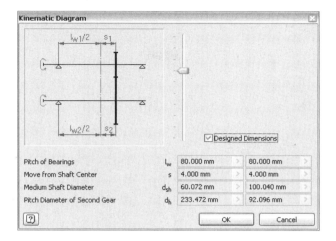

FIGURE 11.29
Gear calculator indi-
cates risk of pitting or
breakage for this design

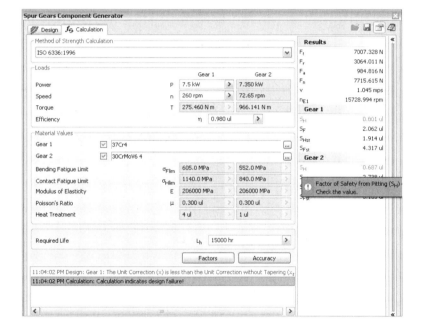

FIGURE 11.30
Gear calculation indicating compliance after changing width and safety factor

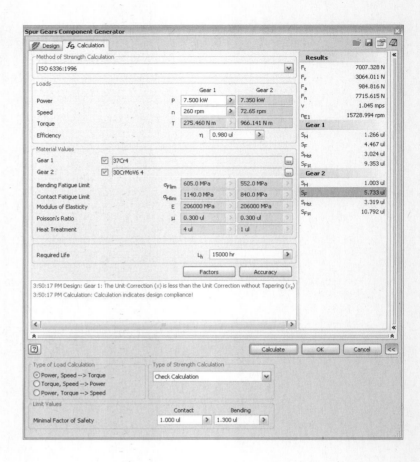

FIGURE 11.31
Finished Gear 1

Key Connections

Key and spline connections are typically used to fasten gears on shafts. In the previous example, you constructed a spur gear set, but the movement of the spur gear set is not yet driven or connected to the other gears. Therefore, you will use keys to make a rigid connection between Spur Gear1 and Gear 4 of Gear Set 2 while trying to solve your design challenge: connect the gear on the shaft with a key connection, and make sure that the connection does not break for a given speed (260 rpm) and given power transmission (7.5 kW).

Open HoistGearBox.iam from the Key Connections folder, and activate the view representation called Gears. Make the spur gears flexible, and verify that you can freely rotate Gear 1 around the axis of the bore hole in Gear 4. Figure 11.32 shows Gear 1 and Gear 4.

FIGURE 11.32
Gear 4 on the left and
Gear 1 on the right

Start the Key Connection Generator (it is one the commands in the Shaft Generator pulldown). In the Key Connection Generator window, select first the key type from the Content Center library, and pick ISO 2491 A. Set the groove type to a groove with two rounded ends. Change the default number of keys from 1 to 3.

When you select the shaft of Gear1 as Reference 1 *and* the end face of the shaft as Reference 2 for the shaft groove, the calculator detects a diameter of 60 mm and proposes a key length of 50 mm. Override the key length by selecting a slightly larger size of 63 mm from the pulldown. You can also more conveniently drag the red size arrows on the graphical screen to change the key size (only sizes available in the library can be selected). The key size shown will be 18 × 7 – 63.

You also make the necessary selections on Gear 4 for the Hub Groove, because the Key Connection Generator by default not only generates the keys but also the necessary grooves in both the shaft and the gear (hub). You can decide which of these three objects to generate by selecting all or a couple of the icons in the Select Objects To Generate section of the dialog box.

The Key Connection Generator automatically chooses an orientation plane for the keys. You can override the orientation by selecting work geometry or origin planes that belong to the respective parts (either the shaft or the gear). You cannot select any of the origin planes of the parent assembly. To determine the orientation and to avoid extra construction, you prefer to select the YZ origin plane for both the shaft and the hub groove. The two YZ origin planes are the two visible planes in the active view presentation, as shown in Figure 11.33.

FIGURE 11.33
Autoresized YZ planes
used for key orientation

You can change the angle of the first key relative to the orientation plane by dragging the red single-sided arrow, as shown in Figure 11.34.

FIGURE 11.34
Using single-sided arrow
to determine orientation

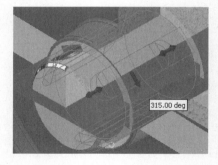

Your design dialog box should now look like in Figure 11.35.

Before you click OK to generate the keys, you want to make sure that your design withstands the speed (260 rpm) and power (7.5 kW) you set forth. Enter the speed and power in their respective fields, and select surface-hardened steel for the key material. Leave the loading conditions at their default values in the Joint Properties panel. When you run the calculation, your design is considered to be safe according to Figure 11.36.

Figure 11.37 shows a cross section of the completed key connection.

FIGURE 11.35
Defining three keys on a gear shaft

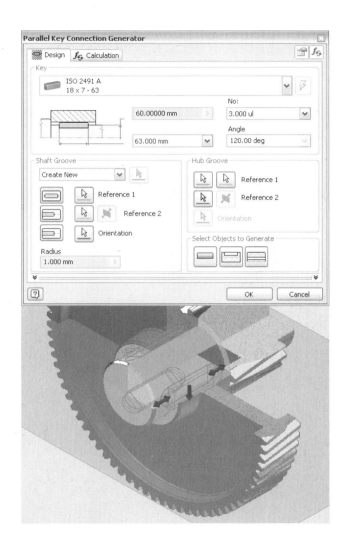

FIGURE 11.36
Key calculation on a
gear shaft

FIGURE 11.37
Completed key
connection

Shaft Generator

Open Hoistgearbox.iam from the Shaft Generator folder, and activate the view representation called Output Shaft.

The design challenge here is to design a shaft that holds the output gear so that it withstands the forces and bending moments generated by the driving gear while lifting a load of 2 ton (20 kN).

Start the Shaft Generator, and you will notice that the generator automatically prepopulates four segments. Remove all except the first segment by using the x icons to the right of the segments. This should result in a situation, as shown in Figure 11.38.

FIGURE 11.38
Default shaft with first
segment active

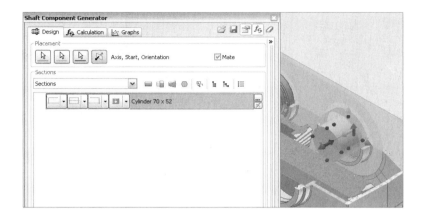

You first carefully pick the start location of the shaft by selecting a cylindrical opening on the housing, a planar face on the housing, and an orientation plane (the only visible plane in the active view representation).

Two sets of arrows are now visible on the shaft. The thin RGB arrows on the shaft depict the X, Y, and Z directions as usual and cannot be dragged. The thicker arrows, however, can be dragged.

Dragging the thick double-sided red arrow changes the length of the active shaft segment, and dragging the red dots allows you to change the diameter (in the image above the first segment is active). You can also enter the diameter and length values manually by clicking the . . . icon (or double-clicking the segment row in the dialog box) and collect the dimensions by measuring the surrounding geometry.

Dragging the thick blue arrow allows you to change the orientation of the shaft. Double-click the thick blue arrow, and orient the shaft to 0 or 360 degrees.

Dragging the thick green arrow allows to create an offset from the housing. Note that by default the Mate icon is checked, indicating that the shaft will be constrained to the housing. Therefore, it is a good idea to create a 0.5 mm offset with the thick green arrow.

Every segment has four sets of pulldown icons. The second set defines the overall shape of the segment, and the other icons add detail such as chamfers, fillets, grooves, reliefs, wrenches, threads, and keyways. Figure 11.39 shows the fourth pulldown set.

FIGURE 11.39
The four icon sets that
define the geometry of a
segment

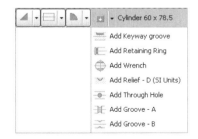

Change the size of the first segment to 60 mm × 78.5 mm, as shown in Figure 11.40. Add a 0.5 mm chamfer to the segment by using the first set of pulldown icons.

FIGURE 11.40
Changing the size of the
first segment

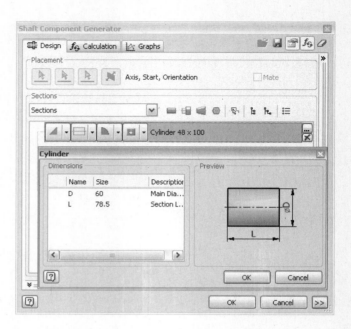

SEAN SAYS: QUICKLY CHANGE DIAMETERS AND LENGTHS

Although you can change the diameter and length of a section of shaft by dragging the grips if you want to quickly change these values or if you want to enter a precise value, click the . . . button next to the section of interest. This opens a dialog box that allows you to enter the diameter and length.

Add four more cylindrical segments to the shaft to accommodate the future bearings and the output gear. Change the size of each segment by measuring the distance in the housing and diameters of the openings. Here are the dimensions of the four extra segments, as shown in Figure 11.41:

68 mm × 64 mm

75 mm × 36.5 mm

80 mm × 20 mm

78 mm × 46 mm

You have now created the geometry of the shaft so that it fits nicely within the confines of the gearbox, but does it also satisfy the load requirements? To find out the forces and moments that are at play on the output gear, you exit the Shaft Generator for a second and edit the Spur Gears subassembly using Design Accelerator and enable the Calculation tab on the Spur Gears component. See Table 11.1 to find out the icon to enable a calculation. Run the calculation on the gear, and consult the calculation results by clicking the Results button in the Calculation tab. From the results (shown in Figure 11.42), you learn that the radial force on the shaft on the output gear location is 3064 N, the tangential force is 7007 N, and the axial force is 984 N.

With this knowledge, you can now start the shaft calculation, and you edit the existing shaft.

FIGURE 11.41
Geometry of shaft with
five segments

FIGURE 11.42
Load results of the out-
put gear

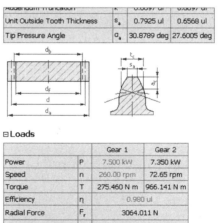

		Gear 1	Gear 2
Power	P	7.500 kW	7.350 kW
Speed	n	260.00 rpm	72.65 rpm
Torque	T	275.460 N m	966.141 N m
Efficiency	η	0.980 ul	
Radial Force	F_r	3064.011 N	
Tangential Force	F_t	7007.328 N	
Axial Force	F_a	984.816 N	
Normal Force	F_n	7715.615 N	
Circumferential Speed	v	1.045 mps	
Resonance Speed	n_{E1}	15728.994 rpm	

☐ Loads

To add a radial force to the middle of segment 2, first activate segment 2 by selecting the middle green dot on segment 2 by clicking either the 2D Preview screen or the 3D graphics. Then select the Loads pulldown. Select the first icon (down arrow) next to the pulldown. The available load types are shown in Figure 11.43; they are radial force, axial force, continuous load, bending moment, torque, and common load.

FIGURE 11.43
The six different load types

The radial force on the gear translates into a force in the X direction on the shaft. Likewise, the tangential force on the gear will result in a force in the Y direction on the shaft situated in the center of segment 2, which is the segment on which the output gear will sit. By clicking the . . . option on the force in the dialog box or by double-clicking the force arrow on the graphical screen, you can change the Forces option to be Forces in X and Y Axes.

Enter Force in x-axis = 3064 N and Force in y-axis = 7007 N. See also Figure 11.44. You can now delete the default radial force on segment 1.

Here are a couple of tips on how to navigate around the shaft preview. The force arrow can be dragged along the shaft so that it snaps to one of the green hotspots. The green hotspots depict the center and the extremities of the segments and are associative with any shaft geometry change. The blue hotspot depicts the active segment (any load or support that is added will be added to the *active* segment). So, it is extremely important to position your blue dot in the right location prior to adding loads or supports!

The force arrows can be reconnected to the green hotspots by double-clicking the arrow and entering a zero distance. When you hold down the Ctrl key, you can rotate the force vector to change its angle.

FIGURE 11.44
Entering the radial and tangential forces and positioning supports for the shaft

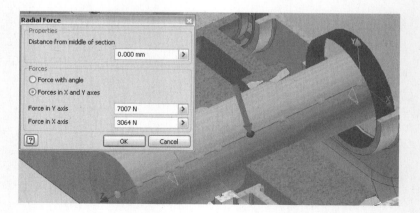

You now concentrate on defining the correct position of the free and the fixed support. If you look at Figure 11.44, the fixed support is the cyan triangle on the left in the middle of segment 4, and the free support is the cyan triangle on segment 1 at 10 mm from the end of the shaft or -29 mm from the middle of segment 1. The two supports are typically provided by bearings.

In Figure 11.45, you can see that the axial force is 948 N. Add this force to segment 2 but with a minus sign.

FIGURE 11.45
Entering data for an
axial force

FIGURE 11.45
Entering data for an
axial force

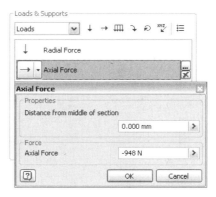

In a similar fashion, we add torque of 966 Nm to segment 2 and -966 Nm to segment 5. Torque is shown with two circular arrow glyphs that are pointing in opposite directions as illustrated in Figure 11.46.

FIGURE 11.46
Adding torque and axial
force to the shaft

The shaft will also undergo some bending because of the axial force on the output gear. Determining the value of the bending moment is relatively simple:

$$Bending\ moment = axial\ force\ on\ output\ gear \times \frac{pitch\ diameter\ of\ output\ gear}{2}$$

The value of the pitch diameter can be found once again in the gear calculation results table (274.673 mm) of Figure 11.42. We enter a bending moment value along the x-axis of 948N*274.673 mm/2 on segment 2, as shown in Figure 11.47.

Finally, you add to segment 5 the actual load that the shaft will have to provide (20 kN). The load is shown as the arrow on the left pointing down in Figure 11.48.

To complete this challenge, inspect several types of graphs on the Graphs tab to see whether stresses remain within reasonable limits. With a 29.2 MPa total stress, as shown in Figure 11.49, this design is considered to be safe.

If you open the HoistGearBox.iam from the Shaft Generator final folder, you can animate the gearbox by driving the Drive Me angular constraint.

FIGURE 11.47
Adding a bending moment to the shaft

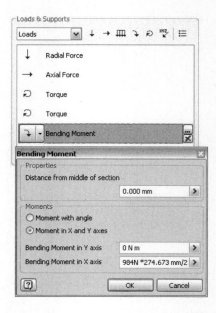

FIGURE 11.48
Adding a 2-ton load completes the load conditions

FIGURE 11.49
Reduced stress graph of the shaft

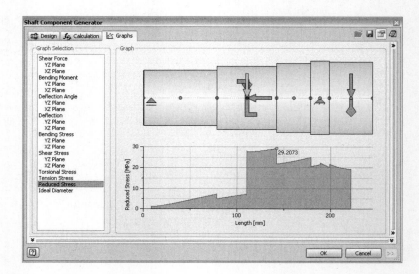

Cam Generator

Inventor has a Linear Cam Generator and a Disc Cam Generator. For the benefit of this challenge, we will use the Disc Cam Generator only.

The challenge in this exercise is to design the camshaft of a special Otto combustion engine: design a camshaft that opens the inlet (and outlet valve) over a distance of 0.7 mm during 1/4 of the full-cycle period. The engine is a four-stroke Otto-type engine running at 1000 RPM.

Open the `Single cylinder 4 stroke engine.iam` assembly from the cam generator folder, and select the cross-section view representation.

SECTIONING OF SHAFT PARTS

You will note that the bearings and the shaft are not sectioned in this view representation. Shafts and fasteners typically do not get sectioned in general in technical drawings. If you still want to section the shaft in the assembly, you can do this by checking the Participate In Assembly And Drawing Sections check box in the Modeling tab of the document settings of the shaft part inside the shaft assembly.

Before you dive into the cam design, we'll point out several important things you need to know about the cam generator:

◆ The updates in the Design tab window are not automatic. You will have to click the Calculate button to update the graph after a change has been made.

◆ When hovering over the graph, the tool tip will give intermediate values.

◆ By default there are two segments in the cam graph. You can add segments by clicking the Add Before or Add After button. Click the Delete button to delete segments. You are not editing all segments all the time. The segment number that is shown in the Actual Segment pulldown is the active segment. All edits will affect only the active or actual segment.

◆ The YZ origin plane of the Disc Cam component corresponds with the 0-degree angle of the graph. This is important to know when you later in the design add Angular constraints to this YZ plane to correctly orient the cam on the shaft.

◆ The start plane of the cam is the plane in which the cam profile sketch is created. The generator extrudes the sketch perpendicular to this start plane to obtain the cam.

◆ In the cam dialog box, you can superpose multiple graphs (torque, pressure, and so on). Figure 11.50 shows the different graph types. Each graph has its own color. For a disc cam, the x-axis of the graph goes from 0 to 360 degrees. For a linear cam, the x-axis represents the length. The vertical axis has no units because all the different cam parameters can be displayed simultaneously on the same graph. This would otherwise result in a ton of different units on the same axis.

FIGURE 11.50
Icons for different graph types

Now let's return to our challenge. To work correctly during the four phases of the Otto cycle, ideally our valves would have to work according to the diagram in Figure 11.51.

FIGURE 11.51
Lift vs. camshaft angle

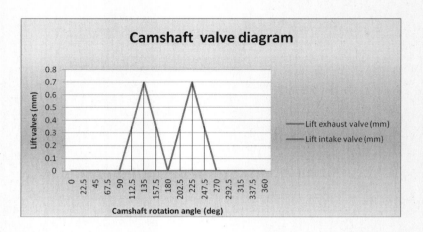

The question is how to follow this ideal diagram as closely as possible within the laws of physics. That is where the Inventor's Disc Cam Generator comes in handy.

Start the Disc Cam Generator, select a cylindrical face, and select one of the two cylindrical rings that are situated on the cam shaft. Select the ring that is closest to the inlet valve. As the start plane, select the side of the ring.

On the Design tab of the inlet cam, enter the geometry data that you can readily measure on the model. Enter the following:

Basic radius $= 4.3/2\,\text{mm} = 2.15\,\text{mm}$

Cam width $= 2\,\text{mm}$

Roller radius $= 0.5\,\text{mm}$

Roller width $= 0.4\,\text{mm}$

For the angle vs. lift data, you enter the data from the camshaft valve diagram pictured in Figure 11.51. Leave the lift at zero for the first two segments covering 0–90 degrees and 90–180 degrees because the peak in our ideal graph would give you excessive forces between cam and cam follower. We prefer to take an harmonic (sinusoidal) transition between zero lift and maximum lift in the third segment and an harmonic transition from maximum lift to zero lift in the fourth segment. Finally, leave the lift at zero in the fifth segment that goes from 270 degrees to 360 degrees. The result should look identical to Figure 11.52.

You can also overlay other graphs like acceleration and torque over the inlet cam shape graph like in Figure 11.53.

A full overview of all calculations and all graphs can be obtained by exporting the results into an HTML-formatted report by clicking the Results icon.

FIGURE 11.52
Inlet cam shape

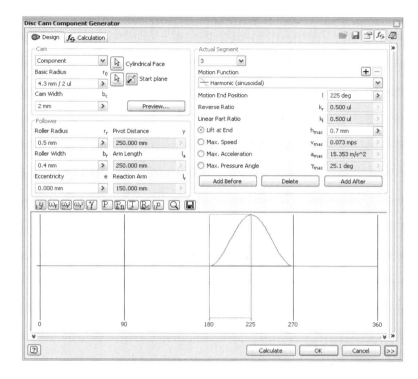

FIGURE 11.53
Inlet cam shape with
acceleration and speed
overlays

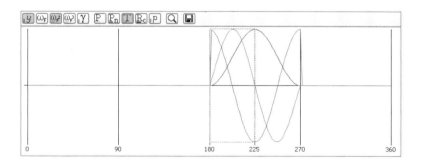

You now move on to the strength calculation of the cam. Figure 11.54 shows the values that need to be entered on the Calculation tab. Here follows the explanation of those values. The camshaft runs at half the speed of the crankshaft, which means it will operate at $1000/2 = 500$ rpm. The force on the roller is calculated around 1 N (see the "Springs" section in this chapter for more details), and the spring rating or spring constant k is 0.544 N/mm. For the material for both the cam and the cam follower, we select Steel SAE 5130 that has an allowable pressure 900 MPa, which is safely higher than the maximum allowable pressure of 607 MPa that the calculator comes up with.

You could easily copy the Inlet cam and rename the copy to Exhaust Cam, but you would not have any Design Accelerator edit capability on the copy. An alternative and far better method is to use Design Accelerator templates. Most of Design Accelerators have a Save icon at the top of the dialog box, and this allows you to create a template file. This is a small file in XML format that allows the reuse of all design and calculation parameters of a previous calculation in subsequent calculations.

FIGURE 11.54
Cam material chosen to meet maximum pressure

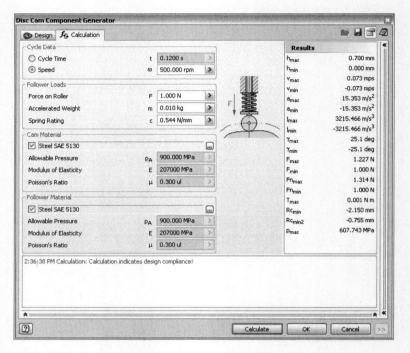

You export the Inlet cam parameters in a file called harmonic.xml and start a new Cam Component Generator dialog box. In this dialog box, you import the harmonic.xml template (use the icon that looks like an open folder), remove the first segment, and reduce the angles of the remaining segments with 90 degrees. Figure 11.55 shows the completed lift graph of the exhaust cam.

FIGURE 11.55
Exhaust cam lift

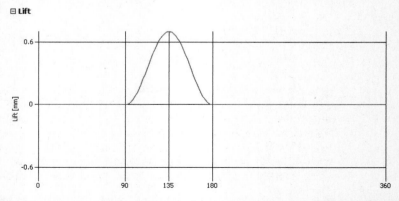

When the piston is placed at its top position (ignition), the two cams are mounted and oriented on the shaft in the position, as shown in Figure 11.56. Use Angular Mate constraints between the cams and between the cams and the shaft to accomplish the correct 90-degree angular shift between the inlet cam and exhaust cam so that the intake phase correctly follows the exhaust phase. This might require some experimentation. You can simulate the entire Otto cycle by driving the constraint that is called Drive Me. If you have problems finding the right constraints, use the Modeling view mode in the assembly browser to group them.

FIGURE 11.56
Position of cams at the ignition point

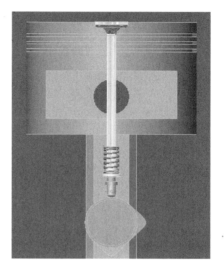

Spring Generator

Inventor can generate four spring types:

◆ Compression springs

◆ Extension springs

◆ Torsion springs

◆ Belleville springs

We will illustrate how to use compression springs to generate the springs that allow you to keep the valves closed. For this exercise, you will use the same `Single cylinder four-stroke engine.iam` assembly from the Springs folder. First you bring the valve in the closed position by placing the Drive Me constraint in a 0-degree position. This allows you to measure the minimum working load length (2.392 mm) of the spring you are about to design. See Figure 11.57 to find out which faces to select during the Measure command.

Start the Compression Spring Generator, and select the axis of the Inlet valve as the axis for the spring and place the start plane of the spring on the end face of the bushing.

To give the spring a sufficient amount of coils and to ensure that the spring fits nicely within the cavity, use a relatively thin wire diameter of 0.15 mm. Set the inner spring diameter to 1 mm so that the spring can slide over the bushing. Because we want to mount the spring in the state when the valve is closed, we take the Min. Load option for the Installed Length pulldown. Set the number of closed end coils and transition coils at 1 for both Spring Start and Spring End. Set the number of ground coils at both ends at 0.5.

FIGURE 11.57
Determining the mini-
mum load spring length

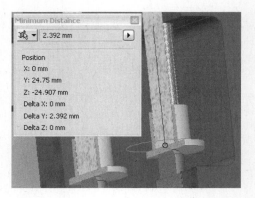

At this point, the only geometrical parameters to define are the coil pitch and the number of coils.

In the Length Inputs field, use the L_0, n --> t option, which allows you to calculate the pitch starting from the loose length and the number of coils. Enter **6** for the number of active coils. For the loose spring length, take a value of 3.5 mm, which is considerably larger than the minimum load length of 2.392 mm so that the spring is sufficiently preloaded to keep the valves shut. You should get a situation similar to Figure 11.58.

FIGURE 11.58
Working load state of
the compression string

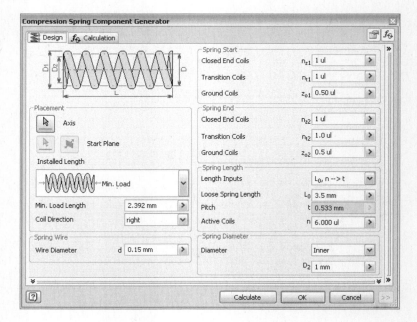

If you clicked Calculate, you would get impossible values for the minimum load length or pitch. This is because you did not define all load conditions yet, and so far, you have no idea if the spring you are designing holds the road when it comes to forces and stresses. To determine this, activate the Calculation tab, select Workforces Calculation, and enter the working conditions of your spring. When you enter the Assembly Dimensions for the spring, this section of the dialog box allows you to obtain the forces that can be exercised with the spring.

The total travel or working stroke of the spring is determined by the lift of the valve, which you know has to be 0.7 mm. You are now ready to enter all assembly dimensions.

Set the assembly dimensions method to H, L_1 --> L_8, and enter the following:

- Minimum load length = 2.39 mm

- Working stroke = 0.7 mm

- Working load length = 2.39 mm

As last step, select Heat Treated Wire Carbon Steel as the spring material, and click the Calculate button. If you look at the calculation results in Figure 11.59, you will notice that the maximum load is equal to 0.984 N. A maximum load of 0.984 N is deemed satisfactory for this design, and the maximum torsional stress t_8 of 854 MPa stays below the allowable torsional stress t_a of 972 MPa of our chosen material.

FIGURE 11.59
Compression spring force calculation with load lengths as input

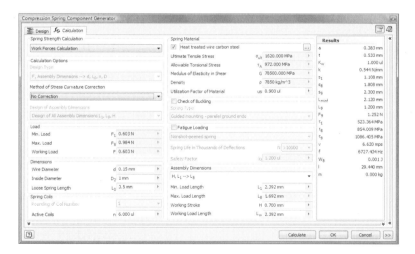

The Spring Generator automatically adds a Mate constraint between the spring axis and the inlet valve axis. You can now simulate the valve open and valve closed positions by editing the spring and displaying the spring in either the maximum load or minimum load installed length state. See Figures 11.60 and 11.61. You finally make a copy of the spring so that you can put the copy around the outlet valve. This concludes the compression spring design.

FIGURE 11.60
Spring position when
inlet valve is closed
(minimum load con-
dition)

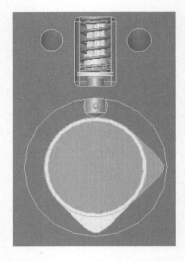

FIGURE 11.61
Spring position when
inlet valve is open (max-
imum load condition)

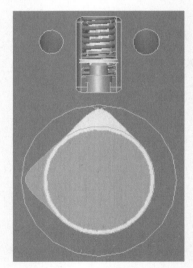

SPRING ANIMATION

If you want to see an animated version of the springs, change your project to Chapter 11
`final.ipj`, and from the Springs final folder, open the `Single cylinder 4 stroke engine.iam`
assembly with the LOD representation called Simplified Springs Activated. This LOD has the
more complex Design Accelerator–generated springs suppressed and has a set of simpler springs
unsuppressed. The simpler springs are made with the Coil command. You can drive the Drive Me
constraint, and the simplified springs will compress during the animation. Cool, isn't it?

The Bottom Line

Use Inventor's Design Accelerators   Design Accelerators and Design Generators allow you to rapidly create complex geometry and the associated calculations that verify the viability of your design.

> **Master It**   Your design needs a bolted connection, but you are not certain about the number of bolts to use to ensure a proper connection.

Use Inventor's Design Calculators   Design Calculators do not create any geometry, but they permit you to store the calculations in the assembly and repeat the calculation with different input values at a later time.

> **Master It**   You need to calculate the size of a weld between two plates to withstand a certain lateral force.

Develop best practices for using these tools   In this chapter, we explained how to use Design Accelerators in the best possible way by providing best practices and tips and tricks concerning the use of templates, exploring the benefits of using a particular type of calculation or connection method for a given scenario, and showing how to select the right material to do the job.

> **Master It**   You need to design a camshaft to activate an inlet valve that needs to respect a specific lift-over-time graph. You also want to reuse the design and slightly modify it for other similar cams like the exhaust valve.

> **Master It**   You want to design a compression spring that operates within very strict dimensional limitations and find a spring material that also satisfies the load requirements.

> **Master It**   Your design needs a gear transmission between two shafts with a predefined position, and you want the gears to be separate components that need to be connected to the shaft.

Chapter 12

Documentation

At any point in your design process, you could choose to begin documenting your design. Although traditionally creating drawings, exploded views, and animations was something that had to wait until the design was fully complete, there are no such restrictions in Inventor. You can start to develop an annotated 2D drawing or a presentation file at any point in your process. It is recommended, however, that you start documenting as late in the design as possible for more predictable results in the documentation environments.

The ultimate goal of this chapter is to illustrate how you can use the Drawing Manager and presentation environments in Inventor to generate both traditional, 2D annotated drawings as well as animated assembly instructions. Each of these finished products can be viewed by downstream design consumers using Autodesk Design Review through the .dwf file format.

In this chapter, you will learn how to:

- ◆ Create an exploded assembly view by creating a presentation

- ◆ Create and maintain drawing templates, standards, and styles

- ◆ Generate 2D drawing views of parts, assemblies, and presentations

- ◆ Annotate drawing views of your model

Working in the Presentation Environment

You can access the presentation environment by opening an existing presentation or .ipn file or by creating a new presentation with the File ➤ New command and starting with a presentation template.

Presentations are generally used to document how an assembly model is put together. Your end result could be as simple as a static explosion that you'll use to generate a 2D view in a drawing or a dynamic video where a design is assembled or disassembled through animation.

When you first create a new presentation file, you'll find the environment looks similar to the other part and assembly modeling environments, but it has a significantly reduced set of commands and tools. The 3D navigation tools detailed earlier in this book (Orbit and View Cube), as well as the browser, are used in presentations as well as in the 3D modeling environments.

Creating a Basic Explosion

Start by creating a new presentation file using the Standard.ipn template.

The first step in creating an assembly explosion is referencing an assembly. A presentation file can reference only one assembly file at a time, but the assembly can be used to generate as many explosions as you might need to properly document your design. For example, you may create one explosion to be used as a 2D drawing view and another explosion to be used as an animation. You may also choose to explode each subassembly in its own explosion.

To create the assembly reference, click the Create View button, the first command in the Presentation tool panel. This launches the Select Assembly dialog box shown in Figure 12.1, which allows you to select any assembly (.iam) file you may already have open in your Inventor session; you can also browse your active project to select an assembly file.

Click the Options button to specify which view, position, or LOD representation of the selected assembly you want loaded into the presentation environment (and whether you want the selected view representation to remain associative between the assembly and the presentation).

If you have a relatively small assembly and it was modeled with a full and robust set of assembly constraints, you may choose to create an automatic explosion in the Select Assembly dialog box and then make minor modifications to meet your needs. Otherwise, use the Manual option, and click OK.

The Arbor Press assembly (Arbor_Press.iam) in the Samples folder is used throughout this section as an example.

You'll now see the selected assembly in your presentation graphics area in its default home view (the top-right isometric unless you changed your .ipn file template).

Now it's time to start adding tweaks using the Tweak Component command on the Presentation tool panel. A *tweak* is simply a stored movement vector for a selected set of one or more components. You can define both linear and rotational tweaks. Clicking the command launches the Tweak Component dialog box shown in Figure 12.2.

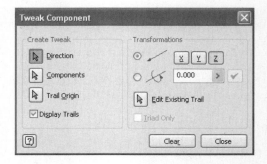

Specifying a linear tweak is a fairly simple three-step process. First, select a piece of geometry to define the direction of the tweak. This is accomplished most easily by selecting a flat face or straight edge anywhere on your model (the geometry you select to define the direction *does not* have to be from the component you eventually want to move through a tweak).

Once you select a piece of geometry to define the tweak orientation, you can specify the direction of the tweak either in the X, Y, or Z direction (Z is always selected by default). You can specify the direction in the Tweak Component dialog box or by selecting the triad arrowhead graphically corresponding to your desired direction.

Next, select the component or components you want to participate in the tweak. You can do this graphically or in the browser. You can use all your 3D navigation tools to rotate, pan, and zoom around your model to facilitate graphical selection.

Each component you select is added to the selection set, and components are deselected by holding the Ctrl key down while clicking. Subassemblies cannot be selected graphically but can be selected in your browser.

Finally, you specify the tweak distance either by keying in a value in the dialog box or by clicking and dragging on the X, Y, or Z direction triad in the graphics screen.

Once you create a tweak, you can continue to tweak additional components by first clicking the Clear button without dismissing the dialog box.

You can add rotational tweaks in much the same way, though rather than indicating the x-, y-, or z-axis for linear direction, the x-, y-, or z-axis is used as an axis of rotation, and the tweak value is entered as degrees of rotation rather than a linear distance.

To add a rotational tweak, click the rotational transformation option before selecting the geometry to indicate the direction.

If you're tweaking only one component at a time and you're comfortable with the selection, orientation, and direction behavior, you can establish direction, choose your component, and input the tweak distance all with one mouse click.

For example, try tweaking the faceplate from the Arbor Press assembly in one click-and-drag motion. Start the Tweak Component command, click the front face of the plate, continue holding the left mouse button while dragging the plate away from the main assembly, and then release the mouse button when you've moved it the desired amount, as illustrated in Figure 12.3.

Trails are added by default. A *trail* is a line (or an arc in the case of a rotation tweak) that is displayed in the graphics area showing the start and endpoints of a particular tweak. By default, the start and endpoints are defined by the three-dimensional geometric center of all the components that are chosen for a tweak. However, an optional fourth step in the tweak creation process is to manually select the tweak points by selecting one or more points on your selected components.

By default, one trail is added per selected component in your tweak. These trails are also visible in drawing views of presentations.

All tweaks can be edited after they're created. As you create tweaks, a browser node representing that tweak is generated in your browser and nested under the selected components that are part of that tweak. By selecting the tweak in the browser, you can enter a new movement value. You can also edit a tweak graphically by clicking and dragging on the endpoint of a tweak trail.

You can delete tweaks, and you can also make them invisible or completely redefine them using the tweak's right-click menu.

If your assembly is large or complex, consider making several explosions and tweaking only a few components per explosion. Additional explosions are added by clicking the Create View command. Each subsequent time the Select Assembly dialog box is shown, a new assembly file *cannot* be specified. You can, however, choose a different view, positional, or LOD representation than your previous explosions.

If the end goal of your presentation is to simply create an explosion that looks good in one or more 2D drawing views, then you already know just about everything you need to know, and you never have to use more than two commands inside the presentation environment. Simply continue to add tweaks as needed, save your file, and move on to creating your drawing.

FIGURE 12.3
Adding a tweak to faceplate

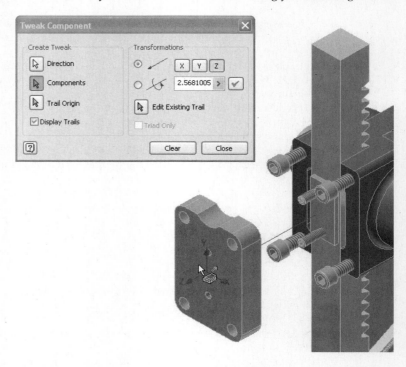

If, however, you want to create an animation, it's important to learn the concepts of grouping and reordering tweaks, editing sequences, saving camera views, and recording animation.

SEAN SAYS: TWEAK A LAYERED ASSEMBLY

When creating a presentation of a part that has many "layers" (imagine an onion), it is typically easiest to select several parts and move them out some distance. Next, select all but the innermost part and tweak them out a distance. Keep repeating this process until the last part is tweaked.

Using the Drawing Manager

Now that you have created your 3D design, you can choose to document it with conventional 2D orthographic drawing views and traditional drafting tools. Creating this kind of documentation is done in Inventor's Drawing Manager environment.

Three high-level Drawing Manager tasks are discussed here:

◆ Creating and maintaining templates and styles

◆ Creating drawing views

◆ Annotating your drawing

Creating Templates and Styles

Although several drawing templates are installed with Inventor, it's recommended that before you begin to document your own designs and models, you create your own custom template or templates to best meet your needs. Most users need to adhere to a specific set of drafting standards dictated by their company, customer, or vendor specifications. These standards are typically derivatives of one of several international drafting standards such as ANSI, ISO, or DIN. As such, Inventor ships with a set of templates and drafting styles configured for the following international standards:

◆ ANSI (both English and metric units)

◆ BSI

◆ DIN

◆ GB

◆ GOST

◆ ISO

◆ JIS

When creating your own custom template, it's best to start with a shipping template that most closely meets your requirements and modify it accordingly.

Creating templates in the Drawing Manager is not unlike creating templates in other applications. Where many applications use a special file format for template files, Inventor uses the conventional part, assembly, presentation, and drawing formats as template formats. Therefore, you can use any `.idw` or `.dwg` file as a drawing template; you just need to indicate that the file is to be used as a template at the application or project level.

By default, Inventor templates are stored in and accessed from `Program Files\Autodesk\Inventor 2009\Templates`. The default location is set on the File tab in the Application Options dialog box under Default Templates.

For stand-alone users, consider using this same location for your design projects. If you're part of a networked workgroup, you should create a template folder on a shared network drive and change the default templates path accordingly.

The default template location can be overwritten on a per-project basis.

CHOOSING A FILE FORMAT

Up until Inventor 2008, the `.idw` file format was the only 2D native file type recognized by Inventor. DWG TrueConnect, introduced with Inventor 2008, enables you to use both `.dwg` and `.idw` as valid file formats in Inventor's Drawing Manager.

Using `.dwg` as your file format enables you to open Inventor DWG files in AutoCAD (or an AutoCAD vertical product such as AutoCAD Mechanical) without going through a translation process. Although the data you create natively in Inventor cannot be manipulated directly in AutoCAD, all of the Inventor data can be viewed, measured, and printed using conventional AutoCAD commands.

Choosing `.dwg` as your default file format allows downstream consumers of your designs to view your 2D drawing documents in AutoCAD without having to purchase or install Inventor or download the Inventor file viewer. Vendors, customers, or other internal personnel can open the native Inventor DWG file; view, measure, and plot the Inventor data; or even add AutoCAD data to the file to create a hybrid document that can be viewed quickly and efficiently in either application.

For Inventor users, there is essentially no difference between using `.dwg` or the traditional `.idw` file format. The native `.dwg` file includes a Layer 0 in the layer list and an AutoCAD Blocks folder in Drawing Resources. These are the only noticeable differences between the two file formats.

An `.idw` file can always be saved as an Inventor DWG, and vice versa, without any loss of fidelity or data. If there's a good chance of someone wanting to see a DWG version of your Inventor file, you might consider choosing `.dwg` as your default file format.

Inventor's Task Scheduler enables you to batch convert a set of IDW files into DWG files.

CUSTOMIZING TEMPLATES

There are three areas of the template that should be customized to conform to your chosen drafting standards and personal preferences: drawing resources, document settings, and document styles.

Drawing Resources

Drawing resources are simply a collection of reusable sketches that are stored in a drawing file. There are four types of drawing resources: sheet formats, borders, title blocks, and sketched symbols. If you've decided to use `.dwg` as your template format, you'll notice that AutoCAD blocks are also managed as Inventor drawing resources.

Drawing resources are accessed from your Drawing browser under the Drawing Resources folder, as shown in Figure 12.4. If you expand the Drawing Resources node, you'll see a folder for each of the drawing resources types listed, and contained in each of the subfolders are drawing resource definitions.

FIGURE 12.4
The Drawing Resources node in the Drawing browser

Double-click any drawing resource to place an instance in your drawing.

You can employ several document management techniques with respect to templates, sheet sizes, borders, and title blocks. Although you could create and maintain separate drawing templates for each sheet size and title block you might need, it's generally recommended that a single drawing template be used to maintain each of these different configurations.

When you start a new drawing from one of the templates installed with Inventor, a specific sheet size is already selected, and a border and title block instance have already been placed.

You can change the default sheet size by choosing Edit Sheet from the sheet's right-click menu in the browser. If you're using the ANSI (in) template, the default sheet size is C. If you change the sheet size to D, the border on the sheet updates automatically to accommodate the change in sheet size.

To have your templates default to an A- or B-sized sheet, simply open your template file, activate the desired sheet size, and then save the document. When you start a new document from the template, this new sheet size will be active.

If needed, you can add sheets to your template, which is recommended if most of your design documents require more than one sheet. To insert a new sheet into your document, click the New

Sheet command in the Drawing Views panel (this adds a copy of your active sheet to the drawing including the border and title block).

Borders

The default border that's instanced on the Inventor templates may not meet your needs. You should first delete the default border from your sheet before creating a new border (choose Delete from the border's right-click menu). To create a new, custom border in your template, choose either Define New Border or Define New *Zone* Border from the Border's right-click menu under Drawing Resources. It is recommended that you always choose the option to create a zone border because this will generate an intelligent border that updates according to sheet size. If you create a new border (not a zone border), the resulting border will be completely static, and you'll need to create a new border for every possible sheet size you may need.

Sketch Formatting

Although model sketches provide you with the ability to format sketch geometry, it is typically more important to apply different line formatting (line weight, color, and linetype) to border and title block geometry.

You can change the format of drawing sketch geometry in one of two ways. You can draw or move your lines and arcs onto a layer configured to your required line formatting, or you can override the layer formatting individually for each piece of sketch geometry.

To draw geometry on a particular layer, start a Draw command (line or arc, for example), and then change the layer from the Layer pulldown on the Standard toolbar before you begin picking points.

You can, alternatively, draw all your geometry on a single layer and then move selected geometry to another layer with different formatting properties. With no command running, select the sketch geometry you want to move to another layer and then choose the desired target layer from the Layer pulldown control.

To override the layer formatting, choose Properties from the geometry's right-click menu and set the color, line weight, or linetype as needed (notice that all properties are initially set to be formatted by layer).

When you're done creating or editing your border sketch, click the Return button on the Standard toolbar, or right-click and select Save Border. You'll be prompted for a border name, which is the name you'll see in your Drawing browser under the Drawing Resources ➤ Borders node.

Title Blocks

Customizing title blocks is done in much the same way as borders. Title blocks typically contain more text-based information than the border, so we'll spend more time talking about creating sketch text in this section.

Create a new border title block with the Drawing Resource Title Blocks browser's right-click menu. Click Define New Title Block to enter the sketch environment to start drawing your custom title block.

Instead of creating a new title block from scratch, consider modifying one of the title blocks in the default templates. Chances are they're already close to what you will need. Right-click the ANSI-Large browser icon under Drawing Resources (the definition) or under the sheet (the placed instance), and choose Edit or Edit Definition.

Setting up a title block raises yet another administrative decision: whether to use file iProperties, prompted text entries, or a mixture of both to fill out required fields on your title block.

From a document management perspective, it's recommended that you try to use iProperties to populate your title block. This method has many advantages: it allows non-Inventor users to sign off on drawings without access to a full Inventor version, and several utilities (such as the Design Assistant) allow you to view properties from a whole set of files as well as copy iProperty data from one to another.

SEAN SAYS: USE MODEL iPROPERTIES

The Red Sox or the Yankees, Chicago or New York pizza, iProperties or prompted entries? Nothing can start a religious war over CAD documents quicker than when you sit down to create your title blocks. Although there is no wrong answer, I strongly suggest you utilize model iProperties to drive your title blocks.

In particular, I suggest you use the model (rather than the drawing) iProperties to house the part information. It is my strong belief that the model is the "master" — the keeper of all the information. The drawing simply is a way to express that information. By filling out the iProperties in the model, you keep that information with the model.

This allows you to use that model in other projects and to retain the iProperty information from project to project. Besides, it will sure save you a lot of typing in those prompted entries.

Edit the ANSI-Large title block definition in the ANSI (in) standard template (.idw or .dwg).

Zoom in on the title block, and notice the existing text in the sketch. For each field, there is both static, readable text that is shown on the sheet itself when outside of sketch mode as well as text that represents attributed iProperty text. This text is shown in the sketch in brackets, as in <CREATION DATE>.

We'll use the same text layout model to create an additional piece of field text for Stock Number, a file iProperty.

First, notice that in every rectangular field area, there is a second set of construction lines for each visible title block line. These are "sketch-only" lines used to constrain and align title block text and are not visible outside sketch mode.

First, let's draw our own sketch-only line along the bottom of the title block, in the empty rectangular field just below the Approved field. Draw it between the two leftmost horizontal *title block* lines (not the construction lines). Next, add a sketch dimension between your line and the bottom title block line, and set it to .03 in (or d25 as the others).

Next, select the line you just drew, and then click the Sketch Only button on the Standard toolbar (next to the Layer and Style pulldowns).

Now, add text by clicking the Text command at the bottom of the Drawing Sketch panel. Click well below the title block to place the text; you'll constrain it into position after it's created.

In the Text dialog box, first make sure the justification settings are set to top and left justified, and then set your text height to .100 in. Then type **COST CENTER** in the text area, and hit OK.

The text you created has a small point in the upper-left corner of the bounding area. This is your justification point and is used to constrain sketch text so that you can line it up with other geometry in your sketch (including other text).

Using the Coincident constraint from the Sketch toolbar, constrain the COST CENTER text justification point to the left vertical construction line in the title block (the same line APPROVED and MFG are constrained to).

Then next, add another .03 in (or 2d5) sketch dimension between the justification point and the horizontal line in this title block field.

Now create a second string of text by clicking the Text command once more. Again, click to start the text below the title block. This time, make sure the justification is set to the bottom left and the text height is set to .125 in. Instead of typing text into the text editor, you'll reference a model iProperty. In the Type pulldown, select Properties – Model; then in the Property control, find COST CENTER, and click the Add Text Parameter button. You then see the iProperty reference <COST CENTER> in the text field. Click OK. Now constrain this new piece of text to the intersection of the leftmost construction line and the construction line you created earlier.

Next, you'll add a prompted entry field for the QA approval. Start the Text command again, set the justification to bottom left, and set the height to .125 in. In the Type pulldown, select Prompted Entry. Replace the <Enter Prompt for Field> text with **QA Signoff**, and hit OK. Drag the prompted entry text into position under the QA text. Figure 12.5 shows the title block sketch.

FIGURE 12.5
Customizing the title block

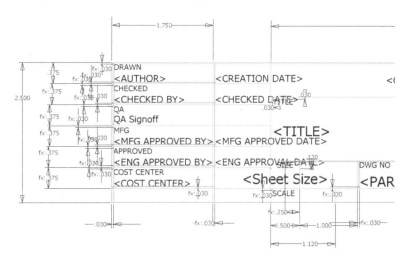

Finally, exit the sketch (right-click, and select Save Title Block), and save the changes. Save and close your drawing template (or choose Save As if you want to preserve your default template file — just be sure to save it in your templates folder).

Now start a new drawing, and use the template you just modified. The title block Prompted Texts dialog box is shown before you can continue. This dialog box allows a user to populate prompted title block entries with values. If the values are intended to be entered later, this dialog box can be dismissed (Cancel) and reaccessed at any time by right-clicking the Field Text browser node under the title block instance under the sheet and selecting Edit Field Text (change the field text filter from All to Prompted Entry).

Other than your prompted entry, none of the title block field information is populated yet. Model iProperty fields are not populated until a model view is placed on the sheet. When referenced in a title block, model iProperties are read from the first model view placed on the sheet. Even though you can create multiple base views on a sheet, only the *first* sheet view populates model iProperty references in the title block.

The other iProperty field references in this title block are drawing iProperties that have not yet been populated in the drawing document iProperties. You can edit drawing iProperties now, or you can check a document option that copies model properties from the first model you reference in your drawing to the drawing iProperties.

In the Format pulldown, select Document Properties, go to the Drawing tab, and select the Copy Model Properties option. Then click the Properties button, and check the All Properties option. Click OK in both dialog boxes.

Open any model file, and select File ➤ iProperties. On the Project tab, enter a value in the Cost Center field. Close the dialog box, and save your changes to the model.

Now return to your drawing, and click the Base View command in the Drawing Views panel. In the Drawing View dialog box, make sure the model file you edited is referenced in the File control, and then click anywhere to place the view.

Many of the title block field references are now populated, but only the Cost Center field is directly referencing the model iProperty. The other fields are still referencing drawing iProperties, but the act of placing a base view copied all of the model property values to the drawing iProperties.

This property copy option is a one-time copy only and not an associative link.

> **SEAN SAYS: KNOW WHEN TO LINK AND WHEN TO COPY PROPERTIES**
>
> The workflow shown here is certainly one way you can "link" these model iProperties to the drawings. Another option is to just allow the title block to directly reference the model iProperties. By doing this, any changes to the model iProperties will automatically update in the title block. By copying the properties, a user can edit the drawing's iProperties and cause a disconnect between the model and the drawing.

Sketched Symbols

Sketched symbols are created, edited, placed, and managed much like other drawing resources, but there is no limit to the number of sketch symbol instances you can place on a sheet. Like other drawing resource definitions, sketched symbols are placed by double-clicking the definition node in the browser or using the Symbols command (at bottom of the Drawing Annotation panel or from the sketch symbol's Definition right-click menu).

Sketched symbols can optionally include a leader. Using a leader, you can associate a sketch symbol with a model so that model-specific properties can be displayed in the symbol. For example, you could create a sketch symbol that calls out a component's mass.

First, start a new drawing using any drawing template. Next, expand the Drawing Resources browser folder, right-click the Sketch Symbol folder, and select Define New Symbol.

Just like you created model iProperty field text in your title block, create sketch text that references a model's mass. First, add static text that simply reads **MASS:**. Next, create a second text object, and in the Text dialog box, select Physical Properties – Model from the Type pulldown in the text editor; then select Mass in the Property control, and click the Add Text Parameter button (you can optionally adjust the precision before adding the property).

You can continue to make this sketch symbol as elaborate as you like, but for the purposes of this exercise, the Mass property reference is all that is required. When finished, choose Save Sketched Symbol from the right-click menu and assign it a name (**Mass**, for example).

Next, open the Arbor_Press.iam file from Samples, and select Update Mass Properties from the Tools pulldown. Return to the drawing, and place a view of the Arbor Press assembly using the Iso Top Right orientation.

Finally, right-click the Mass sketch symbol definition in the Drawing browser, and select Symbols. Make sure the Mass symbol is chosen from the list on the left side of the Symbols dialog box, and select the Leader option. This dialog box enables you to add a scale or rotational value to the sketch symbol instance you're about to place.

SEAN SAYS: TAKE ME TO YOUR LEADER

Remember, if you want a sketched symbol without a leader, you can just double-click the symbol. To place it with a leader, you need to right-click, select Symbols, and then select the leader option from the dialog box.

Hit OK, and then click any model edge in the drawing view; click again for each leader vertex you'd like, and then choose Continue from the right-click menu. Continue to place these additional symbol instances, but be sure to point to a different Arbor Press component each time (as shown in Figure 12.6). Each sketch symbol displays a mass value in accordance to the component being referenced by the leader. You can see these values update when clicking and dragging the leader termination point from one component to another.

FIGURE 12.6
Applying sketched symbols to a drawing view

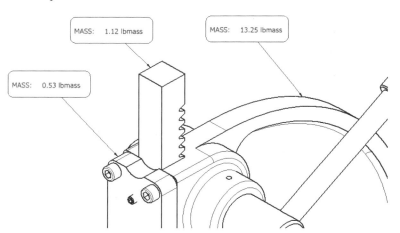

If you need to establish a symbol reference to a model but do not want to see the leader, you can edit the symbol and then select (double-click or select Edit Symbol from the symbol's right-click menu) and uncheck the leader Visibility option.

Sketched symbols can be placed as needed on new documents or placed on the template itself. If there is field text in the sketch symbol, it becomes populated just like title block field text when you create a new drawing.

Sketched symbols placed by double-clicking the definition are set to static by default, and you can set this option prior to placement if you use the Symbols command.

Static sketched symbols cannot be graphically rotated or scaled like nonstatic symbols can. When you mouse over a nonstatic sketch symbol, a single blue hot point is shown on the center top of the symbol, and four yellow hot points are displayed at the four corners of the symbol. Clicking and dragging the blue hot point causes the symbol to rotate, while clicking and dragging any of the yellow hot points enables dynamic scaling.

Sheet Formats

Sheet formats are a preset collection of a drawing sheet, border, title block, sketched symbols, and/or base and projected views. They essentially give you the ability to quickly generate multi-view drawings just by referencing a single model file.

Try inserting one of the sheet formats in the standard drawing template, and notice the results. This technique is ideal if you're detailing similar designs of common size and complexity.

To save your own sheet format, set up your sheet the way you like it with placed drawing resources as well as base and projected views of any model, and then select Create Sheet Format from the sheet's right-click menu in the browser.

Only base and projected views are saved in a sheet format. All other views and annotation are discarded.

You can preload your drawing template as a sheet format as well. Simply open your template, create a base and projected views of any model, and then save and close. When you next use your template for a new drawing, you'll be immediately prompted to reference a model file, and the drawing views are automatically created.

USING THE DRAWING RESOURCE TRANSFER WIZARD

Drawing resources definitions can be copied from drawing to drawing by selecting Copy from the definition's right-click menu; then right-click the appropriate drawing resource node in the target document, and select Paste.

You can use this technique to both add new drawing resources and update existing resources with an updated change.

The copy-paste technique is efficient for single changes or transfers between two drawings, but to push one or more new or updated design resource definitions to multiple drawings, an external application has been developed to facilitate this task.

To start the Drawing Resource Transfer Wizard, first close Inventor; then from the Windows Start menu, select All Programs ➢ Autodesk ➢ Autodesk Inventor 2009 ➢ Tools ➢ Drawing Resource Transfer Wizard.

This utility is a bulk copy-paste command for drawing resources, and the interface is very basic: select a source file, select the drawing resources you want to transfer, select a set of target drawings, and hit Start.

An ideal and practical example for using this utility is for updating title blocks if your company's contact information requires updating (such as a phone number or website address). Simply open your template file to make the required edits to the title block, save your changes, close Inventor, and start the Drawing Resource Transfer Wizard to push the updated title block to any drawing that requires updating.

AREA CODE CHANGES

In 2002, the phone number area code for Rochester, New York, and the surrounding areas changed from 716 to 585. This meant that every manufacturing, engineering, and architectural group in the area suddenly had hundreds and thousands of drawings with the wrong phone number in the title block of working drawings. Many companies that wanted or needed to update their title blocks had to manually copy and paste title blocks on each drawing in their archives (the savvier groups wrote custom application scripts to perform this task). Unfortunately, the Drawing Resource Transfer Wizard was not released until some years later. It would have likely saved thousands of hours of work.

EDITING STYLES AND STANDARDS

Like color, material, lighting, and sheet metal styles in the modeling environment, the Drawing Manager makes heavy use of XML-based styles. The basic framework of drawing styles is no different from those in the modeling environment. Drawing style setting are viewed and edited using the same Style Editor dialog box, they can be shared among a workgroup via the same XML style library as the modeling styles, and they can be imported and exported as a stand-alone XML file.

Drawing styles differentiate themselves from modeling styles more in concept than in practice. Drawing styles are a collection of drafting rules that make up a larger standard.

A standard is a style itself, but in the context of the Drawing Manager, a standard is a high-level regulator of an externally recognized international drafting standard such as ANSI, ISO, or GB.

Object Defaults

The true key to understanding how styles are used to determine the formatting of everything you can create on a drawing sheet is the notion of the Object Defaults style.

When working in the Drawing Manager, only one standard can be active at a time, yet there are no practical limitations on the number of dimensions styles that can be employed as you create dimensions. Coupled with each standard is a single Object Defaults style. Indeed, you can even think of the Object Defaults style as an extension of the standard.

Open an IDW file, start the Style Editor dialog box (select Format ➤ Style And Standard Editor), and click the Object Defaults (ANSI) style node (located under the Object Defaults tree node). You'll see in Figure 12.7 that the Object Defaults Style interface is essentially a mapping table. The leftmost column lists almost every discernable object you can create in the Drawing Manager, from dimensions and tables to view edges and center marks. Each object row is associated with a layer style, and every type of annotation object is associated with an object style as well.

FIGURE 12.7
Object Defaults Style interface

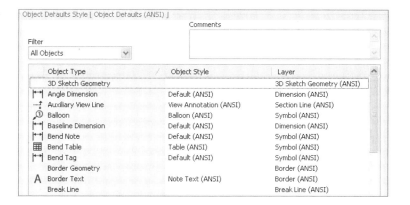

As you create objects in Inventor using the various view and annotation commands, before anything is drawn on your sheet, Inventor looks to this active Object Defaults table and assigns a layer and object style assignment to whatever it is you're creating.

Layers look and behave just like they do in AutoCAD, with the noted exception that Inventor manages its layers like any other style definition.

Every object is drawn on a layer, from which it receives color, line weight, linetype, and visibility formatting. Knowing this, it's easy to appreciate that when Inventor creates drawing views of a part with hidden lines displayed, those hidden view edges are mapped to a layer that's set to a thinner linetype and a dashed line style.

If you were to place a view and then click any one of the resulting view edges, you'll see that in the Layer pulldown on the Standard toolbar the layer assignment is set to By Standard. If you place a dimension on that view and then select the dimension, you'll see that the layer is set to By Standard and the object style is set to By Standard. This term refers to the associativity between the objects you create and the Object Defaults style. It means that your object got its layer and style assignment from the standard via object defaults.

Of course, you can override this style assignment as you create objects or as an edit operation after they're created. For example, if you started the Text command, you'll note right away that it's getting a By Standard text style. Before you click to place the text, you can click the Style or Layer pulldown control and change the associative style.

Objects that have become decoupled from the standard in this way will not update if you make any modifications to the Object Defaults style. If you changed the layer assignment in object defaults for visible view edges to a new layer that was green, your visible view edges would all update because they're associated with that standard. If, however, you changed the text's default layer assignment, you would see no change to the text object you created because it's no longer set to By Standard.

SEAN SAYS: OVERRIDE AND RESTORE STYLES

A quick way to get a set of annotations (for example, a set of dimensions) to use their standard is to window or Ctrl-select the dimensions and then select the new standard. All the dimensions will update to use the newly selected standard.

Styles and Substyles

A basic example of a substyle in the modeling environment is the color style. The color style is a substyle of the material style. Once you apply a new material to a part, not only are you changing its physical parameters but you're potentially changing its color so that it shows the material's color substyle.

The use of substyles in the Drawing Manager is extensive. Almost every kind of annotation you create in a drawing contains some kind of text (dimensions, weld symbols, and parts lists), and many make use of leaders. The text style and leader style, therefore, are frequently used as substyles of other styles. This basically provides one-stop shopping if you wanted to quickly change all the text on your document. If you wanted to change the font for all text, for example, it's unlikely you would have to modify more than two text styles to achieve this goal.

Substyles are coupled with their parent styles, which means a substyle cannot be purged if it's in use by another style. If you cache a high-level style into your document from the library or if you save a high-level style into the library from your file, all substyles participate in those operations.

Styles are an extremely powerful formatting tool that enable you to quickly change the entire face of a document. This also serves as a warning that modifying styles without understanding how they work can quickly generate unexpected results.

SEAN SAYS: TAKE THE TIME TO UNDERSTAND STYLES

I know it's about as interesting as your high-school medieval European history class, but styles are extremely powerful, and you're doing yourself a disservice by not spending some time getting to know them. They are complex, but with the complexity comes a very powerful tool. Play around with changing styles in drawings and seeing how the annotations change. Once you have a good understanding of them, sit down with your design group and come up with a set of standards with which everyone is happy. Apply these styles to your documents and use them for a while. One of the great aspects of the style library is that if you want to make a change, you can make it to the library, and everyone will have access to this new/changed style each time they open a file.

Drawing Style Administration

Each drawing template that comes with Inventor has a full set of styles saved (cached) in the drawing document. Although you can use the style library as a sharing and update tool, there is no direct link between objects on your sheet and styles in your library. Any in-use style is loaded into your document either automatically or manually.

If your project is set to use the style library (Use Style Library setting is Yes or Read Only), then it's important to keep your style definitions in sync between your template file and the library. If your project is using the style library and you have a style in the library that has the same name as a style in your template and those styles have different settings, the definition in the library automatically overwrites the definition in the template each time it's used to start a new drawing (a warning dialog box is shown when this condition is detected).

The best way to ensure synchronization is to open your template file and run either the Update Styles command (which pulls updates from the library) or the Save Styles To Style Library command, depending on which way you want to transfer the styles.

Creating Drawing Views and Annotations

We'll explore the various view creation, editing, and annotation commands in the following sections as we discuss documenting different types of 3D models: part, assembly, sheet metal, weldment, and iPart/iAssembly.

PART DRAWINGS

Drawing views reference part, assembly, or presentation files. The workflows involved in creating and editing views from these different sources are similar, but with some notable exceptions detailed here.

Base and Projected Views

From the Samples directory's Assemblies\Arbor Press\Components folder, open FACE PLATE.ipt, and examine the part. Start a new drawing, and click the Base View command on the Drawing Views panel.

When you see the Drawing View dialog box after clicking the Base View command, you first need to specify the model source for your view. The File list is populated with all the appropriate model types that are open in your current Inventor sessions, but you can also browse to select any part, assembly, or presentation file. If the faceplate is the only model file open in your Inventor session, it should be preselected in this field. If you move your mouse outside the dialog box, you'll see a preview of the drawing view you're about to create.

Most of the options you see in the Drawing View dialog box can be altered later by editing the view, but it's important to set the Orientation properly now because it cannot be changed once placed. We'll choose the Front view orientation for the base view of the faceplate.

If you're using the ANSI (in) drawing template that was installed with Inventor, you may find the 1:1 drawing scale too small for the C-sized sheet, so change the scale to 2:1, and then click the drawing sheet to place the view near the lower-left corner of your sheet.

You can enter any scale value you like in this control rather than picking from the list. This control accepts decimal, fractional, and rational (for example, 2:1) inputs. If you choose to turn on your scale display (View/Scale Label lightbulb icon), the value appears as you entered it.

Next, create two orthographic and one isometric projected view using a single Projected View command. Although you can access the Projected View command in the Drawing Views panel, let's start this command from the base view. Right-click anywhere in the base view, and select Create View ➢ Projected View from the menu.

As you drag your mouse around the base view, notice the view previews that are being generated. From this point, you can click to place as many as eight different projected views (four orthographic and four isometric).

Click and place top, right, and top-right isometric views, and then choose Create from your right-click menu.

Look at your Drawing browser, and notice how it's being populated as you create views (Figure 12.8). The two orthoprojected views are listed underneath the base view that was first created. This shows you that these views are treated as children of the base (parent) view.

FIGURE 12.8
Drawing views in the browser

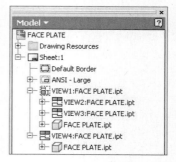

The isometric view is *not* nested beneath the base view. Projected isometric views are treated in many respects as independent base views, though they maintain some associativity to the base view.

You can move drawing views between sheets by dragging and dropping the browser nodes. When projected views are moved to a different sheet than their parent, a removed view annotation is generated automatically on the parent view.

The resulting views inherit certain settings from the base view. The most obvious common setting is the view scale. This can be verified by double-clicking either one of the orthographic views to open the Drawing View dialog box. In the View/Scale Label area at the bottom of the dialog box, notice the Scale From Base option is checked. This option is checked automatically for projected ortho views and links the scale setting in your base view to this view.

Also notice a similar Style From Base option checked on the bottom-right side of the dialog box. This option associates the display style of the base view with child views: hidden lines removed, hidden line view (default for parts), and whether or not the view is shaded.

Cut Views: Sections and Break-out Views

This part has a milled pocket in the center of the front face. The feature information, particularly the depth of the cut, is best shown in either a section view or a breakout view. We'll show how to create both to spotlight each of these view types.

Because the section view you're about to create eliminates the need for the top view, right-click the top view, and select Delete from the context menu. Next, click the Section View command from the Drawing Views panel, and then select the base view. Next, click to draw a single horizontal line across the base view. Don't worry about exact placement of the section line. As you create the sketch line, you're in fact creating a sketch on the drawing view. You can infer sketch constraints as you sketch just like you would when creating a conventional 2D sketch. You can add inferred Coincident, Parallel, and Perpendicular constraints. If you prefer, you can hold the Ctrl key down as you create the section line to turn off the automatic constraint behavior. For example, you might want to avoid the midpoint Coincident constraint to the midpoint of the vertical edge of the part but accept the Perpendicular constraint.

The section line can be multisegmented (lines only; no arcs). Each time you click after clicking your starting point, you're adding a segment. For our purposes, you need only a single, horizontal segment, so after clicking again to establish the second endpoint, right-click and choose Continue.

Configure the settings in the Section View dialog box to meet your needs. You can indicate the depth of the resulting section view in this dialog box. This is especially useful for large assemblies or complex parts by eliminating a lot of unnecessary view edges in the resulting view.

Notice how the placement of the section view is constrained perpendicularly to the section line. You can override this alignment behavior by holding the Ctrl key down before placing the view. Click and place the section view above the base view.

Look at the browser to see how the section view was added as a child view of the base. Also, notice the sketch that was created on the base view listed just above the section view node (Figure 12.9). This sketch is the section line itself and can be edited like any other sketch. You can add or remove constraints (including sketch dimensions) as needed to precisely position the section line around your base view.

The section line annotation on the base view is formatted according to a layer and a View Annotation style. You can verify this by clicking the section line and noting the layer and View Annotation style applied to it from the Layer and Style pulldown menus.

The section line can be moved around your base view provided no coincident constraints were added, and the section view updates immediately to show the new section line placement. Try moving the section line so that it passes through one of the tapped holes in the center of the part.

Any view face that is the result of a cut operation such as a section view can have Hatch automatically applied to it. Hatch is turned on automatically for orthographic views but needs to manually be set for ISO views (edit the view, and check the Hatching option on the Display Options tab).

We defined the section line on the fly during the Section View command. We could also have used an explicit view sketch or even a recovered model sketch to define the section. Let's now create another, slightly more complex section view by drawing our section line sketch first.

To create a sheet sketch, click the base view, and then click the Sketch command on the Standard toolbar. You can now project model edges onto your view sketch and use them to create and constrain your sketched section line.

FIGURE 12.9
Part section view

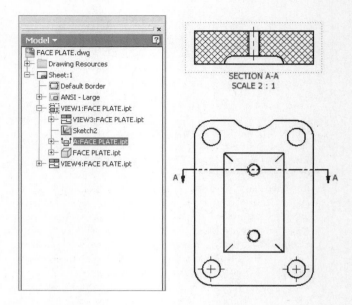

Rather than using a view sketch, you'll create a model sketch and then recover it into the drawing view to be used as a section line.

If the FACE PLATE.ipt model is not already open, open it.

SEAN SAYS: OPEN MODELS QUICKLY FROM DRAWINGS

When you have an IDW or DWG of a model file open, you can open that model file quickly and easily by simply right-clicking any base view and selecting Open. The model file will then open in a new window.

Create a new sketch on the front face of the plate, and draw a series of continuous line segments that pass through both tapped holes (you'll need to project these hole edges onto the plane) and two of the mounting clearance hole (select opposing corners), as shown in Figure 12.10. Exit the sketch, save the part, and then return to the drawing.

To temporarily remove the first section view, right-click the view, and click Suppress. Both the section view and the section line annotation in the base view are made invisible. Also, notice how the section view icon now appears in the Drawing browser. Suppressing a view both removes it and the dependent annotation from the graphics area as well as removes the view from memory (this can both increase performance and increase the memory footprint of the drawing).

To recover the model sketch into the drawing view, the sketch plane must be parallel to the sheet in the drawing view.

In the Drawing browser, locate the FACE PLATE.ipt icon under the base view, right-click the part node, and select Get Model Sketches from the context menu.

To use the recovered model sketch as a section line, click the Section View command again; then select the recovered sketch, and click to place the view (shown in Figure 12.11).

FIGURE 12.10
Section line sketch on
model

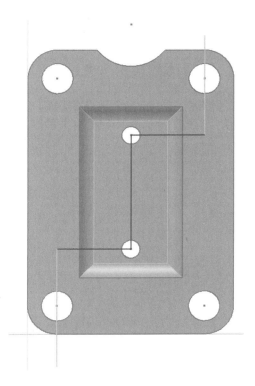

FIGURE 12.11
Section using model
sketch

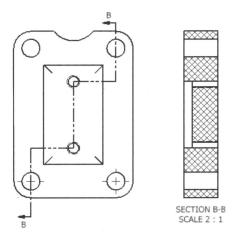

SECTION B-B
SCALE 2 : 1

You can also use a breakout to show a mill cut. Unlike the Section View command that creates
a new view, a breakout is a cut operation you perform on an existing view, such as our right-side
projected view.

Breakouts start with a closed loop profile drawn on a view sketch, so you'll begin there as well.
Select the right-side view, and click the Sketch button on the Standard toolbar.

Use the Rectangle Sketch command to draw a rectangle that encompasses the entire profile of the mill cut on one of the side views of the part file, as shown in Figure 12.11 (you could use a more complex shape, such as a spline, and you could also project model edges into your sketch to use as reference geometry for constraints). Then exit the sketch.

Click the Break Out command on the Drawing Views panel, and then select the right-side projected view. If your view sketch contains only one close-loop sketch profile (like our rectangle), it is automatically selected as your breakout profile (as shown in Figure 12.12). You can select multiple closed-loop profiles for a breakout if needed. Make sure you're zoomed out so that you can view both the base view and the projected view in your graphics area. Change the depth pulldown from From Point to To Hole, and then click either one of the tapped holes in the base view; finally, hit OK.

FIGURE 12.12
Creating a breakout

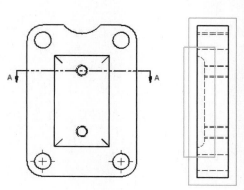

Your profile was used to cut through the model view to the hole, and the hidden view edges that represented the bottom surface of the mill cut are now shown as visible edges.

You can better appreciate how the breakout operation affected your model by right-clicking the right-side view with the breakout and creating a projected isometric view. This view does not contain hatching, but because there are cut faces in the view, you can edit the view to enable hatching. Double-click to edit the new ISO view, and check the Hatching option on the Display Options tab.

If you were using the ANSI (in) template, the hatch pattern you see in all of the cut views is ANSI 31. This is the default hatch pattern used for all views as set in your active hatch style.

Hatch formatting for cut views is modified by right-clicking the hatch and selecting Edit. In the Edit Hatch Pattern dialog box, you can change the hatch pattern, as well as other hatch formatting such as scale, angle, color, and shift.

You can also associate hatch patterns to applied model materials through the standard style.

Go to the Style And Standard Editor, and click your active standard style; then click the Material Hatch Pattern Defaults tab. This table is initially empty but can be populated with various material names, and each can be assigned its own hatch pattern.

Start by importing all the material names from your active style library (if your project is not set to use the style library, click From File, and then browse to the FACE PLATE.ipt in the Arbor Press assembly).

You'll now see all the materials defined in your style library listed in the table. Scroll down and locate Steel, Mild; then change its hatch pattern from ANSI 31 to any other hatch pattern.

Save your changes, and exit from the Style dialog box. The name of the utility you just modified is called Material Hatch Pattern Defaults where defaults means that the material associativity applies only to new cut views and operations.

You can update existing hatches to be configured by material by right-clicking the pattern and choosing Pattern ➤ By Material. Try this now with the hatch in the breakout and section views.

Detail Views

Create a detail view to blow up and segregate a particular portion of a drawing view as a new view. Continuing with the faceplate drawing, click the Detail View command, and then click the base view. In the Detail View dialog box, the default scale value is twice that of the base view. Here you can also change some of the fence and detail annotation formatting options. Other than the shape (circle or rectangle), all of these options can be changed after creation.

Keep all the default settings, and click your view to set the detail view center; then drag out to define the circle diameter. Once you've set the diameter and view letter position how you like it, click to create the detail view, and then click again to place the view. Figure 12.13 shows the resulting view.

FIGURE 12.13
Creating a detail view

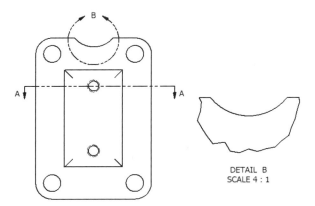

DETAIL B
SCALE 4 : 1

Several detail view formatting options are available in the Detail View dialog box and the detail view annotation's right-click menu. In particular, it shows whether the cut shape is smooth or jagged, circular or rectangular, whether you want the full boundary drawn around the resulting view, and whether you want a connection line between the detail view and the parent view.

Oftentimes, so much model geometry is in your view that an appropriate position for the detail view letter about the detail fence isn't available. For these cases, you can right-click the detail view annotation and choose the Leader option. Once this option is invoked, the next time you drag the annotation text label, a leader is generated from the text back to the fence, enabling you to position the view letter in a less-cluttered area on your drawing.

SEAN SAYS: USE DETAIL VIEW ANNOTATION

Although detail views are created at a scale larger than the base view, Inventor takes this into account when creating dimensions for the detail view. All your dimensions will be to the correct scale. These detail views are useful when you need to show dimensions on a very small feature that is on a larger part.

ANNOTATING PART DRAWINGS

You've now created the appropriate views to document the model, so you can start to add annotation; you'll begin with centerlines and center marks.

The Center Mark command on the Drawing Annotation panel is quite simple: start the command and then click any arc or circular edge, and a center mark is drawn at the center of the selected arc.

Center marks, as well as centerlines, are primarily formatted by the Center Mark style, but there is a distinct difference between how ANSI and non-ANSI center marks are drawn, so be sure your active standard is set properly.

Try adding center marks to the six holes on the front view of the front plate.

Depending on how you want to annotate your drawing views, you may choose to draw full centerlines between the four mounting holes and two more between the tapped holes in the front view.

The Centerline command (accessed from the Center Mark flyout on the Drawing Annotation panel) is used for just this purpose. Delete the center marks you just created, and try using the Centerline command to generate centerlines between the six holes on the front face. When arcs are selected as centerline endpoints, a center mark is drawn on the arc along with the centerline.

SEAN SAYS: WATCH YOUR MOUSE CLICKS DURING CENTERLINE CREATION

The Centerline command is a bit specific in the order it wants to see mouse clicks. After you have selected the final features on which to place the center mark, right-click and select Create. If you do not select Create and continue to select the next hole, you may end up with undesirable results. For example, in Figure 12.14, you'll need to select the top-left and then the top-right holes and then right-click and select Create. If you keep selecting the next lower-right hole, you'll end up with an arced centerline. Also, do not be confused by the Done command. This exits you from the Centerline command without creating any of the centerlines that have not yet been created. It takes a little getting used to, but you'll quickly figure it out.

You can also select edge endpoints and midpoints to define a centerline (center marks are not generated in this case).

The Centerline Bisector command (also found beneath the Center Mark flyout button) generates a centerline between two selected parallel view edges.

Use this command to create a centerline in the top section view along the tapped hole axis. Start the command, and then select either the two hidden tapped edges or the two visible hole edges; notice how the resulting centerline is drawn on the view, as shown in Figure 12.14.

Both centerlines and center marks can be drag-edged to be resized or even moved (though deleting and re-creating them usually generates more predictable results than dragging and moving).

Rather than placing centerlines and center marks manually, you can use the Automated Centerlines command. This command is in the view's right-click menu, and you can run this on multiple views on the same sheet at one time (multiselect views while holding your Ctrl key down before executing the command).

Again, delete the centerlines and center marks on your front view; then right-click and choose Automated Centerlines.

In the Automated Centerlines (ACL) dialog box, you can add center marks to hole features (selected by default) and other kinds of modeling features that result in circular edges such as fillets and revolutions.

Centerline bisectors are also created through this command, and where circular or rectangular patterns are used, centerlines can be drawn between these features as well.

You can input threshold values for circular edges, fillets, and arc angles so you can filter out certain features you may not want to have annotated with center marks.

FIGURE 12.14
Centerline and centerline bisectors

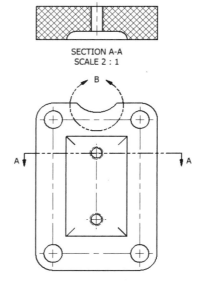

Accept the default values here, and hit OK. Notice that six center marks were created, one on each hole edge in the front view.

You can set the default settings for the ACL command in your template file by selecting Tools ➤ Document Settings and going to the Drawing tab. Click the Automated Centerlines button.

General Dimensions

A significant portion of any detailing job is placing and modifying dimensions, so it's important to become familiar with the various dimension commands and formatting options available in Inventor's Drawing Manager.

The General Dimension command on the Drawing Annotation panel is typically your primary dimensioning tool. It works very much like the Sketch Dimension command discussed earlier in this book in that this single command can generate several different types of dimensions depending on the geometry you select (selecting a linear edge results in an aligned, horizontal, or vertical dimension; selecting an arc or circle results in a radial or diameter dimension; selecting two parallel lines results in an angle dimension; and so on).

A few more types of dimensions are available in drawings than can be generated in sketches using the General Dimensions command.

Once an arc is selected (not a full circle), a radius dimension is created by default, but prior to placement, you can right-click and choose Angle, Arc Length, or Chord Length from the Dimension Type flyout.

Prior to placing linear dimension between two points or two parallel lines, you can create Linear Diameter or Linear Symmetric dimensions from the dimension's right-click menu, Dimension Type flyout. These types of dimensions are used commonly with symmetrical parts, especially turned, cylindrical parts. You can find a good example of these dimensions on the Tire Rim drawing in the Samples directory.

You can change dimension snap settings during the dimension command by holding your Shift key down, right-clicking, and selecting Snap Settings.

Recovering Model Dimensions

Another way to quickly add dimensions to your model views is using the Retrieve Dimensions command. You can access this command from the view's right-click menu or from the Drawing Annotation panel.

This command allows you to recover sketch and feature dimensions that were used to model your part into the drawing view.

Try running this command on the front view of the faceplate. Start the command, select the base view, and then click the Select Dimensions button in the Retrieve Dimensions dialog box. This displays all the relevant sketch and feature dimensions, allowing you to select the ones you want shown in your drawing view (if you want all the available dimensions, multiselect the entire group, and hit OK). You can also filter the available dimensions per selected feature or even per selected part if you're running this command against an assembly view.

Recovered model dimensions behave similarly to regular, placed dimensions with respect to editing and formatting. Recovered model dimensions cannot be detached or reattached from the geometry they're referencing.

Model dimension values can be directly edited from the drawing view, thus changing the model parameter value and affecting size and shape of your model feature. Access the dimension value by selecting Edit Model Dimension from the dimension's right-click menu.

The ability to change model dimension values is set during Inventor installation; the default setting is to have the ability enabled.

SEAN SAYS: EXERCISE CAUTION EDITING MODEL DIMENSIONS SETTINGS

The option to enable edits of model dimension values from the drawing (an install setting, set when installing Inventor), can be *very* powerful and very dangerous. Editing a model dimension from a drawing is a quick way to edit the size and shape of a model, but it is often blind to other issues it may create. For example, if a part is used in an assembly and another part references holes adaptively in that assembly, changing the model dimension may affect this second part without your knowledge. I suggest you always open the assembly to see what else your changes will affect. In my nine-plus years of using Inventor, I have *never* edited a model dimension from the drawing environment.

Once a particular model dimension is recovered in one view, it cannot be recovered again in any other view in the same file. You can move recovered model dimensions between views, however, provided appropriate attachment points exist in the target view.

Baseline and Ordinate Dimensions

Baseline dimensions are a series of linear dimensions that each terminate to a common point (or baseline). The Baseline Dimension and Baseline Dimension Set commands (both in the Drawing Annotation panel) offer a mechanism to quickly add dimensions to a drawing view in an orderly way.

When you execute the Baseline Dimension command, you're left with a series of conventional linear dimensions. This command simply automates what you could do on your own with the General Dimension command. The Baseline Dimension Set command, however, generates a collected group of linear dimensions that are moved (through dragging and editing) as a single group so their spacing remains constant.

Try running each of these commands on the front view of the faceplate (delete any dimensions you may already have placed).

Start either command, click the bottom horizontal part edge (this will be the baseline), and then manually or multiselect additional horizontal features (these can be model edges or center mark legs). When you've selected all the geometry you want to dimension, right-click and click to place the dimensions (shown in Figure 12.15). After you place the dimensions, you can continue to select points on the view (points on geometry rather than explicit geometry), or you can right-click and select Create.

FIGURE 12.15
Baseline dimensions

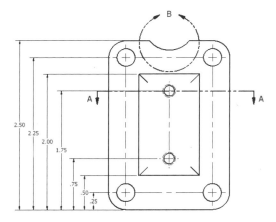

Ordinate dimensions and ordinate dimension sets are created much the same way. Again, a dimension set is managed and formatted as a single, selectable object (with some exceptions), while the Ordinate Dimension command results in independently controlled dimensions.

Another key difference between ordinate dimensions and an ordinate dimension set is that you can have multiple ordinate sets on a single view with different origin points. Once you specify an origin for ordinate dimensions on a view, all ordinate dimensions placed on that view will reference that origin as well as any hole tables referencing that view. The reverse is true as well: once an origin is specified for a hole table, ordinate dimensions on that view share the origin.

Dimensions in Isometric Views

When you use the General Dimension command to add dimensions to an isometric view, the resulting dimensions are fundamentally different than those you place in orthographic views.

This is immediately noticeable when you see how the resulting dimensions are drawn on the sheet: all of the dimension geometry (text, arrowheads, extension lines, and dimension lines) are drawn in 3D space and not in sheet space (like orthographic views). Dimensions generated on isometric views are called *true* (meaning they reflect the true model space dimensional value). Dimensions added to orthographic views are known as *projected* because the dimension value represents the calculated distance or angle between endpoints or geometry projected onto the sheet.

When placing an isometric dimension, Inventor tries to determine an appropriate annotation plane based on your geometry selection. In many cases, particularly with linear dimensions, multiple inferred annotation planes are available. Prior to placing the dimension, you can toggle through these inferred annotation planes by clicking the spacebar.

If none of the inferred work planes meets your needs, you can project the dimension either onto the sheet or onto a model work plane. These options are in the command's right-click menu prior to dimension placement.

The change in dimension behavior (true versus projected) happens automatically depending on the view orientation. Any projected isometric or base isometric view results in True dimensions. As a rule, newly added dimensions to a view are treated as true if none of the model's origin planes is parallel to the sheet (with the exception of auxiliary views).

You can override this rule on a view-by-view basis by right-clicking a view and changing the dimension type (True or Projected).

Isometric dimensions are functionally identical to orthographic dimensions; however, they cannot be "moved." That is, they cannot be detached and reattached to different geometry, and they can't be moved using the dimension Move command on the dimension's right-click menu. All formatting commands and behavior are otherwise identical.

While placing machining dimensions is a relatively unconventional technique, you can, in fact, add almost every dimension needed for fabrication of the faceplate part in one single isometric view. Try adding dimensions to the isometric view in the faceplate drawing (shown in Figure 12.16).

Formatting and Editing Dimensions

All the different types of dimensions discussed in this section are initially formatted by an associative dimension style. Indeed, each different type of dimension can be set to use a different dimension style if needed. Almost every formatting option available for dimensions are set through the dimension style. There are literally dozens of individual style settings — too many to list here. To illustrate how to change dimension formatting through styles, let's walk through setting up a new dimension style to apply a symmetrical tolerance.

From the Format pulldown, start the Style And Standard Editor, expand the Dimension node on the left side, right-click the Default (ANSI) dimension style, and select New Style. Give the style a unique name (we'll use PM5 to indicate a ±.005 tolerance).

On the Tolerance tab, set the method to Symmetric, and then set the Linear Precision to three places. Next, enter **.005** in the value field (Figure 12.17).

Finally, go to the Units tab, and change the Linear Precision setting to 3-place (3.123).

Save your changes, and close the Style Editor dialog box.

To apply this dimension style to an existing dimension, select one or more of the dimensions you've already created on your sheet. Unless you've already changed their style reference, you should see the Style pulldown display By Standard (Default ANSI). If an object (a dimension, a piece of text, or a model edge) is shown as By Standard in either the Layer or Style pulldown, it means that the active Object Defaults style determines the style and/or layer assignment for the object.

FIGURE 12.16
Isometric view
dimensions

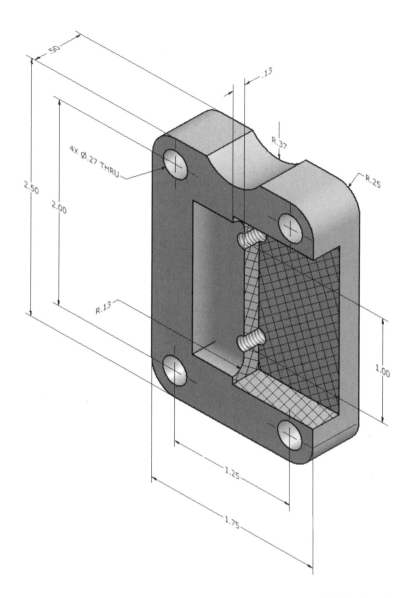

SEAN SAYS: CREATE DIMENSION STYLES

It is a good idea to create all your standard dimension styles before rolling out your style library. By creating standards for all users to use, you eliminate any discrepancy that comes from multiple users all trying to create drawings that look the same. You can create all your decimal place dimensions (one place, two place, three place, and so on), toleranced dimensions, even dowel pin hole toleranced dimension styles that users need only select.

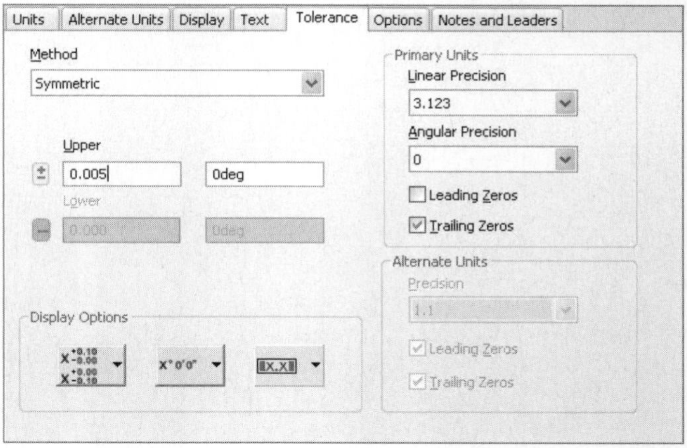

FIGURE 12.17
Dimension style
tolerance settings

From the Style pulldown, choose the new dimension style you just created with the symmetrical tolerance. The selected dimensions immediately update to reflect their new style assignment.

Next, double-click to edit one of the dimensions you just applied the new style to, and click the Precision And Tolerance tab. The ±.005 tolerance setting is reflected here in the Edit dialog box. Change the tolerance value to ±.003.

You've now created two formatting overrides for a single dimension: you changed the Object Defaults Dimension style assignment by setting it to a dimension style (not By Standard) and a tolerance value override from the style itself.

In addition to making style-level formatting changes to dimensions, you can copy and paste dimension formatting between dimension objects on your sheet.

Right-click the dimension you just edited, and select Copy Properties; then click a few other dimensions that have not yet received any edits to format. As you select dimensions, they adopt both the style formatting and the local tolerance value override from your source dimensions. You can configure which properties are copied before selecting the target dimension by right-clicking and selecting Settings after invoking the Copy Properties command.

Hole and Thread Notes

A hole note differentiates itself from a traditional diameter dimensions by calling out feature information beyond just the hole diameter.

The Hole/Thread Note command (found in the View Annotation panel) generates a leadered note that displays all pertinent hole feature information derived from the hole edge that is selected.

For example, a hole note pointing to a simple blind hole appears as ν.27 ξ.75. A hole note pointing to a through tapped hole appears as 10-32 UNF-2B ξ.50. Inventor provides you with the ability to tailor the exact contents of the hole note through your dimension style.

Use the Hole/Thread Note command to add a single note for the mounting hole and tapped hole in the faceplate front view.

You can configure hole notes to display whatever string of description text you prefer as well as set the various hole parameter values' precision and tolerance settings. These preferences are set and stored in the Dimension style.

There are more than 50 types of holes that can be configured in this interface generally corresponding to the different kind of holes you can create using the Hole feature command in part and assembly modeling (''holes'' as a result of circular-extruded cuts, voids, or circular sheet metal cut features are also supported by hole notes).

You can configure hole notes to display the hole quantity as part of the note. Notice the two tapped holes in the faceplate. These are Blind – Depth Thread holes (you can confirm this by double-clicking the hole note and noting the note format).

A quantity note can be added either directly on an individual note through the Edit Hole Note dialog box or at the style level so they appear for all holes of the same type.

To add a quantity note at the style level, make sure you're editing the dimension style associated with the hole notes on your drawing (the best way to ensure this is to access the dimension style from the hole note's right-click menu). Select Blind – Depth Thread in the Note Format pulldown, and then click in the text field so that the curser is in front of the note text; finally, click the button with the # sign on it. This inserts the <QTYNOTE> variable token in front of the note, as shown in Figure 12.18.

FIGURE 12.18
Hole note settings in dimension style

You can customize the quantity note by clicking the Edit Quantity Note button on the dimension style's Notes And Leaders tab. By default, the quantity note is set up as a prefix to the full hole note (4X). This dialog box also lets you determine how the hole quantity is determined (either the number of holes in a feature or pattern or a complete evaluation of identical holes in a view where all the hole axes are normal to the view).

As soon as you save the changes to your dimension style, you should see the hole note for the tapped holes update to include the quantity of holes (2X).

The Notes And Leaders tab on the Dimension style also enables you to preconfigure other kinds of feature notes including chamfer notes (which are actually calculated notes and not feature-dependent), punch notes, and bend notes (both of which are available only for views of sheet metal parts).

Leadered Symbols

Many of the annotations you can apply to a drawing belong to a common class of annotations we'll refer to as *leadered symbols*. These are all grouped together in the Drawing Annotation panel: Surface Texture Symbol, Welding Symbol, Feature Control Frame, Feature ID Symbol, Datum ID Symbol, and five different Datum Target commands. Each of these commands is created the same way, and each is formatted by their own dedicated style.

Let's walk through an exercise of adding some geometric dimensioning and tolerancing symbols to your faceplate drawing.

Start by clicking the Datum Identifier Symbol command; then click the far-right edge of the part in the front view, drag the leader to your desired length, click, and finally right-click and select Continue. Accept the default A value in the text editor, and hit OK.

Add a second datum ID (B) to the bottom edge of the part, and then cancel out of the command (right-click and select Done, or hit Esc).

Next, you'll create a feature control frame (FCF), which can be added to a drawing view with a leader the same way you created the datum IDs.

The FCF can also be attached directly to the model edge in the view without a leader by choosing Continue from the right-click menu after clicking the initial attach point.

Using a FCF in conjunction with a hole note is another common practice. Inventor allows you to attach an FCF to hole notes and other symbols such that they move together because model changes or manual drag-edits to the annotation. This is illustrated in Figure 12.19.

FIGURE 12.19
FCF attached to hole note

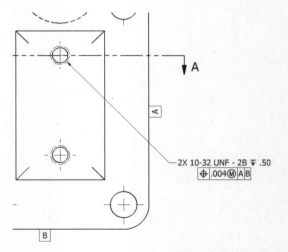

Start the Feature Control Frame command, and mouse over one of the hole notes you placed in the front view. Click when you see a green hot point near the bottom-center of the note (you'll also see your cursor show a Coincident constraint icon). You'll see a leader generated in the preview graphics, but if you right-click and select Continue, a leader is not generated.

Fill out the appropriate fields for a positional tolerance relative to the A and B datums; then hit OK. Now click to select the hole note, and then click and drag the leader landing to move the note. Notice how the FCF remains constrained to the hole note.

Drawing Text

You can add text to your drawing in multiple ways. The Text command (on the View Annotation panel) is used to create general drawing notes. This kind of text is limited because it can't be associated (constrained) to a drawing view and because it offers no control over which component iProperties and parameters are being accessed from.

Leader text provides both view and component association, allowing you to extract and display iProperty and model parameter values from whichever component the leader is attached to.

If view associativity is required but you don't want a leader, create a view sketch (select the view, and then click the Sketch command), and add sketch text.

Each of these commands utilizes the generic Format Text dialog box. This dialog box is used to edit any text-specific annotations as well as other annotations such as hole tags and datum and feature IDs.

The general text formatting for any drawing annotation containing text ultimately comes from a text style. Text style formatting (size, font, color, and so on) can be overwritten in the Format Text dialog box.

Hole Tables

Hole descriptions, quantities, and locations on a view can be documented using a hole table rather than using hole notes. Indeed, the hole table can be used not only to document hole features but sheet metal punches as well. You can even use a hole table to call out locations of recovered work points in your model. This technique can be used to detail specialized features such as slots and bosses.

Hole tables, like most types of annotation in Inventor, are initially formatted by an associative style — a Hole Table style in this case.

The Hole Table style enables you to select which columns you want displayed in your table, format precision and units for the X and Y location column, change line formatting, filter on different hole types, and configure various grouping mechanisms depending on your needs.

Everything about the hole table is formatted by the Hole Table style except for the description string for the hole. The description string uses the same configuration as your hole notes and receives this particular formatting by the hole tag's dimension style (hole tags are created with the hole table and are formatted by a dimension style).

Let's walk through setting up a Hole Table style and creating a hole table for the faceplate.

Start by deleting any hole notes you have on the front view, launch the Style Editor dialog box, expand the hole table, and click in the Hole Table (ANSI) style (shown in Figure 12.20).

Click the Column Chooser, find the Quantity property in the list on the left, and add it to the included list of columns on the right. Move the Quantity column up in the list as you like; then hit OK.

Right-click the XDIM Property in the Default Column Settings frame, and select Format Column. In the Format Column dialog box, change the precision to 3-place, and change the column heading to X LOCATION. Hit OK, and repeat for the YDIM column. Save the changes, and exit from the Style Editor dialog box.

FIGURE 12.20
Hole Table Style
interface

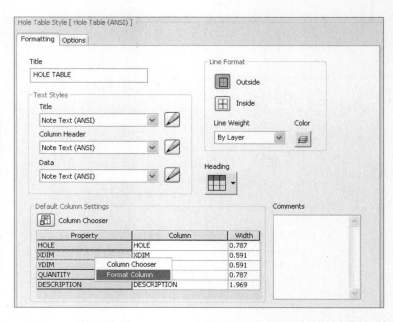

There are three different hole table commands on the Drawing Annotation panel: Selection, View, and Selected Feature. Selection lets you control which holes are added to the hole table by explicitly selecting them as you create the table. View documents all holes in a view (though you can use filters to exclude certain hole types). As holes are added to the part, the hole table update to include them. Selection Feature limits the hole table to one (and only one) hole feature (which could be multiple holes, but all the same type).

For this exercise, choose the hole table's View command, select the front view, place the origin at the apparent intersection at the lower-left side of the part (using point tracking — you may want to zoom in a bit on the view to do this), and then snap the hole table to the lower-left side of the drawing border.

For each individual hole in the view, a hole tag is placed next to the hole edge, and a corresponding row is generated in the hole table. Also notice that because each hole is called out individually in this table, each row has a quantity of 1 (shown in Figure 12.21).

FIGURE 12.21
Hole table

HOLE TABLE				
HOLE	QUANTITY	X LOCATION	Y LOCATION	DESCRIPTION
A1	1	.250	.250	Ø.27 ⍒ .75
A2	1	1.500	.250	Ø.27 ⍒ .75
A3	1	.250	2.250	Ø.27 ⍒ .75
A4	1	1.500	2.250	Ø.27 ⍒ .75
B1	1	.875	.750	10-32 UNF - 2B ⍒ .50
B2	1	.875	1.750	10-32 UNF - 2B ⍒ .50

Double-click the table to edit. On the Options tab, click the Rollup option under Row Merge Settings, and hit OK. The hole table now collapses common holes into a single row, and the quantity columns update accordingly.

You can make direct overrides to hole descriptions by double-clicking the description text, and you can override X and Y location precision by right-clicking an individual cell.

SEAN SAYS: HOLE TABLES SAVE TIME ON LARGE PARTS

For large plates with many different holes, hole tables are a wonderful tool. A large plate could take a half hour or more to fully dimension. Furthermore, it's often difficult for a machinist to tell where all five of the same holes are located if they are not all called out individually. The hole table gives the machinist X and Y locations of the holes that they can use to program their CNC milling machine extraordinarily quickly. Don't be surprised if the machinist asks you to dimension all your parts using hole tables.

ASSEMBLY DRAWINGS

Creating/annotating drawing views of assemblies is not dissimilar than for parts. All the same views and annotation commands discussed in the previous sections can be executed against assembly and presentation models.

The most significant differences between these two types of model views are the view options available for assembly views.

When an assembly file is referenced in the Base View command, notice the set of representation options that become available on the Component tab of the Drawing View dialog box. These controls allow you to specify which assembly view, positional, or LOD representation is displayed in the resulting drawing view.

View representations can optionally be made associative to the view (using the check box at the top of the View Representation control). Specifically, an associative view representation means that as a component's visibility is changed from the assembly, the change is witnessed in the drawing view as well.

SEAN SAYS: MAKE YOUR VIEWS ASSOCIATIVE

Ninety-nine percent of the time you are going to want to make your views associative. If you do not, you'll be scratching your head trying to figure out why the drawing view is not matching your view representation.

If the associative option is unchecked, you can toggle component visibility from the drawing itself.

Start a new drawing using the standard template, and create a base (left-side) view of the Arbor_Press.iam at half scale. Before placing the view on the sheet, make sure the Default View Representation and Closed Positional Representation options are selected and the Associative View Representation option is checked (shown in Figure 12.22).

Open the Arbor Press assembly in another window by right-clicking the drawing view and choosing Open. Make sure the default view representation is active; then right-click the handle caps, and uncheck Visibility. Return to the drawing, and notice that the handle caps are now invisible in the drawing view. In the Drawing browser, expand the base drawing view node and the Arbor Press assembly node beneath it, and notice the handle cap nodes are shown as invisible. If you right-click one of the handle cap nodes, you'll see the Visibility option is disabled.

To reenable the Visibility option for components in the assembly view, double-click the view, and uncheck the Associative View Representation option.

FIGURE 12.22
Assembly base view
creation

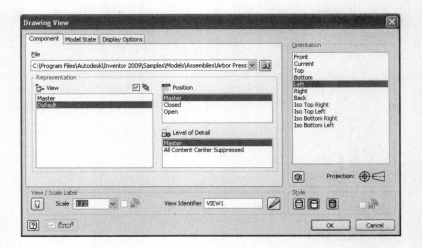

Reference Data in Drawing Views

Assembly components can be designated as Reference. This attribute can be applied as a document setting on the part or assembly file itself or on a per-instance basis when placed in a higher-level assembly.

In addition to being omitted from the assembly mass property calculations, BOM, and subsequent drawing parts lists, reference components are drawn and calculated differently in assembly drawing views.

By default, all reference component edges are mapped to a unique layer with a broken line style (double-dash chain). Hidden line calculation, by default, is run separately for reference components than nonreference components. Finally, reference components do not affect the calculation of the drawing boundary. This means that if you have a reference component well apart from nonreference parts in an assembly, it may not be visible in a drawing view until you increase the reference margin.

You can adjust all of these reference data view behaviors on the Model State tab of the Drawing View dialog box, as shown in Figure 12.23.

Interference Edge Display

As you virtually place and constrain components in an assembly file, it may be necessary to create an interference condition between parts. This is common for press-fit conditions such as pins in undersized holes.

This condition is common in Inventor even when you have a threaded fastener being inserted into an equal-diameter threaded hole. You can see this condition on the Arbor Press assembly. Create an isometric view of the assembly, and notice the set screws inserted into threaded holes in the frame and faceplate. There's clearly a missing edge where you'd expect to see the screw meeting the flat face of the frame or plate.

These edges are designated as interference edges and can be enabled by editing the view and checking the Interference Edge check box on the Display Options tab. Figure 12.24 shows the resulting change to the view.

FIGURE 12.23
Reference data settings

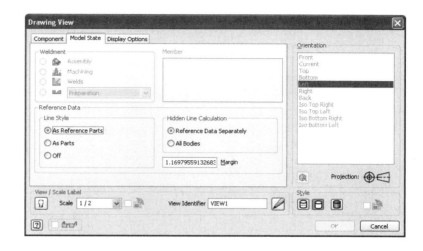

FIGURE 12.24
Interference edge display
on set screws

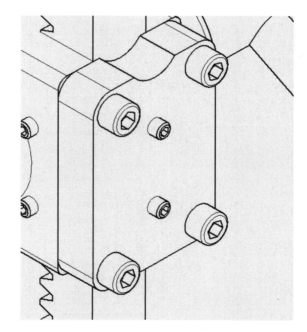

Parts Lists

Parts lists are a formatted, tabulated report of the assembly bill of materials (BOM). Most of the data you see in a parts list is ultimately derived from the assembly BOM, but the BOM and the parts list are managed very differently inside Inventor.

Parts lists have a dedicated formatting style that provides dozens of formatting variations.

We'll walk through a typical parts lists editing and creation workflow to demonstrate what kind of capabilities can be levered in the parts lists.

On the Arbor Press drawing that was started earlier in this section, launch the Style Editor dialog box, expand the Parts List node, and click the Parts List (ANSI) style.

Click on the Column Chooser, then add the Material property, OK out of the dialog, then change the heading placement to Bottom. Save your changes and exit the Style dialog box.

On the Drawing Annotation panel, click the Parts List command. The Parts List dialog box allows you to either click an assembly or presentation drawing view or browse directly to an assembly or presentation file (you can create a parts list on a drawing with no drawing views).

You can choose either a structured (first or all levels) or parts-only part lists. If the parts list is too long for the sheet size you're placing it on, you can also enable the option to wrap the parts lists based on a specified number or rows.

Click OK, and then snap the parts lists to the lower-left corner of the drawing border.

Although you can specify the default column width at the style level, you may need to adjust the width based on the length of the text strings read in from the component iProperties.

You can adjust column width by clicking and dragging the vertical column lines on the parts list on your sheet. Resize the Description column on the Arbor Press parts list to better accommodate the long description text.

The initial item numbering for the components and the row order come from the last save state of the assembly BOM but can be changed by editing the parts list.

Double-click the parts list to launch Parts List dialog box. Click the Sort button, sort by Part Number in descending order, and then click OK. Next, click the Renumber Items button, and notice how new item numbers are assigned based on the sort order.

The new item numbers appear blue and bold in the Parts List dialog box (shown in Figure 12.25). Any change you make to any of the cells in the Parts List dialog box (except for custom rows or custom columns) are treated as overrides to the BOM data. The blue and bold formatting indicates the cell value has been overwritten and is no longer associative to the BOM.

FIGURE 12.25
Parts list with item number overrides

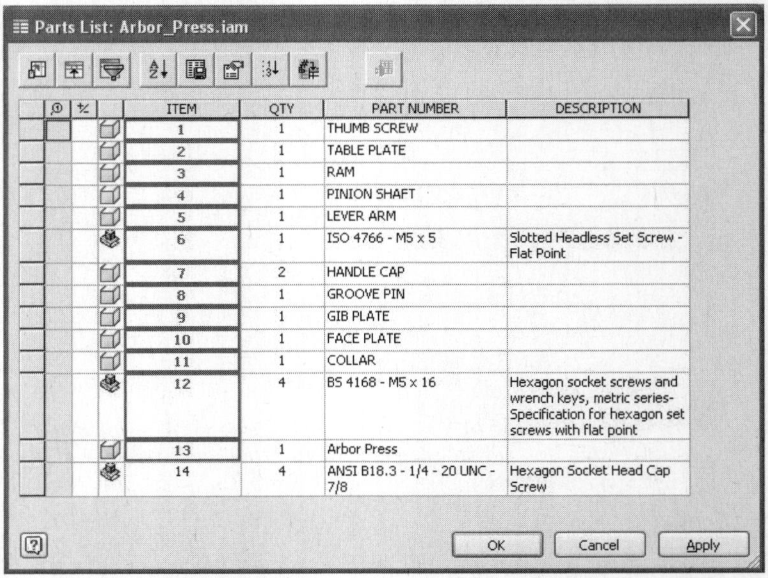

ITEM	QTY	PART NUMBER	DESCRIPTION
1	1	THUMB SCREW	
2	1	TABLE PLATE	
3	1	RAM	
4	1	PINION SHAFT	
5	1	LEVER ARM	
6	1	ISO 4766 - M5 x 5	Slotted Headless Set Screw - Flat Point
7	2	HANDLE CAP	
8	1	GROOVE PIN	
9	1	GIB PLATE	
10	1	FACE PLATE	
11	1	COLLAR	
12	4	BS 4168 - M5 x 16	Hexagon socket screws and wrench keys, metric series-Specification for hexagon set screws with flat point
13	1	Arbor Press	
14	4	ANSI B18.3 - 1/4 - 20 UNC - 7/8	Hexagon Socket Head Cap Screw

Item number changes (and only item number changes) can be saved to the assembly BOM. This can be done cell by cell from the right-click menu or for the entire parts list by running the Save Item Overrides To BOM command by right-clicking the parts list itself on the sheet or on the Parts List browser node.

The Parts List dialog box isn't designed to be an iProperty editor, which is why all cell edits are treated as BOM overrides. If you see an iProperty value in the parts list that you want to change at the component level, right-click the parts list, and choose Bill Of Materials. Edits made in the BOM editor are written back to component iProperties.

The Parts List is not directly associated with any drawing view (if you choose a view when you create the parts list, it acts only as a pointer to the assembly file itself). Assembly drawing views are related to parts lists by ballooning the components in the assembly drawing view.

SEAN SAYS: EDIT IPROPERTIES WITH THE BOM EDITOR

Novice users will likely attempt to change iProperty information in the Parts List. While this does display the correct information in the Parts List the information is no longer associative. The correct method is to use the BOM Editor to change the information in the model file. This way, the Part List only shows what information was assigned to the model and keeps the design intent in the model file.

Balloons

Balloons are perhaps the only type of annotation that are relevant only for assembly views. By default, balloons are set to display a component's assigned item number only, but through changes to the balloon style, a balloon can be configured to display any component iProperty or BOM property.

Continue working with the Arbor Press drawing. Open the Style Editor dialog box, and select the Balloon (ANSI) balloon style for editing. Toggle through the available shapes and, depending on the shape, different iProperties and BOM properties. For example, a circular and hex balloon shape are limited to displaying only one property (item number); a split balloon (circular - 2 entries) can display two properties (item number and quantity); and if you choose no shape, you can display any number of properties.

Click the Property Chooser, remove the QTY selected property, and add the Part Number property; then click OK.

Change the balloon shape to circular – 2 entries, save the changes, and exit the Style Editor dialog box.

Start the Balloon command (on the Drawing Annotation panel), and click any of the component edges in the drawing view of the Arbor Press drawing, and click again to set the length of the leader line. Then right-click and choose Continue.

The balloon is displaying the item and part number as set in the balloon style.

Right-click to edit the balloon you just placed. The Edit Balloon dialog box provides the options to change the balloon shape (you can choose any sketch symbol you have defined in Drawing Resources) or change the item number.

Edit the balloon style again, and set the shape back to circular – 1 entry.

You can string multiple balloons together on a single leader. This is a common technique when ballooning a collection of hardware such as a screw, lock washer, and split washer.

Add a balloon to the one of the handle caps in the front view; then right-click the balloon, and select Attach Balloon. Finally, click the lever arm. The balloon for the lever arm is shown attached to the handle cap's balloon (Figure 12.26). Drag your mouse around the balloon to set the position of the attached balloon, and then click to place it.

FIGURE 12.26
Attached balloons

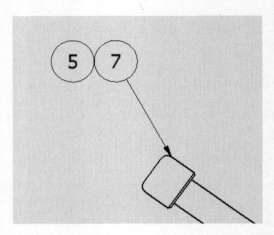

If you need to attach a balloon for a component that can't be selected graphically, use the Attach Balloon From List command on the balloon's right-click menu.

Balloons can be added one at a time, or you can use the Auto Balloon command (under the Balloon flyout) to quickly add multiple balloons to a drawing view.

Start the Auto Balloon command, select the Arbor Press drawing view, multiselect all the components in the view, and then click Select Placement. Before clicking to place the balloons, change the placement options, and notice how the preview graphics update; then click OK.

Overlay Views

If you've defined multiple positional representations in your assembly (as does the Arbor Press), you can use these different positional representations to create an overlay view. First, create another half-scale view of the Arbor Press drawing's right side, and choose the Open positional rep. Right-click this view, and choose Overlay View from the Create View flyout. In the Overlay View dialog box, choose the Closed positional representation; then click OK.

You're given the opportunity to specify a view representation for the overlay view. It's recommended that before you create an overlay view, you create a view representation that visibly isolates only the components that move as a result of the positional representation. Otherwise (as is the case in this example), all of the nonmoving components are redrawn over the same components in the base view.

Center of Gravity Display

You can display the center of gravity (COG) of a part or assembly drawing view as a center mark. Only one COG can be shown per view with the exception of overlay views.

Locate the base view for the overlay view in the browser, expand it, right-click the Arbor_Press assembly icon, and select Center Of Gravity. This command recalculates the model's center of gravity (it does not read the value in from the model's physical properties) and draws a center mark at the calculated location.

Repeat this command on the Arbor_Press assembly icon under the Overlay View icon in the browser.

Finally, dimension the location of these center marks relative to the bottom-left corner of the Arbor Press frame. Double-click to edit one of these dimensions, and add **(COG)** as a suffix to the dimension value on the Text tab of the Edit Dimension dialog box. Use the Copy Properties command to copy this appended text to the other COG dimensions (shown in Figure 12.27).

FIGURE 12.27
Overlay view with recovered COG

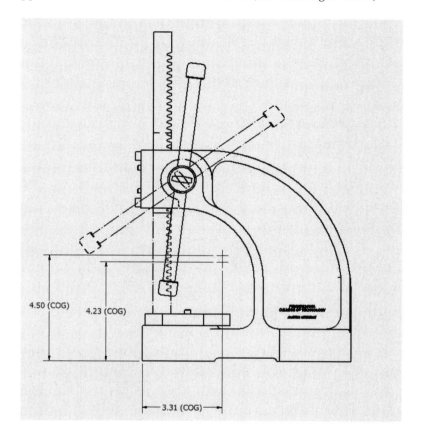

SHEET METAL DRAWINGS

Drawing views of sheet metal parts offer some unique options beyond what are normally available for conventional part files.

Start a new drawing using the standard template, start the Base View command, and browse to select the electrical box.ipt file under the Sheet Metal folder in the Samples directory.

Drawing views can be generated for both the folded sheet metal model as well as its flat pattern (provided that one was created in the part file). On the Component tab in the Drawing View dialog box, select the Flat Pattern option as well as the Recover Punch Center option, and then place the view of the flat pattern on the sheet.

Bend Centerlines and Extents

Bend centerlines are drawn on sheet metal flat pattern views where the center of the bend is located on the material face. Inventor tracks negative and positive bend centerlines independently of one another to enable users to apply different line formatting for these two conditions.

Click the Edit Layers button on the Standard toolbar, create a new layer called Bend Centerline (negative), and set the color to something other than automatic (black).

Remain in the Style Editor dialog box, click the Object Defaults (ANSI) style, and scroll down on the table until you see Sheet Metal Bend Centerline. Set this object's layer to the new layer you just created. Save changes, and exit the Style Editor dialog box.

The four internal bend centerlines on the view are updated to show the formatting from the new layer you created.

Lines representing bend extents can be enabled by editing the flat pattern view and selecting the Bend Extents Display option.

Bend and Punch Notes

There are two sheet-metal-specific annotation commands on the Drawing Annotation panel: Bend Notes and Punch Notes.

Bend notes are placed on bend centerlines in sheet metal flat pattern views and can convey information about the bending operation including the bend radius, direction, angle, and K-factor.

Click the Bend Note command button, and click one of the bend centerlines in the drawing view. You can quickly add bend notes to every bend centerline in the view by multiselecting everything in the view (this command looks only for bend centerlines, so don't be concerned about selecting regular model edges).

By default, the bend notes are drawn adjacent to the bend centerlines, but where the note may be obscured in the view, you can click and drag individual bend notes to flip them to the opposite side of the bend centerline, or you can drag away from the bend centerline, and a leader is generated back to the bend centerline. Try this with the two outermost bend notes on the electrical box flat pattern view (shown in Figure 12.28).

FIGURE 12.28
Bend notes in flat
pattern view

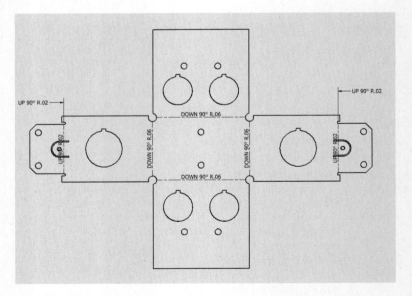

The style formatting and direct editing of bend notes is identical to hole notes. You can pre-configure the contents of the note with the note's dimension style by adding one or more variable tokens for the bend note attributes.

Punch notes (the command is accessed under the Bend Note command flyout) are used to convey information about sheet metal punch features (a special kind of iFeature). Punch notes can be applied only to flat pattern views of sheet metal parts. They can be attached to recovered punch centers (shown as center marks in the flat pattern drawing) or on any model edge generated by the punch.

Punch notes can be configured to display the punch identifier (defined as part of the iFeature definition), the punch angle, the depth, and the direction.

Punch notes are likewise formatted through dimension styles and have a similar editing interface to hole notes.

Bend Tables

Bend information can alternatively be displayed in a table rather than a note.

A Bend Table is generated using the Tables command on the View Annotation panel.

The Tables command basically morphs into several different kinds of tables depending on what you specify as a data source.

If no data source is selected in the Table creation dialog box, you'll end up with an empty table that you can populate manually.

You can also browse and import data from a .csv or .xls file into the table.

The Table command is also used to display model data for sheet metal files (a bend table) or iPart and iAssembly authoring setting (a configuration table).

To create a bend table for our electrical box, first delete any bend notes you created earlier, start the Table command, and select the drawing view (like parts lists, a bend table does not require a view to be created on the drawing; you can browse to select any sheet metal file with a flat pattern to generate a bend table).

Prior to placing the table, you can change the column choices and configure the bend ID format. Click OK, and place the bend table anywhere on your sheet.

A bend table is edited and maintained like a parts list. The Table dialog box is essentially identical, and any changes to the cell data are treated as overrides to the data source (in this case, the bend data stored in the sheet metal file).

The bend identifiers are added to the drawing view and correspond to rows in the bend table. These bend IDs can be dragged and edited just like a bend note to better position them for clarity, as shown in Figure 12.29.

FIGURE 12.29
Bend table

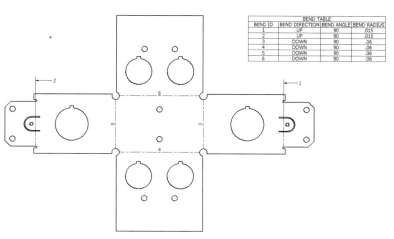

BEND TABLE			
BEND ID	BEND DIRECTION	BEND ANGLE	BEND RADIUS
1	UP	90	.015
2	UP	90	.015
3	DOWN	90	.06
4	DOWN	90	.06
5	DOWN	90	.06
6	DOWN	90	.06

Punch Tables

Punch information can likewise be displayed in a table, but because punches closely resemble holes with respect to the kind of information required to be displayed, a hole table is used to generate tabulated punch data.

Start the Hole Table – View command, select the flat pattern view, and select an origin point. Prior to placing the table, though, change the table's style from By Standard (Hole Table (ANSI)) to Punch Table (ANSI). This hole table style has preconfigured columns for sheet metal punch features and filters out all other hole types. Figure 12.30 shows the Punch table.

FIGURE 12.30
Punch table

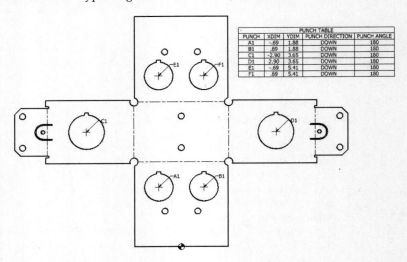

PUNCH TABLE				
PUNCH	XDIM	YDIM	PUNCH DIRECTION	PUNCH ANGLE
A1	-.69	1.88	DOWN	180
B1	.69	1.88	DOWN	180
C1	-2.90	3.65	DOWN	180
D1	2.90	3.65	DOWN	180
E1	-.69	5.41	DOWN	180
F1	.69	5.41	DOWN	180

WELDMENT VIEWS

Weldments are a special kind of assembly model and offer unique drawing view and annotation options in Drawing Manager.

Start a new drawing with the standard template, and browse to select the `Carriage.iam` assembly file under the Weldments folder in Samples. Click the Model State tab, and the drawing view can display any of the weldment states: the base assembly prior to any machining or welding (as assembled), the machining state (default), the weld state, or the preparation state. Further, you can use the Preparation pulldown to isolate any of the top-level weldment components in their preparation state (shown in Figure 12.31).

Click the Display Options tab, and check the options to recover Weld Annotations and Model Weld Symbols; then place the model view.

The weld symbols are recovered exactly as they were generated in the assembly weldment environment, and weld annotations appear in the view to show weld bead end fills and caterpillars (top view of a weld bead). Recovered weld symbols are shown in Figure 12.32.

Customers who don't use the weldment tools in assembly modeling but still need to convey welding information in a drawing can create weld symbols and weld annotations (end fills and caterpillars) manually on the drawing view. Each command is available in the Drawing Annotation panel and is formatted by a dedicated style (the Weld Symbol style and Weld Bead style, respectively).

FIGURE 12.31
Weldment state settings

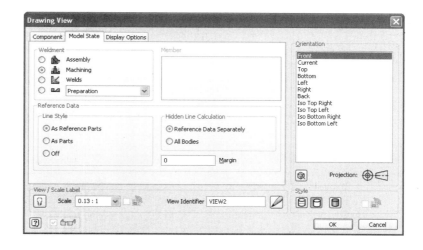

FIGURE 12.32
Weldment drawing with
recovered annotation
and weld symbols

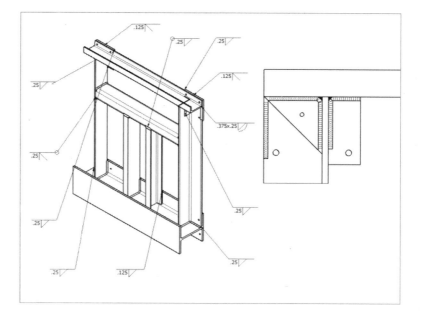

iParts and iAssembly Drawings

When your drawing view references an iPart or iAssembly, you can choose, from the Drawing View Model State tab, which member file you want to document.

Annotations (particularly dimensions) attached to drawing views of iParts and iAssemblies generally remain attached if you edit the base view and change the iPart member on the Model

State tab. This means you can fully annotate just one iPart or iAssembly member and Save Copy As for each unique member after changing the member referenced in the base view.

SHARING YOUR DRAWING OUTSIDE YOUR WORKGROUP

Once your design is fully annotated, there are numerous ways to share the design documents to downstream consumers.

Of course, the traditional hard-copy route is available from the Print command in the File pulldown menu, but there are numerous ways to distribute electronic versions of the document as well.

The native file formats offer several possibilities.

Inventor IPT, IAM, IPN, and IDW files can be viewed in their raw state using the freely distributed Inventor View application. A version of this is already installed with Inventor but can be downloaded for free from the Autodesk website (www.autodesk.com).

As mentioned earlier, if you use DWG as your drawing file format, anyone with a copy of AutoCAD or AutoCAD LT 2007 or later can view, plot, and measure the Inventor drawing. There are object enablers that even allow older versions of AutoCAD to open Inventor DWG files on the Autodesk website.

Using the Publish command from the File pulldown lets you generate a neutral .dwf or .pdf file. The .dwf file can store both your 2D drawing and the 3D models that are referenced in the drawing. DWF files are viewed using Autodesk Design Review, which is available for download from the Autodesk website.

PDF is a popular publishing format that can be read by Adobe Acrobat Reader available for download from Adobe's website (www.adobe.com).

The Bottom Line

Create an exploded assembly view by creating a presentation   Presentation files are used to virtually disassemble an assembly so downstream consumers can better visualize the design. The explosion created in the presentation file can be referenced in an assembly drawing to complement nonexploded assembly views.

Master It   Your assembly design is complex and contains many internal components that can't be visualized in traditional assembly drawing views.

Create and maintain drawing templates, standards, and styles   Inventor provides numerous methods to create, store, and use drawing templates and styles. Careful planning should be considered for how and where to manage these resources. Consideration must be given to how templates are deployed on your network and whether to use the style library.

Master It   Rather than using one of Inventor's out-of-the box drawing settings, you need to set up a drawing template, a drafting standard, and annotation styles to conform to a particular international, industry, or company drafting standard.

Generate 2D drawings views of parts, assemblies, and presentations   The Drawing Manager environment in Inventor enables you to generate traditional 2D drafting views from your 3D solid models.

Master It   You've used Inventor's modeling tools to generate parts and assemblies to meet your design criteria. Now you need to generate drawing views of this design so that it can be communicated to machinists, fabricators, and inspectors.

Annotate drawing views of your model   Drawing Manager provides a rich set of dimensioning tools, special symbols, and tables that enable you to fully annotate part and assembly drawings conforming to several international drawing standards.

Master It   Now that you've generated drawing views of your design, the views must be fully annotated in accordance with your company's or your customer's required drafting standard.

Chapter 13

Inventor Tools Overview

Using tools effectively helps you improve your productivity and get the most out of Autodesk Inventor. Initially, tools require a certain amount of familiarity to be productive; however, they pay off in the long run.

This chapter assumes you have a good understanding of parts, assemblies, and drawings. Some of the tools covered in this chapter assume you have a set of Autodesk Inventor files (templates, parts, assemblies, and drawings) to work with. Two examples of tools are the Design Assistant and the Drawing Resource Transfer Wizard. In this chapter, you will learn the various aspects of Inventor tools and some of the add-ins that are helpful. We will cover the key aspects of the tools and add-ins that come with Autodesk Inventor and some relevant workflows. Many other tools (not covered here) are available on myriad websites that are built using the Autodesk Inventor API.

We will cover various topics in this chapter, including the AEC Exchange, AutoLimits, Design Assistant, Drawing Resource Transfer Wizard, style tools, Supplier Content Center, Task Scheduler, the iProperties command, the Measure tool, CIP, CER, and other miscellaneous tools.

In this chapter, you will learn how to:

◆ Take your models from Inventor to ABS

◆ Create AutoLimits/design sensors

◆ Manage design data efficiently using Inventor tools

◆ Manage styles

◆ Create expressions with iProperties

◆ Measure in assemblies

◆ Give feedback to Autodesk

AEC Exchange

The Architecture, Engineering, and Construction (AEC) exchange is an add-in environment for parts and assemblies. Using the AEC exchange, you can import Inventor models into ABS, which is another Autodesk product used for building design and construction systems. You can use ABS to document the architectural, mechanical, electrical, and plumbing information of designs. You can go to the AEC exchange environment by clicking on Application ➤ AEC Exchange while in parts and assemblies.

A Typical Scenario for the AEC Exchange

ABC Construction specializes in designing commercial and residential buildings. It uses ABS to do the entire building design. Your company uses Inventor and specializes in electrical and mechanical designs, and you have to supply the air conditioner for the building designed by ABC Construction. To minimize the risk in losing information and future rework, you meet with ABC Construction to ensure the interfaces between the motor and the building are all agreed upon. ABC Construction does not care about any internal details of the air conditioner; however, the company is extremely sensitive to any changes in the interfaces. The plan is to design the model and interfaces in Inventor and send the design to ABC Construction. In this case study, we will cover the steps necessary to address this workflow.

The AEC exchange workflow is achieved with the following three steps.

Model Simplification

You start with a part or assembly in Autodesk Inventor. You use Autodesk Inventor's skeletal modeling (Chapter 8) and/or LOD representation (Chapter 9) technology to do model simplification.

Model Authoring

The AEC exchange environment allows you to create connector objects such as cables, conduits, ducts, and pipes on the simplified model. These connector objects define the interfaces. Interfaces are the connection points between Inventor and the AEC model. Autodesk Inventor allows you to create, edit, and delete connector objects.

Model Publishing

A part in the AEC exchange is the basic unit, that is, a specific size of the component placed within a part family. The part has instance-specific properties associated with it, for example, a name and geometric representation. You can publish a family within an ABS catalog. This process creates a family of parts. You can use the ABS Catalog Editor tool to create and manage the catalogs in Autodesk Inventor. A catalog helps you reuse components by creating chapters or families.

In the AEC exchange panel bar, you can use the Save AS DWG Solids command to save an active Inventor model as a dumb solid (no connection or multiviews). You can create a DWG file from the 3D solid. The 3D DWG can be directly manipulated in any AutoCAD version that supports 3D DWG. You can also export to AutoCAD architecture, Revit-based software, and AutoCAD.

AutoLimits

The AutoLimits tool allows you to monitor model changes so that you can reduce errors and engineering changes. You can think of it as a sensor. For example, say you are a plastics manufacturer and want to analyze the situation when the wall thickness of the components becomes too thin. You are a machinist and are concerned if two holes come too close to one another. You want to communicate this information to the designer and ensure that such a situation is caught early in the design. With AutoLimits, the designer can set up these limits and let the system warn you.

AutoLimits are passive and hence do not drive geometry. Another way to look at AutoLimits is as a persistent Measure tool. The Measure tool performs the measurement and the result does not persist, while with AutoLimits the measurement persists. When you open a file, the AutoLimits are not shown unless you activate the AutoLimits panel bar.

AutoLimits monitors the following limits:

1. **Dimensional:** Length, Distance, Angle, Diameter, Minimum Distance

2. **Area-Perimeter:** Area, Perimeter

3. **Physical Property:** Volume, Mass

See Figure 13.1 for the different types of AutoLimits.

FIGURE 13.1
Types of AutoLimits

Feedback is given to the user in terms of shape and color. For example:

◆ A green circle means it is within the boundary limit.

◆ An amber inverted triangle means it is near the boundary limit.

◆ A red square means it is beyond the limit.

Figure 13.2 shows the different types of AutoLimits and their settings. (Click the AutoLimits panel bar and then click AutoLimits Settings to access the AutoLimits Settings dialog box.) You can control the visibility of each AutoLimit type by the On and Off radio buttons shown. In an assembly, only the edited document's AutoLimits are visible in the browser; in other words, AutoLimits at other levels of the assembly are not visible or available unless that component or level is edited.

FIGURE 13.2
AutoLimits Settings dialog box

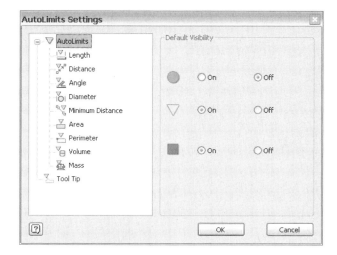

Creating AutoLimits

To create AutoLimits, follow these steps:

1. If you are in a part or assembly environment, click the Part Features or the Assembly Panel pulldown in the panel bar to go to the AutoLimits environment.

2. Click the AutoLimits Settings command, and in the dialog box that appears, as shown in Figure 13.2, select the defaults, boundaries, and so on.

3. Click the Dimensional AutoLimits command in the panel bar, and click Length AutoLimits. Select an edge in the model, and click OK. Based on the geometry selected, some selection buttons may not be available.

4. Figure 13.3 shows the Length AutoLimits example, with two edges selected for Length AutoLimits.

FIGURE 13.3
Length AutoLimits

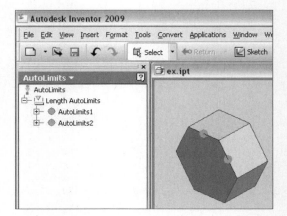

5. In the Dimensional AutoLimits dialog box in the AutoLimits tab you will see a few columns like +/-, Value, Cumulative columns (see Figure 13.4). The Value column shows the total value of the selections for that row. The Cumulative column shows the sum or difference of the rows. In the column to the left of the Value column, select the + or − depending on whether you want to add or subtract the value.

6. Click the Boundary tab to define the lower and higher values. Click the Level column to change the warning level for each highlighted boundary. Click Apply to add the AutoLimits. You can continue to add as many AutoLimits as desired.

Editing AutoLimits

You can edit AutoLimits in the AutoLimits Model browser by selecting each AutoLimits entry and right-clicking it. It is recommended you set the selection filter to Feature Priority, because it will be easier to select the AutoLimits glyphs. You can copy or delete AutoLimits. You can also create a group of AutoLimits that are mainly used to control the visibility of related AutoLimits.

FIGURE 13.4
Dimensional AutoLimits
dialog box

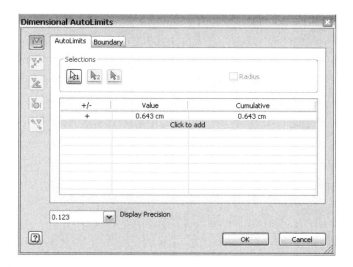

DON'T GO CRAZY WITH AUTOLIMITS

Use only the minimum number of AutoLimits in an assembly to monitor only the critical design information of interest to you. Using more than 10 AutoLimits can begin to impact the processing speed of your model. You can use AutoLimits in all environments except Autodesk Inventor Studio, the AEC exchange, Dynamic Simulation, the construction environment, Solid Edit, the Flat pattern environment, and Engineer's Notebook.

Design Assistant

The Design Assistant helps you find, manage, and maintain Autodesk Inventor files and related documents, spreadsheets, and text files. Say your company is evaluating a new design that involves doing minor changes to an existing design. You have been asked to reuse the parts, assemblies, drawings, and presentations as much as possible. Once you make these changes, you need to send the existing and modified designs to the analysis and packaging department for their input on the overall design. The Design Assistant (DA) and Pack and Go tools can help in this situation. Based on file relationships, you can perform searches, create file reports, and work with links across Inventor files. In addition, you can preview and view the iProperties.

You can launch the DA in three ways:

◆ Within Inventor, select File ➤ Design Assistant while a file is open.

◆ Right-click a file in Windows Explorer, and select the Design Assistant command.

◆ Select Start ➤ Programs ➤ Autodesk ➤ Autodesk Inventor 2009 ➤ Design Assistant.

SEAN SAYS: MANAGE FILES IN THE DESIGN ASSISTANT

Note that the Manage button will not be visible if you open the DA from an actively open file in Inventor. To manage the links, the file must be opened from the DA directly or via Windows Explorer and cannot be open in Inventor.

The Design Assistant 2009 dialog box, as shown in Figure 13.5, contains three buttons in the left column: Properties, Preview, and Manage. You can open files using the File ➢ Open menu. Figure 13.5 shows the result of a File ➢ Open command on the simple assembly `Assembly1.iam` that has two parts: `block.ipt` and `cyl.ipt`.

FIGURE 13.5
Design Assistant 2009 dialog box

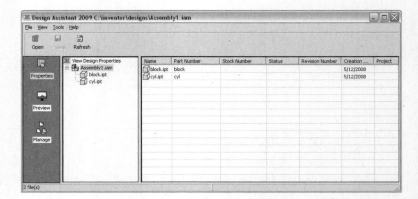

You can right-click any file like `Assembly1.iam` in the DA and select View in Inventor View 1.0, which launches the Inventor View dialog box, as shown in Figure 13.6. In the Inventor View tool, you can use the view functions such as zoom, pan, and rotate.

FIGURE 13.6
Inventor View

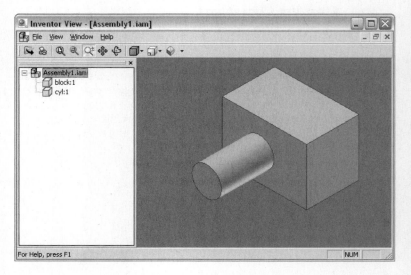

SEAN SAYS: USE THE INVENTOR VIEW

Inventor View is a lightweight version of Autodesk Inventor that can be used to view models and drawings. You can access it from Design Assistant, from the Windows Start menu, or by simply right-clicking a file in Windows Explorer and selecting View with Inventor View. This application is especially useful for nonengineering users who might need to view and print models and drawings but do not have the authority to edit or create models.

To view the preview in the DA, you can click the Preview button in the DA dialog box too, as shown in Figure 13.6. The DA shows the preview for all the files. Figure 13.7 shows the preview of `Assembly1.iam` and `block.ipt` and `cyl.ipt`. You can click `block.ipt` and `cyl.ipt` and click the Preview button to have their previews shown.

FIGURE 13.7
Preview button

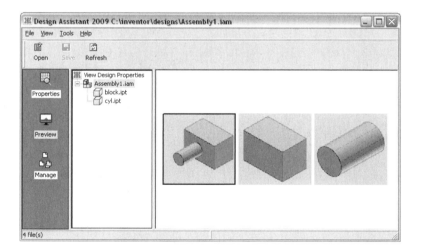

Using the Find Files Command

To use the Find Files command, follow these steps:

1. Click the Manage button shown in the left column, as shown in Figure 13.8.

2. Click the Drawings, Assemblies, and Parts check boxes. These check boxes are located next to the text Include Files Of Type in the Design Assistant 2009 dialog box.

3. You can check Search Subfolders shown next to the Parts check box in the DA dialog box to include subfolders.

4. Find Files will find the files that use `Assembly1.iam`. In this example, `Assembly3.iam` and `Assembly4.iam` use `Assembly1.iam`, and hence they are shown in the lower part of the window in Figure 13.8.

FIGURE 13.8
Using the Find Files
function

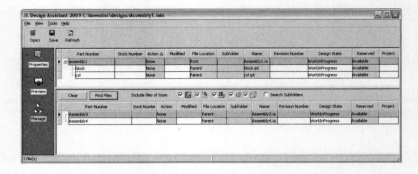

Right-clicking `Assembly1.iam` and selecting iProperties gives you the properties for the selected part or assembly without opening the part or assembly in Inventor, as shown in Figure 13.9.

FIGURE 13.9
iProperties in the DA

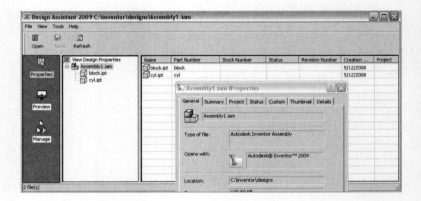

Using the Where Used Command

Selecting the Tools ➤ Find ➤ Where Used command shows all the files that use the current file. For example, to find out the files that use `Assembly1.iam`, you can do the following:

1. Select Tools ➤ Find ➤ Where Used (in the Design Assistant 2009 dialog box). You will see the dialog box shown in Figure 13.10.

2. Select the options in the Where Used dialog box such as Parts, Drawings, Include Subfolders, and so on.

3. Click Search Now.

Under Look In in the Path area, you can add paths that you want to search. In this example, you can click <Click to Add...> and enter **C:\inventor\designs**. You will get the results shown in Figure 13.11. `Assembly3.iam` uses `Assembly1.iam` and hence lists `Assembly3.iam` in its "where used" results. Given a file, it will list all the files where this file is used in some way. File relationships can include but are not limited to derived components and using a part or assembly in an assembly, drawing, presentation, and so on.

FIGURE 13.10
Where Used dialog box

FIGURE 13.11
Results of clicking
Search Now in the
Where Used dialog box

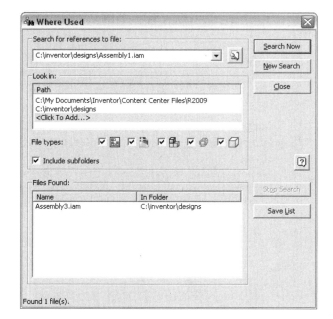

Renaming and Performing Other Operations on Files

To rename a file that is in an assembly, drawing, or presentation, follow these steps:

1. Close Inventor

2. Open the assembly file in the Design Assistant.

3. Click on Manage button. In the Manage browser click to select the component to be renamed. Right-click in the Action column, and select Rename. All occurrences of the component are highlighted.

4. Right-click the Name column, and select Change Name. In the Open dialog box, change the name, and select Open.

5. Click Save (as shown earlier in Figure 13.8) to apply the changes.

If you want to copy a file that is referenced in an assembly or drawing, right-click the Action cell for the component in Step 3 above, and select Copy. This highlights all occurrences of the component. You can right-click the Name cell for the component and then select Change Name. In the dialog box, enter the new filename. The part number, revision or other file attributes can be edited.

If you want to replace a part or assembly file with an assembly, you can right-click the Action cell and then select Replace. Right-click the Name cell for the component, and then click Change Name. In the dialog box, select the replacement file. After a file is replaced, renamed, or copied, other reference files that reference the original file need an update. The Update option will be useful, as shown here:

1. Open the `assembly` file in the Design Assistant.

2. Click Manage, and select files that are being modified from the upper browser.

3. In the lower browser, select the file types you want to include in the update.

4. Click Find Files. The referencing files are displayed in the lower browser.

5. In the lower browser, select the file types you want to include in the update.

6. Click the Save button to apply the changes.

The DA is the preferred mechanism to copy, rename, and replace files. The key point is DA rewires the file connections after the operation. This is the fundamental difference in doing these operations in Windows Explorer (not recommended) and doing them in the DA. The DA cannot make changes in certain circumstances. Examples are when the active project is set to semi-isolated; when the design state of a file is set to released, read-only permissions; when trying to change the workgroup copy of the file; and so on.

SEAN SAYS: THE DESIGN ASSISTANT VS. VAULT

Although DA can make many of the changes discussed here if you find yourself copying designs, changing filenames, and relinking projects, often you owe it to yourself to investigate Vault. Vault can do all of these operations and much, much more.

Using Pack and Go

Use the Pack and Go tool to package an Autodesk Inventor file and the set of referenced Inventor files in a project or folder to a single location. This is a useful feature to typically archive a design and all the files related to the design into a single ZIP file. For example, say `Assembly.iam` has parts `Part1.ipt`, `Part2.ipt`, and `Part3.ipt`. Pack and Go can find the parts `Part1.ipt`, `Part2.ipt`, and `Part3.ipt` for `Assembly.iam` and copy it into a new directory. Files in that new directory can be zipped into a new file to be archived or sent to other users. You can access the Pack and Go tool by right-clicking in Microsoft Windows Explorer or from a Design Assistant session started outside of Inventor. Click the Properties or Preview tab, and right-click the Assembly to access the Pack and Go command.

To use Pack and Go on an assembly, follow these steps:

1. Right-click the `Assembly3.iam` file to open the Pack and Go dialog box, as shown in Figure 13.12.

FIGURE 13.12
Pack and Go dialog box

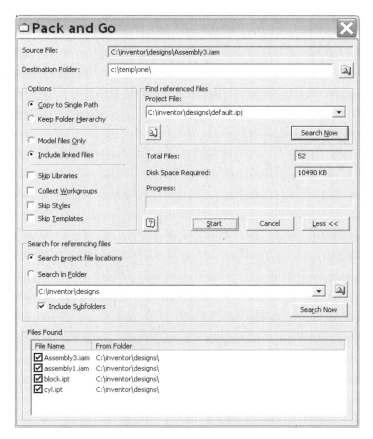

2. Click Search Now to find the IPT and IAM files that link to `Assembly3.iam`. They will appear in the Files Found section of the dialog box.

3. Enter the destination directory, and click the Start button to copy these four files to `C:\temp\one`.

4. The resulting files will be copied to the `C:\temp\one` directory.

5. You can also search the associated drawing files for `Assembly3.iam` and its parts by clicking the Search Now command in the Search For Referencing Files area. This will generate a list of all the drawings, as shown in Figure 13.13.

FIGURE 13.13
Pack and Go referencing
files found

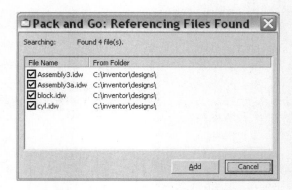

Pack and Go does not modify the source files. When you package Inventor files, they are copied to the new destination. A log file and a copy of the original project file with a .txt suffix are also copied to the destination folder. Changes made to the packaged files do not affect source files.

Uses of Pack and Go include the following:

◆ Archiving so that you can package files on a CD-ROM.

◆ Sending files to another user.

◆ Separating the referenced files from other files in the same source folders.

◆ Copying an assembly to a new location and then creating a design variant by making changes to the copy. The original is unaffected.

SEAN SAYS: USE PACK AND GO AS A CLEANUP TOOL

Pack and Go can be useful as a project cleanup tool. Often a project folder will become clogged with numerous unused files. Use Pack and Go on the top-level assembly and all of the drawings in a secondary location.

Pack and Go uses the active project file. You can change the active project file. If you have files in multiple locations, the project file must specify all those locations.

Drawing Resource Transfer Wizard

The Drawing Resource Transfer Wizard helps copy drawing resources such as borders, title blocks, and sketched symbols from one source drawing to one or more destination drawings. To use the tool, you have to close Autodesk Inventor just to avoid a situation where you are in the middle of modifying a drawing and you want to use that drawing as part of the process for transferring resources.

The wizard is available by selecting Start ➣ Programs ➣ Autodesk ➣ Autodesk Inventor 2009 ➣ Tools ➣ Drawing Resource Transfer Wizard. For example, say your company has hundreds of drawings in Inventor 2009. This year there has been a minor change in the standard. The objective is to transfer this change to hundreds of drawings in an automated fashion. The transfer wizard is an ideal solution to solve this kind of problem.

Use the following steps to use the wizard:

1. Open the tool as shown in Figure 13.14, and click Next.

2. On the Select Source Drawing And Resources screen, select the drawing template, and then click OK. We selected `Standard.idw` in the standard template directory location, as shown in Figure 13.15.

3. This loads the preview (if available) under Preview and shows the available drawing resources hierarchy in the source under Source Resources. You can uncheck the resources you don't want to transfer to destination, as shown in Figure 13.15.

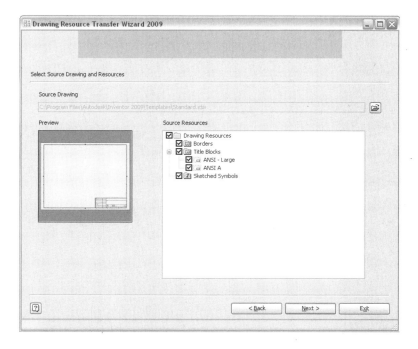

4. Click Next to go to the Select Target Drawings screen, as shown in Figure 13.16. On this page, select one or more drawings (with Shift-select), and click Open. You can click the file or path column name to sort files.

FIGURE 13.16
Selecting destina-
tion drawings

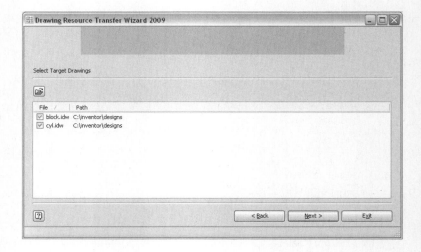

5. Click Next, and select Yes for replacing resources in the target file with the same name as in the source (not shown). Selecting Yes means using the same name as the source for the target file. Selecting No means give a unique name to target drawing resources that have the same name as those in the source file. Copied resource is given the name Copy of (ResourceName). The drawing version in the target retains the original name.

6. Click Start (see Figure 13.17), which shows the progress bar and a Pause button to temporarily halt the process.

7. Click Exit to complete the process.

FIGURE 13.17
Beginning the batch
processing

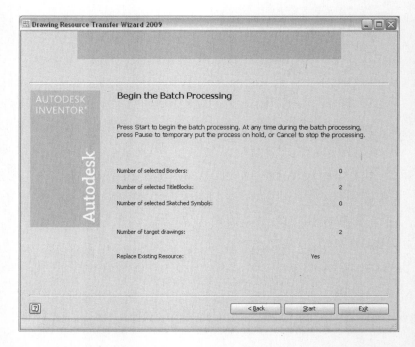

If you have a number of old drawings that you need to bring it up-to-date with a new standard, this tool is very useful.

SEAN SAYS: USE THE WIZARD FOR NEW TITLE BLOCKS

A problem that pops up quite often in manufacturing is changing title blocks. Companies change addresses, change logos, get bought or merged; any number of things can happen to require you to change your title block. This is where the Drawing Resource Transfer Wizard can come in handy. Simply edit the title block as required in your template file and then transfer it out to all your old drawings. Trust me, this sure beats editing them all individually.

If you have hundreds of IDW files that are scattered in different directories and you need to transfer the drawing resources, you could use this trick: search for all the IDW files you need to transfer, select them all, and create a shortcut to a directory. With this you can select all the IDWs in that directory in one click. This helps avoid selecting the files in each individual directory by clicking Select Target Drawings each time in the Drawing Resource Transfer Wizard and selecting the drawing files.

Style Tools

Two helpful Style tools are external to Autodesk Inventor: the Style Library Manager and the Style Management Wizard. You can access them as shown in Figure 13.18, by selecting Programs ➤ Autodesk ➤ Autodesk Inventor 2009 ➤ Tools.

FIGURE 13.18
Style tools

Using the Style Library Manager

You can use this tool to copy, rename, and delete library styles. For example, say you are a CAD administrator or one who rolls out all the standards for the company and you want to ensure that a good library of styles exists for others to use. The style tools come to rescue in this situation. You can create a new style library using the Create New Style Library button, as shown in Figure 13.19 under the Style Library 2 column. Figure 13.19 shows the dialog box for the Style Library Manager. Any changes in the style library are not available in other documents until the current Autodesk Inventor closes and a new session is reopened.

COPYING STYLES

You can reuse your styles by copying them from one style library to another by the following steps:

1. Click the Style Library Manager tool.

2. In Style Library 1, click the pulldown arrow to select the source library styles you want to copy.

3. In Style Library 2, click the pulldown arrow to select the style library for the destination. You can also click the Create New Style Library button.

4. Click one or more styles in Style Library 1, and then click the right arrow button to add them to Style Library 2. Click the right and left arrow to add or remove styles to the destination as desired.

5. Click Exit to save the libraries.

FIGURE 13.19
Style Library Manager

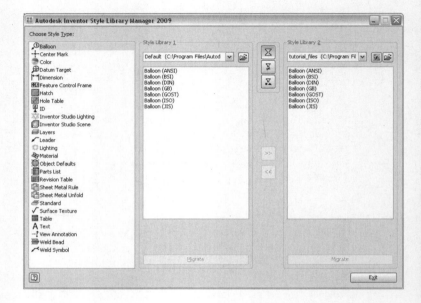

RENAMING/DELETING STYLES

You can rename or delete styles as follows:

1. Click the Style Library Manager tool.

2. Click the arrow or browse to the library whose style you want to rename.

3. In Style Library 1 or 2, you can right-click a style name and select Rename or Delete. A warning will appear that all document links to that style will be broken or the style will be permanently deleted from the style library. Click Yes to continue, and enter a new name. Click No to cancel the Rename or Delete operation. Note that you cannot undo or reverse a deletion.

Using the Style Management Wizard

This wizard helps you go through a set of Inventor files (parts, assemblies, and drawings), collect all the local style definitions within those files, and write them into a new library or append them to an existing style library. Prior to Autodesk Inventor 9, all styles were stored locally in documents. The key point is that this tool helps you collect the scattered styles into one central repository. Your Inventor files need to be migrated to the current release before using this tool.

You can harvest dimensions and text styles directly from your AutoCAD DWG files too. This helps you roll the changes to multiple files in one operation.

HARVESTING STYLES

The source is a group of Inventor files such as parts, assemblies, and drawings, and the destination is a style library. Harvesting styles means you can collect all the styles from these source files and add them to the target style library.

You can select a project and add all its files (by clicking the Add All Files in Active Project button) or select and add individual files (by clicking the Add Specific Files button). You could drag and drop or right-click a file and select all its reference files, which will get you the files that the selected file is dependent on into the list. You could also right-click a file and get all of them or get just the drawings and presentations, as shown in Figure 13.20. You can click the column headings to sort like you do in Microsoft Windows.

FIGURE 13.20
Selecting files to process

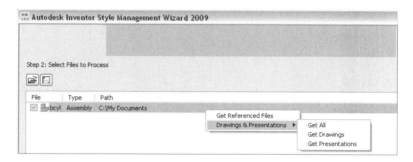

To harvest styles, follow these steps:

1. Select Management Options, and click Harvest Styles Into Target Style Library. You could either create a new style library by clicking the Create A New Style Library radio button or select an existing style library by selecting the Select An Existing Style Library radio button (see Figure 13.21).

2. Click Next.

3. Review the selections you have made, and then click Start to start the process.

4. A log file is generated during processing, and you can halt the process by clicking Pause. You can also click Cancel to stop.

PURGING STYLES

In large files (assemblies), it becomes imperative to keep only the styles that are used. You can specify a group of files such as parts, assemblies, and drawings and remove every unused style in all the documents. This technique is used to remove styles from legacy documents that now use a style library. It is recommended that you back up the styles before you do this operation since the involved styles are permanently deleted. You can use similar steps as in harvest styles to process the files. The major difference for Purge Styles from Harvest Styles is that in step 3, you select Purge All Unused Styles From Files.

FIGURE 13.21
Autodesk Inventor Style
Management Wizard
2009

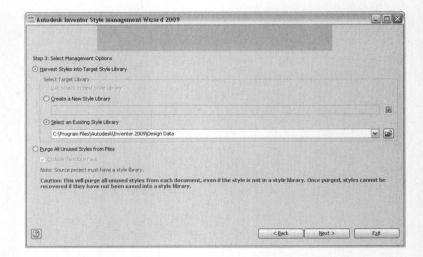

FIGURE 13.21
Autodesk Inventor Style
Management Wizard
2009

Supplier Content Center

The Supplier Content Center is accessible from the Autodesk Tools menu, as shown in Figure 13.22, or from www.autodesk.com/suppliercontent. The main advantages of using the Supplier Content Center are as follows:

◆ Promote design reuse.

◆ Supply Autodesk Inventor native data: parts or 2D views. Also available are Mechanical Desktop and AutoCAD parts and assemblies from commercial suppliers.

◆ Ensure part numbers and metadata are accurate; makes ordering easy and accurate.

◆ Provide reconfigurable parts and assemblies to meet your custom needs.

◆ Keep parts up-to-date.

FIGURE 13.22
Supplier Content Center

These parts are available in native Autodesk Inventor format from more than 100 suppliers. Some supplier contents are listed here:

◆ Part solutions

◆ 3D model space

◆ Traceparts

Figure 13.23 shows the web page that opens when you click Tools ➢ Supplier Content Center.

FIGURE 13.23
Content from suppliers

On the supplier content website you can browse the information by categories such as Bearings, Fasteners, Hydraulics, and so on. You have to log in to download parts and reuse them. You could also do a keyword search and select the category.

To use parts and assemblies from the Autodesk Supplier Content Center, follow these steps:

1. Go to the suppliercontent website, and create an account.

2. Log in with a username and password.

3. Under Settings, click the CAD format you need; it will show parts in this format.

4. Search and navigate the catalogs for the desired part. Configure the part or assembly. You can click the eye icon to preview it.

5. Add the part to My Documents by clicking the shopping cart icon.

6. Download the part by clicking the disk icon.

7. Click the download icon after the generation of the part is finished to save it.

Task Scheduler

A large design repository needs to have a way to manage tasks for efficiency and repeatability. Nonproductive and mundane tasks tend to be expensive and boring for a user. The purpose of the Task Scheduler is to precisely automate such tasks. To access the Task Scheduler, select Start ➤ Programs ➤ Autodesk ➤ Autodesk Inventor 2009 ➤ Tools ➤ Task Scheduler, as shown in Figure 13.24.

FIGURE 13.24
Task Scheduler

Say you are working for a service company that handles outsourcing work for auto suppliers. The supplier works with hundreds of files. The supplier is trying to decide whether to move to Inventor 2009. You have been asked to evaluate this for the supplier. You want to do testing and present quantitative data on the results of migration or some other custom tasks the supplier normally performs on legacy files. The main purpose of the Task Scheduler is to automate the tasks and quickly give you results. The Task Scheduler has the ability to create various tasks such as migrating a set of files from AutoCAD, Autodesk Mechanical Desktop, and Autodesk Inventor software; publishing DWF files; importing files; exporting files; updating parts, assemblies, and drawings; checking out and checking in from Vault; and printing jobs. Users can also create a custom Visual Basic program to do custom tasks.

Creating a Task for Migrating Files

To create a task to migrate files in Task Scheduler, follow these steps:

1. Select Create Task ≻ Migrate Files, as shown in Figure 13.25.

FIGURE 13.25
Create Task menu

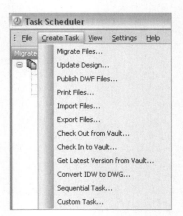

2. In the Migrate Files dialog box (see Figure 13.26), enter the task name, frequency, start time, and start date. If Immediately is checked, the task will start immediately after you click OK. The log file helps to see the output of the task.

3. Click the Add Folder icon, as shown in Figure 13.27.

4. In the Browse for Folder dialog box, select the directory where you have unmigrated files. In Figure 13.28, you can see the Inventor 2008 directory as an example.

FIGURE 13.26
Migrating files

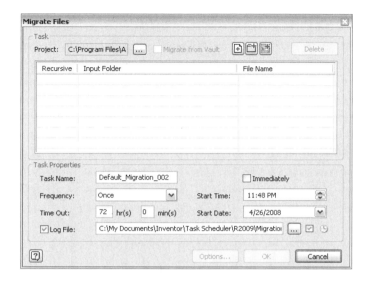

FIGURE 13.27
Adding a folder

FIGURE 13.28
Browsing for a folder

5. Click Options in the Migrate Files dialog box, and the Migration Options dialog box like the one shown in Figure 13.29 will appear. The Total Rebuild option, if checked, will rebuild all the parts and assemblies. Since the second and third boxes have been checked, unresolved and already migrated files will be skipped. Checking Purge Old Versions will rewrite the older version file. The Compact Model History box removes the B-rep history from the model if checked, thus producing reduced file sizes. If you did this, then edits to the model are slower since all features prior to the edited feature must be recomputed. You should check this option only when further changes are unlikely, such as when archiving and releasing the model.

FIGURE 13.29
Migration Options
dialog box

6. Click OK to run the task. When the task is done, you will see the status shown as completed.

Users can run, edit (see Figure 13.30), delete, or disable tasks once they are created. Tasks are also saved so they can be run again. By clicking Task ID and Name columns, you can sort the data by that column.

FIGURE 13.30
Editing a task

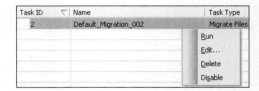

Performing Sequential Tasks

You can create several subtasks to set up multiple tasks and schedule them to run in a specified sequence at a specified time. Custom subtasks can be also used in a sequential task. One subtask can depend on the output of the previous subtask. Examples of multiple subtasks are as follows:

◆ Importing files

◆ Updating designs

◆ Publishing DWF files

◆ Printing files

◆ Generating a cost report (custom task)

Performing Custom Tasks

A form of a COM object that implements the COM interface could be a custom task. For instance, you can use a custom task to open a batch of text files. A type library file called ServiceModuleIntefaceDef.tlb is shipped with the Task Scheduler. To access the COM interface, reference this file within your project. Custom tasks can be created in a programming language that supports COM.

Tweaking Multiprocess Settings

In the Multi-Process Settings dialog box, as shown in Figure 13.31, you can tweak parameters to complete batch jobs in less time by leveraging the multiprocess support in the Inventor Task Scheduler. Up to 16 processes can be run at the same time. You can set the number of processes and the amount of memory to be used.

FIGURE 13.31
Multi-Process Settings
dialog box

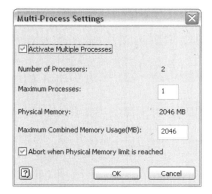

If you are using the task Publish DWF Files and if you have a source filename.ipt, then that becomes the destination filename.ipt.dwf. Some users find this difficult to accept. The motivation to rename it not as filename.dwf is as follows: if Inventor produced filename.dwf, then it can be overwritten if you have two files with the same name but different extensions, that is, filename.ipt and filename.iam. Therefore, the Task Scheduler takes the current filename with the extension (.ipt or .iam) and appends .dwf at the end. There are programs available on the Internet or Windows scripting commands to rename files from filename.ipt.dwf to filename.ipt, which could be used to fix the filenames.

iProperties

Autodesk Inventor files have file-specific properties known as iProperties. The iProperties command helps you specify and view them. You can enter custom data into iProperties, search by those fields, and update your title blocks and parts lists in drawings and bill of materials. You can launch this command by selecting File ➢ iProperties or by right-clicking the root browser node in the Model browser and selecting iProperties. Figure 13.32 shows the iProperties dialog box for a part. The iProperties dialog box in parts and assemblies environment contain seven tabs, while the iProperties dialog box in the drawings environment contain only six tabs (they are missing the Physical properties tab).

FIGURE 13.32
Physical properties with
Aluminum as material

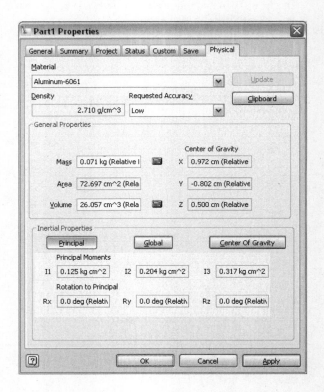

You can also right-click the file in Windows Explorer and use the Design Assistant to work with files outside Inventor to view iProperties. In the Design Assistant, right-click a file in the browser, and then select iProperties. In the iProperties dialog box, you can modify data on the Summary, Project, Status, and Custom tabs. On unsaved files, changing the iProperties using the Design Assistant could lose unsaved changes. You can save any open Inventor files before using the Design Assistant to change iProperties.

The various tabs in the iProperties dialog box are as follows:

◆ The General tab contains fields that cannot be modified by the user.

◆ The Summary tab contains fields that can be modified by the user, such as Title, Subject, Author, and so on.

◆ The Project tab contains important fields such as Part Number, Revision Number, Project, and so on.

◆ The Status tab contains pulldown controls for Part Number, Status, Checked Date, and so on.

◆ The Custom tab helps define your own attributes. These attributes follow the Name, Type, and Value format. For example, you can have Name = Department, Type = Text and Value = Design123.

◆ The Save tab helps you specify whether to save the preview picture of your files so that it can be used as a preview image you see during the File ➢ Open command in the Open dialog box, or you can specify an image file to use for this preview picture.

◆ The Physical tab lets you calculate and display the physical properties (Area, Volume, Inertia, and so on) for a part or assembly. The material selected is used to calculate the mass properties. The Update button on the Physical tab is useful to update the physical properties based on changes to your models.

The Summary, Project, Status, and Custom tabs are used to search files to update the BOM and parts lists.

Figure 13.32 shows an example of iProperties on a simple box part. The Density field cannot be changed in this dialog box. To change the density for this example, select Format ➢ Style And Standard Editor, and under Material find Aluminum 6061, and then change the density.

SEAN SAYS: OVERRIDE MASS AND VOLUME FOR A SIMPLIFIED REPRESENTATION

Sometimes you'll want to model a simplified representation of a part but still need to have an accurate measure of its mass or volume. In these cases, simply type over the mass or volume in the iProperties dialog box. The calculator icon will then change to a hand icon signifying that the mass and/or volume has been overridden. To allow Inventor to recalculate the mass or volume, simply delete all the text from the box. Inventor will then compute the mass and volume based on the size and density of the model.

Copying iProperties to Drawings

You can copy iProperties non-associatively (copied iProperties don't change when source is changed) from a document to drawing files by following these steps:

1. In Drawing document, select Tools ➢ Document Settings, and go to the Drawing tab.

2. Click Properties, which opens the dialog box shown in Figure 13.33.

3. Check the boxes for the properties you want to copy. You can select the All Properties check box at the bottom to copy all the properties.

When placing views, the selected iProperties are copied to the drawing from the source file. Existing iProperties will be overwritten.

FIGURE 13.33
Properties dialog box

Creating Expressions with iProperties

If you have a need to create "stock size" of your parts to be used in your BOM with associativity to model parameters, you can create and manage expressions for iProperties by using the following steps:

1. Click on File ➤ iProperties, and go to the Summary, Project, Status, or Custom tab. Then click a field where an expression needs to be created. Right-click an existing expression, and you can edit the expression.

2. Start with the = sign, and type the text. If you want to include parameters or iProperty names, then simply include them in brackets, as shown here. A detected expression is denoted by *fx*. See Figure 13.34.
   = ANSI 1234 – I 567 <duser1>
   In this example, duser1 is a parameter with value of 4 cm. The expression is evaluated after you click Apply or press Enter as follows:
   ANSI 1234 – I 567 4.000 cm

You can further customize the parameters in the fx:Parameters dialog box to have it displayed differently in iProperties. For example, 4.000 cm could be displayed as 4.0 cm. Right-click the parameter, and select Custom Property Format. In the Custom Property Format dialog box, change Precision to 1.1. Other than this, units and format could be also changed. Currently, iParts, iAssemblies, and Content Center ignore the expressions saved in iProperties.

To promote reuse, create a template file with predefined expressions for iProperties that lets you unify your parts list and other documentation. The Bill Of Materials dialog box provides the Property Expression builder, which helps you to create expressions for iProperties.

FIGURE 13.34
Concatenating text and parameters in iProperties

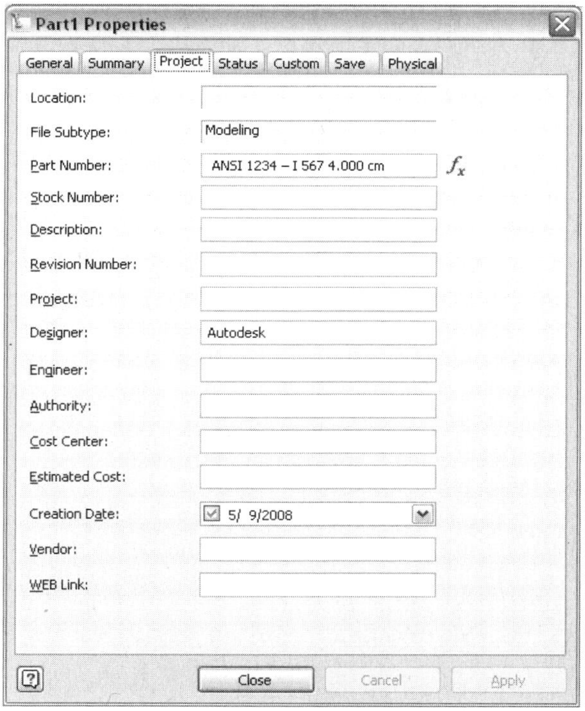

Working with the DA and iProperties

You can use the Design Assistant to copy design properties from one Autodesk Inventor file to another. If the active project is set to shared or semi-isolated, then you cannot copy properties to a file that is checked out to someone else or into the workgroup version of a file. To copy design properties from one source file to another, use the following procedure:

1. In the DA, select Tools ➤ Copy Design Properties to get the Copy Design Properties dialog box.

2. Set the source file in the Copy From box.

3. Select the properties to copy.

4. Select destination files to receive the properties.

5. Click the Copy button.

You can refer to the "Design Assistant" section to learn more about the DA and iProperties.

Creating Design Property Reports

You can use the DA to create design property reports that show only selected iProperties. In the Properties view browser in the DA, you can select the design properties to display for files.

1. While in the Properties view, in the DA select View ➢ Customize, and select the required property group.

2. Select the properties to display. Clicking the Add or Remove button helps you move a property from the Available Properties list to the Selected Property list. You could also double-click it. The Name property is a default property that is mandatory in all displays.

You can reorder the properties list by clicking the Move Up or Move Down button.

Measure Tool

The Measure tool lets you measure distances, angles, loops, and areas. The tool is available by selecting Tools ➢ Measure Distance in Inventor, as shown in Figure 13.35. It is available in these environments: assemblies, parts, sheet metal, flat pattern, construction, and 2D and 3D sketch. You can select sketches, edges, faces, bodies, and work geometry to take measurements.

◆ The Measure Distance command lets you measure length of a line, arc, distance between points, radius, diameter of a circle, distance between two components, two faces, or positions in relation to the active coordinate system.

◆ The Measure Angle command lets you measure the angle between points, edges, or two lines. To measure between points, click two points to define a line and then a third point to measure the angle.

◆ The Measure Loop command gives you the length of the loops. For 2D sketches, it measures open or closed loops. For 3D sketches, it measures only open loops.

◆ The Measure Area command gives you the area of closed regions.

FIGURE 13.35
Tools ➢ Measure
commands

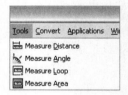

Using Measurement Helpers

Figure 13.36 shows some of the other commands that are useful while using the Measure tool. Measurements can be accumulated, cleared, and displayed in different ways. The Add To Accumulate command adds the current measurement to the total sum. The Clear Accumulate command resets the sum to zero. The Display Accumulate command displays the current sum. The Dual Unit lets you see the measurement in the desired units. The Precision command displays eight formatting values and the option to display all decimals.

One of the advantages of the Measure command is to enter feature parameters by measuring vs. directly entering it. For example, in Figure 13.37, extrusion depth can be entered as a value of

1.0 in. Alternatively, you can select the Measure command from the Depth flyout and then select a model edge. The length of the edge will appear in the Depth control of the Extrude dialog box. This is a convenient way to input dimensions by measuring vs. directly entering it into the dialog box. In the graphics window, click the geometry to measure. The measurement is transferred to the dialog box automatically.

FIGURE 13.36
Measurement helpers

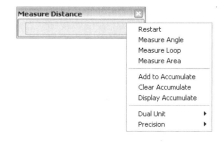

FIGURE 13.37
Measure command and feature parameters

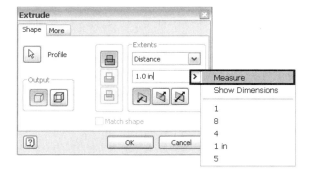

Measuring in Assemblies

In assemblies, since you have faces and components, there is a need to differentiate measuring between them. In the context menu, you can change the selection priority.

When Component Priority is selected, the minimum distance is measured between subassemblies. Part priority signifies measurement between parts only. Faces And Edges Select Priority lets you select only faces and edges, which is the default when nothing is preselected. Changing the selection priority resets any existing selections. Figure 13.38 shows the priority type and the respective choices for the selection filter.

FIGURE 13.38
Selection priority for measurements

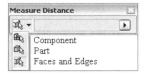

The CIP and CER

The Customer Involvement Program (CIP) aids in collecting your specific use of the Autodesk Inventor software. Customer error reporting (CER) aids in sending information to Autodesk when the software program closes unexpectedly.

Participating in the CIP

To guide the direction of the Autodesk design software in the future, your specific use of the Autodesk Inventor software is forwarded to Autodesk if you participate in the CIP. You can access this by selecting Help Menu ➢ Customer Involvement Program. In the Customer Involvement Program dialog box, you can select a level of participation and then click OK. Information collected includes the following:

◆ Autodesk product version and name

◆ Inventor commands and time spent

◆ Error conditions (catastrophic and nonfatal)

◆ Other information such as system configuration, IP address, and so on

The CIP is committed to privacy protection. It can collect neither drawing or design data nor personal information such as names, addresses, and phone numbers. It will not contact users by email or any other way. The Customer Involvement Program aids in letting Autodesk know about most commonly used commands and features, the most common problem areas, and so on. You can stop participation anytime by accessing the controls from the Autodesk Help menu. Your system administrator can choose to block the CIP.

Participating in CER

Customer error reporting is a process by which Autodesk Inventor users can report crashes to Autodesk. A software crash happens when the software program closes unexpectedly. When you find the unexpected error, Inventor shows a dialog box, and you can choose to send the error to Autodesk. CER records the subset of the code that was in use before the crash. The CER report collects a variety of information such as the following:

◆ Operating system and graphics driver name, version, and configuration

◆ Autodesk software name and version

◆ List of recently used Autodesk commands

◆ Lines in the code where the crash happened

You can enter the step-by-step process that led to the crash. In addition, you can include your email and contact information. The error data is sent to Autodesk using a secure Internet connection in an encrypted form. If you have concerns about security and personal confidential information being sent to Autodesk, please do not send the customer error report.

At Autodesk, an automated system sorts the report based on the code call stack so that the Autodesk development teams can analyze them. Each set of report is prioritized based on the number of users having the same issue and how often the problem happens. If there is no current update, Autodesk will use that information for a future update or major release. When the issue is fixed, it is included in either a future maintenance update or a future release of the product.

Customers who reported the error are notified. If there is a current update (immediate update notification), it is immediately sent to the customer. If not (delayed update notification), customers are notified when their error is addressed in a future software update.

Miscellaneous Tools

In this section, we will cover some miscellaneous tools such as the Inventor Multi-Sheet Plot, the Add-In Manager, and the Project Editor. The following tools are available from this location: Start ➤ Programs ➤ Autodesk ➤ Autodesk Inventor 2009.

Using the Autodesk Multi-Sheet Plot

The Autodesk Multi-Sheet Plot command opens the dialog box shown in Figure 13.39. It allows you to print one or more drawing sheets of various sizes. Clicking Next takes you to another dialog box that allows you to select drawings. Once the drawings are selected, you can schedule to print the multisheet. This tool helps you reduce paper usage and reduce plot setup time. Besides, it optimizes sheet layout on a selected paper size that you can print directly or save as a batch file.

FIGURE 13.39
Autodesk Multi-Sheet Plot dialog box

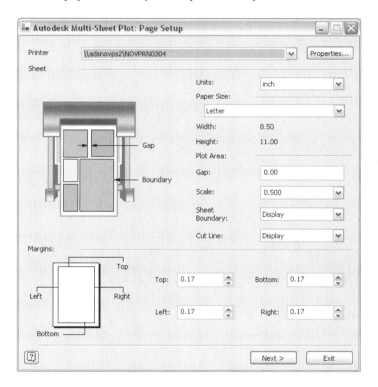

Using the Add-in Manager

The Tools ➤ Add-Ins command opens an Add-in Manager dialog box to make selections on which add-ins you want to load or unload when Inventor starts up. Click the add-in in the

Available Add-Ins area, and at the bottom of the dialog box for Load Behavior, uncheck the Loaded/Unloaded option to unload it.

SEAN SAYS: USE THE ADD-IN MANAGER TO SPEED INVENTOR LOAD TIME

If there are add-ins you know you do not use, then you can use the Add-in Manager to prevent these add-ins from loading when Inventor loads. This will slightly speed up the load time (and amount of RAM) Inventor uses. Be sure you understand what add-ins do because some are required for the proper operation of the software.

Using the Project Editor

The Project Editor command opens a dialog box for Inventor's Project Editor. This is similar to the dialog box that opens after you select File ➤ Projects in Inventor. You can select each project, make changes to it, and save it without having to open Inventor.

The Bottom Line

Take your models from Inventor to ABS   If you frequently have the need to take your Inventor models to ABS, then AEC exchange can help you in this process with three simple steps. Inventor provides a variety of ways to simplify the model and author it. Such models can be published in ABS.

> **Master It**   You can do this with the following three steps: model simplifying, authoring, and publishing. You can also save a DWG as a solid.

Create AutoLimits/design sensors   You use AutoLimits to monitor design parameters in which you are interested.

> **Master It**   How many AutoLimits can you use in an assembly? Use no more than 10. You can customize the AutoLimits and have it set up in the model.

Manage design data efficiently using Inventor tools   There are different tools for managing design data, which is typically distributed across part, assembly, and drawing files. Associated with these can be Excel spreadsheets, text files, Word documents, and so on.

> **Master It**   The Design Assistant keeps the file relationships while copying, renaming, and moving files. Whenever you are sending Inventor files to others, use Pack and Go, which hunts the file relationships, and you can use WinZip software to package it into a single ZIP file. You can delegate many of the tasks in Inventor to the Task Scheduler. You can propagate source drawing template information to several destination drawings using the Drawing Resource Transfer Wizard.

Manage styles   You can use the Style Library Manager and the Style Management Wizard to organize your styles to keep it simple and clean.

> **Master It**   How do you manage your styles? Styles normally need to be copied, edited, and deleted. Use the Style Library Manager. How can you create a central repository of styles? How do you purge styles? Use the Style Management Wizard for these tasks.

Create expressions with iProperties   Property fields can be concatenated to produce desired customized information in BOM and parts lists.

> **Master It**   You can break down for example "stock size" of your parts to be used in your BOM with associativity to model parameters. You can create and manage expressions for iProperties. You can further customize the parameters in the *fx*:Parameters dialog box to have it displayed differently in iProperties.

Measure in assemblies   Click the right Measure command and selection filters to make measurements.

> **Master It**   How do you measure in assemblies? Once you set the selection filter, make the selections, and use the measurement helpers to get complex measurements.

Give feedback to Autodesk   You could participate in the Customer Involvement Program (CIP). Customer error reporting (CER) helps Autodesk know about the issue.

> **Master It**   For the CIP, you can stop participation any time by accessing the controls from the Autodesk Help menu. You could include the steps (if that is known) that led to the unexpected termination of the program. You can skip the CER process.

Chapter 14

Exchanging Data with Other Systems

The need to bring files created by other CAD applications into Inventor is common to many Inventor users. If you design components that others use in their designs, you might need to output files to a standard format so that others can use them with a different software package. If you are a manufacturing job shop, you may receive many different file formats from customers that you need to bring into Inventor. The ability to open and translate files into Inventor 2009 has been improved with the inclusion of native file format translators as well as the ability to open and save out neutral file formats.

In this chapter, you will learn how to:

◆ Import and export geometry

◆ Use Inventor file translators

◆ Work with imported data

◆ Work with Design Review markups

◆ Use Feature recognition

Importing and Exporting Geometry

Essentially, three data types make up a 3D model: curves or wires, surfaces, and solids. A model, if composed of only curves or wires, would lack volume but would have a size and shape. A surface model is composed of wires or curves that define the surfaces. A solid model is composed of wires or curves, which define surfaces, which define the solid. Within each of these data types, translation issues can occur.

Within the category of wires, there are different ways in which wires and curves are defined. If you are translating files that represent wires and curves as NURBS to a format that represents wires and curves as B-splines, then there might be something lost in translation. Likewise, when you translate a surface model, if the surface normal were to get reversed, then you will have translation issues. And so it is with translating solids. If a solid model is translated so that a gap is formed where two surfaces meet, then translation may not be complete.

Translation of curves, surfaces, and solids occur between different packages because different software might use different methods of geometric accuracy. Accuracy controls such things as how close two points in space are before being considered a single point or how close two edges can be before they are considered connected.

To help with translating from one software package that solves curves using one method to software that uses another method, you can create an intermediate or neutral file. Common neutral file formats include IGES, STEP, SAT, and others.

DWG

When an AutoCAD DWG file is imported into Inventor, the file is translated into an Autodesk Inventor part, assembly, and/or drawing file, based on the import settings. The original AutoCAD file is not changed. When exported from Inventor to a DWG, a file is translated into AutoCAD objects. The translated DWG is not associative to the Inventor file from which it was created. Instead, the DWG data is fully editable within AutoCAD.

To import a DWG file, select File ➤ Open, set the Files Of Type pulldown to AutoCAD Drawings (*.dwg), and then select the DWG file you are going to import. Click the Options button, and choose Import. (If you are translating a number of DWG files, you can set Import to be the default by selecting Tools ➤ Application Options and going to the Drawing tab.) Once you've selected Import, as shown in Figure 14.1, click OK. This returns you to the Open dialog box where you will click the Open button to start the DWG/DXF File Wizard. Note the Configuration pulldown box. If you have an import configuration already saved, you can specify it now and click Finish. If you have not yet created a configuration template, then you will click Next to go to the Import Destination Options dialog box.

FIGURE 14.1
Importing a DWG file

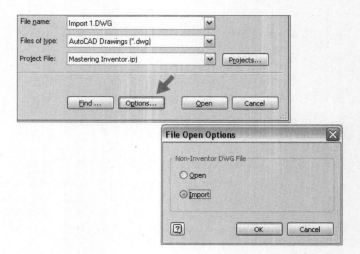

IMPORTING 3D SOLIDS

If the AutoCAD DWG has 3D solids, you can check the 3D Solids check box to translate them into Inventor part files. Use the Solids To Single Part File check box if you want multibody solids to be translated into an Inventor part file. Leave this option unchecked if you want each solid body in the DWG to be created as an individual Inventor part file and automatically placed in an Inventor assembly. Figure 14.2 shows the import options for 3D Solids.

Set the destination folder to a path in which you want to have the part files created and choose Use Default File Names to allow Inventor to name the resulting part files automatically. If you choose this option, the new Inventor parts will be given a name based on the DWG name and be incremented by a value of 1. For instance, if the DWG is named `Engine.dwg`, then each solid in the DWG will be named `Engine1.ipt`, `Engine2.ipt`, `Engine3.ipt`, and so on. If left unchecked, each solid in the DWG will be named `Part1.ipt`, `Part2.ipt`, `Part3.ipt`, and so on.

FIGURE 14.2
3D solids options

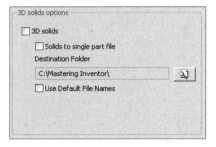

IMPORTING 2D DATA

If the DWG contains only 2D data, then you can leave the 3D Solids check box unchecked and turn your attention to the Destination For 2D Data area of the dialog box, as shown in Figure 14.3. Selecting the New Drawing radio button translates the DWG data to a new Inventor DWG or IDW. If you check Promote Dimensions To Sketch, then the 2D data is placed in a draft view that is created in the Inventor drawing.

FIGURE 14.3
2D data options

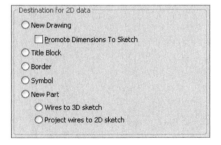

You can use the Title Block radio button to convert an AutoCAD title block DWG into an Inventor title block. When doing this, be sure to click the mapping options to set the layer and font mapping options, as shown in Figure 14.4. You can use the Symbols radio button to translate the 2D data into a sketched symbol for use in an Inventor DWG or IDW file. Use the New Part radio button to translate AutoCAD 2D data into a new IPT sketch. Choose between creating a 3D or 2D sketch within the file.

Inventor has both a decimal and a fractional unit style for dimensions. When dimensions are translated, if Inventor detects that the AutoCAD file employs a scientific, decimal, engineering, or Windows Desktop style, those styles are converted to decimal style. Fraction and architectural are mapped to fractional style.

FIGURE 14.4
Mapping options

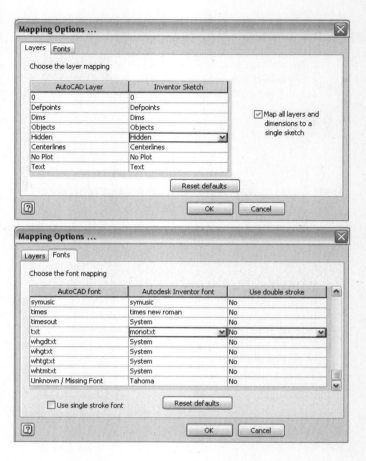

UNITS, TEMPLATES, CONSTRAINTS, AND CONFIGURATIONS

Whether importing to 2D or 3D, you will use the templates area to specify which template to use for each of the file types to translate to. In the Import Files Units area, you can specify the units, if they do not match the units that Inventor detects from the AutoCAD file. The detected unit is based on the INSUNITS system variable in the DWG file.

You can use the Constrain End Points and Apply Geometric Constraints check boxes to allow Inventor to place constraints on sketch entities when it can. Endpoints found to be coincident will be given a coincident constraint; lines found to be parallel will be give parallel constraints; and so on.

Once all these options are configured, you can click the Save Configurations button, as shown in Figure 14.5, to write out a file to use the next time you convert a DWG file. Doing this allows you to convert files more accurately and more quickly.

FIGURE 14.5
More import destination options

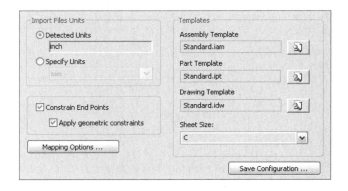

When all the configuration settings have been made and saved, click Finish to start the Import process. Inventor will create the new files based on your configurations and leave the files open in the current Inventor session.

Mechanical Desktop DWG

Mechanical Desktop (MDT) files can be imported into Inventor part and assembly files. If the source files contain geometry or features that are not recognized in Inventor, they are omitted, and the missing data is noted in the browser or the translation log file. No links are maintained to the existing MDT files. Note that the Inventor 2009 suite does not ship with MDT 2009 and must be requested from Autodesk as per the instructions in the installation media in order to install it. There is no extra charge for MDT 2009. You must have MDT 2009 on your computer to import files into Inventor 2009.

You can import MDT DWG files using the Options button in the Open dialog box just as you would a regular DWG. However, if Inventor detects that the file is an MDT file, you are given the option to read the data as a MDT file or as an AutoCAD or AutoCAD mechanical file, as shown in Figure 14.6.

FIGURE 14.6
Reading MDT file contents

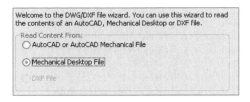

Although many of the options for template, units, and configuration settings are the same as previously described for regular DWG files, the assembly and part options are specific to MDT files, as shown in Figure 14.7.

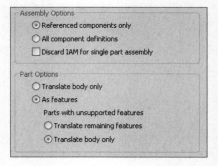

Consider the following items when migrating MDT files to Inventor:

◆ Broken views, base section views, and breakout section views from MDT will be turned into base views.

◆ Exploded views will become unexploded views (no tweaks applied).

◆ Importing discards (AMPARDIMS) from MDT automatically creates associative model dimensions in Inventor.

◆ If Move With Parent is selected in a MDT file, Inventor aligns all views according to the view type.

◆ If a parent view is missing in a MDT file, a child view is not created in Inventor.

◆ Inventor centerlines and center marks are automatically generated during translation; therefore, they might not be the same as in the MDT file.

◆ Radial section views have broken alignment in Inventor

In addition to importing MDT files one at a time, you can use the Inventor Task Scheduler to batch the translation from MDT to Inventor. It is important to ensure that the MDT files are migrated to MDT 2009 files before attempting to translate them into Inventor files.

STEP and IGES

Standard for the Exchange of Product (STEP) model data and Initial Graphic Exchange Specification (IGES) are nonproprietary file formats to write data to in order to exchange data among proprietary software. When opening a STEP or IGES file in Inventor, one part file will be created if the file contains only one part body; otherwise, you can create multiple Inventor part files placed within an assembly file.

Although no links are maintained between the original STEP or IGES file and the Inventor files created from them, when importing an updated STEP or IGES file, Inventor updates the geometry and maintains all modeling constraints and features applied to that STEP or IGES file.

To import a STEP or IGES file, select File ➢ Open, and set the Files Of Type pulldown to STEP Files (`*.stp`, `*.ste`, `*.step`) or IGES Files (`*.igs`, `*.ige`, `*.iges`). Then select the file you intend to import. Click the Options button, and you will be presented with the Import Options. Specify the destination directory for all parts and assemblies created during the import dialog box, as shown in Figure 14.8. By default, the destination directories will point to the same directory as the original STEP or IGES file.

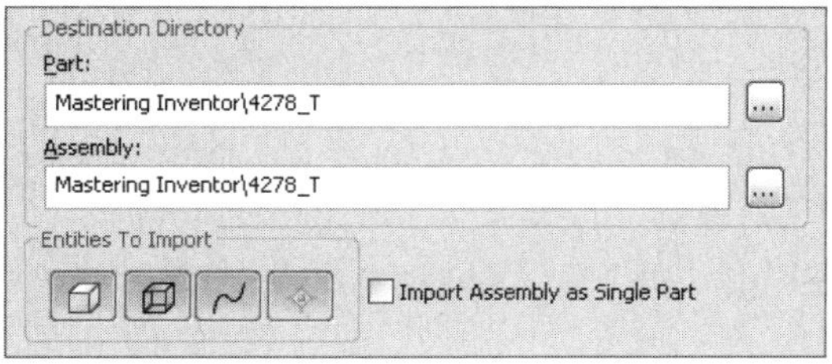

FIGURE 14.8
STEP or IGES import options

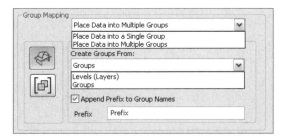

In the Entities To Import area, use the selection buttons to specify the inclusion of solids, surfaces, wires, and points in the import action. Use Import Assembly As Single Part to turn a multibody STEP or IGES into a single part file.

In the Group Mapping area of the Import Options dialog box, you can select Place Data Into Multiple Groups or Place Data Into A Single Group when importing a file. If the Place Data Into Multiple Groups option is selected, then more than one entity is generated. The Place Data Into A Single Group option allows entities to be combined into a single entity. If Place Data Into Multiple Groups is selected when importing an IGES file, you can select between Levels (Layers) and Groups. The Levels (Layers) option is not available for STEP files. Figure 14.9 shows the group mapping options.

FIGURE 14.9
STEP or IGES group mapping options

The two icons on the left in the Group Mapping area are Composite Feature Mapping and Construction Group Mapping. These icons control the way that data is imported within the part.

A *composite* is a collection of surfaces, as opposed to a single quilt of surfaces. A composite can consist of any combination or single or multiple faced surfaces or closed volume surfaces. Oftentimes these surfaces will not be connected even if they appear to be. Composites can be used when many surfaces are imported as an expedient way of getting surface data into Inventor for reference or inspection.

When Construction Group Mapping is chosen for import, imported surfaces and wireframes are always placed in a Construction folder. Objects in the construction folder can then be opened in the construction environment and manipulated manually. Figure 14.10 shows the same file imported in four different ways:

Far Left = Place Data Into Multiple Groups and Construction Group Mapping

Middle Left = Place Data Into Multiple Groups and Composite Feature Mapping

Middle Right = Place Data Into A Single Group and Construction Group Mapping

Far Right = Place Data Into A Single Group and Composite Feature Mapping

FIGURE 14.10
Group mapping comparisons

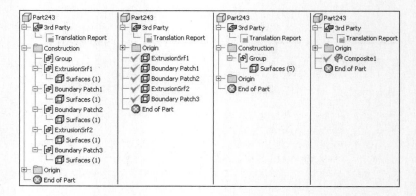

In the remainder of the Import Options dialog box, you have the Save Parts During Load option. If this option is selected, the files are saved to locations specified by the Destination Directory settings. Next is the Import Multi-lump Solids As Assembly options, which allows multibody files to be translated to Inventor assembly files. The new Inventor parts will be given a name based on the filename and incremented by a value of 1. For instance, if an IGES is named 4278_T.igs, then the Inventor parts will be named 4278_T 1.ipt, 4278_T 2.ipt, 4278_T 3.ipt, and so on.

The Check Parts On Import directs Inventor to analyze the surface and solid data when imported. If the parts are determined not to have any errors, they are marked with a green check mark in the browser. If they have errors, they will be detailed in the translation report, as shown in the browser in Figure 14.10. The Check Parts On Import option, as shown in Figure 14.11, will lengthen the time required to open files.

FIGURE 14.11
More import STEP and IGES options

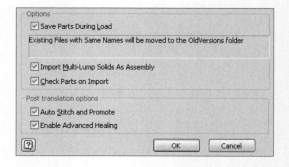

Auto Stitch And Promote allows surfaces to be automatically stitched together in the construction environment. If Auto Stitch And Promote is on and Construction Group Mapping is selected, then the data is stitched for each group. The Enable Advanced Healing option modifies surface geometry, thereby allowing edges to be stitched.

Benefits of STEP

Many Inventor users prefer to send and receive STEP files to and from vendors or clients because they find STEP files import better than other file formats. Here is a list of attributes that make STEP a popular choice:

◆ STEP files can retain the original part names when importing to an assembly.

◆ STEP creates instances for duplicated parts. If you are sent a STEP of an assembly created in another software package and that assembly has 12 instances of a certain screw size, Inventor will typically create just one file for the screw and instance it 12 times, as opposed to creating 12 different files.

◆ STEP files can maintain assembly hierarchy, meaning that subassembly structure can be translated. In other formats, assemblies may be translated with all parts at the top-level assembly.

◆ STEP translates part colors, whereas other formats generally do not contain the information needed to carry part colors across different platforms.

◆ STEP format is governed independently and is not tied to a particular modeling kernel; as a result, it is often considered somewhat of a more standard format.

To export a file as a STEP, select File ➤ Save Copy As, and set Save As Type to STEP Files (`*.stp`, `*.ste`, `*.step`). Click the Options button to set the STEP version. You can also choose to include sketches. Included sketches are translated to the STEP file in named groups.

To export a file as an IGES, select File ➤ Save Copy As, and set Save As Type to IGES Files (`*.igs`, `*.ige`, `*.iges`). Click the Options button to set the IGES output to either surfaces or solids. You can choose to include sketches. Includes sketches are translated to the IGES file in named layers.

SAT

SAT files are files written in the standard file exchange format for the ACIS solid modeling kernel. To import a SAT file, select File ➤ Open, set the Files Of Type pulldown to SAT Files (`*.sat`), and then select the file you intend to import. Click the Options button, and you will be presented with the Import Options dialog box, as shown in Figure 14.12. Specify the destination directory for all part and assemblies created during the import.

The Healer Enabled option detects and attempts to correct imprecise data found in the SAT file during the import. The Auto Stitch And Promote option allows surfaces to be automatically stitched together and promoted to the part environment. Selecting Import Assembly To Single Part will create a part file from a multibody file. File entities can be filtered out by the Solids, Surfaces, and Wires categories by unchecking the corresponding check box in the Entities To Import area.

Some CAD software outputs SAT files in a default unit without regard for the units used to create the original file. Use the Units Of SAT File pulldown to specify the units that the SAT file was exported in. The SAT file will be converted from the specified units to the unit system of your default template. If the original software specified the unit upon output, Inventor uses this during import rather than the units specified here.

If multibody files are to be imported as assemblies in Inventor, you can use this option to allow Inventor to assign part names based on the original SAT filename. For instance, if a SAT is called

Loader.sat, then the Inventor parts will be named Loader 1.ipt, Loader 2.ipt, Loader 3.ipt, and so on. Clearing the check box allows you to specify the filename as each inventor file is created.

FIGURE 14.12
SAT import options

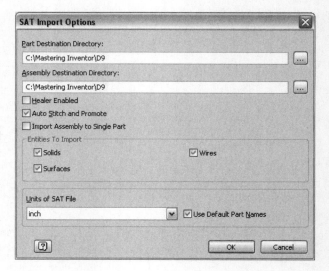

To export a file as a SAT, select File ➤ Save Copy As, and set Save As Type to SAT Files (*.sat). Click the Options button to set the SAT version. The default is version 7.0. You can also choose to include sketches. Included sketches are translated to the SAT ungrouped.

SEAN SAYS: WATCH FOR SAT FILE VERSIONS

As of Inventor release 5.3, Autodesk broke away from the ACIS SAT standard when it created its ShapeManager kernel. This means that Autodesk Inventor cannot read in any SAT file that is newer than version 6.0. Keep this in mind when requesting models from third parties or when downloading them from a vendor's website.

Using Inventor File Translators

With Inventor 2009 you can access files from other CAD systems without downloading an add-in or translating the files to an intermediate format such as STEP, IGES, or SAT. Instead, you simply open the file, and Inventor will translate the file into an Inventor file on the fly.

Pro/ENGINEER

To open models created in Pro/ENGINEER, select File ➤ Open, and set the Files Of Type pull-down to Pro/ENGINEER (*.prt*; *.asm*) or (*.g) or (*.neu*). Then select the Pro/Engineer file you want to open. Click the Options button to adjust the options for the file destination, part save, and import check. Figure 14.13 shows the Pro/Engineer options.

If the Save Parts During Load option is checked, files created during the import process will be saved on the fly to locations specified by the Destination Directory settings. If this option is left unchecked, Inventor creates the files but does not save them until you tell it to do so. It may be slower to open a Pro/E assembly file with this option on.

FIGURE 14.13
Pro/Engineer import options

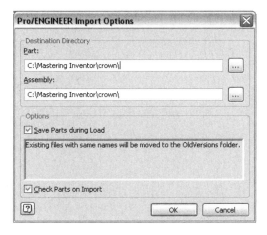

FIGURE 14.13
Pro/Engineer import options

The Check Parts On Import option determines whether the surface and solid data are checked during the import process. If this option is enabled and no errors are found in the file, then the part browser is marked with a green check mark. This option will make opening files slower as well.

To import Pro/Engineer parts or assemblies that contain instances of family tables, the accelerator files (`*.xpr` or `*.xas`) must be saved independently of the Pro/Engineer part and assembly files.

When the files are opened in Inventor, they will consist of a base solid, work features, and a translation report. You can then add features to the base solid using standard Inventor part-modeling tools. Figure 14.14 shows an imported Pro/Engineer file with translated work features.

FIGURE 14.14
An imported
Pro/Engineer part

Unigraphics and Parasolids

You can access Unigraphics and Parasolids files in the same way as described for Pro/Engineer files. Select File ➤ Open, and set the Files Of Type pulldown to Parasolids Text Files (`*.x_t`), Parasolids Binary Files (`*.x_b`), or Unigraphics (`*.prt`). Next browse for the file you want to open. Click the Options button to adjust the options for the file destination, part save, and import check. Figure 14.15 shows the Parasolids import options.

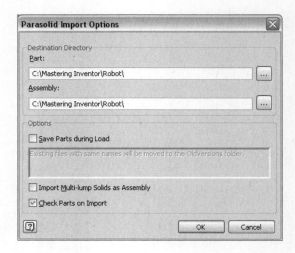

If the Save Parts During Load option is checked, files created during the import process will be saved on the fly to locations specified by the Destination Directory settings. If this option is left unchecked, Inventor creates the files but does not save them until you tell it to do so. It may be slower to open an assembly file with this option on.

Use the Import Multi-lump Solids As Assembly option to convert multibody solids into an Inventor assembly. Part names will come from within the file and follow the original assembly names.

The Check Parts On Import option determines whether the surface and solid data are checked during the import process. If this option is enabled and no errors are found in the file, then the part browser is marked with a green check mark. This option will make opening files slower, because Inventor checks each part during the process.

Solidworks

To open models created in Solidworks, select File ➢ Open, and set the Files Of Type pulldown to Solidworks (`*.prt`, `*.sldpart`, `*.asm`, and `*.sldasm`). Then select the Solidworks file you want to open. Click the Options button to adjust the options for the file destination, part save, and import check.

If the Save Parts During Load option is checked, files created during the import process will be saved immediately to locations specified by the Destination Directory settings. If this option is left unchecked, Inventor creates the files but does not save them until you tell it to do so. It may take longer to open a Solidworks assembly file with this option on.

The Check Parts On Import option determines whether the surface and solid data are checked during the import process. If this option is enabled and no errors are found in the file, then the part browser is marked with a green check mark. This option will make opening files slower as well. Figure 14.16 shows the Solidworks import options.

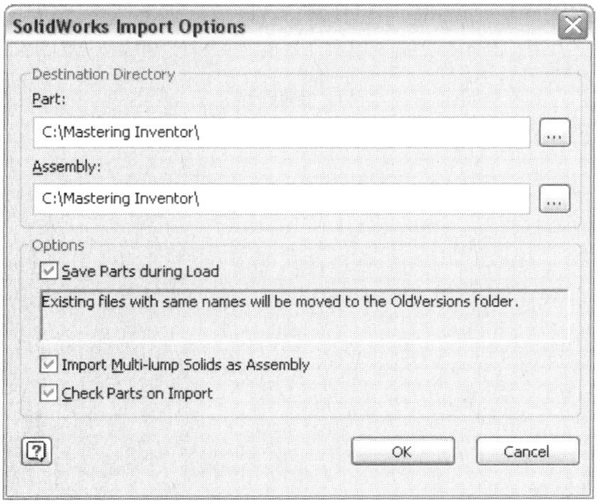

FIGURE 14.16
Solidworks import
options

When the files are opened in Inventor, they are automatically translated into an Inventor IPT file and consist of a base solid and a translation report. You can add features to the base solid using standard Inventor part-modeling tools.

IDF Board Files

Intermediate Data Format (IDF) is the standard data exchange format for transferring printed circuit assembly (PCA) files between printed circuit board (PCB) layouts and mechanical design programs. You can access IDF board files by selecting File ➢ Open and setting the Files Of Type pulldown to IDF Board Files (`*.brd`, `*.emn`, `*.bdf`, and `*.idb`).

IDF board files can be imported into Inventor as assembly or part files. When brought in as an assembly, board components are translated into individual parts, contained in the new assembly. When imported as a part, the board components are translated into sketches and features. Inventor will translate IDF outlines, keepouts, group areas, drilled holes, and components.

Part files are automatically named based upon the information in the existing board file. Once imported, the files can be placed into Inventor assemblies and detailed in Inventor drawings just as you would any other Inventor model. Figure 14.17 shows the IDF import options. You are presented with this dialog box automatically upon opening an IDF board file.

Placing Components from Other CAD Systems

So far you have learned about importing and translating files into Inventor through the Open dialog box in order to convert files into Inventor file. You can also access most of these file types in the assembly environment and place them straight into your Inventor assembly file just as you would any other model.

To place a non-Inventor component into an Inventor assembly, click the Place Components icon in the Assembly panel. In the Open dialog box, select the file type of the component you intend to place, or set the file type to All Files. Locate and select the file, and click the Options button. Configure the options as required, and click OK. Click Open to translate, and place the component into the assembly.

FIGURE 14.17
Importing an IDF board file

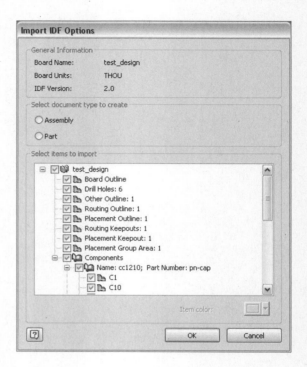

Working with Imported Data

In a perfect world, you would not need to import or export data at all. Instead, all files would exist in one perfect, universal file format. Of course, this perfect world does not exist, and you are probably required to import files created in another program from time to time. In a near-perfect world, imported data would always come in healthy and without any problems. Of course, that isn't the case either.

Instead, importing data can sometimes be a struggle. Typically the biggest struggles come with importing surface models. Inventor provides a construction environment for repairing poorly translated surfaces. Once repaired, imported surfaces must be promoted to the part environment for use in parametric modeling or to be able to see them in an assembly.

Working in the Construction Environment

If you choose Auto Stitch And Promote when importing a surface an IGES or STEP, Inventor will attempt to automatically promote imported surfaces to the part environment. If surfaces cannot be promoted, they are left in the construction environment. With Auto Stitch And Promote turned off, the surfaces open directly in the construction environment.

If a construction folder exists in the browser, you can right-click it and choose Edit Construction to enter the construction environment. If no construction folder is present, you must copy composite features to the Construction folder. You can do this by right-clicking the composite in the browser and choosing Copy To Construction.

To examine the construction tools in action, open the file named `Imported Data.igs` from the Mastering Inventor folder. Remember to set the file type to IGES, as shown in Figure 14.18.

FIGURE 14.18
Opening an IGES file

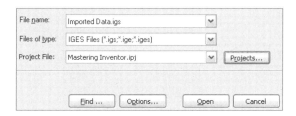

Click the Options button to set the import options as follows. Ensure that all the Entities To Import buttons are selected. Set the Group Mapping option to Place Data Into Multiple Groups. Set the Create Groups From pulldown to Groups. Click the Construction Group Mapping icon. Ensure that the Auto Stitch And Promote check box is not checked. You can leave all the other settings at their defaults. When the specified settings match Figure 14.19, click the OK button, and then click Open.

FIGURE 14.19
Import options

Once the file is open, examine the Model browser to notice the presence of the Construction folder. Expand this folder to reveal that there are 90 surfaces in one group within the folder. Notice you cannot select the surfaces in the graphics area. This is because all the surfaces reside in the construction environment. Note that had you selected the Auto Stitch And Promote option, the surfaces might have been promoted from the construction environment automatically. Depending upon the quality of the surfaces, you might be required to stitch and promote surfaces manually, as you will here.

Examine the model, and notice that there are some missing surfaces. You will need to repair these surfaces in order to promote the surfaces and turn this part into a solid. Figure 14.20 shows the location of the missing and errant surfaces.

FIGURE 14.20
Missing and errant
surfaces

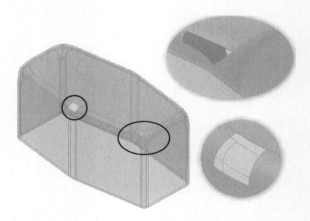

To activate the construction environment, right-click the Construction folder, and choose Edit Construction. This opens the Construction tool panel. Select Stitch Surface from the tool panel, and window select all of the surfaces onscreen. Enter **0.001 in** in the Maximum Tolerance input, and click Apply. You will see the 90 surfaces stitched into a single quilted surface. The gaps created by the missing and errant surfaces are also highlighted, and the remaining free edges are reported in the Stitch dialog box, as shown in Figure 14.21.

FIGURE 14.21
Stitching surfaces

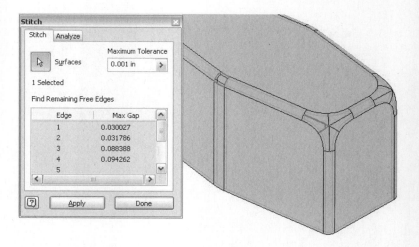

Next you will use the Boundary Patch tool to create a surface to fill in one of the gaps. Zoom in to the area indicated with a circle in Figure 14.20, and notice the missing surface. Choose Boundary Patch from the tool panel, and select the four edges as indicated in Figure 14.22. Use the Stitch tool to stitch the new surface you've just created to the quilted surface created with the previous stitch.

Next zoom to the corner area indicated with an ellipse in Figure 14.20, and notice the missing errant surface. You'll notice two of the surfaces extend beyond the adjacent surfaces and the corner of the surface is cut short leaving a gap. To resolve this, you will first select the surface, and choose Unstitch, as shown in Figure 14.23.

FIGURE 14.22
Boundary patch

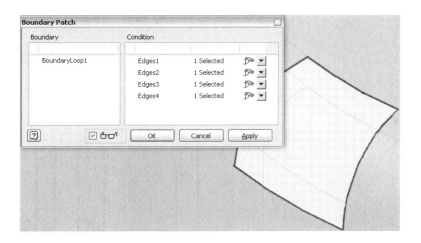

FIGURE 14.23
Unstitching the errant
surface

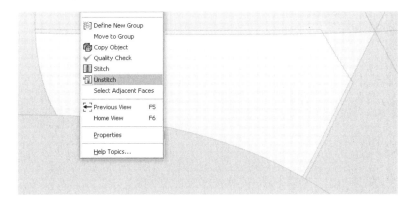

To fill the gap in the surface, select Extend Faces in the tool panel, and choose the edge, as shown in Figure 14.24. Enter **0.026 in** for the distance, and click Apply. This will extend the surface over the existing gap.

FIGURE 14.24
Extending a face

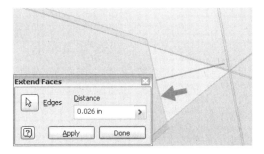

Now you need to trim the surface edges to the adjacent surfaces. To do this, use the Boundary Trim tool in the tool panel, and select the edges of the adjacent faces, as shown in Figure 14.25. Then choose the unstitched surface, and click Apply.

FIGURE 14.25
Using the Boundary
Trim tool

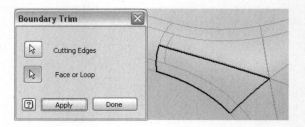

Once the surface is trimmed, you can use the Stitch tool to add it to the surface quilt. Upon doing so you will see the group switch from Surfaces (2) to Solid (1), indicating that you have a surface set that is ready to be promoted to a solid. To do this, choose Copy Object from the tool panel, and select Solids (1) from the model tree. Set the Output to solids, and then click Apply, as shown in Figure 14.26.

FIGURE 14.26
Copying object

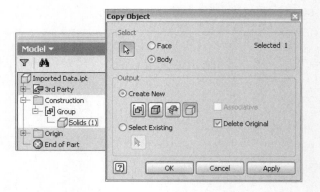

You will now have a base solid in the Model browser, as well as the Construction folder and the third-party translation report. Click the return arrow to exit the construction group, and then you can remove the translation report and construction group by right-clicking them in the browser and choosing Delete.

Editing Imported Data

You can add features to the base solid by sketching any of the desired surfaces and using the standard Inventor part-modeling tools. You can also edit the base solid size by right-clicking it in the browser and choosing Edit Solid. To widen the solid, first turn the visibility of the YZ origin plane on. Then choose the Extend or Contract Body icon from the tool panel. Select the YZ plane, enter a distance of **1.0 inch** in the Distance box, and click OK, as shown in Figure 14.27.

You can also use the Move Face tool to adjust a base solid. To adjust the depth of this part, click the Move Face icon in the tool panel, and select the bottom face of the part. Enter **0.25 in** in the Distance box, click the Flip Direction button so that your preview looks like Figure 14.28, and then click Apply. You will see the depth of the part increase. Had you clicked the Direction button, you could have decreased the depth of the part.

FIGURE 14.27
Extending or contracting
a solid body

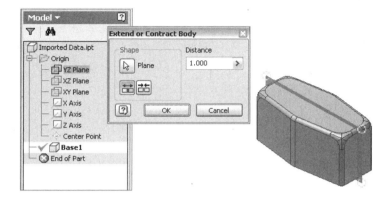

FIGURE 14.28
Moving a face

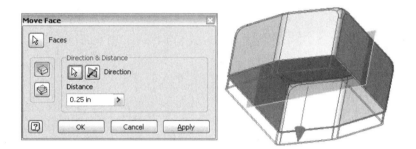

SEAN SAYS: USE EDIT SOLID TO MODIFY PURCHASED PARTS

When building custom machinery, we often run into a situation where we do not know what size air cylinder we might need for a design. Many times we will have downloaded a SAT file of, say, a 3″-long cylinder, and we then discover that we really need a 4″-long model. Rather than download and import a new model, you can take a shortcut by using these Edit Solid tools to make the body of the cylinder longer.

Viewing DWF Markup

Autodesk Design Review offers Inventor users a simple and effective way to view and mark up both 2D and 3D DWF files. Design Web Format (DWF) files are lightweight versions of your Inventor files you can publish from Inventor and email to a collaborator to be viewed and redlined with Autodesk Design Review (ADR). Non-Inventor users can download and install ADR free of charge from the Autodesk website.

The DWF markup process begins from within Inventor where you will publish a DWF from your Inventor files. Once the DWF is published, it is sent to the reviewer and marked up within

ADR. You can then bring those markups into your Inventor file and change the status of a markup, add comments, or accept the markup. With Inventor 2009 you have the additional choice of publishing to DWFx format, allowing reviewers to access the file directly through Internet Explorer 7.0 or Windows Vista.

A typically DWF markup process is as follows:

1. **Publish:** You write out the DWF file from Inventor 2D and/or 3D files.

2. **Receive:** The reviewer receives the DWF file from you and opens it with ADR to check for errors and omissions.

3. **Review:** The reviewer can comment on and mark up the DWF file using callouts, text blocks, shapes, dimensions, stamps, and custom symbols. Then they save those markups to the DWF file.

4. **Return:** The reviewer then sends the markups back to you for your review.

5. **Revise:** You load the marked-up DWF into Inventor and revise the Inventor files as required.

6. **Republish:** After revising, you write out the DWF file from Inventor 2D and/or 3D files again.

PUBLISHING A DWF OR DWFx FILE

With the file you intend to publish open in Inventor, select File ➢ Publish DWF, which opens the Publish dialog box. There are three options for publishing the DWF or DWFx:

◆ **Express:** Select to publish only the active sheet without the 3D model.

◆ **Complete:** Select to publish all sheets and all 3D models except sheets excluded from printing.

◆ **Custom:** Choose sheets and 3D models to publish, depending upon the type of file you are publishing. Extra tabs appear in the Publish dialog box for each file type as required. The following are the descriptions of what is included for each file type when using the Custom option:

  ◆ **Drawing files:** The DWF or DWFx file includes all sheets and tables, as well as the complete referenced 3D models.

  ◆ **Assembly files:** The following assembly options are available:
    ◆ **General:** The DWF or DWFx file includes the assembly with view and positional representations, as well as enabled BOM views.

    ◆ **iAssembly factory:** The DWF or DWFx file includes all members and the iAssembly table with view and positional representations.

    ◆ **iAssembly member:** The DWF or DWFx file includes the assembly with view and positional representations, as well as enabled BOM views.

    ◆ **Weldment:** The DWF or DWFx file includes the assembly with view and positional representations, as well as enabled BOM views, weld beads, and weld symbols.

    ◆ **LOD master:** The DWF or DWFx file includes the assembly with view and positional representations, as well as enabled BOM views.

◆ **LOD nonmaster:** When an assembly is at any other LPD other then the master, only that LOD is published to the DWF or DWFx. All view and positional representations, as well as enabled BOM views are also published.

◆ **Part files:** The following part options are available:

 ◆ **General:** The DWF or DWFx file includes only the part model.

 ◆ **Sheet metal:** The DWF or DWFx file includes the folded model and flat pattern (if one exists).

 ◆ **iPart factory:** The DWF or DWFx file includes all iPart members and the iPart table.

 ◆ **iPart member:** The DWF or DWFx file includes only the iPart model.

 ◆ **Stress analysis:** The DWF or DWFx file includes the model with stress/constraint indicators as well as a stress scale.

◆ **Presentation files:** The DWF or DWFx file includes the presentation views, animations, and assembly instructions, as well as the complete assembly.

DWF or DWFx files can be published with the ability to measure, print, and enable and disable markups. They can be password protected for security also. Figure 14.29 shows the publish options for an iAssembly factory.

FIGURE 14.29
DWF or DWFX publish options

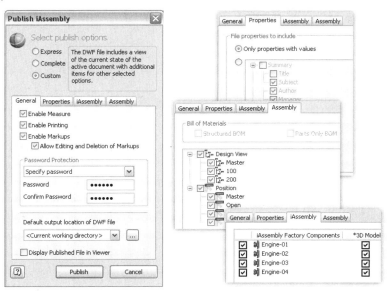

Once you choose the appropriate options, click Publish to specify between DWF or DWFx formats, and specify a location to create the file. The resulting file can be opened in Design Review to create markups.

REVIEWING AND MARKING UP DWF AND DWFX FILES

Once a DWF or DWFx file is open in Design Review, you can create markups in the form of callouts, text blocks, shapes, stamps, custom symbols, and measurements. To access the markup toolbar, if it's not already displayed, select Window ➢ Toolbars, and choose Markup. Figure 14.30 shows the markup toolbar.

FIGURE 14.30
Markup toolbar

From left to right, the markup tools are as follows:

Text: Create text on 2D sheets.

Drawing: Draw shapes such as lines, circles, and rectangles on 2D sheets.

Callout: Draw a callout on 2D and 3D sheets.

Measurement: Add measurements on 2D and 3D sheets.

Stamp: Put a stamp on a 2D sheet.

Symbol: Put a symbol on a 2D sheet.

Snapshot: Take a screen capture, and add it to the DWF file as a 2D sheet.

Grid Snapshot: Take a screen capture of the Grid Data palette for tabled information such as BOMs and iPart tables, and add it to the DWF file as a 2D sheet.

When markups are created, they are listed in the Markups palettes and organized by the sheet upon which they reside. Most markups contain the following collection of properties: Status, Notes, History, Created, Creator, Label, Modified, and Sheet. Drawn markups such as lines do not have properties.

Each markup can have its own status. The status can be <None>, For Review, Question, and Done. When a markup is clicked in the Markups palettes, the screen will zoom to the markup at the same zoom scale at which it was created. Once markups are complete, the DWF or DWFx file can be saved. Figure 14.31 shows a view marked up in Design Review.

FIGURE 14.31
Marked-up view in
Design Review

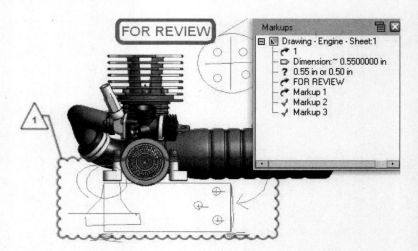

ACCESSING DWF OR DWFX MARKUPS IN INVENTOR

To open a markup set in Inventor, select File ➢ Load Markup Set. The DWF markups will be overlaid onto the Inventor drawing, and the Markups browser displays the markup set in the tree view. The status and properties of each markup can then be edited by right-clicking the markup in the browser, as shown in Figure 14.32.

FIGURE 14.32
Markups loaded into Inventor

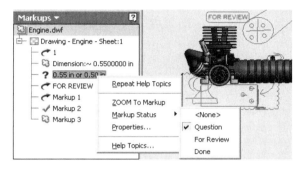

Once you've reviewed all markups, you can save the markups back to the DWF or DWFx file and republish the sheets that are marked up or republish all sheets. You can access these commands by right-clicking the DWF or DWFx filename in the Markups browser, as shown in Figure 14.33.

FIGURE 14.33
Saving and republishing markups

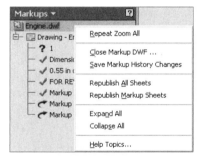

Using Feature Recognition

Autodesk has made the recognition of Inventor features from a base solid a possibility though the use of the Feature Recognition add-in available at Autodesk Labs (http://labs.autodesk.com/). When this tool is loaded, it will attempt to recognize features in any file you import and translate. It is important to note that not all translated files can have their features translated.

To recognize features from neutral solids such as STEP, SAT, and IGES, use the Open dialog box to translate the file. At the end of the translation, you will be asked whether you want to attempt to recognize features from the solid, as shown in Figure 14.34. Clicking Yes to the feature recognition prompt will automatically open the Feature Recognition tool panel. Note that if the file has taken a long time to translate, you might want to click No and start the feature recognition process manually, as described next.

FIGURE 14.34
Feature recognition
prompt

If you are importing files from other modeling platforms, such as Pro/Engineer or Solidworks, you will be prompted to recognize features also. However, because the file types might contain objects that are not recognizable, you should click No to the recognize features prompt shown in Figure 14.34 and initiate the feature recognition tool manually. This gives Inventor a chance to complete translation process and scan for unrecognizable feature types.

To do this, right-click the base solid (typically named Base1), and choose Recognize Features. If unrecognizable features are detected, you will be given a prompt, as shown on the right of Figure 14.35. Typically these will be work features such as planes, axes, and points. If a large number of features are listed as unrecognizable, it might be wise to click No at the prompt and delete the features manually. Then right-click the base solid again, and choose Recognizable.

FIGURE 14.35
Discarding unrecogniz-
able features

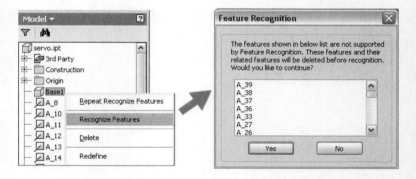

Once the Feature Recognition tool panel is displayed, as shown in Figure 14.36, you can attempt to recognize features automatically or manually by type. This add-in can recognize extrudes, revolves, holes, shells, sweeps, fillets, chamfers, and sculpts.

AUTOMATIC FEATURE RECOGNITION

Click the Automatic Feature Recognition icon to attempt to recognize features automatically and open the dialog box, as shown in Figure 14.37. Inventor will attempt select all the faces of the part and list them in the pane on the right. You can use the check boxes on the left to select the types of features you want to attempt to recognize.

If you prefer, you can select only one feature type at a time, click Apply, then repeat the process for the next feature type, and so on, until all features that have been recognized have been converted to Inventor native features. Or you can select them all and click Apply. Recognizing feature types one at a time gives you greater control over the order and naming of the features. Features are named in the order that they are recognized.

FIGURE 14.36
Feature Recognition tool
panel

FIGURE 14.37
Automatic Feature
Recognition dialog box

You can add faces to the Selected Faces pane by clicking the faces of the part onscreen, and you can remove them by right-clicking them in the list and choosing Delete. You can use the Select All and Clear All buttons as well. For best results, you should attempt to recognize smaller features such as fillets and chamfers before attempting to recognize base feature. Once features are recognized, the remaining solid is reduced in complexity, and base features can be recognized easier.

When the feature types and selected faces have been chosen, click the Apply button to run the recognition tool. You will see the progress bar for each feature type display as Inventor attempts to recognize each feature type, unless you have elected to run the recognition tool for the feature types separately. Figure 14.38 shows the progress bar for the Extrude feature.

FIGURE 14.38
Feature recognition
progress bar

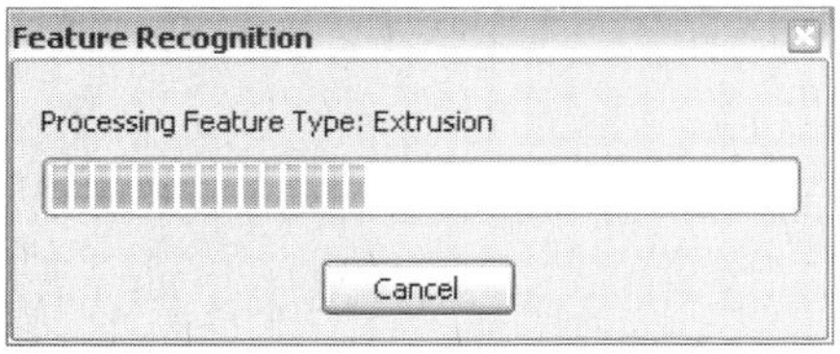

When complete, the recognized features will be listed in the part browser bar, and the Selected Faces pane will be cleared. If no features of the types you specified can be recognized, you will not see any updates in the part browser, and the Selected Faces pane will be cleared. Some recognized features may have multiple solutions. If Inventor recognizes a feature as a hole and you prefer it to be a revolution, you might be able to right-click it and choose Change Type, as shown in Figure 14.39. This option depends upon the geometry and is not available for all features.

FIGURE 14.39
Changing the recognized feature type

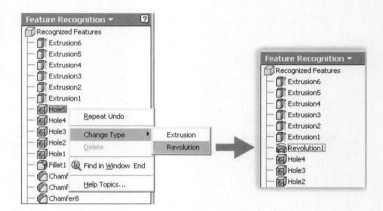

Once all the features that can be recognized are recognized, click the Inventor Return button. You will be prompted that some features have been recognized and given the choice to create them in your model, as shown in Figure 14.40. Click Yes to continue.

FIGURE 14.40
Creating the recognized features

The recognized features will now appear in the Model browser as standard Inventor features. It is important to note that recognized features will be underconstrained and generally lacking in sketch dimensions and constraints; however, you can edit the features and place dimensions and constraints as you normally would.

> **SEAN SAYS: LOCK DOWN RECOGNIZED FEATURES**
>
> As mentioned in this chapter, recognized features are usually underconstrained and undimensioned. It is important to "lock down" these features by editing the resulting sketch and applying dimensions and constraints so that they do no change shape during the design process.

MANUAL FEATURE RECOGNITION

In addition to using the Automatic Feature Recognition tool, you might want to recognize features manually so you can control the way they are interpreted. Or you may want to ensure that the majority of the model stays a base solid and recognize only a certain feature or set of features so that they can be resized or otherwise adjusted.

Typically you will want to remove small, dependant features such as fillets and chamfers first and then work down to large base features. As you recognize features, they will be removed from the model, leaving a simplified version onscreen. Figure 14.41 shows a model before and after fillets are recognized.

FIGURE 14.41
Recognizing fillets

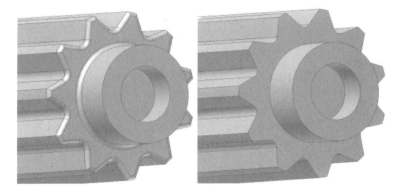

Features that are the same size and are arranged in a pattern can be recognized as such once the patterned feature has been recognized. Figure 14.42 shows four identical holes being recognized as patterned features by selecting them all and right-clicking to choose Recognize Pattern.

FIGURE 14.42
Recognizing patterns

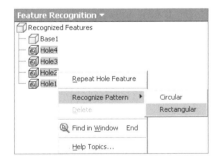

USING FEATURE RECOGNITION WISELY

Although the feature recognition tool is a great help when working with translated files, it is not a substitute for good modeling skills. It is also important to understand that this tool is simply a geometry translator, and as such, it cannot be guaranteed to work 100 percent of the time. You should exercise good judgment concerning how many features of a translated part require recognition. For instance, if you are working on a customer-supplied STEP file and need to redesign a particular set of features in order to accommodate your in-house tooling, you may be able to recognize just those features and translate them so you can easily modify them.

However, oftentimes a complex part might require you to recognize many features you are not concerned with, before getting to the features you are after. In these cases, it might actually be more efficient just to remodel the part from scratch. Using the feature recognition tool selectively and with a purpose will get you much further than using it indiscriminately or as a "shortcut" to sound modeling.

The Bottom Line

Import and export geometry   In the design world today, you most likely need to transfer files to or from a customer or vendor from time to time. Chances are, the files will need to be translated to or from a neutral file format to be read by different CAD packages.

> **Master It**   You are collaborating with another design office that does not use Inventor. You are asked which you would prefer, IGES or STEP files.

Use Inventor file translators   Inventor 2009 offers native file translators for Pro/Engineer, Solidworks, Unigraphics, and other CAD file types. This allows you to access these file formats with Inventor and translate the files into Inventor files directly.

> **Master It**   You are a "job shop" and in the past have been required to have a copy of Solidworks in addition to your copy of Inventor in order to work with customers who send you Solidworks files.

Work with imported data   Using the construction environment in Inventor, you can repair poorly translated surface files. Often a file fails to translate into a solid because of just a few translation errors in the part. Repairing or patching the surfaces and promoting the file to a solid allows you to use the file more effectively.

> **Master It**   You download an IGES file from a vendor website, but when you attempt to use the component in your design, the surface data is found to have issues.

Work with Design Review markups   Design Review offers you and the people you collaborate with an easy-to-use electronic markup tool that can be round-tripped from Inventor. Design Review markups can be made on both 2D and 3D files.

Master It   You want to use Design Review to communicate with vendors and clients in order to save time and resources, but you have found that others are unsure of what Design Review is and how to get it.

Use Feature recognition   The Feature Recognition add-in can be downloaded online for free from Autodesk Labs. This tool allows you to add intelligence to otherwise "dumb" imported solids.

Master It   You receive STEP files from a client but often find that holes and other features need to be resized to accommodate your tooling.

Chapter 15

Frame Generator

The Frame Generator application is an add-in that uses the Inventor API. Since the API does not provide access to all the Inventor functionality, there are some UI differences between add-ins and core Inventor. For example, the edit fields in core Inventor have an extensive flyout menu. The add-ins do not have access to this functionality, so their edit fields are more limited.

Frame Generator creates a reference skeleton model from the selections in an assembly. This allows you to select work geometry, layout sketch geometry, and edges of components. Any selection is added to the reference skeleton, so the frame automatically updates to changes in size or position.

Frame Generator gets structural profiles from the Content Center. In addition to the structural profiles included in the Inventor libraries, you can author and publish your own profiles. This is useful for adding aluminum profiles, since the structural profiles in the Inventor libraries are standard steel shapes.

In this chapter, you will learn how to:

- ◆ Work with frame files

- ◆ Insert frame members onto a skeleton model

- ◆ Add end treatments to frame members

- ◆ Make changes to frames

- ◆ Author and publish structural profiles

Accessing the Frame Generator Panel Bar

The Frame Generator panel bar, shown in Figure 15.1, is available in the assembly environment. It has tools specific to Frame Generator plus the Beam and Column calculator from the Design Accelerators.

The tools fall into four categories: working with frame members, creating end treatments, doing maintenance, and performing analysis. Insert and Change are used to place and replace frame members. Miter, Trim To Frame, Trim–Extend To Face, Notch, Lengthen–Shorten Frame Member, and Remove End Treatments are used to add end treatments to frame members. Frame Member Info and Refresh are maintenance tools. Beam And Column is an analysis tool for frame members.

FIGURE 15.1
The Frame Generator panel bar

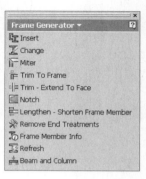

Exploring the Frame Generator File Structure

When you create the first members in a frame assembly, a dialog box prompts you for filenames. Frame Generator creates a subassembly and a skeleton file in the parent assembly. The subassembly does several things. It acts as a container for the skeleton and frame member, isolating them from the assembly constraint solver, and it acts as a filter so Frame Generator commands, such as Frame Member Info, ignore other assembly components. Each frame member is created as a separate file.

Special attributes in the frame subassembly contain references to the parent assembly. This enables the frame skeleton to maintain references to the other assembly components. One limitation is that you can't use copies of the frame in other assemblies and maintain Frame Generator functionality.

Exploring the Anatomy of a Frame Member

Frame Generator initially creates frame members, such as the one shown in Figure 15.2, that are the same length as the selected geometry. When you add end treatments, the length is adjusted to make the member longer or shorter. To accomplish this, the structural profiles are created with a From-To extrusion between two work planes.

FIGURE 15.2
A typical frame member

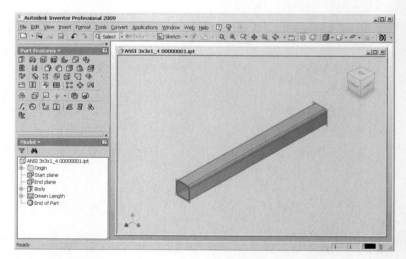

When the part is first created, the start plane is coincident with the XY plane, and the end plane is set to the initial length. When an end treatment is added, the start or end plane is moved to shorten or lengthen the member.

The parameter relationships that control the length are complex. Three parameters drive the length, two parameters are driven by those parameters to determine the length, a reference parameter reports the overall length, and a parameter is used in the BOM, as indicated in Figure 15.3. Table 15.1 lists the length parameters.

FIGURE 15.3

Frame member parameters

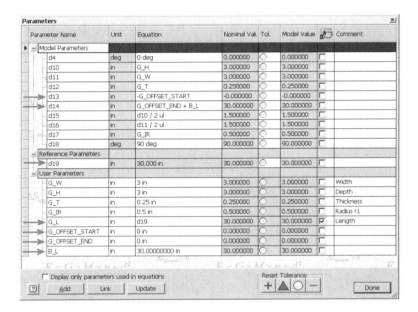

TABLE 15.1: Frame Member Parameters

PARAMETER	DESCRIPTION
B_L	The initial length of the member.
G_OFFSET_START	The offset value of the start work plane.
G_OFFSET_END	The offset value of the end work plane.
d13	The parameter for the start work plane. It is driven by G_OFFSET_START.
d14	The parameter for the end work plane. It is driven by G_OFFSET_END.
d19	A reference dimension that measures the overall length of the part.
G_L	The length parameter that is used in the BOM. It is equal to the reference dimension.

Inserting Frame Members

The process for inserting frame members can be broken down into three basic steps. You select the frame member from the Content Center, select the placement geometry for placing the frame members, and adjust the orientation of the frame members.

Specifying a Structural Shape

The left side of the Insert dialog box, shown in Figure 15.4, has a series of pulldown fields for specifying the structural shape.

FIGURE 15.4
Frame Member
Selection group

You use the Standard, Family, and Size fields to select the member from the Content Center. These fields are progressive, and the update behavior varies. If you select a new standard, the first family is automatically selected. If you select a new family, the size is not automatically selected.

The Material Style and Color Style settings are not pulled from the Content Center. The first time you work with Frame Generator in an Inventor session, the material is set to Default. The material and color styles remember the last setting throughout that session, but they reset when you restart Inventor.

Changing the Orientation

After you have selected the placement geometry, you can change the position and orientation of the member. A thumbnail of the profile is displayed in a grid of radio buttons that control the position of the member, as shown in Figure 15.5. These positions are based on the rectangular bounds of the profile. As a result, the corner positions of a 1-inch by 1-inch square tube are the same as a 1-inch diameter pipe.

FIGURE 15.5
Orientation group

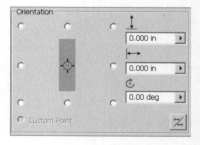

If a part has been authored with an alternate base point, the Custom Point control is enabled. This adds another insertion point to the nine standard ones. The custom point is not displayed in the thumbnail image, so you should confirm the preview is in the expected position relative to the selected edge.

You can fine-tune the position by entering values in the horizontal and vertical fields. You can also rotate the member. For example, food procession equipment frequently has horizontal members rotated 45 degrees so spilled food doesn't build up on top of square tubing.

The Mirror Frame Member button is used for profiles that don't have rotational symmetry, such as C-channel and angle iron.

The orientation changes affect all the members of a select set. Depending on the geometry, it might be more efficient to use a batch select tool and change the orientation of a few members afterward, or you might want to select only those members that have a similar orientation.

Since structural shapes are extruded, Frame Generator needs a method for determining the extrude direction. When an edge is selected, Frame Generator uses the closest endpoint as the start of the extrusion. Depending on where you select an edge, the same radio button can cause the member to be in a different position. The thumbnail is the view of the profile looking at the XY plane. It takes some practice to get a good feel for the relationship between how an edge is selected and the behavior of the radio buttons. Once you understand this relationship, you will be able to predict the behavior and use it to increase your productivity.

To see how this is accomplished, open the `conveyor.iam` file, and refer to Figure 15.6. Specify the Standard, Family, Size, and Material Style settings, as shown in the dialog box. Click the first edge near the bottom, and select the corner radio button to place the member inside the surface.

FIGURE 15.6
Preview of the first member when selected near the bottom

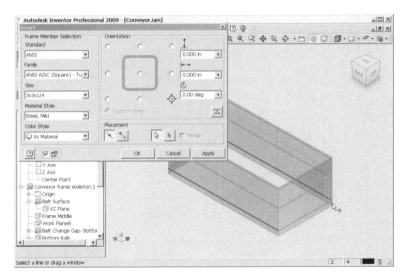

Click the next edge near the bottom, as shown in Figure 15.7, and its relative position is the same as the first member. This places the member outside the surface.

The second member needs to be inside the surface, so deselect the edge, and click the edge near the top, as shown in Figure 15.8. This time, since the extrusion direction was reversed, the member is inside the surface.

FIGURE 15.7
Preview of the second member when selected near the bottom

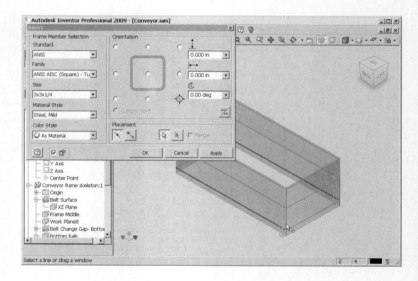

FIGURE 15.8
Preview of the second member when selected near the top

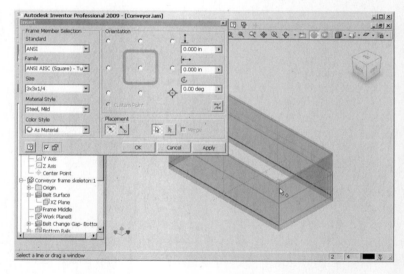

If the profile has an alternate insertion point defined, the Custom Point control is enabled. This point is in addition to the standard insertion points around the profile. Figure 15.9 shows a profile with an alternate insertion point.

Selecting Placement Geometry

When you select placement geometry, you can select edges and lines, or you can select two endpoints. When you select edges and lines, you can insert multiple members. When you select two endpoints, you can place only one member at a time. The most common placement method is by selecting lines and edges. This allows the most flexibility in geometry selection and the use of batch select tools.

FIGURE 15.9
Profile with an alternate
insertion point

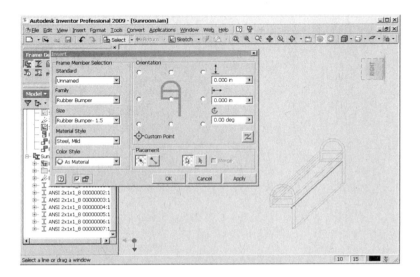

There are two philosophies for placing frame members. Some people like to place frame members individually, making sure each one is in the correct position and orientation. Other people like to place as many members as possible and then edit them as necessary. The method you choose will depend on the type of models you work with, how much effort you put into setting up the skeleton models, and, most important, the way you like to work.

BATCH SELECTION TOOLS

Frame Generator has several tools for selecting geometry. Multi Select is the default selection mode. These are the standard tools for building a selection set: picking, using selection windows, and using the Shift and Ctrl keys to add and subtract. Two additional select modes are available in the context menu shown in Figure 15.10: Chain Select and Sketch Select.

FIGURE 15.10
Select mode context
menu

Chain Select automatically selects all lines and edges that are tangentially connected to the selection. Chain Select will not follow past a point that has multiple lines or edges, even if one of them is tangential.

Sketch Select selects all the lines in a sketch. You can select the sketch in the browser or click a line in the graphics window.

PLACEMENT BY SELECTING LINES AND EDGES

The default selection mode is Insert Members On Edges. You can select any combination of sketch lines and model edges and surface edges. Figure 15.11 shows the conveyor.iam model. The frame skeleton is constructed of surfaces and sketch lines. The power roller is in the correct position, but it needs support members.

FIGURE 15.11
Belt conveyor skeleton
model

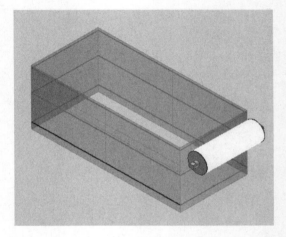

Figure 15.12 shows the conveyor frame populated with ANSI AISC HSS (square) tubing. The legs are 3 × 3 × 1/4 square tubing positioned inside the surface. On one side, the legs have a removable section for installing the belt. Insert the legs in pairs by using the edge selection technique demonstrated in the "Changing the Orientation" section.

FIGURE 15.12
Conveyor frame with all
frame members inserted

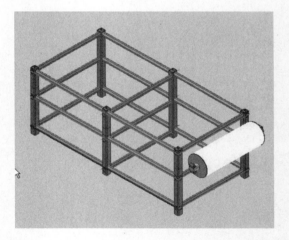

The horizontal members are 2 × 2 × 1/4 square tubing inserted at 45 degrees. Switch to Sketch Select to click the sketches. See Figure 15.13. Once these tubes are inserted, you can turn off the visibility of the conveyor frame skeleton part to reduce clutter.

SEAN SAYS: USE CHAIN SELECT

Use Chain Select to select the four vertical legs as single lines and to place frame members by edge.

FIGURE 15.13
Inserting the horizontal members

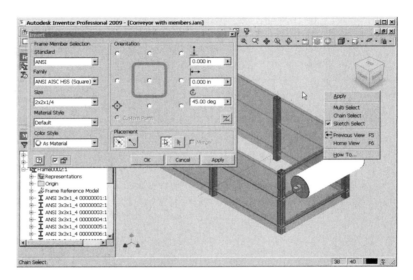

The power roller supports are 1-1/2 × 1-1/2 × 3/16 square tube. The lower support is flush with the flat, and there is a small gap between the upper support and flat. Select the edge of the lower flat, and offset the tube horizontally so it is aligned with the leg. Select the upper edge, and offset it horizontally to align with the lower support and 0.125 inch vertically, as shown in Figure 15.14.

FIGURE 15.14
Inserting the upper power roller support

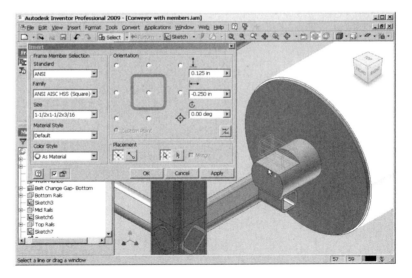

PLACEMENT BY TWO POINTS

In some cases, it can be more productive to select the endpoints rather than create the geometry. The select set is limited to two points, but you can speed up the insertion process by selecting Apply from the context menu and then picking the next pair of points.

In our example, the conveyor frame needs horizontal members in the center. Sketch Select was used to select the perimeter members, and they were offset. Instead of adding sketch geometry and deselecting the lines or changing the orientation of the center members after creation, endpoint selection seemed more productive. Turn the visibility of the conveyor frame skeleton on again. Change the placement method to Insert Members Between Points. Pick the endpoints of the side lines in each sketch, as shown in Figure 15.15, to place the 2 × 2 × 1/4 square tube.

FIGURE 15.15
Inserting the cross members

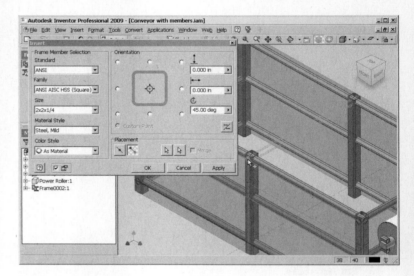

MERGE

The Merge option is enabled when there are connected lines or edges. Merge combines the selections into one member. Although Merge is useful when you want to have one continuous member, you cannot add end treatments to merged members.

Aligning Frame Members

Frame Generator follows two rules to give a frame member its initial orientation. If it is the first member in a select set, the member is aligned to adjacent geometry or the coordinate system. For the rest of the select set, Frame Generator tries to align the members to the first selection. These rules work well for most rectangular machine frames. If part of the frame is at an angle and there isn't a good reference, Frame Generator can select an orientation that doesn't match the design intent.

The frame in Figure 15.16 is the roof for a sunroom. The members for the base and back have already been inserted, and the two angled rafters need to be inserted. When you insert a member on the left line, the orientation is skewed, as shown in Figure 15.17.

On the right side, a reference line was added to the base. If that line is selected first, as shown in Figure 15.18, Frame Generator can align the angled member. Since a frame member isn't needed on the bottom line, it can be deselected, and the angled member is inserted correctly, as shown in Figure 15.19.

FIGURE 15.16
The sunroom roof has angled rafters.

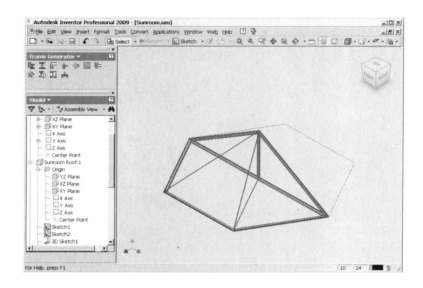

FIGURE 15.17
The left rafter is skewed.

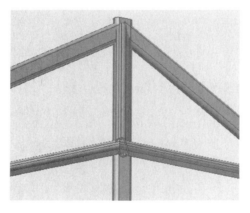

FIGURE 15.18
Selecting a reference line to align the rafter

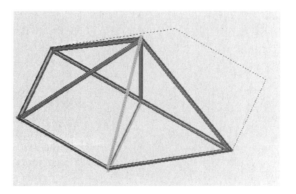

FIGURE 15.19
The right rafter is
aligned correctly.

Using reference geometry for angled frame members is an art. If you regularly create these types of frames, you will develop a feeling for the ways that Frame Generator aligns members, and you will learn when and how you need to add references.

Adding End Treatments

The end treatments are some of the most powerful Frame Generator tools. As you add end treatments, the frame member length automatically updates. The end treatments also carry over if you change the frame member to a different profile.

Miter

The Miter end treatment makes angle cuts on two members. Figure 15.20 shows the Miter dialog box. You can miter multiple members by applying the end treatment to each pair of members.

FIGURE 15.20
Miter dialog box

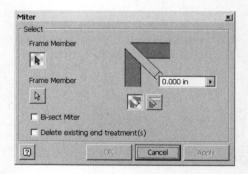

The default selections cut along an angle that results in full-face contact, shown in Figure 15.21, between the members. Bi-sect Miter splits the angle between the members. Figure 15.22 shows the cut is located where the centers of the two members intersect.

FIGURE 15.21
The standard miter joint has full-face contact.

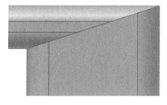

FIGURE 15.22
The optional bi-sect miter cuts both members at the same angle.

You can add a gap between the members. The default gap is split between the two members. If you want to have the end gap on one member, as shown in Figure 15.23, it will be removed from the first selection.

FIGURE 15.23
Miter gap on one member

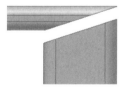

The sunroom assembly has a miter end treatment between the two angled members on the back, and the vertical member needs to be mitered to fit, with a small gap to allow for manufacturing tolerances.

Figure 15.24 shows the first step to create the miter. The gap should be cut only on the vertical member, so it needs to be the first selection.

The vertical member still needs a miter to trim the other side. Repeat the miter, as shown in Figure 15.25, with the same settings.

The resulting miter shown in Figure 15.26 requires two cuts on each member. An alternate method that produces a more cost-effective joint will be shown in a later section.

FIGURE 15.24
First miter cut

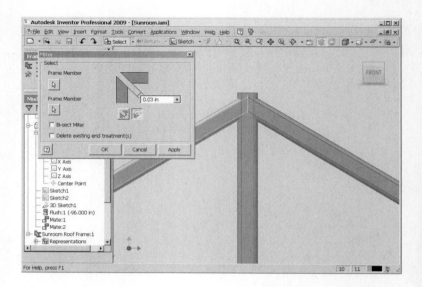

FIGURE 15.25
Second miter cut

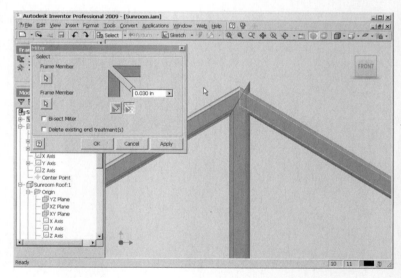

FIGURE 15.26
Resulting miter joint
between the three
members

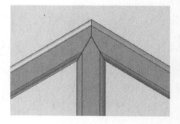

Trim to Frame Member

This end treatment trims or extends both members so they are flush. The first selection is made flush to the second selection, and the second selection butts up to the first. Figure 15.27 shows the selections, and Figure 15.28 shows the results.

FIGURE 15.27
Trim To Frame
selections

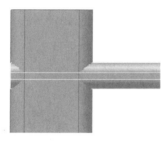

FIGURE 15.28
Trim To Frame results

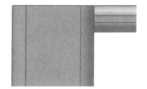

Trim and Extend to Face

This end treatment is the only one that can trim multiple members at once. You select the members you want to trim, and then you select the cutting face. A separate end treatment feature is created for each frame member. If you edit or delete the end treatment for a particular member, it does not affect the other members.

Returning to the conveyor example, the conveyor frame is a typical machine frame. All of the members are perpendicular with simple butt joints. Since you can select multiple members, as shown in Figure 15.29, using Trim and Extend is an efficient way to add details. Since the frame is symmetrical, you can trim the members on both sides at once. If a design change requires an offset leg, it is pretty straightforward to edit the end treatments on the members and change the face selection.

This end treatment can also be used to create miters. Applying miter end treatments to the sun-room frame resulted in a complex joint. Trimming the vertical member to fit the angled members results in the less expensive detail shown in Figure 15.30.

Notch Frame Members

Notch cuts one frame member to match the other. It uses the profile to create a cutting surface. You can't create an offset, so the cut is an exact match. This is simply a cut operation, so the frame member is not shortened or extended before the cut. If you notch the short I-beam shown in Figure 15.31, which extends past the tall I-beam, the extra lump will be left as shown in Figure 15.32. If the members don't intersect, the notch will have little or no effect.

FIGURE 15.29
Trim the horizontal members to a leg

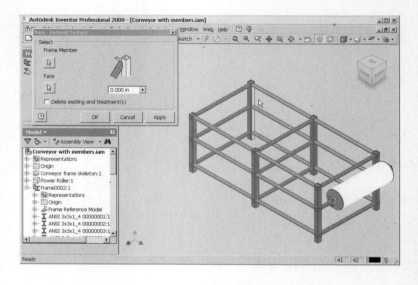

FIGURE 15.30
Creating a miter using Trim

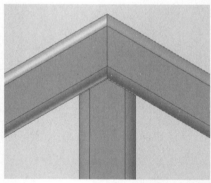

FIGURE 15.31
Frame members before notch

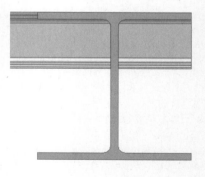

FIGURE 15.32
The result of removing the intersecting material

A notch is frequently a secondary end treatment. For example, if you add a Trim/Extend To Face end treatment first, the notch will remove any intersecting material.

Lengthen–Shorten Frame Member

Sometimes, there isn't another frame member you can use as a reference for an end treatment. For example, the power roller supports on the conveyor are stubs that were placed by selecting the part edges. The power roller is moved to adjust the belt tension, so the tubes need to be extended away from the frame.

The tubes were already extended to the frame. Since the total length of the tube should be a nominal value, measure the length of the tube before starting the command. In this case, the tube is 9.088 inches long. The tube needs to be about 3 inches longer, so the overall length should be 12 inches. Copy the length from the measure dialog box, and build an expression in the Lengthen–Shorten dialog box.

Frame Generator modifies the end that is closest to the pick point, as shown in Figure 15.33. If the pick is closer to the frame, an error will display because there is already an end treatment at that end. Although it isn't obvious at first, this is an intuitive way to select the member, since you are likely to pick the member close to the end you will modify.

FIGURE 15.33
Lengthening the power roller supports

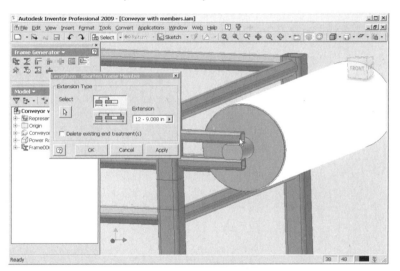

SEAN SAYS: FRAME END TREATMENTS ARE NOT EXEMPT FROM DESIGN INTENT

You should spend time planning your frame design to minimize the number of end treatments required, because each end treatment is an opportunity for the model to fail if a change is made. Methodical analysis of the frame should help you design a frame that utilizes robust end treatments whenever possible.

Maintaining Frames

Maintaining existing assemblies can be time-consuming. Frame Generator provides several tools that help streamline this process.

Remove End Treatments

The Remove End Treatments tool removes all end treatments from a frame member. You can also select multiple members for the batch removal of end treatments. This is handy if you need to change the end treatments on a few members or if you have to rebuild a frame.

Frame Member Information

The Frame Member Information tool is used to query frame members. It displays the family and size information, mass properties, and material. This is a useful tool because it quickly gives you information about a member. For example, it can tell you the wall thickness of a tube. Since the tool filters for frame members, you can use it at any level of the assembly.

Refresh

The Refresh tool is a Content Center tool. It checks the Content Center for the latest revision of the members in the frame. If a newer version is available, it will prompt you to replace it. End treatments are retained during refresh, but other features, such as holes, are not carried over to the new member.

Performing Analysis

Like other Design Accelerator dialog boxes, the message pane at the bottom and the calculation results pane on the right side can be opened and closed by clicking the chevrons. You can drag the splitter bar to resize the panes or double-click it to open or close them.

When you click OK, a component is added to the assembly that contains all the data and results.

USING THE BEAM AND COLUMN CALCULATOR

The Beam and Column Calculator is a Design Accelerator tool that can do a simple stress analysis of a single beam or column. It assumes a uniform cross section, so it does not take into account holes or end treatments. You should refer to a *Mechanics of Materials* book to learn more about section properties and static analysis. An in-depth discussion is beyond the scope of this chapter.

Model Tab

When you select the power roller support, the calculator automatically loads the section properties from the Content Center, as shown in Figure 15.34. Although the Content Center has most of the section properties, some data is missing. You can use several methods for determining the properties.

In Inventor 2009, a tool was added to calculate the properties of a sketch profile. If you want to use this tool for the section properties of a frame member, you can open the frame member, place a sketch on one end, and project the face. Once you have the profile, select Tools ➤ Region Properties. You select the profile you want to analyze and click Calculate. The basic regional properties for any closed loop are calculated. You will need to calculate the rest of the properties based on those results.

The regional properties are calculated with respect to the sketch origin. Depending on the profile, you may have to edit the sketch coordinate system to locate the sketch origin at the center of the profile.

FIGURE 15.34
The section properties
for the power roller
support are loaded from
the Content Center.

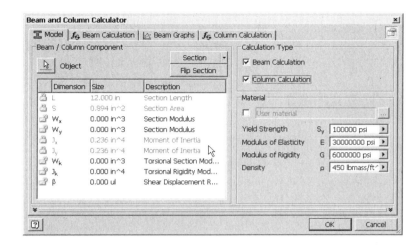

Another option for calculating section properties is to use the Section button. When you click the button, a list of geometric shapes displays. When you select a shape, a dialog box like Figure 15.35 displays for entering dimensions. The calculated properties assume sharp corners and constant thickness, so the results won't be accurate for profiles with tapered flanges.

FIGURE 15.35
Rectangle section
properties calculation
dialog box

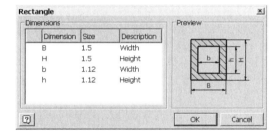

Flip Section is used to change the orientation of the x- and y-axes. The z-axis is always in the direction of the extrusion. Gravity is always in the negative y-axis direction, so it is important to make sure the calculation coordinates match the assembly coordinates. If the beam is at an angle, you have a couple of options for handling gravity. You can place a copy of the beam horizontally in the assembly. If you want to ignore the effect of gravity, there is an option on the Beam Calculation tab to turn the gravity load off.

Both beam and column calculations are available. The beam calculations focus on deflection based on loads and supports. The Column calculation checks for buckling. You can select Beam, Column, or both calculation types. The Calculation tabs are turned on and off based on the selections.

The default material properties do not correspond to an actual material. They give you an example of the required properties. You can enter properties for a particular material, or you can select a generic material. When you check the box, a dialog box displays with materials such as gray cast iron, steel, and aluminum. These properties can be used for initial calculations, but for more accurate results, you should enter the properties for the particular alloy you are using.

This section uses the power roller supports on the conveyor as the example. If you haven't saved your work, you can use the `Conveyor with Members.iam` file. The supports need the end treatments described in the previous section, or you can override the member length.

Follow these steps to enter the member data into the dialog box:

1. Select one of the lower supports for the power roller.

2. If necessary, click the padlock (unlocking it) for Section Length, and change the value to 12 inches.

3. Click Section, and select Rectangle.

4. Enter the tubing dimensions (1.5 inch outside and 1.12 inside), and click OK.

5. Select both the Beam and Column calculations in the Calculation Type group.

6. Click in the material field to launch the material dialog box. Select Steel, and choose OK.

The coordinate system alignment is correct for this example. In this case, gravity could be ignored, but having the correct orientation simplifies adding the loads and interpreting the results.

The dialog box should look like Figure 15.36. Note that all the section properties except Shear Displacement Ratio are calculated. This property is optional for the calculations. Comparing the calculated values with the original ones, the Section Area and Moments of Inertia are close but higher.

FIGURE 15.36
Model data entered into the Beam And Column Calculator

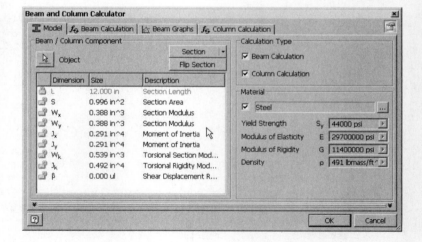

Beam Calculation Tab

The Beam Calculation tab, shown in Figure 15.37, has the controls for defining the loads and supports for beams and columns, as well as calculation options. The Engineer's Handbook (available from the Design Accelerator panel bar or the Help system) contains the equations used in the calculations. You should review those equations before you use this calculator.

FIGURE 15.37
The Beam Calculation tab

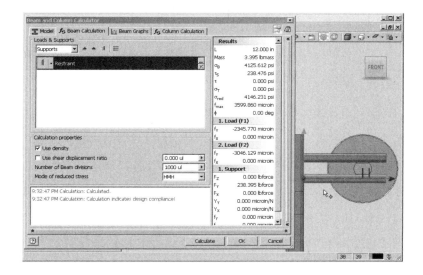

LOADS & SUPPORTS GROUP

The Loads & Supports group contains a browser and controls for adding and removing loads and supports for the frame member. All the controls are available from the tool strip at the top of the group or from the context menu in the browser.

The pulldown menu switches the browser between loads and supports views. The controls, as shown in Tables 15.2 and 15.3, change with the current browser view.

TABLE 15.2:   Loads Buttons

BUTTON	DESCRIPTION
↓	Adds a force.
→	Adds an axial force.
⊞	Adds a distributed force.
↱	Adds a bending moment — a single twisting force perpendicular to the z-axis.
↻	Adds a torque load — a twisting force around the z-axis. Two equal and opposite torque loads are required.
XYZ	Adds a combined load — any of the forces added at the same point on the beam.
☰	Displays the Options dialog box.

TABLE 15.3:   Supports Buttons

BUTTON	DESCRIPTION
⛰	Adds a fixed support.
▲	Adds a free support.
⏚	Fixes one end of the beam.
≔	Displays the Options dialog box.

The Options dialog box shown in Figure 15.38 gives access to visibility controls for the 2D and 3D previews. By default, the size of the loads and supports dynamically update to maintain the same size as the view scale changes. You can turn off the automatic update and set a static scale value. The Options dialog box is the same whether it is launched from the loads or supports controls.

FIGURE 15.38
Loads & Supports
Options dialog box

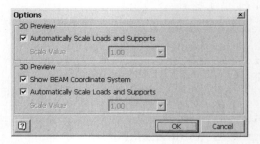

Each load or support can be edited in the browser by double-clicking or by clicking the ... button. A properties dialog box displays that has controls for specifying the location, size, and direction of the force.

THE CALCULATION PROPERTIES GROUP

The Calculation Properties group, as shown in Figure 15.39, has four controls. The controls adjust how the calculations are made.

FIGURE 15.39
The Calculation
Properties group

The Use Density check box adds gravity as a load. This is selected by default.

The Shear Displacement Ratio check box is used when calculating the twist angle caused by torsional loads. The value is determined by the profile shape. It is also called the *form factor of shear*. Textbooks contain formulas for calculating this number. This is selected by default.

The default setting for Number Of Beam Divisions is 1000. Increasing the number of divisions can result in improved accuracy for longer beams. You should experiment with different values to see whether the number of divisions causes a significant change in the results.

Mode of Reduced Stress has two options for modeling the stress distribution. The Huber-Mises-Hencky (HMH) method is based on the maximum-energy-distortion criterion, and the Tresca-Guest method is based on the maximum-shearing-stress criterion. The HMH method is the default selection.

RESULTS

The result pane on the right side updates when you click the Calculate button. Warnings will display in the lower plane if the calculation indicates that stresses are too high.

For the conveyor example, the support is welded to the frame at one end and unsupported at the other. The power roller weighs 150 pounds, and the torque is 40 pounds per feet. The torque causes the power roller to twist between the supports. The edge of the flat is 1.5 inches from the center of the power roller. This means the reaction force at that point is 320 pounds. Both the weight and the reaction force are split between the two sides.

1. For the power roller weight, add a 75-pound radial force at 10 inches (the maximum distance for the power roller).

2. For the torque reaction, add a 160-pound radial force at 11.12 inches.

3. Switch to the Supports browser.

4. Delete the Free support.

5. Click the pulldown arrow for the Fixed support, and select Restraint.

6. Leave Use Density checked.

7. Deselect Use Shear Displacement Ratio since you don't have a value for that property.

8. Click Calculate; the reduced stress is 4126 psi, which is 9.4 percent of the 44000 psi yield stress.

The dialog box should look like Figure 15.40. Note that the forces are displayed in the graphics window. If you hover over a force, a tool tip displays the information. You can drag the force to a different position, or you can double-click the force to display the properties dialog box.

Beam Graphs

The Graph Selection pane allows you to select the results you want to display. The selected graph displays in the bottom of the Graph group. At the top of the Graph group is a schematic of the beam, supports, and loads. You can drag the supports and loads to different positions. If you double-click a support or load, the properties dialog box displays so you can directly edit the data. The Calculate button is not available on the Beam Graphs tab, so you have to switch back to the Beam Calculation tab to update the results.

The Beam Graphs tab is primarily intended for reviewing results. Twenty-two graphs are available on the tab. This example is a pretty simple analysis. You should experiment with other loads (torques and bending moments) and support types and then view the results on the graphs.

FIGURE 15.40
Loads & Supports
data entered into the
calculator

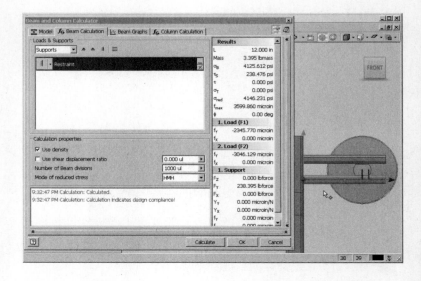

Column Calculator

The Column Calculator tab checks for column buckling. In the Loads group, you enter the axial load and the factor of safety, and you select a coefficient for the end loading conditions. When you click the . . . button, a dialog box displays with four end conditions. If you have different end conditions, you should enter the proper coefficient from a reference book.

You shouldn't have to enter any data in the Column group. The length, section area, and least moment of inertia are carried over from the Model tab. The reduced length value is calculated by multiplying the length by the end coefficient.

For example, let's say that during transport, the frame shifts and the power roller supports slam into the trailer wall. The power roller was removed during shipping, so the supports take all the force from the impact, estimated at 4,000 pounds evenly distributed across the four supports. Set the axial load to 1,000-pound force, and click Calculate to determine whether the supports will buckle. Figure 15.41 shows the results.

HTML Results

When you click the Results button in the upper-right corner of the dialog box, an HTML page displays with all the data, calculation results, and graphs.

Publishing Frame Members

In Inventor 2009, Frame Generator is integrated with the Content Center. The authoring and publishing process is similar to that used for other applications. Since Frame Generator requires specific modeling techniques, the authoring process will make some changes to the model and the parameters.

Authoring a Part

The authoring process for a frame member is similar to component authoring. The Structural Shape Authoring tool, located on the part-modeling panel bar, is used to prepare the part for publishing. The tool identifies the geometry used for placement, sets the parameters, and modifies the part so Frame Generator can use it.

FIGURE 15.41
Column calculator results

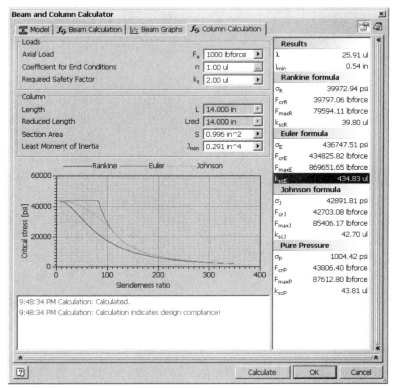

CREATING A RUBBER BUMPER

This example uses the Rubber Bumper.ipt file. This iPart is a rubber bumper that is attached to frames. There are parameters to control the dimensions, but the engineering properties (moments of inertia, and so on) were never calculated. Since this isn't a load-bearing part, these properties aren't required.

When the Structural Shape Authoring tool starts, everything is blank. Once a category is selected, the dialog box will update with the appropriate controls. Since this is an unusual part, select the Other category, as shown in Figure 15.42. Frame Generator looks in the Structural Shapes category only, so you have to select one of the standard categories or create a new one in the Content Center editor. The authoring tool displays current Content Center categories only, so you have to add the category to the Content Center before authoring.

FIGURE 15.42
Selecting the category

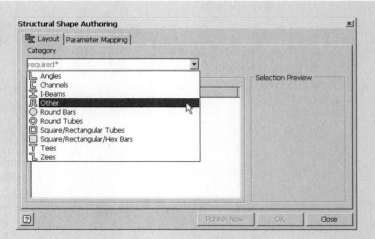

Since there is only one extrusion in the part, the base feature is automatically selected. The default base point is indicated at the center of the profile. For this part, the inside corner of the flanges is the natural insertion point. Click Select Geometry, and select that point in the model, as shown in Figure 15.43.

FIGURE 15.43
Selecting the Default
Base Point

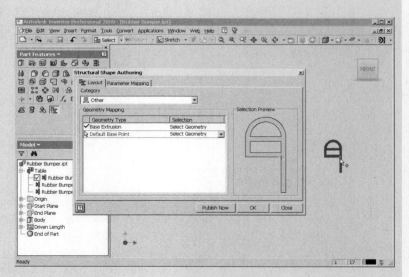

The Parameter Mapping tab has one required field: Base Length. This is the parameter for the extrusion distance. Since this is an iPart, when you click in the field, the iPart properties are listed as shown in Figure 15.44. If this were a regular part, a Part Template Parameters dialog box, as shown in Figure 15.45, would display a browser tree. The rest of the parameters are optional. They are mechanical properties of the profile necessary for calculating loads with the Beam and Column Calculator.

FIGURE 15.44
Specifying the length parameter for an iPart

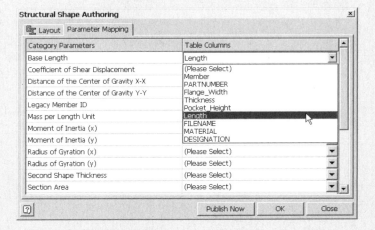

FIGURE 15.45
Specifying parameters for a regular part

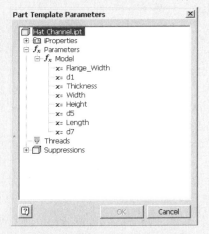

When the geometry and Base Length parameter are mapped, the Publish Now and OK buttons are enabled. Clicking either button will update the part and close the dialog box. Publish Now will also launch the Content Center publishing wizard. When the part is updated, a dialog box displays with information about the changes. A log file, as shown in Figure 15.46, is created in the project directory that lists the changes to the part.

If you inspect the part after authoring, you will see that the browser and parameters have been updated. The details of the model and parameters are discussed in the section "Exploring the Anatomy of a Frame Member."

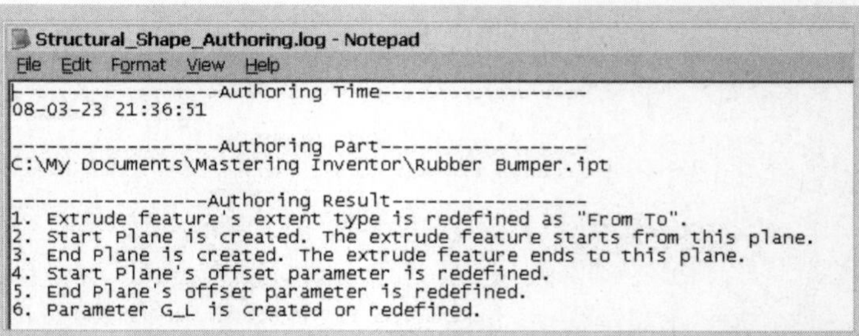

FIGURE 15.46
Log file for an authored
part

```
 Structural_Shape_Authoring.log - Notepad
 File  Edit  Format  View  Help
------------------Authoring Time------------------
08-03-23 21:36:51

------------------Authoring Part------------------
C:\My Documents\Mastering Inventor\Rubber Bumper.ipt

------------------Authoring Result------------------
1. Extrude feature's extent type is redefined as "From To".
2. Start Plane is created. The extrude feature starts from this plane.
3. End Plane is created. The extrude feature ends to this plane.
4. Start Plane's offset parameter is redefined.
5. End Plane's offset parameter is redefined.
6. Parameter G_L is created or redefined.
```

SEAN SAYS: TEST BEFORE YOU PUBLISH

Before you publish the member for use by all your team members, be sure to test it in every conceivable situation. Even a seemingly well-constructed frame member can cause issues after applying end treatments. You'll save yourself a lot of headaches if you test the member before it's released into the wild.

Publishing a Part

The publishing process uses the Publish Guide wizard. Since the part was authored, most of the publishing information has already been added to the file. If you aren't familiar with publishing to the Content Center, you should spend some time learning how to work with libraries before you publish a part.

These publishing steps are important for Frame Generator:

◆ When you define the family key columns, the length parameter must be set as a key column.

◆ In the Family Properties pane, the standard organization is used to categorize the member during insertion. If you leave this field blank, the category selection will be Unknown.

◆ In the thumbnail image pane, a special thumbnail is displayed. Since the thumbnail is used as the orientation image in the dialog boxes, it is important to use the thumbnail Frame Generator creates.

The Bottom Line

Work with frame files   Frame Generator puts all the members at the same level in the assembly.

   Master It   You have a frame that is built up in sections that are welded together. You need to document the manufacturing process.

Insert frame members onto a skeleton model   Frame Generator builds a skeleton model for the frame from the selected lines and edges.

Master It   Since Frame Generator builds its own skeleton model, you don't have to build a master model before you start creating the frame. You can use sketches, surfaces, and model edges to insert frame members.

Add end treatments to frame members   Frame Generator does not support end treatments on merged members.

Master It   Let's assume you are building a stairway and the handrail has curved sections.

Make changes to frames   An existing frame needs to be modified to strengthen it.

Master It   You need to determine the size and wall thickness of the tubing and make it either thicker or larger.

Author and publish structural profiles   Your company uses custom aluminum extrusions in its frames.

Master It   You need to add the profiles to the Content Center so Frame Generator can access them.

Chapter 16

Inventor Studio

The means to communicate your design, to sell your concept or product, is valuable whether your customer is internal or external to your company. Visualization, through static imagery or animation, has the potential to improve that communication by providing your customers with a conceptual or practical demonstration of your design. Inventor Studio, a rendering and animation environment, is a visualization tool built into Inventor assembly and part environments.

With Inventor Studio, you can create and apply surface styles that enhance the realism of your components and create lighting styles that draw attention to specific aspects of your design. Inventor Studio comes with many surface styles and a modest set of lighting and scene styles to use. You can modify the delivered styles or make as many new ones as you need. The goal is to make your image as true to your concept as you want.

Inventor Studio uses assembly constraints and positional representations for animation purposes. You can animate a single part or an assembly.

This chapter will discuss how to use Inventor Studio to create the images and animations that communicate your design to its targeted audience.

In this chapter, you will learn how to:

- ◆ Create and manage surface, lighting, and scene styles

- ◆ Create and animate cameras

- ◆ Start new animations, modify animations, and use the various animation tools

- ◆ Use multiple cameras to create a video production of your animation

- ◆ Use props to enhance your scene

- ◆ Render realistic and illustrative images

- ◆ Render animations and video productions

Exploring the Inventor Studio Environment

The Studio environment contains the tools required for creating realistic imagery and animations of mechanistic movement. This section will discuss the various tools, environment settings, and browser in the Studio environment.

One item of importance before entering Inventor Studio is that you may want to consider what you will be using as resources (diffuse maps, bump maps, decals, and so on) for your images. Inventor comes with a collection of diffuse and bump maps, but if you have any images for textures or bump maps, you will want to include the directories where these reside in your project file. Doing so ensures those resources will be available when you work in Inventor Studio. Then, plan ahead by storyboarding your animation; giving thought to camera positions and settings, lighting, and animation.

The Studio tool panel is divided into three sections: image-related tasks, animation-related tasks, and parameter access.

The Studio Scene browser is a custom browser that contains folder nodes specific to Inventor Studio. Right-clicking a folder node, you are able to create one or more productions, animations, cameras, and local lights within the same document. The instances are maintained in the corresponding folder. The Lighting folder is the active lighting style and its lights. The Local Light folder is for lights not associated with the lighting style; most often this contains your animated lights.

The Animation Favorites folder contains instances of the constraints that have been animated and the parameters that have been nominated for use in the animation.

To enter the Studio environment from either a part file or an assembly file, select the Applications menu and click Inventor Studio. Figure 16.1 shows the browser.

FIGURE 16.1
Inventor Studio browser

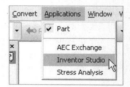

Creating and Managing Studio Styles

Three types of styles are used in Studio: surface, lighting, and scene styles. Each has a different purpose and contributes to the final image you produce. In the style dialog boxes, covered in the following sections, you'll see a set of four common tools and, where applicable, a set of tools for the particular style's dialog box.

Figure 16.2 shows the common tools. From left to right, they are as follows:

◆ Clicking New Style creates a new local style based on the Inventor defaults. Local styles are available in the current document but are not available globally to all documents.

◆ Clicking Purge Style removes the selected local style from the list.

◆ Clicking Update Style updates the selected style from the style library.

◆ Clicking Save To Style Library saves the selected local style to the style library. The style becomes global, available to all components, when saved to the style library.

FIGURE 16.2
Common style tools

Keep in mind that style modifications are applied to the selected style. A style does not have to be active or in use to be modified. We'll cover surface styles first by looking at the Surface Styles dialog box. Then we'll look at the Lighting Styles and Scene Styles dialog boxes.

Surface Styles Dialog Box

Surface styles are the means by which you create color and texture for your components. Many surface styles are combined in collections called *categories*, which are containers for styles. The Surface Styles dialog box has a variety of controls to assign color, reflection, opacity, and diffuse and bump maps, as shown in Figure 16.3.

FIGURE 16.3
Surface Styles dialog box

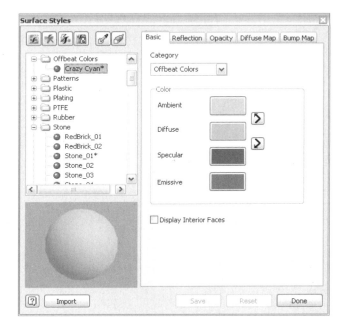

The Surface Styles dialog box consists of the following tabs and sections:

◆ The tool section at the top left of the dialog box is divided into two areas, one for creating and editing the surface style and the other for dealing with the component or face.

 ◆ The group of four icons to the left provides tools for creating, purging, updating the style from the library, and saving a style to the library.

 ◆ The group of two commands are the Get Surface Style command, which is used to interrogate faces for their surface style, and the Assign Surface Style command (aka the paintbrush), which assigns the current style to a component or face.

◆ The surface style list of categories, their styles, and the general styles.

◆ The preview pane that displays the selected surface style, including diffuse and bump maps.

The rest of the controls are on the tabbed sections.

To better show how these controls work, we will walk you through the process of taking an existing surface style, creating a new one based on it, altering its appearance, and placing it in a category.

Here are the steps:

1. Click the Surface Styles icon in the tool panel. To quickly locate the Surface Styles command, right-click in the tool panel and click Display Text with Icons, then click the Surface Styles command.

2. From the general list of colors, select Blue (Sky).

3. To create a new surface style from an existing style, right-click and then select Copy Surface Style. This creates a local copy of the surface style and presents a dialog box so you can name the new style.

4. Specify a new name by typing **Blue Sky (Gloss)**.

5. Next, on the Basic tab, assign a category for the new surface style. In the Category pulldown, enter **Paint**. In this one step, you've created a new category and assigned the surface style to it.

6. Set the colors accordingly (these values are RGB):

   a. Ambient: 0, 20, 129
   b. Diffuse: 0, 20, 129
      Note: If you set Diffuse first, you can click the Copy To button to make Ambient the same value.
   c. Specular: 255, 255, 128
   d. Emissive: 0, 47, 0

7. On the Reflection tab, set Shininess to 61.

8. Click Save to retain this local style.

All three style types, surface, lighting, and scene, have corresponding new and copy commands.

CREATING A SURFACE STYLE

You can produce a new surface style in two ways, in the context menu:

Clicking New Surface Style starts a new style from a default set of values. The style is named Default.

Clicking Copy Surface Style makes a copy of the selected style and names it Copy of [selected style]. The name is presented in a naming dialog box so you can provide the desired name. You cannot have two styles with the same name. When the displayed value is red, the value is invalid and must be changed before continuing.

BASIC TAB

On the Basic tab of the Surface Styles dialog box, you specify the color parameters, the categories, and the display of interior faces.

Categories

As you just experienced, categories either exist or are created at the same time as surface styles. To populate a new category, simply assign a surface style to that named category. In a like manner, by reassigning or deleting all surface styles in a category, you delete the category.

If you create a new surface style that is designed to give a metal appearance, for example, you can set the category for the style to Metals, and the surface style appears in and is accessed through that category folder.

Categories provide a useful means of organizing your surface styles for easy access. To add a new category, simply type the category name and press the Enter key. The current surface style is assigned to that category, and the category is added to the list in the Surface Styles dialog box.

To remove a surface style from a category, empty it of all surface styles and it will be removed.

Colors

Ambient color is the color the component reflects in areas covered by shadow. You can make interesting colors by altering this setting.

You can set the ambient color to match the diffuse color using the button between the two inputs.

Diffuse color is the color the object reflects in direct daylight or artificial lighting. When referring to an object's color, diffuse color is what is meant.

Specular color is the color of the reflections in the object. You can set the specular color to match the diffuse color using the button between the two inputs. Matching the specular color to the diffuse color will reduce the shininess of the object. Specular color changes can provide interesting variations. After you create a diffuse color, experiment with it, adding small amounts of another color using the Specular setting. To clearly see the difference, you should render the scene.

Emissive color is the color given off by an object as if it contained a light source that is projecting light through the color. This color does not interact with lighting styles.

Display Interior Faces

As you define transparent surface styles, determine whether the interior faces will be seen. Consider the simple drinking glasses shown in Figure 16.4; their faces are transparent, so the interior faces are seen. To display interior faces, check the Display Interior Faces option on the Basic tab.

FIGURE 16.4
Displaying interior faces

REFLECTION TAB

The Reflection tab is where you define the style reflectivity or shininess. For objects that have a matte finish or low reflectivity, you'll use numbers less than 50. The lower the number, the more dispersed the lighting is across the surface. If you are looking to make a shiny style such as paint, chrome, and so on, then you will use a setting greater than 50.

To give you an idea of where to set the value, Studio's Chrome styles use a Shininess setting of 88.

For any surface style, you can define a reflection map. Inventor surface styles use the default map that is installed with Inventor. However, if you want the surface style to use a specific reflection map, you must specify the map for that style.

To globally change the reflection map, you can replace the delivered image with one of your choice. If you're overwriting the existing map, you must use the same name as the delivered map, `Car3.bmp`.

Inventor specifies a default reflection map and keeps that map in the Textures directory. For a standard XP install, this is `C:\Program Files\Autodesk\Inventor 2009\Textures`. If you've installed on Windows Vista, the location will differ because of the permission requirements of Windows Vista.

OPACITY TAB

The Opacity tab has two controls, Opacity and Refraction.

Opacity

Opacity defines how impenetrable the surface style is for lighting. An easy way to think of it is as the opposite of transparent. The control reflects that notion as well; 100 percent opaque means light will not shine through an object. As you can see in Figure 16.5, the block's opacity setting is increased from one block to the next, starting on the left: 30 percent, 60 percent, and 100 percent. The amount of light that passes through the object decreases, and the shadow darkness increases as less light makes it through the object.

FIGURE 16.5
Opacity comparison

Refraction

Refraction settings manage the degree to which the light direction is changed when passing through the object. This implies surface style transparency or low opacity. There are preset refractive index values to get you close to where you want to be when using this option. In the dialog box, click the Refraction presets button above the refraction value to display the list.

The name of common items that have that index of refraction helps you relate to the value and quickly choose one that is closest to what you need. You are able to provide your own value up to an index of 3.0.

DIFFUSE MAP TAB

A diffuse map gives the appearance of surface texture without bumpiness. You might liken it to a bowling ball that has multiple colors in patterns around it. The surface is smooth but has an interesting surface appearance.

When specifying a diffuse map, the directory where the map resides should be included in the project file libraries or frequently used folders. If not, you will get a warning message.

You are able to scale the image from 1 percent to 1000 percent. If that amount of scaling is insufficient for your map, you will have to do some extra work in an image editor to change the pixels-per-inch/mm ratio. To increase the relative size of the image — for example, if you are working on a building or ship — lower the pixels-per-inch ratio. To map the image to a very small object, you need to increase the pixels-per-inch ratio.

Let's say you have an image that is 120 pixels per inch and you want to cover a large object with that image. Then you would do the following:

1. Make a copy of the image.

2. Edit the image by changing the pixels per inch (ppi) to 30 ppi, and create another copy at 12 ppi. The net effect is that the 30 ppi image will be 4 times as large on the model, as shown in Figure 16.6, and the 12 ppi will be 10 times larger.

FIGURE 16.6
Increasing the size of a
diffuse map

By using this method, you can enlarge diffuse images. At some point, though, the image will not have enough resolution and can begin to look stretched or out of focus. You may have to create or resample an image to use in such a case.

BUMP MAP TAB

Now that you have a diffuse map, you will want to use a bump map to provide the notion of a textured surface. Inventor Studio has bump maps that match some of the diffuse maps. Figure 16.7 shows the dramatic difference a bump map makes, where the only difference is that the part on the right has a bump map.

FIGURE 16.7
Comparison without and
with bump map

To use a bump map, click the Bump Map tab, and select the Use Bump Image check box. If you want the bump map pattern to match the diffuse map, you can check the Same As Texture option. However, that option may not provide optimal results because displacement is based on the color's lightness (or whiteness, to be more exact). As Figure 16.7 shows, white areas are raised. You can reverse the effect by checking the Invert option just below the percentage of bump to apply, as shown in Figure 16.8.

FIGURE 16.8
Inverting the white areas

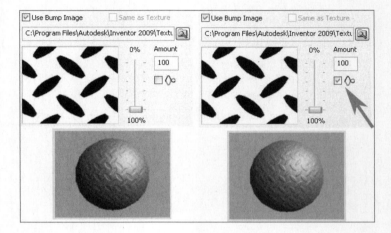

The bump map colors do not affect the diffuse map color, but using a colored bump map does affect the degree of bump you can apply. The more black and white you can define the map, the greater your control over the overall appearance. Therefore, the amount of contrast between the bump map colors plays a part. In Figure 16.9, the middle component is what the component looks like without a bump map. The left component uses a black and white map, which yields the greatest bump contrast. The right component uses a similar but gray and white map. The bump contrast is less visible.

FIGURE 16.9
Map contrast

The control beneath the percentage input field inverts the bump effect. This control is very useful when you specify that the bump map is the same as the diffuse map.

Getting and Assigning Surface Styles

As mentioned earlier in the chapter, the Surface Styles dialog box contains the tools Get Surface Style and Assign Surface Style. After selecting the part or face, use Get Surface Style to find out what style is assigned. The dialog box displays the surface style for editing. Use the Assign Surface Style tool to apply the selected style to the selected face or component.

If you are working on applying surface styles to specific faces or features, you must be working in the part document. To assign a style to an assembly, sublevel or top-level, you must be working in the assembly document.

Creating a Surface Style

We've discussed surface styles; now we'll take a minute to show you how to create one for your use. The style will be brushed stainless steel because this isn't quite the same as the one provided. Let's get started:

1. Activate the Surface Style command. The Surface Styles dialog box appears.

2. In the Metal category, right-click Metal-Steel (Stainless, Brushed) and then select Copy Surface Style.

3. Give the style a new name by typing **Stainless Steel – Brushed**.

4. On the Reflection tab, set Shininess to 15.

5. On the Diffuse Map tab, click the Browse button, and select `Metal_15.bmp`.

6. On the Bump Map tab, clear the Use Bump Image check box. Since this is a finished surface treatment, there should be very little, if any, bump visible.

7. Click Save.

8. If you have an assembly open, click a component to which you want to assign the style. Click the Assign Surface Style tool in the dialog box to assign the style to the component.

There you have it — a new surface style for brushed stainless steel. If you want, continue modifying settings until you get the appearance you want.

Lighting Styles Dialog Box

Several lighting styles are provided with Inventor, and you can use these as is or modify them to meet your needs. You can also create new lighting styles to suit your needs. Lighting styles differ from surface and scene styles. Lighting styles have settings that affect all lights in the style and individual lights have settings for only the selected light. Thus, you will find on some of the light-related tabs the option to have those parameters observe the style settings instead of being individually controlled.

In the Studio tool panel, next to the Surface Styles command is the Lighting Styles command. Click to activate the command and display the Lighting Styles dialog box. The New Light command is next to the common commands. This command adds a new light to the selected lighting style. The new light dialog box displays and you specify the settings.

Next you'll explore the light styles and what they control.

LIGHTING STYLE

In this section, we'll discuss the Lighting style settings. The settings affect all lights in the style. In the Lighting Styles dialog box, a list of lighting styles is presented on the left. Each style has a set of controls; these are:

◆ Brightness

◆ Skylight

◆ Ambience

◆ Bounced Light

◆ Shadows

◆ Orientation

◆ Scale

◆ Position

Note that the active style, currently displayed in the scene and used for rendering, is listed with bold letters, and the selected style, the one whose settings are exposed for editing, has background fill, as shown in Figure 16.10. You can double click a style in the list to edit it. The style does not have to be the active one.

FIGURE 16.10
Active and selected styles

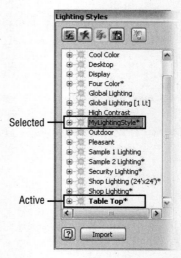

Besides the common style commands, you'll also see a New Light command in the tools area of the Lighting Styles dialog box. This adds a new light to the lighting style you have selected in the list. The new light then is made the active edit target so you can complete the definition.

General Tab

Brightness controls the overall style brightness. This tool affects all lights in the style.

Skylight is the tool that provides uniform, directionless illumination in the scene. When enabled, you are able to specify light intensity and color, or you can use an image for lighting the scene. The image supplies colors for the lighting but should not be confused with high dynamic range image (HDRI) illumination.

Using the Skylight and Bounced Light commands is computationally intensive, and therefore they should be used sparingly, usually for final renders only.

Indirect Tab

The Ambience setting controls the amount of ambient light used in the scene. Setting the value higher increases the amount of light in the scene, so if you have a scene that is lit but is too dark and needs a minor adjustment to get more light, try increasing ambience.

The Bounced Light setting is a component of global lighting and is included when the Skylight option is checked. However, you can use Bounced Light without the Skylight option. Bounced Light provides the lighting that comes from objects as light encounters them and then reflects off the surfaces. With Bounced Light, you have the option of using preset values for the number of rays that are sampled for bounced lighting. There is also a custom setting should you decide you need a value other than those provided.

Shadows Tab

The Shadows tab provides access to the following:

- ◆ Type: You can specify None, Sharp, and Soft.

- ◆ Quality: You can specify Low, Medium, and High.

- ◆ Density: You can specify 0 to 100 percent.

- ◆ Light Parameter: Here you specify the spherical diameter for a soft shadow effect.

If the light casts no shadow, then the type should be set to None, and all other controls on the page are disabled and not used.

Sharp shadows provide a well-defined shadow, where the boundaries of an object define a sharp contrast between shadow and nonshadow areas.

Soft shadows blur the area between shadow and nonshadow areas. The Light Parameter setting, available only for soft shadows, defines the spherical diameter of influence for soft shadows.

Figure 16.11 shows a comparison of the three shadow types: None, Sharp, and Soft shadows.

FIGURE 16.11
Shadow types: None,
Sharp, and Soft

Note that the Light Parameter setting controls the *penumbra* (dispersing shadow around the darkest part of the shadow) and that it is a diameter dimension.

Shadow density provides an additional level of control because you can set the density on a per-light basis. As Figure 16.12 shows, the shadow density increases with the value of the parameter.

FIGURE 16.12
Shadow density at 15 percent, 45 percent, and 75 percent

It is easy to see how working with these settings you can greatly affect the results of your rendered image or animation.

As mentioned earlier, the Light Parameter setting is a spherical diameter value that controls the influence of soft shadows. If you want soft shadows around the whole scene, then the sphere must be set to be somewhat larger than the scene. If the influence is to be limited, you can use a lower setting. A good rule of thumb is to estimate the extents of your assembly and add 10-15 percent for a reasonable penumbra.

Position Tab

The Position tab gives you access to the orientation, scale, and location of the lighting style.

Orientation is derived from one of the following:

◆ Canonical origin planes: XY Plane, XZ Plane, YZ Plane.

◆ Scene style ground planes: Available in the pulldown list.

◆ Any model face or work plane: Use the select button.

If you want reverse the lighting style orientation, can use the Flip command next to the pull-down list and invert the direction of the lighting style.

Scale affects all lights in the style. This allows you to quickly modify your lighting style to fit the model conditions. You can specify any scale factor from 1 percent to 1000 percent.

Lighting style position is expressed in model units and is based on the center of the top-level assembly. If you want to relocate the entire style, position settings allow you to easily reposition the lighting style.

Adding a New Light

To add a new light to an existing style, use the New Light command in the dialog box or context menu in the light style list. Then follow these steps to produce a new light:

1. Specify a face to act as the light target and normal. The face selection determines the light target location and beam direction.

2. After selecting a face, you'll see a straight line proceeding from the target or face; drag your cursor along that line to define the light position.

3. In the dialog box, modify the light parameters to fit your needs.

If you adjust the settings before defining the position, return to the General Tab and select the Target or Position command to begin specifying the light position interactively.

Creating a New Lighting Style

You can create new lighting styles in three ways:

◆ Use the New Lighting Style command, which is also available from the list context menu. The new lighting style contains one each of the three light types with default values.

◆ Copy an existing lighting style. Then edit it to suit your needs.

◆ Import a lighting style from a file.

When you create a new lighting style, you are provided with each of the three types of discrete lights. You can change the light types, add more lights, and modify parameters to achieve the lighting effect you want.

If you copy an existing lighting style, you are able to rename it, modify the parameters, add new lights, or change the light types for the existing lights.

If you have an exported lighting style that you want to import and use, you would use the Import command, which is the button at the bottom of the dialog box; navigate to the appropriate file; and then import it. Be advised, though, that if you import a lighting style with the same name as an existing lighting style, the imported style will overwrite the current same-named style.

DISCRETE LIGHTS

Within each lighting style are discrete lights. These lights can be one of three types: directional, point, or spotlight. Certain controls for the discrete light types differ from the style controls, but shadow parameters can be linked to the style and managed globally for the style from there.

Discrete lights, though three different types, all have but one set of parameters. Based on the light type, access to invalid parameters is blocked. This provides a distinct ease-of-use feature, switching between light types without having to delete and re-create new ones. You can experiment with different light types quickly and determine which is best for your circumstances.

Figure 16.13 demonstrates the difference between a spotlight (left) and a point light (right). The light type is the only difference. The spotlight was set up for the scene, rendered, and then changed to a point light; then no other changes were made, and it was rerendered.

FIGURE 16.13
Spotlight and point light compared

As you can see, the difference can be dramatic. The point light sends light in every direction, whereas the spotlight can be pointed and focused on an area of interest. As you work with lights, experiment so that you learn their characteristics and are able to easily add the type of light you want to a scene.

General Tab

On the General tab, you're able to do the following:

◆ Define the light type; you can choose Directional, Point, or Spot.

◆ Set the on/off condition. This condition can be animated.

◆ Redefine the position and, for the Directional and Spot types, the target.

◆ Flip the light, reversing the target and position locations.

You can copy and paste lights, so once you've set one up, you can quickly duplicate it. You cannot create arrays of lights.

Illumination Tab

The Illumination tab contains controls for light color and intensity. Intensity is a percentage value from 0 to 100 percent.

Light color, as most people realize, helps inject emotion into a scene. Warm colors (yellows, oranges, reds, and so on) evoke a different response than do cool colors (blues, greens, and so on). Let's say you want light in the scene, but would like to give the impression it is turned off at a certain point. However, you want enough light to see the scene clearly. How can you achieve this? Instead of actually turning the light off, you could change the color and intensity of the light from yellow at 80 percent to light blue at 30 percent, giving the impression the light is off while still illuminating the scene.

Shadow Tab

The Shadow tab duplicates the style Shadows tab. Thus, the shadows of any discrete light can be linked to the style shadows and derived from there. If you choose to have the selected light use different settings, remove the check from the Use Style Settings checkbox. Then, specify the settings for the selected light.

Directional Tab

Directional lights provide parallel beams of light from a single direction. The light source is considered as being an infinite distance away. Thus, you could use directional light to simulate sunshine. To add to that metaphor, the positional information for a directional light is defined by longitude and latitude values.

The latitude and longitude controls easily relate to seasonal positioning for lighting. You need to be familiar with where the seasonal lighting is for your geography.

Directional lights do not participate in soft shadow lighting. The control is disabled for any directional light.

Point Tab

Point lights cast light in all direction and therefore have only position parameters for locating the light. The light target is ignored and for all intents and purposes is considered as traveling with the light position. Position values are listed in absolute X, Y, Z values based on the top-level assembly origin.

The light decay controls apply to point lights and spotlights only. These controls have an impact on how real the lighting looks. There are three decay types:

◆ None: This specifies that light energy will not decay over distance. If you want indirect light to remain constant throughout the scene, regardless of the distance between objects, use this setting.

◆ Inverse: Light energy decays at a rate proportional to the distance traveled. Photon energy is $1/r$, where "r" is the distance from the light source.

◆ Inverse Squared: Light energy decays at an inverse square rate. Photon energy is the inverse of the square of the distance from the light source, that is, $1/r^2$.

In the real world, light decays at an inverse square rate. However, for lighting to be realistic, the light values must also be real-world accurate. You'll find that it takes more lights to amply light a scene when you use Inverse Squared for decay.

The rendering cost, in time, increases as you move from no decay to Inverse and again from Inverse to Inverse Squared. For most renders, you can use None or Inverse and have good results based on how you set up your lighting style. When using light decay, you are able to specify the distance from the light source when the decay begins to occur. The greater the decay start distance, the brighter the light will appear to be. This means that if you have a lighting style you prefer but want to make it less bright in some areas, you can change specific lights to use Inverse decay and have a considerable effect on the output. Light decay is a setting that takes experimentation to get a feel for when and how to use it.

Spot Tab

Spotlights provide light in a more focused manner, at a specific location. For spotlights, there are more controls for adjusting the light parameters. You can do the following:

◆ Explicitly position the light target or light source

◆ Specify the light hotspot and falloff

◆ Specify the light decay type and start distance

As discussed thus far, you can modify lighting styles giving explicit values for input. You can also interactively modify lighting styles. For example, you can edit position, target, hotspot, and falloff interactively.

To interactively modify any of these settings, you must first edit the light you intend to change. Place your cursor over the light graphic, the light node in the scene browser, and right-click; then select Edit from the context menu. At this point, place your cursor over the graphical representation of the element you want to edit, and do one of the following:

◆ Click the light source to display the 3D Move/Rotate command for modifying the position or target.

◆ Click and drag the graphic representing the hotspot or falloff to change its size.

◆ Click the line representing the light beam; it connects the position graphic to the target graphic. The 3D Move/Rotate triad is placed over the center of the line, enabling a reposition of the entire light. Click and drag the arrow to move the light in that direction.

LOCAL LIGHTS

Local lights are discrete lights that belong to the scene but not the lighting style. They are useful for control panel lights, and so on, that you may want to animate individually. Thus, local lights come only in the Spot or Point light type. Local lights travel with components, so if you create a lightbulb component, you can specify a local light for use with the bulb object. The advantage is when you animate a component with a local light, the light travels with the component.

Local lights use the same controls as discrete style lights. In fact, you can easily create a local light by right-clicking any style-based discrete light and selecting the command in the context menu.

Local light settings and position can only be animated when the light is at the top level of the assembly or part model.

Scene Styles Dialog Box

Scene styles provide a backdrop for your scene. You can use a single solid color, a gradient color, an image, or a spherical image. What you use depends on how you want to compose your scene.

Scene styles provide a built-in ground plane that eliminates the need for you to add geometry in the model to provide the illusion of ground or a surface on which your assembly is sitting. However, if you have specific needs or use props that replace the ground plane, then it is not necessary to show shadows or reflection. The Scene Styles command is located in the tool panel next to the Lighting Styles command.

BACKGROUND TAB

The Background tab provides access to the various controls for specifying the type of background and location of images to use. You can forego specifying any of this information by selecting the Use Application Options check box. The current Inventor background will be used. There are four background types from which to choose, covered next.

Solid Color

If you want a single solid color background, click the Solid Color button and specify the color to use in the Colors section.

You could use the Solid Color option to produce an image so that the background could be removed or specified as a transparent color. However, there is a much easier method that is discussed when it comes to rendering images.

Color Gradient

Color Gradient is a popular choice because it has the potential to look more like a presentation. Both color controls enable, and you specify the top and bottom gradient colors, respectively. With the environment controls, you can further tune the background, using shadows and reflection, to make the scene style complement your model.

Experiment with different solutions. You'll find some really nice sets of colors that work well together. For example, we've seen a really nice use of dark blue (top) and black (bottom) with reflections on and set to 80 percent. This setting, with the proper lighting, looks very elegant.

Image

The Image setting enables the image controls at the bottom section of the dialog box. When you activate this choice, the Open dialog box is automatically displayed so you can select the desired image. The default location for the image choices is the Textures directory that is created and populated during the Inventor installation. If you plan to use images other than those supplied, you should do one of two things:

◆ Edit the project file to include the directory where the images are located as a library. (This is recommended.)

◆ Place any image you will use in the installed Textures directory.

Figure 16.14 demonstrates the use of the `forrest 2.bmp` background. The proper placement of the assembly relative to the background enhances the end product. Be sure to take the time to analyze your background to see what may need to be adjusted to optimize your output. In this instance, we arranged a lower camera angle and turned on shadows in the scene style. The lighting style was set to produce soft shadows.

FIGURE 16.14
Scene style with image
background

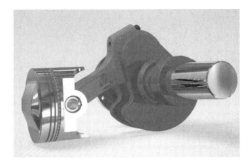

When the image section is enabled, you have three choices of how to use the image in the scene. You can center, tile, or stretch the image. If you choose to tile the image, the Repeat controls are enabled for your use. A little later we'll discuss how to match the model view to your image.

Image Sphere

If you use the Image Sphere option, the selected image is mapped to an environment sphere. The image is stretched to map to the sphere.

ENVIRONMENT TAB

The Environment tab manages the ground plane orientation, shadows, reflection, and environment mapping.

Direction & Offset

The scene style ground plane orientation is based on one of the three canonical assembly work planes. Select the orientation you desire, and specify an offset if any is required to position the plane at the proper height for your model. Negative values position the ground plane below the assembly plane to which it is parallel.

Show Shadows

The option to show shadows is useful when the scene style is acting like a ground plane for the assembly, in other words, not using any prop models or other model to serve as a floor. The Show Shadows setting specifies whether shadows are cast on the scene style ground plane.

Show Reflections

If your scene style is serving the purpose of a model ground plane and you want to reflect the model in the ground plane, select the Show Reflections option and adjust the percentage of reflection you want in the rendered image. The higher the numbers, the more reflection you see in the ground plane. If set to 100 percent, it will reflect the assembly as if it were sitting on a mirror.

Reflection Image

The Use Reflection Image setting is there for you to specify an environment image map. This is the image you will see reflected in those parts having reflectance in their surface style when rendered. Depending on the image, it can have minor to major influence on the rendered outcome. Here again, experimentation is the best teacher.

Collect or produce a set of widely different images, and make new scene styles using the images for reflection mapping. Render the same model with the different styles to see what sort of influence the image produces.

MATCHING YOUR CAMERA TO AN IMAGE

If you want to match your model up to a photograph, use the Image Background type for the scene style. Analyze the photo you will use for the background. Determine where the light is coming from and how much shadow is being cast. Then, set your view to use a perspective camera. Orient the model so that its horizon and vanishing point are similar to the image. Next, create or modify a lighting style so that it produces light and shadows similar to those in the photo. Do a few test renders, and refine the camera position and lights until you're able to get something that looks like you want.

Here's an example and the workflow we used:

1. Select the Inventor A-Platform.iam sample file.

2. Select an image, such as Figure 16.15, to fit the theme, and make a scene style using the Image background type.

FIGURE 16.15
Mountain scene selected for background

3. Orient the model, as shown in Figure 16.16, to look like it fits into the scene.

FIGURE 16.16
Model orientation

4. Use the Outdoor lighting style, and scale it to fit the scene. To make sure the shadows are close, modify the style orientation to match the shadow angles on the mountains. Do a test render, make a couple of tweaks to the style position, and then render the image, as shown in Figure 16.17.

FIGURE 16.17
A-Platform.iam with
background

In the next example, Figure 16.18, we used an existing Inventor background, centered in the scene. We used a previous release Inventor sample model — an engine assembly. This time, we wanted to produce an image more for marketing purposes. So, to help make the product (the sample assembly) emerge from the image, we oriented the assembly and made it large enough to extend beyond the background image, giving the illusion of it protruding from the image. We then rendered the image.

FIGURE 16.18
Scene style example

Composing and Rendering Images

Although it is good to know how to use the tools to produce the styles, it is also important to know the purpose of the image you are composing and rendering. What is its use? Who is the target audience? The type of image you compose and render will be different based on the answers to those questions. For example, if you are producing imagery for an assembly or repair manual, as used by technicians, you may elect to use an illustration style of output as opposed to a realistic style. The noncritical content may be simplified to a degree. However, if you are presenting a product to a group of investors or potential customers, you may want to compose an image showing the product in its anticipated environment. The use of props can add context to your image or animation and possibly more realism.

Since you are using an engineering assembly to create an image, it is likely you do not want to alter the engineering models for the sake of the image — not adding prop content to an engineering model. So, the recommended step is to place the product model into a "wrapper" assembly.

Wrapper assemblies are simply a level higher and can contain nonengineering content that serves as props for composing the final rendered images or animations. Let's say you are producing a product that is used in a machine shop. You place the product's final assembly in a wrapper assembly and add shop content, such as walls, tables, tools, and so on, to set the stage for the rendered image or animation, as shown in Figure 16.19.

FIGURE 16.19
Wrapper assembly
with props

As you can see, there is nonessential content in the scene, but when combined, those items contribute to communicating a purpose for the items in the image. Even the surface style on the tabletop evokes a sense of a well-used workbench. It is small touches such as these that enhance your image.

CREATING AND USING CAMERAS

Although you might conclude that cameras would be best used for animations, they are also very useful for working with images. Cameras make it easy to recall view orientation, and they can be animated. There are two methods for creating cameras: the camera command and the view context menu.

Camera Command

To use the Camera command, located in the Studio tool panel, do the following:

1. Click the Camera command.

2. Select the target, a component face. The camera direction line is presented normal to the face preview and selection. Click to select the target. The command then cycles to the camera position input.

3. Specify the camera position by moving the cursor over the camera direction line and moving it along the line. When the preview is satisfactory, click to select the camera position.

4. If you check the Link Camera To View check box, the camera graphics are hidden, and the view is changed to what the camera sees. Unchecked, the camera graphics are restored. This gives you an easy way to check your settings.

5. Set the Camera Zoom value to fit your requirements.

6. New in Inventor 2009, Depth Of Field provides two methods of setting the range of focus, Focus Limits and f-Stop.

The Focus Limits setting provides you with near and far values, in model units. Content between the near and far values will be in focus. Content outside those values will be proportionally out of focus. f-Stop, the other method, uses an f-Stop value and a Focus Plane setting.

To make setting up the camera a little easier, you can link the focus plane to the camera target. Then, whenever the target is moved, the depth of field adjusts to fit with the camera. That makes less work when it comes to updates.

7. Click OK, and the camera is created. You can rename the camera with the browser node slow-click method.

Current View

The graphic region context menu method is useful for rapidly creating a camera using the current view. To access the other camera settings, you must edit the camera after creating it. To use the graphic region context menu method, simply orient the view so it displays what you want the camera to show, right-click, and click Create Camera From View. A camera is added for this position. You can edit the other camera parameters via the Camera dialog box.

It is not unusual to have 8 to 10 cameras defined when you consider the various vantage points from which you might look at a product.

RENDERING IMAGES

Now that the stage is set, the lighting selected, and the model positioned, you're anxious to render something to see how it's coming. You can always render using the current view. So, whatever position you set the view to, you can render and get results. It is not required that you have a camera defined in order to render. However, repeatability getting back to that same camera location, settings, and so on, really requires that you define a camera. So, quickly before discussing rendering, we'll talk briefly about setting up a camera.

The easiest method, by far, is to orient your model, choose orthographic or perspective viewing, and then in the graphic region right-click and select Create Camera from View. That's it! You have defined a camera. Now, you can easily recall that camera should you change the view orientation. As with any Inventor browser, you can click the node twice and rename it. We recommend naming your camera(s) for ease in selecting, recalling, or animating them.

The Render Image command presents the Render Image dialog box with three tabs: General, Output, and Style. The following sections will briefly discuss the controls and use of the Render Image command.

General Tab

The General tab contains controls for sizing the image and for specifying the camera, lighting style, scene style, and render type to use in producing the image. Active styles prepopulate the style choice fields.

The size controls, Width and Height, provide you with explicit image size control up to 3000 × 3000 pixels. Directly to the right is a pulldown list of predefined image sizes that are typical in the industry. Beneath the pulldown list is a check box for locking the image aspect ratio. If you determine that a specific image size is consistently used, you can enter the values, lock the aspect ratio, and then create images at that ratio but at any size within the permitted limits. This makes scaling an image, post-rendering, easy.

As mentioned earlier, the camera choices include those you have defined and Current View. If you are doing test renders at a low resolution by moving the camera around to see where the best shot will be taken from, use Current View. It's simple and straightforward. Once you determine the camera locations, you can then define and refine those positions and camera settings.

The Lighting Style pulldown lists all the available lighting styles, local (document) and global (style library), including those you have made and maintained locally or in the style library. If you have activated a lighting style, it is preselected. Specify the desired lighting style.

As with the lighting style, the same is true of the scene style. Make your selection based on available local and global styles.

As you were composing the scene, likely you determined whether the end result would be rendered as a realistic or illustration image. Here is where you set that choice. The choice dictates what controls are available on the Style tab.

Output Tab

The Output tab contains controls for where the image is saved and whether to use antialiasing and to what extent to use it.

If you want to save the image, check the Save Rendered Image box. When you do so, the Save dialog box displays. You specify the location and name for the image. If you don't specify this in advance, you are still able to save the image from the render window.

The antialiasing tools include the following choices, from left to right:

◆ None: Antialiasing is not used. This selection requires the least render time and provides the coarsest results.

◆ Low: This specifies a low antialias setting. This eliminates the major coarseness seen in the None selection but still displays a degree of coarseness.

◆ High: This specifies a high antialias setting. This setting virtually eliminates all signs of coarseness in the image. For final renders, in scenes without soft shadows, this selection performs very well.

◆ Highest: This specifies the highest antialiasing setting. This setting is provided particularly for use with refining the image's soft shadows.

With each selection there is an increase in quality accompanied by an increase in render time. Thus, when you select the Highest setting, recommended for soft shadow use only, the quality is increased as is rendering time. It is up to you to determine what meets your need.

Style Tab

When using the Realistic style, there is only one control on the Style tab, True Reflections. When checked, this option ensures that the objects in the scene are seen in reflective surfaces. If unchecked, the image map specified in the surface style or scene style is used.

When using the Illustration style, there are several settings that yield a variety of results. We'll cover some of these next.

To render a line art illustration like you might see in a technical or assembly manual, do the following:

1. Set the graphics display to use the Presentation color scheme. Color scheme selection is located in the Applications Options dialog box on the Colors tab.

2. In Studio, set up the model conditions to fit your requirements. If you want to show something in the state of moving, then use an animation and select a time position that illustrates the condition.

3. Activate the Render Image command, and specify the Render Type as Illustration.

4. On the Style tab, set Color Fill Source to No Color, as shown in Figure 16.20. Since there is no color, you likely want the exterior and interior edges to show. Check both options in the Edges section.

FIGURE 16.20
Render Type:
Illustration, settings

5. Render the scene. The results will be something like Figure 16.21.

FIGURE 16.21
Render Type:
Illustration, No Color
option

Take some time to experiment with these settings because you can come up with some very interesting imagery. For example, make the following changes to the illustration rendering type settings:

1. On the Style tab, set Color Fill Source to Surface Style.

2. Set Levels to 5 (midway across the slider).

3. Activate the Show Shiny Highlights option.

4. On the General tab, set the lighting style to Table Top.

5. Render the scene. The results will look something like Figure 16.22.

FIGURE 16.22
Render Type:
Illustration, Surface
Style option

As you can see, with just a few changes, you can get dramatic differences. Using the same settings, render the scene with a different scene style. The results really start to get interesting.

Animating with Studio

Inventor Studio was designed to use assembly constraints to produce the mechanistic movement within your assemblies. You should consider the following basic concepts when it comes to animating with Inventor Studio:

◆ When you enter the Inventor Studio environment, the model is considered to be in model state, that is, whatever the condition the model was in when you left the part or assembly environment. This means when you exit Inventor Studio, modify the assembly, and then reenter Inventor Studio, the assembly changes are reflected in the model state. That includes view representations, positional representations, component visibility, position, color, and so on. For animations, the model state represents frame zero. Therefore, all modifications affecting the model state also affect all animations in that document because frame zero has changed.

◆ Modifications made in frame 0 of the animation become the starting point for that animation. For example, component1 in animation1 is flush with component2. In animation2, the flush constraint for component1 is offset by 1.5 inches. By changing the constraint in frame 0 for animation2, you don't cause a change in animation1. Had you changed the flush offset in the assembly or Studio model state, animation1 would also be affected.

◆ Because Inventor Studio animates constraints, the free-form movement of a component, part, or assembly may require suppressing constraints that limit movement or the component's degrees of freedom.

◆ Animation actions are a result of modifying constraints; thus, any component that is constrained to a moving object will also move.

◆ The Animation Favorites folder contains all the constraints that have been animated in the active animation. It also contains any parameters you have nominated to appear there. This makes it easier to locate any parameters intended for animation and those constraints that have been animated.

◆ Animation dialog boxes have a common workflow through the dialog box — specify the animation parameters, and specify the time parameters. Based on the animation action target (component, light, camera), the dialog box presents controls relative to the target.

◆ Editing an animation action uses the same dialog box and therefore has virtually the same workflow.

Using Animation Commands

All animation commands are applicable to assemblies. However, in part models only cameras, lights, and parameters can be animated. The Studio tool panel is divided into three sets of controls: image related, animation related, and parameter related. Animation commands are grouped in the animation related division.

Animation Timeline

The Animation Timeline command appears first in the division of animation commands. The animation timeline is where animation actions for any object are maintained and managed. Anytime you use an animate command, it results in an animation action that is placed in the timeline. Animation actions can be interactively changed using the start or end handle, as well as action's location along the timeline by using the middle section of the action graphic or by editing the animation action.

To edit an animation action, use the action's context menu or double-click the action graphic in the timeline.

Animation Timeline Layout

The playback commands are along the top left of the window. These are similar to other timeline or video playback controls you have used. These and the other timeline controls are described in Figure 16.23.

FIGURE 16.23
Animation timeline

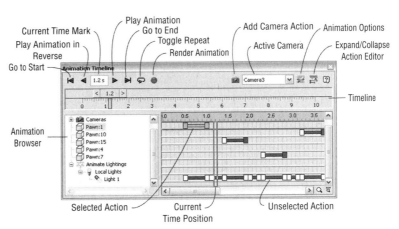

The commands provided are as follows:

◆ Go To Start: Moves the timeline slider to frame 0 and updates the graphics region to show frame 0.

◆ Play Animation In Reverse: Is just as the name implies. You move slider to a point in time, click the command, and the animation plays in reverse.

◆ Current Time Mark: Specifies the current time position. You may type into the field to explicitly change to another time position. The graphics region updates content to show what the animation looks like at that time.

◆ Play Animation: Does what the name implies; plays the animation forward from its current position.

◆ Go To End: Puts the time slider at the end of the animation. The graphics region updates content to show what the animation looks like at that time.

◆ Toggle Repeat: Turns on the repeat command. When you play the animation, it will automatically repeat until you click Stop.

◆ Record Animation: Activates the Render Animation command and displays the dialog box.

You can edit selected actions with the dialog box by double-clicking the action in the track section, where the action bars appear, or by right-clicking the context menu and selecting Edit.

You can edit action duration without going to the dialog box; just hover the cursor over the start or end handle and then click and drag the handle to change the position. Hovering over the center of the action and then clicking and dragging moves the entire action in the timeline.

Animation Favorites

Animation Favorites is a folder that contains any animated constraint or parameter that you have nominated for animation. The purpose is to make it easy to find those animation targets when you need to see or used them.

To populate the folder with a parameter, the parameter must be nominated by you. To do this, activate the Parameters Favorites command. The Parameters Favorites dialog box, shown in Figure 16.24, displays, and you select the box in the row of any parameters that you plan to animate.

FIGURE 16.24
Parameters Favorites
dialog box

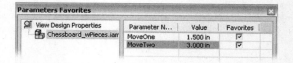

This causes the parameter to populate the Favorites folder. From there you can use the animate parameters command as you'd like.

Common Animation Controls

In each animation command dialog box is a section entitled Time.

The Time section contains all the controls to manage an animation action's time allocation. You specify whether the action starts from the end of a previous action, is a specified time range, or is instantaneous.

Based on the time method, you are able to specify a start time and duration, duration and end time, start time and end time, or simply an end (instantaneous only). The default method is From Previous, which starts the action at frame 0 if there is no previous action defined; otherwise, the new action begins at the end of the previous action.

The other common commands are those on the Acceleration tab.

The Velocity Profile setting defines how rapidly an action starts, proceeds, and ends. You can specify an action to occur at a constant speed. The default option specifies that the action starts with zero velocity and then takes 20 percent of the action duration to achieve complete acceleration. The next 60 percent of the duration is at full acceleration. The last 20 percent of the duration decelerates until it reaches zero at the end of the action. The longer the action, the more observable this becomes.

Think in terms of an electric motor, when power activates the field to which the armature responds, acceleration is not immediate but occurs over a period of time, however long or short.

When the power is off or removed, the armature decelerates and eventually comes to a halt. This is essentially what occurs with the animation action based on the Velocity Profile setting.

The values presented in the dialog boxes are in the document's units.

The appropriate animation command can be accessed from the context menu of the item that is to be animated. For example, you can right-click a constraint and select Animate Constraints to animate the selected constraint. The same is true of the other animation commands and their corresponding browser node.

As we discuss the individual animation commands, we won't include the common sections.

Animate Component

The Animate Component command is located next to the Animation Timeline command in the Studio tool panel. Animate Component is used for the unconstrained animation of parts or assemblies. Think of it as animating a component's degree of freedom. Note that if a component does not move when you create an animation action for it using Animate Component, it likely has a conflicting constraint.

The Animate Component controls are as follows:

◆ Select Components: This is active (default) when initiated; select the component, part, or assembly that will be animated.

◆ Position: This displays the 3D Move/Rotate triad to allow you to implicitly move or rotate the component as desired. Selecting the arrowhead indicates a move vector. Selecting an axis, between arrowhead and intersection, indicates a rotation axis.

◆ Distance: This is where you enter the distance value. Specify this value after selecting the vector on the Position triad.

◆ Rotation: This is explicit input in degrees for a rotation action. Select the axis to be used for rotation.

◆ Revolution: This is explicit input for the number of revolutions the animated component will make. This is an alternate way to input rotation.

◆ Path: This has two options, Sharp and Smooth. Sharp uses no smoothing between the start, duration, and end values. Smooth uses a continuous motion curve between the start, duration, and end values.

Animate Fade

The Animate Fade command is next to the Animate Component command in the Studio tool panel. The Animate Fade setting changes the opacity of a component over time. The parameters allow for this to happen over any defined period of time or instantly if you desire. You can animate to any level of opacity, from 100 to 0 percent.

This command is useful for fading components to reveal interior components while still giving a sense of the overall envelope, as shown in Figure 16.25.

Animate Fade is not associated with a component's visibility state; rather, it is a separate control for animating component opacity. This means you must create an instantaneous action in frame 0 for the component to start out with less than 100 percent opacity.

For example, if you were to start an animation of a transmission with the housing at 10 percent opaque, you must create the action at frame 0 for the opaque value. Then, during the animation, you could create a different action to increase the Opacity value in order to make the housing 100 percent opaque.

FIGURE 16.25
Faded exterior

The Animate Fade controls are as follows:

◆ Select Components: Active (default) to allow selection of the objects to fade

◆ Start: The component's percent Opacity value at the start of the action

◆ End: The component's percent Opacity value at the end of the action

Animate Constraints

The Animate Constraints command is next to the Animate Fade command in the Studio tool panel. Assemblies are built using constraints that remove degrees of freedom and cause components to remain in place with relation to one another. They also work as engines to cause mechanistic movement. Thus, constraints make it easy to animate objects.

The Animate Constraints command is used to modify a constraint over time. The component's orientation changes as constraints are modified.

The constraint's current value is the starting value, and the value you give the end parameter determines the degree to which the object, and those constrained to it, responds.

When animating with constraints, there will be times when something does or does not respond. This is most often caused by other constraints causing a conflict with the animated constraint. One way to overcome this condition is to suppress the conflicting constraint if that doesn't cause a radical change in the animation or its purpose.

Animate Parameters

The Animate Parameters command is next to the Animate Constraints command in the Studio tool panel. If you have used parameters in your assembly and want to animate the parameters, this is the command you will use. The parameter must first be added to the Animation Favorites folder, as discussed earlier.

You can also use Animate Parameters with part parameters. As a result, you can morph the physical shape of a part given the right set of parameters and animation actions. For example, let's say you are designing a vascular stent. As part of the product presentation you want to show the degree to which the stent can expand and perform its function. How would you do this?

1. Create a stent diameter parameter in the part model.

2. In Studio, use the Parameter Favorites command to nominate the parameter for animation use.

3. Set the timeline to two seconds.

4. Use Animate Parameters and change the stent diameter thereby demonstrating the expansion the product undergoes.

If you've used parameters on a part or assembly, you can access the parameters and animate them with these basic steps.

Animate Positional Representations

The Animate Positional Representations command is next to the Animate Parameters command in the Studio tool panel. Positional representations (aka PosReps) use constraints to locate components while respecting the other constraints. You could conclude they work almost like keyframes for a Studio animation. And, in fact, Inventor Studio treats them almost like that. Studio allows you to animate between positional representations.

All that is required is specifying the two PosReps and time over which the transition is made. Studio does the rest. To animate a positional representation that is "deep," meaning it is deeper within the assembly hierarchy, you will need to set the subassemblies, between the top level and the component owning the positional representation, to Flexible. You do this using the component's context menu. The top-level PosRep must cause the "deep" PosRep to be activated.

You can also activate a "deep" PosRep by creating PosReps in each of the subsequent subassemblies. Each higher-level assembly has a PosRep that calls the child subassemblies' PosRep. This is repeated for each subsequent subassembly.

Editing a PosRep animation action is like any other action, but there is a bonus. If you select the PosRep and expand the node in the Animation browser, you will see the participating members of the PosRep. Each of the members has an action bar, and you can edit their duration and position interactively. The values must stay within the bounds of the defined PosRep. Initially, all members occupy the full span of the action, but you can change that by editing the PosRep. When you edit the PosRep, the members enable so you can adjust them. For an example of what this would look like, see Figure 16.26.

FIGURE 16.26
Editing a positional representation

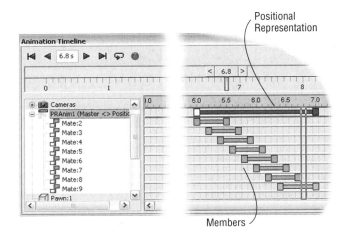

Animate Camera

The Animate Camera command is next to the Animate Positional Representations command in the Studio tool panel. When animating a camera the current camera parameters are used as the "from" parameters of the animation action. Using the Animate Camera controls you define the "to" parameters for the animation action. With these controls you can do the following:

♦ Change the Camera Definition interactively or through a dialog box.

♦ Use the view commands to position the camera, and snapshot it as a keyframe using the Add Camera Action command in the Animation Timeline window.

♦ Use the turntable functionality.

♦ Define a path, and have the camera and/or target follow the path.

In the Animate Camera dialog box, you select the camera to animate from the pulldown list. Then, using one of two methods, you define the end position of the camera for that animation action.

Camera Definition

The first method is to use the Definition command. To access the dialog box, just click the Definition button in the Camera section. The steps are the similar to when you define a camera using the dialog box, such as setting the target and position selection, as well as additional animation options.

When you click the Definition button, the Camera dialog box displays, and you are able to specify the following:

♦ Target placement

    ♦ Fixed: The target does not change positions.

    ♦ Floating: The target maintains positional relationship to camera.

    ♦ Path: The target follows a path made of 2D or 3D sketch geometry.

♦ Camera position

    ♦ Fixed: The camera does not change positions.

    ♦ Floating: The camera maintains positional relationship to target.

    ♦ Path: The camera follows a path made of 2D or 3D sketch geometry.

♦ Roll angle: This defines rotation around the camera to the target axis, displayed as a line between the camera components.

♦ Zoom: This defines a horizontal field of view.

Current View

The second method for defining camera animation is to use the current view. The steps to do this are as follows:

1. In the Timeline Active Camera list, select the camera you want to animate.

2. Position the timeline slider at the time position representing the end of the action you are defining.

3. In the scene browser, right-click the camera you specified in the list, and click Animate Camera in the context menu. Alternatively, you can select the camera in the graphics region.

4. Use the view commands to orient the graphics region to the view you want to see at that time position.

5. Click the Add Camera Action (camera button) next to the Timeline Active Camera list. You will see the view briefly revert to the last known position and then update to the current position.

Repeat steps 2, 4, and 5 as much as is needed for as many cameras as you want.

Turntable

If you simply want a camera to travel around your part or assembly in a circle, the turntable function makes this very easy.

To use the Turntable functionality, do the following:

1. Right-click the camera you want to use as a turntable camera, and click Animate Camera. Alternatively, use the view commands to set the camera to its initial position, right-click, and click Create Camera From View.

2. In the Animate Camera dialog box, select the Turntable tab.

3. Select the Turntable check box to enable the turntable controls. A graphic preview of the current axis is displayed in the graphics region. In the Axis list, select from any of the canonical axes or the current camera horizontal (Camera-H) or vertical (Camera-V) handles.

4. Specify the direction of rotation around the selected axis.

5. Specify the number of revolutions.

6. Qualify the number of revolutions by selecting the literal ($+/-$), per minute, or per second option. For partial turntable effects, use a value less than 1.

7. In the Time section, select whether to loop the camera, or use a time period to define the length of the action.

Path Animation

As mentioned earlier, when you select the camera definition method, you have the option to specify that the target or camera follows a path.

If you are planning on animating a camera along a path, you must define the path geometry, in advance. You do this in a separate part file using 2D or 3D sketch objects. The part file is added to the assembly and positioned where you want it before ever entering Studio. You can, of course, add the path file later and then animate the camera associating it to the path.

Note that in order for the path part file to be hidden from the bill of material, the part should be designated as a reference part.

When you select the Path option, move your cursor into the graphic region, and select the path you want to use. The command searches for sketch geometry, so there are no conflicting inputs when you are in the graphics region.

After you select the path geometry, two handle glyphs appear on the path (Figure 16.27): a green triangle at the beginning of the path and a red square at the end of the path. The glyphs perform two functions:

◆ They tell you the direction the camera is traveling along the path.

◆ Also, the glyph can be moved along the path serving as a limit setting for how much of the path is used. To adjust the glyph position, place the cursor over the glyph, click and drag along the path. Release the mouse button to accept the location.

FIGURE 16.27
Path edit handles

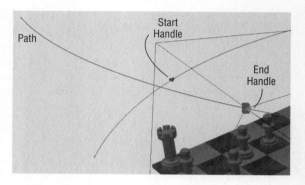

Animate Light

The Animate Light command is next to the Animate Camera command in the Studio tool panel. You can approach animating lights in a few ways. You can animate the lighting style, lights within a style, or local lights. When animating lights, the Animate Light dialog box has the same controls that were used to create or edit the lights. When defining an animation action for a light, you specify the light parameters as they will be at the end of the action. Studio commands use the previous parameter values as the starting point of the animation action and the new parameter values as the ending point of the animation action. You specify the time period over which the action occurs.

The first steps for animating a light are the same regardless of the object to be animated:

1. Activate the Animate Light command. Alternatively, select the object to be animated, and use the context menu entry, Animate Light. The Animate Light dialog box displays.

2. If nothing was selected to start, specify the lighting style, style light, or local light to be animated. The Select command is active by default.

3. Click the Definition button.

4. The corresponding dialog box displays, and only parameters capable of being animated are enabled.

5. If a style is selected for Lighting Style, you are able to animate the style brightness and ambience parameters.

6. For a local light or a light in a style, a variety of parameters are enabled for animating. Specify the values you want represented in the animation at the selected time position.

7. Click OK to commit to the values for the animation. An action is added to the timeline.

Local lights, when defined in components deeper in the assembly, are not accessible at the top-level assembly for animation. Local lights are meant to be light sources that travel with components. Thus, if you define a local light to be in a part used in the top-level assembly, that light will be lighted and be a source of light in any renders or animations. The local light is part of the component, and wherever the component goes, the light goes also. Examples where local lights might be used are lighted gauges, switches, headlights, and so on.

Figure 16.28 shows a sequence of frames at time positions 2.3, 2.6, and 2.8. The local light has both intensity and position animated.

FIGURE 16.28
Animated local light

Time: 2.3   Time: 2.6   Time: 2.8

Lights within lighting styles can provide animated scene lighting. Examples of uses are gallery lights, showroom lighting, and so on. Exploring the various ways to animate lights is worth the effort, not only for experience but also for getting an idea of how much light affects everything in the scene.

Dynamic Simulation to Studio

If you use Dynamic Simulation, part of Inventor Professional and Inventor Simulation, you will see the Create Studio Animation command in that environment's tool panel, which allows you to render your simulation in Inventor Studio. The command is used after you have run a simulation but before you leave run mode. You *must* run the simulation before using the command.

The command initiates the studio environment, creates a new animation called `Dynamic_Simulation`, and adds a new parameter called `Simulation_timeline`. The parameter is placed in the Animation Favorites folder and is ready to animate. The parameter represents the time steps used in the simulation. For this reason, it is recommended that you use the same number for the parameter value that is used for the images in the simulation. This way, you will be able to relate the animation to the simulation.

Animate the parameter, using the Animate Parameters command, to see your simulation. Then use the other Studio tools, such as lighting and scene styles to help enhance the animated result. When you're ready, render the animation.

Using Video Producer

Video Producer, new in Inventor Studio, provides the ability to compose a single animation from one or more animations. You are able to select from all cameras that you have set up, whether animated or not. Reasonably, to provide content for a production, you must create one or more cameras and usually at least one animation.

Video Producer supports the following:

◆ Multiple cameras in the same animation

◆ Camera transitions

◆ Multiple productions in the same assembly document

◆ Interactive modification of camera shots and transitions

It is also possible to create a production of still shots using a variety of cameras.

Video Producer is presented in a window similar to the Animation Timeline window, but with different controls.

The playback controls are the same as those found in the Animation Timeline and most other playback or player software.

The composing timeline and tabbed browser on the left are where you will find the shots and transitions. *Shots* are the cameras that have been defined in Studio, whether animated or not. *Transitions* are available to use between shots. Transitions are overlays over the shots and not segments between shots. Therefore, transitions extend into the shot in one or two directions. This means that when you plan to use transitions, you will need to specify enough shot time to allow for the transitions.

When you activate Video Producer, all cameras are collected, and all image representations are made and listed in the Shot browser. This action is session based. Thereafter, only the cameras that change will be updated when you return to the Video Producer during that Inventor session.

Four transition types are available, but five possibilities exist when you consider "no transition" as an option. The transitions are as follows:

◆ Fade: From color to shot, shot to shot, shot to color

◆ Gradient Wipe: From left to right

◆ Swipe Left: Moves from left to right

◆ Swipe Right: Moves from right to left

VIDEO PRODUCER WORKFLOW

You can compose with Video Producer in two ways: via a dialog box or by dragging and dropping. Each has its own advantage. First we'll discuss the dragging and dropping, or the interactive means of creating and editing. This method's advantage is fast production layout. Note that the composition is an additive process, starting from the beginning of the production.

Interactive Create and Edit

Using the interactive method, you simply determine the camera shot you want to use and then drag and drop it onto the production track. You change the length of the shot by positioning the cursor over either end, horizontally, and click and drag. Figure 16.29 shows an example of each of these techniques.

FIGURE 16.29
Interactive edit handles

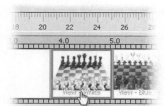 

You can also drag and drop to reorder the shots in the timeline. For more precise control over the time used and shot segment, double-click the shot and edit the parameters. Alternatively, use the Edit command in the context menu.

Transitions behave in a similar manner. You simply drag and drop one onto the track and then adjust them as needed. Double-clicking or using the context menu to select Edit will give you explicit control over parameter values through dialog boxes.

To make it easier to edit contiguous production timeline members, you can select one and then move your cursor over the neighboring member that is to be edited. The selected member displays a cyan highlight, and the new select target gets a red highlight, as shown in Figure 16.30. When both are highlighted, click and drag the boundary between them; they edit and update simultaneously.

FIGURE 16.30
Multimember edit

Shot Editing

In the Shot dialog box there are two sections: Animation Footage and Shot Footage. Animation Footage refers to what the camera records in the animation. Shot Footage is the portion of animation footage that is used in the active production.

In the production timeline, the shot footage displayed is the amount of time in the production that footage is displayed. Any portion of the selected camera, from the designated animation footage, can be displayed during that shot duration.

Transition Editing

In the Transition dialog box, you can edit the type of transition and its parameters.

Transitions that start or finish a production use color as the secondary member for the transition. Use the color selection to change the selection.

Edit Shots and Transitions

After placing a shot or transition into the Video Producer timeline, right-click and select Edit to display the Shot or Transition dialog box. In the Shot dialog box you can edit the following:

◆ Specify the animation from which the footage came

◆ The point in time in the footage to begin using it

◆ The particular camera to get footage from

◆ The time frame of the camera footage to use

In the Transition dialog box you can edit the following:

◆ Specify the transition type

◆ Specify the transition color

◆ The start, duration, and end timeline position

These are the same parameters that are being edited when you do so interactively.

Rendering Video or Animations

It is important to note that if a production is active when you use the Render Animation command, the active production, and *not* the animation, will render. If you want to render a single animation and you have productions, be sure to deactivate the production before rendering.

The available animation formats are WMV and AVI, which will be discussed in more detail in a moment.

The Render Animation dialog box is used whether rendering an animation or production. With productions, you have already selected the camera(s), so that field is disabled. If you are rendering an animation, the camera input is enabled.

The General and Style tabs of the Render Animation dialog box use the same controls as the Render Image dialog box.

The Output tab, shown in Figure 16.31, has controls that specify the various parameters for the rendering the animation.

FIGURE 16.31
Animation output

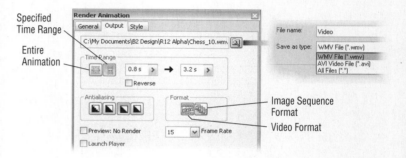

On the Output tab you specify the name for the file(s) that is created. If you use a video format, you can choose from WMV (Windows Media Video) or AVI (Audio Video Interleave). Based on the file type selection and after the OK button has been clicked, you are asked to specify the final parameters before rendering:

◆ WMV Format: You are asked to specify ASF (Advanced Systems Format) Export properties, in particular, the network bandwidth. If you use one of the default choices and the output is not to your liking, use the custom setting and start with 700 Kbps and increase from there.

◆ AVI Format: You are asked to specify the video codec of choice. One or more codecs may have been delivered with the computer software. However, these at times may not produce the desired results.
Over the past few years, two video codecs have emerged as ones that routinely give good-quality results with small to medium AVI file sizes. Although this is not an endorsement, it is good to know that the TechSmith (www.techsmith.com) and DivX (www.divx.com) codecs provide very good results.

In the Time Range section, specify whether the entire animation or a time range will be rendered. If time range is selected, the timeline fields enable so you can specify the start and end times. If you want to reverse the rendered animation, select the Reverse check box.

Note that the controls on the right side of the input fields give access to the most recent values specified for the command.

The Antialias settings are the same as those used in the Render Image dialog box; from left to right they are None, Low, High, and Highest.

The Format section is where you specify whether the animation is output in video format or as a list of frame sequences. If frame sequence is specified, the name provided has incremented numbers appended as images are created. If you plan on adding comments within the video or if you do not have enough disk space, you can output as images and then composite them later. This allows you to move the images to another location and continue rendering.

Then, specify the number of frames per second the video will output with. You will find that 24 and 30 frames per second (fps) are commonly used in broadcast and film media. A 15 fps animation may look good to you. Try it at 24 or 30 fps; you will notice the improvement.

A major concern of anyone rendering is the amount of time it takes to generate an image or animation. Rendering an animation without some idea of what it will look like is a potentially expensive proposition at best. To enable better decision-making processes, you are able to create a preview render; just check the box. Preview renders do not use lighting styles and render quickly. This gives you a means of determining whether any adjustments are needed before committing to rendering over a lengthy period of time.

These are the tools and concepts to accomplish rendering and animation in Inventor Studio. The creative part is up to you. Spend time experimenting, and you'll find you can create compelling imagery.

The Bottom Line

Create and manage surface, lighting, and scene styles   Inventor doesn't have the surface, lighting, or scene style you need for a rendering.

Master It   You need to create a surface style that portrays black bumped plastic.

Create and animate cameras   You need to create a camera and animate it.

Master It   You decide to use the most expedient means to capture camera keyframe positions.

Start new animations, modify animations, and use the various animation tools   You need to start a new animation of an assembly.

Master It   You have an existing animation but want to do a variation on it. You want to copy and edit an existing animation.

Use multiple cameras to create a video production of your animation   Video Producer provides the means to combine camera shots into a single video output. You want to use this feature.

Master It   You created several cameras, animated and static, and want to make a composite animation.

Use props to enhance your scene   Inventor assemblies can be combined with other components to create a more realistic scene for rendering.

Master It   You have completed a design and want to render a realistic image of it in its working environment.

Render realistic and illustrative images   Inventor provides the means to render both realistic and illustrative images.

Master It   With your new product nearing completion, the marketing department has asked for rendered images for marketing collateral and technical documents such as white papers.

Render animations and video productions   Inventor provides the means to render animations and video productions.

Master It   You've created a wrapper assembly and set up the scene with cameras, lighting, and a scene style. Now you want to render an animation for design review and a video production for a multidiscipline review or marketing use.

Appendix A

The Bottom Line

Chapter 1: Inventor Design Philosophy

Manage toolbars in Autodesk Inventor In this first chapter, you learned how the Inventor interface is designed to function efficiently, with tool panels that switch depending upon the stage of design and the environment in which you are working. The Inventor interface is designed for simplicity, ease of use, and ease of learning.

Master It You find that using the scroll bars in the tool panels to access commands is tedious and a bit difficult to keep track of which command is where.

Solution Right-click anywhere in the tool panel and remove the Display Text with Icons check mark so that only the icons display, thereby condensing the tools so that no scroll bar is required.

Utilize the Inventor Model browser The Inventor Model browser displays information about the model in a hierarchy. When working with parts, features are listed in the browser in the order they were created, providing an evolutionary timeline of the model. In the Assembly environment, parts are organized in the model browser in subassemblies for organization and performance. Even in the drawing environment, we have browser to organize the hierarchy of views.

Master It You wish to explore an existing part model to get a better understanding of how it was created and how it might be improved.

Solution Activate any feature in the Model browser for editing and all successive features will be suspended so that the model exists as it did at the time that feature was created. You can also use the end-of-part maker to roll back the model and view it is as was during its creation.

Understand the various file types used in Inventor You have learned that Inventor supports many different file types in its native environment, separating tasks and files to improve performance and increase stability.

Master It You have decided to use the native Inventor DWG format for all your drawing files so that you can email files without translating when sending files to customers and vendors who do not have Inventor. But you notice that when you start a new drawing, it is always an IDW file.

Solution You can set the default drawing type by selecting Tools ➢ Application Options and clicking the Drawing tab. In the default section, click the drop-down arrow for Default Drawing File Type and set this to Inventor Drawing (*.dwg).

Understand basic principles of parametric design   Parametric design is simply a method design in which you link dimensions and variables to geometry in a way that allows the part to change by modifying the dimensions. The power of this approach lies in the fact that we can design parts, building the intent of their function right into them, as we create the model.

Master It   You need to create a model based on key inputs, and want to see how changing the value of those inputs affects the relationship of the features and parts within the model.

Solution   Create your models in Inventor, driving the model off of key parameters you've identified. Set the model up with the intention of editing the features to interrogate the validity of your design. Aim to build a digital prototype rather than just a 3D drawing.

Understand the differences between solid and surface modeling   Over time, as computing technology has progressed, so too has the way that programs approach 3D design. While surface models initially allowed the designer to visualize a design and even manufacture it from digital file, the desire to be able to extract data for calculations concerning mass and center of gravity required a solid model. The need to easily edit and modify designs without having to start over pushed solid modeling to the next step: parametric solid modeling.

Master It   You need to create models that are functionally and esthetically sound.

Solution   Learn to use the solid and surfacing tools in Inventor and use the two methods in concert to create designs that are as functional as they attractive.

Develop best practices for using Autodesk Inventor   You were introduced to some of the best practices in using Autodesk Inventor as your design tool. You would do well to review these best practices from time to time as you progress toward mastering this powerful design tool.

Master It   You want to ensure that your implementation of Inventor is successful and in line with industry best practices.

Solution   Seize the opportunity for change, to evaluate how you arrived at your current file management and general design practices. Don't convince yourself that new software will solve bad habits and poor organization. Develop a plan with a total design and file management solution in mind, and understand that how you manage the files you create with Inventor should facilitate design work, not interfere with it. Find out how others in the industry are tackling the same challenges by visiting the Autodesk Inventor Discussion Groups at http://discussion.autodesk.com.

Chapter 2: Data and Projects

Create an efficient data file directory structure   Create clear paths for support, data, and library files. Be sure to support a unique filename for each assembly and part.

Master It   Earlier in the chapter, you looked at a sample job-based directory structure. Now, consider a directory structure for a product-type-based directory structure to serve customers in the automotive industries. Create a directory structure.

Solution   Compare your directory structure with the one shown here. Do you have clear paths for support, data, and library files? Have you made it easy to locate parts? Does your structure support unique file and folder names?

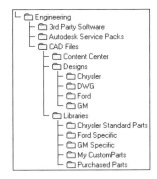

Create efficient search paths Keep your search paths isolated. For instance, keep libraries in the library path, data in the project path, and so on. Organize and group your library parts into logical folders without duplication. Make it easy to find and maintain unique parts.

> **Master It** Consider the location of the libraries in the following directory structure. How is this structure inefficient? Why is it more likely that duplicate parts will be created? How would you improve the search paths in this directory structure?

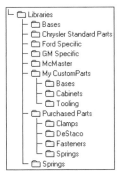

> **Solution** Locating reusable library files in the data area makes them difficult to find, could lead designers to believe that the parts are intended to be edited, and will slow search and file resolution functions. For example, a designer working on optical components might not realize that the hex screw she's looking for has been filed away under in the motor parts area, buried in a gear library, which was filed in the Springs library. If the library were in the library path with other fasteners, the designer would not need to waste time re-creating the part, pulling a part number, and so forth. To improve efficiency, all libraries should be organized according to the type of part that should be located in that folder.

Understand how Inventor uses data, library, and Content Center files Your project file is a XML file that lists the locations and functions of each search path. Part loads and searches begin in the library search path, then move to the local workspace, and finally move to any workgroups. Keep your paths simple to reduce search and load times. Use library files to share designs and automatically protect parts and assemblies from inadvertent revision.

> **Master It** What are the advantages of library files?

Solution   Library parts and assemblies are loaded first. Library paths are searched first and used first during part resolution. They are read-only and can be shared without worries about inadvertent editing.

Determine the best project type for your work   These include the following:

Single-user projects: Single-seat or single-designer projects.

Vault projects: Single- or multiple designer workflows to track work, maintain version control, and facilitate design reuse.

Productstream: Replaces Vault and adds BOM management, item master, revision control, and change management tools to Vault type projects.

Shared projects: Require fast server and fast network connections. Legacy project support that may not be continued.

Semi-isolated projects: Similar to Vault projects, but without the advantage of database searches and management.

Master It   For a complex product that will be worked on by several design teams and updated twice a year for the next five years, which project type would you choose?

Solution   The best choice would be a Vault project, and Productstream might be well worth consideration, given the number of revisions, engineering change orders, and updates anticipated and the fact that multiple design teams will work on the project. A single-user project would require that design team members work sequentially, vastly increasing the design time.

Create single- and multiuser projects   Use the Inventor Project Wizard. Customize the default settings for your work. Include only the paths and files you expect to use. You can always add more later as needed. Use a master project if you frequently create similar projects.

Master It   Why not include every library and data file in your project? What is the benefit of including a master project file?

Solution   Limiting the files and library/data paths you include in your project reduces part and assembly loading, searching, and file resolution times. Using an include file to add a master project file to your project automatically sets the project configuration to preset values from the master project. This ensures consistent projects and saves project setup time.

Evaluate existing parts and assemblies for inclusion in a new design   Be methodical and thorough. Make sure that any changes made to the existing parts or assemblies will not adversely affect other products. Always consider where exiting parts and assemblies are used before revising them.

Master It   What would you do if you needed to make minor changes to an existing part for it to be used in your new project, but the changes would make the part unusable in some of the previous designs that use the same part?

Solution   If using Vault you can run what is called a "Where Used" search to efficiently evaluate which previous designs use the part in question. If it is determined that making a change to the existing part would cause problems in the existing designs, then use Vault to copy the part file to a data directory for the new design and give it a unique name. Then make changes to the model as required. The existing part remains intact for the existing designs. Advanced search functions such as a "Where Used" is just one of the benefits of using a Vault project to manage your Inventor design work.

Chapter 3: Sketch Techniques

Create a new part file from a template   In this chapter, you learned how to choose an appropriate template for creating a new part file. You also explored the Application Options and Document Settings options that control sketch-related settings in Inventor.

Master It   Let's assume you have opened an inch-based template file to create a new part and have created some sketches and features within the file. You now realize that this should have been a metric part and that you should have opened a metric-based template.

Solution   Instead of re-creating a new part using a metric-based template, you will select Tools ➤ Document Settings and go to the Units tab and change the units of measure from inches to the required metric unit. Existing dimensions will automatically update to the new measurement standard.

Preserve model design Intent   Establishing and preserving design intent is a powerful benefit of 3D design. Every design should be created with the possibility that the design will be modified at a later date, and changes to the design may not affect only a particular part; the changes may also affect the function of an entire machine or related components.

Master It   You have created a flange part used to join one 2-inch pipe to another section of 2-inch pipe. Future designs will call for many variations of this design.

Solution   Using construction geometry and dimensional formulas to relate one dimension to another allows variations to be generated quickly by modifying key parameters. Save a copy of the original part file to the templates directory so that you can open this template, update the parameters as needed, and save the new variation without risk of saving over you previous files.

Perform the basic 2D sketching process   We explored sketching in Inventor by concentrating on the use of sketch constraints on sketch objects to establish relationships between them and on the use of parametric dimension to then drive the sketch entities. Recall that you can have both driving and driven dimension in a sketch.

Master It   You have been tasked with redesigning a shop fixture from a previous design but are unsure of some of the dimensions at the onset of your design.

Solution   Create a conceptual sketch for study and concept testing. Add more 2D constraints to properly control the shape of the part. Once the sketch has been fully constrained, you will add dimensions to adjust the size of the part. Leave off dimensions that are currently unknown, or create them as driven dimensions. Come back and add dimensions as they become available, and watch your model adjust according to your design intent. You will finish the sketch by anchoring the sketch to the part centerpoint origin.

Import and convert AutoCAD drawings to Inventor sketches   This chapter discussed reusing and importing existing AutoCAD files into Inventor for part creation.

Master It   You have many existing 2D AutoCAD drawings detailing legacy parts. You want to reuse these designs as you convert to 3D modeling. You need to create numerous features within the model so that the model can be easily edited while preserving design intent.

Solution   Insert AutoCAD geometry into an active Inventor part sketch. Once completed, the sketch can be copied or shared to create additional features. Circles in AutoCAD should be converted to hole features in the Inventor part. Imported sketches should be edited to remove fillets and chamfers from the corners of parts so that fillet and chamfers features can be created in the model.

Create 3D sketches in a part file   Much of working with a 3D parametric modeler can be done by sketching in a two-dimensional plane and then giving depth to the sketch to create 3D features. However, sometimes you need to create paths or curves that are not planar. In those cases, you use the 3D sketch tools.

Master It   You need to create a three-dimensional sketch for a complex model. The design of this model precludes the exclusive use of 2D sketches.

Solution   Consider the design issues that you have with a complex part. You may need to control the shape and the orientation of a sweep or loft path. Using a 3D sketch is the only solution that will create a part. You will need to determine how that 3D sketch will be utilized and controlled to maintain design intent. Once the workflow for creating the part has been determined, you can proceed with the solution.

Chapter 4: Basic Modeling Techniques

Create basic part features   In this chapter, you learned how to plan a workflow that allows you to create stable, editable parts that preserve design intent.

Master It   You need to create a fairly complex part consisting of many extrusions, revolves, sweeps, or lofts. In addition, you will need to create holes, fillets, chamfers, and other part modifiers. This part may need significant modification in the future by you or by other designers.

Solution   Determine how this part will be manufactured. Think about how the part might be designed to minimize production costs, while still fulfilling the intent of the design, by determining how many machining operations will be required. Determine the design intent of this part and how your approach will affect stability and any future edits or modifications.

Create and use work features in part mode   Using work features, work planes, work axes, and work points enable you to create virtually any part or feature. Work features are the building blocks for sketch creation and use.

Master It   Your design will require creating features on spherical and cylindrical faces. You need to precisely control the location and angle of these features.

Solution   Using existing origin features, created model features and edges, sketch objects, and other existing geometry within the file will permit you to create parametric work features as the basis for additional geometry creation.

Place and configure hole features   There are several approaches for creating and modifying existing holes.

Master It   You are required to design a part with several types of clearance and threaded holes, some of which may be custom thread designations and all of which are likely to change in size, designation, or fit.

Solution   Spend some time exploring the various options and settings in the Hole dialog box. Back up the Excel spreadsheets located in the Design Data folder. Use Microsoft Excel to edit the spreadsheets to include the custom hole information.

Pattern and mirror features In this chapter, you looked at how to pattern and mirror features on a part. Using both commands can streamline your part design.

Master It You are tasked with creating a complex part with a group of features that are not only symmetrically distributed across the part center but are also evenly spaced along the length of the part.

Solution Learn how to create rectangular and circular patterns. Explore all the options available in the Rectangular Pattern dialog box, including the ability to pattern a feature along a path. Learn how to isolate and suppress pattern components. Determine when patterns and mirrored features are appropriate and when additional features should be created instead.

Modify existing part features History-based modeling provides access to previously created sketches and features for ease of editing.

Master It You are collaborating on designing a new variation of a standard component. You anticipate changes to your design as the collaborative team collects information and works through design challenges.

Solution Learn how to determine dependent features or sketches by systematically deleting a feature further down the model tree. Examine the dialog box that appears to determine whether other features are dependent upon the deleted feature. Develop a workflow to break or modify dependencies while still preserving design intent.

Chapter 5: Advanced Modeling Techniques

Create complex sweeps and lofts Complex geometry is created by using multiple work planes, sketches, and 3D sketch geometry. Honing your experience in creating work planes and 3D sketches is paramount to success in creating complex models.

Master It You want to model a piece of twisted flat bar.

Solution Create the flat bar profile in a base sketch. Then create a work plane offset from the original sketch the length of the bar. Create the profile sketch on this work plane at a rotated orientation to match the degree of twist needed. Create a 3D sketches, and connect the corners of the first profile to the appropriate corners of the second profile. Use the Loft command to loft from one profile to the other, using the 3D sketch lines as rails, to produce the twisted part.

Design turned parts and threads Turned parts and threaded features can be developed using revolves or extrudes. Both have advantages and disadvantages in usage.

Master It You need to cut a profile out of a part as it would be done in the shop using a radial face cutter.

Solution Create the cutter profile section, and use the Revolve command with the Cut option to digitally replicate the same process that the shop uses.

Utilize part tolerances Dimensional tolerancing of sketches allows the checking of stack-up variations within assemblies. By adding tolerances to critical dimensions within sketches, parts may be adjusted to maximum, minimum, and nominal conditions.

Master It You want to create a model feature with a deviation so that you can test the assembly fit at the extreme ends of the tolerances.

Solution　Use the Parameters dialog box to set up and adjust tolerances for individual dimensions. In the Parameters dialog box, set the tolerance to the upper or lower limits for the part and then update the model using the Update button. Check the fit of the feature against its mating part or parts in the assembly environment and then edit the part to set it back to the nominal once done.

Understand and use parameters and iProperties　Using parameters within files assist in the creation of title blocks, parts lists, and annotation within 2D drawings. Using parameters in an assembly file allow the control of constraints and objects within the assembly. Exporting parameters allows the creation of custom properties. Proper usage of iProperties facilitates the creation of accurate 2D drawings that always reflect the current state of included parts and assemblies.

Master It　You want to create a formula to determine the spacing of a hole pattern based upon the length of the part.

Solution　Set up a user parameter that calls the part length and divides by the number of holes or the spacing and then reference this user parameter in the hole pattern feature.

Analyze parts and work with base solids　Inventor provides tools to analyze translated geometry. These tools provide a quality check on the geometry and permit repair or modification of geometry within the construction environment.

Master It　You need to import a part from a vendor file and remove features in the part.

Solution　Copy the geometry to the construction environment, and unstitch the features you want to discard. Use boundary patch to mend the surfaces and then stitch them back together. Then copy the geometry back out to the model environment, and add features as requited.

Troubleshoot modeling failures　Modeling failures are often caused by poor design practices. Poor sketching techniques, bad design workflow, and other factors can lead to the elimination of design intent within a model.

Master It　You want to modify a rather complex existing part file, but when you change the feature, errors cascade down through the entire part.

Solution　Position the End of Part marker just under the feature you intend to modify. Then move it back down the feature tree one feature at a time, addressing each error as it occurs. Continue until all features have been fixed.

Chapter 6: Sheet Metal

Take advantage of the specific sheet metal features available in Inventor　Knowing what features are available to help realize your design can make more efficient and productive use of your time.

Master It　Of the sheet metal features discussed, how many require a sketch to produce their result?

Solution　Five sheet metal features consume a sketch: Contour Flange, Face, Cut, Punch, and Fold. Since Inventor has well-established paradigms for how sketches can be manipulated, knowing which features consume sketches may allow you to develop designs that are flexible and parametrically configurable.

Understand sheet metal templates and rules   Templates can help get your design started on the right path, and sheet metal rules and associated styles allow you to drive powerful and intelligent manufacturing variations into your design; combining the two can be very productive as long as you understand some basic principles.

Master It   Name two methods that can be used to publish a sheet metal rule from a sheet metal part file to the style library.

Solution   Rules and styles can be published or written to the style library from either in Inventor of by using the Style Management Wizard (the harvester). Using the native Inventor method, right-clicking a given rule/style produces a command called Save To Style Library. Using the harvester, you can select a specific file and add its style information to your existing style library or create a new one.

Author and insert punch tooling   Creating and managing Punch tools can streamline your design process and standardize tooling in your manufacturing environment.

Master It   Name two methods that can be utilized to produce irregular (nonsymmetric) patterns of punch features.

Solution   Sketch center marks can be patterned within the insertion sketch as a symmetric array. During Punch tool insertion, the Centers control on the Geometry tab can be used to deselect center marks where you want a tool to be placed. The feature-patterning tools can also be used to create irregular patterns after a punch feature has been created. This method is accomplished by first creating a symmetric pattern of punch features and then expanding the child pattern occurrences in the feature browser and individually suppressing them. Both methods prevent the feature from being displayed in the folded and flat pattern as well as omit the Punch tool information in the flat pattern punch metadata.

Utilize the flat pattern information and options   The sheet metal folded model captures your manufacturing intent during the design process; understanding how to leverage this information and customize it for your needs can make you extremely productive.

Master It   How can you change the reported angle of all your Punch tools by 90°?

Solution   The flat pattern's orientation infers a virtual x-axis for punch angle calculation, so rotating the flat pattern by 90° will change all the punch angles by the same amount. The flat pattern can also affect the bend and punch direction (up or down) by flipping the base face, and reported bend angles can be changed from Bending Angle to Open Angle by changing options in the Bend Angle tab of the Flat Pattern Definition dialog box.

Understand the nuances of sheet metal iPart factories   Sheet metal iPart factories enable you to create true manufacturing configurations with the inclusion of folded and flat pattern models in each member file.

Master It   If you created sheet metal iPart factories prior to Inventor 2009, any instantiated files contain only a folded model. Name two methods that you could use to drive the flat pattern model into the instantiated file.

Solution   Once you have opened, migrated, and saved a legacy sheet metal iPart factory, you can decide between two methodologies for obtaining the flat pattern model within your instantiated files: push or pull. The push method is accomplished from within the iPart factory by using the context menu command, Generate Files, which is associated with the member filename. This method pushes out a new definition of the member file including the flat pattern model. The pull model requires you to using the Inventor command, Rebuild All, followed by saving the factory file. Now that the factory has been rebuilt, any time you open one of the instantiated files associated with the factory, it will see that it's out of date and will trip the update flag. Selecting Update will pull the flat pattern model into the instantiated member file.

Model sheet metal components with non-sheet-metal features   Inventor doesn't always allow you to restrict yourself to sheet-specific design tools; understanding how to utilize non-sheet metal features will ensure that your creativity is limitless.

Master It   Name two non-sheet-metal features that can lead to unfolding problems if used to create your design.

Solution   As discussed in the chapter, Loft and Shell can lead to numerous problems during unfolding because of non-developable curvature introduced by Loft and non-uniform thickness introduced by Shell.

Work with imported sheet metal parts   Understanding the way in which Inventor accomplishes unfolding as well as how to associate an appropriate sheet metal rule are keys to successfully working with imported parts.

Master It   Name the one measured value that is critical if you want to unfold an imported part.

Solution   The measured sheet thickness is the most important geometric measurement in an imported sheet metal part. Ensuring that the thickness of your imported part matches the active Thickness parameter means the difference between success and frustration. Although you can change the active rule (or create a new one) to match all the geometric conditions of your imported part, these will affect only new features or topology that you introduce; Thickness is the key.

Understand the tools available to annotate your sheet metal design   Designing your component is essential, but it's equally important to understand the tools that are available to efficiently document your design and extract your embedded manufacturing intent.

Master It   What process is required to recover flat pattern width and height extents within your Drawing Manager parts list?

Solution   By creating custom iProperties within your sheet metal part file set equal to <FLAT PATTERN LENGTH> cm and <FLAT PATTERN WIDTH> cm, flat pattern extents can be referenced by your parts list by adding these new properties using the Column Chooser command. To make this process more efficient, you can predefine the custom iProperties in your sheet metal template file, and the custom properties can be authored into a custom Drawing Manager parts list template for quick application.

Harvest your legacy sheet metal styles into sheet metal rules   Using the harvesting utilities provided, you can extract your legacy sheet metal styles and publish them into style library sheet metal rules, preassociated to material styles, sheet thickness values, and sheet metal unfold rules.

Master It How can you extract sheet metal style information from a legacy part files or template files for the purpose of publishing it with a Sheet Metal Rule?

Solution By launching the Style Management Wizard application (also known as the Harvester) from Program Files ≻ Autodesk ≻ Autodesk Inventor 2009 ≻ Tools ≻ Style Library Manager, individual files or entire project directories can be processed to extract sheet metal styles information and automatically publish it to a new or existing Sheet Metal Rule and Sheet Metal Unfold Rule XML files for use by your style library.

As a reminder, while it is possible to harvest sheet metal rules that contain references to model parameters and linked external files, this is simply a result of the harvester's inability to detect these conditions. The extracted rule information will be broken, and the rule will not be usable. By default, the sheet metal document will leverage some programmatic values to keep your model from being corrupted, but once you open the Style and Standard Editor dialog box, you will see errors that must be resolved. To avoid this situation, it is recommended that you preview the contents of files before utilizing them for harvesting. If you need to be able to reference model parameters or external files to drive your sheet metal rule, define these rules within your template file.

Chapter 7: Part and Feature Reuse

Create iParts from existing designs iParts are the solution to creating parts that allow for an infinite number of variations without affecting other members of the same part family already used within your designs.

Master It You use a purchased specialty part in your designs and would like to create the many size configurations that this part comes in ahead of time for use within assembly design.

Solution Create or use an existing model, edit the parameter list to name specific parameters to logical names. Add the configuration table by creating an iPart from this model. Configure the parameters in the table and add rows according to variations needed. And finally, test the newly created iPart by inserting all variations of the part into a blank assembly.

Create and use iFeatures Creating a library of often used features is essential to standardization and improved productivity within your design workflow.

Master It You want to be able to place common punches, slots and milled features quickly, rather than having to generate the feature sketch every time.

Solution Extract iFeatures from existing standard and sheet-metal parts, and place them in user-defined folders within the Catalog subfolder. Using your custom-created iFeatures as well as standard iFeatures, practice placing them into your designs to see how they behave and how they can be modified.

Copy sketches and part features to create additional features and designs You do not have to create iFeatures in order to reuse various part features in your designs. If a part feature will have limited use in other designs, it is often better to simply copy it from part to part or from face to face on the same part.

Master It   You have the need to reuse features within a part or among parts. You consider iFeatures, but realize that reuse is often specialized and doesn't lend itself to setting up an iFeature.

Solution   Practice copying features to other faces on the same part. Determine the difference between creating dependent and independent features. Open different part files, select Arrange All in the Window pulldown, and copy/paste features from one part to another. Copy sketches and paste them on various work planes and part faces. Explore how copying sketches creates independently controlled parameters within the same part file. Copy a sketch and paste the sketch into a new part file.

Configure, create, and access Content Center parts   Content Center provides a great opportunity to reuse database-created geometry within assemblies and within functional design modules. The Content Center Editor provides the means to add custom content into Content Center. Custom libraries can be created within the Autodesk Data Management Server Console and added to your current project file. Content Center performance can be improved by creating selective project files that load only certain Content Center libraries.

Master It   You would like to change the part numbers in some Content Center components to match the part numbers your company uses. You would also like to add proprietary components to the Content Center, so that the design team can access them from the same place.

Solution   Create a Custom Content Center library within the Autodesk Data Management Console. Configure your project file, and create new project files to limit loading of Content Center libraries to specific job types. Utilize the Content Center Editor to create new categories within your custom Content Center library. Convert an iPart to a Content Center component using the Publish option.

Chapter 8: Assembly Design Workflows

Organize designs using structured subassemblies   Subassemblies add organization, facilitate the bill of materials, and reduce assembly constraints; all this results in better performance and easier edits. One of the habits of all Inventor experts is their effective use and understanding of subassemblies.

Master It   You need to hand off an accurate BOM for finished designs to the purchasing department at the end of each design project.

Solution   Organize parts in subassemblies in a real-world manner matching the way that components are assembled on the shop floor. Use phantom assemblies when structuring parts merely for the purpose of reducing assembly constraints. Set subassemblies as Purchased or Inseparable when you want multiple components to list as a single item in the BOM. And then export the BOM from the assembly to an Excel spreadsheet or other intermediate format to give to purchasing.

Use positional reps and flexible assemblies together   Often you may need to show a design in various stages of motion to test interference and/or proof of concept. Copying assemblies so that you can change the assembly constraints to show different assembly positions becomes a file management nightmare. Instead, use flexible subassemblies and positional representations.

Master It   You need to show your assembly in variations dependent upon the position of the moving parts and the task the machine is accomplishing at given stages of its operation.

Solution   Leave subassemblies with parts that determine their position based on the relationship with parts within another subassembly to be underconstrained. Set them to be flexible to allow them to be mated to other parts and used in different positions within the same top-level assembly. Create positional representations to show the design in known kinematic states, such as fully opened, closed, or opened at a given angle, and so on. As an added benefit, animating assemblies in Inventor Studio is very simple when positional representations have been set up in the model.

Copy designs   Because of the live linked data that exists in Inventor assemblies, using Windows Explorer to copy designs and rename parts is difficult and often delivers poor results. Using the tool provided in Inventor will allow you to copy designs and maintain the links between files.

Master It   You need to duplicate an existing design in order to create a similar design.

Solution   Use the Copy Components feature in the assembly environment to copy designs and choose which parts to copy and rename, reuse, or omit from the new design. Use Autodesk Vault to take it to the next level and include all of the 2D drawings in the copy design.

Substitute a single part for entire subassemblies   Working with large assemblies, particularly where large, complex assemblies are used over and over as subassemblies within a top-level design, can tax most any workstation if not approached in the correct manner.

Master It   You would like to swap out a complex assembly for a simplified version for use in layout designs or to use in large assemblies in an attempt to improve performance.

Solution   Create LOD representations to suppress components when not in use during the design cycle. Create single substitute parts from large, complex assemblies to be used as subassemblies within the design. Enjoy the benefit of referencing fewer files while maintaining an accurate bill of materials.

Chapter 9: Large Assembly Strategies

Select a workstation   Having the right tool for the job is the key to success in anything you do. This is true of selecting a large assembly workstation. You have learned that for optimal performance you should strive to keep your system working in physical memory (RAM).

Master It   You notice that your computer runs slowly when working with large assemblies and want to know whether you should consider a 64-bit system.

Solution   Evaluate the amount of time you spend working on large assemblies and the amount of that time you spend waiting on your workstation to decide whether your system is adequate. Monitor your RAM usage and decide whether upgrading to 64-bit system is a good solution for your needs. You should plan for hardware upgrades in your budget to make them more manageable.

Adjust your performance settings   You have learned that there are many settings in Inventor and in Windows that you can use to configure the application to work more efficiently with large assemblies.

Master It You want to make your current workstation run as efficiently as possible for large assembly design.

Solution Disable the unneeded Windows visual effects and discontinue the use of screen savers, large resolution screen sizes, and desktop wallpapers. Learn the location of the Application Options settings within Inventor that will provide performance gains.

Use best practices for large assembly Knowing the tools for general assembly design is only half of the battle when it comes to conquering large assemblies. Understanding the methods of large assembly design and how they differ from a general assembly design is a key to success.

Master It You want to create adaptive parts so that you can make changes during the initial design stage and have several parts update automatically as you work through the details. But you are concerned about how this will adversely affect your assembly performance.

Solution Create adaptive relationships between parts as you normally would, but ensure that the adaptivity is turned off once the initial design is done. If the parts require an update, turn adaptivity back on, make the edits, and then turn adaptivity back off.

Manage assembly detail Inventor includes several tools to help manage assembly detail so that you can accomplish your large assembly design goals.

Master It You want to reduce the number of files your large assembly is required to reference while you are working on it and yet maintain an accurate bill of materials.

Solution Use substitute LOD representations to derive a subassembly into a single part file. Place multiple instances of the subassembly into the top-level assembly at the substitute level of detail.

Simplify parts Creating highly detailed parts may be required for generating production drawings or Inventor Studio renderings, but using those high-detail parts in large assemblies may have an adverse affect.

Master It You want to create a lower level of detail part files for common parts to be reused many times over in your large assemblies but are concerned about managing two versions of a part.

Solution Create an embedded link between the two versions so that you can easily locate and access the other version if the first version requires an edit.

Chapter 10: Weldment Design

Select and use the right weldment design methodology I have shown you three weldment design methodologies. Before starting on any weldment design, it is imperative to keep the documentation, interference analysis, mass properties, and other design criteria in perspective and select the right design methodology.

Master It What is the right weldment strategy for you? If you don't need to document the weldment design stages, you could consider the part files and part features methodology or the weldment assembly and derived methodology. With the weldment assembly methodology you get to document the different stages of weldment design and reap the benefits of any new enhancements.

Solution Talk to your machine shop and then choose the right one that best suits you. Use the weldment assembly design methodology if you can't decide.

Create and edit weld preparations and machining features Following the weldment methodology, you need to plan on creating the gaps needed (weld preparations) to deposit the weld beads. You need to create post weldment machining features that go through the weld beads.

Master It Where can you find these and when do you use it? Weld preparations and machining features are similar to part modeling features. Based on the weld bead shape needed, you need to plan for creating the preparations in advance. Once the welds are done, you need to create the features for the machining processes.

Solution Double-click Preparations or Machining command in the assembly Model browser to go into those environments. Chamfer and Move Face are most commonly used. Most groove welds require some kind of weld preparations.

Create and edit different kinds of weld beads such as cosmetic, fillet, and groove I have described the relative advantages and disadvantages of cosmetic and solid weld beads. Weldment design involves the optimal mix of these weld beads based on needs and requirements.

Master It You have the need to only create the weld annotations in drawings without any need to create them in the model. You have weld subassemblies which only needs lightweight representation in both model and drawings. In situations involving accurate interference and mass properties you need accurate weld beads. The question is: What type of weld beads should you use?

Solution Double-click Welds in the assembly Model browser, and choose the desired weld bead type. For lightweight representation with no interference and accurate mass properties, use cosmetic welds. For interference and accurate mass properties, use the solid representation. Use a combination of fillet and groove welds as needed to generate the desired weld bead shape. Use split technique in cases where precise control is needed. Observe that you can use a single weld symbol to callout multiple weld beads.

Document weldment stages in drawings Welds need to be documented in assemblies or drawings. It is important to show the different stages of weldment design in drawings to get a good idea of how to manufacture the weldment. You can use the drawing tools effectively to annotate the welds in drawings. This will help the welder to understand the design intent better.

Master It What are the different tools used for weld documentation? You can annotate the welds in assemblies. If you prefer to document the welds in drawings, you could document the four stages of weldment design: As-assembled, As-prepped, As-welded and As-machined stages in drawings. Besides, you could use other drawing manager tools to customize weld documentation.

Solution While creating a drawing view, on the Model State tab of the Drawing View dialog box, select Assembly, Machining, Welds, or Preparation. Use the End Fill tool to customize the weld bead process shape. The Weld Caterpillars is another useful tool to shows welds in a drawing.

Generate and maintain a consistent set of BOM's across welded assemblies, drawings, and presentations You have been shown how to generate and maintain a consistent bill of materials for weldment assemblies and a parts list in drawings. Mark parts or assemblies as Inseparable to designate them as weldments.

Master It   How do you generate the BOM and parts list for your weldment? You can generate the bill of materials and mark the components as Inseparable. In the drawing you generate the parts list for the weldment assembly.

Solution   Click the BOM command in a weldment assembly. In the Structure column, you can set each part to be inseparable. Use the parts list command and appropriate table wrapping options to generate the parts list.

Chapter 11: Functional Design

Use Inventor's Design Accelerators   Design Accelerators and Design Generators allow you to rapidly create complex geometry and the associated calculations that verify the viability of your design.

Master It   Your design needs a bolted connection, but you are not certain about the number of bolts to use to ensure a proper connection.

Solution   Use the Bolted Connection Generator to determine the optimum amount of bolts for a given material choice.

Use Inventor's Design Calculators   Design Calculators do not create any geometry, but they permit you to store the calculations in the assembly and repeat the calculation with different input values at a later time.

Master It   You need to calculate the size of a weld between two plates to withstand a certain lateral force.

Solution   Use the Fillet Weld Calculator to determine the size, type, and material of the weld bead.

Develop best practices for using these tools   In this chapter, we explained how to use Design Accelerators in the best possible way by providing best practices and tips and tricks concerning the use of templates, exploring the benefits of using a particular type of calculation or connection method for a given scenario, and showing how to select the right material to do the job.

Master It   You need to design a camshaft to activate an inlet valve that needs to respect a specific lift-over-time graph. You also want to reuse the design and slightly modify it for other similar cams like the exhaust valve.

Solution   Use the Disc Cam Generator to design the shape of the cam; then use a template to export the design, import it, and reuse it for a new design like the exhaust valve.

Master It   You want to design a compression spring that operates within very strict dimensional limitations and find a spring material that also satisfies the load requirements.

Solution   Use the Spring Generator to select the combination of pitch, wire diameter, and material that withstands the applied force without being fully compressed.

Master It   Your design needs a gear transmission between two shafts with a predefined position, and you want the gears to be separate components that need to be connected to the shaft.

Solution   Use the Spur Gear Generator to construct the gears, and use the Module option. Use the Key Connection Generator to connect the gears to the shafts.

Chapter 12: Documentation

Create an exploded assembly view by creating a presentation   Presentation files are used to virtually disassemble an assembly so downstream consumers can better visualize the design. The explosion created in the presentation file can be referenced in an assembly drawing to complement nonexploded assembly views.

Master It   Your assembly design is complex and contains many internal components that can't be visualized in traditional assembly drawing views.

Solution   Create a new presentation file, reference an assembly, and tweak parts and subassemblies away from their constrained positions. Add as many tweaks as necessary to communicate the design affectively. You may choose to create several explosions in one presentation file to achieve this goal.

Create and maintain drawing templates, standards, and styles   Inventor provides numerous methods to create, store, and use drawing templates and styles. Careful planning should be considered for how and where to manage these resources. Consideration must be given to how templates are deployed on your network and whether to use the style library.

Master It   Rather than using one of Inventor's out-of-the box drawing settings, you need to set up a drawing template, a drafting standard, and annotation styles to conform to a particular international, industry, or company drafting standard.

Solution   Use one of the drawing templates that are installed with Inventor, and re-configure it to meet your or your company's requirements. Edit the drawing resources to customize your title block, border, and sketched symbols. Define annotation styles such as Dimension and Parts List styles, and determine how best to share them across your workgroup.

Generate 2D drawings views of parts, assemblies, and presentations   The Drawing Manager environment in Inventor enables you to generate traditional 2D drafting views from your 3D solid models.

Master It   You've used Inventor's modeling tools to generate parts and assemblies to meet your design criteria. Now you need to generate drawing views of this design so that it can be communicated to machinists, fabricators, and inspectors.

Solution   Generate drawing views of your model using the Drawing Views panel in Inventor's Drawing Manager. Generate as many projected and cut views as necessary to fully communicate your design.

Annotate drawing views of your model   Drawing Manager provides a rich set of dimensioning tools, special symbols, and tables that enable you to fully annotate part and assembly drawings conforming to several international drawing standards.

Master It   Now that you've generated drawing views of your design, the views must be fully annotated in accordance with your company's or your customer's required drafting standard.

Solution   Use the Drawing Annotation panel to place dimensions, tables, and symbols on your part or assembly views to fully communicate the design. Use styles to help create consistent drafting techniques and conformity to drafting standards.

Chapter 13: Inventor Tools Overview

Take your models from Inventor to ABS   If you frequently have the need to take your Inventor models to ABS, then AEC exchange can help you in this process with three simple steps. Inventor provides a variety of ways to simplify the model and author it. Such models can be published in ABS.

Master It   You can do this with the following three steps: model simplifying, authoring, and publishing. You can also save a DWG as a solid.

Solution   Simplify using derived technology. Author it with cables, conduit, ducts, or pipe. Create part families and catalogs.

Create AutoLimits/design sensors   You use AutoLimits to monitor design parameters in which you are interested.

Master It   How many AutoLimits can you use in an assembly? Use no more than 10. You can customize the AutoLimits and have it set up in the model.

Solution   Create the AutoLimits, and set up its boundaries. Limit the number of AutoLimits to around 10.

Manage design data efficiently using Inventor tools   There are different tools for managing design data, which is typically distributed across part, assembly, and drawing files. Associated with these can be Excel spreadsheets, text files, Word documents, and so on.

Master It   The Design Assistant keeps the file relationships while copying, renaming, and moving files. Whenever you are sending Inventor files to others, use Pack and Go, which hunts the file relationships, and you can use WinZip software to package it into a single ZIP file. You can delegate many of the tasks in Inventor to the Task Scheduler. You can propagate source drawing template information to several destination drawings using the Drawing Resource Transfer Wizard.

Solution   In the Design Assistant, click the Manage button. Right-click the file in the Action column, and select Action. Right-click the file in the Name column, and select Change Name. Click Save Changes. Right-click the file in Windows Explorer to use Pack and Go. In the Task Scheduler, use the Create Task menu to create your task. In the Drawing Resource Transfer Wizard, select Source resources, uncheck any unwanted resources, and propagate it to destination drawings.

Manage styles   You can use the Style Library Manager and the Style Management Wizard to organize your styles to keep it simple and clean.

Master It   How do you manage your styles? Styles normally need to be copied, edited, and deleted. Use the Style Library Manager. How can you create a central repository of styles? How do you purge styles? Use the Style Management Wizard for these tasks.

Solution   You can create a new style library using the Create New Style Library button in the Style Library Manager. You can copy styles by clicking Style Library 1 and then clicking Style Library 2. To delete styles, right-click the style in the Style Library Manager, and then rename or delete the style. You can harvest styles by adding files and then clicking Harvest Styles Into Target Style Library. You can select an existing style library or create a new library by clicking Start. You could also purge styles in a library by clicking Purge All Unused Styles From Files in the Style Management Wizard.

Create expressions with iProperties   Property fields can be concatenated to produce desired customized information in BOM and parts lists.

Master It   You can break down for example "stock size" of your parts to be used in your BOM with associativity to model parameters. You can create and manage expressions for iProperties. You can further customize the parameters in the *fx*:Parameters dialog box to have it displayed differently in iProperties.

Solution   You can create expressions on the Summary, Project, Status, or Custom tab. Start with the = sign, and type in the text. To include parameters or iProperty names, include them in brackets. A detected expression is denoted by *fx*. You can create a template file with predefined expressions for iProperties that lets you unify your parts list and other documentation.

Measure in assemblies   Click the right Measure command and selection filters to make measurements.

Master It   How do you measure in assemblies? Once you set the selection filter, make the selections, and use the measurement helpers to get complex measurements.

Solution   Use the measurement helpers to accumulate measurements. Click the correct selection filter in the assembly's environment to get the measurement between components, parts, or faces and edges.

Give feedback to Autodesk   You could participate in the Customer Involvement Program (CIP). Customer error reporting (CER) helps Autodesk know about the issue.

Master It   For the CIP, you can stop participation any time by accessing the controls from the Autodesk Help menu. You could include the steps (if that is known) that led to the unexpected termination of the program. You can skip the CER process.

Solution   Participate in the Customer Involvement Program. Send the CER report.

Chapter 14: Exchanging Data With Other Systems

Import and export geometry   In the design world today, you most likely need to transfer files to or from a customer or vendor from time to time. Chances are, the files will need to be translated to or from a neutral file format to be read by different CAD packages.

Master It   You are collaborating with another design office that does not use Inventor. You are asked which you would prefer, IGES or STEP files.

Solution   Request a STEP file over IGES when you have the choice. Take advantage of the extra intelligence concerning assembly structure and filenames that can be retained in the STEP file format.

Use Inventor file translators   Inventor 2009 offers native file translators for Pro/Engineer, Solidworks, Unigraphics, and other CAD file types. This allows you to access these file formats with Inventor and translate the files into Inventor files directly.

Master It You are a "job shop" and in the past have been required to have a copy of Solidworks in addition to your copy of Inventor in order to work with customers who send you Solidworks files.

Solution Use Inventor 2009 to access the customer's files directly and convert them to Inventor files for your in-house use. Use Save Copy As to export the file back out as a Solidworks file to send to the client for review.

Work with imported data Using the construction environment in Inventor, you can repair poorly translated surface files. Often a file fails to translate into a solid because of just a few translation errors in the part. Repairing or patching the surfaces and promoting the file to a solid allows you to use the file more effectively.

Master It You download an IGES file from a vendor website, but when you attempt to use the component in your design, the surface data is found to have issues.

Solution Open the file and copy the surfaces to the construction environment. Use Stitch Surface to create composite surfaces, and identify the gaps in the surface data. Use the construction tools to delete, patch, and extend surfaces in order to close the gaps and promote the data to a solid. Before getting started on this, evaluate the amount of time required to repair the surface data. You may find that you can model the vendor component, by using catalog specs or by measuring an actual part, faster than you can repair some surface models.

Work with Design Review markups Design Review offers you and the people you collaborate with an easy-to-use electronic markup tool that can be round-tripped from Inventor. Design Review markups can be made on both 2D and 3D files.

Master It You want to use Design Review to communicate with vendors and clients in order to save time and resources, but you have found that others are unsure of what Design Review is and how to get it.

Solution Suggest using Design Review to the people you collaborate with and mention to them that this application is a free download. Send them the link to download the application and the online demonstration found in the Design Review's Help menu. Continue to offer your collaborators the review material in PDF, DWG, or any other traditional file type in case they end up in a time crunch, but send them DWF file as well. If they use Internet Explorer 7, consider sending them DWFx files, and mention to them that they can open those file directly in a web browser.

Use Feature recognition The Feature Recognition add-in can be downloaded online for free from Autodesk Labs. This tool allows you to add intelligence to otherwise "dumb" imported solids.

Master It You receive STEP files from a client but often find that holes and other features need to be resized to accommodate your tooling.

Solution Use the Feature Recognition tool to recognize just the features you are interested in modifying. Once the features are recognized, edit the sketch to ensure that the feature is anchored. Then edit the feature, and change the size and configuration as required.

Chapter 15: Frame Generator

Work with frame files   Frame Generator puts all the members at the same level in the assembly.

Master It   You have a frame that is built up in sections that are welded together. You need to document the manufacturing process.

Solution   Use Demote to create subassemblies of frame members. Select the frame members in the browser. From the context menu, select Component ➤ Demote Frame Generator Components. This preserves the Frame Generator relationships.

Insert frame members onto a skeleton model   Frame Generator builds a skeleton model for the frame from the selected lines and edges.

Master It   Since Frame Generator builds its own skeleton model, you don't have to build a master model before you start creating the frame. You can use sketches, surfaces, and model edges to insert frame members.

Solution   Use layout sketches and surfaces to design the basic frame shape. Position the components that will be mounted to the frame in the assembly, and reference edges on the parts. As you make changes to the assembly such as the overall size or the position of components, the frame will automatically update.

Add end treatments to frame members   Frame Generator does not support end treatments on merged members.

Master It   Let's assume you are building a stairway and the handrail has curved sections.

Solution   You can handle this situation in several ways:

◆ When you create the frame member, don't select the Merge option. This creates individual files for each segment. You can add end treatments to the end segments and document the details in the assembly drawing.

◆ Create the sketches so the ends of the curved member terminate at the face of another member. If the mating member has a flat face, you don't need an end treatment.

◆ Add short linear segments that aren't merged with the rest of the curved member. You can document that the length of the curved member does not include end treatments.

◆ Manually create end treatments using part-modeling commands. Frame members are created as custom parts that can be edited.

Make changes to frames   An existing frame needs to be modified to strengthen it.

Master It   You need to determine the size and wall thickness of the tubing and make it either thicker or larger.

Solution   Use the Frame Member Info tool to get the properties for the frame members. Then, you can use the Change tool to increase the wall thickness, increase the size, or select a different structural profile.

Author and publish structural profiles   Your company uses custom aluminum extrusions in its frames.

Master It   You need to add the profiles to the Content Center so Frame Generator can access them.

Solution   Use the Structural Shape Authoring tool to prepare the parts for publishing. Use the Publish Part tool to add the parts to the Content Center.

Chapter 16: Inventor Studio

Create and manage surface, lighting, and scene styles   Inventor doesn't have the surface, lighting, or scene style you need for a rendering.

Master It   You need to create a surface style that portrays black bumped plastic.

Solution   Here is the preferred way to create a new surface style:

1. Copy the Black surface style, giving the new style an appropriate name, such as Plastic (Black–textured).
2. On the Diffuse tab, click Use Texture Image.
3. In the list of images, select one of the Plastic image textures.
4. On the Bump tab, click Same As Texture, and set the percent value to 50 percent.
5. Save and apply the texture to the component.

Here is the preferred way to create a new lighting style:

1. Copy the lighting style containing most of what your new style needs, giving the new style an appropriate name.
2. On the various tabs, modify the lighting parameters.
3. Click OK.

Here is the preferred way to create a new scene style:

1. Copy the scene style that has similarities to the new style, giving the new style an appropriate name.
2. On the various tabs, modify the scene parameters.
3. Click OK.

Create and animate cameras   You need to create a camera and animate it.

Master It   You decide to use the most expedient means to capture camera keyframe positions.

Solution   To create a new camera, do the following:

1. Use the view orientation tools to position the view to show what the camera would see in the first frame.
2. Right-click, and select Create Camera from View.

To animate the camera, do the following:

1. In the Animation Timeline window, in the pulldown list, select the new camera by name.

2. In the Animation Timeline window, set the time slider to the time position representing when you want the camera to be in another location.

3. In the Scene browser, right-click the new camera node, and click Animate Camera.

4. In the graphics region, use the view orientation tools to position the view to show what you want at that time position.

5. In the Animation Timeline window, click Add Camera Action.

Repeat as needed.

Start new animations, modify animations, and use the various animation tools You need to start a new animation of an assembly.

Master It You have an existing animation but want to do a variation on it. You want to copy and edit an existing animation.

Solution Copy the animation:

1. In the Scene browser, expand the Animations node.

2. Right-click the animation for which you want to make a variation, and click Copy Animation.

3. Right-click the Animations folder, and click Paste Animation.

4. The Animations folder populates a new animation based on the selected animation.

Modify the animation:

1. Right-click the new animation, and click Activate.

2. In the Animation Timeline window, make modifications to actions as needed.

3. Add new actions as needed using the animation commands.

Use multiple cameras to create a video production of your animation Video Producer provides the means to combine camera shots into a single video output. You want to use this feature.

Master It You created several cameras, animated and static, and want to make a composite animation.

Solution Do the following:

1. In the Scene browser, expand the Productions node.

2. If no production exists, right-click the Productions node, and click New Production.

3. The cameras are loaded into the Video Producer window and ready for use.

4. Drag and drop shots into the timeline, and set their parameters.

5. Drag and drop the desired transitions between the shots.

Use props to enhance your scene Inventor assemblies can be combined with other components to create a more realistic scene for rendering.

Master It You have completed a design and want to render a realistic image of it in its working environment.

Solution Do the following:

1. Create a new assembly that will be used as a wrapper assembly.

2. Place your product assembly in the new assembly.

3. Add any props, other parts, and other assemblies that make the scene more realistic.

Render realistic and illustrative images Inventor provides the means to render both realistic and illustrative images.

Master It With your new product nearing completion, the marketing department has asked for rendered images for marketing collateral and technical documents such as white papers.

Solution To create a realistic rendering, do the following:

1. Prepare the scene with what you want to render.

2. Click the Render Image command.

3. In the Render Image dialog box, select Realistic as the render type.

4. Specify the camera, lighting, and scene styles to use.

5. Click Render.

To create an illustration rendering, do the following:

1. Prepare the scene with what you want to render.

2. Click the Render Image command.

3. In the Render Image dialog box, select Illustration as the render type.

4. Specify the camera, lighting, and scene styles to use.

5. On the Style tab, specify the appropriate settings for your rendering.

6. Click Render.

Render animations and video productions Inventor provides the means to render animations and video productions.

Master It You've created a wrapper assembly and set up the scene with cameras, lighting, and a scene style. Now you want to render an animation for design review and a video production for a multidiscipline review or marketing use.

Solution To render the animation, do the following:

1. In the Scene browser, select and activate the animation you want to render.

2. Deactivate any active production.

Remember: When a production is active, it is the render target. To render a single animation, you must deactivate any active production.

3. In the Studio tool panel, click Render Animation.

4. Specify the various styles to use and the render type.

5. Specify the output file type and other parameters.

6. Render the animation.

To render a production, do the following:

1. In the Scene browser, select and activate the production you want to render.

2. If you have not completed composing the production, you should do so.

3. In the Studio tool panel, click Render Animation.

4. Specify the various styles to use and the render type.

5. Specify the output file type and other parameters.

6. Render the animation.

Index

Note to the Reader: Throughout this index **boldfaced** page numbers indicate primary discussions of a topic. *Italicized* page numbers indicate illustrations.